WALL PAINTING, CIVIC CEREMONY, AND SACRED SPACE IN EARLY RENAISSANCE ITALY

Wall Painting, Civic Ceremony, and Sacred Space in Early Renaissance Italy investigates how mural paintings affirmed civic identities by visualizing ideas, experiences, memory, and history. Jean Cadogan focuses on four large mural decorations created by celebrated Florentine artists between 1377 and 1484. The paintings adorn important sacred spaces – the Chapel of the Holy Belt in the cathedral of Prato, the monumental cemetery in Pisa's Cathedral Square, and the cathedral of Spoleto – yet extol civic virtues. Building on previously unpublished archival documents, primary sources, and recent scholarship, Cadogan relates the architectural and institutional histories of these sites, reconstructs the ceremonies that unfolded within them, and demonstrates how these sacred spaces were central to the historical, institutional, and religious identities of the host cities. She also offers new insights into the motives and mechanics of patronage and artistic production. Cadogan's study shows how images reflected and shaped civic identity, even as they impressed through their scale and artistry.

JEAN CADOGAN is Professor of Fine Arts at Trinity College, Hartford, Connecticut. A graduate of Wellesley College and Harvard University, she was previously curator of European art at the Wadsworth Atheneum, Hartford. Her publications include *Wadsworth Atheneum Paintings II: Italy and Spain* (1991); *Domenico Ghirlandaio: Artist and Artisan* (2000); as well as numerous articles on drawings, mural paintings, and artisan families in Renaissance Florence.

WALL PAINTING, CIVIC CEREMONY, AND SACRED SPACE IN EARLY RENAISSANCE ITALY

JEAN K. CADOGAN
Trinity College

CAMBRIDGE
UNIVERSITY PRESS

CAMBRIDGE
UNIVERSITY PRESS

Shaftesbury Road, Cambridge CB2 8EA, United Kingdom

One Liberty Plaza, 20th Floor, New York, NY 10006, USA

477 Williamstown Road, Port Melbourne, VIC 3207, Australia

314–321, 3rd Floor, Plot 3, Splendor Forum, Jasola District Centre, New Delhi – 110025, India

103 Penang Road, #05–06/07, Visioncrest Commercial, Singapore 238467

Cambridge University Press is part of Cambridge University Press & Assessment, a department of the University of Cambridge.

We share the University's mission to contribute to society through the pursuit of education, learning and research at the highest international levels of excellence.

www.cambridge.org
Information on this title: www.cambridge.org/9781009535229

DOI: 10.1017/9781009535267

When citing this work, please include a reference to the DOI 10.1017/9781009535267

First published 2025

Printed in the United Kingdom by CPI Group Ltd, Croydon CR0 4YY

A catalogue record for this publication is available from the British Library

Library of Congress Cataloging-in-Publication Data
NAMES: Cadogan, Jean K., author.
TITLE: Wall painting, civic ceremony, and sacred space in early Renaissance Italy / Jean K. Cadogan, Trinity College, Connecticut.
DESCRIPTION: Cambridge ; New York, NY : Cambridge University Press, 2025. | Includes bibliographical references and index. | Summary: "Focusing on four large mural decorations created by celebrated Florentine artists between 1377 and 1484, this book investigates how mural paintings affirmed civic identities by visualizing ideas, experiences, memory, and history. It offers new insights into the motives and mechanics of patronage and artistic production"– Provided by publisher.
IDENTIFIERS: LCCN 2024057760 (print) | LCCN 2024057761 (ebook) | ISBN 9781009535229 (hardback) | ISBN 9781009535236 (paperback) | ISBN 9781009535267 (epub)
SUBJECTS: LCSH: Mural painting and decoration, Renaissance–Italy–Themes, motives. | Mural painting and decoration, Italian–Italy–Themes, motives. | Painting, Early Renaissance–Italy–Themes, motives. | Art and society–Italy–Florence–History–To 1500.
CLASSIFICATION: LCC ND2755 .C33 2025 (print) | LCC ND2755 (ebook) | DDC 751.7/3094509024–dc23/eng/20250127
LC record available at https://lccn.loc.gov/2024057760
LC ebook record available at https://lccn.loc.gov/2024057761

ISBN 978-1-009-53522-9 Hardback

This publication is supported by the William Ravenel Peelle, Jr. and Agnes Stroud Peelle Art History Endowment of Trinity College.

CONTENTS

ACKNOWLEDGMENTS

It is a great pleasure to thank the many friends and colleagues who helped me research and write this book. My interest in mural painting was fostered by visits to scaffoldings during conservation projects. In Santa Croce in Florence, I was guided by Cecilia Frosinini and Maria Rosa Lanfranchi of the Opificio delle Pietre Dure, whose expertise and patience are unlimited. In Prato Cathedral, Mark Gittens of CBC Conservazione Beni Cultuali revealed the complexities of Filippo Lippi's mural technique. Paolo Virilli of Tecnirico in Spoleto shared his expertise and images of the restoration of Lippi's murals in the cathedral and Isabella Lapi Ballerini of the Ministero per i Beni Culturali the conservation report for Agnolo Gaddi's murals in Prato. The Rome conference "Materiali e Tecniche nella Pittura Murale del Quattrocento" in 2002 was an inspiration to further research.

I have been welcomed in many archives and libraries, to whose professional staffs I am indebted. These include, in Prato, the Archivio di Stato and the Biblioteca Roncioniana; in Spoleto the Archivio di Stato; and in Pisa the Archivio di Stato, Archivio Capitolare della Primaziale, the Biblioteca di Filosofia e Storia of the University of Pisa, and especially the Archivio Storico Diocesano, Archivio Capitolare, whose archivist, Dottoressa Elisa Carrara, was unfailingly helpful. In Florence, I consulted the Archivio di Stato and the Archivio Storico dell'Opera di Santa Maria del Fiore, where Lorenzo Fabbri welcomed me. The Kunsthistorisches Institut as always was indispensable for my research, enabled by the kindnesses of Director Emeritus Alessandro Nova.

My colleagues Diane Cole Ahl, Paul Balolsky, Livio Pestilli, and Barbara Wisch read all or parts of the manuscript and offered incisive criticism. The two scholarly reviewers for Cambridge University Press read the manuscript with exceptional care and gave invaluable advice. Professor Dario Del Puppo and the late Jeffrey Kaimowitz, curator of the Watkinson Library at Trinity, helped with translations. Maria Ausilio Pisano provided the transcription of Filippo de' Medici's testament. Julia Damiano-Vicidomini copyedited an earlier version of the text, and Amanda Matava, Digital Archivist at Trinity College Library, assisted with images. I thank Beatrice Rehl at Cambridge

University Press for her advice and encouragement and Liz Davey for her stewardship of the project.

I am grateful to Trinity College and the Fine Arts department for the many research leaves devoted to travel and writing. The William Ravenel Peelle, Jr. and Agnes Stroud Peelle Art History Endowment generously supported publication, allowing color illustrations and extensive appendices.

Last but not least, I thank my family, especially my husband, Alden Gordon, and Alex, Alden, Anna, Maya, Jessie, Asher, Aaron, and Talia for their love and support. This book is dedicated to them.

INTRODUCTION

Artists have painted monumental images on walls throughout time. Images as diverse as the stampeding bulls and horses in the prehistoric caves of Lascaux, Dordogne, France (c. 17000 BCE, Figure 0.1), the enigmatic scenes at the pre-Columbian Maya site of San Bartolo in Guatemala (c. 300 BCE–50 CE), and the languid Bodhisattvas from the fifth century in the Ajanta cave 1 in India (Figure 0.2), decorated tombs, shrines, temples and houses.[1] Fragmentary survivals from Greece, Crete, Rome, and early Christian Europe attest to a continuous tradition of mural painting in the West. Wall paintings reflected profound social change by embracing new imagery, formats, and styles. Striking examples survive in the late Roman catacombs. Murals in the catacomb of Saints Peter and Marcellinus in Rome from the late third or early fourth century CE were painted in a simplified Roman technique and depict images, such as the Good Shepherd, that appealed to pagan, Jewish, and Christian worshippers.[2] Stories from classical mythology and the Hebrew Bible grace the chambers in the Via Latina catacomb from the mid-fourth century.[3] In early Christian basilicas, fourth-century Old Saint Peter's and Saint Paul outside the Walls, the lives of Jesus and the saints unfolded in expansive narrative images above the nave arcade, these sadly lost to us but known from copies.[4]

Today murals as expressions of racial and ethnic identity cover the walls of buildings in cities around the world. In the United States, public art has been long been associated with social activism. Studies of the *Wall of Respect*, a mural

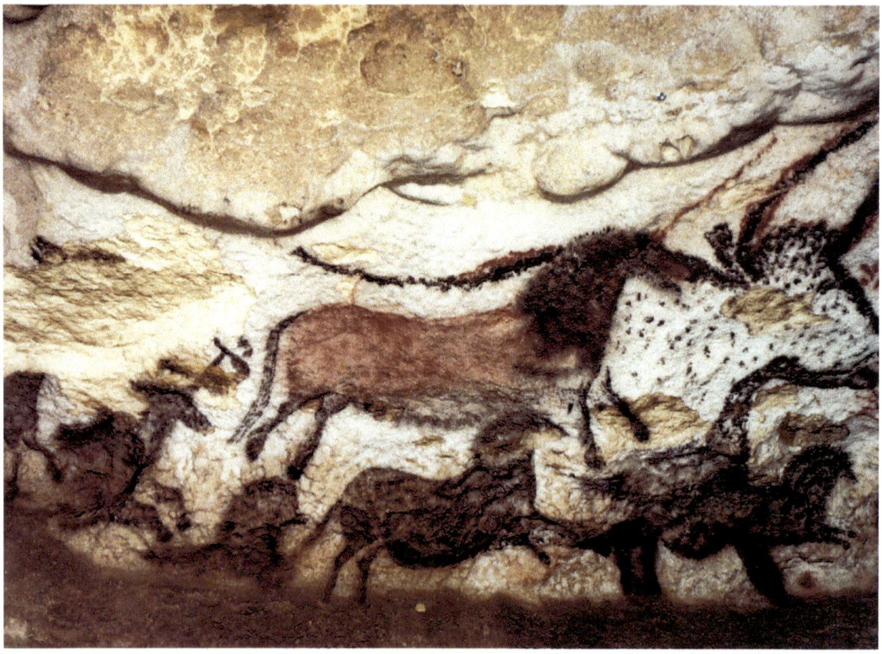

0.1. Hall of Bulls, c. 17000 BCE, Lascaux Caves/Montignac/Dordogne/France. Photo: © Ministère de la Culture / Médiathèque du Patrimoine, Dist. RMN-Grand Palais / Art Resource, NY.

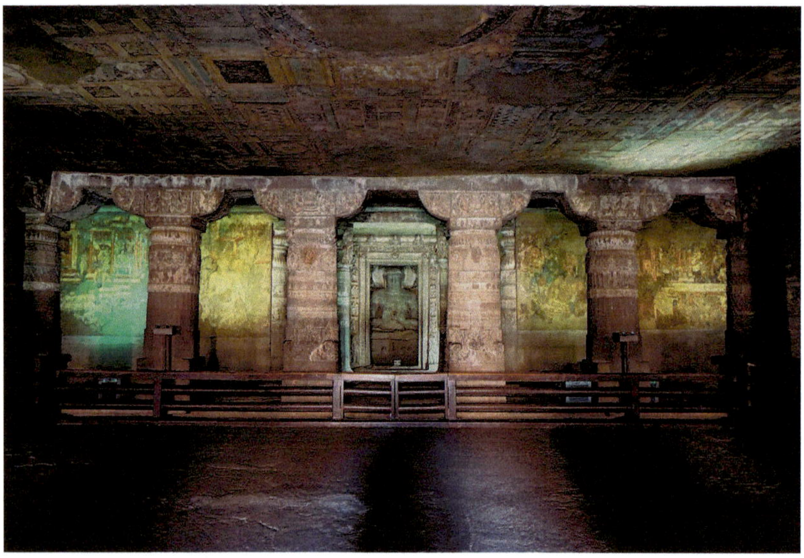

0.2. Main shrine with murals, Cave 1, c. 477 CE, Ajanta, India. Photo: Author.

painted in Chicago in 1967, have highlighted its role in the civil rights movement as a visualization of African American identity.[5] During the 1930s, New Deal agencies, the Public Works of Art Project (1933–34) and the Works Progress Administration's Federal Art Project (1934–43), sponsored

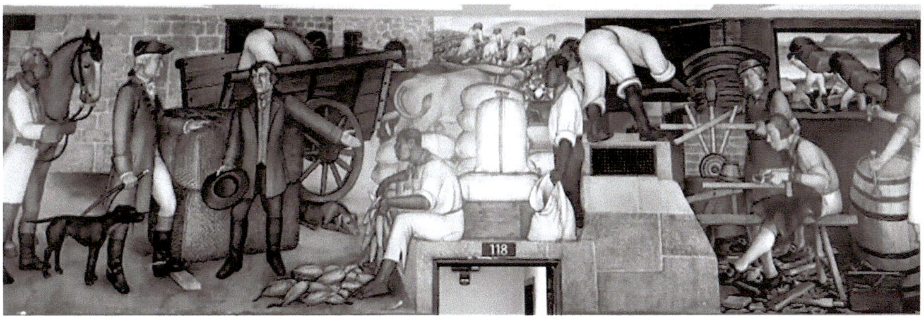

0.3. Victor Arnautoff, Washington at Mount Vernon, 1935–36, George Washington University High School, San Francisco, California. Photo: Jim Wilson/The New York Times.

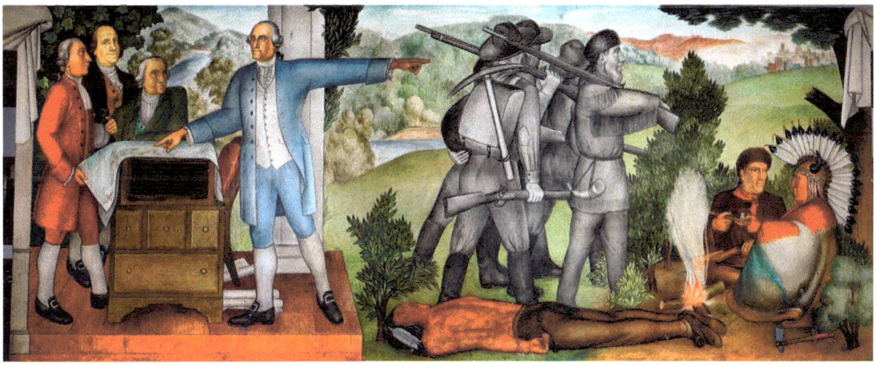

0.4. Victor Arnautoff, Washington Points West, 1935–36, George Washington University High School, San Francisco, California. Photo: Jim Wilson/The New York Times.

mural projects in public buildings, employing out-of-work artists and sparking a dramatic revival of monumental wall painting in the United States.[6] One such project, the *Life of George Washington* in the George Washington High School in San Francisco, has today aroused controversy.[7] The murals, painted in 1935–36 by the Russian émigré artist Victor Arnautoff (1896–1978), depict Black African slaves and the corpse of a Native American (Figures 0.3–0.4).[8] Unremarked at the time, today such images have prompted calls for their destruction.

The passionate debate over the Washington High School murals reminds us of the power of monumental images to shape ideas, experience, memory, and history. *Wall Painting, Civic Ceremony, and Sacred Space in Early Renaissance Italy* focuses on two interconnected themes. The first is how monumental wall paintings in the fourteenth and fifteenth centuries visualized and shaped cities' histories and identities. As social, political, and economic conditions changed, they were reflected in monumental civic images. The paintings discussed here adorn important sacred spaces – the chapel of the Holy Belt in the *pieve* (baptismal church) of Prato, the Camposanto in Pisa, and the cathedral of Spoleto.

The Virgin's Holy Belt in Prato, the hallowed ground of Pisa's monumental cemetery, and the sacred image of the *Madonna Avvocata* in Spoleto were central to the historical, institutional, and religious identities of the host cities. The mural paintings examined here visualize hallowed legends and contemporary realities. The second theme investigates the artists who traveled outside their native city to paint these murals. The exceptional stature and importance of the sacred spaces that these murals adorned led patrons to seek famous artists from abroad for these projects. Florentine artists Agnolo Gaddi, Andrea Bonaiuti, Benozzo Gozzoli, and Fra Filippo Lippi painted the murals between 1377 and 1484 at the invitation of patrons in Prato, Pisa, and Spoleto. The demand for Florentine artists was evident much earlier in the Trecento. Giotto's (c. 1267–1337) peripatetic career spanned the Italian peninsula, working in Assisi, Padua, Rome, and Naples as well as Florence. Agnolo Gaddi's father, Taddeo (c. 1300–66), completed an altarpiece for the city of Pistoia in 1353, for which the commission documents reveal the prestige attached to artists from Florence in the eyes of provincial patrons.[9] Taddeo Gaddi replaced the obscure local painter who had started the altarpiece after consideration of the most famous painters of the day in Florence and Siena. In the wake of the Black Death (1348), the patrons felt it necessary to demand a higher level of quality and prestige. In 1338, the Pratesi had also turned to the Florentine artist Bernardo Daddi (active c. 1312–48) to paint an altarpiece for the new altar housing the relic. The following chapters, centering on specific mural cycles, probe the civic value of monumental images and describe how they came to be made and how they were understood by contemporary viewers. Wedded to architecture, the murals discussed here adorned spaces for public ritual that fostered civic pride and perpetuated memory of historical events, even as they impressed through their scale and artistry. In contrast to panels painted in an artist's workshop, mural paintings were the result of artists' collaboration with scores of workers on a construction site – carpenters, masons, stonecutters, and others. Working on site, the artists were, of necessity, traveling artists, who brought assistants with them, but who also collaborated with local artisans. Documents offer a compelling picture of the complex relationships between the artists and their patrons, on the one hand, and the organization of the worksite, cooperation between local and "foreign" artisans, and adaptation to local traditions, on the other. Close reading of these documents sheds light on the meaning these murals had to multiple audiences. Mural painting, as part of the surging demand for church furnishings in the early Renaissance, adapted to its new role as public imagery by embracing new subjects and a new visual language.[10] The monumental and public nature of wall paintings such as these was a primary reason that mural painting flourished in the early Renaissance and that its practitioners were valued socially.

My research on the murals in this book is informed by the contemporary debate about the role of monumental painting in the public sphere. The vast literature about public art, including mural painting, considers it from multiple points of view, which are, in many cases, the same as those adopted in the following chapters.[11] Then as now, the site defines public art, implying monumental scale and broad access. It is bounded by architecture and linked to the urban fabric. The design of the space controlled how public images were seen, but the urban setting also determined how viewers approached the space, both physically and psychologically. Mobile viewers' visual experiences take place in time, so that the images unfolded within a larger spatio-temporal context.

The audience for public art, both intended and not, considers who has access to the art and the form and degree of their engagement and participation. Public images, such as those considered here, we can assume addressed a broad audience, including all classes of society. Examining the social roles of spaces in the civic and religious lives of cities lends insight into the make-up and reactions of audiences.

Ceremonies, both civic and liturgical, take place in public spaces. Processions penetrated the surrounding spaces and tied dedicated spaces to the wider city. These rituals, where they can be reconstructed, shed light on the form and meaning of wall painting, as described in several of the following chapters.

Patronage – who commissions and pays for the art – is especially revealing for public art. Who has the authority to determine which forms, subjects, and artists will address the public? What kind of process results in a public work or art? Recent accounts of Renaissance patronage envision it as a collaboration between the patron and his client.[12] What is the nature of that relationship, and what is the artist's share? What technical and logistical challenges confronted the artist in the execution of monumental images in each site, and how did he or she meet them? What role does the patron have in the execution of the project?

Beyond the questions involving site, audience, patron, and artist, issues in contemporary mural art might seem irrelevant to fourteenth- and fifteenth-century murals, the subject of this book. Modern and contemporary mural painting, particularly in its populist, collaborative, and temporary aspects, offers few comparisons. Certainly today, expectations for public art are different from those of the fourteenth and fifteen centuries, and art itself is utterly changed in materials, technique, style, and social function. Similarly, contemporary audiences are more diverse. In early Renaissance Italy, Jews, Muslims, slaves, and other marginal groups were not considered as potential viewers, not least because sacred stories addressed an overwhelmingly Christian audience. While the wall paintings studied here were directed at elite and non-elite audiences, the conditions of access to them were controlled through communal statute and religious practice. Even so, public art reflects the social structures, beliefs, and values of its time and place. Aspects that shaped meaning in the murals of the past are explored in the following chapters.

Renaissance mural painting began with the restoration of early Christian murals in Roman basilicas in the late thirteenth century.[13] During Pope Nicholas III Orsini's two and a half-year papacy (1277–80), the Roman artist Pietro Cavallini (c. 1240–after 1330) restored and enlarged the mural decoration of the basilica Saint Paul outside the Walls as part of an ambitious program to rejuvenate venerable early Christian sites. Nicholas's patronage included the decoration of the Sancta Sanctorum in the Lateran palace and work in Old Saint Peter's and the Vatican palace. Cavallini decorated Santa Cecilia in Trastevere with the *Last Judgment*, the most dramatic, surviving example of the new idiom to emerge from this experience, probably in the early 1290s. There, in true fresco, the artist painted massive figures rendered in vigorous chiaroscuro and brilliant color. With his contemporary Jacopo Torriti (active c. 1270–1300), author of the mosaic apses in the Lateran (1291) and Santa Maria Maggiore (1296), Cavallini may have worked in the vast decoration in the upper church of San Francesco in Assisi, which involved Tuscan artists such as Cimabue (c.1240–before 1302) and – according to some scholars – Giotto, as well as Roman ones.[14] The new style emanating from Assisi owed a substantial debt to Roman painting and patronage.

The new visual language and technique, most associated with Giotto, accompanied a new treatment of subject matter. As Belting explains, if the narrative scenes in Assisi render the life of a recent saint with telling details, the murals Giotto painted in the Arena Chapel in Padua in 1305 cast the events of Christ's life as a "drama of souls."[15] Both invite the audience's empathy and affective participation. In this, the new imagery responded to the new social function of narrative. Narrative images and monumental allegories according to Belting, "no longer told a story but served other ends: [they] became a way of arguing, of phrasing topics of general interest, a reading device." The new rhetorical function of narrative emerged at the same time as communal governments in northern and central Italy.[16] Contemporaneously, in the thirteenth century, mendicant orders such as the Dominicans and the Franciscans sprang up to serve the urban faithful.[17] Charismatic preachers told stories of the lives of Christ and the saints, appealing to worshippers' experiences and emotions. Murals lining the walls of the newly built basilicas modeled and reflected viewers' personal relationships with holy figures.

Today mural painting is most commonly associated with the Italian Renaissance, celebrated in the exhibition *The Great Age of Fresco: Giotto to Pontormo*, shown in Europe and America following the 1966 Florence flood, and Eve Borsook's *The Mural Painters of Tuscany*, first published in 1960, revised in 1980.[18] Since then a vast outpouring of books, articles, film, and digital media on mural painting has followed and is unabated today. General studies, such as the multivolume work *Italian Frescoes*, by Joachim Poeschke, Steffi Roettgen, and others, have focused on the production history, imagery, and authorship of select mural painting complexes in Italy.[19] Specific works, often following significant restoration projects, such as Michelangelo's murals in the Sistine Chapel, the murals of the life of Saint Francis in Assisi, and Giotto's Bardi and Peruzzi chapels in Santa Croce in Florence, have highlighted technical discoveries and revealed heretofore unknown aspects of their original appearance.[20]

Previously neglected in histories of mural painting, murals' social role has begun to engage scholars through investigations of patrons and audiences. Most recently, George Bent's *Public Painting and Visual Culture in Early Republican Florence* studied a broad class of public pictures in Florence from the late thirteenth until the early fifteenth century.[21] By "public" Bent means images that people belonging to all classes – from the landed aristocracy (magnates), to merchants, bankers, and artisans (the *popolo*), to the manual laborers (*sottoposti*) – would have been able to see. These included images on exterior walls of buildings and in street tabernacles, and in secular and sacred structures to which a broad public had access, such as guildhalls, confraternity meeting rooms, government offices, and spaces accessible to the laity in churches. Conversely, altarpieces and mural decoration in privately funded chapels, primarily in the mendicant churches, were blocked from public access through grilles or curtains, or they were located beyond the rood screen that sequestered spaces for the clergy. Female viewers, regardless of class, were often barred from these spaces as well. Bent's nuanced readings of public images such as Bernardo Daddi's *Madonna* in Orsanmichele (1347) and Orcagna's opulent tabernacle, which encloses it (1359), consider viewer access and response and deepen our understanding of the many ways images were seen in late medieval Florence.

Many studies of individual patrons have revealed the history of specific commissions in detail. Books and essays on Medici patronage abound; Dale Kent's study of Cosimo de' Medici and the scholarship of F. W. Kent, Laurie Fusco, and Gino Corti, on Lorenzo de' Medici, are only a few among many in a distinguished group.[22] The patronage and collecting of prominent families in and outside Florence include studies of the Spinelli and Tornabuoni among recent contributions.[23] The magisterial *The Roman Crucible* by Julian Gardner is one of the most recent studies of papal patronage.[24]

Accounts of the patronage and use of images by monastic orders, especially the mendicants, have been revelatory. Not surprisingly for an order identified with its charismatic founder, the Franciscans pioneered the use of narratives and images of its founding saint. The hagiographic scenes of Saint Francis's life in San Francesco in Assisi reestablished the centrality that monumental narrative images had enjoyed in the early Christian basilicas. Classic studies of Assisi by Belting, Stubblebine, Romano, and, most recently, Donal Cooper and Janet Robson have mined, but not exhausted, this rich topic.[25] Focused studies of Franciscan patronage by Julian Gardner and Cooper have revealed details of production and reception of specific works.[26]

Joanna Cannon's *Religious Poverty, Visual Riches* reveals a slightly different picture of Dominican patronage in central Italy in the thirteenth and fourteenth centuries.[27] Cannon's rich study addresses mural painting in the naves, apses, and private chapels in Dominican churches. She finds that monumental narrative decorations were located in the choir, where the laity had only restricted access. Private sponsorship of murals in the main chapels of Dominican churches, in contrast to that of altarpieces, was sparse. Sporadic evidence of narrative cycles survives, but variety, not consistency, characterizes these images. In private chapels, where mostly wealthy laypersons held sway, narrative murals were favored, especially in Santa Maria Novella in Florence.

My study differs from previous works in numerous ways. In the first place, the murals examined here are all civic commissions that adorn the most important sacred spaces in the city – in Prato, a reliquary chapel in the *pieve*; in Pisa, the monumental cemetery; in Spoleto, the cathedral apse. Social and political conditions in the host cities and the motivations of the patrons – insofar as they can be reconstructed – reveal how these images were understood by multiple audiences, including the clergy, the laity, civic officials, and the public. In addition, they were all painted by celebrated Florentine artists of the time, including Agnolo Gaddi, Andrea Bonaiuti, Benozzo Gozzoli, and Fra Filippo Lippi. These artists were working outside their native cities on prestigious civic commissions – the reason that patrons sought well-known artists from abroad. These works are less studied than those in Florence by scholars writing in English, and they lead us to consider the renown of individual artists, the civic value of artistic skill, and the role of artists as cultural ambassadors and instruments of civic prestige.

These projects also reveal the artisan networks that the artists deployed to execute each project. In each case, documents and the works themselves allow an in-depth, comparative study of mural painting that has not been done before. Existing records have been newly transcribed and are presented in the Appendix. Overlooked and unpublished entries offer correction and amplification to previous historical accounts and telling insights. Examining specific major fresco commissions from this perspective leads to a detailed picture of the design and execution of individual works, which, by comparison with less well-documented cycles, allows a general view of mural painting practice. Historians' discoveries about the personal and professional relationships of artisans during the period shed light on the conditions under which these mural paintings were made. Models for my work exist in the literature, such as William Wallace's account, *Michelangelo at San Lorenzo: The Genius as Entrepreneur* (1994), and his recent study, *Michelangelo, God's Architect; The Story of his Final Years and Greatest Masterpiece* (2019), although the wealth of documentation Wallace analyzes – in particular, Michelangelo's letters – does not exist for the period of my study.[28] Using technical and archival information, Wallace reveals the role stone cutters and other craftsmen played in Michelangelo's projects. This account of the cooperative enterprise of mural painting in the fourteenth and fifteenth centuries considers issues such as the relationship of the artist to his artisan collaborators as well as to his patrons.

The method adopted here is to examine selected murals in the context of their architectural setting, investigating history, technique, and procedure. In keeping with current methodologies in art history, patronage circumstances of each project, and, where possible, the audience response, are described. These case studies argue for a conception of patronage as a social negotiation among parties and the work of art as a product of contingencies that are generalizable up to a point.[29] Stakeholders, such as members of boards of works (*operai*); political leaders such as Pietro Gambacorta; clerics such as Filippo de'Medici and Berardo Eroli; masters and local artisans – played roles in the enterprise that led to the final work of art. Close reading of the documentation lends insight into how participants came together to complete these projects and allows an in-depth picture of collaboration that has not been previously available.

Chapter 1 examines Agnolo Gaddi's work between 1392 and 1395 in the chapel in Prato Cathedral, which was built to house the Virgin's Belt, the most important relic in the city. Primary sources allow reconstruction of the ceremony during which the precious relic of the Virgin's Belt was displayed to the public. The monumental narratives of the origins of the Holy Belt and its journey to Prato celebrated Prato's favored status as custodian of the relic. Detailed surviving payments, here published in full for the first time, reveal a narrative of the chapel's construction and decoration and bring to light how the artist, Agnolo Gaddi, collaborated with Florentine and Pratese artisans in the enterprise. Agnolo's professional and personal connections with the Pratese Opera, and the social identities of its members, expose a rich network of relationships in which the commission unfolded.

Chapters 2 and 3 focus on the extensive decoration of the Camposanto in Pisa, the monumental cemetery adjacent to the cathedral complex. Ceremonies associated with death, burial, and remembrance animated the vast spaces. Unlike previous assumptions of a single program that guided the mural decoration from the beginning, I propose that the wall paintings, completed during three discrete periods, reflected the changing social and religious significance of the Camposanto as a communal burial space open to all classes of Pisans. Chapter 2 examines the murals of the life of the Pisan patron Saint Rainerius, begun by Andrea Bonaiuti and completed by Antonio Veneziano in 1386. Commisssioned by Pietro Gambacorta, the *Signore* of Pisa, they celebrate Pisa's identity as a vibrant polity with a venerable history, against the backdrop of a fast-changing political reality. Chapter 3, by contrast, describes the imagery and production of the murals of the Old Testament, completed by Benozzo Gozzoli in 1484. Archbishop Filippo de' Medici's role in the commission is placed in the context of his patronage and diplomacy throughout a long career. These murals, painted during Pisa's subjection to Florence, enhanced an impressive locus of Pisan identity and pride, while signaling the political reality of Florentine control.

Chapter 4 pivots to Umbria, where Fra Filippo Lippi painted the apse decoration in the cathedral of Spoleto between 1466 and 1469. Here again, primary and secondary sources reveal the ceremonies that took place in the cathedral and highlight the relationship of the apse paintings and the venerated Madonna icon of the cathedral. The bishop of Spoleto, Berardo Eroli, played a leading role in the commission, which is set in the context of his art patronage in Umbria and Rome. From the copious documentation for the Spoleto project – here published in full for the first time – emerges evidence that Eroli conceived the Coronation murals as a magnificent setting for the Madonna icon of the cathedral and its display on holy days, especially the feast of the Virgin's Assumption on August 15. In his vision and his active involvement in the project during its execution, Eroli sought to link the Spoleto Duomo visually and liturgically with the venerable basilica of Santa Maria Maggiore in Rome.

Common themes emerge that link the chapters. All the projects decorate spaces that were stages for public ritual, in the case of Prato and Spoleto focusing on relics and icons central to the religious and civic identities of the state, and in Pisa for ceremonies for the dead. In reconstructing the ceremonies where possible, a clearer idea of multiple audiences and their degrees of engagement and participation emerges. The imagery of the murals resonated with civic meaning, particularly in the scenes from Saint Rainerius's life in Pisa and the narratives of the translation of the Virgin's Belt to Prato. Their rhetorical function in fostering civic identity and perpetuating memories of singular historical events in civic history was reinforced by monumental scale and compelling style. In the case of Pisa and Prato, the projects were carried out against the background of Florentine state building during the late Trecento and Quattrocento. Cultural patronage, often seen as a hallmark of

Lorenzo the Magnificent's reign in the late fifteenth century in Florence, extended back to the founding of the territorial state in the mid fourteenth century.[30] In Spoleto, by contrast, the visualization of its ties to Rome was a powerful determinant of the commission.

All of the projects were supervised by *Opere del Duomo*, the lay boards of works that oversaw the fabric of the cathedral complexes.[31] While the structure of the *Opere* differed from city to city, their common purpose unites the disparate projects. The *Opere* brought together clerical and lay actors, merchants, and craftsmen. The interchange of skills and ideas that took place within the deliberative bodies of the *Opere* may be a reason for the extraordinary novelty and significance of their projects. What historians of technology have called "trading zones" might be attached to these bodies and their effects part of the newly emergent phenomenon called the Renaissance.[32] Within institutional structures, individuals emerge as powerful drivers of the commissions: Pietro Gambacorta and Archbishop Filippo de' Medici in Pisa and Bishop Berardo Eroli in Spoleto. Seen through the lens of patronage, the form and meaning of the resulting decorative ensembles take on new significance.

The artists that created the murals examined here were all Florentine, and, of necessity when working on walls, they were working outside their native city. The written documentation that exists for three of the projects clarifies in vivid detail the organization of their workshops, the interaction of Florentine and local collaborators, and their networks of specialist suppliers. The artists' adaptability to specific demands of the site, local custom, and new iconographies, as much as their technical and organizational capabilities, was crucial to their appeal. Artists' identities as Florentine were demonstrably a factor in two instances, Agnolo Gaddi in Prato and Benozzo Gozzoli in Pisa; and Florentine expansion into Tuscany provides a context for these cases. Contemporary viewers in Prato and Pisa would have understood the imagery and the narrative idiom as linking the sites to Florence. Patrons sought Florentine artists for the prestige that accrued to them, both in the territorial state and in Spoleto, located in the Papal States. These prestigious projects reveal the conditions for artists' rising social stature, confirmed by documents, and they set the stage for theoretical discussions of the social role of art that would be taken up in the late fifteenth and sixteenth centuries.

NOTES

1 For the caves at Lascaux, see Norbert Aujoulat, *Lascaux: Movement, Space, and Time*, New York: Abrams, 2005. The murals of San Bartolo are discussed in William Saturno, Karl Taube, and David Stuart, *The Murals of San Bartolo, El Petén, Guatemala Part 1: The North Wall. Ancient America 7*, Barnardsville: Boundary End Archaeology Research Center, 2005; and Karl Taube, William Saturno, et al., *The Murals of San Bartolo, El Petén, Guatemala, Part 2: The West Wall. Ancient America 10*, Barnardsville: Boundary End Archaeology Research

Center, 2010. The Ajanta caves are discussed in Ratan Parimoo et al., eds: *The Art of Ajanta*, 2 vols, New Delhi: Books & Books, 1991.

2 Lawrence Nees, *Early Medieval Art*, Oxford: Oxford University Press, 2002, pp. 31–61.

3 William Tronzo, *The Via Latina Catacomb: Imitation and Discontinuity in Fourth-Century Roman Painting*, University Park, PA: Penn State University Press, 1986.

4 Herbert Kessler, "'Caput et Speculum Omnium Ecclesiarum': Old St. Peter's and Church Decoration in Medieval Latium," in William Tronzo, ed., *Italian Church Decoration of the Middle Ages and Early Renaissance*, Bologna: Nuova Alfa, 1989, pp. 119–46.

5 Michael Harris, "Urban Totems: The Communal Spirit of Black Murals," in James Prigoff and Robin Dunitz, eds., *Walls of Heritage, Walls of Pride: African American Murals*, Rohnert Park: Pomegranate Communications, 2000, pp. 24–30, 63; Rebecca Zorach, *Art for People's Sake: Artists and Community in Black Chicago*, 1965–1975, Durham: Duke University Press, 2019, pp. 56–84.

6 Marlene Park and Gerald Markowitz, "New Deal for Public Art," in Harriet Senie and Sally Webster, eds., *Critical Issues in Public Art: Content, Context and Controversy*, Washington DC: Smithsonian Institution Press, 1992, pp. 128–41; Cher Krause Knight, *Public Art: Theory, Practice and Populism*, Oxford: Basil Blackwell, 2008, pp. 1–8.

7 "San Francisco Will Spend $600,000 to Erase History," *New York Times*, June 28, 2021, www.nytimes.com/2019/08/14/arts/san-francisco-murals-george-washington.html. This decision has been reversed: "San Francisco School Board Reverses Vote on Mural Removal," *New York Times*, June 23, 2022, www.nytimes.com/2022/06/23/arts/design/san-francisco-george-washington-mural.html.

8 Suzanne Woodbury Lombardi, "Politics and Humanism in the Depression Era Frescoes of Victor Arnautoff," MA thesis, University of California, Berkeley, 1984, pp. 33–46; Robert Cherny, *Victor Arnautoff and the Politics of Art*, Urbana: University of Illinois Press, 2017, pp. 108–10.

9 Andrew Ladis, *Taddeo Gaddi*, Columbia: University of Missouri Press, 1982, pp. 58–61, 159–66, cat. no. 19; p. 255, doc. 49.

10 Richard Goldthwaite, *Wealth and the Demand for Art in Italy, 1300–1600*, Baltimore: Johns Hopkins University Press, 1993, pp. 70–81.

11 Cher Krause Knight and Harriet Senie, "A Companion to Public Art: Introduction," in Cher Krause Knight and Harriet F. Senie, eds., *A Companion to Public Art*, Cichester: John Wiley & Sons, 2016, pp. 1–22.

12 Jonathan Nelson and Richard Zeckhauser, "Patrons, Artists and Audiences," in Jonathan Nelson and Richard Zeckhauser, eds., *The Patron's Payoff: Conspicuous Commissions in Italian Renaissance Art*, Princeton: Princeton University Press, 2008, pp. 17–35.

13 Serena Romano, *Apogeo e fine del medioevo 1288–1431*, Milan: Jaca Book, 2017, pp. 13–24; Julian Gardner, *The Roman Crucible, The Artistic Patronage of the Papacy 1198–1304*, Munich: Hirmer Verlag, 2013, pp. 245–302; see also Eve Borsook, *The Mural Painters of Tuscany*, 2nd ed., Oxford: Clarendon Press, 1980, pp. xxii–xxiv.

14 Bruno Zanardi, *Giotto e Pietro Cavallini*, Milan: Skira, 2002; Donal Cooper and Janet Robson, *The Making of Assisi*, New Haven and London: Yale University Press, 2013, p. 12, have proposed the period from May 1288 to May 1297 as the chronological range for the nave murals – including the vaults, Old and New Testament scenes and the Life of Saint Francis – in San Francesco.

15 Hans Belting, "The New Role of Narrative in Public Painting of the Trecento: *Historia* and Allegory," in H. Kessler et al., eds., *Pictorial Narrative in Antiquity and the Middle Ages*, Washington, DC: National Gallery of Art, 1985, pp. 51–170; see also Joachim Poeschke, "On the Perception and Effect of Images in the Age of Giotto," in *Italian Frescoes: The Age of Giotto 1280–1400*, New York: Abbeville Press, 2005, pp. 9–13.

16 Helene Wieruszowski, "Art and the Commune in the Time of Dante," *Speculum*, vol. 19, 1944, pp. 14–33; Hans Belting and Dieter Blume, eds., *Malerei und Stadtkultur in der Dantezeit: Die Argumentation der Bilder*, Munich: Hirmer Verlag, 1989.

17 The literature on the visual culture of the mendicant orders is vast; see for the Franciscans, Dieter Blume, *Wandmalerei als Ordenspropaganda: Bildprogramme in Chorbereich franziskanischer Konvente Italiens bis zur Mitte des 14. Jahrhunderts*, Worms: Werner'sche Verlagsgesellschaft, 1983; Louise Bourdua, *The Franciscans and Art Patronage in late Medieval Italy*, Cambridge: Cambridge University Press, 2004. Studies of Dominican patronage have focused on specific monuments such as Santa Maria Novella in Florence; see most recently Andrea De Marchi, ed., *Santa Maria Novella; La Basilica e il Convento*, vol. 1, Florence: Mandragora, 2015.

18 Millard Meiss, Ugo Procacci, et al., *The Great Age of Fresco: Giotto to Pontormo*, New York: The Metropolitan Museum of Art, 1968; Eve Borsook, *The Mural Painters of Tuscany*, 2nd ed., Oxford: Clarendon Press, 1980.

19 Poeschke, *Italian Frescoes: The Age of Giotto 1280–1400*; Steffi Roettgen, *Italian Frescoes*, trans. Russell Stockman, 2 vols., New York: Abbeville Press, 1996–1997; Julian Kliemann, Michael Rohlmann, et al., *Italian Frescoes: High Renaissance and Mannerism, 1510–1600*, trans. Steven Lindberg, New York: Abbeville Press, 2004; Steffi Roettgen, *Italian Frescoes: The Baroque Era 1600–1800*, trans. Russell Stockman, New York: Abbeville Press, 2007.

20 Fabrizio Mancinelli et al., *Michelangelo: La Cappella Sistina*, 3 vols., Città del Vaticano: Edizioni Musei Vaticani, 1994; Carlo Pietrangeli et al., *The Sistine Chapel; A Glorious Restoration*, New York: Abrams, 1994; Leonetto Tintori and Millard Meiss, *The Painting of the Life of St. Francis in Assisi, with Notes on the Arena Chapel*, New York: New York University, Institute of Fine Arts Conservation Center, 1962; Bruno Zanardi, *Il cantiere di Giotto: Le storie di San Francesco ad Assisi*, Milan: Skira, 1996; Cecilia Frosinini, ed., *Progetto Giotto: Tecnica artistica e stato di conservazione delle pitture murali nelle cappelle Peruzzi e Bardi a Santa Croce*, Florence: Edifir, 2016–17.

21 George Bent, *Public Painting and Visual Culture in Early Republican Florence*, Cambridge: Cambridge University Press, 2016.

22 Dale Kent, *Cosimo de' Medici and the Florentine Renaissance: The Patron's Oeuvre*, New Haven and London: Yale University Press, 2000; Francis W. Kent, *Lorenzo de' Medici and the Art of Magnificence*, Baltimore and London: Johns Hopkins University Press, 2004; Laurie Smith Fusco and Gino Corti, *Lorenzo de' Medici, Collector and Antiquarian*, Cambridge: Cambridge University Press, 2006; Francis W. Kent, *Princely Citizen: Lorenzo de' Medici and Renaissance Florence*, ed. Carolyn James, Turnhout: Brepols, 2013.

23 Other studies of family patronage include Maria DePrano, *Art Patronage, Family and Gender in Renaissance Florence: The Tornabuoni*, Cambridge: Cambridge University Press, 2018. Individual patrons such as Giovanni Rucellai, Tommaso di Lionardo Spinelli, and Francesco Sassetti have been the focus of books by Francis W. Kent, Brenda Preyer, and others; Philip Jacks and William Caferro and Eve Borsook and Johannes Offerhaus, respectively.

24 Gardner, *The Roman Crucible.*

25 Hans Belting, *Die Oberkirche von San Francesco in Assisi: Ihre Dekoration als Aufgabe die Genese einer neuen Wandmalereien*, Berlin: 1977; Joachim Poeschke: *Die Kirche San Francesco in Assisi und ihre Wandmalereien*, Munich: Hirmer 1985; James. H. Stubblebine: *Assisi and the Rise of Vernacular Art*, New York, 1985; Serena Romano, *La basilica di San Francesco ad Assisi: Pittori, botteghe, strategie narrative*, Rome: Viella, 2001; Cooper and Robson, *The Making of Assisi.*

26 Julian Gardner, *Giotto and His Publics: Three Paradigms of Patronage*, Cambridge, MA: Harvard University Press, 2011; Donal Cooper, "Redefining the Altarpiece in Early Renaissance Italy: Giotto's 'Stigmatization of Saint Francis' and Its Pisan Context," in *Art History*, vol 36, 2013, pp. 686–713.

27 Joanna Cannon, *Religious Poverty, Visual Riches: Art in the Dominican Churches of Central Italy in the Thirteenth and Fourteenth Centuries*, New Haven and London: Yale University Press, 2013.

28 William Wallace, *Michelangelo at San Lorenzo: The Genius as Entrepreneur*, Cambridge: Cambridge University Press, 1994; William Wallace, *Michelangelo, God's Architect; The Story of his Final Years and Greatest Masterpiece*, Princeton: Princeton University Press, 2019.

29 Creighton Gilbert, "What Did the Renaissance Patron Buy?," *Renaissance Quarterly*, vol. 51, 1998, pp. 392–93.

30 Caroline Elam, "Art and Diplomacy in Renaissance Florence," *RSA Journal*, vol. 136, 1988, pp. 813–26.

31 See in particular Margaret Haines, ed., *Opera: carattere e ruolo delle fabbriche cittadine fino all'inizio dell'età moderna*, Florence: Olschki, 1996.

32 Pamela O. Long, *Artisan/Practitioners and the Rise of the New Sciences 1400–1600*, Corvallis: Oregon State University Press, 2011, pp. 94–96.

CHAPTER ONE

"LARGER, MORE ORNATE, AND MORE SEEMLY"

Agnolo Gaddi and the Chapel of the Holy Belt in Prato

On Palm Sunday, 4 April 1395, Alberto di ser Bartolomeo, the vicar of the church of Santo Stefano in Prato, transported the relic of the Virgin's Belt from a cramped space in the south aisle of the church across the nave to a newly built and sumptuously decorated chapel. Accompanied by song and blazing candles, Bishop Andrea Franchi then displayed the Belt to the attending officials of the city and church and to visiting bishops and clerics from near and far. Throngs of worshippers from Florence, Lucca, Pistoia, Arezzo, and other towns in the Arno valley flocked to witness the event and to enjoy the indulgences granted by Pope Boniface IX (r. 1389–1404) in its honor.[1]

The inauguration of the new chapel was the culmination of a decades-long effort by church and city officials to construct a secure and decorous setting for the display of Prato's most precious relic. This chapter presents a narrative of the chapel's construction and decoration, concentrating on murals by Agnolo Gaddi (active 1369–96) of the *Life of the Virgin* and the *Legend of the Holy Belt*.[2] A close reading of the surviving documentation, published in full for the first time in the Appendix, shows how Agnolo collaborated with an expansive network of artisans and laborers to complete his task. They also describe Agnolo's relationship to the patron of the chapel, the lay board of works of the church. Agnolo's earlier career in Florence set the stage for his employment in Prato by forging ties with patrons and other artisan contemporaries and, most importantly, by establishing his stature as one of the foremost mural painters in Florence.

In addition to the history of the chapel construction and decoration, surviving primary and secondary sources divulge the principal ceremonies that took place in the chapel and adjacent spaces. These rites show that the chapel was the stage for the most important civic rituals that celebrated Prato's history and identity. The narrative decoration visualized the commune's special relationship with the Virgin, whose Holy Belt was preserved in the chapel. The gift of the Belt was the unifying idea in the chapel imagery, reflecting the nexus of favor and obligation that gift giving activates. Agnolo's images relate to other prestigious Marian shrines in Tuscany, particularly in Florence, drawing the Holy Belt into a network of Tuscan relics and miraculous images and signaling the political reality of Prato's absorption into the Florentine regional state.

THE HOLY BELT AND ITS ALTAR

The Virgin's Belt was not the only relic in the church of Santo Stefano (Figure 1.1), but it was the most venerable. Its history dates to biblical times, when, according to legend, as the Virgin ascended to heaven, she gave it to the doubting apostle Thomas as proof of her corporeal presence.[3] In 1141, a Pratese pilgrim brought the Belt from Jerusalem to Prato. On his death about 1170, he entrusted the relic to the provost and canons of the *pieve* (baptismal church) of Santo Stefano.[4] Devotion to the Holy Belt grew throughout the thirteenth century, especially focused on 8 September, the Virgin's birthday, when the relic was displayed to the faithful.[5] At the same time, the ostentation of the Holy Belt became an important civic celebration that coincided with the three-day Prato fair; both events attracted farmers, tradesmen, and worshippers from all over Tuscany.[6] The ceremony, described by Giovanni Miniati in the sixteenth century as a "pompous, honorable and devout spectacle," in which city officials, clerics, and lay members of the board of the cathedral took part, "with a quantity of torches, candles, lamps and incense," is celebrated in Prato to this day.[7] In commissioning a new chapel to house the relic, the *operai* (overseers) of the Sacra Cintola were concerned to provide a secure storage for the Belt and to accommodate the ceremony of the ostentation and its multiple audiences.

From the late thirteenth century, the Holy Belt rested in the "altar of the Virgin" in the *pieve*, in front of the choir, near the pulpit *in cornu evangeli*, that is, on the left or north side.[8] From this altar it was also shown on 8 September and at Easter. In 1301, payments were recorded for a temporary wooden pulpit to be constructed on the exterior south wall of the *pieve*, near the campanile, for display of the relic to worshippers assembled in the piazza.[9] In this way, the throngs of the devout, only fractionally accommodated in the *pieve*, could participate in the rite.

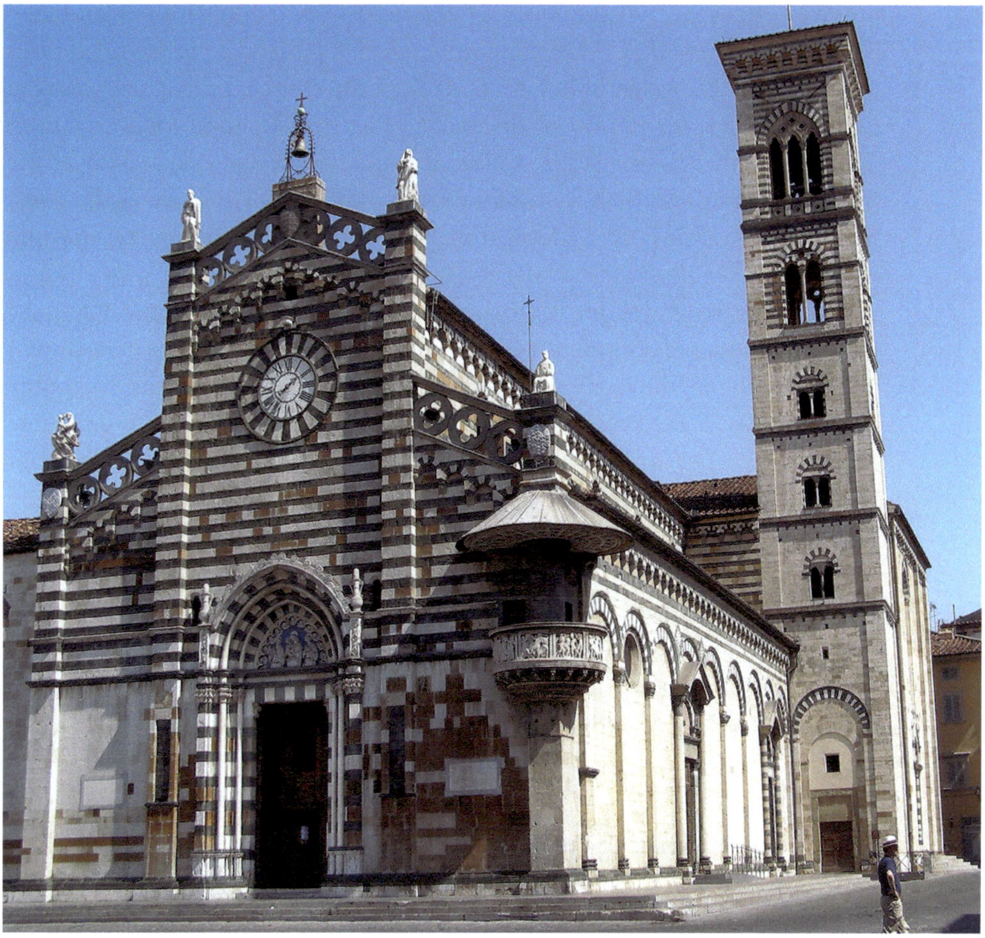

1.1. Duomo di Santo Stefano, Prato. Photo: Sara Mannelli/Creative Commons Attribution-Share Alike 4.0 International.

In 1312, an attempted theft of the relic dramatically revealed the old altar's inadequacy. The unsuccessful theft confirmed the power of the Belt and focused civic attention on its physical housing and display.[10] The incident, described in detail in poetry and prose, involved Giovanni di ser Landetto, called Muschiattino, from Pistoia.[11] The day after the trial of Muschiattino, 29 July 1312, the General Council of the commune decided to construct a new altar for the safe custody and display of the Sacred Belt. They planned to enlarge the *pieve* dramatically by extending the tribune to the east and by constructing more ample transepts. Scholars debate the exact location of the new altar for the Belt, but we know it was to be in the renovated eastern spaces of the church.[12] Payments for the work on the enlarged *pieve* and construction of the new altar for the Holy Belt extended from 1317 to 1322, and the work may have gone on much longer.[13] By 1338, however, when a new altarpiece by Bernardo Daddi was installed – the predella and pediment of which survive – the relic and ceremonies connected with it must have been transferred to the new altar.[14] Documents between 1330 and 1339 recorded plans for a new marble pulpit on the south flank of the church, probably toward the western corner, for display of the Belt.[15] The new location for ostentations likely responded to the newly enlarged piazza to the west and south of the church. This structure was not finished, but by 1360 a marble pulpit there was recorded. Remains of a door from the interior to the pulpit are still discernable.[16]

The enlarged setting for the Belt was used for only a short time. After the commune assumed control in 1346, the relic and its altar were transferred away from the tribune, the locus of clerical activity, to a chapel in the first bay of the south aisle, near the pulpit used for its display.[17] The new location had more than convenience to recommend it, however; it also signaled the ascendant power of the commune, located to the south several blocks at the Piazza Comunale, newly constructed in the late thirteenth century. The new chapel for the Holy Belt was, however, much smaller than the previous chapel. Indeed, the agreement between communal authorities and the clergy alluded to a future enlarged and embellished setting for the relic. An inventory of the chapel, datable to 1390, listed quantities of objects in the space of a single aisle bay, giving rise to the impression of a cramped, provisional space.[18]

THE OSTENTATION CEREMONY

Apart from secure storage for the Belt, the new chapel would have to accommodate the attending officials mandated by statute during ostentations, as well as repeated displays to the crowds of devout. No eyewitness account of the ostentation ceremony and the festivities connected to the fair survives from the time of chapel construction, but evidence gathered from communal records, statutes, chronicles, guidebooks, and literary works permits a general view (Figure 1.2).[19]

On 7 September, the first day of the fair and the vigil of the Virgin's birthday,[20] representatives of Tuscan towns, including the Florentine signoria, honored the communal officials of Prato, the Eight *Difensori* and the *Gonfaloniere di Giustizia*.[21] Seated under the loggia of the Palazzo Comunale,[22] the officials and the attendant crowds heard the musical tributes of trumpeters and pipers attired in brightly colored dress.[23] Special guards for the palace, from the village of Montalbiolo near Carmignano, carried the arms of the Pratese commune, a golden lily on a red field. In the evening, at vespers, a procession comprising secular and regular clergy, the musicians of the commune and surrounding towns, the guilds, the Eight, the *Gonfaloniere*, the *Podestà*, and other magistrates progressed from the *pieve* through the city.[24] An eighteenth-century source describes the itinerary: from the *pieve* to the

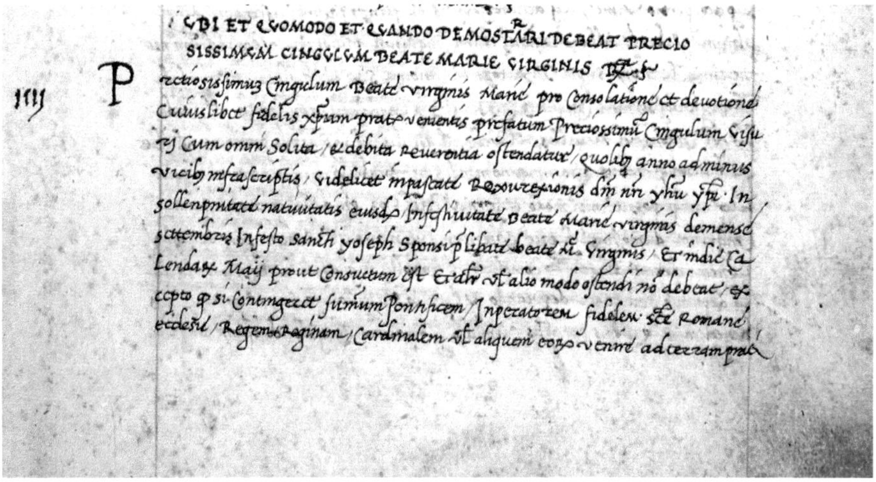

1.2. Communal Statutes, Prato, 1505, Rubric 4: Ubi e Quomodo et Quando Demostrari Debeat Precioissimum Cingulum Beate Marie Virginis (detail); Florence, Archivio di Stato, Statuti delle comunità automome e soggette, 568, c. 3 recto. Photo: Florence, Archivio di Stato.

bishop's palace (formerly the Palazzo della Propositura), to the Canto alla Fortuna (part of current-day via Cesare Guasti from the Piazza San Domenico to the intersection of via Luigi Muzzi and via Banchelli) through Banchi (also part of via Guasti), via delle Carceri (part of the present-day via Benedetto Cairoli from the Piazza Comunale to the via Pugliesi, just opposite Piazza Santa Maria delle Carceri) to Pozzo Nuovo (part of current day via Giuseppe Verdi between the vicolo Fior di Vetta and via Cairoli), Cantaccio (the intersection of present-day via Garibaldi with the via dei Tintori), through the Borgo al Cornio (via Garibaldi), and back to the Duomo (see map, Figure 1.3).[25] This route passed by civic and religious landmarks of the city, including the churches of San Domenico and Santa Maria delle Carceri, the Piazza Comunale, the city prison, as well as the residences of prominent citizens.[26] While the actual route may have varied over time, the linking of prominent sites with the communal and religious power centers was a constant.[27]

On their return to the church, the officers of the villages of the countryside placed their offerings of large wax candles on the altar of the Cintola.[28] Finally, the *pieve* remained open for the entire night to allow the veneration – and the lodging – of the crowds. Specially designated citizens elected by the commune kept order, while others tended specially erected torches in the piazza outside.[29]

The next day, the feast of the *Madonna del Settembre*, a similar procession with musicians accompanied the magistrates from the Palazzo del Podestà to the *pieve* for the solemn function of the ostentation. As they reached the chapel of the Cintola, the Eight, the *Gonfaloniere di Giustizia*, and the officers of the

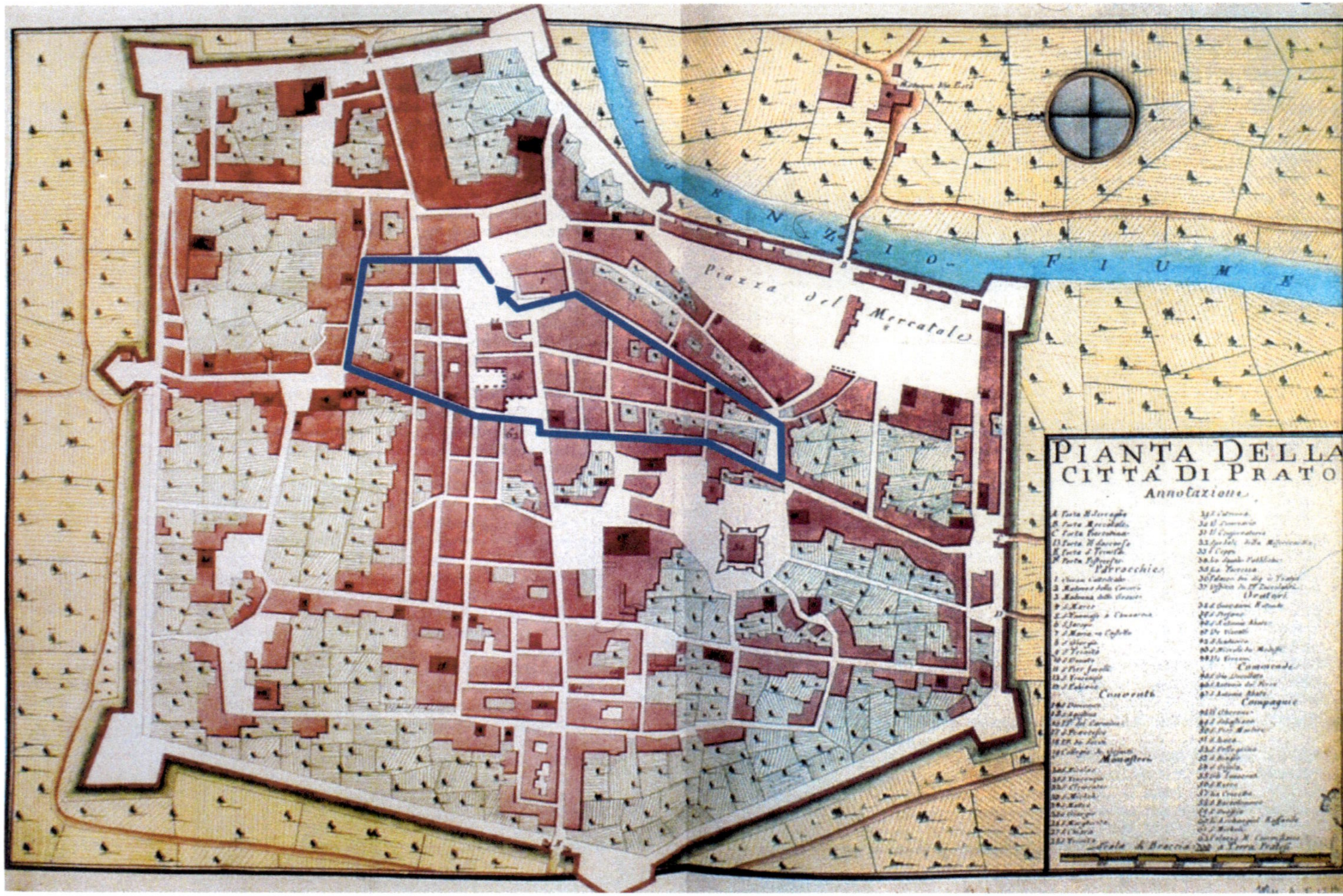

1.3. Map of Prato, mid-eighteenth century, Manoscritti, A. 1. 13[14], Biblioteca Nazionale Centrale, Florence, with processional route. Photo: Creative Commons Attribution-Share Alike 4.0 International CC-BY-SA-4.0.

guilds and neighborhoods of the city placed offerings of wax and coin on the altar.[30] The ceremony of the ostentation followed the offerings. To meet the clamor of the devout, the ceremony was repeated three times, at the canonical hours prime, terce, and vespers (6 and 9 a.m. and 6 p.m., respectively).

The ostentation ceremony evolved into a civic ritual imbued with political significance. The pomp of the ceremony and the splendor of the setting reflected and shaped Prato's identity as guardian of the Sacred Belt by providing a focus for community pride and religious devotion and by constructing and sustaining social memory.[31]

From earliest times, city statute rigidly prescribed participation in the ostentation ceremony to balance communal and clerical roles.[32] While statutes from the late thirteenth century suggest the primary role of the provost and canons of the *pieve* (collectively called the *prepositura*),[33] by 1330, statutes codify the shared responsibility for the security and ostentation of the relic.[34] According to these, only the provost of the *pieve*, with two of the most ancient and worthy canons, and two other clerics elected by the *Gonfaloniere* and the Eight *Difensori*, as well as the Eight and *Gonfaloniere* themselves, were permitted to assist in the rite. Only those permitted by the *Gonfaloniere* and *Difensori* could touch the relic, on pain of a 100 lire fine and loss of office.

The careful division of responsibility meted out by the statute of 1330 ruptured in 1346, when secular authorities wrested control of the relic from the provost of the *pieve*.[35] Motivated by "zeal and devotion" to the relic, this group secured its possession for the "commune and the all the people of the city of Prato." The desire to control what had become the symbol of Prato's civic identity as much as to claim the rich stream of offerings made by the faithful inspired the move.[36] Pope Clement VI (r. 1342–52) intervened, sending a letter from Avignon on 1 September 1350 to a commission formed to mediate the dispute and set new terms for the conservation of the Holy Belt.[37] Also because of this event, the Opera della Sacra Cintola was created.[38] The Opera was the lay board that directed the operations of the baptismal church of Santo Stefano and controlled its relic, the Virgin's Belt. The commune elected four *operai* and charged them with the custody of the relic and the management of the alms and bequests made in its honor. As laypersons or clerics external to the *pieve*, their responsibilities vis-à-vis the *prepositura* were stipulated in an agreement reached in 1351.

THE NEW CHAPEL

The Opera began construction of a new chapel in 1385 to enhance and legitimize its control of the relic. Land to the north of the *pieve* was given to the Opera in order to "build a new chapel and sacristy in honor of God and his blessed mother the Virgin Mary and to honor her most precious Belt."[39]

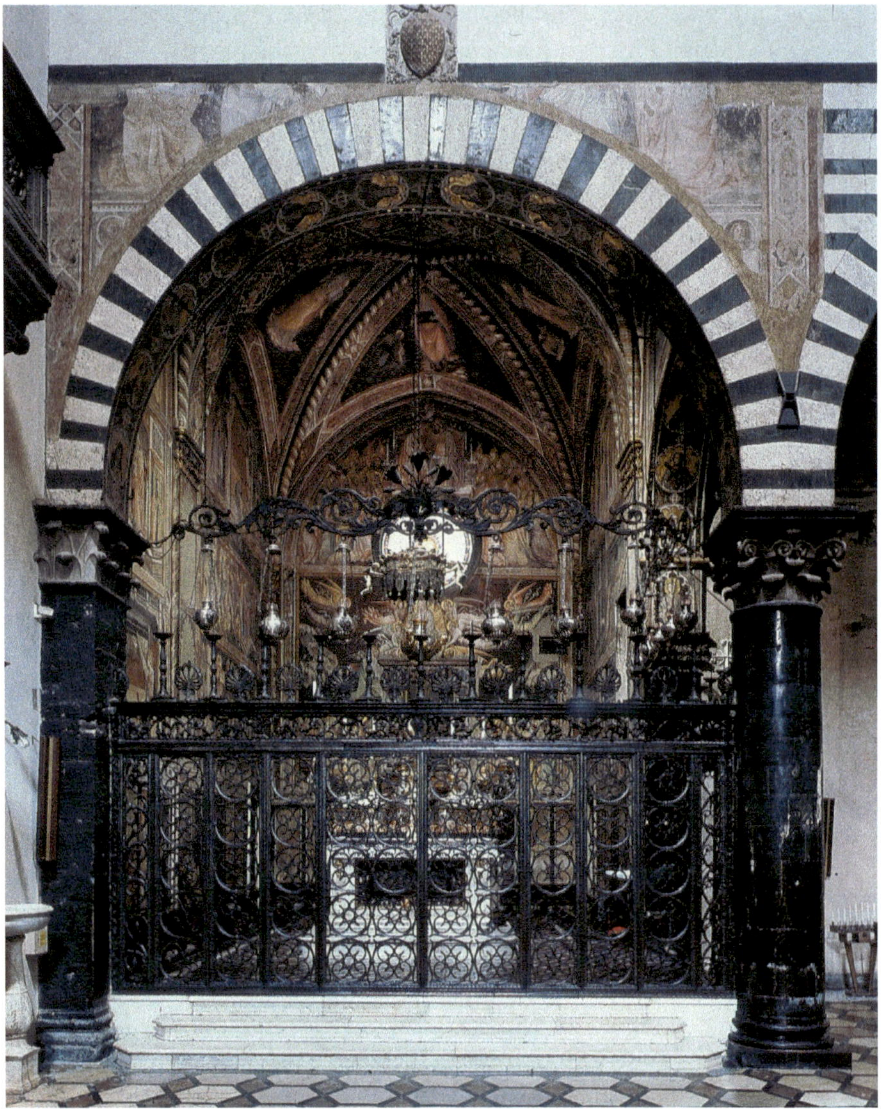

1.4. Chapel of the Holy Belt, 1386–95, Duomo di Santo Stefano, Prato. Photo: Author.

Documents kept by the Opera della Sacra Cintola record construction of the chapel beginning in January 1386.[40] The new chapel, directly across the nave from the previous one, comprised two groin-vaulted bays, the northern one larger than the southern, entrance bay, whose dimensions were fixed by the preexisting aisle (Figure 1.4). The arched entrances to the central nave and the north aisle were open. The location and function of the chapel recalled in its design that of San Jacopo in Pistoia, which housed the relic of Saint James. Provost Bartolomeo Franchi may have wanted to link the Holy Belt to prestigious relics in Pistoia, of which Prato was a dioscese and where his brother was bishop.[41]

Originally, the chapel was lit by a double window in the north wall, the remains of which are still seen on the outside wall. A door in the west wall led to a corridor that connected the chapel with the external pulpit on the southwest angle of the church, as well as an internal pulpit on the inner façade, while another door on the east wall led to the new sacristy.[42]

By 1390, the structural parts of the chapel were finished, but work continued with the construction of a new altar and the decoration of the walls with mural painting.[43] The consecration of the chapel was celebrated on Palm Sunday, 4 April 1395, with the translation of the Holy Belt to its new setting. In attendance were Andrea Franchi, the bishop of Pistoia, among other bishops and abbots, the provost Bartolomeo Franchi, the other canons and chaplains, as well as the *Podestà*, *Gonfaloniere*, Priors, and Counselors. The altar itself, made of marble and including a recess accessed from a door at the side, was consecrated five months later, on 5 September 1395.[44]

THE PRATO OPERA AND ITS ARTISANS

The festive inauguration of the new chapel of the Holy Belt marked the conclusion of major work on the construction and decoration, and the *operai* may have felt that their needs had been well met: the new chapel was a sumptuous setting for the preservation of the relic and a worthy theater for the civic ritual of its display. The documents detail the progress of construction and decoration and reveal the identities of the artisans involved.

Beginning in January of 1386, led by the *operai* Nicholaio di Bernardo and Ridolfo di Nicolaio Manassei, the Florentine architect Lorenzo di Filippo, who was *capomaestro* (foreman) of the Loggia della Signoria from 1378 to 1395 and became *capomaestro* of the Florentine cathedral in 1384, came to Prato to consult on preliminary work for the new chapel.[45] An engineering specialist at Florence cathedral, he supervised the erection of the piers of the octagon and the construction of the arches. In Prato, his first task was to design piers supporting the walls of the new chapel and sacristy to the north of the existing aisle bay where the new chapel was to be built.[46] On 20 January, he returned to inspect the foundation of the piers, which had been constructed by masons from Prato.[47] This pattern of design oversight by artisans from Florence, with the labor of construction carried out by local craftsmen, continued throughout the construction of the chapel. Lorenzo would come for a few days to Prato, usually accompanied by an assistant. For example, he returned on 11 February 1386, "in the service to the Opera," and on 15 April, "to see the work in the chapel."[48] On 3 May 1386, he returned for two days to "prepare the work and to mark out the design."[49] He came back with other masters on 25 August 1386 "to build a stone wall to mark out the said work," and again on 23 February 1387 for two days "to prepare certain things for the chapel."[50]

The summer was occupied with vaulting the chapel: Lorenzo came for two days in July "to prepare the work of the vaults with his companion [Michele Pavoli] who is making the capitals," for two days in September for the same purpose, and for two days in November "to survey how it might be possible to make the vault of the chapel higher."[51] In December 1387, Lorenzo came to Prato "to see how high the roof and the compartment [compasso] of the chapel must go." For most of 1388, work centered on the vaults, roof, and windows; Lorenzo appeared only 13 July 1390 after the *operai* sent for him "to inform themselves of certain things in the chapel."[52] By then, the structural work had been completed, but Lorenzo again was sought by the *operai* on 30 April 1392 "to place and determine the foundation of the door of the chapel," and on 21 July 1394, when he came to Prato "to consult on the altar and the entrance of the chapel."[53] Lorenzo's supervision was continuous, though not intrusive, during the more than eight-year period of construction.

Florentine artisans carved the chapel's architectural details as well. We find listed in the payment records Giovani *lastraiuolo* – the sculptor Giovanni d'Ambrogio, who succeeded Lorenzo as Florentine cathedral *capomaestro* in 1401 – who, between 1386 and 1389, was paid for carving various architectural components for the door frames, arches, and stairs of the new chapel and sacristy, as well as "for two shields with the arms of the commune."[54] He had no need to come to Prato, as he worked in Florence and shipped the completed pieces to Prato. On several occasions he did come, however, to install the frame for the window in the chapel, to give advice on the design of pilasters, to take measurements for capitals, to consult on the design of the altar - the latter in company of Lorenzo di Pietro – and, in May of 1395, to install the altar.[55] Giovanni, one of the major stone carvers at the Florentine Duomo, who later worked on the Porta della Mandorla, may have worked after drawings by Lorenzo, who as *capomaestro* was responsible for producing designs and templates. Other carvers, including the Florentine stone carver Michele Pavoli, who was paid for two capitals and two bases of *pietra forte* in 1386, and a certain Romolo da Firenze, who carved figurative marble elements in the same year, certainly did.[56] Their names occur repeatedly in the documents through the period of construction, up to 1390, while the records make clear that Lorenzo invented the designs and supervised the work. In one payment to Michele Pavoli, the Opera chamberlain acted "according to how the master Lorenzo da Firenze decided."[57] While the carvers were paid by the piece or by the length, Lorenzo earned a daily salary, plus his expenses for transportation and housing.

The employment in Prato of artisans drawn from the Florentine cathedral worksite was not unusual in the fourteenth century. The Florentine Opera del Duomo, a board of trustees made up of secular citizens, was charged with the supervision of the cathedral and other city monuments, but it also functioned as a "public works" institution.[58] Artisans employed by the Opera, including *capomaestri* of the Florentine Duomo, participated in projects such as the construction of fortifications and new towns in the Florentine countryside.[59] Lorenzo di Filippo, in a document reinstating him as *capomaestro* after a brief suspension, was specifically required to reside in the city.[60] Conceivably this provision was invoked in response to his work in Prato.[61] Local Pratese masons and stonecutters undertook more routine tasks. The documents list other masters, such as "Giacheri master, Domenicho Ghuiduci, Piero delle Donne, all stone masters."[62] A certain Jacopo da Como also worked as a stonecutter.[63] Wallers Chimenti del maestro Ghino e compagni, from a group of wallers employed on Prato's city walls, also helped build the walls of the chapel and installed the coats of arms that were above the arch of the chapel.[64]

Unlike the workers charged with the chapel construction, the painters engaged to decorate the new chapel worked in a completely different way, mainly because the work had to be done on site. In addition, the artisans employed were not "on loan" from the Florentine Opera but directly employed by the Pratese Opera della Sacra Cintola. While the Florentine Opera del Duomo employed masons, stonecutters, and carpenters, often over many years, it employed no painter continuously, as far as we can tell from extant records.[65] Painters were engaged for specific tasks that were often widely spaced in time. The rare exception to this pattern was for painters acting in other capacities, as, for example, Giotto, who was *capomaestro* during the construction of the cathedral and the beginning phases of the campanile. Giotto's appointment as *capomaestro* on the death of Arnolfo di Cambio in 1334 was likely an expression of his enormous prestige as an artist, more than his technical skills as a builder or carver.[66] In the period that predates the emergence of architecture as a profession, Giotto's skills in design, which may have included mastery of the constructive geometry used by medieval builders, and in the management of a large workshop, were seen as transferable to a building site.[67] As architectural historians have noted, in Italy beginning in the thirteenth century, design expertise was separated from construction know-how; the architect was responsible for aesthetic choices, while the master builder was in charge of construction.[68] Builders of the cathedrals of Siena, Orvieto, and Florence were sculptors or painters rather than building professionals. In Florence, once the final design for the cathedral nave and tribune was established in 1367, the *capomaestro* acted more like the supervisor of the building workforce than a designer.[69]

The varying terms of employment among sculptors and painters at the Opera seem to have resulted from the nature of the work undertaken in the cathedral in the late Trecento, which was focused on architectural and sculptural projects.[70] The possibility of long-term employment offered to sculptors and builders by the Opera del Duomo was a distinct career advantage they enjoyed that was not open to painters.[71]

We know from copious documentation that survives in the Florentine Opera archive that the workforce was highly structured. Sculptors of large-scale figures, either in the round or set into an architectural matrix, were hired on a project-by-project basis and paid a fixed sum, while carvers of architectural moldings or figurative ornament worked by the day or were paid on a piecework basis.[72] The terms of these elite sculptors' employment seem closer to those of the painters, except that they frequently worked from designs supplied by painters, signaling a standing in the Opera bureaucracy closer to the stone carvers of decorative moldings, who followed the *capomaestro*'s designs. Payment to figurative sculptors and painters were computed in gold florins rather than silver or copper coin, also suggesting their enhanced status.[73]

Agnolo's employment by the Florentine Opera del Duomo – both before and after his work in Prato – seems to be typical of the relationship the Opera had with painters. He performed a variety of services from 1383 until just before his death in 1396. Primarily, he supplied designs for work in sculpture or stained glass. The earliest dates from 1383, when Agnolo was paid for designs for figures of Virtues to serve as models for sculpture to be placed on the Loggia della Signoria (Figure 1.5).[74] They were set in trilobe frames against a backdrop of blue mosaic supplied by the glass master Don Leonardo di Simone, a Vallombrosan friar who would also collaborate with Agnolo in the chapel of the Holy Belt in Prato.[75]

Agnolo also supplied designs for the Duomo façade. In 1387, he designed a figure to be carved by Piero di Giovanni Tedesco, part of a series of apostles for the Duomo, and in 1395, he also supplied designs for four figures sculpted by Piero di Giovanni Tedesco and Niccolò di Pietro Lamberti, part of a different campaign of figurative sculpture.[76] Also for the Duomo, Agnolo designed figures and chose the colors for stained-glass windows.[77] In 1395, he and his associate, Nerio d'Antonio, collected the considerable sum of fifteen florins for painting, presumably in fresco, the splay for a window that had been made by Don Leonardo.[78] In the same year, he collaborated with Giuliano d'Arrigo, called Pesello, to supply designs for the new funerary monument to John Hawkwood (who had died in 1394) and the rebuilt monument to Pietro Farnese, a *condottiere* active in the Florentine war against Pisa in the 1360s.[79]

Agnolo's work for the Opera was wide-ranging and concentrated on design work. While the records are sometimes ambiguous, it seems clear that the Opera sought his expertise in figure design and color and that he was relatively well paid for it. How closely sculptors followed his drawings is open to question, but it seems unlikely that they entirely disregarded Agnolo's inventions.[80] Analysis of the role of drawings at the Opera, as well as visual inspection of figures Agnolo designed, point to his authorship. Taken together,

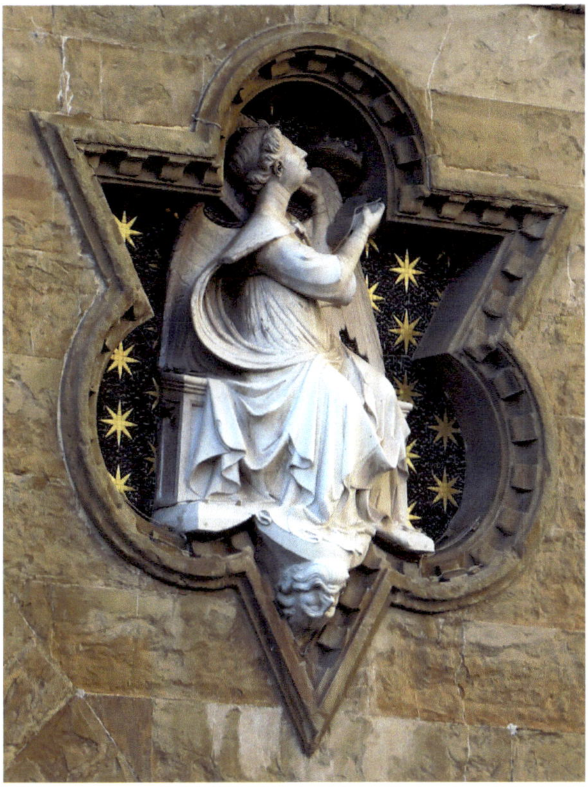

1.5. Designed by Agnolo Gaddi, 1383, carved by Jacopo di Pietro Guidi, 1384–85, *Hope*, Loggia della Signoria, Florence. Photo: Sailko / Creative Commons Attribution 3.0 Unported.

Agnolo's work for the Opera was more significant for the connections he derived from it and the prestige that accrued to him rather than from the volume of work he undertook. Lorenzo di Filippo, the *capomaestro* for the Loggia and most likely the designer of the attic section and cornice for which Agnolo supplied the Virtue designs, likely recommended Agnolo to the Pratese *operai* in the first place.[81] Agnolo would also work at Prato with Giovanni d'Ambrogio and with Piero di Giovanni Tedesco, both of whom carved Virtues he had designed.[82]

Agnolo's working relationship with the Pratese Opera was fundamentally different from that which he enjoyed with the Florentine Opera, owing to the nature and scale of the project and the need to work on site. Although there is no known contract that would have spelled out the details of his employment in Prato, payment records that do survive reveal their general outlines (see Appendix I). These payments were published selectively in 1932 by Giovanni Poggi, who was primarily interested in the activities of the principal artisans, especially Agnolo. In republishing the complete documentation, I have restored the chronological order of the payments and included many that record the mundane activities of lowly craftsmen and laborers about whom we know little else. Their tasks bring to life the teaming activity of the worksite and make apparent the collaborative nature of the enterprise.[83] Against this backdrop, Agnolo's relationships with artisans and laborers take on special significance.

Agnolo first appeared in June of 1392, when he received the considerable sum of 605 lire and seven soldi (equal to about 157 florins). This payment, a record culled from the *libro lungo* – most likely a detailed ledger that does not survive – was for his *faticha* – that is, his labor – as well as for gold, tin, rope, and the blue pigment called azurite, from 19 June 1392 until 25 April 1393 – a period of about ten months.[84] It was also noted that he was reimbursed 106 lire and 15 soldi for two pounds and seven and a half ounces of ultramarine, a deep blue pigment, and for tin. His arrival coincided with furious activity between May and September 1392 to build the scaffolding, presumably with Agnolo's input.[85] The surviving accounts record expenses for lumber and its transport, including taxes, as well as for nails, and payments to various workers to saw the lumber and hammer the nails. The first coat of plaster must have also been applied at this time, as expenses for purchase, transport, and preparation of lime are also recorded.

Work proceeded steadily, with one notable interruption, until March of 1395, when the interior frescoes were finished. Agnolo then completed an *Assumption of the Virgin* in the star-shaped recess on the façade, a task apparently not included in the initial agreement.[86] This motif was perhaps inspired by the trefoils of the Loggia della Signoria, also a collaboration between Lorenzo di Filippo and Agnolo.[87]

Terms of his employment emerge from the surviving records of payments. The painter was paid at regular intervals not only for his labor but also for materials, which it must be surmised he was charged with securing. Costly materials such as gold and ultramarine were supplied by specialist suppliers, often located far afield; in this instance, these materials primarily came from Florence. Large pieces of wood for the scaffolding were bought from Pistoia and transported to the work site.

The Opera relied on local sources, however, for more mundane construction materials and implements. The accounts name stationers, kilnsmen, ironworkers, carpenters, and many other tradespersons who supplied rope, sand, lime, bricks, nails, hooks, buckets, and other items needed in building the chapel. The manual laborers who sawed and planed wood, dug foundations, slaked lime, and transported materials were also local. The sacristan of the chapel, Piero di Guelfo, undertook the task of coordinating the work of the local laborers and the visiting artisans from Florence. Piero appears continually in the accounts in various capacities, charged with securing materials and food for Agnolo and his assistants an helping them in a general way.

Moreover, the payments record that the patron, the Opera, assumed the costs of Agnolo and his helpers while they were working. Payments for food, including bread, wine, meats, and salad are referred to in the payments, as well as for rent, woolen cloth, and unspecified expenses, denoted "for his reasons." There is also a record that the merchant Francesco di Marco Datini (1335–1410), the "Merchant of Prato," for whom Agnolo had worked previously, loaned him some bedding in November of 1393.[88] The final price for the murals was not fixed in advance, however. In April 1394, when they were nearing completion, Ridolfo di Lanfranco, one of the overseers, traveled to Florence for two days at Opera expense. His task there was to view "certain works that Master Agnolo made in Florence" (these probably included the decoration of the Castellani chapel in the church of Santa Croce, which are referred to in the records and which the Opera had measured in January of 1395) and to do an estimate for his work in Prato.[89] A summary of payments recorded the estimate of 535 florins, and Agnolo and his assistants received their final payment for the decoration of the chapel from the Opera on 25 May 1395.[90] It is difficult to calculate whether the 535 florin payment was solely for Agnolo's work or whether it included materials such as gold and pigment, as was usual.[91] The records are vague on this point (presumably the lost *libro lungo* provided more detail), although the total cost of the decoration was about 1,000 florins.

The payments also reveal that, when Agnolo was arrested by a judicial official in November 1392, and required to appear before a Florentine court for non-payment of a 600-lire fine (levied when he assaulted a tax collector), the Opera incurred an expense of fifty-eight lire and change for the *zufa* or scuffle. What this was for, either damages to equipment or medical supplies and treatment, is not detailed.[92] These expenses – and they are not unique in these projects – though unforeseen, were evidently part of the cost of doing business.

AGNOLO GADDI AND THE PRATO COMMISSION

Agnolo's reputation as a difficult personality, attested to by documented incidents in Florence in the early 1390s, and alluded to by the sixteenth-century biographer Vasari, may have been known to the Pratese *operai*, and yet they commissioned him for this highly important project, surely the most prestigious commission in the city of Prato.[93] Presumably, the Opera was satisfied with Agnolo's work in the end, for, after work on the chapel itself was finished, they commissioned him to paint an *Assumption* in the decorative star-shaped recess in the new façade facing the piazza. Other than technical and aesthetic competence, what did Agnolo bring to the relationship with his Opera patrons?

Either one or several of the *operai* probably knew Agnolo, directly or indirectly, in the early 1390s. At that time, as in the past, the *operai* were Pratesi drawn from the old landed families or the merchant elite, especially wool traders; some *operai* were members of both groups. In the 1390s, there were four *operai* elected for twelve-month terms; two were elected on 1 February and two on 1 August each year. For the period when Agnolo was in the Opera's employ, a typical member of the board was Ser Piero di Paolo Rinaldeschi, a member of a magnate family whose fortunes, while still respectable, were in decline in the late fourteenth century.[94] Ser Piero di Paolo was a doctor of law, judge, and neighbor of Francesco Datini.[95] He could have known that Agnolo executed decorative painting in Datini's palace just before the painter's appointment with the Opera.[96] On 1 August 1393, one of the new *operai* was Francesco Datini, long-standing acquaintance and sometime patron of Agnolo (despite their stormy relationship) and business associate of Agnolo's brother, Zanobi di Taddeo Gaddi, in Venice.[97] His service on the Opera is noteworthy because Datini was notoriously reluctant to assume public office (he declined the office of Prato's Gonflaoniere di Giustizia in 1386, escaping to Florence).[98]

Hence, the *operai* were in general successful and well-connected Pratesi, many active as notaries or wool merchants and many with ties to Florence.[99] Some of them, such as Piero di Paolo Rinaldeschi and Datini, may have been acquainted with the *operai* of the Florentine Opera del Duomo. The Florentine Opera was, unlike the Pratese Opera, under the management of the Arte della Lana (the Wool Guild), and the *operai* were frequently wool merchants like those in Prato with whom they may have done business.[100]

The Pratese *operai* were aware of Agnolo's work both in Prato and in Florence, and they likely commissioned the murals in the chapel of the Holy Belt with his accomplishments firmly in mind. Indeed, Agnolo's previous work in fresco, especially in Santa Croce, qualified him as executor of the Prato project. While the precise dates of Agnolo's activity in Santa Croce are not known, scholars generally agree that his work in the Castellani and Alberti chapels preceded his work in Prato.[101] In fact, the payment registers for Agnolo's work in Prato refer to one or both of these chapels as touchstones for the evaluation of the chapel of the Holy Belt.[102] The "cappella di messer Vanni" mentioned in the record for May 1395 is almost certainly the Castellani chapel that Agnolo painted, probably in collaboration with other artists, in the years just after 1383.[103] The Castellani chapel may also be the chapel measured the previous January, as it is similar in structure and dimensions to the chapel in Prato.[104]

The other chapel in Santa Croce that the *operai* may have used as a touchstone for the commissioning and evaluating of Agnolo's work in Prato is the *cappella maggiore* (main chapel), located diagonally across from the

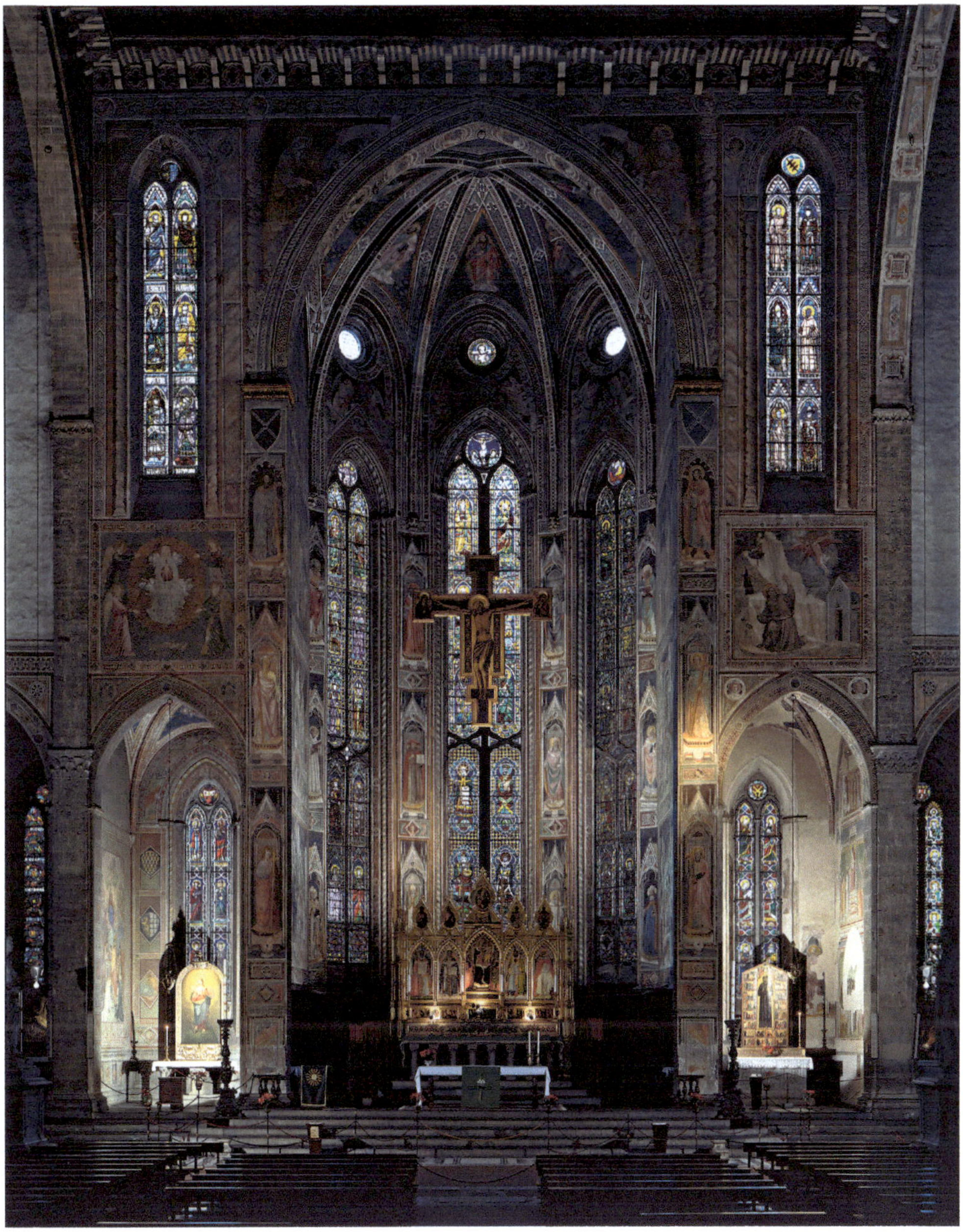

1.6. *Cappella Maggiore* (Alberti chapel), Santa Croce, Florence. Photo: Scala / Art Resource, NY.

Castellani chapel, and to which the patronage rights were owned by the Alberti family (Figure 1.6).[105] The Alberti, unlike the Castellani, were a very old Florentine family, who, while richer than the Castellani, were somewhat differently positioned politically. In the 1380s, however, the families' allegiances to the Guelph party may have brought them together.[106] We know also that the Alberti and Castellani were allied by marriages in 1362 and 1384.[107] The Alberti were an extremely large family, with many different branches; one branch had been allied with the populist regime of 1378–82. Exactly which branch of the family commissioned the decoration of the chapel, however, is not known; their known association with the chapel dates to the 1348 testament of Alberto del fu Lapo degli Alberti, who left 500 gold florins to Santa Croce for the building and decoration of a funerary chapel for himself and his dependents. The details of the will are confusing; especially as the *cappella maggiore* had long since been constructed in 1348; moreover, the decoration, for which precise documentation again is lacking, dates to at least thirty years later.

The main chapel is a polygonal apse with a six-part vault, and it is larger in its footprint than the newer chapel. The friars, not the patrons, probably chose the subject of the murals, the story of the True Cross. The Franciscans dedicated Santa Croce to the Holy Cross, and they acquired a splinter of the True Cross as a most sacred relic.[108] While infrequently depicted in visual art, the history of the True Cross received its first monumental depiction in Agnolo's murals and served as the impetus to a long and rich visual tradition.[109]

The story follows the wood of the cross from the time of Adam to the seventh century CE, adapting the account of *The Golden Legend* by Jacobus de Voragine.[110] In devising the murals for this extremely large and complex decoration, Agnolo had to invent compositions for which few visual models existed. By organizing the narratives on facing walls, those scenes depicting the finding of the Cross on one side, and those with its rescue and restoration on the left, each wall is associated with particular feast days. The Invention of the Cross was celebrated on 3 May and the Exaltation of the Cross on 14 September. As late as the eighteenth century, Santa Croce's fragment of the True Cross was shown in procession on these days.[111]

In form, Agnolo's True Cross frescoes bear scant relation to his earlier work in the Castellani chapel.[112] Set in exotic locations, Gaddi painted deep, panoramic landscapes, frequently punctuated by rivers that lead the viewer's eyes to vistas of hills crowned with churches and castles. Throngs of figures enact the story, choreographed to focus attention on the protagonists and ensure legibility. In some cases, as in the *Wood Being Pulled from the Piscina Probatica and the Making of the Cross* (Figure 1.7), incidents of the narrative merge. In this scene, an extensive architecture of a hospital at the left and a church at the right fill the background.[113] An odd disjunction of scale exists; the seated figures in the loggia of the hospital are larger than the workers in the foreground, who labor to retrieve the cross from the pool and construct the cross at the right. The hospital is larger than the church just next to it. Yet in the subsequent scene, the *Invention of the True Cross* (Figure 1.8), showing two incidents – the finding of the Cross and its Proof – the cast of figures has been

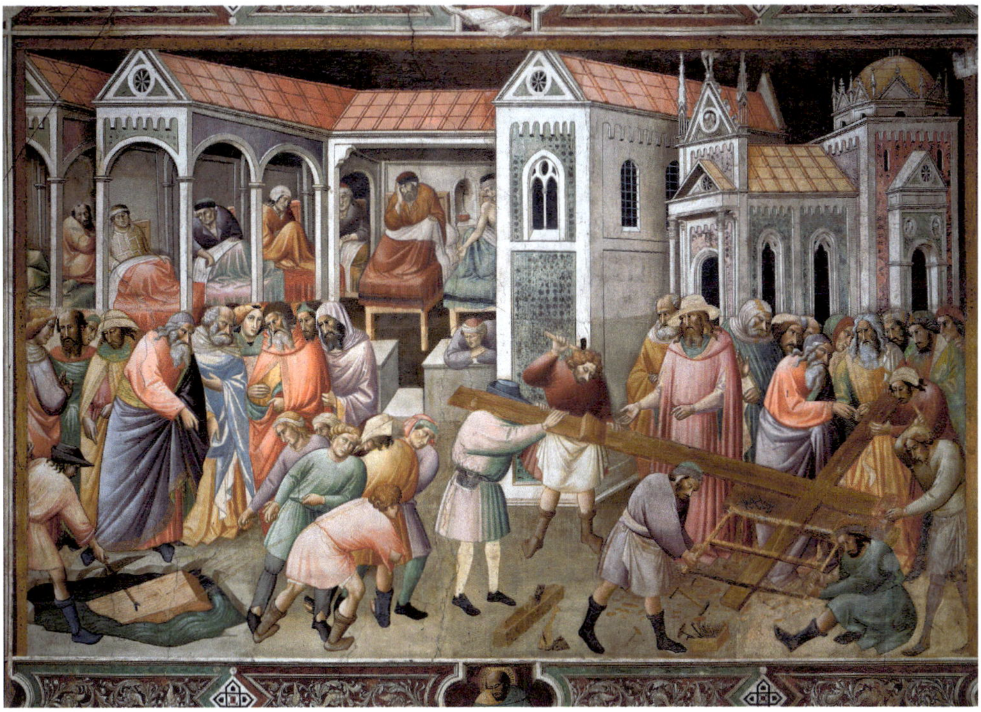

1.7. Agnolo Gaddi, *Wood Being Pulled from the Piscina Probatica and the Making of the Cross*, mid 1380s, Santa Croce, Florence. Photo: Scala / Art Resource, NY.

deftly organized by the great geometric shapes of the two Crosses. In the first scene of the left wall, *Saint Helena Returning the Cross to Jerusalem*, the walled city of Jerusalem at right extends far into the distance. The city, prominent in the narrative, held special significance for the Franciscans, who were charged with custody of the holy sites.[114]

In Santa Croce, Agnolo's choice of colors subtly evolved, from the pinks, greens, and yellows in the Castellani chapel and on the top scenes of the Alberti chapel, to a richer, more saturated palette that he employd on the lower levels. Nonetheless, in the *cappella maggiore*, Agnolo's inventive compositions and deployment of light and color rejected Giottesque precedent. His narratives, in which perspective is abridged and figural groups scattered across a vast surface, are akin to contemporary allegories such as those in the chapter house in Santa Maria Novella by Andrea Bonaiuti, discussed in Chapter 2. His stories, set in the distant past and in exotic locations, take on the aura of fantastic tales.[115]

Yet the Alberti murals in *cappella maggiore* must have impressed the Pratese *operai* more than simply through their grandiose scale and decorative style. For the narratives celebrate the story of the precious relic of the church, the True Cross, in the way that the Prato murals highlight the story of the precious relic stored in the *pieve*, the Holy Belt.[116] The points of contact in the histories of

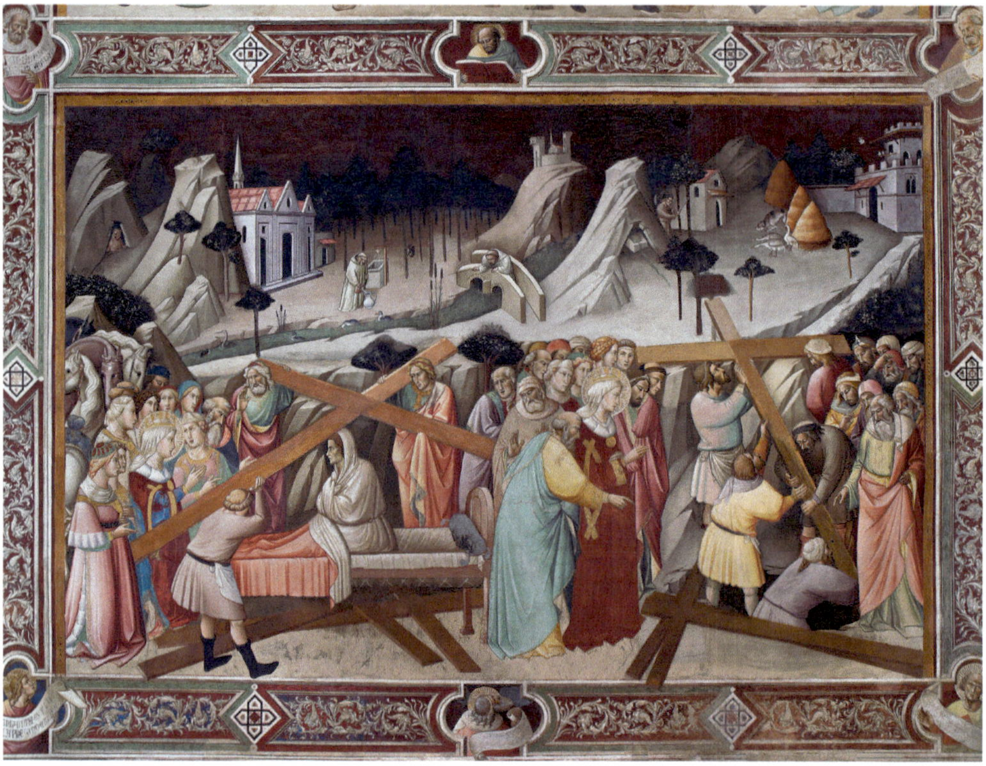

1.8. Agnolo Gaddi, *Invention of the True Cross*, mid 1380s, Santa Croce, Florence. Photo: Scala / Art Resource, NY.

the two relics are numerous. Each visualizes the origin of the relic, the miracles it performs, and the story of its transfer to its present location. In both chapels, the task of the painter was to visualize relic legends, specifically translation and theft legends. If, as Baxandall says, the artist is a "professional visualizer of holy stories," then Agnolo's monumental achievement in the *cappella maggiore* of Santa Croce would have been a powerful incentive to the Pratese to employ them for their project as well.[117]

Agnolo's link to the Pratese *operai* directly, as with Datini, or indirectly, thorough the Florentine *operai* and the wool guild, may have been a factor in his securing the Prato commission. The possible role of Datini has, however, been overstated. We know that in 1391 Datini acted on behalf of other artists, the painters Niccolò di Pietro Gerini and Tommaso del Mazza, then in his employ, to secure the Prato commission.[118] By early in 1392, Francesco seems to have recommended a different painter, possibly Spinello Aretino.[119] Datini, however, may have overvalued his influence with the cathedral officials. He did not join the Opera until 1 August 1393, when Agnolo's work was well underway. His recommendations may have carried less weight with the *operai* than the recommendations from Florentine associates, who would have known Agnolo's Florentine works and their prestigious patrons. In fact, Datini's later efforts to secure work for Gerini and Lorenzo di Niccolò in the chapel of Ridolfo Manassei in the *pieve* came to nothing.[120]

Agnolo's relations with other artisans employed by the Florentine Opera del Duomo may have also been significant. As with the employment in Prato of stone carvers from the Florentine Opera del Duomo, secured and supervised by Lorenzo di Pietro, Agnolo brought with him from Florence numerous assistants, some of whom went on to have known careers, such as Neri d'Antonio and Bartolomeo di Fruosino.[121] The task of sorting out which assistant painted what has not, however, produced illuminating results.[122] In collaborative enterprises such as mural painting, the master's style and technique dominated in the result; assistants assumed the master's style, as required for a unified effect. The master was also responsible for the competence of his collaborators, which ensured a consistently high level of execution.[123]

Connections of another sort, however, with a network of artisans and suppliers of precious materials such as pigment and gold, were an asset he brought to the project. Specialized materials for painting flowed from the larger city, and Agnolo was frequently the agent by which these were secured.[124] The quality of materials, especially the expensive gold leaf and ultramarine, varied considerably, and patrons had to monitor their supplies carefully. The merchant Francesco Datini took care to secure materials for the painters working for him; he showed an almost obsessive concern to have the best quality at a good price. With his far-flung trading empire, Datini was in a good position to secure materials from distant sources.[125] He did not trust painters to supply material, remarking, "About the blue, that it costs less than that in Venice is good. Take the sort that the Maestro advises but be careful that he hasn't come to an agreement with the dyer, that he isn't cheating you."[126]

The *operai* of the *pieve*, however, mostly relied on Agnolo for materials. His first payment of 605 lire, seven soldi was "for his labor in gold, blue, tin, and rope," between 19 June 1392 and 25 April 1393.[127] For the period from 30 July 1392 to 14 September 1393, Agnolo was paid for two pounds seven and a half ounces of ultramarine for the sum of 10 florins a pound (equal to 760 soldi per pound) and for tin. The reason for the overlapping pay periods is probably owing to the different account books from which these entries were copied. Of the named suppliers, one of the most important was the *speziale* (pharmacist) Donato di Bonifazio, who was first cited in the records for payments made between 3 September 1392 and 20 November 1393. Because the account book is a summary, the specific dates of payment are not included, but the materials he supplied are: a pound and a half for *azurro oltramarino finisso* for 80 lire per pound (equal to 1,600 soldi to the pound),

120 lire for 2,000 piece of gold, and 18 soldi for tin, in all a payment of 186 lire.[128] Donato was paid again for the period 6 June 1393 to 29 July of the same year for blue and gold; while Agnolo was also paid for *azzuro*, gold, and tin for a similar period, from 17 May to 23 July.[129] In the summary of expenses for these precious materials between 21 July 1394 and 23 April 1395, we learn that Donato supplied blue and gold on numerous occasions.[130] He was not the sole supplier of these materials, however; in the same summary, a certain pharmacist named Francesco was paid for three sheets of tin on 20 November 1394. He was perhaps a local pharmacist who could be trusted with a less precious material. Occasionally, local apothecaries supplied materials, such as Francesco di Vanni, who was paid on 3 May 1395 "for several things taken from his shop," or a certain Lorenzo *speziale*, who was paid on 5 May 1395, for nine pounds of rope for the lamps.[131]

Another supplier of gold was from Florence; this was Maffio di Giovanni Palmieri *battiloro*, who supplied beaten gold sometimes through Agnolo's assistants, Vittorio and Massaio, and through one of the *operai*, Nicholao di Bernardo.[132] Vittorio was also paid for a pound of blue that he brought from Florence, but this was perhaps the less costly German blue, as it cost only two lire and eight soldi, compared to the eighty lire a pound blue purchased from Donato. The Opera sent the *operaio* Ridolfo di Lanfrancho on 27 September 1395 to purchase blue pigment in Florence, to see the chapel painted by Agnolo in Santa Croce, and to have Agnolo brought to Prato.[133]

These payments make clear that, as with artisan expertise, the most precious and costly materials came from Florence, while less expensive materials were from local suppliers. Donato di ser Bonifazio was an artisan of a certain stature; he had matriculated in the Guild of Doctors and Apothecaries at an unknown date, but after 1358,[134] and he was elected prior in Florence several times.[135] His descendants would continue the trade of *speziale*, supplying pigments to many painters who were collaborators or assistants of Agnolo such as Giuliano d'Arrigo and Massaio di Jacopo.[136] In 1460, the heirs of Bonifazio di Donato supplied pigments to Filippo Lippi, then at work in the *pieve*.[137] Maffio di Giovanni, who matriculated in the guild on 9 August 1378, also supplied Florentine painters.[138] As with Lorenzo di Pietro for the architectural and sculptural components of the chapel, Agnolo was instrumental in bringing his connections with specialist suppliers with him to Prato. Moreover, as he was certainly responsible for the quality of his assistants in painting the chapel, he was probably to some extent a guarantor of the quality of materials supplied by these sources.

Artists from Florence had long dominated the artistic scene in Prato, so it is not surprising that, when the Pratese *operai* sought a master to fresco the new chapel of the Holy Belt, they would look to the dominant city on the Arno.

That an artist from Florence brought not only skill, honed in the competitive and demanding art market of the city, but also prestige was undoubtedly important to potential employers. As we have seen, when it came time to build the sumptuous new chapel for the Holy Belt, the Pratese *operai* again turned to Lorenzo di Filippo, the *capomaestro* of the Florentine Duomo and Loggia della Signoria, for the design and structural work, and to the stone carvers, such as Giovanni d'Ambrogio, for the architectural details. In employing Agnolo, the *operai* followed the tradition of patronage at the *pieve*, thereby confirming the continuing high reputation of Florentine artists. Agnolo's expertise in the design and execution of wall paintings, his experience in the organization of a large workshop, and his links to networks of specialist suppliers were amply demonstrated by the *cappella maggiore* murals in Santa Croce, the commission that had probably been completed shortly before the Prato project and was the most impressive mural decoration in Florence of the late Trecento. In employing Florentine artists, the *operai* would have also modeled their behavior on that of their Florentine counterparts, whose goodwill they courted in the period of Florentine political dominance.

AGNOLO'S MURAL TECHNIQUE

Material evidence gathered during a recent restoration confirm what detailed payment records reveal about the murals' materials and work progress.[139] The scaffolding, which was moved and reconfigured several times according to the payments, must have covered the entire chapel and allowed for the execution on all the walls at once from the top down.[140] The pattern of *giornate*, the daily patches of fresh plaster, conforms to traditional practice of mural painting. They vary in size corresponding to the motif; the areas of sky or landscape are generally larger than those for figures, and for the figures, groups of heads were executed together, as were draperies.[141] Some *giornate* spread to adjacent walls, again suggesting a scaffolding that allowed access to all walls at once. Evidence of design transfer through pricked cartoons occurs in the architectural framing. Direct incisions using a straight edge and compass, and snapped cords using a plumb line, guided the design of architecture and other geometric shapes such as haloes. Glimpses of hastily sketched underdrawings where the *intonaco* (the top level of plaster) has fallen away suggest preliminary graphic preparation for figures, while the careful delineation of architecture implies a fully worked out design, probably in small scale, before painting began.[142] The murals are in a technique that mixes fresco and *secco* (on dry plaster) application. Many of the figures, draperies, and landscape elements were applied to fresh plaster, while pigments like ultramarine, made from lapis lazuli, were applied *a secco* and have disappeared. The restoration revealed the fluid brushwork and transparent paint film in the areas of flesh tones in the faces and hands of the figures.

Agnolo's love of colors such as pinks, greens, and violets, often in combination with the pigment called *giallorino* (lead-tin yellow), is apparent. The lavish use of gold, applied as leaf and as liquid (shell gold), sometimes over tin, was evident, although little of the original gilding has survived. In general, Agnolo's technique corresponds to the precepts of Cennino Cennini's *Libro dell'Arte*, a manual of painting techniques; this correspondence is not surprising as Cennino was Agnolo's student, although he had probably left Agnolo's workshop before the Prato project.[143]

THE CHAPEL OF THE HOLY BELT AS A SETTING FOR RITUAL

The "larger, more ornate, and more seemly" chapel was the manifestation of Pratese prestige and devotion to the Sacred Belt.[144] As a locus for the conservation of the Belt, as well as daily Masses[145] and public and private ostentations, the chapel was the setting for displays of public unity.[146] The celebration of the relic expressed a model of ideal relationships characterized by harmony and clearly articulated power structures.[147] The chapel, as well as the adjacent spaces of the nave and the surrounding piazza, was the staging ground for the idealized interaction of church and city, clergy and magistracy, the powerful and the *popolo*.

Recent historians, guided by anthropologists, view ritual as revealing fundamental social structures and values of a culture.[148] Lively debate questions our ability to interpret the meaning of ritual in this period, however. Written accounts and images that are used to reconstruct ceremonies and events, as referenced here, are themselves hardly objective; they are narratives crafted to specific ends. Moreover, rituals themselves have multiple meanings for participants – some contradictory or subversive.[149] They mirror the social order from a particular point of view; they cannot encompass changing social relationships over time or the variety of individual experience. And yet, the concept of ritual, either narrowly focused on church liturgy, or more broadly interpreted as "mental rituals," is a useful prism through which to view how individuals in a society relate to one another.

From the outset, the procession that preceded ostentations choreographed these associations.[150] The cortege, itself a symbol of civic unity forged by the Belt, started at the Piazza Comunale and ended at the chapel, spatially and temporally linking the civic authority of the commune with the spiritual center of the *pieve*. The location of the chapel, as mentioned above, at the furthest extreme from the main altar off the nave just to the north from the western portal, physically telegraphed the shared custody of the Belt by church and commune. We do not know the order of the procession for regular ostentations in the fourteenth century, but a detailed description of the translation of the relic to its new location provides a clue. A legal instrument drawn up by the chancellor of the commune makes clear that the entire civic and clerical hierarchy of the city was involved in the translation ceremony.[151] On such occasions, we might imagine that the clergy lead the procession, either the bishop, as at the consecration, or the provost or his vicar. The lay participants followed, with the communal officials ranged according to rank. All would have carried the candles dictated by statute for offering at the altar of the Holy Belt.[152]

Entering the church, the procession would have turned to the left under the broad arch flanked by the green serpentine pier and pilaster. The new altar, located in the center of the space under the transverse arch of the newly vaulted chapel, was also described in the translation document: "an altar, constructed in the middle of this chapel with sculpted marbles on every side, decorated with the story of the same Glorious Virgin, of her death, her Assumption into heaven, and of other glories, in which, henceforth, in most holy and appropriate place [the relic] will be preserved."[153] The arrangement of the clergy on this occasion is not known. Choir stalls around the perimeter of the chapel occupied by officials and clergy were constructed only later, but it is likely that laity and clergy were grouped on either side and at the back of the chapel, as seen in later depictions of the ostentation.[154] Provisions of earlier statutes mandating minimum viewing distances of three *braccia* (about 175 centimeters) from the relic also suggest that the arrangement of spectators was prescribed.[155]

The translation document describes the ostentation:

> By command of the said Lord of the *Podestà* and the Defenders and the Vicar of the Lord Provost, the aforementioned Lord Alberto, Vicar of said Lord Provost, with the permission, will, and consent of the said office of Eight Lord Defenders and the Standard-bearer of Justice of the land of Prato, and in their presence, openly, with solemn songs and with devout mind in honor and reverence and glory of God and of the glorious Virgin Mary and in reverence of said Belt, transported, transferred, and translated this precious Belt of the Virgin Mary from said old chapel to this above named new chapel of the Virgin Mary, and there in said new chapel, beside the altar of this new chapel on the front side, after said Holy Father Lord Andrea, Bishop of Pistoia, in the presence of the People standing near, unfolded and devoutly displayed this Belt, Lord Alberto [his] Vicar, in the presence of myself, a Notary, and said witnesses, reverently refolded [it] and, after folding [it], wrapped [it] in its accustomed cloths, and thus wrapped, he placed [it] inside its accustomed little ivory box [reliquary], and finally he placed and enclosed this little box with the Belt contained and being inside it in a box of wood and iron chained on this new altar of this new chapel, and in this way he left and released it closed in said box and said box enclosed with said Belt on said altar and secured [them] with several keys and locks, and shut the recess of the altar for the secure protection and preservation of said Belt.

> Of which keys, part remained with said Vicar, and the remainder with this office of the Defenders and Standard-bearer.[156]

This description highlights the delicate ballet of shared custody and participation in the rite of ostentation evolved over more than a century. The senior lay official, the *Podestà*, with the consent of the Eight and the *Gonfaloniere di Giustizia*, mandated the transfer, validated by the legal document. In their presence, the Vicar of the Provost solemnly transferred the relic to the new chapel. From the new chapel, in front of the altar, the bishop displayed the relic before the assembled officials. The Vicar then reverently refolded it and wrapped it in the "veils" and put it inside an ivory casket, deposited the casket inside another of wood and iron secured with chains, and finally placed the relic inside the new altar, the cavity of which was secured with several keys and locks. Of the keys, part remained in the custody of the Vicar, and the other part that of the office of the Eight and the *Gonfaloniere*.

The architecture of the new chapel contained and shaped the ceremony while imbuing it with multiple meanings. The impressive scale of the new chapel could accommodate the privileged viewers with greater ease than the inadequate chapel across the nave. While the procession and ceremony included the entire communal and clerical hierarchy of Prato, probably only the clerical and lay elite entered the chapel.[157] In the fourteenth century, a screen in gilt wood enclosed the chapel, replaced in the fifteenth century by the elegant wrought iron grille we see today. Although in part a security measure, designed to thwart attempted theft such as that of Musciattino, the grille also marked off the sacred space from the rest of the church, controlling access to only the worthiest. Probably during the ostentation, the gate remained open to allow viewing by spectators not admitted to the chapel itself.

The altar in the center of the space facilitated viewing of the precious relic during the ceremony. While the previous chapel probably had an altar against the south wall of the *pieve*, the provision of a vaulted space in the new chapel reinstated the freestanding location of the altar and improved viewing conditions for the gathered officials. The sculpture of the *Virgin and Child* by Giovanni Pisano, with its spiraling figures, brought from the earlier altar and reinstalled on the new one, would have been visible to the spectators (Figure 1.9).[158] The translation document stated that the bishop performing the ostentation stood in front of the altar. The ostentation itself, though not described, as we know from later sources consisted in draping the Belt over the celebrant's extended hands and raising it above his head.[159] The parallels with the consecration of the host at the altar during Mass are striking and present in other relic celebrations of the time.[160] The document does not specify whether the priest turned his back to the altar or was facing it, as in the elevation of the

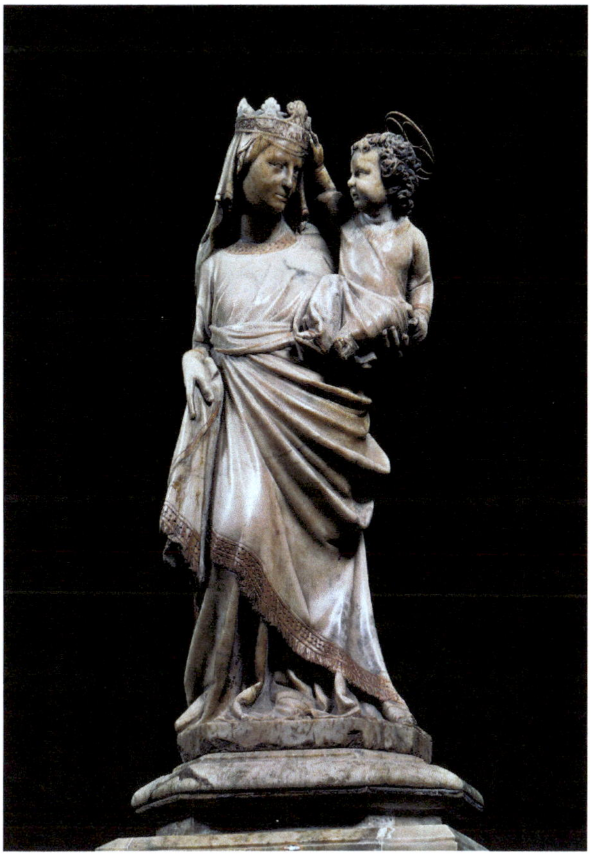

1.9. Giovanni Pisano, *Virgin and Child*, c. 1312, Chapel of the Holy Belt, Duomo di Santo Stefano, Prato. Photo: Scala / Art Resource, NY.

consecrated host; but later depictions of the ceremony suggest that the celebrant faced the spectators.[161]

The central position of the altar probably also facilitated the procession of the celebrant to the indoor and outdoor pulpits for public viewing during regular ostentations. The provision of a door in the west wall, giving onto the corridor constructed between the old and new facades that led to the pulpits, also ensured a secure and decorous unfolding of the ceremony.[162]

CHAPEL FURNISHINGS AND DECORATION

Music, song,[163] and a great quantity of candles and torches accompanied the ostentation ceremony.[164] In addition to the wax offerings of various officials, chapel and altar were lit by several lamps that are referred to in the documents.[165] Francesco Datini would also leave provisions in his testament of 1410 for twelve silver lamps for the altar of the chapel.[166] The dazzling spectacle of flickering candlelight, remarked upon in later guidebooks, was enhanced by the somewhat dark prospect of the chapel at other times. Originally, the chapel had been lit by a double arched window in the north wall, but, during the mural decoration, the window had been replaced by a smaller round one filled with stained glass. The new window allowed greater scope for the mural decor but it may also be that diminished natural light was sought. Stoneworkers received payments for a green marble frame for a star-shaped recess on the west wall, facing the piazza, in December of 1387, but this was not for a window but a decorative element in the wall.[167] Recent considerations of the lighting of pilgrimage churches suggest that dimly lit interiors were associated with miracle-working images and other Marian shrines. By contrast, a round window above the old chapel across the nave from the new, was inserted in the south flank of the church in 1395. This window allowed for direct illumination of the chapel altar on the winter solstice, 21 December.[168]

As the communal and clerical worthies of Prato passed under the entrance arch, where Agnolo painted a *Maestà* on the exterior wall of the chapel facing the nave (now fragmentary), and through the open grille into the newly constructed chapel for the translation ceremony, they would have been dazzled by the freshly painted murals surrounding them. Kneeling at the altar in veneration of the relic, they would have lifted their eyes to the scene of the Virgin's *Assumption* and *Coronation* (Figures 1.10–1.11). The central image of

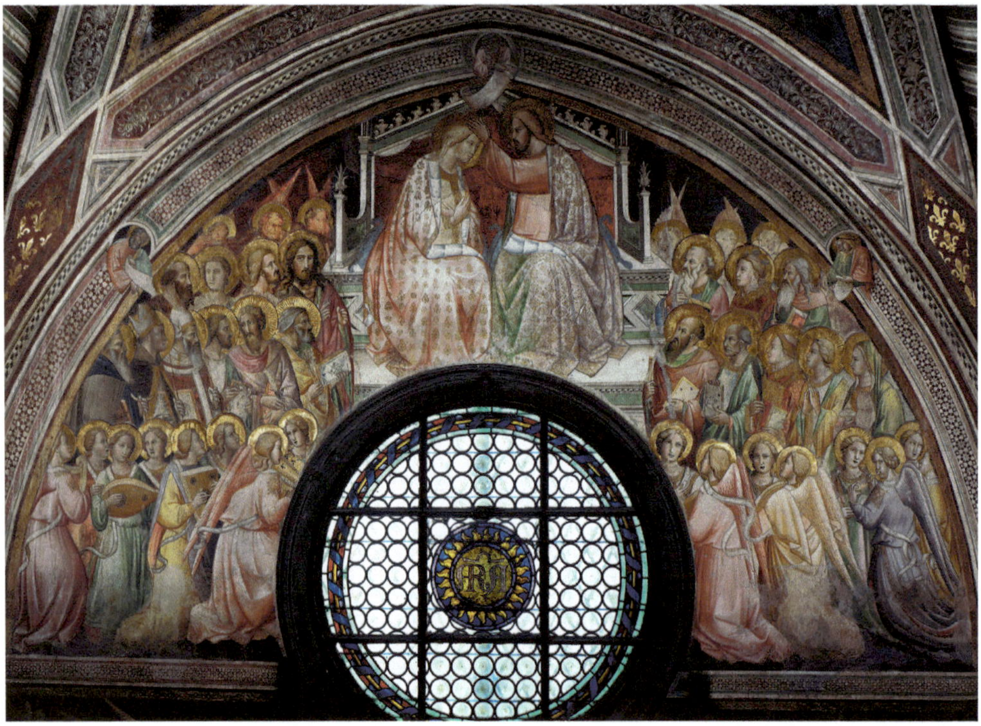

1.10. Agnolo Gaddi, *Coronation of the Virgin*, 1392–95, Chapel of the Holy Belt, Duomo di Santo Stefano, Prato. Photo: Scala / Art Resource, NY.

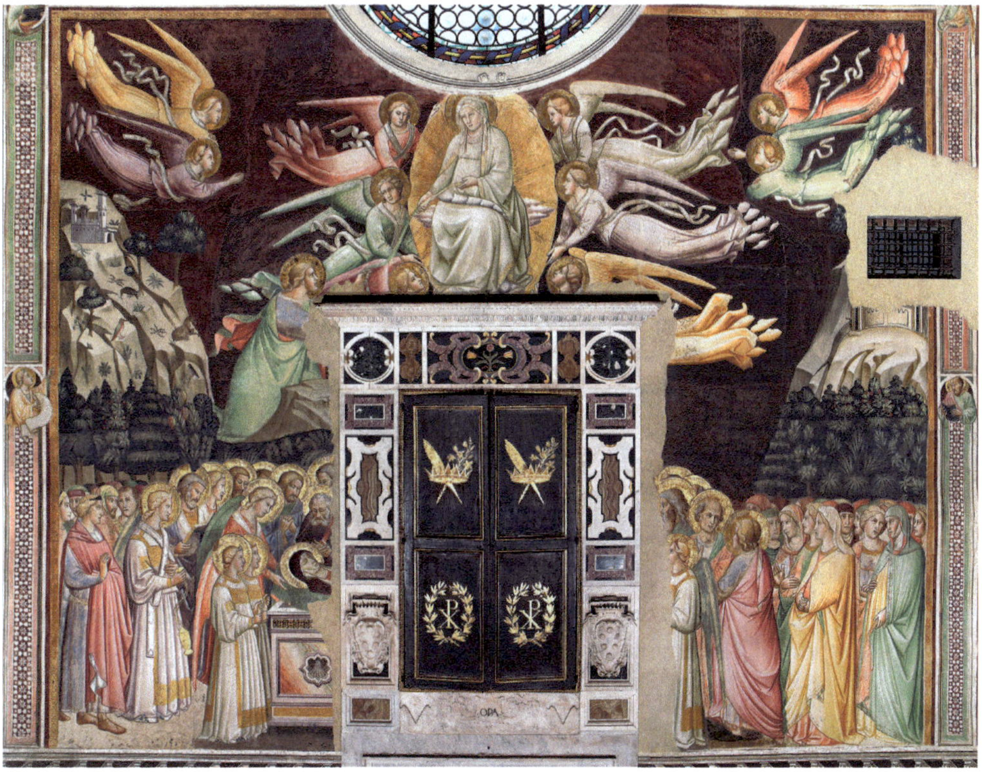

1.11. Agnolo Gaddi, *Death and Assumption of the Virgin* (fragmentary), 1392–95, Chapel of the Holy Belt, Duomo di Santo Stefano, Prato. Photo: Scala / Art Resource, NY.

the Virgin, seated on a cloud within a shining mandorla, turning to the left and handing her Belt to Thomas, who grasps it in his upheld hand, was striking. The images depicted the sacred origin of the relic conserved in the altar before them and reiterated the link of the Belt both to an ancient, sacred past and to the distant Holy Land. The *Coronation* would also remind worshippers of the future, of the promise of eternal salvation, and the role of the Virgin as chief intercessor, not just to the skeptical Thomas but to the assembled faithful as well. Just as the Virgin's body was reunited with her soul at the Assumption, so too could the participants hope for salvation at the Last Judgment. Her special favor, made tangible by the presence of the Belt in their midst, resonated in the context of the ritual unfolding in the sacred space, in which offerings were made and the relic displayed.[169]

Turning to their left, they would have seen the story of the Virgin, the generous donatrix, on the west wall of the chapel, and to their right, the story of the precious gift (*dono*) of the Belt to the Pratesi on the east wall. The idea of the Belt as a gift, first from the Virgin to Thomas, and then from Michele, the Pratese pilgrim, to the city of Prato, pervades the literary sources and is the organizing principle for the murals' imagery.[170] Discovery and transfer of the Holy Belt signified above all God's mercy and here, that of his Mother, who had judged Prato to be deserving of the gift.[171] The relic was the tangible proof of a special relationship with the Virgin, who protected and unified the Pratesi. Early accounts of the legend, telling of the gift of the Belt to Thomas, its translation from the Holy Land to Prato, and the miracles it performed, refer to the Belt as a *dono* or *donum*.[172] Gift imagery is especially prominent in the poem, *Il Cincturale*, written in celebration of the relic in 1340 by the Pratese scholar Duccio di Amadore. He begins the poem with "Celesti quodam de dono"; and elsewhere, "Qualiter hoc donum Pratum suscepit."[173] Indeed, this poem, most likely a civic commission, is remarkable among the early literary sources in putting equal emphasis on the civic and institutional meaning of the relic, as much as its miraculous nature.[174]

The theme of the gift giving is also fundamental to the imagery of the chapel's murals. The images of the *Assumption*, the *Gift of the Belt*, and the *Coronation* receive pride of place on the north wall, in ascending sequence in accord with their meaning. The histories of the Virgin on the left, and the journey of her Belt from Jerusalem to Prato on the right, underscore the generosity and mercy of the Virgin and the favored status of Prato as the recipient of her precious gift. The ritual unfolding in the sacred space amplified the theme of gift exchange. In a society in which patron-client relationships defined community, gift giving was the manifestation of these relationships.[175] Similarly, the participation of city officials in the sacred rite emphasized the civic importance of the Belt's presence in Prato. The attendance of the officials and their offerings, mandated by statute, underscored the obedience offered by the Pratesi in homage to the Virgin and in thanks for her favor and protection.

Agnolo's presentation of the *Death*, *Assumption*, and *Coronation of the Virgin* conformed to an imagery of the Virgin's last days that had evolved in Tuscany in the late Trecento, largely in tandem with the growing renown of the Holy Belt in Prato.[176] The mural was severely reduced when the window in the center of the wall was enlarged and a reliquary chest inserted, obliterating the center scene of the Virgin on her bier and the lower part of the *Assumption* and *Consignment of the Belt*. We can assume that the missing parts replicated earlier representations of the Virgin's last days.[177] Depictions of the gift of the Belt existed in the thirteenth century, when the pose of the Virgin was generally frontal, hieratic, and unresponsive to the figure of Thomas below, who somewhat passively received it from her. In the early fourteenth century images in Tuscany, the Virgin became more animated, turning to hand down her Belt to the doubting Thomas, who variously knelt or lunged forward to grasp it from her.[178] Her active pose and her response to the saint underscored her mercy and her humanity; the Belt itself was proof of her corporeal presence during the Assumption. As it is tangible – brought home by the eager grasp of the saint – so the Virgin herself was assumed body and soul into heaven.[179] The emphasis on the Virgin's corporeal Assumption, a subject of theological debate that was not made part of church doctrine until the twentieth century, resonated in the area in which the cult of the Holy Belt was widely recognized, corroborated by its presence in the altar of the chapel. Spectators, with their faces uplifted and necks craned as they observed the Belt held high above them during public ostentations, either from the altar in the chapel, from the interior pulpit, or from the external pulpit, could identify with the active figure of Thomas. The images responded to trends in late medieval devotion emphasizing sensory experience, especially visual experience of the holy – the consecrated host, relics, and holy images.[180] The images emphasized tangible evidence of the Virgin's special role as Mother of God and Queen of Heaven, and they contributed to the widespread popularity of the cult of the Belt.

The setting of the scene emphasized the real presence of the Virgin during the Assumption and the real presence of the Belt in the chapel. In early images of the *Assumption of the Virgin*, as in Daddi's altarpiece, the Virgin was encased in a mandorla with little background or landscape (Figure 1.12).[181] Even with the figure of Thomas, the background was often gilded.[182] Agnolo sets the events of the last days of the Virgin in a mountainous landscape, complete with castles, flora, and fauna. The details evoked the Holy Land where these

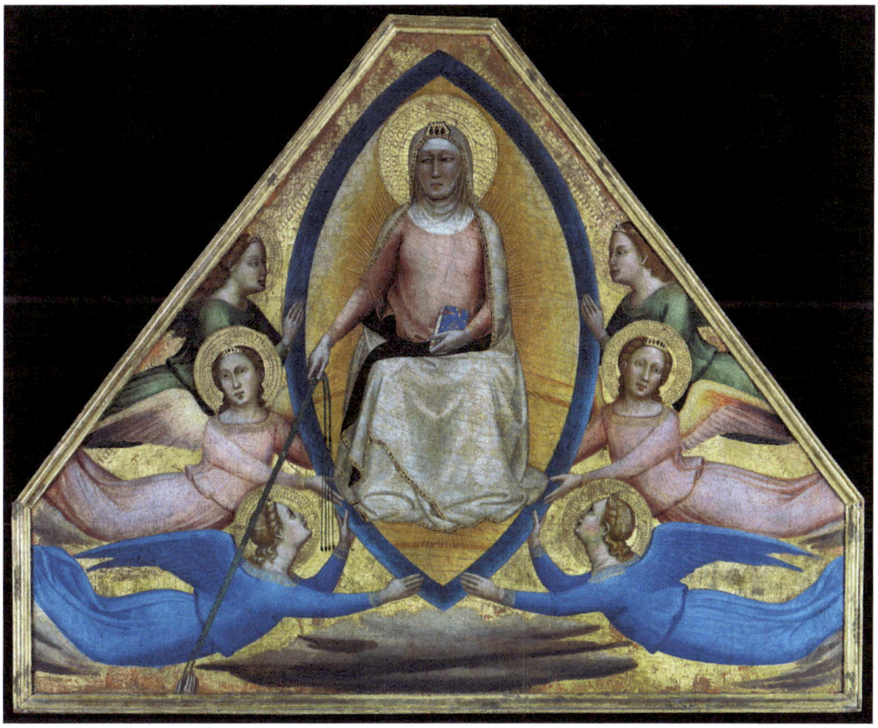

1.12. Bernardo Daddi, *Assumption of the Virgin* (fragment), 1337–39, Robert Lehman Collection, The Metropolitan Museum of Art, New York, 1975.1.58. Photo: The Metropolitan Museum of Art.

momentous events took place.[183] According to the early legends, the disciples, except for Thomas, buried the Virgin in the rocky Valley of Josaphat.[184] Thomas arrived after her death and burial and beheld the Virgin's Assumption into heaven from the Mount of Olives; there he received the Belt from her. In the *Cincturale*, Duccio described the earth swelling to a small mountain at the place Thomas rested his feet.[185] Agnolo evokes the topography of the Holy Land, reiterating the link of Prato with the *terra santa*, made explicit by the presence of the Holy Belt in the *pieve* of Santo Stefano.[186]

The murals on the east wall of the chapel recount the translation of the sacred relic from the Holy Land to its final resting place in the very chapel in which the viewer stood. In visualizing these momentous events, Agnolo drew on the rich literary tradition of translation legends, themselves part of the hagiographic tradition that had its origins in the early Christian cult of the saints.[187] Translation legends glorify saints and demonstrate their sanctity; their accounts include literary topoi and follow an established sequence of events.[188] These include the discovery or origin of the relic (*inventio*); the transfer of the relic from its place of discovery to a new location (*translatio*); miracles through which the saint makes known his or her assentation to the transfer and miracles performed by the relic during and after the transfer, either in the face of danger, neglect, or skepticism (*miracula*); the ceremonial welcome of the relic (*adventus*), including the procession to the church and deposit of the relic in a suitable receptacle (*deposito* or *elevatio*); and finally its presentation (*ostensio*).[189]

Translation legends differ from hagiography in that they describe action in a specific time and place. Due to their importance to church history, feasts commemorating relic translation took on public, ritualistic, and communal dimensions; processions and relic display through spectacle and song recalled history and reinforced communal memory.[190] Written translation legends of the Holy Belt and the visual history presented in Agnolo's murals share hagiographic and historical meanings.

Written accounts of the Holy Belt and its translation to Prato date to the second half of the twelfth century. They shared with other translation narratives a sequence of episodes: the Virgin's gift of the Belt to Thomas (*inventio*), his voyage with it to Prato (*translatio*), the miracles through which its authenticity was made known (*miracula*), its installation in the *pieve* (*adventus, elevatio*), and finally, presentation to the public (*otensio*).[191] Agnolo's murals depict all of these elements, creating the first monumental presentation of the translation legend in visual form. Bernardo Daddi had illustrated the legend in the predella of his altarpiece, and it may have been depicted in the lost murals executed on the north wall of the *pieve*. However, Agnolo's murals, by virtue of their scale and location in the chapel where the relic was preserved, assumed a prominent role in the perpetuation of Pratese identity with the relic. A closer look at the murals reveals this role more clearly.

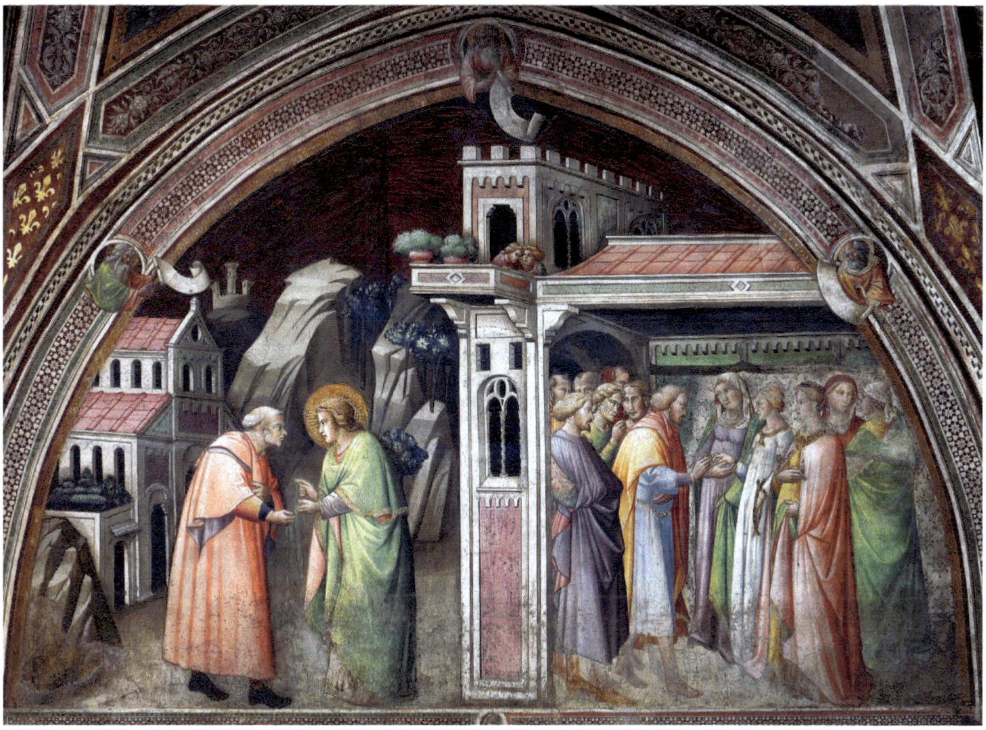

1.13. Agnolo Gaddi, *Thomas entrusts the Belt to a Pious Man*; *Marriage of Michele and Maria*, 1392–95, Chapel of the Holy Belt, Duomo di Santo Stefano, Prato. Photo: Scala / Art Resource, NY.

The first events in the translation legend are shown in the lunette high on the northeast wall: Thomas, before his return to missionary work in India, entrusted the Sacred Belt to a pious man for deposit in a church to be constructed in the Valley of Josaphat (Figure 1.13).[192] The prominent basilican church seen to the left of the mural, in a rocky, wooded landscape, alludes to this church, which was never constructed. The form of the depicted church evokes the *pieve* itself, as does the church in the same scene in Daddi's predella. The Belt passed from this holy man through his descendants to a priest. The Pratese Michele, having journeyed to the Holy Land, fell in love with the priest's beautiful daughter Maria and sought her hand in marriage. Michele received the Holy Belt as a dowry from Maria's mother, unbeknownst to her husband, the bride's father, as an expression of her consent to the match. The mural depicts the marriage of Michele and Maria, in the presence of her mother, but the relic is nowhere to be seen.[193] Agnolo shows the marriage ceremony, done in secret according to the legend, as a public event. Cognate elements in the *Marriage of the Virgin* mural on the opposite wall include the grooms' sliding rings on the fingers of the two Marias, while the officiating high priest in the *Marriage* and the mother of the bride in the Prato scene occupy central positions (Figure 1.14). In each, witnesses crowd the wedding

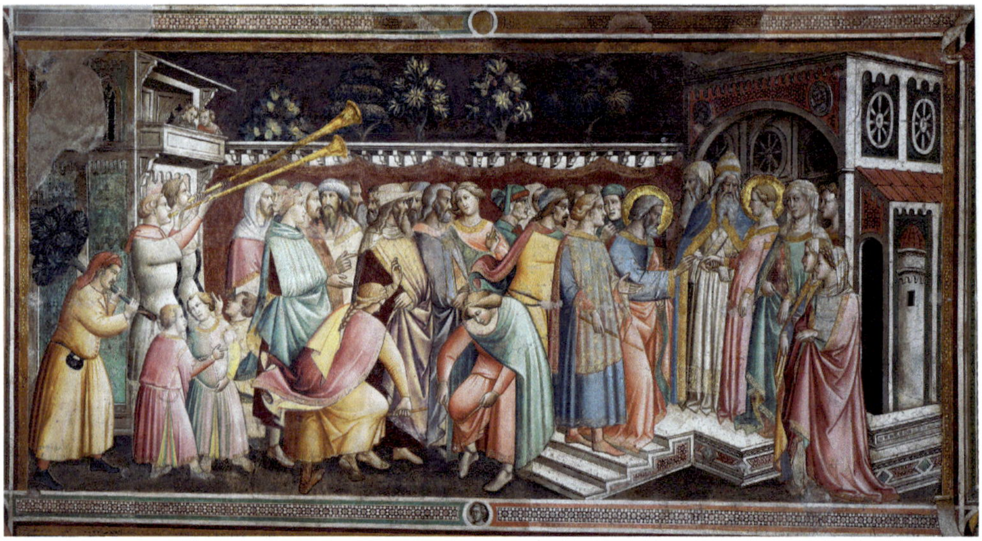

1.14. Agnolo Gaddi, *Marriage of the Virgin*, 1392–95, Chapel of the Holy Belt, Duomo di Santo Stefano, Prato. Photo: Scala / Art Resource, NY.

pair, including, in each case, a disappointed suitor beating the groom on the back. Agnolo perhaps altered the textual source in order to draw narrative parallels with the Virgin's history on the opposite wall, or he may also have depicted the transfer of the relic to Michele as a public event to foster credence of its holy provenance. In Daddi's predella, by contrast, the marriage scene depicts only the wedding couple and the mother; the consignment of the relic occupies a separate scene.

Above the smaller entrance arch from the north aisle, the spectator observes the sea voyage of Michele and Maria from Jerusalem to Prato (Figure 1.15). The newlyweds sit in the boat, the reliquary casket held between them, while other figures tend to the sails and rudder. In this upper horizontal sequence of murals, the events that take place in the Holy Land conclude. The links with pilgrimage, including the sea voyage that during the Trecento was the necessary mode of transport to the East, are plain for all to see.[194]

On the next level down, Michele, now without Maria but clutching the casket with the relic, arrives at the gate of Prato (Figure 1.16). The city is seen with its distinctive elements: the Porta della Mercatale, with its bridge over the Bizenzio river, which had recently been rebuilt. High, crenellated walls, completed in 1388, hem the city center, perhaps alluding to the role of the Belt as its defender and protector, found in literary works such as the *Cincturale* and devotional literature celebrating the Virgin as patron of the city of Prato.[195] The *pieve* di Santo Stefano, with its ancient, gabled façade and campanile, are both identified by striped revetment on the walls and window frames. The Palazzo del Popolo is visible to the left of the *pieve*. The cityscape

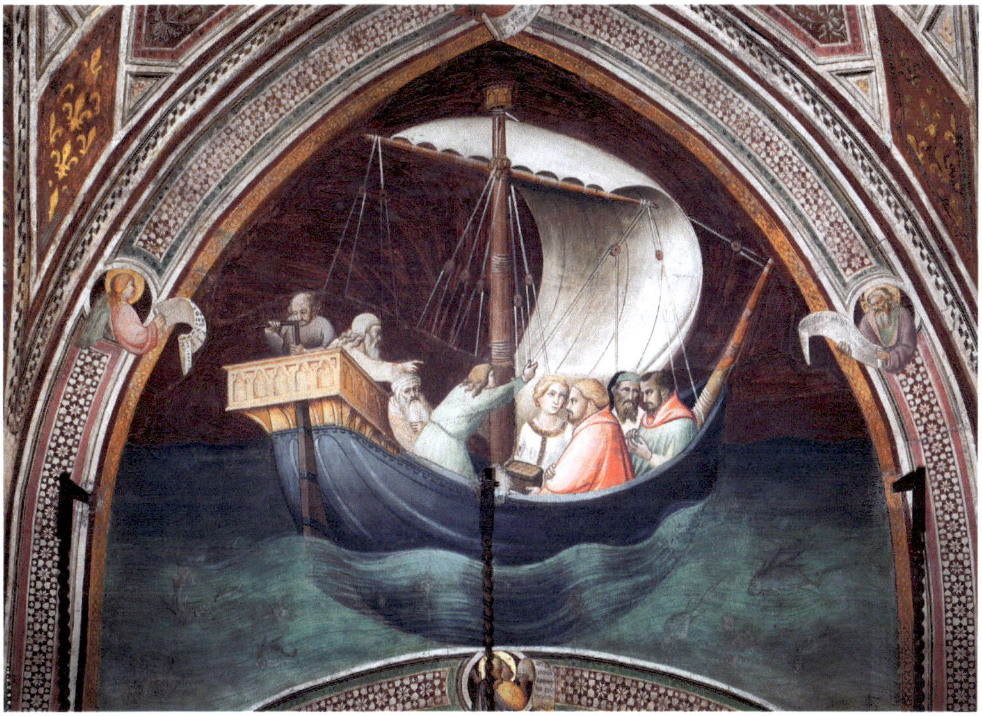

1.15. Agnolo Gaddi, *Journey of Michele and Maria to Prato*, 1392–95, Chapel of the Holy Belt, Duomo di Santo Stefano, Prato. Photo: Scala / Art Resource, NY.

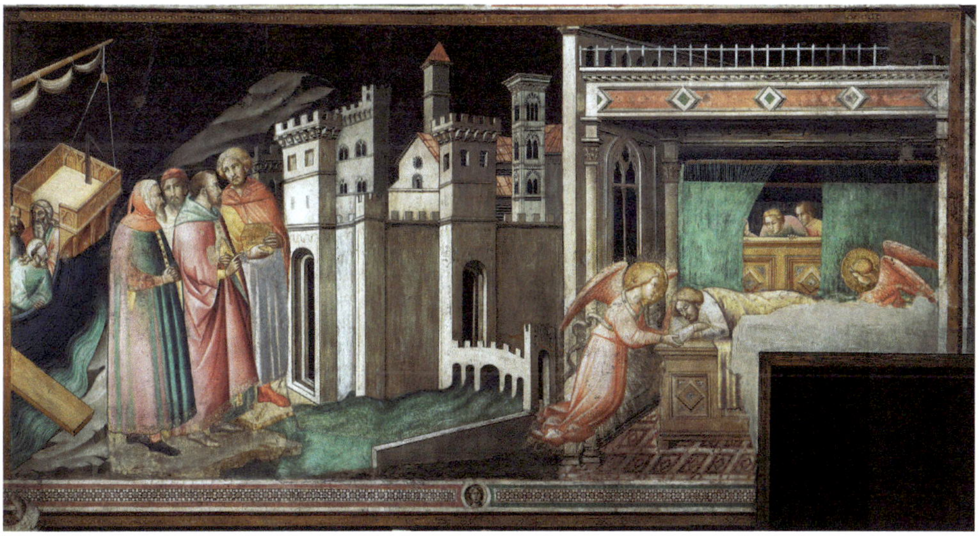

1.16. Agnolo Gaddi, *Michele arrives in Prato; a Miracle of the Belt*, 1392–95, Chapel of the Holy Belt, Duomo di Santo Stefano, Prato. Photo: Scala / Art Resource, NY.

depicted in this mural, absent from its counterpart in Daddi's predella, identifies the holy site of the *pieve* and town where the relic comes to rest, and in its depiction of actual place conforms to the historical character of written translation legends.[196] Assembled dignitaries see the holy presence of the Virgin, and the city that enjoys her favor, as evidence of the matrix of favor and obligation engendered by the Holy Belt, in which they play an essential role.

The first of the miracles associated with the relic is shown next to the arrival scene.[197] Relic translation legends from earliest times included accounts of the many miracles attributed to the relics as proof of their power and authenticity. A core group of seven miracles is recounted in the earliest histories of the Belt. By the mid-fourteenth century, the number had increased – the *Cincturale* records sixteen – and by the end of the fifteenth century the number would expand to thirty-one.[198] In Agnolo's mural, Michele sleeps on a richly carved chest or daybed, depicting the miracle in which Michele, having hidden the Sacred Belt in the chest, slept on top of it to prevent theft.[199] As his servants (or apprentices) Gottifreddo and Porco peer through parted curtains, angels place the sleeping Michele on the floor in order not to dishonor the relic by resting on top of it.

Many years later, Michele is shown on his deathbed. Propped up in his bed, he hands the Cintola, still in its rushed casket, to Uberto, the provost of the *pieve*, while other clerics look on. At the right, Uberto carries the precious casket in procession to the church (Figure 1.17).[200] In the textual sources, a

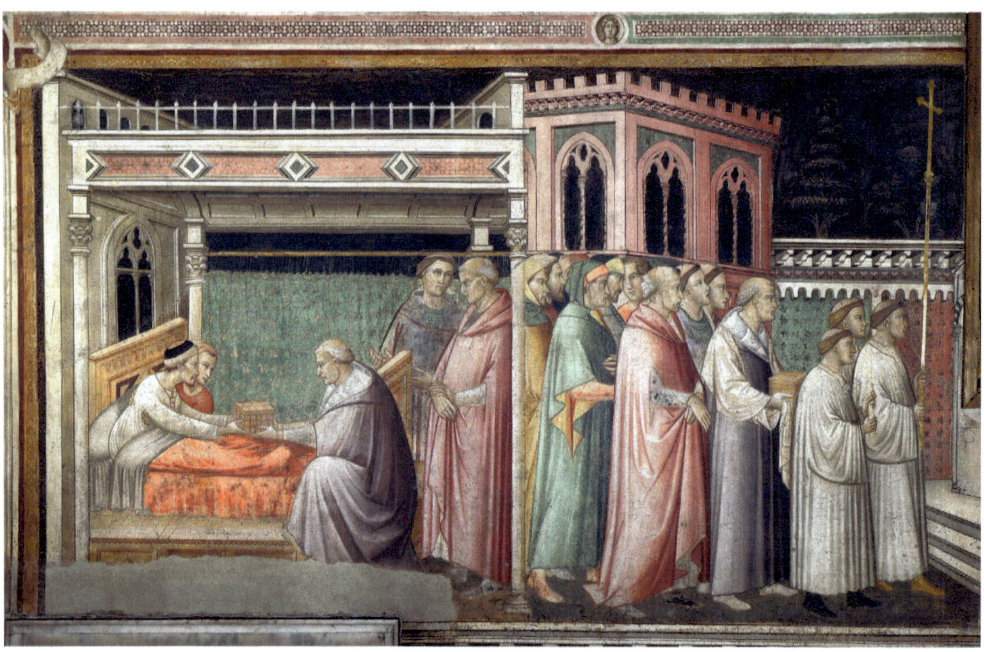

1.17. Agnolo Gaddi, *Death of Michele; the Belt is brought in Procession to the Pieve*, 1392–95, Chapel of the Holy Belt, Duomo di Santo Stefano, Prato. Photo: Scala / Art Resource, NY.

series of miracles unfolds between these two events, in which the provost, initially skeptical of the Belt's authenticity, comes to understand its true nature. Demands of visual narrative and restricted wall space determined Agnolo's abridgement of the textual account. That he devoted an entire scene to the procession, which is not described in the *Cincturale* – and only briefly related by written sources – is significant: it indicates the exemplary function of the murals, mirroring as they do the ceremony of celebration that took place in the chapel. Again, we see the *pieve* itself: just to the right we catch a glimpse of a slim engaged pilaster and part of the striped arch of the façade; the rest of the mural was mutilated by the later insertion of an organ.[201] The palace looming over the procession, with its elegant gothic windows, may also allude to the Palazzo della Propositura, just to the north of the *pieve*.[202] The specificity of the setting reminded viewers of the Prato's favored status as custodian of the sacred relic past and present.

The procession of the assembled dignitaries, led by acolytes carrying a processional cross and candles, may also mirror the actual ceremony of translation recorded in the document of 1395, as well as the processions formed during public ostentations. Here the provost, shown now with an embroidered white stole draped over his shoulders, the ends of which cover his hands holding the relic, precedes the gray-haired cleric, perhaps his vicar, in red. Tonsured brothers, two holding candles, one opening his mouth in song, accompany them. Following them are lay figures in contemporary dress. The mural thus visualizes the alliance of clergy and magistracy charged with the custody of the relic in real time. The celebration in song and light underscores the spectacle of the event.

The incidents of the Belt's translation to Prato shown in the murals were completed by the ceremony of the ostentation itself, as *elevatio* was followed in textual sources by *ostensio*. References to the original translation of the relic to the *pieve*, its relocation in the new altar, and the commemoration of these events during the yearly ostentation created a richly textured frame of reference for spectators and participants in the rite. By commemorating the translation of the relic, the murals fixed these events in memory and embedded them in the daily life of the community.

In visualizing the translation legend, Agnolo's murals can be read on many levels, much as their literary counterparts were. The relic is the vital link of Heaven and Earth, and of past, present, and future. As evidence of the Virgin's corporeal presence at the Assumption, it also demonstrates her real presence in Prato and the city's privileged status conferred by her gift. It collapses geography; the distant Holy Land is evoked as the relic descends to Thomas on the Mount of Olives and is transported by Michele the pilgrim vast distances to its current holy place. The procession to the *pieve*, both past and present, reenacts that pilgrimage and its sacred outcome, the translation of the relic, and inscribe it in the communal memory, thereby perpetuating and propagandizing the favored relationship of the city to its heavenly patron.[203] And as the miracles performed by the Belt demonstrated the power of the relic, so the depiction of the procession recalls the collective obligation of Pratesi to venerate their special patron. The cortege mirrors the social hierarchy of the town and choreographs the power relationships among clergy, magistracy, and *popolo* in Trecento Prato, while presenting its citizens as ordered, decorous, and unified. As dignitaries assembled in the chapel on the most solemn occasions of the civic and religious calendar gazed upon the murals of the east wall, they read a visual foundation history fundamental to the identity of Prato itself.

The same spectators, viewing the murals on the west wall of the chapel depicting the life of the Virgin, contemplated images by then familiar to worshippers. The story begins with the double scene of the *Expulsion of Joachim from the Temple* and the *Annunciation to Joachim* above the entrance arch through which the worshipper entered the chapel. It proceeds on the west wall with the *Meeting of Joachim and Anna at the Golden Gate* and the *Birth of the Virgin* on the top register. In the second register and reading from left to right are shown the *Presentation in the Temple* and the *Marriage of the Virgin*, while on the lowest register are depicted the *Annunciation* (Figure 1.18) and, in one

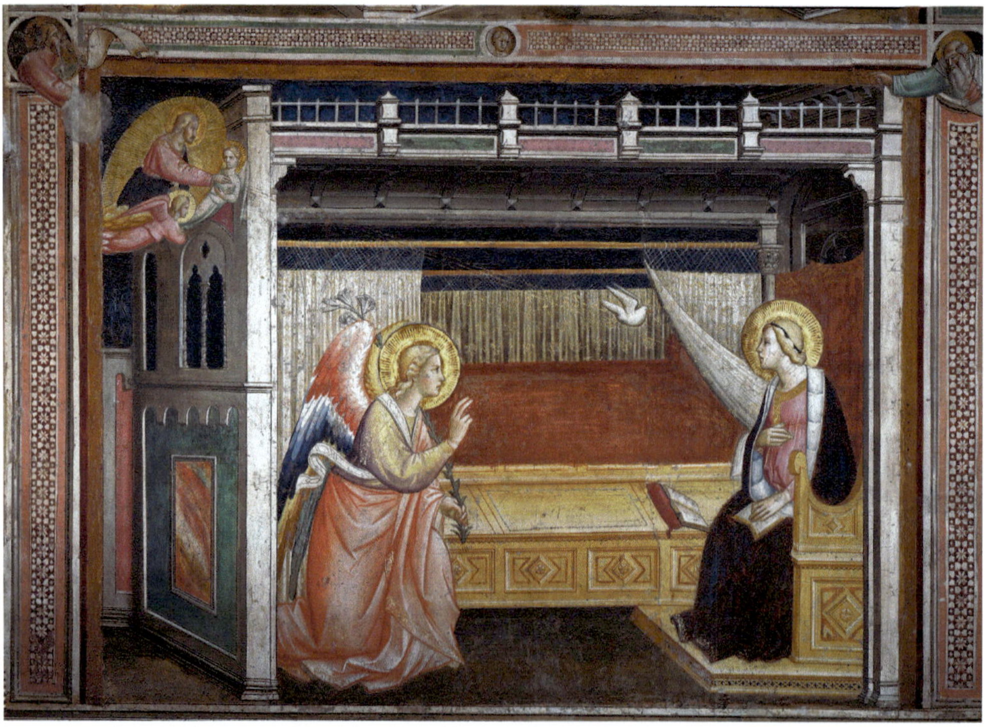

1.18. Agnolo Gaddi, *Annunciation*, 1392–95, Chapel of the Holy Belt, Duomo di Santo Stefano, Prato. Photo: Scala / Art Resource, NY.

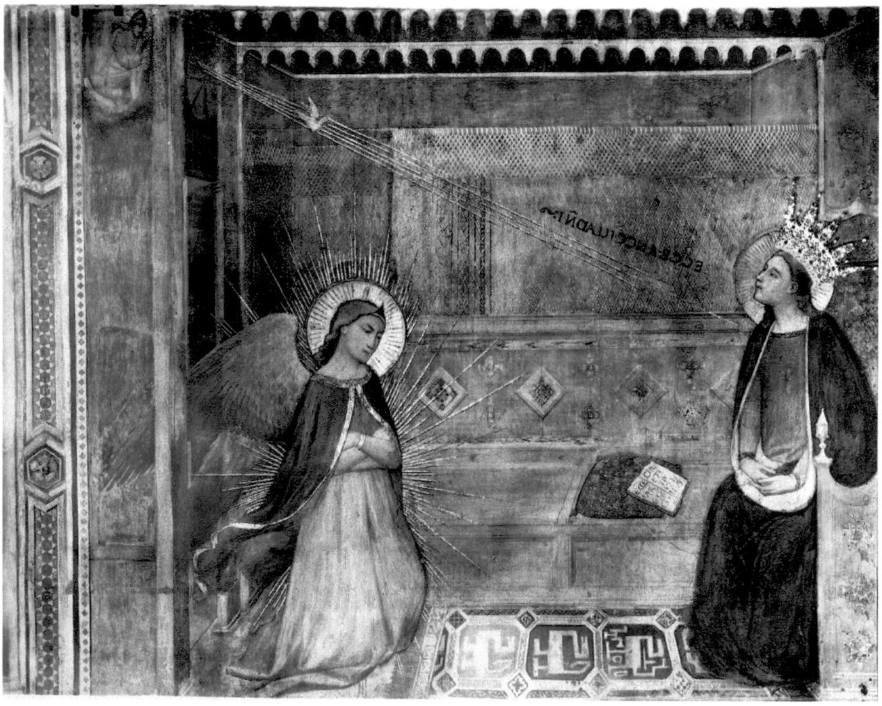

1.19. *Annunciation*, early fourteenth century, SS. Annunziata, Florence. Photo: Scala / Art Resource, NY.

scene, the *Nativity* and *Annunciation to the Shepherds*. In these murals, Agnolo followed precedents well known in Florentine cycles of the life of the Virgin, especially those established by his father, Taddeo Gaddi, in the Baroncelli chapel in Santa Croce.[204] Perhaps for that reason, and owing to the reduced scale of the fields and condensed narrative of their subjects, the Prato murals signaled a retreat from the exuberant complexity of the True Cross cycle. Agnolo moved toward a more sober color palette in Prato, and his compositions have fewer figures and simplified architecture. Continuities with the earlier cycle include the deep landscape, the elegant figures artfully arranged in groups that act out the stories, and the proliferation of observed detail, whether of everyday life or of the flora and fauna of the natural world.[205]

The *Annunciation* (Figure 1.18) is shown on the lowest level just to the left of the entrance arch, visible from the nave and from the aisle looking west. Viewers in the chapel would immediately have recognized the allusion in Agnolo's mural to the miracle-working fresco of the *Annunciation* in the church of the Santissima Annunziata in Florence (Figure 1.19). The elements evoking the sacred Florentine image are the interior view of the Virgin's chamber, in which the event takes place, with the bed surrounded by curtains, and the seat on which Mary sits, her prayer book propped up next to her.[206] While the gestures of the figures differ, the postures and placement of the figures, the angel kneeling and the Virgin seated facing her, are similar in the two scenes.[207] The details of God the Father in a mandorla, held up by angels, and the rays of light, by which the dove traverses the space toward the Virgin, recur. Visitors familiar with the Florentine image would have also noted that the mural occupies a place in the *pieve* like that in the Florentine church, that is, on the interior façade, directly to the left of the entrance portal. The arrangement of the space in the church of the Santissima Annunziata in the late fourteenth century is conjectural, owing to the renovations to the church in the early fifteenth century and the construction of the marble tabernacle in the 1440s. It is likely, however, that the spaces surrounding the miraculous image were previously marked off in some way to create a sanctuary for the veneration of the image.[208] The Prato image, in its form and spatial relationship to the architecture of the church, evokes the Florentine work.

The Santissima Annunziata inspired multiple copies in the late fourteenth century, many of them, like that in Prato, located on the entrance façade to the left of the main portal.[209] The original location perhaps reflects the action of worshippers, who recited prayers to the Virgin on entering and exiting the sanctuary; or it may have conformed to traditional narrative cycles of the life of Christ.[210] The Prato image is, at least as far as I can tell, unique, however, in interpolating the image of the Santissima Annunziata into a monumental narrative cycle.[211]

The evocation of the Florentine image in the Prato cycle is unusual because, since the beginnings of Christian art, isolated images (*imagines*) and narrative scenes (*historiae*), in addition to formal and material differences, have had different functions, carried different meanings, and established different relationships with spectators.[212] The didactic and historical function of the narrative cycle differs, at least in theory, from the devotional role of the icon. Yet transformations, from icon to narrative, and from narrative to icon, occurred in Italy – especially from the thirteenth century on – when a revolution in the form and meaning of images was underway. The way in which these different image types were "read" – the *imago* a focus of prolonged meditation, the *historia* as a station within a sequence – have implications for their form and meaning; in the shifting boundaries between icon and narrative a layering of content ensued.[213] As pointed out by Belting, certain narratives changed into "stations of contemplation," through either compositional change or selective presentation of narrative elements.[214] A fifteenth-century devotional handbook urged the worshipper visualizing a narrative of Christ's Passion, for example, to "Move slowly from episode to episode, meditate on each one, dwelling on each single stage and step of the story. And if at any point you feel a sensation of piety, stop: do not pass on as long as that sweet and devout sentiment lasts."[215] Baxandall proposed that painted images played off viewers' interior visualizations of holy stories; if so, we might suppose that visual narratives were subject to the same attention.[216] How, then, did the dignitaries assembled in the chapel in Prato for the solemn ceremony of the ostentation understand the inclusion of the Santissima Annunziata in the history of the Virgin cycle?

They may have first perceived the sanctity of the space. The miraculous image of the Santissima Annunziata, apart from depicting the initial and most important event in the Incarnation, the moment when Christ assumed human form so that humankind would be saved from eternal damnation, was significant as a miracle-making image. By legend, the image was completed by an angel and hence was different from an image made by mere human hands.[217] So too was the chapel of the Holy Belt, by virtue of the relic it housed, pervaded by the presence of the sacred, the Virgin herself.[218] In addition, spaces that housed images and relics were objects of pilgrimage and places of devotion. The chapels were vessels in a sense for the intense piety directed to the Santissima Annunziata or to the Holy Belt during ostentations.[219] Agnolo's inclusion of the image of the Santissima Annunziata within his cycle of the Virgin's life may have acknowledged the special nature of the chapel he was decorating and the devotional behavior that took place within it. Its placement on the inner façade wall may have been a means of animating a "memory of place" associated with the Santissima Annunziata and thereby enhancing the efficacy of his own image.[220] He may have hoped to extend viewers' intense, lingering contemplation associated with the Santissima Annuziata to the rest of his narrative images.

Worshippers would perhaps recall other Marian shrines they had visited. Their proliferation in the fourteenth century was well known; the Florentine author Franco Sacchetti, writing in the same years in which the chapel of the Holy Belt was constructed, mockingly proclaimed his bewilderment:

> How many changes have taken place in my city in the figure of Our Lady! At one time everyone ran to Santa Maria da Cigoli, then to Santa Maria delle Selve, then Santa Maria di Impruneta was most famous, then Santa Maria Primerana at Fiesole, and then Our Lady at Orsanmichele; then, they abandoned all and ran to the Annunziata of the Servites ... and the people behaved as if Our Lady would have more power to convey her favors in one place than in another.[221]

Sacchetti satirizes the competition among these Florentine shrines, a competition that extended beyond the city limits. Agnolo's allusion to the Florentine image in his murals may have been a bid to enhance its prestige by association with the Pratese relic.[222] For at this time, the Holy Belt in Prato was the more established shrine, the Santissima Annunziata having come to prominence only in the last quarter of the fourteenth century, as Sacchetti alludes.[223] These newer images responded to popular devotional currents and derived authority from local, secular institutions as much as from the Roman church and association with cult images and relics of Rome.[224] Linking the Santissima Annunziata with the Holy Belt evokes a specifically Tuscan group of Marian shrines perhaps as a counterpart or alternative to those of the Eternal city.

Florentine shrines were linked with the Pratese relic in the sumptuous tabernacle in Orsanmichele. Center of a civic cult much like that of the Holy Belt, the tabernacle housing the miraculous image has on its reverse a relief of the *Assumption of the Virgin* that includes the gift of the Belt, as a general acknowledgment of a powerful relic and prestigious site of Marian devotion in Tuscany.[225] Interlocking references to Marian shrines are also seen in the altarpiece painted by Pietro Nelli and Niccolò di Pietro Gerini in 1375 for the Collegiata at Impruneta, home of the famous miraculous image of the Madonna and Child.[226] In the upper register of the altarpiece, next to the depictions of the *Death*, *Assumption* (with the gift of the Belt to Thomas), and *Coronation of the Virgin*, is the image of the *Annunciation*, like that at Prato modeled on the Florentine image.

The lunette of the Assumption with the gift of the Belt would later grace the Porta della Mandorla of the Florentine Duomo, completed in the second decade of the fifteenth century. This was the door, close to the via dei Servi, through which the annual procession to the church of the Santissima Annunziata passed at the feast of the Annunciation.[227] In calling to mind worshippers' experience of sacred objects and spaces of devotion, these images weave a tissue of allusions to disparate and distant shrines that may have been an effort to isolate religious emotion from other experiences, much the way ciboria, chapels, and tabernacles isolate the spaces of prayer from that of quotidian action.[228]

Additionally, as Sacchetti suggested in his parody, the multiplication of sites of Marian devotion in the late Trecento underlined the special nature of the Virgin as a holy person. Unlike the saints, the Virgin left no corporeal remains, as she was assumed body and soul into heaven. The Virgin's Belt at Prato is a contact relic – it had once clothed her body, and it served as a substitute for that body, now in heaven. Instead of fragmenting the Virgin's body, as the dispersal of bodily relics might, the spread of relics such as her Belt or images of her at various shrines did not undermine her powers – Sacchetti mocks the idea that the Virgin would be more powerful in one shrine than in another. The diffusion of her power is based on the very lack of her bodily presence on earth, the "aching void at the center of Marian devotion," as it has been called; the Prato relic, as a proof of her bodily presence in the Assumption, is also at the same time a reminder of her absence from the world.[229] It is perhaps as a focus of longing that the relic inspired such devotion among the faithful.

As the many miracles associated with the Holy Belt suggest, even a secondary relic possessed a power associated with touch and presence that an image did not, and they elicited different behavior.[230] Weather miracles associated with the Virgin of Impruneta required taking her to Florence; while those performed by the Santissima Annunziata, and later, the Madonna delle Carceri in Prato, frequently took place elsewhere and resulted in vows to visit the shrine.[231] Of the miracles associated with the Holy Belt, most, such as exorcisms or healings, occurred in the presence of the relic or through objects – a thread or a cross – that had been in touch with it. In tandem with miraculous images of the Virgin, the Holy Belt stood at the center of what might be called a topography of Marian devotion diffused throughout Tuscany.[232]

We might also read the conflation of the prestige of the Holy Belt with the Santissima Annunziata as a subtle effort to draw the Pratese relic into the Florentine orbit of Marian shrines and thereby place a Florentine stamp on the cult of the Holy Belt. As an act of appropriation, the repetition of the Florentine image may not have conferred simply prestige or sanctity on the Pratese chapel but Florentineness – *fiorentinità*.[233] By insinuating the Florentine image into the space where the symbols and rituals of Pratese history and identity were preserved and enacted, that identity was inflected to signify the political realities of a Prato that at the end of the fourteenth century chafed under Florentine political control. The participation of the civic magistrates, among them the Florentine *Podestà*, in the processions and ostentation ceremony underscored that reality for spectators.

Even the style of Agnolo's frescoes, in which the composition, figure type, and imagery is reminiscent of Giottesque tradition, would contribute to a Florentine presence. Agnolo's recall of Taddeo's compositions, as, strikingly, in the *Marriage of the Virgin*, may have placed before the assembled dignitaries of Prato his own prestigious artistic lineage and that of Florence itself.[234] A student of Agnolo Gaddi, Cennino Cennini, in his *Libro dell'Arte*, written at just about this time, celebrated that lineage and tradition.[235] In this light, the references to Giottesque tradition in Florentine trecento painting, which has been seen as an aesthetic choice, might have taken on a deeper cultural meaning.[236]

FLORENTINE CULTURAL PATRONAGE

Building and decorating the new chapel of the Holy Belt might then be seen as the cultural counterpart of Florentine state-building in Tuscany in the second half of the fourteenth century. During that time, Florence embarked on a program of expansion that resulted in a vast territorial state.[237] Prato, only ten miles to the northwest of the city, was sold to the Florentines by Giovanna of Anjou in 1351 and was one of the first of the Tuscan republics to fall. Formerly allied with the German emperors, whose fortress stood at the point where a major pass through the Apennines met the valley of the Bisenzio river, Prato's strategic and economic importance to Florence was evident. After 1351,

Florence left many of the local political institutions and offices unchanged but retained ultimate political authority. Local traditions, codified in municipal statutes, were left intact, so that political domination was leavened by the outward forms of autonomy.[238] And yet the Pratesi, famously proud, resisted Florentine dominance; in 1391, 600 Pratesi protested against heavy taxation, and political opposition to Florentine rule emerged sporadically in the late Trecento and early Quattrocento into the Medici regime starting in 1434. While Pratese resistance was less overt than in Pisa, as described in Chapter 4, it continued through the fifteenth century, only abating with the emergence of the Medici duchy in the sixteenth century.

Many Pratese historians have marveled that the Florentines failed in "Florentinizing" the cult of the Holy Belt or even removing it to Florence.[239] The rebuilding and redecorating of the chapel of the Holy Belt in the late fourteenth century might, however, be seen as part of a Florentine effort to subjugate the countryside and consolidate its holdings. The provost of the *pieve*, and the presiding bishop, his brother, during the time the new chapel was built and decorated, were both Pistoiesi with close ties to Florence.[240] As we have seen, the primary artisans charged with the design and execution of the new chapel and its decoration were either employed by or long associated with the Florentine Opera del Duomo.[241] The documents detailing the progress of the chapel construction are replete with importations of both material and expertise from Prato's powerful neighbor. While culturally Prato had long been in Florence's shadow, the new chapel of the Holy Belt takes on the aura of a concerted effort by the Florentines to control access to and presentation of the prestigious relic, emblem of civic identity. Their insistent demands during the fifteenth century for special ostentations of the Belt to visiting dignitaries signaled a growing sense of ownership.[242] Carlo de' Medici, the natural son of Cosimo de' Medici (1389–1464), was appointed provost of Santo Stefano in 1460 and retained the position until his death in 1492. Lorenzo de' Medici's (1449–92) intervention during the 1480s in Santa Maria delle Carceri, a new site of a Marian worship in Prato, was also foreshadowed by the project to build the chapel of the Holy Belt. In the context of Florentine territorial expansion, as well as the fierce competition for pilgrims among Marian shrines, the new chapel of the Holy Belt can be seen as an early instance of Florentine cultural patronage, one that set the stage for the policy of the Medicean regime in the fifteenth century.

NOTES

1 A description of the ostentation ceremony is contained in a legal document validating the translation, found in Prato, Archivio di Stato (hereafter ASP), Patrimonio Ecclesiastico (hereafter PE), 1002, c. 7 (see below). Sandro Marcovaldi reported the indulgences in his *Cronaca*, published by Ruggero Nuti in *Archivio storico pratese*, vol. 18, 1940, pp. 49–69.

2 Aspects of this chapter have been presented in several lectures and in Jean K. Cadogan, "The Chapel of the Holy Belt in Prato: Piety and Politics in Fourteenth Century Tuscany," *Artibus et Historiae*, vol. 60, 2009, pp. 107–38. This chapter presents an expanded discussion and full presentation of the supporting documents.

3 While the Assumption of the Virgin became Catholic dogma only in 1950, the depiction of the Virgin being assumed into heaven and crowned by Jesus was widespread in the visual arts from the twelfth century. For the textual tradition of the Assumption of the Virgin, which is not mentioned in the gospels, see Marina Warner, *Alone of All Her Sex: The Myth and the Cult of the Virgin Mary*, New York: Knopf, 1976, pp. 3–33, 81–102; Mary Clayton, *Cult of the Virgin Mary in Anglo-Saxon England*, Cambridge: Cambridge University Press, 1990, pp. 1–24; Manuela de Giorgi, *Il Transito della Vergine*, Spoleto: Centro Italiano di Studi sull'alto Medioevo, 2016, pp. 65–89; Andrea De Marchi, "Prato e la sacra Cintola: Mitopoiesi civica e nuove forme della devozione, all'incrocio fra la chiesa e il mondo," *Iconographica*, special issue, 2021, pp. 21–22.

4 Already by 1276–79, the ostentation was referred to in a fragmentary communal statute, while statutes datable between 1285 and 1294 devote an entire rubric to the Belt's preservation; see Renzo Fantappiè, "Nascita e sviluppo di Prato," in *Prato, storia di una città*, vol. 1, part 1, Bagno a Ripoli: Le Monnier, 1991, pp. 245–46, note 29; Renzo Fantappiè, "Storia e 'storie' della Cintola," in Claudio Martini, ed., *La Sacra Cintola nel Duomo di Prato*, Prato: Claudio Martini, 1995, p. 54, note 8.

5 The ostentation ceremony was first documented to 1255, when the bishop of Pistoia granted indulgences to worshippers on 8 September; Renzo Fantappiè, "Per la storia del Sacro Cingolo," *Archivio storico pratese*, vol. 87, 2011 [2013], pp. 151–52, doc. no. 1. The celebration of the birth of the Virgin on 8 September has been known in the Eastern Church since the seventh century and in Rome dates to the second half of the seventh century. Pope Sergius (687–701) instituted processions like that on 2 February, the feast of the Purification, on 25 March (Annunciation), 15 August (Assumption), and 8 September; Clayton, *The Cult of the Virgin Mary*, pp. 28–29; Dominique Iogna-Prat et al., ed., *Marie: Le culte de la Vierge dans la société Médiévale*, Paris: Beauchesne, 1996, pp. 17–18.

6 The Prato fair has existed at least since 1239; Ruggero Nuti, *La Fiera di Prato attraverso i tempi*, Prato: Associazione turistica pratese, 1939, pp. 14, 37.

7 Giovanni Miniati, *Narrazione e disegno della terra di Prato di Toscana* [1594], Prato: Vestri, 1827, pp. 71–72. On the ceremony of ostentation generally, see Nicole Herrmann-Mascard, *Les Reliques des saints: Formation coutumière du'un droit*, Paris: Klincksieck, 1975, pp. 206–16.

8 Giuseppe Bianchini, *Notizie istoriche della sacratissima cintola*, Prato: Vestri, 1822, p. 45; Gioacchino Pelagatti, *Il Sacro Cingolo Mariano in Prato*, Prato: Giachetti, 1895, p. 8. See also Claudio Cerretelli, "Tre cappelle per la sacra Cintura," in Isabella Lapi Ballerini, ed., *Agnolo Gaddi e la Cappella della Cintola; La storia, l'arte, il restauro*, Florence: Polistampa, 2009, pp. 63–73.

9 Ruggero Nuti, "Aspetti di Prato nel Medioevo: La Piazza della pieve," *Archivio storico pratese*, vol. 27 (1934), p. 50; Fantappiè, "Per la storia del Sacro Cingolo," pp. 142–43.

10 Patrick Geary, *Furta Sacra*, 2nd ed., Princeton: Princeton University Press, 1990.

11 By some accounts, Musciattino intended to sell the relic to Florence; by others, he wished to carry it to his native city of Pistoia; Bianchini, *Notizie istoriche*, pp. 39–40, 44–53; Pelagatti, *Il Sacro Cingolo*, pp. 107–22; Claudio Cerretelli, "Musciattino tra storia e leggenda," *Prato; Storia e Arte*, vol. 112, December 2012, pp. 103–15. A fourteenth-century history in Latin is published by Anna Imelde Galetti, "Storie della Sacra Cintola (Schede per un lavoro da fare a Prato)," in Franco Cardini, ed., *Toscana e Terrasanta nel Medioevo*, Florence: Alinea, 1982, p. 335. Documents from Musciattino's trial are published in Bianchini, *Notizie istoriche*, pp. 49–52; Galetti, p. 335; and Fantappiè, "Per la storia del Sacro cingolo," pp. 155–63, doc. no. 5.

12 Fantappiè, "Storia e 'storie' della Cintola," pp. 55–56, notes 28, 29, quotes the deliberations from 29 and 31 July 1312.

13 Fantappiè, "Storia e 'storie' della Cintola," p. 56, note 29. For the construction and the attribution of the design to Giovanni Pisano, see Giorgio Vasari, *Le vite de' più eccellenti pittori scultori e architettori*, ed. Gaetano Milanesi, Florence: Sansoni, 1906, vol. 1, p. 318; Giuseppe Marchini, *Il Duomo di Prato*, Milan: Electa, 1957, pp. 33–45. Giuseppe Marchini, *Il Tesoro del Duomo di Prato*, Prato: Cassa di Risparmi, 1963, pp. 55–58, argues for a protracted period of construction, publishing documents for the vaulting of the transepts dating to 1365–68; see also pp. 95–99, docs. 2–7, 18. For the various locations of the altar, see Pelagatti, *Il Sacro Cingolo*, p. 43; Marchini, *Il Duomo di Prato*, p. 35; and Claudio Cerretelli, L'architettura della chiesa," in Claudio Cerretelli and Renzo Fantappié, eds., *Il Duomo di Prato*, Florence: Le Lettere, 2009, pp. 63–65; Claudio Cerretelli, "La sacra cintola e il suo scrigno: La pieve di santo Stefano dal XII alla fine del XIV secolo," in Andrea De Marchi and Cristina Gnoni Mavarelli, eds., *Legati da una cintola: L'Assunta di Bernardo Daddi e l'identità di una città*, Florence: Mandragora, 2017, pp. 44–45, 47–53.

14 G. Giani, "Documenti su antichi pittori pratesi," *Archivio storico pratese*, vol. 2, 1917, p. 74; Marchini, *Tesoro*, p. 97, doc. 13; Marchini, *Il Duomo di Prato*, p. 35; Claudio Cerretelli, "La Pieve e la Cintola: Le trasformazioni legate alla reliquia," in Martini, ed., *La Sacra Cintola nel Duomo di Prato*, p. 89. On the altarpiece, see Andrea De Marchi, "Prato 1338: Una pala risarcita di Bernardo Daddi, una città che cresce sotto il segno della cintola," in De Marchi and Mavarelli, eds., *Legati da una cintola*, pp. 13–28 and 122–31, cat. nos. 4–6; De Marchi, "Prato e la sacra Cintola: Mitopoiesi civica e nuove forme della devozione," pp. 15–24.

15 Marchini, *Tesoro*, pp. 63–64, 96, doc. 9; Fantappiè, "Per la storia del Sacro Cingolo," pp. 143–44.

16 Cerretelli, "Tre cappelle," p. 64; Cerretelli, "La sacra cintola e il suo scrigno," pp. 43–51.

17 Bianchini, *Notizie istoriche*, p. 75; Marchini, *Tesoro*, p. 98, doc. 15.

18 Marchini, *Tesoro*, pp. 60, 100, doc. 25; the original is in ASP, PE 1002, cc. 60 verso–62 verso. Listed are liturgical objects and vestments, sculpture, paintings, a tabernacle, votive objects, tapestries, and other objects. Marchini supposed that the inventory referred to the new chapel being built at that time, but Cerretelli, "La Pieve e la Cintola," p. 91, correctly notes that it must refer to the older chapel. Cerretelli reconstructs this chapel, based on the inventory, as a vaulted chapel enclosed by a low parapet surmounted by a wooden grate with two doors. Furniture included two benches or pews and various cupboards. An altar abutting the wall was covered with liturgical vessels, statues, and paintings. Another structure above housed "unum altare super volta cappelle," and may refer to an internal pulpit for the display of the Belt, connected to the outdoor pulpit referred to in documents of 1359–60 and reached by a stairway against the wall; see Cerretelli, "La Pieve e la Cintola," pp. 90–91; Cerretelli, "Tre cappelle," p. 64; Cerretelli, "La sacra cintola e il suo scrigno," pp. 46–47; and Giampaolo Ermini, "Per la cappella 'intermedia' della Cintola nel Duomo di Prato (post 1346–1395). Note sulla costruzione e sulla struttura del pulpito esterno," *Iconographica*, special issue, 2021, pp. 138–58.

19 Giampiero Nigro, *Il Tempo liberato: Festa e svago nella città di Francesco Datini*, Prato: Istituto Internazionale di Storia Economica "F. Datini," 1994, p. 56, reasonably attributes this lack to the widespread familiarity of the event. A general account is available in the 1505 statutes, Florence, Archivio di Stato (afterward ASF), Statuti delle comunità autonome e soggette, 658 (Prato, 1505), cc. 3 recto–6 recto; see also Fantappiè, "Per la storia del Sacro cingolo," pp. 135–38; and the rubric from the 1297 statutes in De Marchi and Mavarelli, eds., *Legati da una cintola*, p. 118 cat. no. 2.

20 Nuti, *La Fiera di Prato*, pp. 15, 38.

21 This description follows that in Nuti, *La Fiera di Prato*, pp. 17–18. The communal structure of the Pratese government took shape in the late thirteenth century. Although Prato remained under nominal imperial control, communal and popular institutions evolved to include, by the late thirteenth century, a *Podestà* and the *Capitano del Popolo*, both foreigners, and a *Gonfaloniere di Giustizia*, a Pratese citizen. The legislative function was exercised by a *Consiglio Generale*, presided over by the *Podestà*, and a *Consiglio del Popolo* (or *dei*

Quaranta), presided over by the *Capitano del Popolo*. The organ that provided the leadership for political and administrative life of the commune was the *Consiglio degli Otto Difensori* and the *Gonfaloniere di Giustizia*, both popular, who were the most important citizen magistrates. When Prato was absorbed into the Florentine dominion in 1351, the structure continued, though ultimate authority rested with Florence, exercised through the *Podestà*, a Florentine, and, like political developments of the late Trecento in Florence, power was increasingly concentrated in the hands of the economic elite. See detailed accounts in Emilio Cristiani, "Il Libero Comune di Prato," and Guido Pampaloni, "Prato nella Repubblica Fiorentina," in *Storia di Prato*, Prato: Edizioni Cassa di Risparmi, 1980, vol. 1, pp. 363–412, vol. 2, pp. 3–21; Sergio Raveggi, "Protagonisti e antagonisti nel libero comune," in *Prato: Storia di una città*, vol. 1, part 3, pp. 614–759. For a history of the institutional structure, see Guido Bisori, "Gli ordinamenti di un comune toscano nei primi del 1500," *Archivio storico pratese*, vol. 5, 1925, pp. 104–26.

22 On the structure and building history of the Palazzo Comunale, see Ruggero Nuti, "Aspetti di Prato nel Medioevo, II: Il Palazzo del Popolo," *Archivio storico pratese*, 29, 1953, pp. 25–48; and Claudio Cerretelli, "La piazza ed il palazzo del commune dal XIII agli inizi del XIV secolo," *Prato, storia e arte*, no. 77, 1990, pp. 7–44.

23 Payments to musicians from Lucca, Pistoia, Pisa, San Gimignano, and Montalbiolo are listed in an entry of 9 September 1538 in the *Diurno*, in ASP, Comunale 130, c. 25 recto. Ruggero Nuti, in Count Giuseppe Maria Casotti, "Lunario istorico pratese," ed. R. Nuti, *Archivio storico pratese*, 10, no. 3, 1930, p. 164, note 1, quotes the text from a communal state of 1498 describing the payments, or "mancia," paid by the commune to the musical representatives from the various towns. Listed are delegations from the signoria of Florence, the *Capitani* of the Parte Guelfa, and from the *signorie* of Siena, Lucca, Pistoia, Volterra, Colle, San Gimignano, San Miniato, Pescia, and Monte Robbiolo.

24 An entry in the *Diurno* of 7 September 1538 describes the procession; ASP, Comunale 130, c. 24 verso. The procession formed at the 22nd hour (two hours before sunset) and included the secular and monastic clergy; the Eight and Standard-bearer, the *Podestà*, and other magistrates assembled in the Palazzo Comunale and progressed to the altar of the Holy Belt, where solemn offerings were made. See also Casotti, "Lunario istorico pratese," pp. 103–4; Nuti, *La Fiera di Prato*, p. 18.

25 Casotti, "Lunario istorico pratese," p. 163; for the ancient street names see Enrico Fiumi, *Demografia movimento urbanistico e classi sociali in Prato*, Florence: Olschki, 1968, pp. 510–15, and the website www.comune.prato.it/storiastrade/. A procession in 1484 to the site of the image of Santa Maria delle Carceri is discussed in Robert Maniura, *Art and Miracle in Renaissance Tuscany*, Cambridge: Cambridge University Press, 2018, pp. 98–101.

26 The procession passed by houses of the feudal lords the Mazzinghi, in Borgo al Cornio, and the Milanesi, on the via Mazzoni near the Palazzo Comunale. The Mazzinghi had a tower (still extant) at the beginning of the via del Borgo al Cornio by the fourteenth century. See also Fiumi, *Demografia movimento urbanistico e classi sociali in Prato*, pp. 426, 433–34.

27 In the fourteenth century, the church of Santa Maria delle Carceri did not exist. However, the prisons, from which the church takes its name, were located near there, and release of prisoners was a custom on the Virgin's birthday; see Bianchini, *Notizie istoriche*, pp. 92–94.

28 These offerings were dictated by statute; see Bianchini, *Notizie istoriche*, pp. 64–65.

29 Fantappiè, "Storia e 'storie' della Cintola," p. 56, notes 38, 39, cites payments from 1293 for these services.

30 Bianchini, *Notizie istoriche*, pp. 64–65; Bianchini noted that the offerings in wax had in more recent times been discontinued in favor of coin. The compulsory offerings of wax are detailed in the 1505 statute, Florence, ASF, Stauti delle comunità autonome e soggette, 658 (Prato, 1505), cc. 4 verso–6 recto, rubric 6, on the offerings of the Eight and the Standard-bearer, rubric 7, the offerings of the villages of the Pratese contando, and rubric 8 the offerings of the guilds. The offerings run from the half-pound wax of the Eight, worth at least 30 soldi, to a range from 32 to 10 soldi for the towns, and from 2 to 1 soldi for the

guilds. Bisori, "Gli ordinamenti di un comune nei primi del 1500," p. 144 and 157, note 155, noted that the expense for the wax candles offered by the Eight on 8 September was borne by the commune, which purchased them from the Opera of the Sacra Cintola. Income from the sale of candles, sold from a desk in front of the chapel by an employee of the Opera, was one of the main sources of support for the activities of the cult. See also Diana Toccafondi, "Legati da una Cintura: Devozione, culto e potere a Prato dal medioevo all'età contemporanea," in Martini, ed., *La Sacra Cintola nel Duomo di Prato*, pp, 64–65.

31 The use of ritual in Italian city-states has been widely discussed; see Edward Muir, *Ritual in Early Modern Europe*, 2nd ed., Cambridge: Cambridge University Press, 2005; and Diana Webb, *Patrons and Defenders: The Saints in the Italian City-states*, London: Tauris Academic Studies, 1996. On the concept of social memory, see Maurice Halbwachs, *The Collective Memory*, trans. Francis Kitter and Vida Ditter, New York: Harper and Row, 1980; Pierre Nora, "Mémoire collective," in J. Le Goff, R. Chartier, and J. Revel, eds., *La Nouvelle Histoire*, Paris: Retz, 1978, pp. 398–401; Pierre Nora, "Between Memory and History: Les Lieux de Memoire," *Representations*, vol. 26, Spring, 1989, pp. 7–24; Patrick Geary, "The Historical Material of Memory," in Giovanni Ciappelli and Patricia Rubin, eds., *Art, Memory, and Family in Renaissance Florence*, Cambridge: Cambridge University Press, 2000, pp. 17–25.

32 Fantappiè, "Storia e 'storie' della Cintola," pp. 42–43, 54–55, notes 8, 21–23. A fragmentary statute from c. 1285–94 stipulated that the Belt was not to be shown by city officials without the express permission of the provost of the *pieve*; Bianchini, *Notizie istoriche*, pp. 46–47; Pelagatti, *Il Sacro Cingolo*, pp. 100–101; Marchini, *Tesoro*, pp. 54, 95, doc. 1, publishes the text. Ten "buonomini" were charged with assisting the captain in the management of the relic. The casket in which the relic was kept was locked with two keys that were in the possession of the commune. During the ostentation, only clerics were permitted to touch it, but the statutes required that they wear silk gloves embroidered with gold threads. During the ceremony, the *Podestà*, the *Capitano del Popolo*, the eight *Difensori*, and the *Gonfaloniere di Giustizia*, with their "families" (that is, their administrative staffs) were in attendance, but they were forbidden to touch the relic, or to advance to within three braccia of it, under pain of a penalty of 25 lire. Initially the Belt was shown twice a year, on 8 September, the nativity of the Virgin, and at Easter. In 1382, Christmas was added, and also in the late fourteenth century the 1st of May; in 1494, the feast of Saint Joseph was added, but by 1628 the occasions were reduced to the initial four; see Toccafondi, "Legati da una Cintura," p. 65.

33 Pelagatti, *Il Sacro Cingolo*, p. 100; Toccafondi, "Legati da una Cintura," p. 65.

34 Marchini, *Tesoro*, pp. 96–97, doc. 10, publishes the text of the deliberation dated 20 October 1330; Bianchini, *Notizie istoriche*, pp. 57–58, also publishes a similar text from 8 October 1330. See also Pelagatti, *Il Sacro Cingolo*, p. 133.

35 Bianchini, *Notizie istoriche*, pp. 59–63.

36 Marchini, *Tesoro*, p. 54; Fantappiè, "Storia e 'storie' della Cintola," p. 46.

37 Marchini, *Tesoro*, pp. 97–98, doc. 15, publishes this letter; Bianchini, *Notizie istoriche*, pp. 73–83, publishes a similar agreement between the commune and the provost, dated 28 January 1351/2, in which the division of responsibility is precise: that the *proposto* of the *pieve* was the titular possessor of the relic and that he had custody of half of the keys to its altar and casket; if he was away, the possession of the keys passed to his vicar and to the chapter of the *pieve*. It was determined that the other half of the keys were in the hands of the magistrates and *Gonfaloniere di Giustizia* of the commune. If ever the altar and the chapel in which the relic was housed were to be enlarged or enriched, this would be done with the approval of the provost. Also, the chaplain or chaplains who were deputized to serve at the altar of the relic were to be elected by the Eight and *Gonfaloniere* of the commune and confirmed by the provost or his representatives; hence they were independent of the *pieve* but also bore certain obligations to it. For the subsidy and maintenance of those who served the altar and other affairs of the relic, a portion of the offerings of the

chapel were to go to the clerics; a third of the oblations, legacies, and alms offered to the chapel were for the provost, and the rest, according to the statutes of the commune, would go to the *camarlingo* of the commune.

38 The document with the names of the first *operai* and the summary financial statement of the Opera is in ASP, PE 1002, c. 181. In 1374, the Opera della Cintola and the Opera della Pieve were merged; see Toccafondi, "Legati da una Cintura," pp. 65, 73, note 14. For a description of the Opera della Sacra Cintola, see Bianchini, *Notizie istoriche*, pp. 84–85. Renzo Fantappiè, "Da pieve a cattedrale," in Cerretelli, Fantappiè, et al., eds., *Il Duomo di Prato*, pp. 18–21, describes the organization of the clergy.

39 Cerretelli, "La Pieve e la Cintola," p. 150, note 23, taken from notebooks of Martino Benelli in Prato, Biblioteca Roncioniana (hereafter BRP), Ms. U IV, 2, V, c. 44.

40 The documents were published in summary form by Giovanni Poggi, "La Cappella del Sacro Cingolo nel Duomo di Prato e gli affreschi di Agnolo Gaddi," *Rivista d'arte*, 14 (1932), pp. 355–76. Cerretelli's accounts of the chapel construction, in "La Pieve e la Cintola," pp. 92–96, and "Tre cappelle," pp. 64–67, also refer to the documents. The construction documents are in ASP, PE 960, and for the paintings and furnishings in ASP, PE 44–48, transcribed here in Appendix I.

41 Lapi Ballerini, "Per onorare la sua preciossima cintola," p. 26; Lapi Ballerini, "La cappella della cintola," pp. 59–60. Franco Cardini, "Identità cittadina, mariodulia e culto delle reliquie. Il 'caso' pratese," in Paola Maffei et al., eds., *"Honos alit artes": Studi per settantesimo compleanno di Mario Ascheri*, Florence, 2014, vol. 2, pp. 177–85. On the Franchi as patrons of art, see Giacomo Guazzini, "Commissioni artistiche tra Prato e Pistoia, anno 1400: Un'apertura per il vescovo Andrea Franchi ed il fratello Bartolomeo," in Paolo Benassi et al., eds., *Officina Pratese: Tecnica, stile, storia*, Florence: Edifir, 2014, pp. 211–28. Despite the provost's and bishop's support for building the new chapel in Prato, there is no evidence of their direct intervention in its design or decoration, as Guazzini notes, pp. 216–17.

42 The new façade, which was begun in 1385 and probably reached the height of the external pulpit by 1389, was completed only in 1457; see Cerretelli, "La Pieve e la Cintola," pp. 97–100, and "Tre cappelle," pp. 69–70.

43 In the course of 1388 and 1389, the new spaces were vaulted, a roof constructed, and the sacristy furnished with benches, cupboards, and a glass window, while the chapel was paved with glazed tiles; Cerretelli, "La Pieve e la Cintola," p. 93.

44 The act of translation was published (with some omissions) by Bianchini, *Notizie istoriche*, pp. 81–83, and in an Italian translation (based on Bianchini) by Gioacchino Pelagatti, *Il Sacro Cingolo Mariano*, 2nd ed., Prato: Bechi, 1937, pp. 59–62. The original is in ASP, PE 1002, c. 7. Payments for the altar extend from 21 July 1394 to 26 January 1395; the act of consecration was published by Ruggero Nuti, "La consacrazione dell'altare del Sacro Cingolo," *Archivio storico pratese*, 12, no. 2, 1934, pp. 73–75; the original is found in Prato, Archivio dell'Opera del Duomo, Capitolo, Diplomatico, 5 September 1395.

45 ASP, PE 960, c. 2. On Lorenzo, see Cesare Guasti, *Santa Maria del Fiore: La costruzione della chiesa e del campanile*, Florence: M. Ricci, 1887, pp. 261–97; Howard Saalman, *Filippo Brunelleschi: The Cupola of Santa Maria del Fiore*, London: Zwemmer, 1980, pp. 55–56, 182, 185.

46 For what follows see Poggi, "La Cappella del Sacro Cingolo," pp. 358–62; Cerretelli, "La Pieve e la Cintola," pp. 92–94; and Appendix I.

47 ASP, PE 960 c. 3, 20 January 1385/6.

48 ASP, PE 960, cc. 10 verso, 16 verso.

49 ASP, PE 960, c. 20.

50 ASP, PE 960, cc. 25, 35.

51 ASP, PE 960, cc. 44, 46 verso, 50.

52 ASP, PE 42, c. 97.

53 ASP, PE 44, c. 28 verso; PE 47, c. 20, Appendix I.1, p. 348.

54 "Per 2 schudi dell'arme del Comune"; ASP, PE 960, cc. 7, 21 verso, 50 verso, 65 verso, 82; PE 46, c. 4 verso and 8 verso, Appendix I.2, pp. 339, 343; PE 47, cc. 18 recto and 20 recto, Appendix I.3, pp. 346–48; PE 48, c. 20 recto, Appendix I.4, p. 361. See also Gert Kreytenberg, "Giovanni d'Ambrogio," *Jahrbuch der Berliner Museen*, vol. 14, 1972, pp. 5–32. One of these coats of arms is illustrated in Cerretelli, "Tre cappelle per la sacra Cintura," p. 66, fig. 6.

55 ASP, PE 46, c. 1, 10 June 1393, c. 4 verso, 9 December 1393, Appendix I.2, pp. 334, 339; PE 47, c. 20, 21 July 1394, c. 23 verso, 25 May 1395, Appendix I.3, pp. 348, 355 (when he was accompanied by his son, Lorenzo di Giovanni; for the latter, see Gert Kreytenberg, "Giovanni Fetti und die Porta dei Canonici des Florentiner Domes," *Mitteilungen des Kunsthistorischen Institutes in Florenz*, vol. 20, 1976, pp. 155–56).

56 Michele di Pavolo: ASP, PE 960, c. 6 verso, 43, 44, 50 verso; Romolo di Benozzo: ASP, PE 960, c. 8; PE 47, c. 18, Appendix I.3, p. 347.

57 ASP, PE 960, c. 50 verso.

58 Saalman, *Filippo Brunelleschi*, pp. 181–85. In the fifteenth century, the Opera supervised such varied projects as the maintenance of the palazzo and Loggia della Signoria and of the Studio Fiorentino and the construction and furnishing of the papal apartments in Santa Maria Novella. The fortifications in the countryside and the security works connected with the conquest of Pisa were also supervised by the Opera; see Margaret Haines, "Firenze e il finanziamento della cattedrale e del campanile," in T. Verdon, ed., *Alla riscoperta di piazza del Duomo in Firenze, 3: Il Campanile di Giotto*, Florence: Centro Di, 1994, pp. 82–83. This aspect of the Opera has not been systematically studied; see Antje Middeldorf Kosegarten, "Situazioni conflittuali nei rapporti tra artisti, committenti e operai intorno al 1300," in Margaret Haines and Lucio Riccetti, eds. *Opera: Carattere e ruolo delle fabbriche cittadine fino all'inizio dell'età moderna*, Florence: Oschki, 1996, pp. 371–92; and Friedman's review of the volume in *Ricerche storiche*, vol. 27, 1997, pp. 185–87. See also Francis.W. Kent, "Lorenzo de' Medici at the Duomo," in Timothy Verdon and Annalisa Innocenti, eds., *La Cattedrale e la Città: Saggi sul Duomo di Firenze*, Florence: Edifir, 2001, vol. 1, pp. 341–68.

59 David Friedman, *Florentine New Towns: Urban Design in the Late Middle Ages*, Cambridge, MA: MIT Press, 1988, pp. 3–49, 147–66.

60 Guasti, *Santa Maria del Fiore*, pp. 261–62.

61 The documents reveal a total of only slightly more than twenty days he spent in Prato between 1385 and 1392, so this conclusion seems unlikely; see Cerretelli, "La Pieve e la Cintola," p. 92.

62 ASP, PE 960, c. 6.

63 ASP, PE 960, c. 52.

64 ASP, PE 46, c. 6, Appendix I.2, p. 340. On this company of wallers, see Richard K. Marshall, *The Local Merchants of Prato*, Baltimore: Johns Hopkins University Press, 1999, p. 121. Chimenti Ghini, aged thirty-four, with his wife and three sons, are listed in the 1372 estimo and assessed fifty lire; Florence, ASF, Estimo 215 (Capo di Famiglia, Quartiere di Santa Maria Novella [contado], 1371/2), c. 604.

65 Documents for Florence cathedral are published in Guasti, *Santa Maria del Fiore*; Giovanni Poggi, *Il Duomo di Firenze: Documenti sulla decorazione della chiesa e del campanile, tratti dal'archivio del'opera*, ed. Margaret Haines, 2 vols., Florence: Edizioni Medicea, 1988. Those for the Loggia della Signoria are in Carl Frey, *Die Loggia dei Lanzi zu Florenz*, Berlin: Hertz, 1885. The original documents are in Florence, Archivio dell'Opera del Duomo (henceforth AOD). For an analysis of the role of artisans at the Opera, see Jean K. Cadogan, "Agnolo Gaddi's Career and the Opera del Duomo in Florence," in Cecilia Frosinini, ed., *Agnolo Gaddi and the Cappella Maggiore in Santa Croce in Florence: Studies after Its Restoration*, Milan: Silvana Editoriale, 2014, pp. 55–71.

66 The document announcing the appointment of Giotto calls him "experienced and famous" (*expertus et famosus*), "qualified" (*sufficientior*), and celebrates his "science and knowledge" (*scientia et doctrina*). No mention is made of previous building experience; ASF, Provvigioni, XXVI, 84; Guasti, *Santa Maria del Fiore*, pp. xlv–xlvi.

67 James Ackerman, "'Ars sine Scientia Nihil Est' Gothic Theory of Architecture at the Cathedral of Milan," *Art Bulletin*, vol. 31, 1949, pp. 84–112; Howard Saalman, "Early Renaissance Architectural Theory and Practice in Antonio Filarete's 'Trattato di Architettura,'" *Art Bulletin*, vol. 41, 1959, pp. 89–106; Saalman, *Filippo Brunelleschi*, pp. 178–81.

68 Franklin Toker, "Building on Paper: The Role of Architectural Drawings in Late-Medieval Italy," *L'art et les révolutions: XXVIIe Congrès international d'Histoire d'art*, vol. 8, Strasbourg, 1992, p. 43.

69 Saalman, *Filippo Brunelleschi*, pp. 180–81.

70 For an overview of this period, see Howard Saalman, "Santa Maria del Fiore: 1294–1418," *Art Bulletin*, vol. 46, 1964, pp. 471–500; Gert Kreytenberg, *Der Dom zu Florenz: Untersuchungen zur Baugeschichte im 14. Jahrhundert*, Berlin: Gebr. Mann, 1974; Francesco Gurrieri et al., *La Cattedrale di Santa Maria del Fiore a Firenze*, Florence: Giunti, 1994, I, pp. 35–79; for an overview of the sculptural decoration, see Gert Kreytenberg, "La Decorazione del Duomo nel Trecento e la genesi della scultura," in Margaret Haines, ed., *Santa Maria del Fiore: The Cathedral and Its Sculpture*, Fiesole: Cadmo, 2001, pp. 47–58.

71 Antje Middeldorf Kosegarten, "The Origins of Artistic Competitions in Italy," in *Lorenzo Ghiberti nel suo tempo: Atti del convegno internazionale di studi*, Florence: Olschki, 1980, vol. 1, pp. 167–86, describes early artistic competitions in the thirteenth and fourteenth centuries. See also Richard Goldthwaite, *The Building of Renaissance Florence*, Baltimore: Johns Hopkins University Press, 1980, pp. 297–301, on the instability of employment in the construction trades.

72 For an extended discussion, see Cadogan, "Agnolo Gaddi's Career and the Opera del Duomo in Florence," pp. 55–56.

73 Michelle O'Malley, *The Business of Art*, New Haven and London: Yale University Press, 2005, pp. 13–15.

74 For the history of the Loggia and documentation for the sculpture, see Frey, *Die Loggia dei Lanzi*, pp. 35–39 and 302–5, docs. 13, 16, 23, and 30. The documents are in Florence, AOD, II-1-16 (Deliberazioni, stanziamenti, etc., bastardello del notaio, 1382–83), c. 29 verso (27 June 1383); II-1-17 (Deliberazioni, etc, August–December 1383) c. 9 verso (29 December 1383); II-1-18 (Deliberazioni, etc. 1383/4–June 1384), c. 6 recto (11 February 1383/4); II-1-19, c. 6 recto (12 August 1384); II-1-21 (Deliberazioni, etc., 1385–86), c. 15 verso (27 March 1386). For further discussion of Agnolo's designs for the Opera, see Cadogan, "Agnolo Gaddi's Career and the Opera del Duomo in Florence," pp. 56–71.

75 Florence, AOD, II-1-21 (Deliberazioni, etc., 1385–86) c. 21 verso (4 May 1386); II-1-22 (Deliberazioni, etc., July–December 1386), c. 6 verso (20 July 1386); Frey, *Die Loggia dei Lanzi*, pp. 38–39.

76 For this cycle, see Gert Kreytenberg, "Tre cicli di apostolic dell'antica facciata del Duomo fiorentino," *Antichità viva*, vol. 16, 1977, pp. 13–29; Florence, AOD, II-1-36 (July–December, 1395), c. 12 verso (21 October 1395); Poggi, ed. Haines, *Il Duomo di Firenze*, vol. 1, p. 19, doc. 112. Poggi identified the four figures as doctors of the church carved between August, 1395 and August, 1399 by Niccolò di Piero Lamberti and Piero di Giovanni Tedesco, which are now, much altered, in the Museo dell'Opera del Duomo; Poggi, ed. Haines, vol.1, pp. xxxii–xxxv; see also L. Becherucchi and G. Brunetti, *Il Museo del'Opera del Duomo di Firenze*, Milan: Electa, 1971, vol. 1, pp. 254–55, nos. 106–9. Bruce Cole, *Agnolo Gaddi*, Oxford: Oxford University Press, 1977, p. 69, questioned the attribution of the design of the extant sculptures to Agnolo, and the identification has been investigated by Antje Middeldorf Kosegarten, "Florentiner Statuen von 'Uomini illustri' aus dem frühen Quattrocento: Versuch über die Fassade von S. Maria del Fiore," in Marion Ackermann et al., eds., *Kunst und Geschichte: Festschrift für Karl Arndt zum siebzigsten Geburtstag*, Munich: Deutscher Kunstverlag, 1999, pp. 41–91, who identifies the figures as famous poets Homer, Virgil, Petrarch (?), and Dante (?), carved by Giovanni d'Ambrogio in 1410–18. See also Gert Kreytenberg, "Piero di Giovanni Tedesco: Ein Deutscher

Bildhauer in der Florentiner Dombauhütte am Ende des 14. Jahrhunderts," *Städel-jahrbuch*, n.f. vol. 20, 2009, pp. 72–76. The four saints, or doctors, referred to in the documents are untraceable.

77 Florence, AOD, II-1-34 (Deliberazioni, etc. July–December, 1394), cc. 3 verso–4 recto (6 August–14 October 1394); Poggi, ed. Haines, *Il Duomo di Firenze*, vol. 2, pp. 87–88, doc. 456.

78 Florence, AOD, II-1-37 (Deliberazioni, etc. January 1395/6–June 1396) c. 20 recto (7 April 1396); Poggi, ed. Haines, *Il Duomo di Firenze*, vol. 2, p. 93, doc. 484.

79 Florence, AOD, II-1-36 (Deliberazioni, etc. July–December 1395), cc. 17 verso–18 recto (2 December 1395); Poggi, ed. Haines, *Il Duomo di Firenze*, vol. 2, pp. 127–28, doc. 2068. See Eve Borsook, "The Power of Illusion: Fictive Tombs in Santa Maria del Fiore," in Haines, ed., *Santa Maria del Fiore, The Cathedral and Its Sculpture*, pp. 62–63. Yael Even, "Paolo Uccello's John Hawkwood: Reflections of a Collaboration between Agnolo Gaddi and Giuliano Pesello," *Source: Notes in the History of Art*, vol. 4, 1985, pp. 6–8, speculates that in the original Hawkwood monument, Agnolo designed the upper, figural parts, and Pesello the lower, decorative parts.

80 For this opinion, see Wundrum, "Jacopo di Piero Guidi," p. 202; Kreytenberg, "Die Figurekonsolen der Loggia dei Lanzi," p. 280, note 1; Kreytenberg, "Piero di Giovanni Tedesco," pp. 59–60, has conceded that differences in the style of the apostles carved by Piero di Giovanni Tedesco in 1387–90 may be owing to stylistic differences in the designs supplied by Lorenzo di Bicci, Spinello Aretino, and Agnolo Gaddi.

81 Frey, *Die Loggia dei Lanzi zu Florenz*, p. 32; Francesco Vossilla, *La Loggia della Signoria: Una galleria di scultura*, Florence: Edizioni Medicea, 1995, pp. 25–26.

82 Frey, *Die Loggia dei Lanzi zu Florenz*, pp. 38–39.

83 Alessio Monciatti, "'With Much Mastery of Handling but Not with Much Design': Notes toward the History of a Wall-painting Worksite at the End of the Fourteenth Century," in Frosinini, ed., *Agnolo Gaddi and the Cappella Maggiore in Santa Croce in Florence*, pp. 86–87, discusses Agnolo's participation at other worksites and provides valuable comparison to the situation in Prato. See also Jean K. Cadogan, "Agnolo Gaddi and his Family: A Florentine 'Success Story,'" *Zeitschrift für Kunstgeschichte*, vol. LXXIV, 2011, pp. 153–76, for Agnolo's murals (now fragmentary) in the refectory of the convent of San Domenico al Maglio from 1376–77.

84 ASP, PE, 45, c. 28 verso, Appendix I.1, p. 332. To put this amount in context, economic historians have estimated the average daily wage rate for skilled laborers – masons, stonecutters, and so forth – at this time to be about seventeen soldi, an amount that fluctuated but remained fairly constant through the first quarter of the sixteenth century; see Goldthwaite, *The Building of Renaissance Florence*, pp. 435–39. Agnolo's payment of 605 lire, at 20 soldi to the lire, was 12,100 soldi, which, if he worked for six days a week for ten months, would equal a daily wage rate of about 50 soldi per day (or about 16 florins a month). Even if the amount is reduced to consider costs for materials and assistants (but not his living expenses), he was still making far more than a skilled laborer. In fact, the laborers who were paid for building the scaffolding were paid about 13 soldi a day and the assistants only about 5 soldi a day. Also of course, Agnolo was paid a salary, as was Lorenzo di Filippo, rather than a daily rate as a laborer. See also the analysis of payments for Agnolo's work as a junior member of a team of painters, with his brother Giovanni Gaddi and Giottino, in the Vatican palace in 1369 in Sonia Chiodo, *Painters in Florence after the "Black Death": The Master of the Misericordia and Matteo di Pacino*, in Offner and Steinweg, et al., eds., *A Critical and Historical Corpus of Florentine Painting*, sec. 4, vol. 9, Florence: Giunti, 2011, pp. 87–93 and 97–106. The comparison is imperfect owing to the very different nature of the decoration (most likely nonnarrative) and the short duration of the project, as well as the many artisans involved. Also, the Vatican documents use papal florins, valued at twenty-six soldi each, rather than Florentine florins, valued at sixty-six soldi in 1369, according to Goldthwaite, *The Building of Renaissance Florence*, p. 429. By contrast, the

Florentine accounts for the painters Nardo and Jacopo di Cione in the Oratory of the Misericordia in 1363 and 1369 that Chiodo discusses reveal that for a decoration that included narrative scenes, the painters received approximately 12 and 13 florins a month. See also William Levin, "A Lost Fresco Cycle by Nardo and Jacopo di Cione at the Misericordia in Florence," in *Burlington Magazine*, vol. 141, 1999, pp. 75–80.

85 ASP, PE 45, passim, Appendix I.1, pp. 311–334.

86 ASP, PE 47, c. 25 recto, Appendix I.3, pp. 357; PE 48, c. 20 verso, Appendix I.4, p. 361.

87 Cerretelli, "Tre cappelle," p. 67.

88 Cole, *Agnolo Gaddi*, p. 64, doc. 23.

89 ASP, PE 46, c. 8 recto, Appendix I.2, p. 343.

90 ASP, PE 47, c. 17, Appendix I.3, p. 344.

91 O'Malley, *The Business of Art*, pp. 74–75, 90–96. See also the analysis of Chiodo, *Painters in Florence after the "Black Death,"* pp. 87–93.

92 ASP, PE 45, c. 29 recto, Appendix I.1, p. 333.

93 Cole, *Agnolo Gaddi*, pp. 63–64, docs. 21–22.

94 Fiumi, *Demografia movimento urbanistico e classi sociali in Prato*, pp. 97 and 463–66; see also ASF Estimo 215 (Capo di Famiglia, Quartiere di Santa Maria Novella [contado], 1371/2), c. 620: Ser Piero di Paolo, aged thirty-five, lived with his wife, Donna Simona, aged twenty-five in the Furia neighborhood, his patrimony was assessed at 250 lire. In the 1402 Estimo, ASF Estimo 287 (Libro del Quartiere di Santa Maria Novella [contado]), c. 92 verso (new numbering), he is listed, taxed four soldi on an assessment of nine lire, nine soldi, ten denari; this estimo does not provide information on the household. In 1423, Piero di Paolo, by now quite elderly, complained to the Pratese Consuls that he could not pay his tax bill without selling his possessions; see F. Sznura, "Edilizia privata e urbanistica in tempo di crisi," in Braudel et al., eds., *Prato, storia di una città*, vol. 1, part. 1, p. 342, note 64. The tax districts, the *ottavi*, took their name from the city gates; see the map in Maniura, *Art and Miracle in Renaissance Tuscany*, p. 16, fig. 6. A prosopographical analysis of *operai* at the time of Agnolo's work in Prato include the following: Ser Tommaso di Ser Arighetto, a notary, whose family was also active in the wool guild, from the Gualdimare neighborhood; Fiumi, *Demografia movimento urbanistico*, pp. 97 and 290–91; ASF Estimo 215 (Capo di Famiglia, Quartiere di Santa Maria Novella [contado], 1371/2), c. 596. Ridolfo di Nicholaio Manassei, a *ritagliatore* recorded in the 1402 Estimo as living in the San Giovanni quarter. His family had been politically active since the thirteenth century and prospered during the second half of the fourteenth century primarily through activities in the wool trade. In 1395, the painters Niccolò Gerini and Bartolomeo di Bertozzo sought Datini's aid in securing the commission to decorate the family chapel in the *pieve*, an effort in which they were not successful; Simonetta Cavaciocchi, "Francesco Datini and the Painters," in Giampiero Nigro, ed., *Francesco di Marco Datini: The Man the Merchant*, trans. Isabelle Johnson, Florence: Florence University Press, 20210. p. 221. Francesco di Piero Cambioni, from a *popolare* family in the porta Leone (Porta Fuia) neighborhood, joined the board on 1 August 1392. Their social and economic position rose appreciably in the second half of the fourteenth century. Francesco di Piero was a member of the wool guild in 1380. His son Bartolomeo was a close friend and partner with Francesco Datini and managing director in a bank in Florence in 1398; see Fiumi, *Demografia movimento urbanistico*, p. 336; Melis, *Aspetti*, p. 212. On Bartolomeo di Francesco Cambioni's relationship with Datini, see Michele Cassandro, "Aspects of the Life and Character of Francesco di Marco Datini," pp. 27, 36; Giampiero Nigro, "Francesco and the Datini Company of Florence," pp. 236–37; Giampiero Nigro, "The Banking Company," pp. 522–26, in Nigro, ed., *Francesco di Marco Datini*. Paolo di Vanni Saccagnini had been elected as *operaio* in 1389 and reelected in 1392. A member of one of the richest and most powerful *popolano* families of Prato, Paolo di Vanni was a merchant with ties to Datini and Florence; See Melis, *Aspetti*, pl. XLV, note 15; and Fiumi, *Demografia movimento urbanistico*, p. 474. Piero

di Gieri di Ghetto Buonristori, from the Tiezi neighborhood and belonging to one of the richest families of wool merchants in Prato, was elected 1 February 1393; see Fiumi, *Demografia movimento urbanistico*, pp. 97, 329–30; Michele Cassandro, "Commercio, manifatture e industria," in *Prato, storia di una città*, vol. 1, part 1, pp. 433, 440–41. ASF Estimo 215 (Capo di Famiglia, Quartiere S. Maria Novella [contado], 1371/2), c. 634.

95 Cesare Guasti, *Lettere di un Notaro e un Mercante del secolo XIV*, Florence: Le Monnier, 1880, vol. 1, pp. 51, 78, 127, 137, 139, 198, 201, 204, 208; vol. 2, p. 20. Piero di Paolo also advised Datini in 1394, when he was pressured by the tax officials in the district of his Florentine residence to pay taxes as a resident of Florence, not Prato. Rinaldeschi appealed to the Difensori of Prato to support Datini's efforts to remain a Pratese resident; but the Eight apparently feared the Florentines (among whom numbered members of the powerful Strozzi and Rucellai families), some of whom owned land near Prato. Eventually Rinaldeschi advised, and Datini accepted, that Datini should become a citizen of Florence. In addition, Datini loaned money at low interest to Piero di Paolo from time to time, and he helped Piero di Paolo pay for the dowry and the marriage ceremony of his daughter in 1394. See Carolyn James, "A Woman's Work in a Man's World: The Letters of Margherita Datini (1384–1410)," pp. 67–69, Giampiero Nigro, "The Merchant and his Wealth," p. 89, and Nigro, "The Banking Company," p. 516, in Nigro, ed., *Francesco di Marco Datini*.

96 Bruce Cole, "The Interior Decoration of the Palazzo Datini in Prato," *Mitteilungen des Kunsthistorischen Institutes in Florenz*, vol. 13, 1967, pp. 61–82. The identity of the "Agnolo dipintore" cited in the relevant documents with Agnolo Gaddi has been questioned by Margherita Romagnoli, "La dimora di un mercante pratese nel XIV secolo, parte II," *Arte Cristiana*, vol. 97, 2009, pp. 22–23; and by Simonetta Cavaciocchi, "Francesco Datini and the Painters," in Nigro, ed., *Francesco di Marco Datini*, p. 217. However, Agnolo and Bartolomeo di Bertozzo had a long-standing professional relationship, dating back to at least 1376; see Cadogan, "Agnolo Gaddi and His Family," pp. 160, 169–76. Moreover, nowhere in the documents is the painter Agnolo designated as in a junior position related to Bartolomeo.

97 On Datini's relationship with Zanobi di Taddeo Gaddi, see Melis, *Aspetti*, pp. 216–21; and Reinhold Mueller, *The Venetian Money Market: Banks, Panics, and the Public Debt, 1200–1500*, Baltimore: Johns Hopkins University Press, 1997, p. 159. Datini is listed in the 1372 estimo: ASF Estimo 215 (Capo di Famiglia, Quartiere S. Maria Novella [contado], 1371/2), c. 619: Franchescho di Marcho anni xxx, he has no family and is assessed 50 lire; at this time he was living in Avignon. Melis, *Aspetti*, p. 219, lists correspondents of Datini in Venice between 1383 and 1410, the year of Datini's death. Datini visited the chapel of the Holy Belt in the Prato Duomo with Leonardo Dandolo, Venetian ambassador to Florence, in 1397, a visit arranged by Zanobi shortly after his brother Agnolo had finished painting the murals in the chapel; Melis, *Aspetti*, 57, note 9, and 73–74.

98 Melis, *Aspetti*, 54–55; Armando Sapori, *La mercatura medievale*, Florence: Sansoni, 1972, p. 64. Melis publishes an extract from a letter of 16 February 1387 in which Datini complains of having to accede to the office despite his reluctance.

99 On the social makeup of the ruling group in the late thirteenth and early fourteenth centuries, see Sergio Raveggi, "Protagonisti e antagonisti nel libero comune," in Braudel, ed., *Prato, Storia di una città*, vol. 1, part 2, pp. 643–69.

100 For the financing of the Opera del Duomo, see Haines, "Firenze e il finanziamento della cattedrale," pp. 71–83.

101 Cole, *Agnolo Gaddi*, p. 21; Sonia Chiodo, "Comparative Analysis and Historical Context," in Frosinini, ed., *Agnolo Gaddi and the Cappella Maggiore in Santa Croce in Florence*, pp. 73–81.

102 For example, the payment on 30 April 1393 to Ridolfo di Lanfrancho, "per ii dì ch'andò a Firenze, in servigio dell'Opera a informarsi di cierti lavorii ch'avea fatto il maestro Angnolo in Firenze, e d'altri per fare la stima de quello della pieve, l. tre"; ASP, PE 46, c 8 recto,

Appendix I.2, p. 343; "a Nicholaio di Bernardi, dì xxvi di gennaio [1394/5] l. una, per uno dì chandò a Firenze a recharge la misure della chappella di Santa Croce, che dipinse il maestro Agnolo"; ASP, PE 47, c. 21 verso, Appendix I.3, p. 351. "A lui detto [Ridolfo di Lanfrancho, camarlingo dell'Opera] per uno dì ch' andò a Firenze mandato dagl'operai a comperare azzurro e vedere la chapella di Messer Vanni e fare che'l Maestro Agnolo venisse a dipignere fu fine dì 27 di settembre, l. una"; ASP, PE 47, c. 24 recto Appendix I.3, p. 357.

103 This could refer to Vanni di ser Lotto, the father of Michele, whose bequest paid for the construction of the chapel.

104 The Castellani chapel is one of a series of large chapels appended to the original transepts of Santa Croce in the fourteenth century. They were all private commissions of wealthy families, they are generally elevated above the pavement level of the transepts themselves, and they are generally larger and display finer architectural carving than the chapels flanking the east end of the transepts. See Marvin Trachtenberg, "On Brunelleschi's Old Sacristy as Model for Early Renaissance Church Architecture," in Jean Guillaume, ed., *L'Eglise dans l'architecture de la Renaissance*, Paris: Picard, 1995, p. 13; and Ena Giurescu, "Trecento Family Chapels in Santa Maria Novella and Santa Croce: Architecture, Patronage, and Competition," PhD dissertation, New York University, 1997, pp. 100–2.

105 For a summary, see Giurescu, "Trecento Family Chapels," pp. 85–94; Costanza Cipollaro, *Agnolo Gaddi e la leggenda di Santa Croce: La cappella maggiore e la sua decorazione pittorica*, Foligno: Cartei & Bianchi, 2009; Annamaria Bernacchioni, "Family Alliances, Merchant Companies: The Alberti, Agnolo Gaddi and the Cappella Maggiore of Santa Croce," in Frosinini, ed., *Agnolo Gaddi and the Cappella Maggiore in Santa Croce*, pp. 35–45.

106 Chiodo, "Comparative Analysis and Historical Context," pp. 80–81.

107 Susanna Foster, "The Ties That Bind: Kinship Association and Marriage in the Alberti Family 1378–1428," PhD dissertation, Cornell University, 1985, p. 749.

108 Nancy Thompson, "The Franciscans and the True Cross: The Decoration of the Cappella Maggiore of Santa Croce in Florence," *Gesta*, vol. 43, 2004, p. 61.

109 Barbara Baert, *A Heritage of Holy Wood: The Legend of the True Cross in Text and Image*, trans. Lee Preddy, Leiden: Brill, 2004; Takaharu Miyashita, "The Narrative Structure of the Cycle of the Legend of the True Cross by Agnolo Gaddi," in Frosinini, ed., *Agnolo Gaddi and the Cappella Maggiore in Santa Croce in Florence*, pp. 113–21.

110 Jacobus de Voragine, *The Golden Legend*, trans. William Ryan, Princeton: Princeton University Press, 1993, vol.1, pp. 277–83, vol. 2, pp. 168–73. Giovanni Paolo Maggioni, "The Literary Sources for the *Legenda aurea*," in Frosinini, ed., *Agnolo Gaddi and the Cappella Maggiore in Santa Croce in Florence*, pp. 123–35, analyzes the literary sources.

111 Thompson, "The Franciscans and the True Cross," p. 69.

112 The Castellani murals may have been executed by a partnership of masters, a *compagnia*, rather than a single workshop, as they show considerable variation in style; see Cole, *Agnolo Gaddi*, pp. 9–20.

113 Francesco Benelli, "Painted Architecture in the Frescoes of the Cappella Maggiore," in Frosinini, ed., *Agnolo Gaddi and the Cappella Maggiore in Santa Croce in Florence*, pp. 149–53.

114 Alessandra Malquori, "On the Margins of the Invention of the True Cross," in Frosinini, ed., *Agnolo Gaddi and the Cappella Maggiore in Santa Croce in Florence*, pp. 165–69.

115 Hans Belting, "Das Bild als Text: Wandmalerei und Literatur im Zeitalter Dantes," in Hans Belting and Dieter Blume, eds., *Malerei und Stadtkultur in der Dantezeit: Die Argumentation der Bilder*, Munich: Hirmer, 1989, pp. 23–64.

116 For the connection of the Holy Belt with the Crusades, see Raoul Manselli, "Istituzioni ecclesiastiche e vita religiosa," in Braudel, ed., *Prato, storia di una città*, vol. 1, part 2, pp. 812–13. Franco Cardini, "La cultura," in Braudel, ed., *Prato, storia di una città*, vol. 1, part 2, p. 850, also remarks on the shared theme of relic legends between the Prato and Alberti chapel decoration.

117 Michael Baxandall, *Painting and Experience in Fifteenth-Century Italy*, 2nd ed., Oxford: Oxford University Press, 1988, p. 45; see also Creighton Gilbert's remarks on artists' roles in the selection and visualization of subject matter, in "What Did the Renaissance Patron Buy?," *Renaissance Quarterly*, vol. 51, 1998, pp. 399–405.
118 Cavaciocchi, "Francesco Datini and the Painters," p. 226, note 44.
119 Cavaciocchi, "Francesco Datini and the Painters," p. 226, note 47.
120 Joseph Patrick Byrne, "Francesco Datini, 'Father of Many'" PhD dissertation, Indiana University, 1989, pp. 317–23; Cavaciocchi, "Francesco Datini and the Painters," p. 221. Some of the letters are printed in Guasti, *Lettere di un notaro ad un mercante del secolo XIV*, vol. 1, pp. 401–6; and Renato Piattoli, "Un mercante del trecento e gli artisti del tempo suo," *Rivista d'arte*, ser. 2, vol. 12, 1930, pp. 572–73.
121 For the assistants and followers of Agnolo, see the discussion by Cecilia Frosinini, "Agnolo Gaddi," in Martini, ed., *La sacra cintola del Duomo di Prato*, pp. 229–33; and Monciatti, "'With Much Mastery of Handling but Not with Much Design,'" in Frosinini, ed., *Agnolo Gaddi and the Cappella Maggiore in Santa Croce in Florence*, pp. 87–111.
122 Cole, *Agnolo Gaddi*, pp. 32–39; see also the comments of Miklós Boskovits in his review of Cole in *Art Bulletin*, vol. 60, 1978, p. 707–11, and Lapi Ballerini, "Per onorare la sua preziosissima Cintola," pp. 39–41.
123 O'Malley, *The Business of Art*, pp. 90–96.
124 O'Malley, *The Business of Art*, pp. 47–76.
125 Cavaciocchi, "Francesco Datini and the Painters," pp. 217, 225, note 23. See also Julia A. DeLancey, "Shipping Colour: *Valute*, Pigments, Trade and Francesco di Marco Datini," in Jo Kirby et al., eds., *Trade in Artists' Materials: Markets and Commerce in Europe to 1700*, London: Archetype, 2010, pp. 74–85.
126 ASP, Datini, Firenze-Prato, Francesco Datini, 1 August 1391; Cavaciocchi, "Francesco Datini and the Painters," p. 217.
127 "Per sua faticha di oro, azurro, stagno e in funi"; ASP, PE 45, c. 28 verso, Appendix I.1, p. 332.
128 ASP, PE 45, c. 28 verso, Appendix I.1, p. 333.
129 ASP, PE 46, c. 2 verso, Appendix I.2, p. 337.
130 ASP, PE 47, c. 17 verso, Appendix I.3, pp. 345–46.
131 "Per più cose tolte dalla sua botteghа"; ASP, PE 47, c. 23, Appendix I.3, p. 354.
132 ASP, PE 47, cc. 17 verso, 26, Appendix I.3, pp. 346, 359–60.
133 ASP, PE 47, c. 24, Appendix I.3, p. 357.
134 ASF, Arte dei Medici e Speziali, 9 (Matricole, 1358–), c. 3 recto.
135 ASF, Tratte 595, c. 107 verso (27 February 1379/80): Donatus Bonifaci spetarius; ASF, Tratte 596, c. 3 verso (29 December 1381). He perhaps died in office as a special election was held 11 March 1381/2 to elect someone in his place, c. 6.
136 ASF, Catasto 32 (quartiere S. Croce, Gonfalone Lion Nero), 1433, cc. 250 verso–252 verso, return of Bonifazio di Donato di Bonifazio; see also Alessandro Guidotti, "Battiloro e dipintori a Firenze fra Tre e Quattrocento: Bastiano di Giovanni e la sua clientele (dal Catasto del 1427)," in Cristina De Benedictis, ed., *Scritti di storia dell'arte in onore di Roberto Salvini*, Florence: Sansoni, 1984, pp. 239–49, especially p. 244, note 8.
137 Eve Borsook, "Fra Filippo Lippi and the Murals for Prato Cathedral," *Mitteilungen des kunsthistorischen Institutes in Florenz*, vol. 19, no. 1, 1975, p. 123, doc. 406.
138 ASF, Arte dei Medici e Speziali, 9 (Matricole, 1358–), c. 67 recto (9 August 1378).
139 Alessandra Popple, "Il restauro della cappella della cintola," in Lapi Ballerini, ed., *Agnolo Gaddi e la Cappella della Cintola*, pp. 135–57.
140 The scaffolding was constructed starting in May 1392; ASP, PE 45, cc. 16 recto–17 verso, Appendix I.1, pp. 311–14. It must have been somewhat complex; it included a *sopponte*, perhaps a lower level, and "cavaletto sopra il ponte" and a "sopponte sopra il balco." On 9 August 1493, Cristofano di ser Francia was paid "a disfare e rifare il ponte della cappella"; ASP, PE 46, c. 2 recto, Appendix I.2, p. 336.

141 Some of the *giornate* that unusually intersect these areas, such as in the foliage to the right and left of the *Dormition*, probably result from the position of the scaffolding; see the *giornate* diagram in Popple, "Il restauro della Cappella della Cintola," p. 134.

142 On the use of preparatory drawings for mural painting, see Cecilia Frosinini, "Design, Planning and Drawing in the Legend of the True Cross," in Frosinini, ed., *Agnolo Gaddi and the Cappella Maggiore in Santa Croce in Florence*, pp. 217–33.

143 For comparison with Agnolo's technique in the *cappella maggiore* in Santa Croce, and its relationship to Cennino's text, see Fabrizio Bandini, "A Comparison of Agnolo Gaddi's Painting Technique in the Fresco Cycle of the *Cappella Maggiore* with Cennino Cennini's Il libro dell'arte," in Frosinini, ed., *Agnolo Gaddi and the Cappella Maggiore in Santa Croce in Florence*, pp. 271–82; and the many essays in this volume concerning Agnolo's mural technique.

144 "Maior, et ornatior, atque decentior," as the chapel was described in the translation document; see Bianchini, *Notizie istoriche*, p. 81 and below.

145 Bianchini, *Notizie istoriche*, pp. 87–88, records that Mass was to be celebrated at the altar of the Holy Belt every morning, a sung Mass every Saturday evening, and on Sunday evening the confraternity of the Arcangelo Raphael sang the office of the Virgin. These rites were in addition to Masses at various times throughout the year provided for by legacies to the chapel.

146 Richard Trexler, "Ritual Behavior in Renaissance Florence: The Setting," *Medievalia et Humanistica*, new series, vol. 4, 1973, pp. 126. Peter Brown *The Cult of the Saints: Its Rise and Function in Latin Christianity*, Chicago: University of Chicago Press, 1981, pp. 36–49, 93–105, discusses the social dimensions of ceremonies of relic translation and celebration in late antiquity. For the role of city authorities in encouraging the cult of saints in Italy during the thirteenth and fourteenth centuries, see André Vauchez, "Patronage of Saints and Civic Religion in the Italy of the Communes," in Daniel Bornstein, ed., Margery Schneider, trans., *The Laity in the Middle Ages*, Notre Dame: University of Notre Dame Press, 1993, pp, 153–68; and Webb, *Patrons and Defenders*.

147 Brown, *The Cult of the Saints*, pp. 93–105. Whether such rituals fostered unity or masked conflict is open to discussion; see Muir, *Ritual in Early Modern Europe*, pp. 253–54, 261–62.

148 On ritual, see Muir, *Ritual in Early Modern Europe*, pp.1–11; Philippe Buc, *The Dangers of Ritual: Between Early Medieval Texts and Social Scientific Theory*, Princeton: Princeton University Press, 2001; Geoffrey Koziol, "Review Article: The Dangers of Polemic: Is Ritual Still an Interesting Topic of Historical Study?," in *Early Medieval Europe*, vol. 11, 2002, pp. 367–88; Alexandra Walsham, "Review Article, *The Dangers of Ritual*," in *Past and Present*, vol. 180, 2003, pp. 277–87; Frances Andrews, "Ritual and Space: Definitions and Ways Forward," in Frances Andrews, ed., *Ritual and Space in the Middle Ages*, Donington: Shaun Tyas, 2011, pp. 1–29.

149 See Miri Rubin, *Corpus Christi: The Eucharist in Late Medieval Culture*, Cambridge: Cambridge University Press, 1991, pp. 265–67.

150 On processions generally, see Muir, *Ritual in Early Modern Europe*, pp. 256–60; his bibliography, pp. 287–93, lists numerous specialized studies.

151 The chancellor was ser Nicola di Jacopo di Montecatini; witnesses included Paolo di Guelfo dei Landi, the Opera sacristan, and Francesco di ser Diotaiuto di ser Lapo di Prato. The document reads: "Idcirco congregatis Reverendissimo in Christo patre et domino Andrea Francisci de Pistorio Dei et Apostolice Sedis gratia Episcopo Pistoriensi, et aliis pluribus Reverendisimis Episcopis et venerabilibus Abbatibus, et Prioribus, et Magistris, et Fratibus et religiosis, et venerabili viro Domino Alberto Ser Bortolomei de Prato Vicario Generali Reverendssimi Patris, et Domini, Domini [*sic?*] Preposti Bartolomei Francisci de Pistorio Dei et Apostolice Sedis gratia prepositi Pratensis, et venerabilibus viris Canonicis et Cappellanis, et presbiteris dictis Plebis, et aliis presbiteris et Chericatu Pratensi, et nobilibus viris Potestate Octo defensoribus populi, et Vexillifero iustitie terre Prati, et populo

Pratensi in multitudine copiosa in dicte Plebe." (Therefore, after bringing together the most Holy Father in Christ [and] lord Andrea Franchi of Pistoia, by the grace of God and the Holy See Bishop of Pistoia, and also many other most holy bishops, and venerable abbots, priors, masters, brothers and religious; and the venerable lord Alberto di Ser Bartolomeo di Prato, vicar general to the most Holy Father and Lord [the Lord] Provost Bartolomeo Franchi of Pistoia, by the grace of God and the Holy See Provost of Prato, and the venerable Canons, Chaplains, and priests of the parish, and other priests and the Pratese clergymen, and the noble men the *Podestà*, the Eight Defenders of the People, and the Standard-bearer of Justice of Prato, and the people of Prato in great numbers in said parish.) ASP, PE 1002, c. 7; Bianchini, *Notizie istoriche*, pp. 81–83; Pelagatti, *Il Sacro Cingolo Mariano*, 2nd ed., pp. 59–62.

152 An image of a procession in Siena, published in Diana Norman, *Siena and the Virgin*, London: Yale University Press, 1999, pl. 100, shows clergy in the lead, followed by secular officials, all carrying candles.

153 "Altare constructum inmedio ipsius cappelle circumcircha lapidibus scultis ystoria eiusdem virginis gloriose tam eius mortis, quam assumptionis in celum et aliis honorificentiis decoratum." ASP, PE 1002, c. 7.

154 The new choir stalls were commissioned in September 1395; a Florentine woodworker, Marco di Boninsegno, was charged with completing the twenty-nine stalls within a year, for a price of 290 gold florins. They were to be modeled on those of the Florentine Baptistery and richly carved. However, the worker did not fulfill the contract, and in July of 1397, having collected most of the payment, he fled. The next year, the work was consigned to another workman, this time a Pratese who had made the stalls in the choir and who finished the work in 1400. See Poggi, "La Cappella del Sacro Cingolo," p. 376; Cerretelli, "La Pieve e la Cintola," p. 152, note 47; the documents are in ASP, PE 51, cc. 48, 49v, 50, 51, 53v, 54, 55; and PE 52, cc. 4, 7, 8v; no. 53, cc. 22, 23. Seventeenth-century depictions of the ostentation are reproduced in De Marchi and and Mavarelli, eds, *Legati da una cintola*, pp. 218–25, cat. nos. 51b and 52.

155 From a statute dated May 1297; cited in Fantappiè, "Storia e 'storie' della Cintola," p. 55, note 22; De Marchi and and Mavarelli, eds., *Legati da una cintola*, p. 118, cat. no. 2.

156 "De mandato dicti Domini potestatis et defensorum et Vicarii Domini Prepositi, prefatus Dominus Albertus Vicarius dicti Domini Prepositi de licentia, voluntate, et consensu dicti ofitii dominorum Octo defensorum, et Vexilliferi iustitie terre Prati, et in eorum presentia patenter, cum solepnibus canticis, et cum mente devota, ad honorem, et reverentiam, et gloriam, Dei, et gloriose Virginis Marie et dicti cinculi reventia translatavit transtulit et transmutavit ipsum pretiosum cingulum Vergine Marie de dicta veteri cappella in ipsam novam cappelam Virginis Marie superius nominatam, et ibidem in dicta cappella nova circa altare ipsius novae Cappellae ex latere anteriori ipsum Cingulum extensum, et devote demonstratum per dictum reverendum Patrem Dominum Andrea Episcopum Pistoriensam coram dicto astanti Populo ipse Dominus Albertus Vicarius coram me Notario, et dictis Testibus reverenter replicavit et replicatum involvit in velis eius solitis, et sic involutum immisit in Capsectina eius solita eburnea, et demum ipsam Capsectinam cum ipso Cingulo in ea recluso, et existente et ipsum Cingulum in ipsa Capsectina reclusum immisit et clausit in capsecta lignea ferrata, et in ipso novo Altari dictae novae Cappellae incatenata et sic clausum in dicta Capsecta, et dictam Capsectam cum dicto Cingulo in dicti altari inclusam dimisit, et relaxavit, et cum pluribus clavibus, et serraminibus communivit, ac firmavit hostiola Altaris eius pro secura costodia, et conservatione Cinguli prelibati. Quarum clavium pars remansit penes ipsum Vicarium, et reliqua pars penes ipsum Officium Defensorum, et Vexilliferi." ASP, PE 1002, c. 7.

157 The number of persons housed in the chapel during the ostentation is difficult to fix precisely. Of the communal authorities, we know the Standard-bearer, the Eight, the Captain of the People, and the *Podestà* were present, a total of eleven, possibly also with their administrative staffs (the "famiglie"), whose numbers varied but ranged from

about seventeen to more than fifty. We know from documents that the chapel was furnished with twenty-nine choir stalls, but other officials, either standing or seated, could have also been accommodated in the new chapel; Cerretelli, "La Pieve e la Cintola," p. 152.

158 The so-called Madonna della Cintola, whose authorship and date are undocumented but widely attributed to Giovanni and dated toward the end of his career, c. 1312, is listed in the 1390 inventory of the chapel and was installed on the new altar, as payments for painting and gilding the sculpture and construction of a pedestal attest; see Poggi, "La Cappella del Sacro Cingolo," p. 375; ASP, PE 48, c. 22 recto, Appendix I.4, p. 362: "Vettorio dipintore, adì detto [25 October 1495] per horo e dipintura la figura della Vergine Maria, e basa e piedistallio, la quale stae in suso l'antare, l. quatordici." See also Maria Grazia Trenti Antonelli, "La Madonna col Bambino di Giovanni Pisano," in Martini, ed., *La Sacra Cintola nel Duomo di Prato*, pp. 235–45; Claudio Cerretelli, "La Madonna della Cintola a Prato," in Antonio Paolucci, ed., *Colloqui davanti alla Madre: Immagini mariane in Toscana tra arte, storia e devozione*, Florence: Mandragora, 2004, pp. 81–90.

159 A painting by Giovan Pietro Naldini from c. 1633 of the *Ostentation of the Sacred Belt* in a private collection in Prato shows the celebrant with gloved hands lifting the Belt above his head; see Cerretelli, "La Pieve e la Cintola," p. 109; De Marchi and Mavarelli, eds., *Legati da una cintola*, pp. 224–25, cat. no. 52.

160 On the "elevatio" of the consecrated host during Mass, see Rubin, *Corpus Christi*, pp. 49–58; Godefridus Snoek, *Medieval Piety from Relics to the Eucharist: A Process of Mutual Interaction*, Leiden: Brill, 1995, pp. 54–60 and 278–95.

161 The Naldini painting shows the priest with his back to the altar; see note 159.

162 Cerretelli, "La pieve e la cintola," p. 98; Cerretelli, "La sacra cintola e il suo scrigno," p. 53.

163 The musical component is alluded to in the song attributed to L'Acquattino: "Ritornammo alla pieve, chè mostrare / La santa orliqua n'era la stagione; / E 'n su la piazza stando a riguardare, / Quella vedemmo in man del sacerdote mostrar con suoni e con dolce cantare." See Giovanni da Prato, called "L'Acquettino," (Untitled song), in Domenico Guerri, *La corrente popolare nel rinascimento*, Florence: Sansoni, 1931, p. 158. The solemn chanting is also referred to in the translation document, cited above.

164 See Rubin, *Corpus Christi*, pp. 60–63; and Snoek, *Medieval Piety*, pp. 227–36, on the use of light and incense in ceremonies honoring relics and the Eucharist.

165 These included four lamps left in bequest by a certain Filippo di ser Giovanni, fabricated and painted in 1391, and others painted by Vittorio, an assistant of Agnolo Gaddi, in 1395; Pelagatti, *Il Sacro Cingolo Mariano*, p. 58; for the documents, see Poggi, "La Cappella del Sacro Cingolo," pp. 362, 375; ASP, PE 42, c. 106 verso and 47 c. 23 verso.

166 For transcription and translation of Datini's will, see Byrne, "Francesco Datini, 'Father of Many,'" p. 340. The lamps were to cost 300 florins.

167 Cerretelli, "La Pieve e la Cintola," pp. 93 and 151, note 34, who notes that the "compasso" would not let light directly into the chapel in any case, since the wall of the chapel was covered by the the new façade, then in construction.

168 Paul Davies, "The Lighting of Pilgrimage Shrines in Renaissance Italy," in Erik Thunø and Gerhard Wolf, eds. *The Miraculous Image in the Late Middle Ages and Renaissance*, Rome: Erma di Bretschneider, 2004, pp. 57–80. Later efforts to increase the lighting in the chapel of the Holy Belt included an enlargement of the window, perhaps first in 1403–4, and again in 1660; see Marchini, *Tesoro*, p. 101, doc. 33; Cerretelli, "La Pieve e la Cintola," p. 96. For the oculus in the south wall, see Lapi Ballerini, "Per onorare la sua preziosissima Cintola," pp. 31–32; and Piero Ranfagni, "Sole mariano nel Duomo di Prato, calcoli e considerazioni," in Lapi Ballerini, ed., *Agnolo Gaddi e la Cappella della Cintola*, pp. 58–61. Payment related to the window is in ASP 47, 2 April 1395, c. 22 recto (see Appendix I. p. 352).

169 The function of relics of joining Heaven and Earth has been treated by Brown, *The Cult of the Saints*, pp. 1–22. Since the Virgin was assumed body and soul into heaven, she left no bodily remains as relics, and hence "secondary relics," such as her tunic at Chartres, or her

Belt, were venerated instead. Brown also describes the way in which relics secured the physical presence, or "praesentia," of the holy person in a particular place; see pp. 86–105.

170 The theme of gift giving, and the bestowal of favor, has been part of the cult of relics since late antiquity; Brown, *The Cult of the Saints*, p. 91. On the anthropology of gift-giving, see Marcel Mauss, *The Gift: The Form and Reason for Exchange in Archaic Societies*, trans. W. D. Halls, New York: W.W. Norton, 1990; but see also Patrick Geary, "Gift Exchange and Social Science Modeling: The Limitations of a Construct," in Gadi Algazi et al., eds. *Negotiating the Gift: Pre-Modern Figurations of Exchange*, Göttingen: Vandenhoeck and Ruprecht, 2003, pp. 129–40.

171 Brown, *The Cult of the Saints*, pp. 92–94.

172 Giuliano Guizzelmi, *Historia della Cinctola della Vergine Maria*, ed. Cesare Grassi, Prato: Società Pratese di Storia Patria, 1990, p. 92 (c. 13 recto): "Veduta la Assumptione della gloriossissima Vergine Maria, et della sua pretiosissima cinctola el dono facto a S. Thomaso."

173 Duccio di Amadore, *Il Cincturale*, ed. and trans. Cesare Grassi, Prato: Società Pratese di Storia Patria, 1984, p. 30, line 1; p. 70, line 77.

174 Duccio di Amadore was a teacher of grammar in Prato, a contemporary of the better known Convenevole da Prato (master of Petrarch and author of the *Regia Carmina*, a Latin poem in praise of Robert of Anjou, the *Signore* of Prato, written in 1320). Little information about Duccio has come to light; the last notice of him is in November of 1343. Considering Duccio's employment by the Commune of Prato, and also the civic and contemporary tone of the poem, the conclusion that it was a civic commission seems reasonable. See Grassi's introduction to his translation of the poem, Duccio di Amadore, *Il Cincturale*, pp. 7–8; see also Convenevole da Prato, *Regia Carmina*, ed. and trans. Cesare Grassi, Cinisello Balsamo: Silvano, 1982.

175 Brown, *The Cult of the Saints*, pp. 45–46.

176 The literature on the iconography of the Death, Assumption, and Coronation of the Virgin is vast; see L. Réau, *L'Iconographie de l'art chrétien*, Paris: Presses universitaires de France, vol. 2, 1957, pp. 597–635; Penelope Dunford, "Iconografia della dormizione e dell'Assunzione della Vergine Maria nell'arte rinascimentale italiana," *Arte Cristiana*, vol. 63, 1975, pp. 284–98; Daniel Russo, "Les représentations mariale dans l'art d'Occident: Essai sur la formation d'une tradition iconographique," in Iogna-Prat et al., eds., *Marie: Le culte de la Vierge dans la société Médiévale*, pp. 173–291; and Jean-Claude Schmitt, "L'Exception corporelle: À propos de l'Assomption de Marie," in Jeffrey Hamburger and Anne-Marie Bouché, eds., *The Mind's Eye: Art and Theological Argument in the Middle Ages*, Princeton: Princeton University Press, 2006, pp. 151–85. Henk Van Os's essay, "The Assumption in Sienese Painting," in *Studies in Early Tuscan Painting*, London: Pindar, 1992, pp. 123–279, offers a useful summary of the relationship between theological concepts and visual imagery. For the iconography of the gift of the Belt to Thomas, see Richard Offner et al., eds., *A Critical and Historical Corpus of Florentine Painting*, section 3, vol. 7, New York: New York University, 1957, pp. 48–49; Marchini, *Il Duomo di Prato*, p. 35; Brendan Cassidy, "The Assumption of the Virgin on the Tabernacle of Orsanmichele," *Journal of the Warburg and Courtauld Institutes*, vol. 51, 1988, pp. 174–80 (see p. 180, note 34, for a listing of Florentine representations of the Assumption with the Gift of the Belt); Marco Ciatti, "Gli affreschi della Cappella della Cintola," in Martini, ed., *La Sacra Cintola nel Duomo di Prato*, pp. 177–92. See also Alick McLean, *Prato: Architecture, Piety and Political Identity in a Tuscan City-State*, New Haven and London: Yale University Press, 2008, pp. 173–93.

177 Presumably a prominent model for Agnolo's image would have been the altarpiece by Bernardo Daddi installed on the high altar in 1338. A gabled panel of the *Assumption of the Virgin* in the Lehman Collection has been identified by Miklós Boskovits, *A Critical and Historical Corpus of Florentine Painting*, sec. 3, vol. 9, *The Painters of the Miniaturist Tendency*, Florence: Barbèra, 1984, pp. 72–73, as the upper part of the altarpiece from Prato

(fig. 1.12). John Pope-Hennessy, *The Robert Lehman Collection I: Italian Paintings*, New York: The Metropolitan Museum of Art, 1987, pp. 48–50, argued that the main part of the original altarpiece was a single panel rather than a polyptych. Offner, *A Critical and Historical Corpus of Florentine Painting*, section 3, vol. 7, pp. 48–50, pl. XVI, suggested that a miniature from Impruneta reflects the lost main panel of Daddi's altarpiece; see also *Legati da una cintola*, pp. 162–63, cat. no. 21, attributed to the Master of the Dominican Effigies. The predella for the altarpiece, which is now in the Museo Civico in Prato, is the earliest surviving narrative sequence of the translation legend. In it, the incident when Thomas showed the disciples gathered around the empty grave the Belt as proof of her corporeal Assumption is included. See most recently on the altarpiece, Andrea De Marchi, "Prato 1338: Una pala risarcita di Bernardo Daddi, una città che cresce sotto il segno della cintola," in De Marchi and Mavarelli, eds., *Legati da una cintola*, pp. 13–29 and pp. 122–31, cat. no. 5.

178 Similarly, the image of the *Assumption and Gift of the Belt* in a relief by Niccolò di Cecco del Mercia, possibly from an outdoor pulpit c. 1360 and now in the Museo dell'Opera del Duomo in Prato, shows a more animated interaction of the Virgin and Thomas; see Renzo Fantappiè and Claudio Cerretelli, eds., *Sacre Suggestioni: Museo dell'Opera del Duomo di Prato*, Prato: Cariprato, 2001, pp. 31–32, no. 31; Lapi Ballerini "Per onorare la sua preziossima Cintola," pp. 21–24; and Cerretelli, "Tre cappelle," p. 64; Cerretelli, "La sacra cintola e il suo scrigno," pp. 48–51; and De Marchi and Mavarelli, eds., *Legati da una cintola*, pp. 164–66, cat nos. 22 a–c.

179 The theme of touch associated with the relic is raised in a miracle related by Duccio in which one of the buttons or knots on the Belt, having come loose, was about to be repaired by a tailor. When the man went to sew it, he found it had healed itself; see Duccio di Amadore, *Il Cincturale*, pp. 32–37. Touch was also a way of conferring sanctity on other objects, such as the *brandea*, strips of cloth lowered to touch the graves of martyrs.

180 For discussion of the role of sensory experience in late medieval religious devotion, see Thomas Lentes, "'As Far as the Eye Can See . . .': Rituals of Gazing in the Late Middle Ages," in Hamburger et al., eds., *The Mind's Eye*, pp. 360–73.

181 Van Os, "The Assumption in Sienese Painting," p. 129 and figs. 6, 7, 17, 20–28, 31–35.

182 The gilt background is prominent in Daddi's image of the *Assumption*, though the loss of the lower part of the panel renders a comparison with Agnolo's landscapes impossible. In the predella, however, the gilt backgrounds recur, and the landscapes in the *Apostles at the Tomb* and the *Consignment of the Belt* are limited to barren hills.

183 Brown, *The Cult of the Saints*, p. 87, discusses how the cult of relics collapses distances. The storage of the Belt in the altar under lock and key, and its ceremonial removal and display during the ritual of ostentation, was part of the carefully controlled access to the relic that was fundamental to its power; see also Toccafondi, "Legati da una Cintura," pp. 63–68.

184 The Valley of Josaphat lay outside the Golden Gate of Jerusalem and was traversed by the Cedron River. See the map of Jerusalem in *Géographie de Ptolémée*, trans. Jacopo d'Angiolo de Florence (late fifteenth century), ed. H. Omont, Paris: Catala frères, 1926, pl. 73; illustrated in Malquori, "On the Margins of the Invention of the True Cross," in Frosinini, ed., *Agnolo Gaddi and the Cappella Maggiore in Santa Croce in Florence*, p. 168, fig. 3.

185 Duccio di Amadore, *Il Cincturale*, pp. 64–67, lines 520–24. The exact spot where Thomas received the Belt was marked by a rock, now in the garden of the Russian church of Santa Maria Maddalena, Jerusalem; see Michele Bacci, "La Cintura della Vergine nell'oriente mediterraneo," in *Iconographica*, special issue, 2021, pp. 31–32.

186 The miniature in Impruneta also shows the Assumption taking place above a rocky, wooded landscape; and this topography is also alluded to in Orcagna's relief on the tabernacle in Orsanmichele. Another panel of the *Assumption* by Maso di Banco in Berlin, by contrast, shows the Virgin standing rigidly in a mandorla carried aloft by angels against a gold background. Thomas kneels and reaches for the Belt in a barren landscape; see Miklós Boskovits, *Gemäldegalerie Berlin, Frühe Italienische Malerei*, Berlin: Gebr. Mann, 1988, pp. 109–12, no. 42, pl. 164–66; Cristina Gnoni Mavarelli, "L'Assunta e la cintola:

Exempla di un'iconografia in Toscana dal XIII al XVI secolo," in *Legati da una cintola*, pp. 72–85.

187 On translation legends generally, see Geary, *Furta Sacra*, pp. 9–15; Martin Heinzelmann, *Translationsberichte und andere Quellen des Reliquienkultes*, Turnhout, Belgium: Brepols, 1979. Heinzelmann, pp. 46–52, relates how translations were from earliest times assimilated into the liturgical celebrations of saints. On translations of relics generally, see Herrmann-Mascard, *Les Reliques des saints*, pp. 175–92; and Robert Bartlett, *Why Can the Dead Do Such Great Things? Saints and Worshippers from the Martyrs to the Reformation*, Princeton: Princeton University Press, 2013, pp. 282–96.

188 Heinzelmann, *Translationsberichte*, pp. 52–53.

189 On the different stages of translation included in legends, see Heinzelmann, *Translationsberichte*, pp. 46–83, and Geary, *Furta Sacra*, pp. 125–28.

190 Herrmann-Mascard, *Les Reliques des saints*, pp. 194–205; Heinzelmann, *Translationsberichte*, pp. 57–62; Geary, *Furta Sacra*, pp. 11–15, 125–28; Muir, *Ritual*, pp. 252–55.

191 For a detailed textual analysis of the manuscript sources and arguments for their date, see Grassi's introductions in Duccio di Amadore, *Il Cincturale*, pp. 11–15; and in Guizzelmi, *Historia della Cinctola della Vergine Maria*, pp. 8–16; as well as Grassi's essay "La Storia del Sacro Cingolo," in Martini, ed., *La Sacra Cintola nel Duomo di Prato*, pp. 23–39.

192 The versions of the legend vary in detail. I have drawn this account from those that seem to be closest in date to the murals: the *Cincturale* of Duccio (1340) and the history copied by Guizzelmi in 1493. For more on Guizzelmi and his history, see Maniura, *Art and Miracle in Renaissance Tuscany*, pp. 13–27, 71–94.

193 Grassi, "La Storia del Sacro Cingolo," p. 37, note 6, observes that Agnolo's mural misrepresents the marriage of Michele and Maria, because according to most versions of the legend, the wedding was performed in secret, without the consent of the bride's father. See also Ciatti, "Gli affreschi della Cappella della Cintola," p. 192.

194 See Franco Cardini, *In Terrasanta: Pellegrini italiani tra medioevo e prima età moderna*, Bologna: Il Mulino, 2002, on accounts of fourteenth- and fifteenth-century pilgrims to the Holy Land, with maps of their itineraries, pp. 197–296; see also Michele Bacci, "Portolano sacro: Santuario e immagini sacre lungo le rotte di navigazione del mediterraneo tra tardo medioevo e prima età moderna," in Thunø and Wolf, eds., *The Miraculous Image*, pp. 223–48.

195 Duccio di Amadore, *Il Cincturale*, pp. 38–39, lines 125–29.

196 Daddi's predella may allude to the *pieve* in the scene of Thomas giving the Belt to a priest. The gift takes place in front of a Romanesque church portal with a decorative stone inlay above the lintel characteristic of Tuscan Romanesque revetment; see Alick McLean, "Sacred Space and Public Policy: The Establishment, Decline and Revival of Prato's Piazza della Pieve," PhD dissertation, Princeton University, 1993, vol. 1, p. 208 note 354.

197 The prominence of many miracles in the early translation legends of the Belt raise the question of why only one is depicted here. The answer may be that, after the attempted theft of Musciattino, the commune commissioned the painter Bettino di Corsino to depict the event and its aftermath in ten scenes on the walls of the *pieve*. The payments were authorized on 31 May 1313, "pro decem ystoriis per eum depictis in plebe de Burgo pro miraculo cinguli beate Marie"; see Fantappiè, "Storia e 'storie' della Cintola," p. 55, note 27; the document is in ASP, Comune, Diurni, 71, c. 421 verso. The document suggests that Bettino depicted other miracles associated with the Belt; so the scene of the angelic transfer of Michele in the chapel might have alluded to the miracles on view just outside. Fragments of mural painting on the north wall of the church may be the remains of this cycle, partially destroyed during the construction of the new chapel; see Lapi Ballerini, "Per onorare la sua preziosissima cintola," pp. 16–18; and Claudio Cerretelli, "Bettino, la cintola, e la prima veduta del Duomo di Prato," in *Prato, storia e arte*, vol. 121, June 2017, pp. 17–31.

198 Grassi, "La Storia del Sacro Cingolo," pp. 23–33.

199 Duccio's *Cincturale* omits this miracle.

200 The house of Michele, where the Belt was preserved for many years, was thought to have been in the ancient Piazza della Pieve and to have been demolished during the renovations to the piazza in the late thirteenth century. In the early fourteenth century, either by 1301 or in 1333, a column was erected at communal expense marking the location; see Ruggero Nuti, "Aspetti di Prato nel Medioevo: La Piazza della pieve," *Archivio storico pratese*, vol. 27, 1951, pp. 64–65; McLean, *Prato*, pp. 152–53.

201 Cerretelli, "La Pieve e la Cintola," p. 96. The organ was installed in 1454 (Filippo Lippi, then employed in the *pieve*, was paid in that year to restore the damage) and enlarged in the eighteenth century.

202 The ancient Palazzo della Propositura, later Palazzo Vescovile, has entirely disappeared owing to later alterations. See Nuti, "La piazza della pieve," pp. 61–63. Miniati's guidebook, *Narrazione e disegno della terra di Prato* [1594], p. 76, refers to the palazzo as having loggie, terraces, windows with stone moldings, etc. However, a drawing of the palazzo from 1596 published by Guazzini, "Commissioni artistiche tra Prato e Pistoia, anno 1400," p. 219, pl. 12, does not accord with this description. The fresco by Piero di Miniato in the Palazzo Pretorio again shows a large palace next to the *pieve*, which, though the windows are different, may allude to the Palazzo della Propositura.

203 Rita Tekippe, "Pilgrimage and Procession: Correlations of Meaning, Practice, and Effects," in Sarah Blick and Rita Tekippe, eds., *Art and Architecture of late Medieval Pilgrimage in Northern Europe and the British Isles*, Leiden: Brill, 2005, pp. 693–751. Hartmut Kühne, *Ostensio Reliquiarum: Untersuchungen über Entstehung, Ausbreitung, Gestalt und Funktion der Heiltumsweisungen im römisch-deutschen Regnum*, Berlin: de Gruyter, 2000, pp. 528–34, discusses the historical link of relic ostentation with translation ceremonies, citing many examples.

204 Miklós Boskovits, *Pittura fiorentina alla vigilia del Rinascimento 1370–1400*, Florence: Edam, 1975, pp. 121–23; Cole, *Agnolo Gaddi*, pp. 32–39; Ciatti, "Gli affreschi della Cappella della Cintola," pp. 211–14.

205 Chiara Nepi, "Le piante negli affreschi della Cappella della Cintola," in Lapi Ballerini, ed., *Agnolo Gaddi e la Cappella della Cintola*, pp. 125–33.

206 As Lapi Ballerini has remarked, the presence of two prayer books – one in the Virgin's lap and another on the bench beside her – is unusual. The second book on the bench may have been added to make the links to the Florentine image more explicit; Lapi Ballerini "Per onorare la sua preziosissima Cintola," p. 35.

207 The inconsistencies in the replicas, especially in the position of the Virgin's head, are cited by Megan Holmes, "The Elusive Origins of the Cult of the Annunziata in Florence," in Thunø and Wolf, eds., *The Miraculous Image*, pp. 111–12, as evidence for a retrospective elaboration of the image as "not made by human hands."

208 For the building history, see Walter and Elisabeth Paatz, *Die Kirchen von Florenz*, vol. 1, Frankfurt: Klostermann, 1940, pp. 158–59; see also Francesco Petrucci, *Santissima Annunziata*, Rome: Fratelli Palombi, 1992; Eugenio Casalini, *Michelozzo di Bartolommeo e l'Annunziata di Firenze*, Florence: Convento della SS. Annunziata, 1995, pp. 52–58; Eugenio Casalini, *Una icona di famiglia*, Florence: Convento della SS. Annunziata, 1998; Timothy Verdon, "La Santissima Annunziata: Storia, arte, spiritualità," in Timothy Verdon, ed., *Alla riscoperta delle chiese di Firenze; 4. Santissima Annunziata*, Florence: Centro Di, 2005, pp. 9–32.

209 Giacomo Prampolini, *L'Annunciazione nei pittori primitivi italiani*, Milan: Hoepli, 1939, pp. 11–50; Stefanie Renner, *Die Darstellung der Verkündigung an Maria in der florentinischen Malerei von Andrea Orcagna bis Lorenzo Monaco*, Bonn: Lemmens, 1996, pp. 103–8; Timothy Verdon, "L'Incarnazione e la città del fiore: L'Annunciazione nell'arte fiorentina," *Arte cristiana*, vol. 88, 2000, pp. 227–30. Replicas include those in Santa Maria Novella, attributed to Pietro di Miniato c. 1400, Paaztz, *Die Kirchen von Florenz*, 3, p. 701; in San Marco (this fresco now to the right of the entrance portal, Florentine, fourteenth century)

Paatz, *Die Kirchen von Florenz*, vol. 3, p. 25; in Ognissanti (attributed to the Master of Barberino, formerly inscribed with the date 1369, now transferred to the sacristy), Paatz, *Die Kirchen von Florenz*, vol. 4, p. 418; in Santa Lucia sul Prato (on the left wall, attributed to the manner of Nardo di Cione, c. 1360), Paatz, *Die Kirchen von Florenz*, vol. 2, p. 623; and a lost fresco on the right wall in San Pancrazio, possibly fourteenth century, Paatz, *Die Kirchen von Florenz*, vol. 4, p. 571. In Prato, panels evoking the Florentine image are found in Santo Spirito, attributed to Jacopo di Cione, and in Calenzano, near Prato, in San Niccolo, attributed to the school of Jacopo di Cione. These images show slight variations. The phenomenon of replication of a sacred image in the Renaissance as a reflection of its temporal plurality is considered by Alexander Nagel and Christopher Wood, *Anachronic Renaissance*, New York: Zone Books, 2010, pp. 13–14 and 29–34.

210 Louise Bulman, "Artistic Patronage at SS. Annunziata: 1440–1520," PhD dissertation, Courtauld Institute, 1971, p. 10; Michele Bacci, *Pro remedio animae: Immagini sacre e pratiche devozionali in Italia centrale*, Pisa: Edizioni ETS, 2000, p. 59.

211 Trecento mural cycles of the life of the Virgin generally locate the Annunciation in a prominent place, isolated from the other narrative scenes, as Giotto's two-part scene above the altar arch in the Arena chapel in Padua; Taddeo Gaddi's mural in the Baroncelli chapel, the murals in the Collegiata in San Gimignano attributed to Barna da Siena, the mural in Volterra, Palazzo dei Priori, Sala del Consiglio, attributed to Jacopo di Cione and Niccolò di Pietro Gerini; and in Toledo Cathedral, the chapel of San Blas, attributed to the circle of Antonio Veneziano.

212 See Erwin Panofsky, "Imago Pietatis," in *Festschrift für M.J. Friedlander zum 60. Geburtstag*, Leipzig: Seemann, 1927, pp. 261–308; Sixten Ringbom, *Icon to Narrative: The Rise of the Dramatic Close-up in Fifteenth Century Devotional Painting*, Abo: Abo Akademi, 1965; Hans Belting, *The Image and Its Public in the Middle Ages: Form and Function of Early Paintings of the Passion*, trans. Mark Bartusis and Raymond Meyer, New Rochelle, NY: A. D. Caratzas, 1990, pp. 41–59; Julian Gardner, "The Louvre Stigmatization and the Problem of the Narrative Altarpiece," in *Patrons, Painters, and Saints: Studies in Medieval Italian Painting*, Aldershot: Variorum, 1993, pp. 217–47; Alexander Nagel, *Michelangelo and the Reform of Art*, Cambridge, MA: Harvard University Press, 2000, pp. 38–41; and Megan Holmes, "Miraculous Images in Renaissance Florence," *Art History*, vol. 34, 2011, pp. 432–64.

213 Just how visual narratives were understood by spectators in the late Middle Ages has been much discussed; see, for example, Paul Barolsky, "The Visionary Experience of Renaissance Art," *Word and Image*, vol. 11 1995, pp. 174–81; Lina Bolzoni, *The Web of Images: Vernacular Preaching from Its Origins to St. Bernardino da Siena*, trans. C. Preston and L. Chien, Aldershot: Ashgate, 2004.

214 Belting, *The Image and Its Public*, pp. 46–47.

215 *Zardino de Oration*, quoted in Baxandall, *Painting and Experience*, p. 46; Belting, *The Image and Its Public*, pp. 47–48.

216 Sixten Ringbom, "Devotional Images and Imaginative Devotions: Notes on the Place of Art in Late Medieval Piety," *Gazette des Beaux-Arts*, ser. 6, vol. 73, 1969, pp. 159–70; David Freedberg, *The Power of Images, Studies in the History and Theory of Response*, Chicago: University of Chicago Press, 1989, pp. 161–91; Jeffrey Hamburger, "The Visual and the Visionary: The Image in Late Medieval Monastic Devotions," *Viator*, vol. 20, 1989, pp. 161–82; and J. Oliver, "Image et dévotion: Le Rôle de l'art dans l'institution de la Fête-Dieu," in André Haquin, ed., *Fête-Dieu (1246–1996): Actes du colloque de Liège*, Louvain: Collège Erasme, 1999, vol. 1, pp. 153–72.

217 R. Trexler, "Florentine Religious Experience," pp. 7–41; Megan Holmes, *The Miraculous Image in Renaissance Florence*, New Haven and London: Yale University Press, 2013, pp. 80–81.

218 See Brown, *The Cult of the Saints*, pp. 86–105, on "praesentia." The concept of "aura," in the sense it is used in Walter Benjamin, "The Work of Art in the Age of Mechanical Reproduction," *Illuminations*, New York: Harcourt, Brace & World, 1968, pp. 217–51, has

also been used in this context; see Christof Diedrichs, "Wahrnehmung des mittelalterlichen Kirchenraums," in Christina Lechtermann and Carsten Morsch, eds., *Kunst der Bewegung: Kinästhetische Wahrnehmung und Probehandeln in virtuellen Welten*, Bern: Lang, 2004, pp. 267–84.

219 For the concept of ciboria and chapels creating "spaces of prayer" before miraculous images, see Timothy Verdon, "Michelozzo e lo spazio della preghiera: il 'Tempietto' della Santissima Annunziata," in Gabriele Morolli, ed., *Michelozzo scultore e architetto (1396–1472)*, Florence: Centro Di, 1998, pp. 171–77. Holmes, *The Miraculous Image*, pp. 211–18, discusses these spaces and other framing devices.

220 Holmes, "The Elusive Origins of the Cult of the Annunziata," p. 110, discusses the importance of "contact" in the dissemination of miraculous powers of relics and sacred images. See also Brown, *The Cult of the Saints*, pp. 87–89, on *brandea* and contact relics generally.

221 "Quanti mutamenti sono stati nella mia città pur nella figura di Nostra Donna! E' fu un tempo che a Santa Maria da Cigoli ciascun correa; poi s'andava a Santa Maria della Selva; poi ampli la fama di Santa Maria in Pruneta; poi a Fiesole a Santa Maria Primerana; e poi a Nostra Donna d'Orto San Michele, poi s'abbandonorono tutte, e alla Nunziata de' Servi ogni persona ha concorso con gran cerimonia a la quale, or per un modo, or per un altro sono state poste e apicate tante imagini .... È cosi la gente, e Dio il sa quanto netta di peccati; come se Nostra Donna avesse più di forza a far le grazie in uno luogo che in un altro." Franco Sacchetti, *La battaglia delle belle donne, Le lettere, Le sposizioni di vangeli*, ed. Alberto Chiari, Bari: Laterza, 1938, p. 103. Pisa also possessed a relic of the Virgin's Belt; see Francesca Dell'Acqua, "Trame mariane. Le cintole di Maria nella Toscana medievale – prodromi," in Saverio Lomartire, ed., *Il pane di segale: Diciannove esercizi di storia dell'arte presentati ad Adriano Peroni*, Varzi: Guardamagna, 2016, pp. 67–83.

222 Bacci, *Pro remedio animae* p. 10, notes the movement of the shrines enumerated by Sacchetti over time from the outskirts toward the center of Florence.

223 Official accounts of the miracles associated with the Santissima Annunziata date only from the late fifteenth century. Communal intervention in the cult began in 1401, though references to the image and chapel began in the 1360s; see Giuseppe Richa, *Notizie istoriche delle chiese fiorentine* [1759], [reprint Rome: Multigrafica Editrice, 1972], vol. 8, pp. 9–12; Bacci, *Pro remedio animae*, pp. 58–61; Antonio Paolucci, "L'Annunciazione della Santissima Annunziata a Firenze," in Paolucci, ed., *Colloqui davanti alla Madre*, pp. 15–19; Holmes, "The Elusive Origins of the Cult of the Annunziata," pp. 97–108. Indulgences were granted to worshippers by Pope Innocent VI in 1361, and the altar was consecrated in 1370. These dates contrast with concession of indulgences to Pratese pilgrims by John XXII in 1318, renewed in 1362, 1380, 1394, on the occasion of the translation to the new chapel, and in 1435; see Fantappiè, "Storia e 'storie' della Cintola," p. 54, note 19.

224 Holmes, "The Elusive Origins of the Cult of the Annunziata," pp. 118–19; see also Vauchez, "Patronage of Saints and Civic Religion," pp. 157–61, on the uneasy relationship of local cults of saints to the Roman church. The Holy Belt itself had been coupled with the most ancient and venerated acheiropoieta in Rome, the Vera Icon, as early as the *Cincturale* (1340). This image of Christ's visage had been imprinted on the cloth used by a pious woman to wipe Christ's face on his way to Calvary. Housed in Saint Peter's, it was a major focus of pilgrimage. Duccio di Amadore asserted that, after the Veronica, or Vera Icon, the Holy Belt in Prato was the most potent and popular cult object; *Il Cincturale*, pp. 80–81, lines 725–28. See also Herbert Kessler, Joanna Zacharias, *Rome 1300: On the Path of the Pilgrim*, New Haven and London: Yale University Press, 2000, pp. 210–12.

225 Cassidy, "The Assumption of the Virgin on the Tabernacle of Orsanmichele," pp. 177–80. A history of the shrine is given in Diane Zervas, "Orsanmichele from Its Origins to the Eighteenth Century," in Diane Zervas, ed., *Orsanmichele a Firenze*, "Mirabilia Italiae," Modena: Panini, 1996, vol. 1, pp. 11–179; for the painting by Bernardo Daddi, see most recently Holmes, *The Miraculous Image*, pp. 145–51.

226 Franco del Grosso, "Origine del culto alla Madonna d'Impruneta e suoi rapporti con la città di Firenze," in *Impruneta, una pieve, un paese*, "Quaderni di storia urbana e rurale," vol. 2, Atti del convegno di Studi 20–22 maggio, 1982 (Florence, 1983), pp. 33–77; Rosana Caterina Proto Pisani, "Una pieve, un rurale, un santuario," in *Il Museo di Santa Maria all'Impruneta*, Florence: Salimbeni, 1996, pp. 14–21. On the altarpiece, see Boskovits, *Pittura fiorentina alla vigilia del Rinascimento*, p. 59, pl. 61.

227 Bulman, "Artistic Patronage at SS. Annunziata," pp. 13, 29 note 18; see also Lamberto Crociani, "Culto mariano in Santa Maria del Fiore," in Timothy Verdon and Annalisa Innocenti, eds. *La cattedrale e la città: Saggi sul Duomo di Firenze*, Florence: Edifir, 2001, vol. 1, part 1, pp. 431–39.

228 Verdon, "Michelozzo e lo spazio della preghiera," pp. 171–77.

229 See Robert Maniura's discussion of the sacred image at Santa Maria delle Carceri and its relationship to the Holy Belt in "Persuading the Absent Saint: Image and Performance in Marian Devotion," *Critical Inquiry*, vol. 35, 2009, pp. 629–54. Late medieval concepts of vision, which admit a tactile quality to sight, tended to elide the effects of sacred images and relics; see Christof Diedrichs, "Desire for Viewing: 'A Deluge of Images' in the Middle Ages," in Eyolf Østrem et al., eds., *Genre and Ritual: The Cultural Heritage of Medieval Rituals*, Copenhagen: University of Copenhagen Press, 2005, pp. 115–17.

230 On the role of the Giovanni Pisano sculpture giving a tangibility to a relic hidden most of the time from public view, see Petra Janke, *Ein heilbringender Schatz: Die Reliquienverehrung am Halberstädter Dom im Mittelalter*, Munich: Deutsche Kunstverlag, 2006, pp. 16–22. See also Nagel and Wood on the difference between images and relics in *Anachronic Renaissance*, 2010, p. 31; and further discussion in Holmes, *Miraculous Image*, pp. 235–36.

231 Trexler, "Sacred Image," pp. 11–20. Pierre-André Sigal, *L'Homme et le miracle dans la France médiévale (XIe–XIIe siècle)* Paris: Cerf, 1985, sees the change in devotional behavior as a historical evolution.

232 Stephen Campbell, *The Endless Periphery: Towards a Geopolitics of Art in Lorenzo Lotto's Italy*, Chicago: University of Chicago Press, 2019, pp. 32–33, discusses "heterotopic" – or imaginary, non topographic – landscape as a way of drawing connections across a wide geographic area. The replications of the Santissima Annunziata created such a landscape.

233 Robert Nelson, "Appropriation," in Robert Nelson and Richard Shiff, eds., *Critical Terms for Art History*, 2nd ed., Chicago: University of Chicago Press, 2003, pp. 160–73. See also Franco Cardini's remarks in Braudel, ed., *Prato, Storia di una città*, vol. 1, part 2, p. 850; Richard Trexler, *Public Life in Renaissance Florence*, Ithaca: Cornell University Press, 1980, pp. 4–8; and Maniura, *Art and Miracle in Renaissance Tuscany*, pp. 92–94. Mayu Fujikawa, "Florence's Territorial Hegemony in the Eyes of foreign Dignitaries: The Cappella della Sacra Cintola in Santo Stefano, Prato," in Lilian Zirpolo, ed., *The Chapels of Italy, from the Twelfth to the Eighteenth Centuries: Art, Religion, Patronage, and Identity*, Woodcliff Lake, NJ: WAPACC Organization, 2010, pp. 177–203, discusses how Florence used ostentations of the Holy Belt as a diplomatic tool.

234 The triple portrait of the Gaddi family in the Uffizi is a visualization of that lineage; see Cadogan, "Agnolo Gaddi and his Family," pp. 153–76.

235 Cennino Cennini, *Il libro dell'arte*, ed. and trans. Lara Broecke, London: Archetype, 2015, pp. 19–20.

236 Cole, *Agnolo Gaddi*, pp. 46–50; Chiodo, "Comparative Analysis and Historical Context," pp. 78–79.

237 See Giorgio Chittolini, *La formazione dello stato regionale e le istituzioni del contado*, Turin: Einaudi, 1979, pp. 292–352; Guido Pampaloni, "Prato nell Repubblica fiorentina, secolo XIV–XV," in *Storia di Prato*, vol. 2, pp. 3–18; Guido Pampaloni, "L'autonomia pratese sotto Firenze (1351–1500)," in Braudel, ed., *Prato, Storia di una città*, vol. 2, pp. 377–62; and the various contributions to the volume *Florentine Tuscany: Structures and Practices of Power*, ed. William Connell and Andrea Zorzi, Cambridge: Cambridge University Press, 2000.

238 Pampaloni, "L'autonomia pratese sotto Firenze," in Braudel, ed., *Prato, Storia di una città*, vol. 2, p. 741; Francis W. Kent, "Prato and Lorenzo de' Medici," in Carolyn James, ed., *Princely Citizen. Lorenzo de' Medici and Renaissance Florence*, Turnhout: Brepols, 2013, pp. 281–98. For general remarks on the maintenance of civic cults in subject communes, see Webb, *Patrons and Defenders*, pp. 13–14.

239 For example, Fantappiè, "Storia e 'storie' della Cintola," p. 46. Vauchez, "Patronage of Saints and Civic Religion," p. 165, notes examples of the removal of relics from the countryside as part of the "cultic policy" of Italian communes.

240 Andrea Franchi (1335–1401), who became Bishop of Pistoia in 1381, served until 1400; his brother Bartolomeo Franchi was apostolic protonotary to Urban VI; he was provost of the *pieve* di Santo Stefano in Prato between 1373 and 1400; see Eugenio Marino, "Iconologia del ciclo via Paradisi di Giovanni di Bartolomeo Cristiani," in *Memorie domenicane*, vol. 8/9, 1977, pp. 269–72; R. Agresti, *Dizionario Biografico degli Italiani*, vol. 50, 1998, pp. 83–85; and Franco Cardini in Braudel, ed., *Prato, Storia di una città*, vol. 1, part 2, p. 850.

241 See Poggi, "La Cappella del Sacro Cingolo," pp. 356–76; and Cerretelli, "La Pieve e la Cintola," pp. 92–94. These artisans included Lorenzo di Filippo, who supervised the construction of the Loggia della Signoria in Florence and was later *capomaestro* of the Duomo, Giovanni d'Ambrogio, Michele di Giovanni da Firenze, and of course Agnolo Gaddi. The association with the Florentine Opera predates building the new chapel; in February 1368, Giovanni di Lapo Ghini and Francesco Talenti, *capomaestri* of the Florentine cathedral, were paid for advice on the final construction of the new eastern end of the *pieve*; Cerretelli, "La sacra cintola e il suo scrigno," pp. 50–51.

242 Fujikawa, "Florence's Territorial Hegemony," pp. 178–80, describes Florentine requests for special ostentations of the Holy Belt to visiting foreign dignitaries.

CHAPTER TWO

"A MOST DEVOUT PLACE"

The Camposanto from Cemetery to Civic Space in Fourteenth Century Pisa

The Camposanto in Pisa has been widely identified from the beginning of its history as a monument of civic identity and pride (Figure 2.1). Today the vast corridors, lined by tombs, are a pantheon of elite Pisans. This arrangement, however, is a product of the nineteenth century.[1] From earliest times, the Camposanto's function was quite different, and the choice to be buried there was an act of humility. This chapter outlines the early history and social role of the Camposanto as a prelude to a new reading of the fourteenth-century mural decoration. Previous accounts assume that the imagery, on the east and south walls, was part of a comprehensive decorative program, devised in the early fourteenth century, on themes of sin, penance, and redemption. The later Trecento paintings depicting Pisan saints are, however, distinct in imagery and meaning. The murals of the life of Saint Rainerius, painted by Andrea Bonaiuti (also called Andrea da Firenze; active 1346–79) and Antonio Veneziano (active 1369–1419) between 1377 and 1386, were part of a conscious campaign by civic leaders in the wake of the Black Death to reclaim the Camposanto as a communal space. Taken up in the second half of the fourteenth century to counter the rapid growth of private burial spaces in the mendicant churches, the murals on the southwest wall were completed during the signoria of Pietro Gambacorta (r. 1369–92). Their imagery celebrated Pisa's patron saint as a layman whose life was lived in the late medieval city, a theme with which spectators could identify. Pisa was presented as a locus of sacred and secular activity that brought material and spiritual wealth to

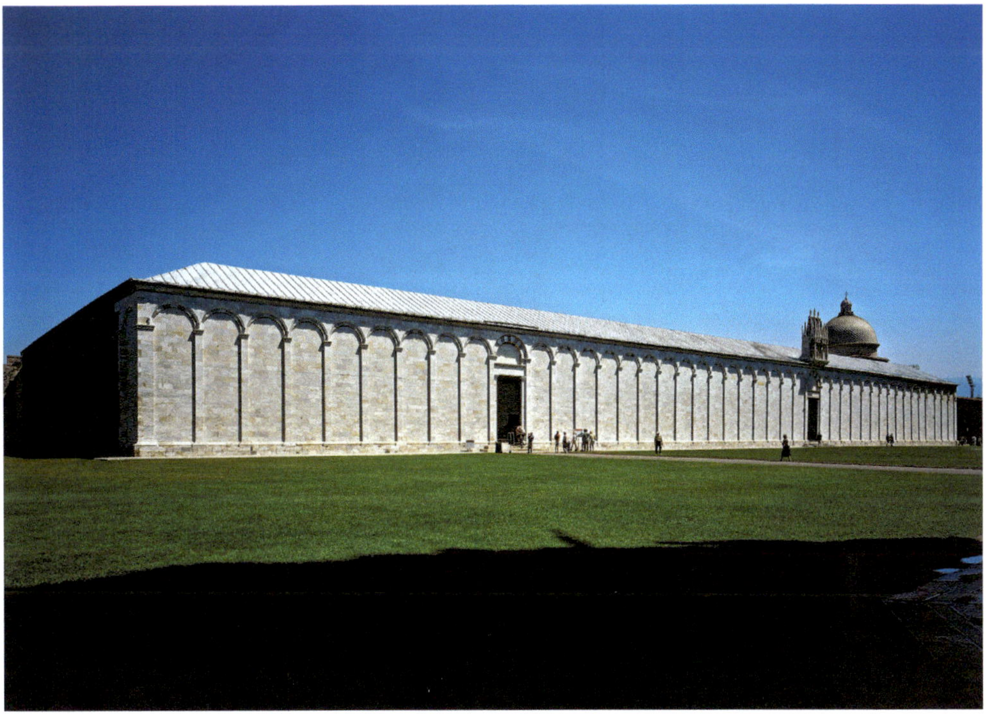

2.1. Camposanto, Pisa. Photo: Scala / Art Resource, NY.

all its citizens. In addition, the scenes of the journey of Saint Rainerius to the Holy Land referenced the history of the Camposanto itself, built as a giant reliquary for the sacred earth brought from the Holy Land to Pisa and deposited there. The vast expanse of the *Death and Burial of Saint Rainerius* mural depicted funerary rites and commemorative Masses celebrated in the Camposanto throughout the liturgical year. These murals continued the theme of the murals depicting the Old Testament story of Job in the southwest corner, completed sometime between the 1340s and 1360s, which recalled the Office of the Dead, whose texts were taken almost exclusively from the Book of Job.

EARLY BUILDING HISTORY OF THE CAMPOSANTO

About 1430, an anonymous chronicler described the Camposanto in Pisa,

> And between the Duomo and San Giovanni there is the Campo Sancto, covered with lead, where there is a great quantity of tombs on a marble floor, with marvelous stories painted on the wall and many tombs in relief.[2]

Despite its considerable attractions, Pisa's monumental cemetery was in the early fifteenth century incomplete, its vast decoration begun in the fourteenth

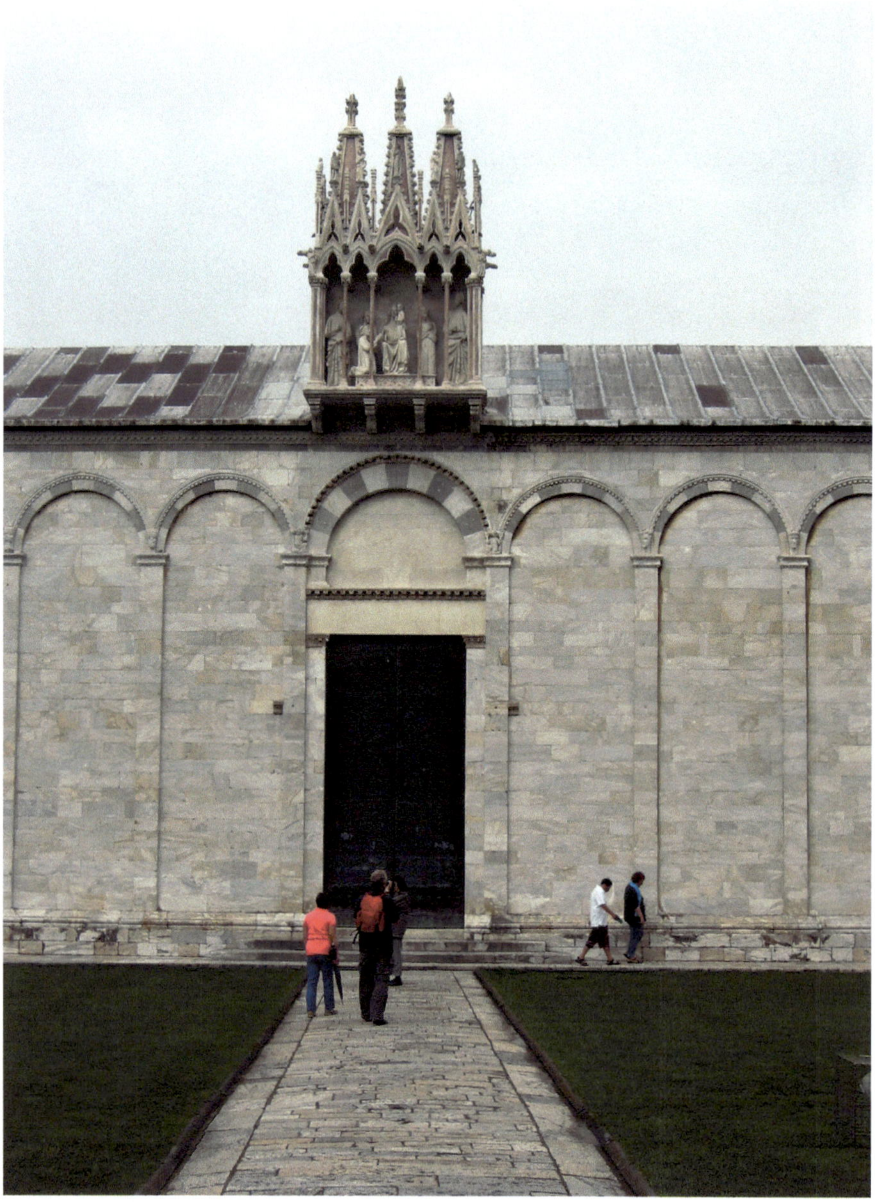

2.2. Eastern Door, Camposanto, Pisa. Photo: Author.

century unfinished. A visitor traversing the path from the west façade of the Duomo (Figure 2.2), passing through the main door surmounted by the tabernacle with the Madonna and Child on the exterior and the frescoed lunette of the *Assumption of the Virgin* within, would find him or herself in a vast cloister, 200 by 67 steps, as reported by the chronicler (see plan Figure 2.3).[3] In the center, the "sacred field" (Figure 2.4), where soil from the Holy Land, transported in Pisan galleys during the Crusades, had been

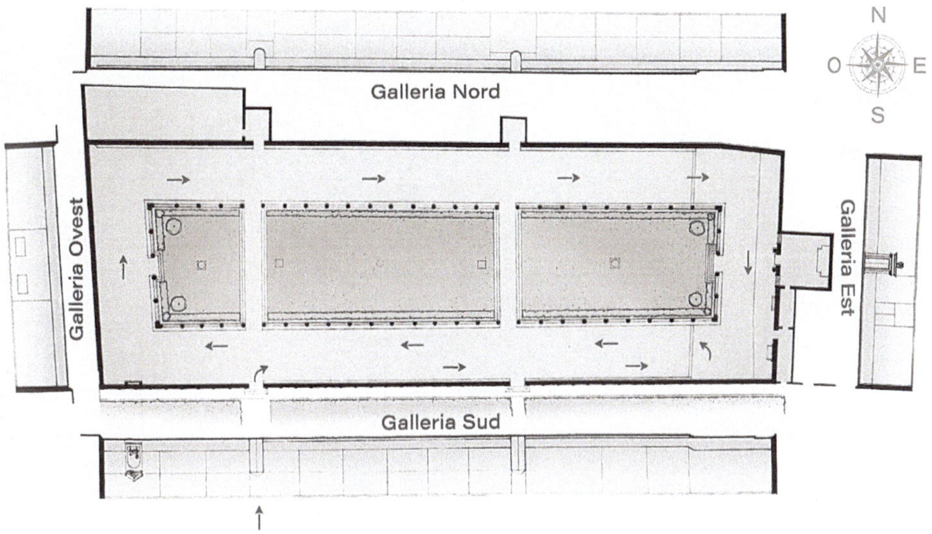

2.3. Plan of Camposanto, Pisa. Photo: Stefano Renzoni, *Il Camposanto monumentale di Pisa*, Pisa: Pacini Editore, 2020, p. i.

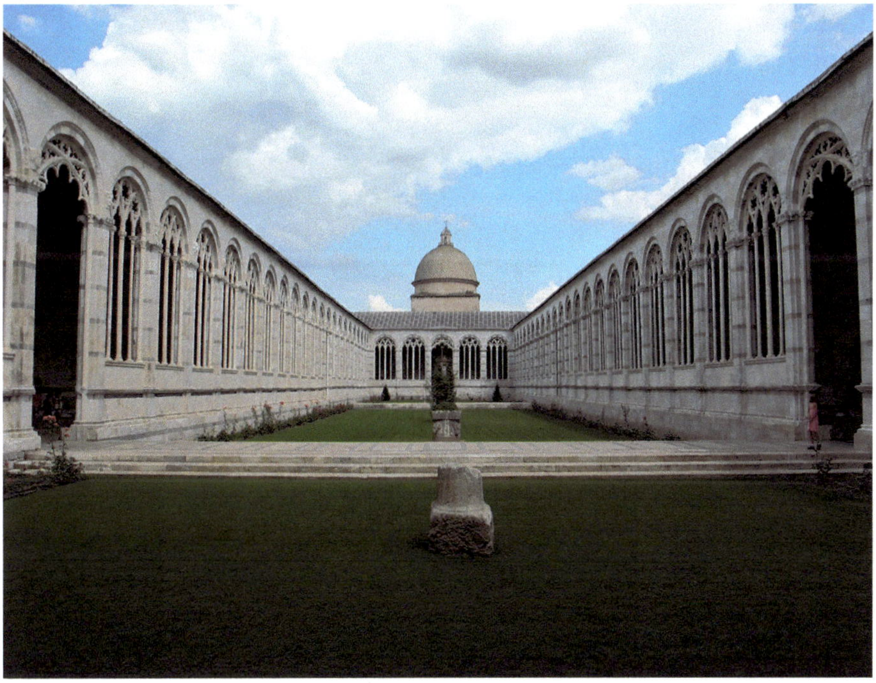

2.4. Interior view, Camposanto, Pisa. Photo: Author.

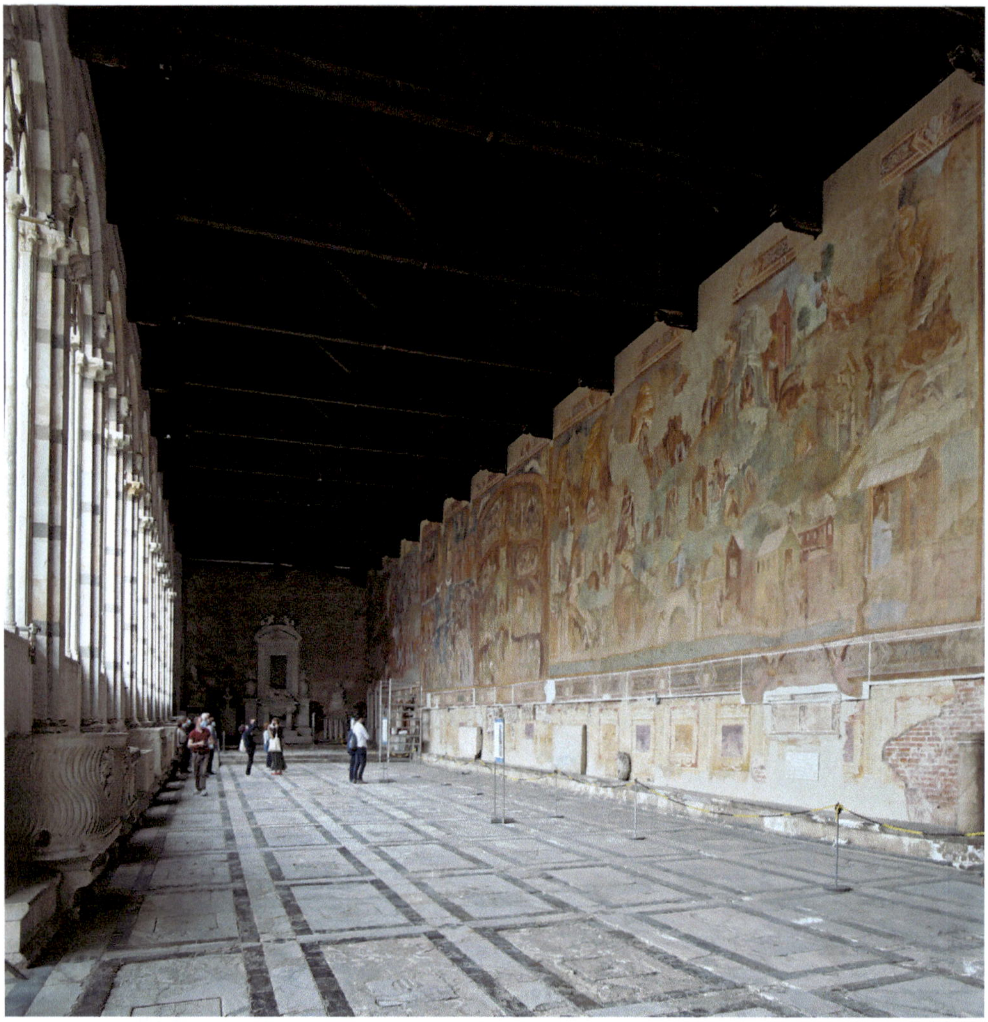

2.5. View of the south corridor, Camposanto, Pisa. Photo: Author.

deposited, our visitor would discover "in the open air placed on the ground, many tombs in relief" brought there from the areas surrounding the cathedral. Following the vista down the corridor to his right, he would have been drawn to a giant mural of the *Crucifixion* on the southern end of the east wall. As he traversed the marble pavement, comprising tomb slabs marked out by black limestone frames, he would have seen visions of the *Lives of the Hermit Saints*, then *Hell*, the *Last Judgment*, and finally, the *Triumph of Death* unfolding before him (Figure 2.5). Arriving at the eastern "corridor," to the left of the altar dedicated to All Saints, with its great frescoed altarpiece of the *Crucifixion*, scenes of the *Resurrection*, *Revelation of the Stigmata to Saint Thomas*, and the *Ascension* would conclude the history of Christ's earthly life.[4] Our spectator might then retrace his steps to the entryway and proceed west, taking in the

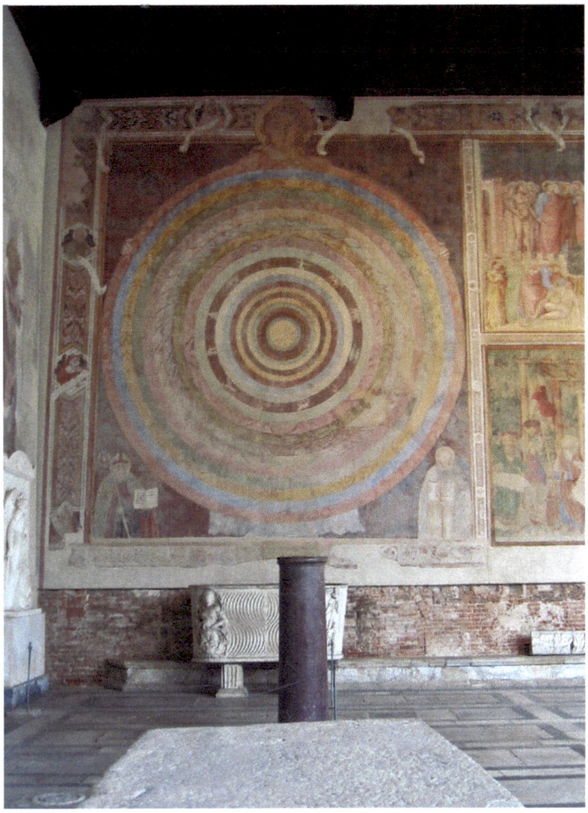

2.6. West Corridor, view toward the north wall, Camposanto, Pisa. Photo: Author.

histories of Pisan Saints Rainerius, Ephysius, and Potitus; and, to the right of the western door, the story of Job. Pausing at the southwest corner, he might have glimpsed across the undecorated west corridor, the monumental image of the Cosmos on the north wall opposite (Figure 2.6). Abutting this striking image, histories of Adam and Eve, Cain and Abel, and Noah adorned the upper part of the wall, but below and to the east the decoration ended abruptly.

Beginning in the late thirteenth century, the construction and decoration of the Camposanto proceeded in sporadic bursts of activity for over one hundred and fifty years. In 1277, when Archbishop Federigo Visconti donated land to the north of the cathedral for the formation of the Camposanto, he expressed the desire to systematize the area around the Duomo, then encumbered by tombs and graves.[5] The archbishop's plan to enhance the dignity of the church and its surroundings and to secure its use for the public provided for a new cemetery, removed from the immediate proximity of the Duomo and enclosed by walls.[6] Among the monuments of the Piazza del Duomo, the Camposanto was a complement to the Baptistery; baptism initiated souls into the faith; death released them to eternal life. The vast façade of the

Camposanto formed a harmonious backdrop to the processions and ceremonies of the piazza, tethered to the other monuments by its strategically located portals, the east-most linked directly to the Duomo façade, the western portal aligned with the main door of the Baptistery. The Camposanto was managed by the Opera del Duomo, a civic body subordinate to the magistrates of the commune that since the twelfth century had responsibility for the construction and maintenance of the structures.[7]

To the left of the Camposanto's main portal an inscription records the date 1278, which has been understood to mark the structure's inception.[8] Yet recent research has revealed its building history to be complex and protracted. An attentive re-reading of the building fabric and archival documentation has led some scholars to propose that the Camposanto as it is known today was a replacement for an original structure on the site, not built *ex novo*.[9] Whatever its precise origins, records of burials and religious ceremonies indicate that the south and east corridors of the Camposanto had been built and to some extent decorated by the 1330s.[10] The monumental murals of the east wall, the *Crucifixion*, *Resurrection*, *Revelation of the Stigmata to Saint Thomas*, and the *Ascension*, and of the south wall, *Lives of the Hermit Saints Hell*, the *Last Judgment*, and the *Triumph of Death*, are undocumented and the subject of vast commentary in the art historical literature. They have more recently and persuasively been dated to the 1330s and early 1340s, that is, before the devastating plague of 1348.[11]

Documents testify to continued construction of the south and west corridors of the Camposanto from the 1340s to 1369, but they do not, however, permit a detailed chronology.[12] The north corridor was also probably begun by the late 1360s and was completed by the early 1390s, as suggested by payments for materials and labor in the accounts. Although by then the essential structure was complete, the fashioning of elaborate tracery to fill the internal arcades continued into the next century, while work on the tomb slabs and pavement continued until the end of the decade.

The mural decoration of the southwest wall is, in some cases, documented. By October 1377, Andrea Bonaiuti (active 1346–79) had painted three scenes from the life of Saint Rainerius on the upper register between the two portals. Antonio Veneziano (active 1369–c. 1419) painted three further histories of the saint on the lower level in 1384–86.[13] Spinello Aretino (c. 1350–1410) painted the scenes from the lives of Saints Ephysius and Potitus in 1391–92.[14] The story of Job, attributed by Vasari to Taddeo Gaddi in the first edition of the *Lives*, and to Giotto in the second, completes the mural decoration of the south wall. The Job scenes, to the west of the westernmost door, could have been painted as early as the 1340s, or they may have been executed as late as the 1360s, but in any case predate the murals between the two doors.[15]

Mural decoration for the north wall seems to have begun shortly after its construction; payments to the Orvietan painter, Piero di Puccio, between 1389 and 1391 were for his *Theological Cosmos*, *Stories from Genesis*, and *Coronation of the Virgin* in the northwest corner. Not until the late fifteenth century, in 1484, were the murals of the north wall completed by Benozzo Gozzoli (the subject of Chapter 3).

THE PIAZZA DEL DUOMO AS A PUBLIC SPACE

The Camposanto's institutional history is as complex as that of its physical structure. The last monument to be built in the Piazza del Duomo, its vast façade forms the north perimeter of the piazza, paralleling the city walls and stretching from the Baptistery to the north transept of the cathedral (Figure 2.7).[16] The façade of the Hospital of Santa Chiara (founded in 1258), comprise the southern flank, while city walls to the west and the campanile and archbishop's palace mark the eastern boundary. The tall, blind arcade of the Camposanto's gleaming marble façade harmonizes with the Romanesque

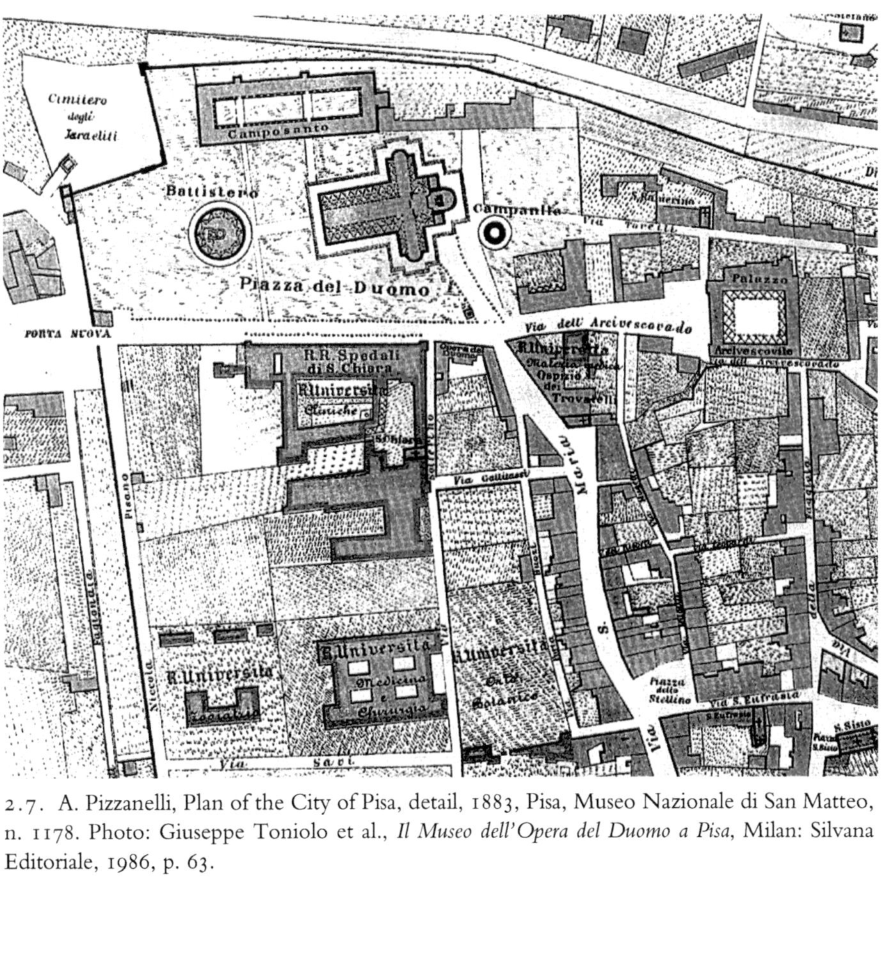

2.7. A. Pizzanelli, Plan of the City of Pisa, detail, 1883, Pisa, Museo Nazionale di San Matteo, n. 1178. Photo: Giuseppe Toniolo et al., *Il Museo dell'Opera del Duomo a Pisa*, Milan: Silvana Editoriale, 1986, p. 63.

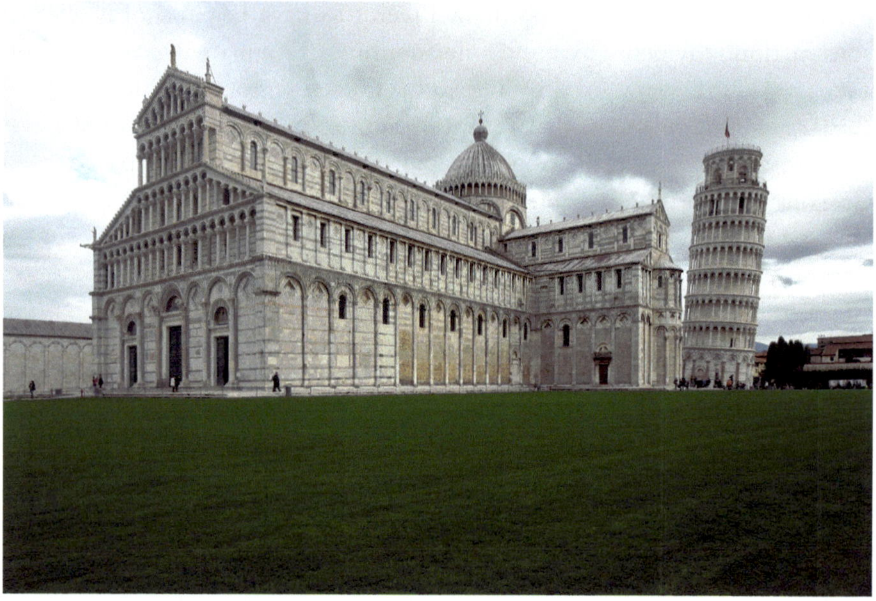

2.8. Piazza del Duomo, Pisa. Photo: source: © José Luiz Bernardes Ribeiro / Creative Commons Attribution-Share Alike 3.0 Unported CC BY-SA 3.0.

elevations of the other buildings, sharing with them white and gray marble revetment and classicizing details (Figure 2.8).[17] Though built over a period from 1063 to 1464, the construction of the structures overlapped and was carried out by Opera workshops dedicated to their realization. The continuous existence of the workshop and the conservatism of its traditions are probably responsible for the harmony of the site, rather than a preexisting plan that envisioned the final design.

The most striking aspect of the piazza today, the broad, green lawn from which the buildings rise in stark isolation, was probably realized only in the sixteenth century.[18] Earlier, the piazza housed pilgrims' hostels, private residences, shops, a well, and olive trees.[19] Roads traversed the space, while pilgrims traveling the via Francigena from the North to Rome entered the city through the Porta del Leone in the western wall. As a public space the piazza must have been populated at all times of day with a mix of religious and secular, commercial and communal, mundane and festive activities.

The piazza was the locus for the public life of the city, much as was the Piazza del Duomo in Prato, discussed in Chapter 1. Individually, the monuments were built for specific religious uses: the Duomo for the performance of Masses, the Baptistery for baptism, the campanile to call the devout to worship, and the Camposanto for burial.[20] Strategically placed in the piazza, they comprised a spacious theater for the performance of important religious rituals. As at Prato, these ceremonies involved civic authorities as well as clerical participants. Pisa, much like Prato, had a communal government, comprising various councils of magistrates; unlike Prato, however, Pisa was an independent state until the end of the fourteenth century. A major feast was 15 August, the Assumption of the Virgin, Pisa's primary patron saint. On the vigil of the feast, processions of city officers departed the communal palace, in the current-day Piazza dei Cavalieri, and followed the via Santa Maria toward the piazza del Duomo.[21] Joined by clergy and citizens, they traversed the great expanse of the piazza to the cathedral, where they made offerings of candles.[22] The Pisan statutes of 1255 prescribed the ceremony. On the vigil of the feast, the *Podestà*, his *famiglia* (staff), and the members of the Senate and Council of the Credenza, accompanied by the *capifamiglia* of the people and the heads of subject communities in the countryside, proceeded to the cathedral and offered a candle "to the honor of God and the Most Holy Virgin Mary."[23] Participation of both clerical and secular segments of the population clearly established the communal control and civic nature of the celebration. The statutes decreed that neither on the vigil of the feast nor the feast day itself were carts or temporary wood structures permitted on the via Santa Maria or on any part of the piazza. It further stipulated and that two pavilions of red cloth were to be erected for the *Podestà* and the *Anziani*, the principal governing body.[24]

In addition to religious celebrations, political events were also staged in the Piazza del Duomo. One of the earliest of these, perhaps the "inauguration" of the piazza as a public space, occurred 17 March 1312, when the Holy Roman Emperor, Henry VII of Luxembourg, received the pledges of allegiance and fealty of the *Anziani* and the *sindicus* and *procurator* on behalf of the entire populace in front of the cathedral.[25] Ranieri Sardo's chronicle described further momentous political events taking place in the piazza, including King Charles of Bohemia's entrance into the city in 1355.[26] Ten years later when a peace treaty was signed with Florence, crowds gathered to rejoice in the piazza.[27] Many other events that Sardo relates make clear that the spatial and symbolic functions of the piazza were well established by the time the Camposanto was nearing completion at the end of the fourteenth century.

THE CAMPOSANTO AS A PUBLIC AND SYMBOLIC SPACE

The Camposanto had multiple uses and symbolic roles in late medieval Pisa. In the preamble to his decree of 1277 cited above, Archbishop Federigo Visconti envisioned a walled cemetery as part of the public arena but also distinct from it spatially. Access to it – both physically and visually – was to be restricted. From its earliest form, it shaped the great theater of the Piazza del Duomo. Yet it is a building that is inward turning, its façade relatively simple and unadorned compared to the other structures in the piazza, preparing its visitors little for the character of the spaces within.

Deacon Rolando's descriptions of Holy Week ceremonies in about 1200 reveal the Camposanto's role in public ceremonies.[28] In the celebration of Palm Sunday, the piazza and its monuments became a metaphorical Jerusalem as the clergy and laity reenacted Christ's entry into Jerusalem. Architecture and ritual evoked the sacred topography of Jerusalem, and the city of Pisa was transformed into an elision of the earthly and heavenly Jerusalem – in other words, into Paradise.[29] In ceremonies such as these, the unity of the piazza and its monumental structures, of worshippers and clergy, of the city and the Holy Land, and of biblical past and contemporary reality was vividly displayed.

FUNERARY RITE: THE ENTRY INTO PARADISE

The tradition of inhumation around major churches dates to early Christianity; indeed, the first churches were built near cemeteries, which were outside city walls following pagan practice, to accommodate funerary and memorial ceremonies.[30] With the rise of the cult of the saints, the desire for the faithful to be buried "ad sanctos," close to the graves of martyrs and saints – the "very special dead" – gradually eroded the prohibitions against intramural and interchurch burial.[31] Burials in atria, cloisters, and adjacent graveyards were common, and by the ninth century, the widespread practice of allowing clergy and certain laypersons to be buried within church walls was legitimized. In Pisa, a cemetery to the south or southeast of the cathedral of Santa Maria existed from the tenth century. The cathedral's monopoly on funerary and burial functions ended in the mid-twelfth century; however, those primarily monastic churches that were granted funerary privileges were required to give a quarter of funerary bequests to the cathedral.[32]

Guillelmus Durandus (c. 1230–96), author of the influential liturgical treatise *Rationale Divinorum Officiorum* (*Manual of Divine Offices*) (1286), defined the medieval cemetery as a sacred space, consecrated by the church and sanctified by God.[33] As such, those buried in the cemetery were limited to baptized Christians, although sinners, heretics, the excommunicated, and victims of crimes were excluded, as were unbaptized, stillborn children.[34] Cities too ensured the sanctity and dignity of cemeteries.[35] The Camposanto, moreover, enjoyed exceptional status as a sacred place by the deposit of the *terra santa* brought back by Archbishop Ubaldo Lanfranchi in the late twelfth century from the Third Crusade in the Holy Land (1189–92), probably to the north of the Duomo.[36] This sacred field was devoid of private monuments, its ground covered with simple markers and symbolic plants; it may be identified with the woods next to the city walls, acquired by Ubaldo in 1202–3, perhaps as a future site for the cathedral cemetery.[37] Much later, olive trees grew in the central, uncovered space of the Camposanto, perhaps a link with the earlier character of the site. The churchyard evoked a walled garden, emblem of Paradise, and alluded to the universal hope for salvation.[38] The link of the sacred earth with Jerusalem, and the Revelation imagery of Paradise as a Heavenly Jerusalem, reinforced by the Easter ceremonies, perhaps also informed the experience of the devout in the central uncovered space of the Camposanto.[39]

Medieval funerary rituals prescribed actions from the deathbed to the grave and after. Although we have no account of the Pisan rite during the fourteenth and fifteenth centuries, a general account follows.[40] A "good death" was preceded by confession, communion (viaticum), and extreme unction, sacraments administered to the dying by a priest in the company of family and friends. Pisan sumptuary law of 1350 underscored the public nature of the death by limiting the number of nonfamily, lay observers to ten during the administration of extreme unction. The reading of all or part of Christ's Passion from the Gospel was included in the deathbed ceremony if the dying person were lettered.[41] The dying lay on his or her back, and a cross was placed at the feet, so that, as Durandus says, the dying would be more contrite. The last rites secured the safe journey of the deceased's soul to God and ended with the blessing, the *Commendatio Animae* (*Recommendation of the Departing Soul to God*). The death bell sounded once the dying had ceased breathing to inform and to solicit the prayers of the community' a practice curtailed by Pisan sumpturary law in 1350.[42] The corpse was then lowered to the floor and placed on a bed of ashes and straw.[43] It was washed and clothed, for a cleric in the robe of his or her order, for a layperson in clothes appropriate to his or her profession or confraternal membership.[44] The bier was surrounded by candles and then made available for viewing by mourners in the home.

After this period of viewing, a procession accompanied the body from the house to the church. The priest and other clerics carried a cross, while men carrying candles processed two by two in front of the bier. Durandus is strict about the composition of the procession: the body must be carried by men from the same profession; if a cleric, by clerics of the same rank; if a member of a confraternity, by other members. On no condition were women to carry the defunct.[45] Behind the bier, the widow and finally the women followed. These processions, with the participation of female mourners who performed the *pianto* or *planctus* (weeping or mourning) were, in contrast to the previous events, public spectacles that entailed dramatic lamentations. Both the *pianto* and the dazzling display of candles became objects of sumptuary legislation.[46] The procession wound its way through the neighborhood, the clergy chanting, the community responding in farewells.[47] Pisan law permitted the ringing of bells in the district of the deceased, as well as those in the churches of his neighborhood and along the processional route and in the church where he was buried.[48] At the church entrance, the body was carried feet first to rest in the nave, while clerics' bodies were placed in the restricted area of the choir.

Once in church, the clergy celebrated the Vigils of the dead, the requiem Mass, and the blessing of the body. Vespers (the first of three liturgical hours that comprise the Office of the Dead) were performed over the bier by clerics hired by the family or provided for by the deceased's confraternity on the evening before the funeral.[49] Socially prominent families might be joined by city magistrates, but in Pisa this practice was expressly forbidden in the 1313 statutes.[50] Family members prayed the office from their books of hours. Matins and Lauds were prayed by the same clerics on the morning of the funeral. The Office of the Dead – distinct from the texts of the funeral Mass or the rites for burial – comprised psalms and readings from the book of Job in the Old Testament; Job's story was understood as an allegory of earthly life and the trials of purgatory.[51] Vespers began with the antiphon "Placebo Domino in regione vivorum" ("I will please the Lord in the land of the living"; Psalm 114:9), followed by the chanting of Psalms 114, 119, 120, 129, 137, and 145, and the Magnificat (Luke 1:46–55). The Latin antiphon for Matins began with the words "Dirige, Domine, Deus meus, in conspectus tuo viam meam" ("Direct, O Lord, my God, my steps in your sight"; Psalm 5:9); and was followed by Psalms 5, 6, 7, 22, 24, 26, 29, 39, and 41. Next were recited the nine lessons for Matins from the book of Job.[52] The longest of the three hours of the office, Matins was divided into three nocturnes, the first recited at 9:00 p.m., the second at midnight, and the third at 3:00 a.m. Lauds was usually recited just after Matins and consisted of Psalms 50, 64, 62, 148, 149, 150, and 129, and the canticles *Ego Dixi* (Isiah 38:10–20) and *Benedictus Dominus* (Luke 1:68–79).

The requiem Mass followed, with readings on themes of the Last Judgment. The *Dies Irae* ("That day of wrath, that dreadful day, when heaven and earth shall pass away"), a hymn written in the mid-thirteenth century, preceded the Gospel reading and underscored the fate of all humans at the end of time. After the Mass, the body was blessed, censed, and sprinkled with holy water. The cleric then sang the "Libera me, domine, de viis [or, de morte]," in which the Last Judgment was again invoked. Following the ceremonies, the pallbearers bore the corpse in procession to the cemetery for burial. During the procession, the clergy chanted the *In Paradiso,* marking the deceased's transition from this world to the heavenly Jerusalem: "May the angels lead you into Paradise; may the martyrs receive you at your coming and take you into the holy city Jerusalem. May the choir of angels receive you and may you find eternal rest with Lazarus, no longer poor."

At the cemetery, all but family members departed. The priest sprinkled holy water to ward off demons and poured the spent cinders from the censer into the open grave. The ashes resisted decomposition and identified the grave long after the body had been consumed. The corpse was placed with its head at the west and feet toward the east, in preparation for Judgment Day. Aromatic herbs might have been added to conceal odors and to recall the biblical account of Christ's entombment. At the head of the grave, a cross was placed to protect against demons.[53] After a final prayer, the clergy returned to the church, while the family members commended the deceased to God with prayer, repetitions of the *Pater Noster*, and *Ave*. Following these lay devotions, the family returned home in procession for a funeral meal; these banquets became subject to sumptuary laws, an indication that they were opportunities for the wealthy to indulge in the ostentatious display of food and drink. An integral part of the funeral was the alms or bread distributed by the family of the deceased to the poor. This practice too drew official scrutiny: the 1350 sumptuary law in Pisa forbade payments to clergy or members of religious confraternities, unless these were directly connected to the deceased's place of burial.[54]

With the widening currency of the concept of Purgatory – an interim period the soul passed in purgation before entering heaven – commemorative Masses for the dead became common. Prayers to the Virgin and the saints by the living expedited the soul's passage; requiem Masses for the soul of the dead, often provided for by testators in wills, were most efficacious. Durandus explained that since the dead cannot perform good works nor pray for themselves, "For those who . . . are in limbo, our prayers are favorable to them or cause a softening of their sorrows . . . or serve them to obtain a complete remission or certainly render their condemnation more tolerable."[55] Such prayers were useful to the dead and the living, for they fostered devotion. Masses were said on the third day after burial, on one-week, one-month, and yearly anniversaries. These were occasions for the family to gather and for women to perform the *pianto*; memorial banquets often followed. At regular Sunday Mass, the celebrant said prayers for the dead before the Canon. During the church year, the feast of All Souls Day, 2 November, Masses for the dead were often followed by processions to the cemeteries to bless the graves.[56]

Provisions in testaments analyzed by Cohn and others shed light on Pisan practice.[57] While many wills were composed on testators' deathbeds and witnessed by the parish priest, others were drawn up with the aid of a notary; in either case, Pisan statutes regulated the form and legality of the document.[58] The testamentary formula gave prominence to funerary expenses, treating at the very beginning the place of burial and stipulations for wax, alms, commemorative Masses, and donations. Although many testators stipulated the amounts for these funerary expenses, others, especially at the end of the fourteenth century, left the exact sums to the discretion of families and heirs.[59] Increasingly common in the later fourteenth century were requests that members of lay confraternities assist at funerals. Members of lay sodalities often requested burial in the robes of the confraternity.[60]

THE CAMPOSANTO AS A COMMUNAL BURIAL SPACE

Architecturally, the Camposanto is a unique structure without clear typological antecedents.[61] A recent interpretation links its form to the Akeldama burial ground in Jerusalem, the likely source of the sacred soil Archbishop Ubaldo deposited on the site of his new cemetery.[62] More generally, the Camposanto's rectangular, arcaded form recalls a cloister or atrium, which had been used for Christian burial for many centuries, especially for clerics, as well as for laypersons with a particular devotion to an order.[63] Most burials of the general populace were in churchyards next to the parish churches. Archbishop Visconti's plan entailed the removal of tombs from the area, many of them ancient sarcophagi reused for Christian burial, which had been clustered around the external walls of the Cathedral, their inscriptions still legible in some cases.[64] Yet many other graves were unmarked, and indeed, anonymity was the norm in early medieval burial practice. In the earliest configuration in the Camposanto, the sarcophagi removed from the cathedral precinct were placed on the original *terra santa* along the perimeter of the central, open space of the new cemetery.[65] Because many of these sarcophagi were separated from the identifying inscriptions carved into the walls of the cathedral, they, too, would be anonymous, the remains identified only later through painstaking research.[66] In the center, marked perhaps only by a cross, were the graves of the poor that – true to the legend that the holy earth consumed cadavers in three days – soon disappeared. Remains exhumed from overflowing tombs were also buried there, as well as deceased who had specifically requested the most humble and anonymous resting place. These latter were often mendicant friars, who begged alms at the portal, as well as pious laypersons.[67] Tomb slabs located in the arcades of the Camposanto offered more modest sites for display and remembrance than sarcophagi and greater practicality for the living.[68] The earliest of these date only to the 1330s and are located in the southeast corner, the probable original nucleus of the current structure.[69]

While burial was the primary function of the Camposanto, documents often referred to it as a church until the early fourteenth century. Although the term often encompassed the surrounding spaces, including the cemetery,[70] in Pisa the term *ecclesia*, in connection with the Camposanto, may lie with Archbishop Visconti's dedication of the site to the Holy Trinity and the celebration of the feast of the Trinity there, as documents from the late thirteenth century attest.[71] References to construction work in the Camposanto, contained in the archival series of the Opera del Duomo, under whose auspices the cemetery was built and administered, often refer to "ecclesia S. Trinitatis de campo sancto" or simply "ecclesia campi sancti."[72] The inscription placed on the façade of the Duomo by the administrator Burgundio di Tado claimed that he had "Had the church of the Camposanto made from the arcade up."[73] And the act of election of the new *operaio* of the Duomo Giovanni Rosso in 1319 referred to the Camposanto as "cemetery or mortuary or church and chapel of the mortuary or cemetery."[74] In its prolixity, the passage underscores the multiple functions of the Camposanto, as well as the various spaces contained within the structure. We can imagine tombs, both "in relief" – perhaps the sarcophagi transported from around the Duomo – and more modest graves in the "sacred field" and tomb slabs in the covered pavement.[75] We can also image various altars constructed against the external walls, often referred to as chapels. Altars dedicated to Ognissanti in the southeast corner, below the *Crucifixion* mural on the east wall, and to the Trinity, just below the *Ascension* mural on the same wall, were used for commemorative Masses for defunct *operai*, buried immediately adjacent, and other testators who left funds for memorial services.[76]

These altars were used eventually for purposes in addition to funerary and commemorative Masses. The feast of the Holy Trinity, celebrated on the first Sunday after Pentecost, was said in the Camposanto already in 1299.[77] The major feast day for the commemoration of the dead, All Souls' Day, 2 November, was celebrated in the Camposanto at the altar of Ognissanti, for which the account book of the Opera records revenues from sales of candles to the faithful.[78] This ceremony continued in later centuries, as recorded by Giuseppe Sainati in the *Diario Sacro Pisano*.[79]

Burial of all classes of citizens further emphasized the civic nature of the monument. While the earliest tombs in the Camposanto were those transported from the area around the Duomo, burials are recorded in the new cemetery itself from around 1300.[80] During the fourteenth and fifteenth centuries, until 1467, the wealthy elite often chose to be buried in repurposed ancient sarcophagi, like those in the central open field.[81] These included both family and individual tombs for members of the old Pisan nobility, as well as members of the emerging popular families. In addition to the ancient sarcophagi, tombs of contemporary manufacture imitated the ancient style.[82]

Burials in the covered cloister, by contrast, are recorded in large numbers only from the 1330s, but there is evidence to suggest that the practice began in the first years of the fourteenth century. The building history, adumbrated by the records from the Opera del Duomo, and the analysis of the inscriptions on the tomb slabs in the south and east corridors, support the view that most of the burials in the pavement occurred from the second quarter, and in large part from the second half, of the fourteenth century.[83]

The social identity of persons buried in the pavement also reveals that most were not from the nobility or even the upper bourgeoisie.[84] Rather, tombs of clerics associated with the cathedral, with the archbishop, or with the Opera del Duomo were especially prevalent and appear to have been individual burial sites rather than extended family tombs. The tombs of the east corridor include some of the oldest, including that of the *operaio* Giovanni Rosso, who founded the altar of the Ognissanti on the southeast wall. His tomb slab, marked with the arms of the Opera, was formerly inscribed with his name and dated 1333, the year of his death.[85] His successor, Giovanni Scorcialupi, likewise founded an altar and was buried nearby.[86] Collective tombs for the cathedral clergy, the chaplains, archbishops, and canons were located here as well, arranged, with that of Giovanni Rosso, in a cross-shaped pattern.[87] A common tomb for the *operai* may have been located here at one time.[88] The singularity of the eastern location, and its elevation above the pavement level of the south and north corridors, conferred a privileged status on this area. It is often referred to in documents as a "*coro*" or "*presbiterio*," in accordance with the designation of the structure as a church. The arrangement of the tombs, with the cruciform group at the center and its orientation to the exterior walls, also suggests that these tomb slabs predate the homogeneous design of the pavement that distinguishes the northern extension of the east corridor and the other corridors as well.

Tombs probably from the first half of the Trecento are also found along the south corridor proceeding from east to west. The earliest is not a slab but the tomb of Frate Giovanni "Soldato" or "della Pace," a penitent who died around 1331 and was a founder or adopted patron of a flagellant confraternity, with ties to the Dominican monastery of Santa Caterina and the archbishops Giovanni di Poli (r. 1299–1312) and Simone Saltarelli (r. 1323–42) (Figure 2.9).[89] His tomb, a

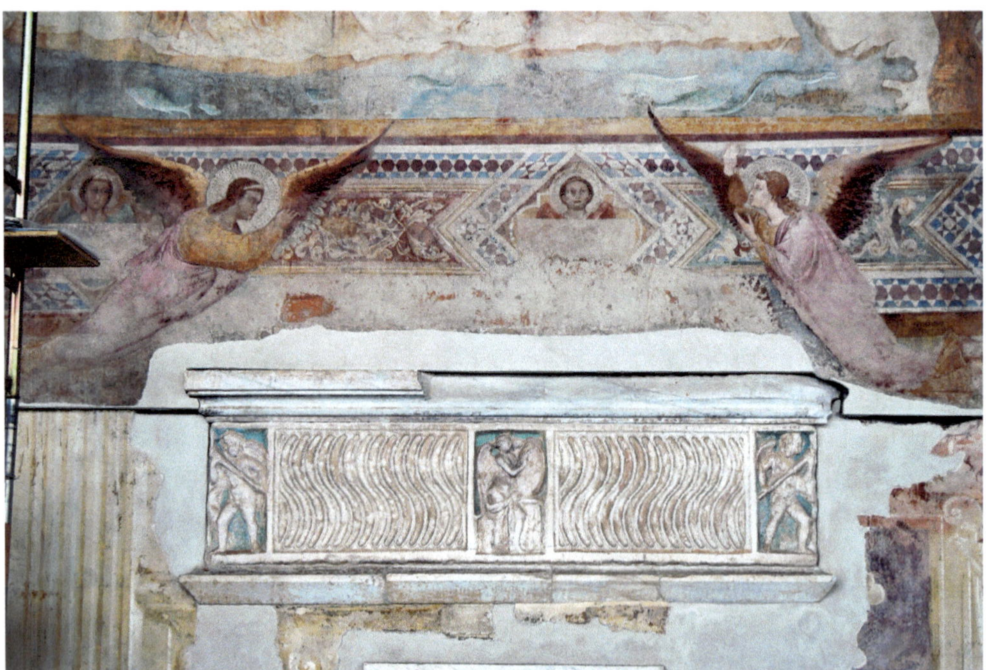

2.9. Sarcophagus of Frate Giovanni "Soldato," first half of the fourteenth century, southeast wall, Camposanto, Pisa. Photo: Author.

strigulated sarcophagus from the second half of the third century, was immured in the external wall, just to the right of the eastern entrance, so that it would have been one of the first monuments a visitor encountered.[90] It was marked by an arched canopy constructed in wood, and the collective tomb for his sodality was at its foot.[91] Giovanni's tomb is only one of several for lay penitents.[92] Their tombs in the pavement were marked by reliefs of kneeling penitents shown in the act of self-flagellation; flagellants, later altered to angels, also hovered over the sarcophagus of Fra Giovanni (Figure 2.10).[93] Documents from this time describe processions of *battuti* (self-flagellants) entering the portal and proceeding toward the altars in the east and attest to the popularity of the Camposanto as a burial location for such groups.[94]

Individual and family tombs in the southeast corridor were also established in the first half of the Trecento.[95] By the mid-fourteenth century, then, the Camposanto would have begun to fulfill the function that Archbishop Visconti had envisioned so many decades earlier: of a monumental, decorous burial ground for all Pisans, from the poor to the nobility to the cathedral clergy.

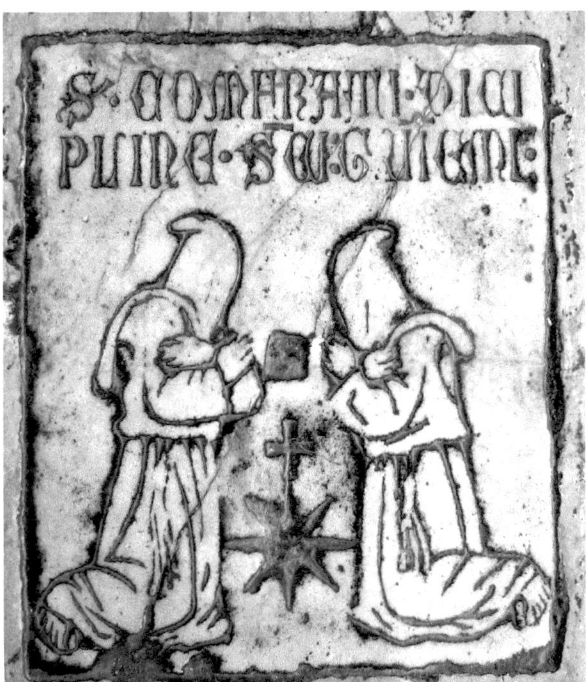

2.10. Tomb slab (detail), Camposanto, Pisa. Photo: Author.

THE FIRST MURALS IN THE CAMPOSANTO

The murals of the *Crucifixion* and theophanies of Christ on the east wall and the *Triumph of Death, Last Judgment, Hell,* and *Lives of Hermit Saints* on the southeast walls of the Camposanto also date to the first half of the fourteenth century, contemporary with the initial construction and first burials. The murals on the east wall celebrate Jesus's triumph over death and manifestations of His divinity and therefore seem entirely appropriate for the burial function of the Camposanto – modeling for the dead and living enduring faith and aspirations for eternal life in Paradise. Those on the southeast wall, by contrast, have been understood as didactic and exhortatory. The murals' imagery has been linked to the teachings of Dominican friars at nearby Santa Caterina, the monastery of the Order of Preachers. Both in form and meaning, scholars have argued, the murals reflected the monastic and eremitic ideals that underlay the writings of Fra Domenico Cavalca (1270 –1342), such that the images comprise a visual sermon.[96] These ideals were made explicit to the literate through the inclusion of numerous inscriptions in Latin and the vernacular, now almost entirely effaced but partially preserved in manuscript.[97] The vanity of earthly pursuits, the ubiquity of death, and the terrors of eternal damnation are depicted with searing urgency and detail in the *Triumph of Death, Last Judgment* and *Hell.* In contrast, in the *Lives of the Hermit Saints*, the pious hermit saints of the Thebaid, the desert realm of Upper Egypt near the ancient city of Thebes, inhabit a mountainous terrain removed from the world, confronting demons and temptresses in their pursuit of a life of simplicity and prayer (Figures 2.11–2.13). The imagery of the mural relates directly to Cavalca's vernacular edition of the *Vitae Patrum, Le Vite de' Santi Padri*, and it reflects the movement of penitential piety then sweeping the Italian peninsula.[98] St. Onuphrius, in his conversation with Paphnutius, described the lives of the desert fathers: "I am removed from every thing, only hope in God remains. In them is true chastity and humility, and in them there is no other thought or battle, but how they can fast and make sacrifice to God."[99] The hermits' reward of eternal life in Paradise was in stark opposition to the fate of the damned, depicted in the adjacent mural.

Recurring motifs in the lives of the desert saints visualize ideals of piety and asceticism.[100] Most obviously, all of the saints have rejected civilization, specifically, the life of the city, symbolized by the city gate and walls, with a glimpse of its secular monuments within, just visible in the lower left of the *Lives of the Hermit Saints.*[101] Paphnutius, whose conversation with Saint Onuphrius is seen in the middle right of the mural, sought a "deeper solitude," leading him to journey further into the legendary region.[102] Rejection of society often entails a quest, often in search of a holy man, as in Saint Anthony's search for Paul the Hermit, seen in the upper left corner of the mural.[103] Abbot Zosimus, who gave communion to Saint Mary of Egypt at

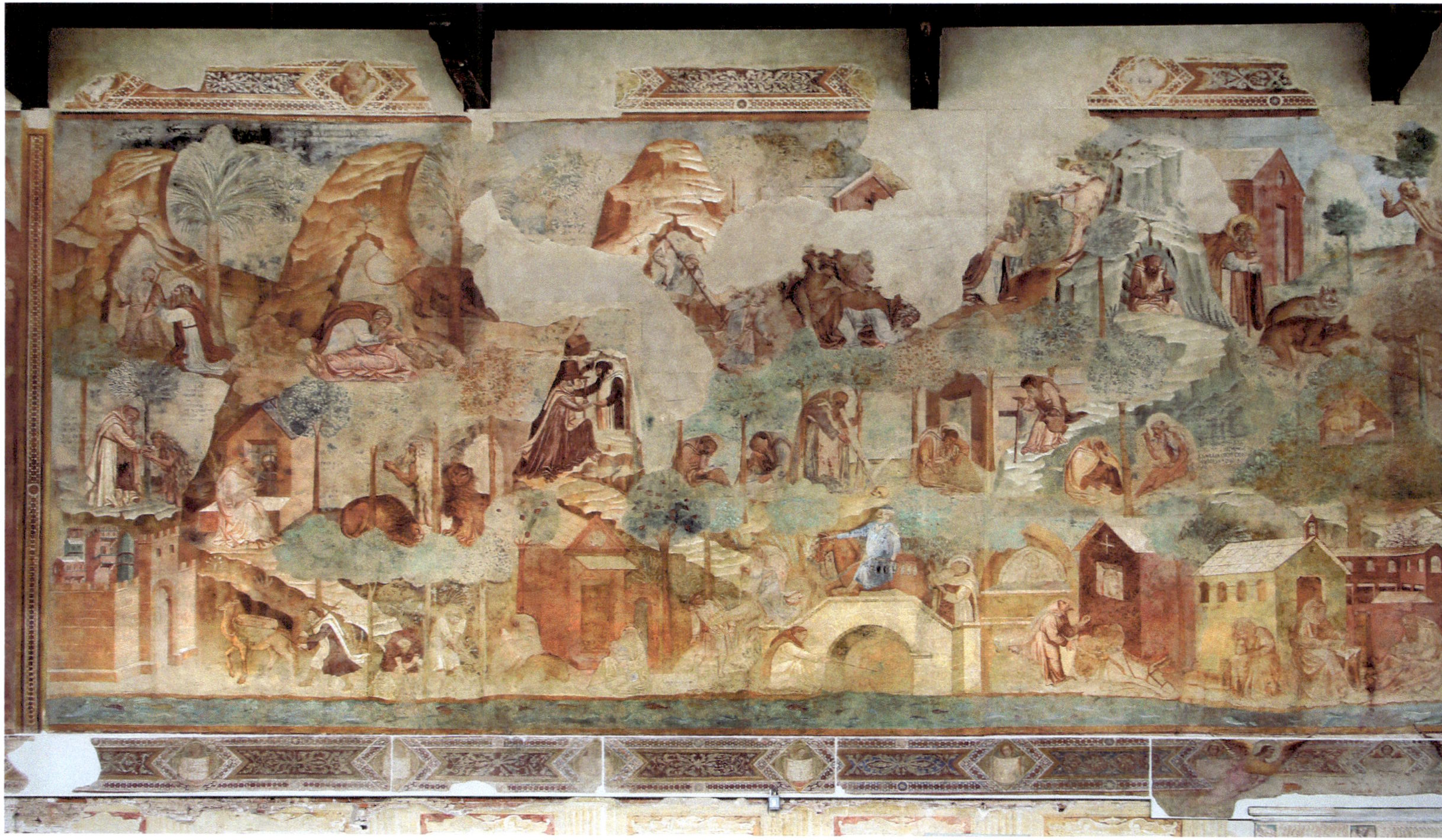

2.11. Attributed to Buonamico Buffalmacco, *Lives of the Hermit Saints* (*Vite de' Santi Padri*), 1330s, southeast wall, Camposanto, Pisa. Photo: Author.

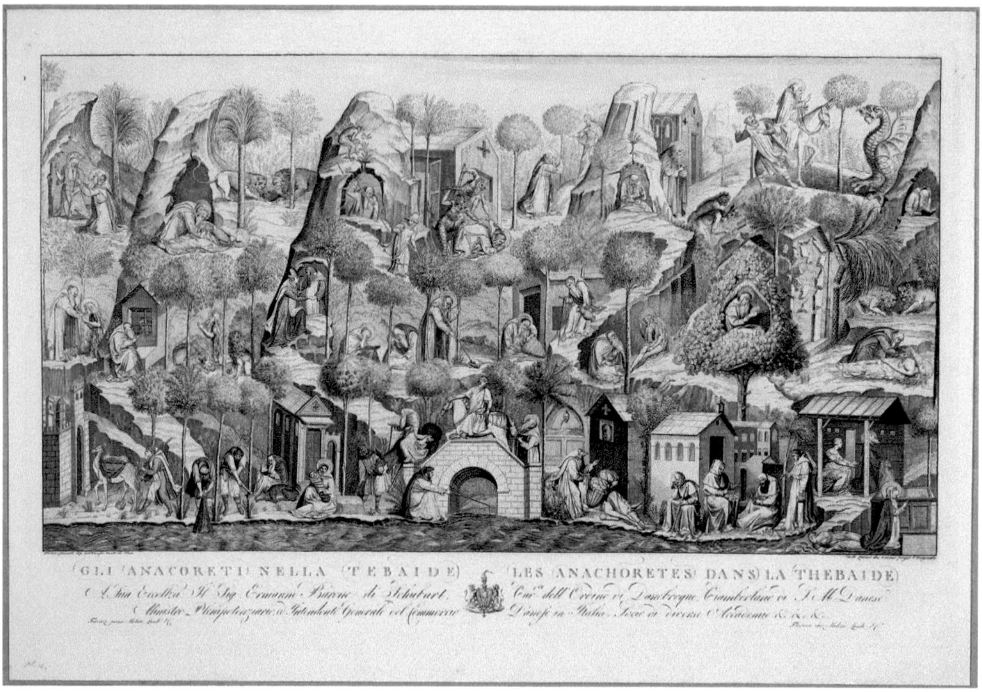

2.12. Carlo Lasinio, engraving (1812), after Buffalmacco, *Lives of the Hermit Saints* (*Vite de' Santi Padri*), 1330s, Harvard Art Museums/Fogg Museum, gift of William Gray from the collection of Francis Calley Gray, G2151. Photo: © President and Fellows of Harvard College.

the left on the middle level, desired to find someone holier than he, for which he ventured into the wilderness.[104] In the desert, they inhabited caves, "natural" abodes, in stark contrast to the highly articulated forms of urban architecture. Hovels hewn from rocks punctuate the landscape. There they abjured the company of other humans: Saint Hilarion, seen confronting a dragon in the upper right corner, fled from place to place in search of solitude.[105] Other saints rejected cultural norms. Saint Macarius the Roman fled from his bride on his wedding night.[106] They often dressed in unconventional vestments; Ornuphrius and Paul the Hermit clothed themselves in tunics of plaited palm fronds; Anthony, too, adopted the habit after Paul's death.[107] Their appearance was uncivilized. Saint Mary of Egypt's skin was dark and shriveled from the sun, and her long, unkempt white hair covered her naked body.[108] Macarius's hair and beard were white like milk, covering his chest, and his brows hid his eyes; his finger- and toenails were overgrown.[109]

The hermits' rejection of culture resulted in embrace of nature – not physical nature but a spiritual realm – the "peaceable kingdom" lost by Adam at the Fall.[110] Aspects of the Thebaid setting, such as the cave where Anthony discovered Saint Paul, recalled physical characteristics of the lost Paradise. Calvalca's *Vita* described a large palm whose fronds extended to the sky growing through an opening in the cave. In the upper left corner of the

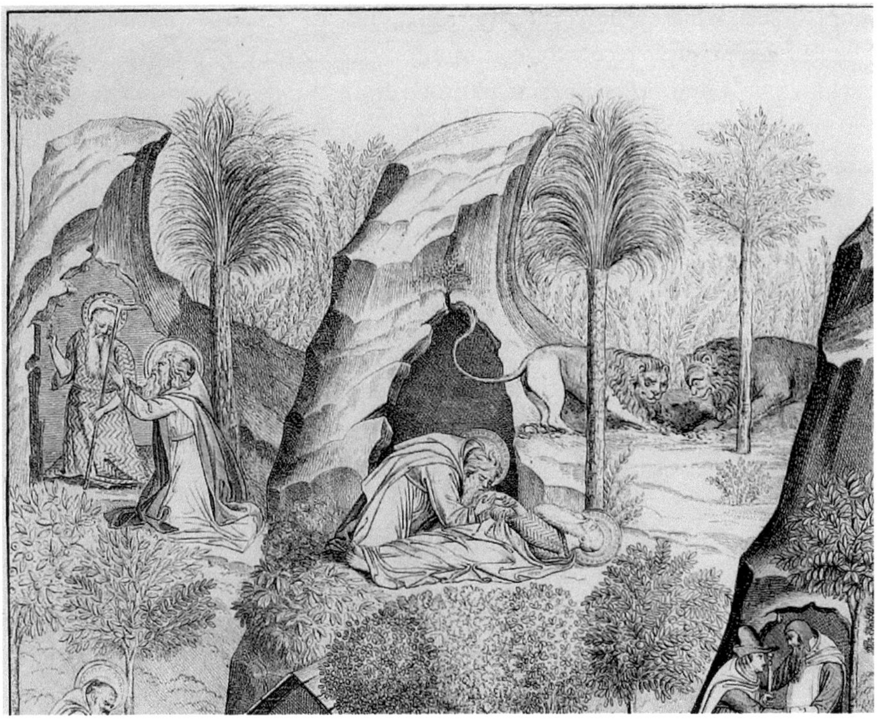

2.13. Carlo Lasinio, engraving (1812), after Buffalmacco, *Lives of the Hermit Saints* (*Vite de' Santi Padri*), detail, 1330s, Harvard Art Museums/Fogg Museum, gift of William Gray from the collection of Francis Calley Gray, G2151. Photo: © President and Fellows of Harvard College.

mural, two large palm trees flank Saint Paul's cave.[111] The river running all along the lower border of the mural alludes to the springs and fountains of clear water associated with Paradise.

The hermits' relationship with animals, especially with lions, recreated the Edenic harmony of man and beast.[112] At the far right of the mural, lions dig the grave in which Saint Paphnutius buried Onuphrius.[113] Lions appeared miraculously before Anthony, digging the grave in which he buried Saint Paul's body, as seen in the upper left corner, while the lions that Saint Macarius nurtured after discovering their dead mother are seen snuggling the praying saint in the center left of the mural.[114] A wolf guides Saint Anthony to Saint Paul's cave.[115] A vanished inscription told how Paul was nurtured by a crow that brought him bread for forty years.[116]

Several scenes hint at the attainment of Paradise through eremitical life. Anthony exclaims to his disciples, "I have seen Elijah, I have seen John the Baptist, and truly I have seen Paul in Paradise."[117] Upon his return to Paul's cave, he witnessed the saint's soul ascending to heaven. He was later privileged to see God. Paphnutius described his vision of God receiving the soul of Saint Onofrius in Paradise.[118] Macarius lived close to Paradise; the inscription next to him explained, "This is Saint Macharius the Roman, who did great penance in the desert, which is near to Paradise at a distance of twenty miles."[119] Saint Mary of Egypt, after receiving communion from Zosimus, was assumed into Paradise.[120] When other hermits returned from the desert and reentered the urban society they had left, they brought tangible benefits: Saint Anthony returned with Pauls's tunic;[121] Paphnutius returned with a tale to tell, written down in a book; perhaps that is the significance of the hermit reading in the tree to the left of the saint's burial.[122] In this sense, the hermits' travels are like a pilgrimage; indeed, Mary of Egypt's conversion to an eremitic life occurred while on pilgrimage to Jerusalem.[123]

Participants of funerals or memorial services in the Camposanto might have viewed the deaths and burials of saints depicted in the Thebaid with special immediacy. In the *Lives of the Hermit Saints*, a modest burial in the earth is depicted in two scenes. In the upper left, Saint Paul, the first of the hermit saints, having received Saint Anthony at his desert abode where he has lived for sixty years, is laid out for burial while two lions dig his grave.[124] Similarly, at the right in the middle register, Saint Onuphrius, having recounted to Paphnutius his life of solitude as an anchorite, is buried by his companion in a ditch dug by two lions.[125] Cavalca's *vita* upholds the humility of Paul's burial as exemplary: "Paul was buried basely in the earth, and will arise in glory; you with your marble tombs and resplendent funerals, will arise in grief."[126] Owing to the burial practices associated with the Camposanto's "sacred field," and to the exemplary lives of the penitents buried in the south corridor, these scenes of humble burial would resonate with viewers. As they entered the cemetery, they confronted the sacred field; as they turned to the right, they trod on the slabs of penitents; as they viewed the mural, ancient history and current practice became one.

In addition to the specific scenes of death and burial, all the eremitic saints experienced a symbolic death, in the form of self-imposed isolation, and, implicitly, they achieved spiritual rebirth. Hence, we see Saint Paul's cave at the upper left, from which he only reluctantly emerged to greet Saint Anthony, or just below, a devil disguised as a pilgrim tempting a hermit from his barred cell. To the right, Saint Macarius is seen in his cave, where a demon disguised as a female traveler (Macarius's jilted bride) tries to seduce him and is ultimately unsuccessful. After he drives her from his cave, seen above, the *vita* tells us that he atoned for his sins by spending the next three years buried up to his neck – an even more onerous, death-like existence than confinement to his cave.[127] In the lower level, we also see a disguised demon mounted on a horse who tries to tempt a hermit from his cell. Temptations such as these or, more directly, the demons that torment Saint Anthony at the center top of the Camposanto mural threaten physical and spiritual death. Saint Hilarion, a disciple of Anthony, confronts a snarling dragon in the upper right corner and defeats it with the sign of the Cross, as was recounted in the inscription.[128]

The rhymed inscription formerly appended to the vignette of Paphnutius and Onuphrius in colloquy in the center of the mural alluded to the physical and spiritual trials they suffered and exhorted the viewer to "Then follow their holy life / To make of the field a better game."[129] Such an exhortation conceivably resonated with the devout, particularly with those venerating the tomb of Fra Giovanni "Soldato" immured in the wall at the lower right of the mural. The *disciplinati* of San Giovanni, who met in Santa Caterina, where Cavalca resided, enjoyed special relations with the Dominicans, under the leadership of the Dominican archbishops Giovanni di Poli and Simone Saltarelli, who shared their ideals of a penitential life.[130] The prominence of Fra Giovanni's tomb and the ideals expressed in the *Lives of the Hermit Saints* are paired expressions of the spiritual life of Pisa in the early fourteenth century, centered on the convent of Santa Caterina.

At the same time, the role of the established church and its sacraments is alluded to only occasionally in the mural, in the communion of Saint Mary of Egypt, the "confession" of Onuphrius to Paphnutius, and the conversation of Saint Macarius with the skull of a pagan, whose soul is in hell.[131] The composition of the mural, with its multiple vignettes embedded in the vast expanse defined by the painted frame, might also be keyed to this audience of penitents and worshippers as they entered the east door and progressed along the corridor toward the great *Crucifixion* mural and its altar. The mural was impossible to view in one glance, owing to its physical location, and could only be regarded piecemeal, from one incident to the other, as the spectator moved through the space.[132] This structure, too, has been likened to that of Cavalca's sermons, where exempla mediate between theological precepts and the daily experiences.[133]

The themes of the *Lives of the Hermit Saints* mural also illuminate aspects of the Camposanto itself. In particular, the overarching theme of humility in the *Vita de' Santi Padri* is echoed in the pavement, with its row upon row of tomb slabs (Figure 2.14). This pavement, the design of which was established probably by the 1340s, comprises white marble tomb slabs of equal dimensions (230 x 87 cm) framed with narrow sheets of black limestone (18 cm). In the upper half of the slab, a trap door (*chiusino*) is closed with a smaller slab on which the obituary in several lines, often surmounted by a coat of arms, or, in the case of a collective tomb, the insignia of the confraternity, is incised. While variations in inscriptions and emblems exist, the overwhelming effect of this arrangement is of vastness and uniformity. The scene reminds the visitor that all are equal before death, as the central inscription on the scroll held up by putti in the *Triumph of Death* mural warned.[134] Durandus's allegorical interpretation of a church pavement suggests that this leveling effect was understood at the time: "The pavement is humility, about which the Psalmists says: 'My soul clings to the pavement.'" He elaborates further: "The pavement of

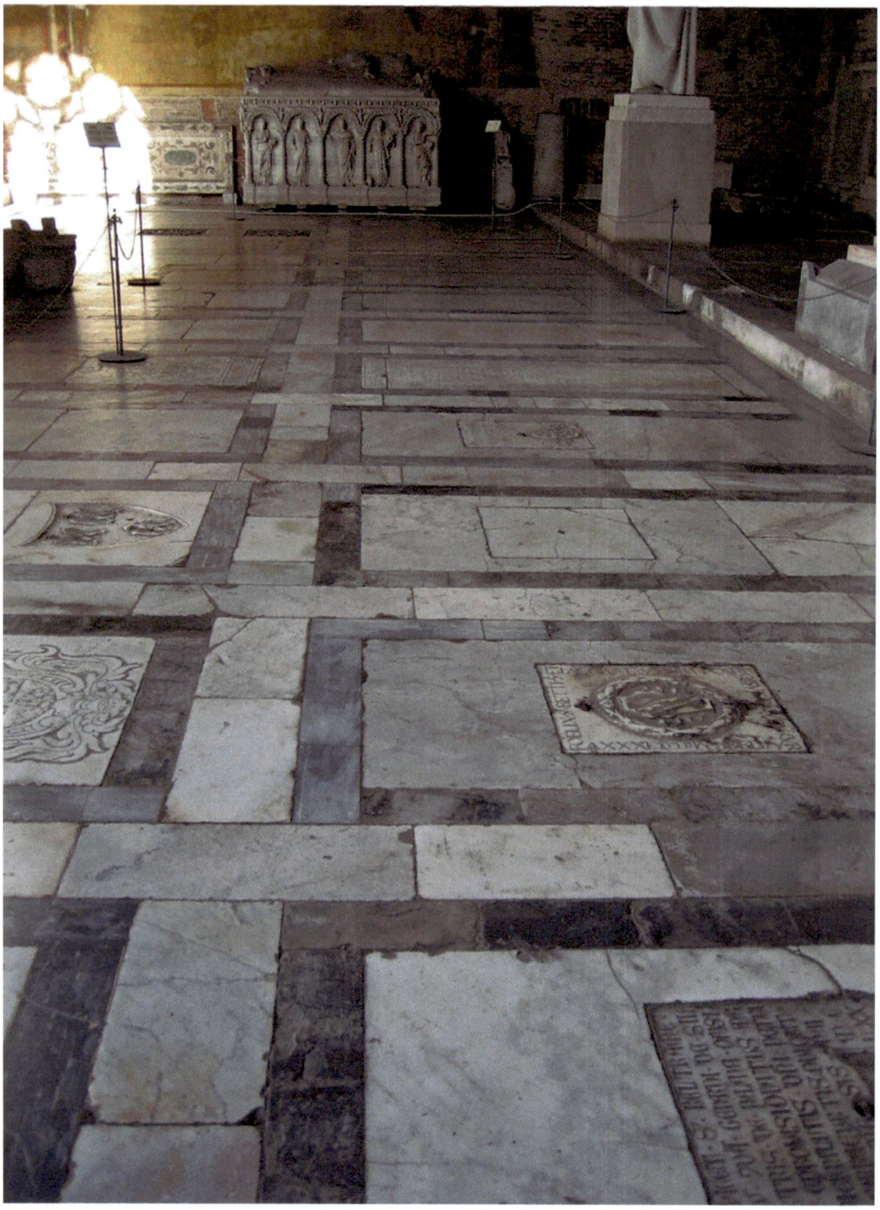

2.14. Pavement, Camposanto, Pisa. Photo: Author.

the church is the foundation of our faith; that is, in the spiritual Church, the foundation is Christ's poor ones, namely those who are poor in spirit, who humble themselves in all things, which is why their humility is likened to pavement."[135]

The collective identity of the hermit saints as depicted in the *Lives of the Hermit Saints*, where individual activity is subsumed in a vast terrain, also approximates the mendicant ideal, especially as exemplified by Saint

Dominic, whose persona was fused with the identity of his order.[136] The mendicants' goal, to suppress individual and family identity and to instead celebrate pious deeds and humility, was voiced in their chronicles and necrologies.[137] The choice of tomb slabs in the pavement by persons from the aristocracy, eschewing the more grandiose family tombs in parish and mendicant churches that perpetuated family memory, can then be understood as an act of humility.

The universal aspiration of the Santi Padri to Paradise resonated with the great cloistered space of the Camposanto itself. Durandus again reminds us "Just as the Church building symbolizes the Church Triumphant, so is the cloister a symbol of the heavenly paradise, a paradise where all will live together with one heart, rooted in the love and will of God."[138] This identification of the cloistered cemetery with Paradise was reinforced on every occasion of a burial, in particular during the chanting of the antiphon "In paradisum deducant te angeli." The words, "May the angels lead you into paradise; may the martyrs receive you at your coming, and take you into the holy city Jerusalem," were sung as funerary processions approached the cemetery. And the hermit saints' exemplary penitence was also echoed by the words of the penitential Psalm 50, *Miserere mei* sung as verses to the antiphon beginning Lauds: "Be gracious to me, O God, in thy true love, in the fullness of thy mercy blot out my misdeeds . . .. I will teach transgressors the ways that lead to thee, and sinners shall return to thee again." This promise fulfills the exhortation of the inscription attached to saints Onuphrius and Paphnutius to "Follow their saintly life."

The series of murals in the extreme western part of the southern corridor of the Camposanto depicting the story of Job also relate to the funerary function of the Camposanto and themes of humility seen in the *Lives of the Hermit Saints*. The Old Testament story of Job is the model of the penitent, who suffers trials, yet retains his faith in God.[139] The penitential theme of the Job murals is compatible with that of the hermit saints; but the story of Job also plays a major role in the liturgy of Christian burial. Verses from Job comprise the nine readings for Matins in the Office of the Dead, following the use of Rome.[140] It is likely that the faithful would have known most intimately these verses from Job, rather than the narrative in the Book of Job.[141]

The Job murals, traditionally attributed to Taddeo Gaddi and dated to the early 1340s, are today in a ruinous state of preservation, yet a general idea of the cycle arises from nineteenth-century engravings after the murals and written descriptions, as well as murals by Bartolo di Fredi in San Gimignano, which closely follow Pisan models.[142] The first mural includes scenes of Job's prosperous life: a banquet in his palace takes center stage, while on one side we see Job distributing alms and the other a view of Job's herds of cattle. In the second scene, the devil's pact with God is seen first, followed by the destruction of Job's herds and army and the rain of fire. The third scene, now largely disappeared, shows the theft of Job's camels and the collapse of his house, killing all his children except one, who brought the terrible news to Job. At the right, Job thanks God: "Naked I came from the womb, naked I shall return whence I came. The Lord gives and the Lord takes away; blessed be the name of the Lord" (Job 1:21–22). The fourth scene, on the next level down at the left, is destroyed; no descriptions or engravings after it exist. Conceivably, the second encounter of God with the devil and the further torments visited on Job were depicted in this scene. In the center of the lower level is the scene of Job depicted naked, his body covered by sores, seated on ashes. He seems to make a gesture of humility or distress, his forearm across his torso, his hand pointing to his chest.[143] He is visited by three friends, and their colloquy contains an extended lament by Job, from which the passages in the Office of the Dead are taken. Finally, God speaks directly to Job, who answers, "I knew of thee then only by report, but now I see thee with my own eyes. Therefore I melt away; I repent in dust and ashes" (Job 42:5–6). To the right, God enjoins the friends to make an offering to atone for having spoken badly, and he promises that he will heed Job's intercession for them. In the last scene, destroyed, God restores to Job his family and possessions.[144] Hence, the narrative emphasizes the triumph of Job's sorely tested faith over bitterness and doubt. Literate viewers would have been able to read vernacular inscriptions that accompanied the scenes that have entirely vanished today.

While the Job story ultimately reaffirms the suffering faithful on earth, the verses in the Office of the Dead include Job's rebellious torrent of complaint.[145] Only gradually is this searing tone modified; the last reading, from Job 19:20–27, was understood in the Middle Ages to prophesize the resurrection of Christ:

> My bones stick out through my skin, and I gnaw my under-lip with my teeth. Pity me, pity me, you that are my friends; for the hand of God has touched me. Why do you pursue me as God pursues me? Have you not had your teeth in me long enough? O that my words might be inscribed, O that they might be engraved in an inscription to be a witness in hard rock! But in my heart I know that my vindicator lives, and that he will rise last to speak in court; and I shall discern my witness standing at my side, and see my defending counsel, even god himself, whom I shall see with my own eyes, I myself and no other.

In the office, the plaint of Job is shared by the defunct. As viewers recalled these verses and remembered their participation in funerary offices – and perhaps imagined their own deaths – they identified closely with the biblical figure of Job, who gave voice to their own suffering, fears, and hope for salvation.[146] The psalms recited as part of the office also emphasized penance and faith in God's justice.[147] The words of the penitential Psalm 129, recited twice, at Vespers and Lauds, perhaps best captures the tenor of emotion attached to the Office of the Dead:

> Out of the depths have I called to thee, O Lord; Lord, hear my cry. Let thy ears be attentive to my plea for mercy . . .. But in thee is forgiveness, and therefore thou art revered. I wait for the Lord with all my soul, I hope for the fulfillment of His word. My soul waits for the Lord more eagerly than watchmen for the morning. Like men who watch for the morning, O Israel, look for the Lord. For in the Lord is love unfailing, and great is his power to set men free.

Reflecting faith in God's mercy as expressed by the Psalms, the lament of Job is colored by a more hopeful tone. Details from the Job story, such as the naked Job perched on a bed of ashes, recalled aspects of the funerary rite, in particular, the washing and preparation of the corpse. Perhaps viewers of the Job murals understood their meaning in the context of their own experiences, as spectators of the *Lives of the Hermit Saints* might recall sermons they had heard from charismatic fourteenth-century preachers, such as Giordano da Pisa or Giovanni Dominici.

THE CAMPOSANTO AFTER THE BLACK DEATH

The Black Death in Pisa in the summer of 1348 had calamitous effects, including dramatic population decline, as elsewhere in Europe. The grim mortality also resulted in a crisis of burial space; Giovanni Boccaccio describes in the *Decameron* (1349–52) how

> Such was the multitude of corpses brought to the churches every day and almost every hour that there was not enough consecrated ground to give them burial, especially since they wanted to bury each person in the family grave, according to the old custom. Although the cemeteries were full they were forced to dig huge trenches, where they buried the bodies by hundreds. Here they stowed them away like bales in the hold of a ship and covered them with a little earth, until the whole trench was full.[148]

The event seems also to have prompted a rethinking of official burial policy in Pisa and with it the civic function of the Camposanto.

When the Camposanto was created in the late thirteenth century, burial in and around the cathedral had been restricted. Yet the prestige of burial in or near the cathedral continued.[149] On 27 February 1349, the Opera del Duomo issued an ordinance reaffirming the prohibition of burial in the cathedral owing to the enormous numbers of dead. This ordinance called for the removal of unauthorized altars there and restricted the tombs in the

Camposanto to the tomb slabs in the pavement. The *Ordinamenta Opere Sancte Marie Maioris ecclesie* declared that

> so that the laudable use of the cemetery or burial ground of the Camposanto as a place of devotion shall not be abused or neglected, it is provided that no one, either man or woman, of whatever rank or condition, may or will be buried in the above mentioned major church of Pisa, in any kind of tomb that is made below the *parvis* [that is, the space in front of the façade], or upon its pavement, or on the walls or sides of this church; and that the *operaio* of the abovementioned church who is now in charge or will be in charge in the future may not (or may not allow) concede or permit to anyone directly or indirectly to bury or to place any cadaver in the abovementioned church, or on the marble pavement or the walls or sides of the Camposanto.[150]

The "neglect" alluded to in the declaration may also be taken to mean that not only was the fabric of the monument in disrepair but also the practice of citizens' seeking burial in the Camposanto had declined. As an indication perhaps of the varied – and unsanctioned – uses to which the Camposanto had been put in the years preceding the plague, the ordinance continues. It states that "no one, man or woman, either humble or powerful, is allowed to play at throwing stones on the tombs or the slabs of the marble pavement of the Camposanto, throwing them on the above-mentioned pavement."[151]

Contemporary with this forcefully articulated burial policy and renewed attention to the monumental cemetery as a civic monument, there is evidence of a concerted effort to complete the construction of the Camposanto. Although precise details of the progress of the work are lacking, the documents of the Opera del Duomo reveal intense activity. From the end of March 1349, a team of stonemasons worked on the walls of the Camposanto; there are payments for bricks, for wood and lead plates to construct a part of the roof, for rubble fill for the walls, and the strips of limestone framing the tomb slabs of the pavement.[152] Caleca supposes this refers to the northern extension of the eastern corridor, where the first burial in the systematized pavement to the north dates from 1349.[153]

Ten years later, there is evidence of progress in the extension of the Camposanto walls northward, toward the city walls. The *Anziani* formed a committee of citizens to decide on "the procedure to follow in the construction of the foundation and the walls of the Camposanto, on the side of the walls of the city of Pisa."[154] But already in 1354, the *Anziani* had instructed the *operai*, before proceeding with the north wall, to finish what they had begun. They ordered the *operai* "to complete the tomb slabs in the process of being made ready in the Camposanto, to proceed with the work of the roof, to reinforce an arch that was in need of repair, and to complete the paintings" and, in general, "to do the work that may seem to them useful."[155] The construction of the north wall, undoubtedly preceded by that of the short west wall, must have proceeded apace, for the account books of the Opera del Duomo record intense activity from this time through the 1380s.[156] The work was done in sections, with the external walls, cloister arcade – including the elegant tracery of the "marble windows" – pavement, and completed roof sequentially, probably from the northwest toward the east.[157]

By June of 1359, the north wall must have advanced enough for the executors of the estate of the medical doctor Ligo Ammannati to commission an altar and sculpted marble tomb. This altar, still extant, occupies a small, private chapel constructed off the north wall, directly opposite the western door of the Camposanto and on axis with the westernmost path traversing the central open space (Figures 2.15–2.16). Ammannati, professor at the University of Pisa, a doctor of medicine and philosophy and one of the *Anziani* from 1346 to 1354, died 18 August 1358, having made his will two days earlier. Although the will is untraced, a later document records the execution of the testamentary bequests. Most prominent among them are two thousand *libbre* for a chapel, to be dedicated to Saint Gregory, in which an altar and tomb for himself were to be constructed.[158]

The construction of this funerary chapel is surprising, for it seems to contradict the provision issued by the Opera in 1349 prohibiting anything but tomb slabs in the Camposanto. The chapel was, perhaps, agreed to in negotiations between the Opera and the executors of Ammannati's testament. The will stipulated that the "most beautiful" chapel be located either in the cathedral, or the platform surrounding it, or in the Camposanto, "in a venerable and decorous place."[159] If, as we have seen, there is evidence that the Camposanto had been in need of measures to ensure its decorousness as a place of burial, perhaps the executors felt that only a separate chapel for the tomb of the deceased could fulfill the will's provisions. In addition, the *operai* may have realized that, in order to enforce the ban on tombs in and around the Duomo, space had to be made available in the Camposanto to accommodate the larger, more grandiose tombs that illustrious and wealthy citizens desired.[160] Furthermore, there is ample evidence to suggest that, if citizens could not erect tombs in the communal cemetery, they were welcomed in mendicant churches.[161] The tomb of the Dominican Archbishop Saltarelli (d. 1342), for example, was erected in Santa Caterina in the 1340s.[162] Many of the nobles of Pisa who were buried in the Camposanto were interred in individual, not family tombs; those nobles who had family tombs in the Camposanto, such as the Scorcialupi, also possessed family mausolea in other churches, including Santa Caterina.[163] Those buried in the Camposanto were often civil servants, such as *operai* of the Duomo or Baptistery, or churchmen – cathedral canons (traditionally a stronghold of the nobility), vicars, or archbishops – or professors at the university like Ligo Ammannati.[164] Furthermore, almost all of the tomb

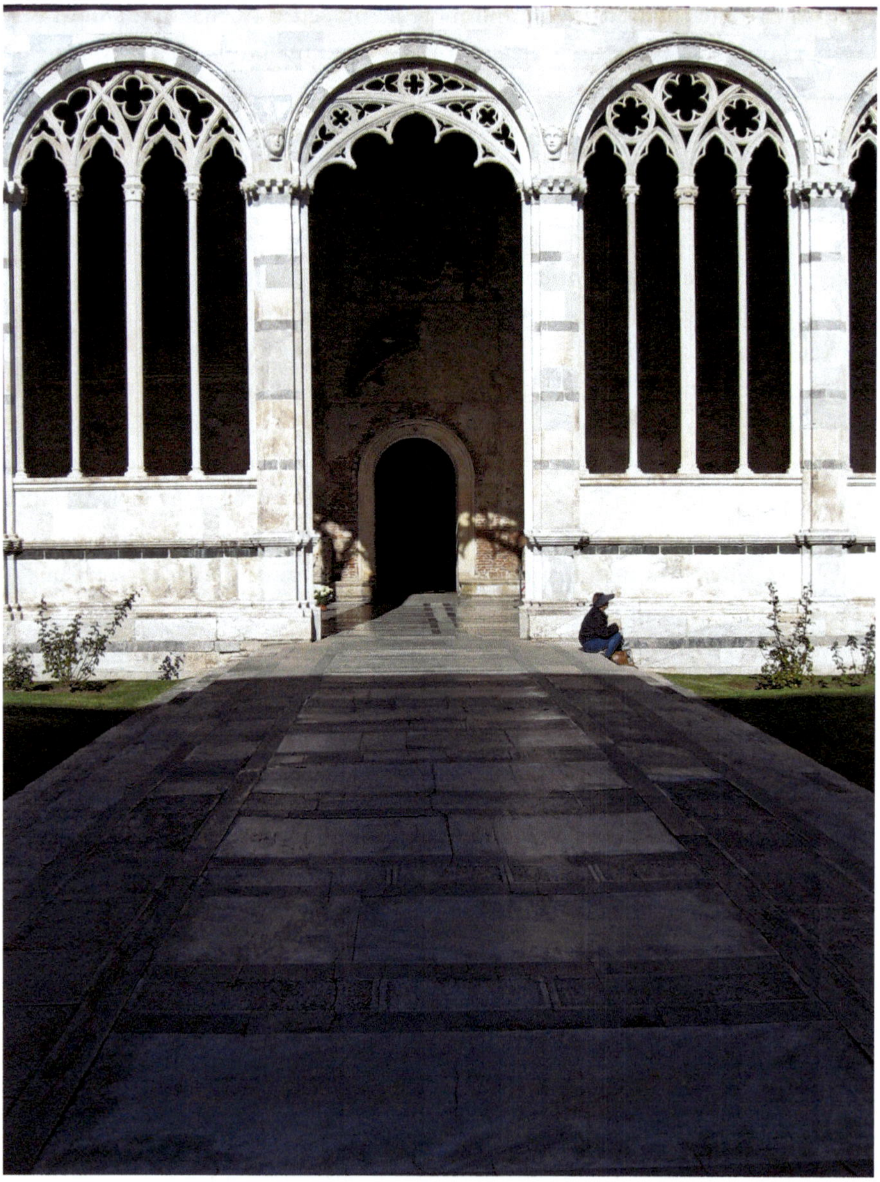

2.15. Western walkway, Camposanto, Pisa. Photo: Author.

slabs with portraits of the defunct, sought primarily by socially ambitious members of the middle class, including mercenaries, educators, and exiles, were also located in mendicant churches. In the Camposanto there is only one, in the northeast corner, of Pietro di Antonio di Santopietro (d. 1429), who was a canon of the cathedral (Figure 2.17).[165] The *operai* may have felt constrained to offer the possibility of private chapels and monumental tombs to staunch the flight of well-to-do testators from the communal cemetery to the churches and graveyards of the mendicants and with it the rich bequests that accompanied

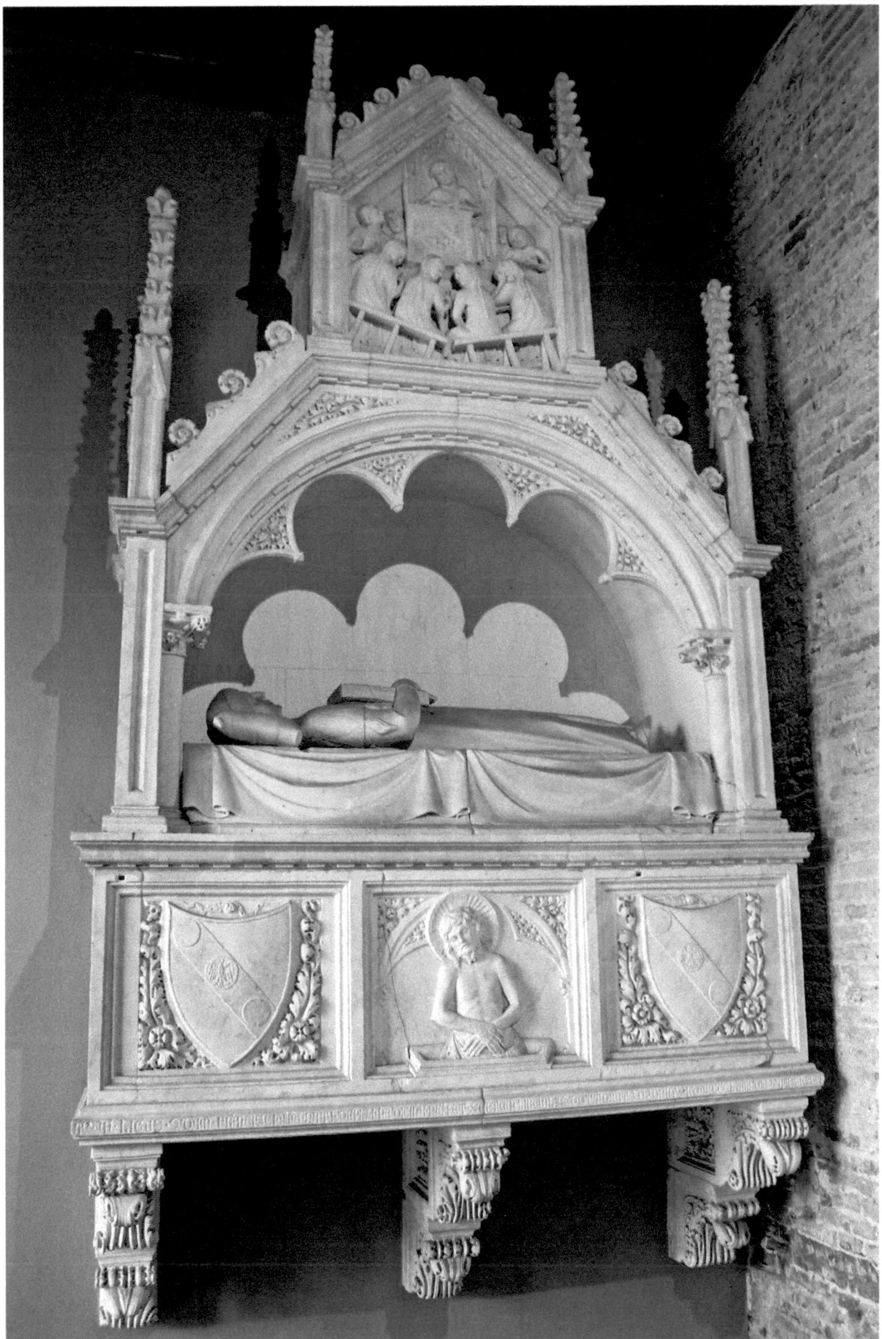

2.16. Tomb of Ligo Ammannati, 1360, Camposanto, Pisa. Photo: Miguel Hermoso Cuesta/ Creative Commons Attribution-Share Alike 4.0 International.

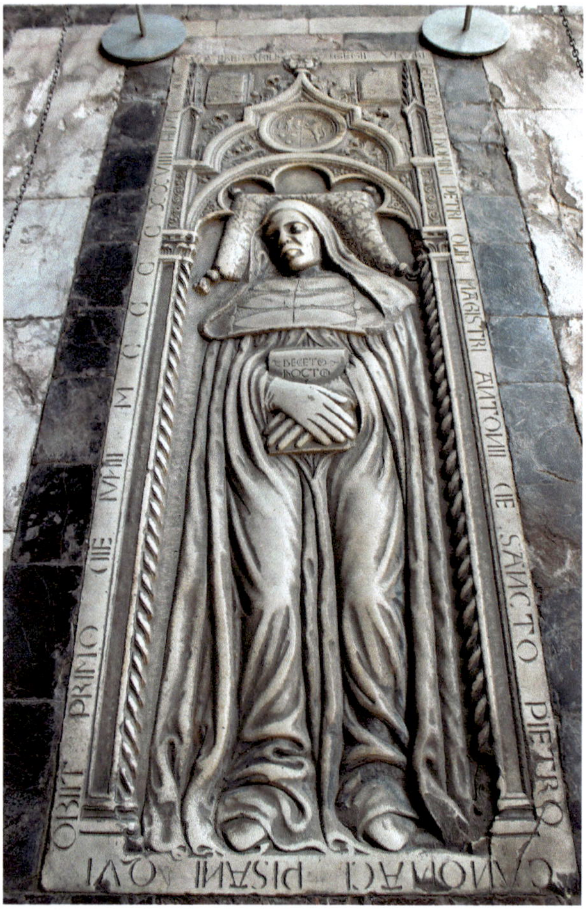

2.17. Tomb of Pietro di Antonio di Santopietro, 1429, Camposanto, Pisa. Photo: Dimitris Kamaras/ Creative Commons Attribution 2.0 CC-By-2.0.

them. Elsewhere evidence suggests that the mendicants welcomed the patriciate's desire for individual and family memory.[166]

The tomb chapel of Ligo Ammannati accommodated the new burial policies in the wake of the Black Death, designed to secure the prestige and holiness of the Duomo complex and the Camposanto, in particular, and the changing funerary habits of the Pisan populace in the late Trecento. That other chapels off the north wall of the Camposanto were planned is suggested by ten arches clearly visible in the north wall before the murals were reinstalled (Figure 2.18). Now filled in, they have the appearance of being part of the original structure, constructed between the 1350s and the 1390s. Only one additional chapel of the merchant Giovanni di Simone da Fauglia was constructed in the fifteenth century.

In January 1359, the *Anziani* issued another ordinance reiterating the prohibition against anyone playing games of stones or dice inside the Duomo or the Camposanto, or outside the Duomo, or throwing stones or

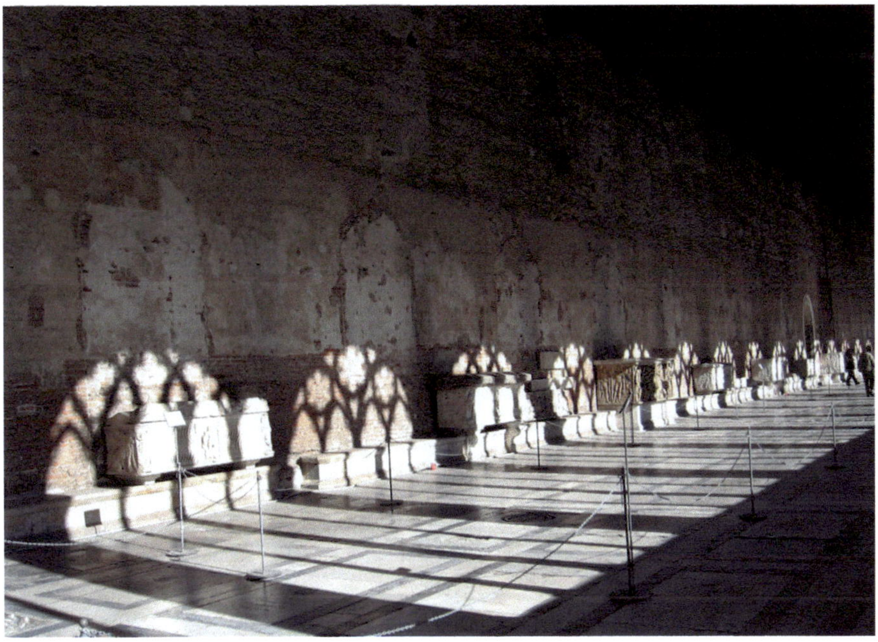

2.18. North Corridor, Camposanto, Pisa. Photo: Author.

sticks at the wax candles hanging inside the Duomo.[167] This ordinance aimed to secure the conservation and reverence due to the cathedral and its environs against anyone who would dare to damage them. In the Camposanto, it was further prohibited to play games on the tomb slabs of the pavement, or on the steps or portals or on the marble benches of the cloisters.[168]

The campaign to re-present the Camposanto as a worthy resting place to the populace seems to have been successful, at least in the short run. A notable acceleration in the purchase of the tombs in the pavement of the Camposanto is evident in the second half of the fourteenth century, mostly concentrated in the south corridor, spreading from east to west.[169] Of the tombs dated or datable to the second half of the fourteenth century in Banti's catalogue, the range of persons buried in the tombs of the pavement is notable.[170] There are artisans and notaries,[171] as well as tradesman such as wine sellers, dyers, and bakers.[172] A striking number of graves are for women, such as the wives of the masters of the Opera del Duomo.[173] Many others came from the suburbs and countryside or from foreign lands, such as Bernardo Ladom, a citizen of Majorca.[174] Especially noteworthy are common graves of confraternities, such as the confraternity of the Holy Cross, or the adjacent tomb of the flagellant company of Santa Margerita, or of the Confraternity of Saint Gregory, among many others.[175]

The extraordinary diversity of social classes buried in the tombs was fostered by the relatively accessible price: in the late fourteenth century, the tombs were sold for three florins apiece. Hence, in the middle of the fourteenth century, to bolster the prestige of the Camposanto, the communal authorities made a conscious effort to appeal to all classes of Pisan society, in keeping with the original conception of the Camposanto as the preeminent burial ground for the city of Pisa. That the city officials were perhaps not entirely successful in this endeavor is indicated by by the persistent desires expressed by Pisan testators for burial in the cathedral.[176] Again, in 1386, the *Anziani* threatened penalties against ball playing in the Camposanto, though the *operaio* did permit the spreading of linen cloth for drying and bleaching.[177] An ordinance of 1540, however, suggests that the erection of monumental tombs in the Camposanto continued. It resolved "To take away all the tombs of the dead that are beneath the roof and chapels of the said Camposanto, because for many years they have been placed there, so that some are ruined . . . and part block the chapels, and in the choir between the altars, with the result that, apart from the ugliness, the administrators cannot reach said altars and chapels."[178] In its reference to ancient tombs immured in the walls or resting on the pavement, impeding access to the altars for celebration of Mass, this provision conjures up an image of a dense, unattractive, and undecorous ambience; precisely what the Trecento officials had sought to avoid.

THE MURALS OF THE SOUTHWEST CORRIDOR: *THE LIFE OF SAINT RAINERIUS*

The earliest evidence we have of the drive to complete the mural decoration of the southwest corridor, as directed by the *Anziani* already in 1354, is in the 1370s. In 1371, Opera ledgers record payments to a group of painters including Francesco di Neri da Volterra for painting and restoring pictures. These payments may relate to the completion of the Job cycle.[179] Only in October of 1377 is there documentation of Andrea Bonaiuti having painted murals of the life of Saint Rainerius on the wall between the east and west portals of the south wall. As we learn from a payment document of 13 October 1377, Pietro Gambacorta, *Signore* of Pisa between 1369 and 1392, had himself drawn up the agreement between Andrea Bonaiuti and the *operaio* of the Duomo to paint the cycle of Saint Rainerius on the south wall of the Camposanto.[180] Gambacorta (c. 1319–92) was from a prominent merchant family, who served multiple times in the *Anziani*, and as ambassador to Emperor Charles IV of Luxembourg in 1354.[181] He assumed the head of one of the political factions of the populace, the Bergolini, but was exiled from Pisa in 1354 in the conflict with the rival faction, the Raspanti. Pietro spent his exile mostly in Florence, reentering Pisa in 1369 and reclaiming his position as head of the faction at a time of political turmoil. He was eventually named Captain of War and Defender of the People, with effective power over the traditional communal bodies, including the *Anziani*.

Gambacorta's direct involvement in the Saint Rainerius cycle is unusual and has been explained in different ways. His choice of a Florentine painter is hardly remarkable, given the participation of Florentines Buffalmacco, Stefano da Firenze, and Taddeo Gaddi (all of these traditional but undocumented attributions) in the Camposanto from the early fourteenth century. As in Prato, artists from Florence had long been active in Pisa. Yet Pisa, unlike Prato, during the fourteenth century had strong ties to Florence but was still politically independent. As an important port city, it was a center of commercial exchange with contacts across the Mediterranean. Non-Florentine painters Antonio Veneziano, Spinello Aretino, and Piero di Puccio would also work in the Camposanto in the fourteenth century. Artisans working in stone, wood, metal, and other materials from Siena, Lucca, Perugia, Como, Sicily, and further afield were active in Pisa, creating a lively milieu that fostered exchange and innovation.[182]

Some scholars have seen Gambacorta's commission of the Saint Rainerius murals as an *ex voto* for his recovery from a serious illness in 1374, underscoring the saint's role as a miracle worker and protector of Pisa's citizens.[183] Others have understood his personal involvement as a product of close relations with the friars of Santa Caterina. The Domenicans' influence, especially Cavalca's *Vite de' Santi Padri*, was, as we have seen, especially strong in the murals in the southeast corridor of the Camposanto.[184] Gambacorta would have been acquainted with the murals Andrea Bonaiuti painted in the chapter house of Santa Maria Novella in Florence during Gambacorta's exile that celebrated the Dominican order, and it is likely that Andrea came well recommended by the friars there. Pietro Gambacorta also contributed to the establishment in 1384 of San Domenico, where his daughter Beata Chiara (1362–1419) founded a reformed Dominican convent.[185]

A broad view of Gambacorta patronage provides context for Pietro's actions.[186] Vasari says Taddeo Gaddi painted the main chapel in the church of San Francesco, where the Gambacorta family tombs were located, in August, 1342, commissioned by Pietro's father Andrea.[187] Perhaps Pietro sought to place himself in a family tradition of patronage by completing the wall murals next to the Job cycle Taddeo had begun in the Camposanto, discussed above. Family members made gifts to Pisan churches, especially the Duomo, and they supported civic institutions such as the Studio.

Very likely far more important in Pietro's role in the Camposanto, however, was his support for the efforts to reclaim the Camposanto as a prestigious site of Pisan civic identity, articulated, as we have seen, as early as 1349. As studies of the history of the church in Pisa have shown, from the middle of the Trecento, with the archbishopric of the Florentine Simone Saltarelli, there emerged a policy of the *chiesa cittadina* much like in Prato, which balanced the roles of clerical and communal authorities.[188] While the Dominicans of Santa Caterina retained the privileged status that they had enjoyed in the early Trecento, they no longer dominated.[189] A broadened civic outlook of the Pisan church continued under the long archbishoprics of Giovanni di Scarlatto (1348–62) and his nephew Francesco Moricotti (1363–78), who were from a non-aristocratic, merchant family.[190] The cathedral canons were increasingly open to new families in the course of the Trecento.[191] With the election of Pietro's nephew Lotto Gambacorta as archbishop, in 1380, and with the assent of the papacy – which in the turmoil of the Western Schism hoped to curry favor with Pisa – the links between Gambacorta and the cathedral were strengthened by bonds of kinship.

Pietro Gambacorta's policies toward various political factions within the city and with foreign states reinforced his efforts to balance sacred and secular interests.[192] The Bergolini faction, of which Pietro was head, comprised marine merchants and ship owners, and Gambacorta pursued a pro Florentine policy. This policy protected the mercantile interests of his supporters, especially by preserving the role of Pisa as the major port of Tuscany – mainly by conferring privileges on its most important clients, Florentine merchants, and favoring their goods with advantageous taxation policies.[193] At the same time, Gambacorta tried to mediate between the competing forces of imperial factions – continuing Pisa's traditional Ghibelline allegiances – and those of papal sympathizers. His role as a mediator, designed to secure the peace that was essential to the economic health of Pisa, was ultimately unsuccessful in the face of the continuing incursions of the Visconti dynasty, rulers of Lombardy, in Tuscany. Matters were made worse by the continuing decline of Pisan trade, onerous taxation, and depopulation in the city and countryside caused by plague and emigration. A treaty with Florence in 1388, which disadvantaged artisans, led to the loss of their support. At the same time, an anti-Florentine faction, encouraged by the Visconti, reemerged to become a powerful political force, led by Jacopo d'Appiano (c. 1322–98), formerly the chancellor of the *Anziani*.[194] In 1392, Gambacorta's regime, built on a carefully constructed web of contacts and alliances, collapsed, he and his sons were brutally executed, and his nephew the archbishop fled Pisa, paving the way for the signoria of Jacopo d'Appiano, the possession of the Visconti, and the bitter capitulation to Florence in 1406.[195]

In this context, the decision to depict the events of Saint Rainerius's life in the Camposanto can be seen as far more than simple nostalgia for a glorious past; it also addressed current realities. The choice of a saint who was from a merchant family reflected Gambacorta's family identity as well as that of his political constituents, including communal authorities and many clerics – not least, the archbishop and some cathedral canons. The depiction of Rainerius as a pilgrim to the Holy Land also emphasizes his lay status and the public nature of his penitence; indeed, the archbishop Moricotti had made a pilgrimage to the Holy Land, returning in 1375.[196] The theme of pilgrimage recalled Pisa's glorious maritime past and participation in the Crusades – often characterized as "armed pilgrimages" – as well as the origins of the Camposanto itself. The prominent depiction of the secular clergy, including its ceremonies, relics, and shrines, celebrates the role of the *chiesa cittadina* in the public life of late medieval Pisa. And the emphatic siting of events in the contemporary city of Pisa appealed with great immediacy to the experiences and collective memory of Pisan citizens who gazed on the monumental scenes in the Camposanto.

Andrea Bonaiuti completed the first three scenes of the Rainerius cycle, for which he was paid in October 1377, before returning to Florence to make his will in December 1377 and dying there shortly afterward.[197] In June of 1379, a Pisan delegation was sent by the *operaio* Piero Sampanti to Genoa to induce the painter Barnaba da Modena to complete the murals, evidently without success.[198] Not until 1384 did the painter Antonio Veneziano, possibly Venetian by origin but active in Siena and Florence, undertake to complete the last three scenes of the Saint Rainerius murals, payments for which last until 1386.[199]

The murals of the history of Saint Rainerius represent a sharp reorientation in the imagery of the Camposanto compared to an earlier time; and they respond to the civic function of the monument as forcefully asserted in the years following the Black Death. Saint Rainerius lived from 1117 to 1160.[200] His family was from the merchant class, and he passed his youth frivolously. After a chance encounter, he converted to a saintlier life. In the murals, comprising twenty-three episodes in six fields, we see the panoply of Rainerius's life, from his conversion to his pilgrimage to the Holy Land, his return to Pisa, and his death, burial, and posthumous miracles.

Today the Saint Rainerius murals are in poor condition, having suffered from deterioration, as have all the works in the Camposanto. All but the earliest mural in the Camposanto, the *Crucifixion*, rested on walls prepared with thick mats of woven cane that had been nailed to brick. The first rough layer of plaster, the *arriccio*, was spread over cane mats, which were intended to insulate the paintings from moisture seeping into the walls, but which instead absorbed it.[201] As a result, adhesion of the *arriccio* and the upper layer of plaster, the pigmented *intonaco*, normally chemically bound together, was compromised. The persistent humidity of the site, in addition to the infiltration of rainwater, caused the conversion of the lime plaster from calcium carbonate into calcium sulphate. In the process of sulferation, crystals of calcium sulphate migrated to the surface of the *intonaco* and caused the colors to lift.[202] By the early eighteenth century, the murals had been subjected to repainting, and several of them were described as ruined.[203]

Further devastation came with the bombing of the Piazza del Duomo on 27 July 1944. The incendiary bombs melted the lead roof of the Camposanto, causing the molten lead to drip down the walls, with disastrous results to the

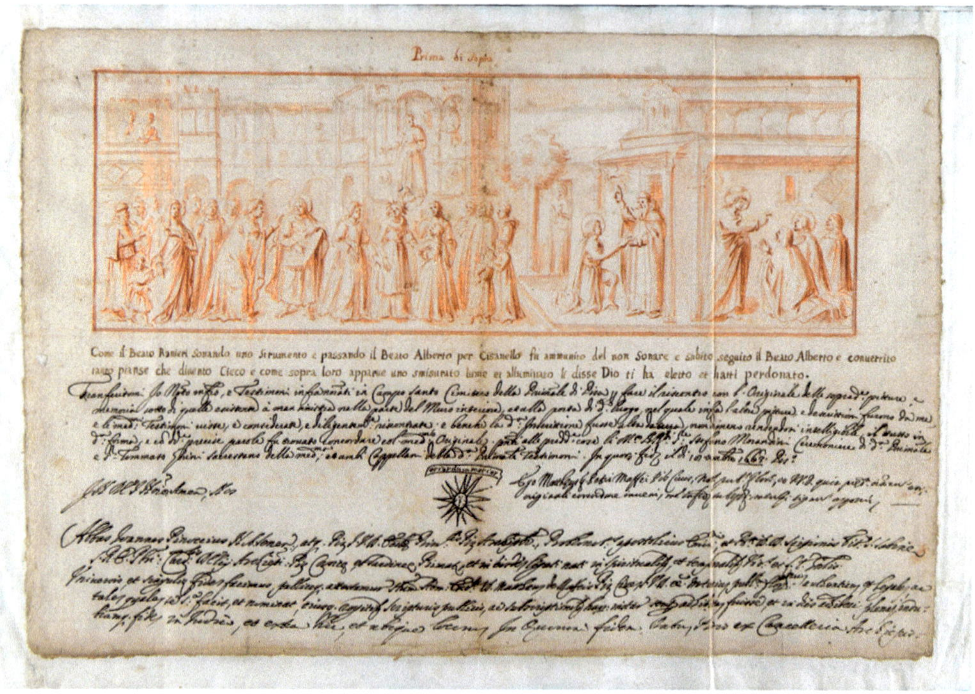

2.19. Anonymous draughtsman after Andrea Bonaiuti, *Conversion of Saint Rainerius* (1376–77), 1662, Manoscritti, C 93/95, Archivio Storico Diocesano, Archivio Capitolare, Pisa. Photo: Archivio Storico Diocesano, Archivio Capitolare.

murals. Beginning in 1947, the murals of the Life of Saint Rainerius that had not already been detached from the walls were remounted on canvas and consolidated. Today, most of the murals have been returned to their original location after further conservation. Although they are now only pale reflections of their original splendor, their sheer scale, particularly when seen in the spaces for which they were designed, hints at their original impact. Earlier reproductions aid our reading of them. While most scholars have relied on engravings by Carlo Lasinio (1759–1838) published in 1812, red chalk drawings made in 1662 provide additional details and the inscriptions that originally accompanied them.

These drawings form part of a volume, now in the Archivio Storico Diocesano, Archivio Capitolare in Pisa, that was to be sent to Rome by officials of the cathedral (Figure 2.19).[204] An anonymous artist drew them in red chalk and red wash on white paper measuring approximately 12 x 39 cm. Their purpose was to have the facts of Saint Rainerius's life and the antiquity of his cult in Pisa confirmed by the Holy See.[205] Whether they wished to support the canonization of the saint is unknown; in any case, Saint Rainerius was never officially canonized. The accuracy of each drawing was corroborated by witnesses and certified by a notary, Matteo di Pietro Maffei, who penned an

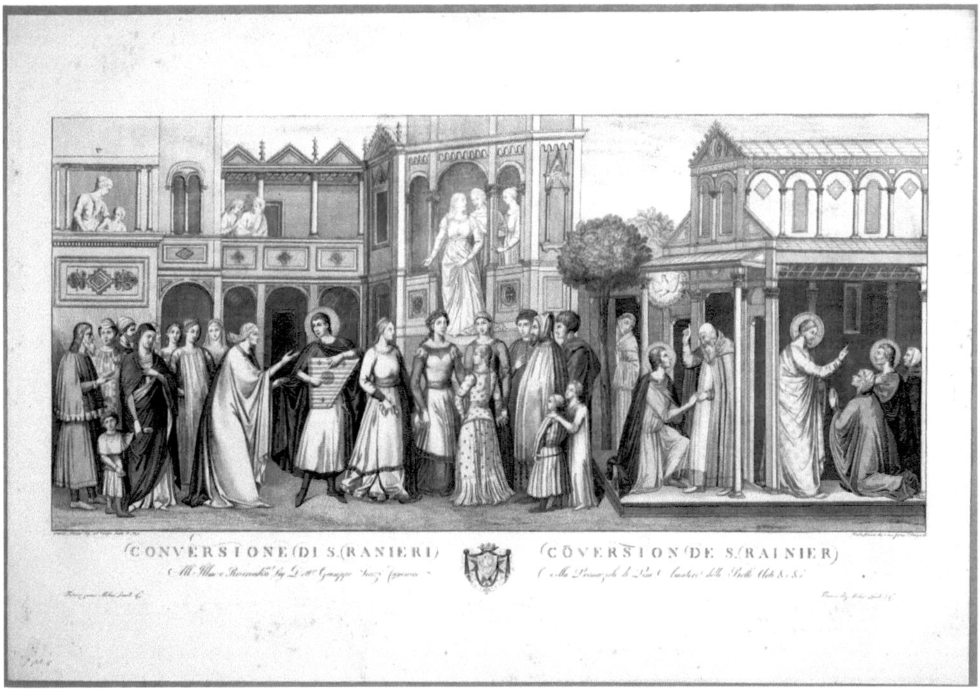

2.20. Carlo Lasinio, engraving (1812), after Andrea Bonaiuti, *Conversion of St. Rainerius* (1376–77), Harvard Art Museums/Fogg Museum, gift of William Gray from the collection of Francis Calley Gray, G2145. Photo: © President and Fellows of Harvard College.

inscription beneath each drawing, complete with his signature, sign, and the date 18 October 1663 (1662 modern style). The volume also included a drawing for a new tomb for the saint in the cathedral.

The restored murals, the nineteenth-century engravings, and the red chalk drawings provide a point of departure for my reading of the St. Ranierius cycle. Similarities with the earlier murals in the Camposanto exist; but the later cycle presents a very different model of sainthood: the saint as an urban layman, rather than as an ascetic or a hermit.[206]

In the first place, the saint, except for brief episodes, engages with the modern world, the world of the city, instead of rejecting it. From a merchant family, Rainerius's activity takes place in the city; the success of his family's ventures is visible in the magnificent palazzo with its arcaded courtyard in which the scene of Rainerius's conversion takes place (Figures 2.20–2.21).[207] The palace was the most desirable and visible of the earthly goods sought by the urban merchant class, as is acknowledged by contemporary sources. Giordano of Pisa alludes to this reality of everyday urban life in his sermons; he urges the faithful toward heaven, "If you could easily enter a beautiful city or a beautiful palazzo, and you chose not to, this would be great negligence."[208] This sentiment is in direct contrast to the exhortations of Saint Anthony, as recounted in Cavalca's *Vite de' Santi Padri*: "I like to ask, after reading this legend, rich and powerful men of the

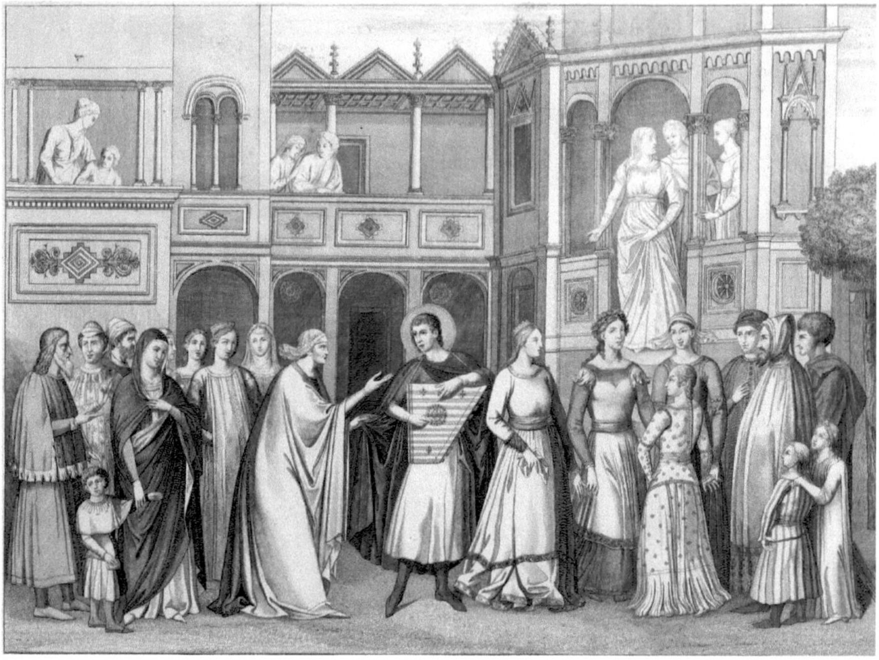

2.21. Carlo Lasinio, engraving (1812), after Andrea Bonaiuti, *Conversion of Saint Rainerius*, detail (1376–77), Harvard Art Museums/Fogg Museum, gift of William Gray from the collection of Francis Calley Gray, G2145. Photo: © President and Fellows of Harvard College.

world, who do not know how to use their riches well, who have grand palaces of marble and gold, and who buy many farms and great possessions: what did this poor, old man, Paul, lack?"[209]

Saint Rainerius is consistently identified as a Pisan, as seen, for example, from the coats of arms of the Pisan *popolo* on the stern of the ship that takes him to the Holy Land (Figures 2.22–2.23).[210] In the 1662 drawing, an eagle, symbol of the justice of the signoria and the seal of the city-state up to 1268, is seen in the central insignia of the ship and above the prow. It alludes to the saint's vision of an eagle bringing him a flaming torch to enlighten men, perhaps a foreshadowing of his future status as patron saint of Pisa.[211]

The urban settings of many of the Saint Rainerius scenes are detailed and identifiable as monuments in Pisa, most notably the monuments from the cathedral complex seen in the last two murals of the lower level (Figures 2.27–2.31).[212] By contrast, in the scenes of the saint in the Holy Land, in the church of the Holy Sepulcher, the Church of the Virgin in Nazareth, and at Mount Tabor, the settings are fanciful and nonspecific, responding to the remoteness and lack of tangible experience the artist – and undoubtedly most of his audience – had of the sacred sites (Figures 2.22 and 2.24). Since the reconquest of Jerusalem by the Khwarismian Turks in 1244, Christian pilgrims' access to the holy sites had been restricted.[213] From 1309, the Mamelukes granted custody of the sacred sites to the Franciscans, who guided Christian pilgrims

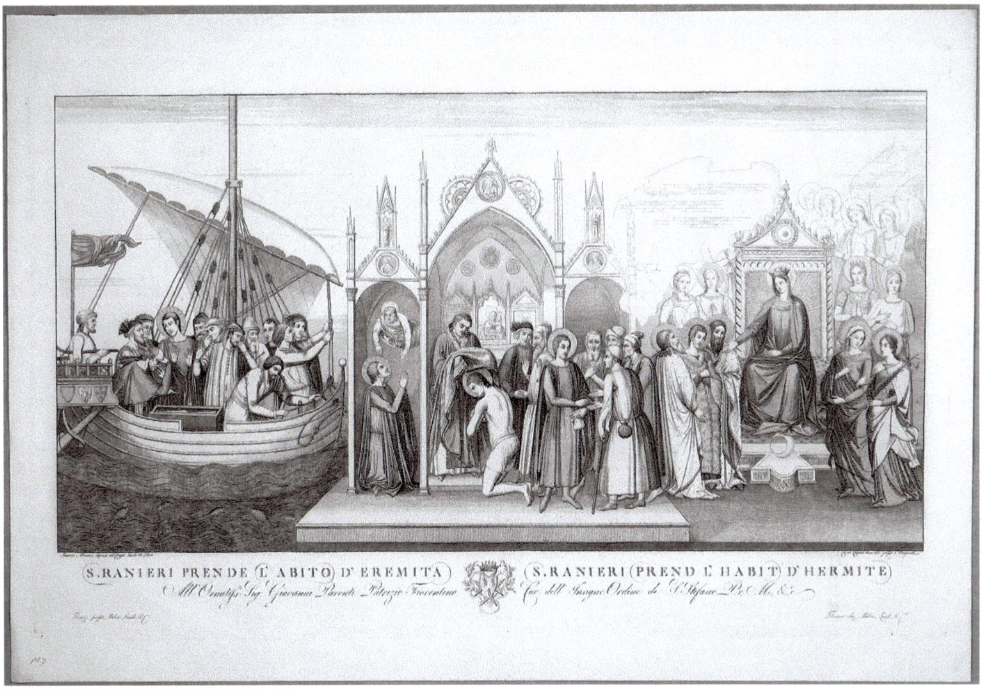

2.22. Carlo Lasinio, engraving (1812), after Andrea Bonaiuti, *Saint Rainerius in the Holy Land* (1376–77) Harvard Art Museums/Fogg Museum, gift of William Gray from the collection of Francis Calley Gray, G2146. Photo: © President and Fellows of Harvard College.

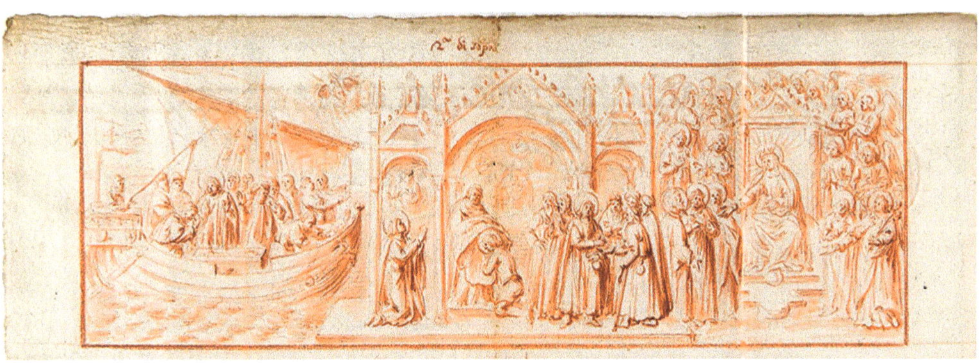

2.23. Anonymous draughtsman after Andrea Bonaiuti, *Saint Rainerius in the Holy Land* (1376–77), 1662, Manoscritti, C 93/95, Archivio Storico Diocesano, Archivio Capitolare, Pisa. Photo: Archivio Storico Diocesano, Archivio Capitolare.

on organized tours departing from Venice and offered visits to sacred sites on a number of different itineraries, but pilgrimage remained arduous and expensive.[214] One of the better-informed authors of guidebooks to the Holy Land was Burchard of Mount Sion, whose *Descriptio Terrae Sanctae* (c. 1283) includes an extensive description of the Church of the Holy Sepulcher based on firsthand experience. The "Place of the Skull" was a two-storied chapel, the upper floor called Calvary and its lower floor Golgotha. A rock to the west rose to just above the floor of the upper chapel.[215] Burchard described the

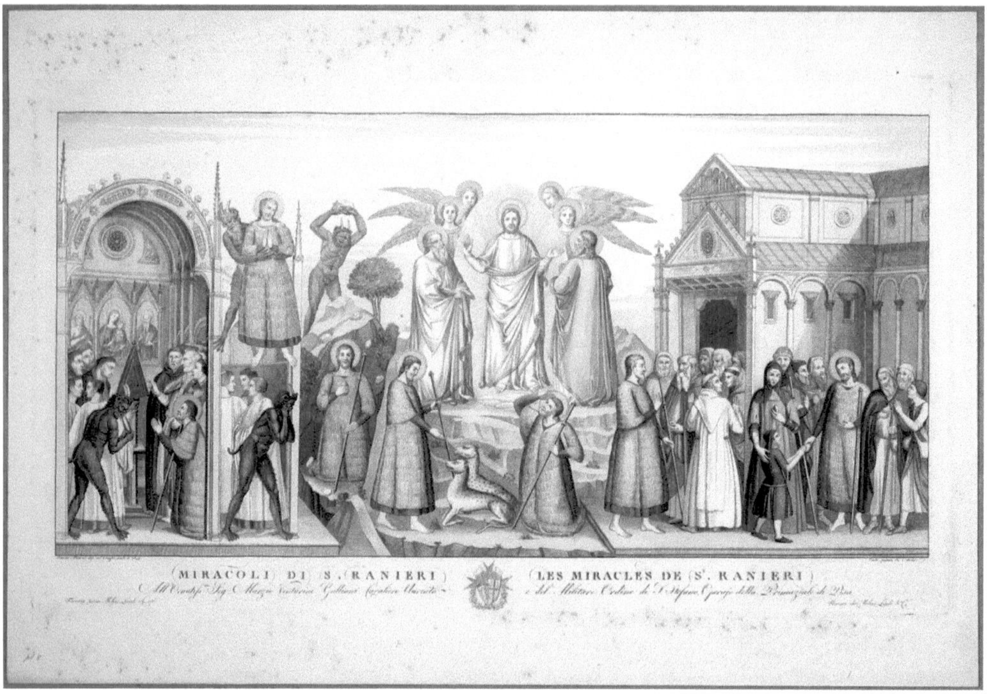

2.24. 20 Carlo Lasinio, engraving (1812), after Andrea Bonaiuti, *Temptation and Miracles of Saint Rainerius* (1376–77), Harvard Art Museums/Fogg Museum, gift of William Gray from the collection of Francis Calley Gray, G2147. Photo: © President and Fellows of Harvard College.

Calvary chapel as eighteen feet above the paved floor of the church and "entirely paved with marble, [and] its walls are covered with marble and adorned with mosaic work of the purest gold."[216] The Pisa mural shows Rainerius receiving his pilgrim costume in the Calvary chapel, rendered as a truncated, gabled chapel (Figures 2.22, 2.24). There is no indication of the two-storied elevation, the rock, and sumptuous revetment reported by Burchard. Only in the rendition of Jerusalem in the mural of Rainerius's return to Pisa, which shows at the left a view of the city cinched by massive walls, might the large-domed building, adjacent round turret, and square tower allude to the Church of the Holy Sepulcher (Figure 2.25). These forms would have been derived from a visual tradition of representation, rather than actual experience.[217]

The architectural "portraits" of Pisan monuments in the murals of the *Death and Funeral of Saint Rainerius* and the *Posthumous Miracles of Saint Rainerius*, however, appealed to the viewer's experience of the urban fabric of contemporary Pisa and served to situate the events depicted in the mural in time and space.[218] Goro Dati, in his *Istoria di Firenze*, described Pisa in the late Trecento: "The town is enclosed by thick walls and inside it has very beautiful and straight streets with beautiful and great tall houses and the view of the houses along the Arno is the most beautiful sight there is to see anywhere."[219] The

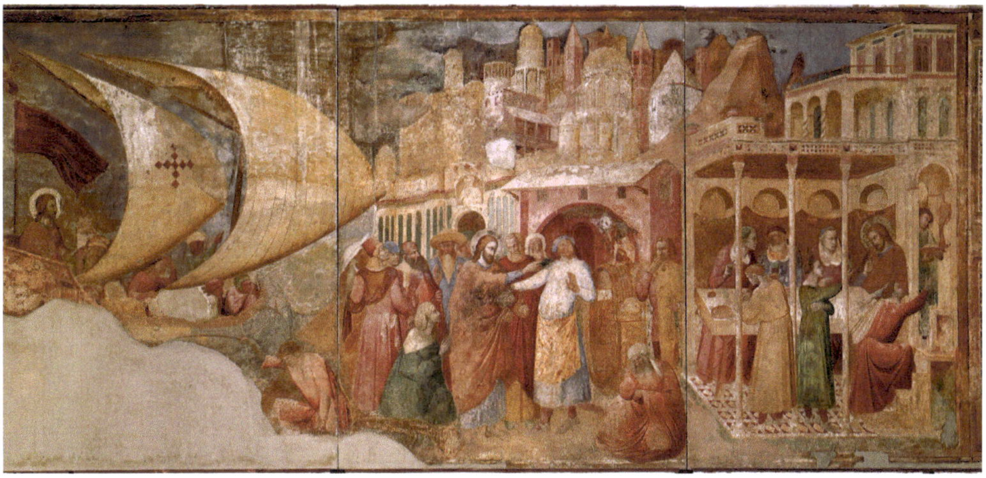

2.25. Antonio Veneziano, *Saint Rainerius Returns to Pisa*, 1384–86, southwest wall, Camposanto, Pisa. Photo: Scala / Art Resource, NY.

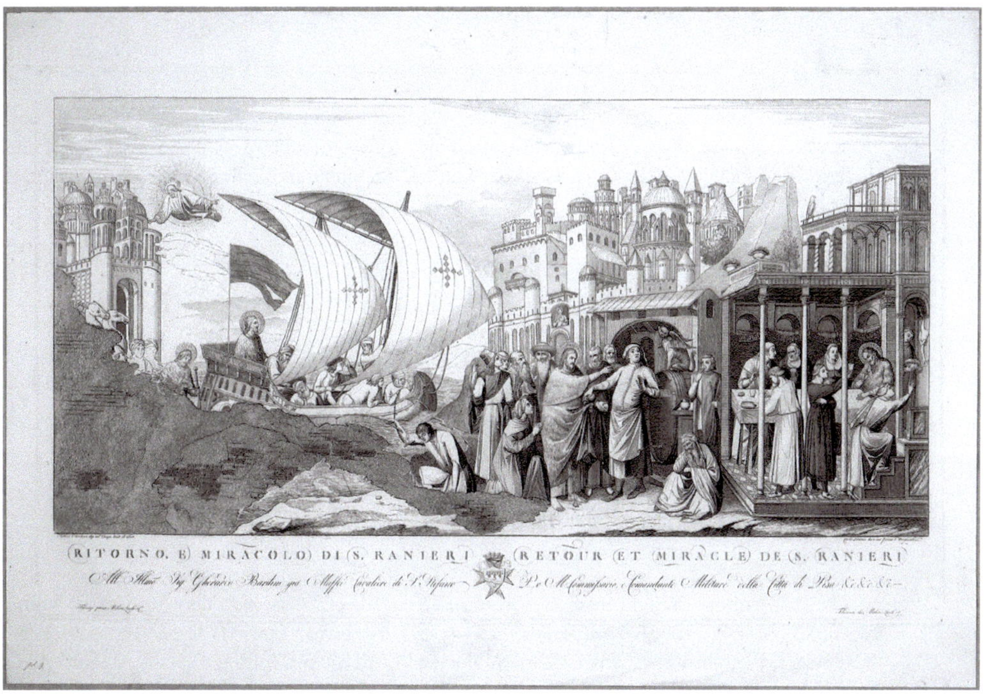

2.26. Carlo Lasinio, engraving (1812), after Antoinio Veneziano, *Saint Rainerius Returns to Pisa*, 1384–86, Harvard Art Museums/Fogg Museum, gift of William Gray from the collection of Francis Calley Gray, G2148. Photo: © President and Fellows of Harvard College.

Piazza del Duomo features prominently in the murals. In the mural of the *Death and Funeral of Saint Rainerius*, the Duomo, its west façade removed, offers a view into the interior, and the campanile with its distinctive tilt – transposed to the north of the cathedral – are rendered in detail (Figures 2.27, 2.28). If the

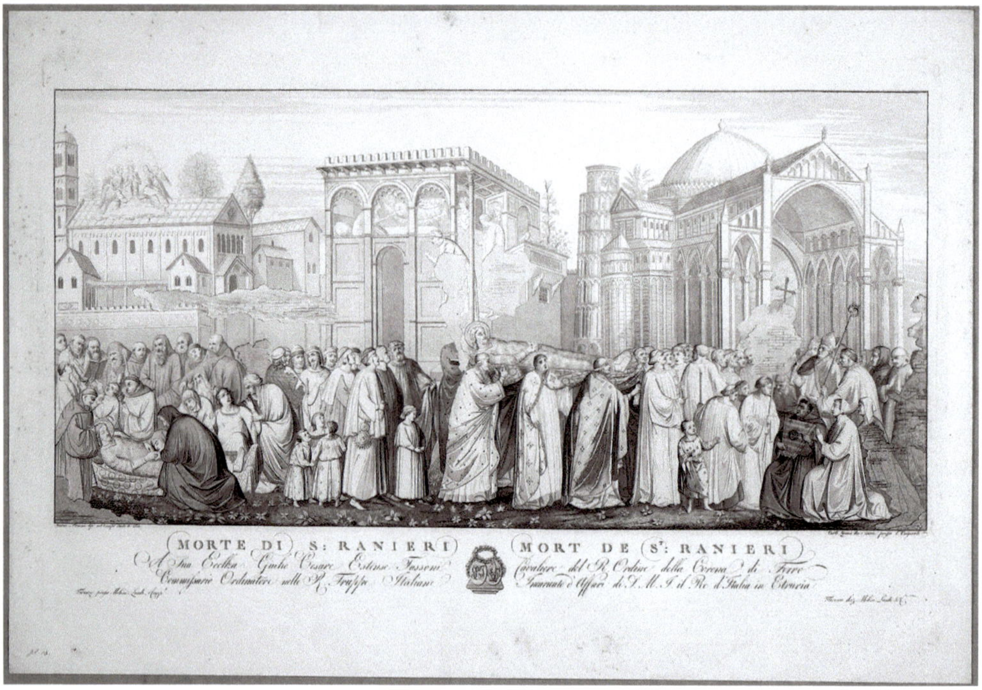

2.27. Carlo Lasinio, engraving (1812), after Antoinio Veneziano, *Death and Funeral of Saint Rainerius,* 1384–86, Harvard Art Museums/Fogg Museum, gift of William Gray from the collection of Francis Calley Gray, G2149. Photo: © President and Fellows of Harvard College.

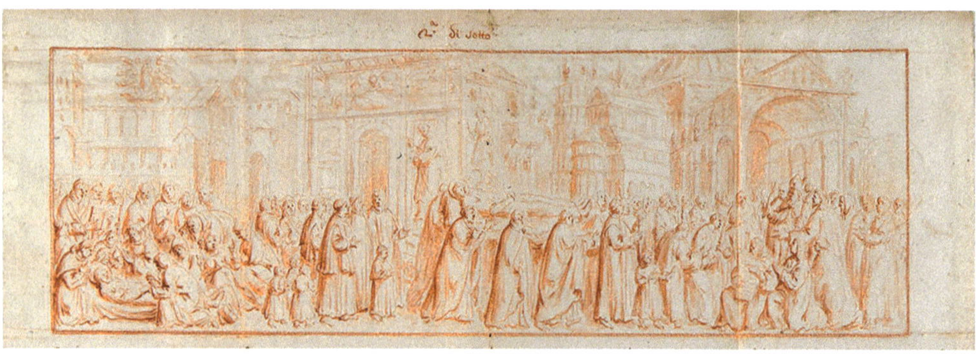

2.28. Anonymous draughtsman after Antoinio Veneziano, *Death and Funeral of Saint Rainerius* detail (1384–86), 1662, Manoscritti, C 93/95, Archivio Storico Diocesano, Archivio Capitolare, Pisa. Photo: Archivio Storico Diocesano, Archivio Capitolare.

elevation of the north flank of the Duomo is not exact, the massing of the north transept and the broad curvature of its cupola is faithfully presented. In the mural of Saint Rainerius's posthumous miracles, the elevation of the Baptistery omits the clerestory level, with its upper cornice that bends over the windows, forming a gable (Figures 2.29, 2.31). While it is not precise in its rendering of monument, which was, in any case, not entirely finished at this time, the allusion is unmistakable.[220] The Baptistery was modeled on the rotunda of the Church of the Holy Sepulcher.[221] Finally, the monumentality

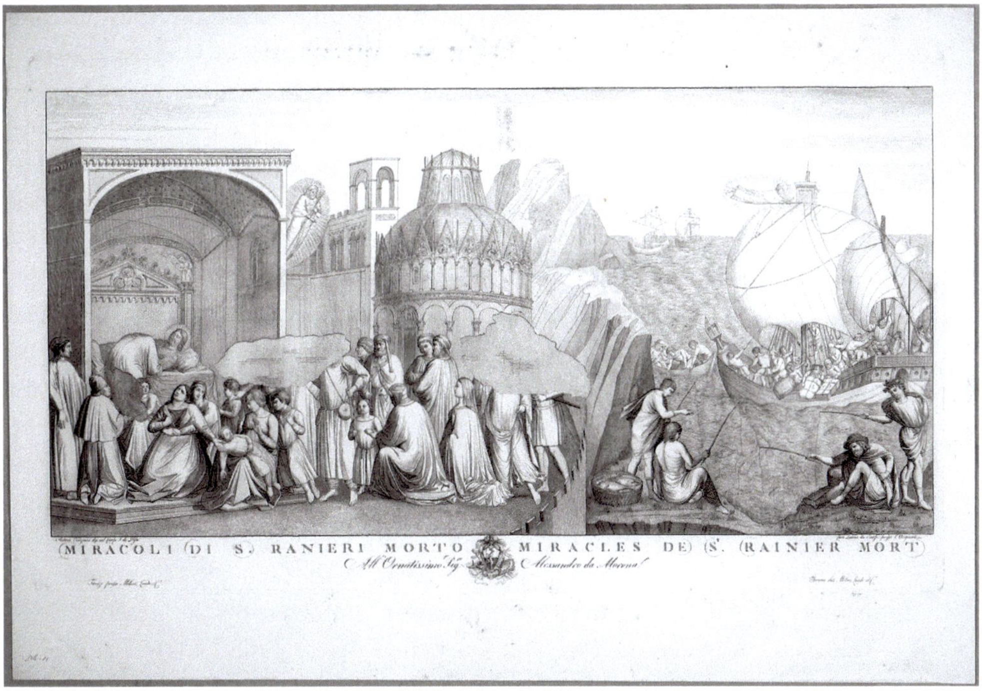

2.29. Carlo Lasinio, engraving (1812), after Antoinio Veneiano, *Posthumous Miracles of Saint Rainerius* 1384–86, Harvard Art Museums/Fogg Museum, gift of William Gray from the collection of Francis Calley Gray, G2150. Photo: © President and Fellows of Harvard College.

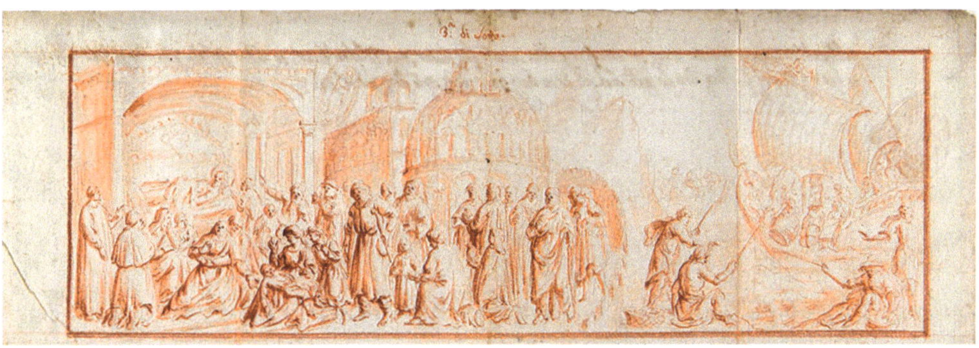

2.30. Anonymous draughtsman after Antoinio Veneziano, *Posthumous Miracles of Saint Rainerius* (1384–86), 1662, Manoscritti, C 93/95, Archivio Storico Diocesano, Archivio Capitolare, Pisa. Photo: Archivio Storico Diocesano, Archivio Capitolare.

and great height – compared to the figure scale – and oblique angles from which the Pisan monuments are seen perhaps evokes the viewer's views of the urban built environment as he or she experienced it in daily life moving through the city.[222] Incidents in Rainerius's life, especially his chance encounter with Blessed Alberto, could only have happened in the dense urban fabric of the late medieval city.

The connection with contemporary Pisa underscores another difference between this cycle and the earlier murals. Rainerius lived in the relatively

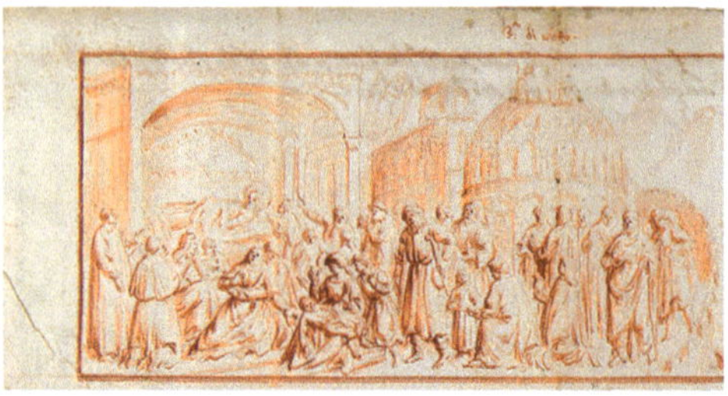

2.31. Anonymous draughtsman after Antoinio Veneziano, *Posthumous Miracles of Saint Rainerius* detail (1384–86), 1662, Manoscritti, C 93/95, Archivio Storico Diocesano, Archivio Capitolare, Pisa. Photo: Archivio Storico Diocesano, Archivio Capitolare.

recent past, and, while certainly no one viewing the murals in the Camposanto could have had known him, his memory, through his interaction with places and institutions still extant, would have been more accessible to contemporaries than that of the distant saints of the *Lives of the Hermit Saints*. That saints from the recent past had resonance for urban laymen was acknowledged by Archbishop Federico Visconti as early as 1261 in a sermon on Saint Francis: "How welcome it must be to the merchants to know that one from their ranks, the blessed Francesco, was himself a merchant, and has been made a saint in our time. What a capital hope it must be for the merchants, to have a merchant such as he for their intercessor with God."[223] Contemporary memory of saints from the recent past was reinforced by the observance of Rainerius's feast day in Pisa, still celebrated on 17 June.[224] The statutes of 1286 and 1313 provided for criers to announce the ceremonies at the saint's tomb in the Duomo.[225] Rainerius remained a layman, and while his life was filled with extremes of devotion and saintliness, his piety was nonetheless a type that characterized the communal saints of the late Middle Ages.[226]

Additionally, whereas the eremitical saints of the earlier mural pursued a solitary, private penance, Rainerius's life, even after his conversion, was lived largely in a populated, urban environment. There he performed charitable acts, as when he distributed alms before the church of the Holy Sepulcher, or he fed ten paupers with one loaf that miraculously did not diminish. Like Saint Francis, he embraced voluntary poverty. His supreme act of penance was going on pilgrimage, a form of public penance attractive to laypersons.[227] While in the church of the Holy Sepulcher in Jerusalem, Rainerius, in imitation of Christ on Calvary, took off his garments and donned the *pilurica*, as a sign of his conversion. This garment is quite different from the costume of plaited palms worn by Saint Paul or Saint Anthony in the *Lives of the Hermit Saints* mural. While the *pilurica*[228] referred to a rough, hairy, woven garment associated with the poor, in the visual tradition, Rainerius is shown wearing something more akin to an animal skin, much like that commonly portrayed on Saint John the Baptist.[229] That the *pilurica* Rainerius wears is associated with a pilgrim, not a hermit, is made clear by showing him with the pilgrim's staff (Figures 2.32–2.33). A similarly attired pilgrim, equipped with a staff and pilgrim's hat, adorned with pilgrim's badges of the cockle shell of Saint James and the Vera Icon, is seen among the figures in Andrea Bonaiuti's *Church Militant and Triumphant* mural in the chapter house of Santa Maria

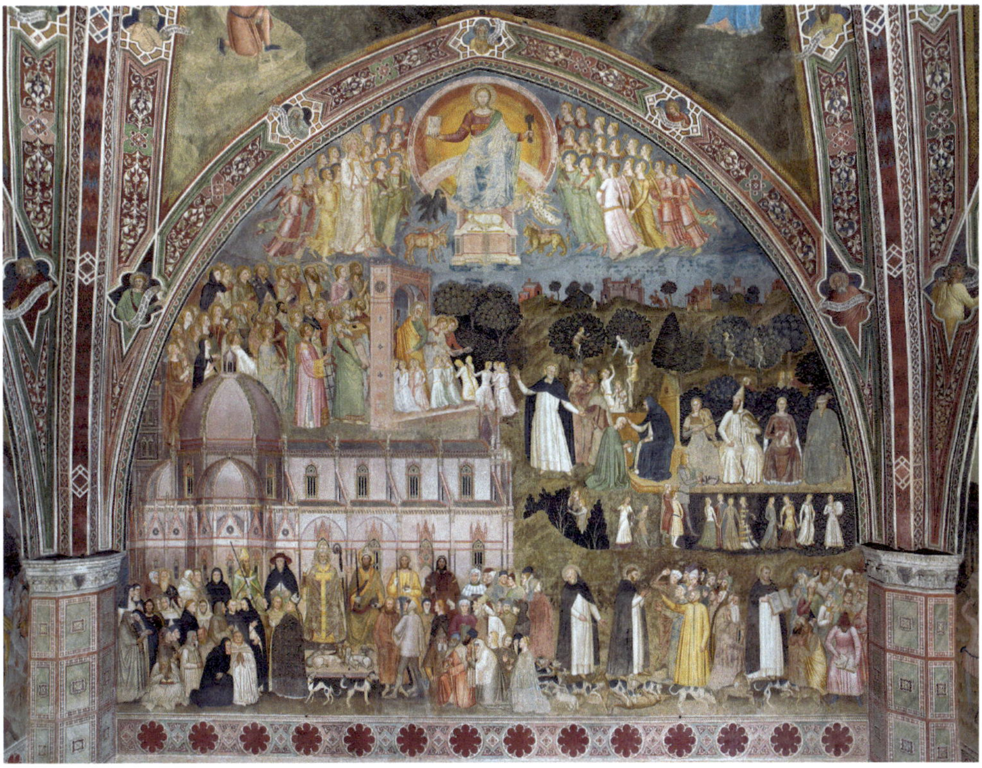

2.32. Andrea Bonaiuti, *Church Militant and Triumphant*, 1366–68, Chapter House, Santa Maria Novella, Florence. Photo: Scala / Art Resource, NY.

Novella in Florence (Figures 2.32–2.33). Also, unlike the desert saints, Rainerius wears a blue tunic, complete with buttons on the sleeve, beneath his *pilurica*, perhaps as a reminder of his former – and future – life as a layman in his native city of Pisa.

Rainerius's travel to foreign lands and his change of clothes signaled his rejection of past sins and his new, saintly life. That life, as depicted in the mural, consisted of acts of charity, service to the poor, visions, and miracles – a life lived in society, not removed from it, as the eremitic saints of the *Lives of the Hermit Saints*. Rainerius's travels take him not far into the desert, beyond the reach of civilization, but to the venerated sites of the Holy Land – the Holy Sepulcher, Nazareth – and the colonies of maritime Pisa, including Messina. In only one instance, in the third mural on the top level, is Rainerius shown wandering in the desert, where the Devil assaulted him. This act, too, was part of his pilgrimage as an *imitatio Christi* – he fasted for forty days on Mount Tabor in remembrance of Christ's forty days in the desert, and he was privileged with a vision of the Transfiguration (Figure 2.24).[230] Throughout his saintly life, however, Rainerius remained a layman who lived his life in the contemporary world.

The new emphasis in the Rainerius cycle leads to a different treatment of subject matter. The Rainerius cycle is a biographical treatment of a single,

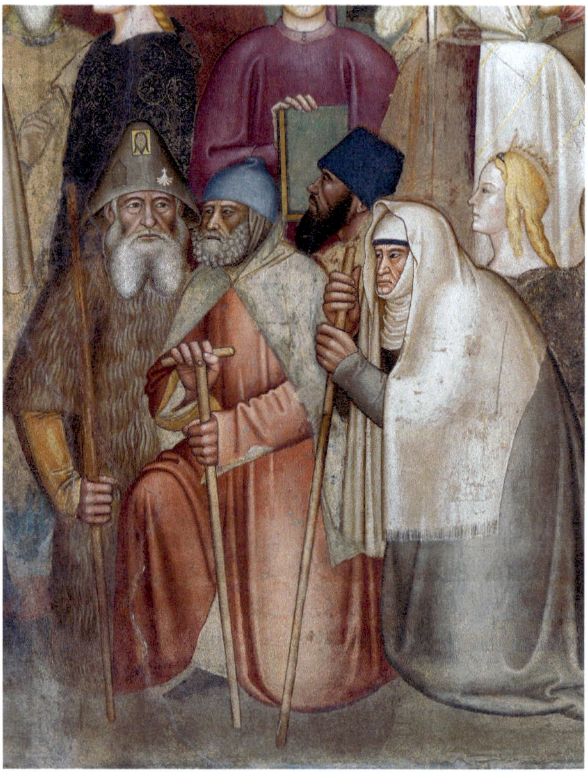

2.33. Andrea Bonaiuti, *Church Militant and Triumphant,* detail, 1366–68, Chapter House, Santa Maria Novella, Florence. Photo: Scala / Art Resource, NY.

historical figure, while the *Lives of the Hermit Saints* mural shows vignettes, episodes in saints' lives that function in the way that *exempla* – brief, moral narratives in contemporary sermons – served as organizing principals and vivid examples of everyday life, fostering empathy in lay viewers.[231] The (largely) chronological treatment of Rainerius's life is organized in scenes, with multiple incidents in each, framed and juxtaposed. They are "read" sequentially by the viewer, aided by the inscriptions in the fresco field and in the border. The *Lives of the Hermit Saints* is one vast landscape with the individual episodes embedded within it, ordered into three levels by the landscape, rocks, and paths.[232] In its simultaneity and rejection of spatial illusionism, the *Lives of the Hermit Saints* mural (and the others from the 1340s) are akin in their message and form to the great allegorical works of the mid-fourteenth century, such as Andrea Bonaiuti's *Church Militant and Triumphant* in the chapter house of Santa Maria Novella (Figure 2.32). The Saint Rainerius cycle, by contrast, adopts the language of the historical narratives of the Giottesque tradition.[233]

The return to biographical narratives in the Camposanto acknowledges the role of narrative in popular religious practice and in the cult of the saints broadly.[234] Modern saints' biographies, efforts to rewrite the hagiographical corpus for educational use, emerged in the thirteenth century as integral to the cult of the saints, as promoted by the mendicant orders.[235] The lively narrative from the mid-fourteenth century by Benincasa, a Pisan canon, describes Rainerius's life with colorful detail, fully embedded in the quotidian life of the medieval city.[236]

The Job cycle in the Camposanto is a dramatic narrative, like that of Saint Rainerius, and its probable design by Taddeo Gaddi, Giotto's most faithful pupil, was an accessible model for Andrea to follow in designing the later cycle.[237] And yet, as far as we can tell in its current condition, the Job cycle did not present to the spectators of the late Trecento a model of communal sanctity, such as the cycle of Saint Rainerius. As we have seen, Job is the model penitent, but his trials are primarily personal and solitary. As he rests on his dung heap, outside the city walls, he is visited by his friends; but ultimately Job's penance does not entail engaging in acts of charity or carrying on any semblance of his life before his affliction. Moreover, Job was a biblical figure, living in ancient Uz, sometimes located in Chaldea, near the southern Euphrates River. The figures' split beards, braided hair, and conical hats conform to images of Mongol peoples in contemporary accounts.[238] While observers may have sympathized with Job's plight, and shared his plaint, he was not a product of a modern, urban society as they were.

Finally, another way in which the Rainerius cycle differs from the earlier ones is in the role played by the communal church, its ceremonies, and its monuments. The earliest source for the saint's life was written by Benincasa, who became the saint's close disciple and, as a constant attendant of the saint's tomb, a witness to the many miracles performed. As this account seems to be the principal source for the legend, the emphasis on the cathedral as a place of pilgrimage and locus for miracles is not surprising.[239]

In particular, the vast area in the murals given over to the death, funeral procession, and exposition of the body of Rainerius in the Duomo contrasts with the visualization of death in the *Lives of the Hermit Saints* mural, in which the penitents, such as Paul or Saint Onuphrius are buried unceremoniously in earthen graves. Rainerius's death, by contrast, is a "good death" – a very public affair, with the rites of the church and the participation of the clergy and populace prominently depicted. We see, for example, outside San Vito, a large crowd of clerics and laypeople gather around Saint Rainerius's bier (Figure 2.27). One woman kisses Rainerius's folded hands, another raises her hands in a gesture of despair, perhaps alluding to the *pianto*. Another woman approaches his feet, while a friar approaches his head. Rainerius's body is clothed in the *pilurica*, following the practice of clothing the dead in keeping with his social identity – here, the pilgrim's garment that marked his conversion in the Holy Land.

The cortege bearing his bier is headed by tonsured clerics and acolytes carrying tall candles, followed by, no doubt, prominent laymen, one of whom carries a pilgrim's flask (Figures 2.27–2.28). Several open their mouths in song. The clerics carrying the bier wear embroidered garments. The procession passes by the archbishop's palace where, in the upper floor the Archbishop Villani is miraculously cured by the saint, who appears to him in a vision.[240] The inscription formerly beneath the scene tells us of the ringing of bells, explicitly permitted by Pisan law; the campanile of the cathedral is shown prominently in the background.[241] As the cortege approaches the cathedral, bearing the dead saint feet-first according to custom, the now-healthy archbishop welcomes him. Rainerius has come home to rest in the sumptuous cathedral, which looms above the group, as foretold by the Virgin: "Your body will rest in my church which is in Pisa" – as the inscription formerly accompanying the central mural in the upper row related.[242] For Pisans, the Virgin's promise to Rainerius was proof of the city's special relationship with her, much as was the Holy Belt to Pratesi. It bolstered Rainerius's shared status as the city's patron saint. It also reinforced the cathedral as the Virgin's church and the place of the saint's burial. The friar kneeling before the archbishop makes music on a harp exactly like that played by the young Rainerius in the first scene, stressing that his life has come full circle.

In the last scene, *Posthumous Miracles of Saint Rainerius*, the body of Saint Rainerius rests in a space that represents the choir of the cathedral, in keeping with his elevated status (Figures 2.29–2.31).[243] Perhaps the emotional gestures of those who surround him – the women, in particular – allude to the searing emotional tenor of the Office of the Dead, the psalms, and the laments of Job. They seek the healing power of the saint; one woman faints into the arms of another, pointing to the limp body of a child. On the right, Rainerius appears to pilgrims assembled outside the church, the Pisan Baptistery prominently depicted behind them, underscoring the cathedral complex, and the saint's tomb in particular, as a place of pilgrimage. On the far right, Rainerius performs twelve miracles at sea. As the patron saint of a city whose prestige and prosperity depended on its maritime trade, the emphasis on travel by ship, and its potential dangers, is not surprising.[244]

Not depicted is Rainerius's burial in the cathedral (though it is mentioned in the inscription accompanying this scene), but this event had been shown on the reliefs on the tomb of the saint that reposed in the left nave (Figure 2.34). This tomb, by Tino di Camaino from the early fourteenth century (completed c. 1306), was a replacement for an earlier tomb that had been erected in a corner of the cathedral and that had been provided by the consuls of Pisa, as stressed by the hagiographic accounts of his life and prophesized by Rainerius himself.[245] A combination of tomb and altar, it was a focus of the cult of the saint, and it possibly housed a reliquary with the saint's head. The tomb, in altered form, was removed from the cathedral to the Museo dell'Opera del Duomo. The gabled shape of the tomb is evoked in the murals in the gabled

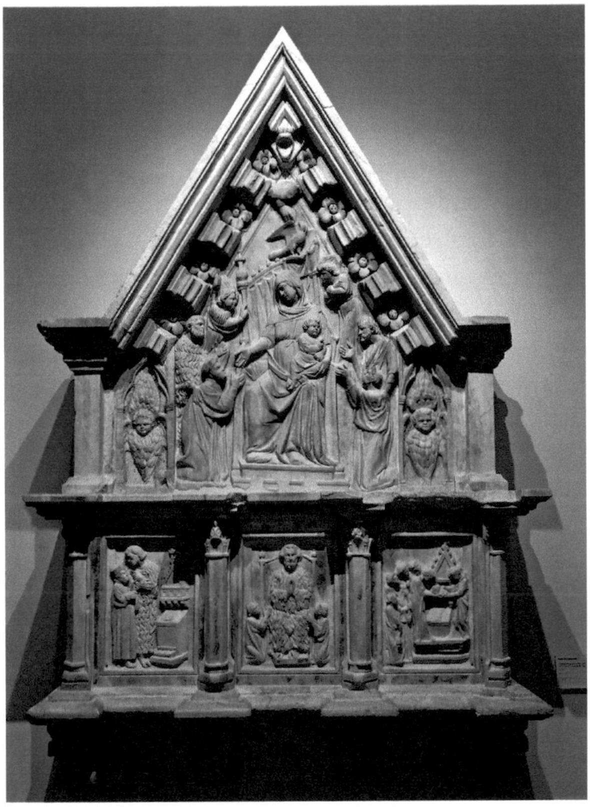

2.34. Tino da Camaino, Tomb of Saint Rainerius, c. 1306, Museo dell'Opera del Duomo, Pisa. Photo: Sailko / Creative Commons Attribution 3.0 Unported.

form of the Virgin's throne in Tyre, as well as the bier on which the body of the saint rests in the last mural of the cycle (Figures 2.22, 2.29, 2.30). Hence, the imagery firmly associates the Virgin with Rainerius as a patron of the city of Pisa and the tomb with her prophecy in Tyre.

The mural of Saint Rainerius's death prominently depicts the official celebration of sacraments and the ceremonies, as evolved in the funerary practices of late medieval Pisa. Here the specificity of the architectural setting leaves no doubt that the cathedral clergy is in charge and that lay citizens are prominent participants. The inscription of the central field in the lower level stressed the collective effort of the clergy and citizens to bring the body to the Duomo, "with an infinite number of lights in hand." While mendicants such as Cavalca celebrated the eremitic piety of the hermit saints, here the cathedral canons and archbishop, in concert with civic magistrates, model civic virtues by honoring Rainerius, a virtuous layman and urban saint whose cult is centered on the spiritual center of the city, the Piazza del Duomo. Although Rainerius was converted at the Benedictine convent of San Vito and returned there after his pilgrimage to the Holy Land, and it was there that he died, his cult remained independent of the mendicant orders. The mural celebrates the lay, civic piety of Rainerius, rather than the private, eremitical piety of the hermit saints.[246]

For the late fourteenth century Pisan viewer, the murals would have been understood against the continuing tension between Pisa's traditional Ghibelline loyalties and papal demands.[247] The depiction of these incidents underscored Rainerius's patronage and protection of the Pisan clergy, especially of the archbishop and cathedral canons, and the harmonious balance among sacred and secular authorities in the city, hence presenting an ideal, if ultimately unrealized, view of Pisan urban life.[248]

The emphasis on the civic identity of the saintly models presented in the Camposanto conforms to the drive to reinforce the Camposanto as a civic institution. Indeed, it is perhaps revealing that, after completing the Rainerius murals, Antonio Veneziano was engaged in repairing the mural of the *Lives of the Hermit Saints*, especially the area around the tomb of Giovanni "Soldato." The wooden baldacchino was removed, and the lacunae filled with scenes that are more urban than those in other areas; a dense group of buildings is visible in the area to the left of the incident of the temptress. Additionally, Antonio changed the flagellant figures flanking the tomb of Giovanni to angels with censers (Figure 2.9). Did this change signal a renewed attempt to reorient attention from the intense piety of the *disciplinati*, with their emphasis on private penance, toward an urban, civic piety as represented by the cathedral church hierarchy?[249] Was it also an attempt to deflect the spiritual control of the Camposanto from the influence of the mendicants, especially the Dominicans, and bring it back firmly under the wing of the city officials and urban clergy? The mendicants' presence in the Rainerius murals is scarce.[250] We know that the *operaio* at the time, Parasone Grasso, who employed Antonio, was an adherent of the *disciplinati*; hence the change cannot be owing to his personal preferences.[251] It seems most likely, then, that the penitential aspect of Giovanni's tomb in the Camposanto was diminished as part and parcel of its new civic identity, emanating from the secular authorities of the commune – of which the Opera del Duomo was a part – as well as from the archbishop and the cathedral chapter.

CONCLUSION

The murals on the south wall of the Camposanto show with especial vividness how monumental civic images reflected and shaped the actions and ideas of contemporary viewers throughout the fourteenth century in Pisa. Responding to the Camposanto's multiple roles as a place of burial and a public theater for sacred ceremony, the murals visualized the virtues of piety, humility, and penance and modeled pious behavior. The evolution of the imagery and narrative style of the murals from the earlier to the later fourteenth century traced in this chapter mirrored the changes in the social function of the Camposanto, the burial customs of the citizenry, and the political realities of Pisa as the era of its independence ended. In the fifteenth century, when the structure and the decoration of the Camposanto were finally finished, its civic function again changed, and with it the imagery and meaning of the murals, a subject explored in Chapter 3.

NOTES

1 Roberto Paolo Ciardi, "Da cimitero a famedio: L'età moderna," Claudio Casini and Fulvia Donati, "Il Camposanto come galleria," Fernando Mazzocca, "Fortune ottocentesche," and Ettore Spalletti, "La continuità della memoria: I monumenti funebri dell'Ottocento," in Clara Baracchini and Enrico Castelnuovo, eds., *Il Camposanto di Pisa*, Turin: Eiunadi, 1996, pp. 147–200.

2 "E apresso tra'l Duomo e San Giovanni sì v'è il Chanpo Sancto, choperto di pionbo, dove sono grandisime quantità di sepolture in sul piano di marmo, chon maravigliose istorie nelle mura dipinte ed èvi grandi quantità di sepolture di rilievo"; Florence, Biblioteca Nazionale Centrale, Codice Magliabechiano, Classe XXV, 8, c. 491; published in I. Benvenuto Supino, *Arte Pisana*, Florence: Alinari, 1904, p. 307; see also Mauro Ronzani, *Un'idea trecentesca di cimitero: La costruzione e l'uso del Camposanto nella Pisa del secolo XIV*, Pisa: Edizioni Plus-University Press, 2005, pp. 91–93.

3 Supino, *Arte Pisana*, p. 307.

4 Augustine Thompson, *Cities of God: The Religion of the Italian Communes 1125–1325*, University Park: Pennsylvania State University Press, 2005, p. 346, reports that worshippers entered the church and turned to the right, moving around the church counter-clockwise This is also the viewing sequence followed by early accounts such as the *Descrizione del Camposanto pisano in forma di dialogo*, from 1593, Manuscript C. 43 in Pisa, Archivio Storico Diocesano, Archivio Capitolare, c. 8. Michelagnolo di Cristofano da Volterra's poem of 1488, however, begins his description with the murals to the left of the door, then turns right to those of the hermit saints; Michelagnolo di Cristofano da Volterra, "Le Mirabili et inaldite belleze e adornamenti del Camposanto di Pisa," in I. B. Supino, *Il Camposanto di Pisa*, Florence: Alinari, 1896, pp. 301–17.

5 In Pisa, the new year began on the feast of the Annunciation, 25 March, but until 1749 its calendar ran one year ahead of common style dating. Hence the dates between 1 January and 24 March accord with common style dates, but those between 25 March and 31 December are one year ahead. Dates in the text are in modern style. For the early history of the Camposanto, see Clemente Lupi, "Sulle origini del Camposanto di Pisa," *Notizie d'arte*, vol. 2, 1910, p. 18, note 35 d.; and Mauro Ronzani "La formazione della Piazza del Duomo (secoli XI–XIV)," in *Bollettino dell'Istituto storico artistico orvietano*, vol. 46–47, 1990–91 [1997], p. 113, note 189.

6 Ronzani, *Un'idea trecentesca di cimitero*, p. 23.

7 Mauro Ronzani, "L'Opera del Duomo nel Medioevo," in Gabriella Garzella et al., eds., *La Cattedrale di Pisa*, Pisa: Pacini Editore, 2014, pp. 37–44; and more exhaustively, Marta Battistoni, *L'Opera del Duomo di Pisa: Il patrimonio e la sua gestione nei secoli XII–XVI*, Pisa: Pacini Editore, 2013.

8 "+ A(nno) D(domini) MCCLXXVIII T(em)P(o)R(e) D(omiNI FEDIERIGI ARCHI / EP(iscopi) PIS(ani)/ ET D(omi)NI TERLLATI POTESTATIS OP(er)ARIO ORLLANDO / SARDELLA (et) IOHANNE MAG(ist)RO AEDIFICA(n)TE" (A.D. 1278 at the time of Lord Federick Archbishop of Pisa, Lord Terlati Podestà, Orlando Sardella Operario, Master John Builder.) Ottavio Banti, "A proposito del 'Iohanne magistro edificante' 'architetto' del Campo Santo di Pisa," in *Critica d'arte*, 8th

ser, vol. 75, nos. 53–54, 2013 [2015], pp. 101–8, has analyzed the epigraphy of the inscription and dates it to considerably later, perhaps to the sixteenth century; this idea has been contested by Rahel Meier, "Ein Witz und eine grinsende Fratze an der Südfassade des Camposanto zu Pisa?," in Michele Bacci et al, eds., *Journeys of the Soul; Multiple Topographies in the Camposanto of Pisa*, Pisa: Edizioni della Normale, 2020, pp. 111–28.

9 Ronzani posits the existence of an earlier church dedicated to the Holy Trinity and servicing an adjacent open-air cemetery on land donated to the Opera del Duomo in 1277 by Archbishop Visconti; Ronzani, *Un'idea trecentesca di cimitero*; see also Emilio Tolaini, "Camposanto di Pisa: Progetto e cantiere," *Rivista dell'Istituto Nazionale d'archeologia e storia dell'arte*, 3rd ser., vol. 17, 1994, pp. 101–46 [reprinted, with slight revisions in Emilio Tolaini, *Camposanto di Pisa: progetto e cantiere: La forma architettonica e la decorazione plastica*, Pisa: Edizioni ETS, 2008]. This church, occupying the southeast corner of the present structure, was subsumed in the current fabric during construction, which began, according to Ronzani, in the second decade of the Trecento. Also see Antonio Caleca, "Costruzione e decorazione dalle origini al secolo XV," in Baracchini and Castelnuovo, eds., *Il Camposanto di Pisa*, pp. 13–48, who asserts that the extant southeast corner had been built and was functioning by 1299; see pp. 17–18.

10 Caleca, "Costruzione e decorazione," pp. 20–21 and 42–43, notes 57, 69, 70; Ottavio Banti, *Le iscrizioni delle tombe terragne del Camposanto di Pisa*, Pontedera: Bandecchi and Vivaldi, 1998, pp. 55, no. 11 [1337], 71, no. 73/6 [1313], 157, no. 363 [1337], 158–59, no. 366 [1333]. Ronzani, *Un'idea trecentesca di cimitero*, pp. 32–36, discusses earlier references to burials.

11 Discussion of the frescoes have centered on issues of attribution and date, spurred largely by Millard Meiss's classic discussion in *Painting in Florence and Siena after the Black Death*, Princeton: Princeton University Press, 1951. The current view of authorship among Italian scholars is the following: *Crucifixion* by Francesco Traini, *Resurrection, Ascension, Revelation of the Stigmata to Thomas, Triumph of Death, Last Judgment, Hell*, and *Lives of the Hermit Saints* by Buonamico Buffalmacco; *Assumption of the Virgin* by Stefano da Firenze; three scenes from the life of Saint Rainerius by Andrea Bonaiuti (Andrea da Firenze); three lower scenes from the life of Saint Rainerius by Antonio Veneziano; lives of Saints Ephesius and Potitus by Spinello Aretino; and Stories of Job by Taddeo Gaddi, finished by Francesco Neri da Volterra. For recent views, see Caleca, "Costruzione e decorazione," pp. 20–27; Hayden B. J. Maginnis, *Painting in the Age of Giotto: A Historical Reevaluation*, University Park: The Pennysylvania State University Press, 1997, pp. 164–76; Mariagiulia Burresi and Antonio Caleca, *Affreschi medievali a Pisa*, Pisa: Pacini Editore, 2003, pp. 85–130; Joseph Polzer, "Who Is the Master of the Crucifixion in the Camposanto of Pisa?," *Studi di storia dell'arte*, vol. 21, 2010, pp. 9–40; Linda Pisani, *Francesco Traini e la pittura a Pisa nella prima metà del Trecento*, Cinisello Balsame: Silvana Editoriale, 2020, pp. 180–83, cat. no. VIII.

12 Caleca, "Costruzione e decorazione," pp. 29–32, 44–46, notes 129, 144 and 146–47.

13 For Andrea see Johannes Tripps, *Tendencies of Gothic in Florence: Andrea Bonaiuti*, section iv, vol. vii, part I, of Richard Offner, Kara Steinweg, et al., eds., *A Critical and Historical Corpus of Florentine Painting*, Florence: Giunti, 1996; and for Antonio, see L. Tanfani Centofanti, *Notizie di artisti tratte dai documenti pisani*, Pisa: Enrico Spoerri, 1897; reprint Bologna: Forni, 1972, pp. 34–40; and James Czarnecki, "Antonio Veneziano: A Florentine Painter of the Late Trecento," PhD dissertation, Indiana University, 1978.

14 See Stefan Weppelmann, *Spinello Aretino und die toskanische Malerei des 14. Jahrhunderts*, Florence: Edifir, 2003, pp. 62–64 and 367, docs. 15–18.

15 Piero Sampaolesi, Mario Bucci, and Licia Bertolini, *Camposanto Monumentale di Pisa: Affreschi e sinopie*, Pisa: Opera della Primaziale Pisana, 1960, pp. 93–102; Andrew Ladis, *Taddeo Gaddi: Critical Reappraisal and Catalogue Raisonné*, Columbia: University of Missouri Press, 1982, pp. 247–50.

16 For the early history of the piazza, see Christine Smith, *The Baptistery of Pisa*, New York: Garland, 1978, pp. 13–23; Ronzani, "La formazione della Piazza del Duomo," Marco Frati,

"La piazza del Duomo di Pisa. Un millennio di miracoli," in Garzella et al., eds., *La Cattedrale di Pisa*, pp. 47–59.

17 Smith, *The Baptistery of Pisa*, pp. 19–20; see also Caleca, "Costruzione e decorazione," pp. 16–17.

18 The piazza had perhaps assumed its present aspect by about 1540; a drawing by Francisco de Holanda shows the main monuments free of intervening structures; Smith, *Baptistery of Pisa*, p. 20, fig. 8.

19 Smith, *Baptistery of Pisa*, p. 23; Fabio Redi, *Pisa come'era: Archeologia, urbanistica e strutture materiali (secoli V–XIV)*, Naples: Liguori, 1991, p. 384.

20 Smith, *Baptistery of Pisa*, p. 30.

21 For the early seat of the communal bodies, see Redi, *Pisa com'era*, pp. 320–34.

22 Paolo Tronci, *Memorie istoriche della città di Pisa*, Livorno: Bonfigli, 1682; repr., Bologna: Forni, 1967, pp. 269–71, describes a procession of 1292.

23 "Ad honorem Dei et sanctissime Virginis Marie"; Francesco Bonaini, *Statuti inediti della Città di Pisa dal XII al XIV secolo*, Florence: G. P. Vieusseux, 1854, vol. 1, pp. 45–51; see also Pietro Vigo, *Una festa popolare a Pisa nel Medioevo. Contributo alla storia delle costumanze italiane*, Pisa: Mariotti, 1888, p. 45; Ronzani, "La formazione della Piazza del Duomo," pp. 111–12.

24 Ronzani, "La formazione della Piazza del Duomo," p. 112.

25 *Monumenta Germaniae Historica, Legum, s. IV: Constitutiones et acta publica imperatorum et regum*, vol. 4, pt. 2, ed. I. Schwalm, Hannover, 1909–11, nos. 753–54, pp. 743–45, as cited in Ronzani, "La formazione della Piazza del Duomo," p. 118.

26 He entered though the Porta del Leone, where he was met by the archbishop. Proceeding to the Duomo, he made an offering of gold florins, then his entourage continued down the via Santa Maria to the Arno. For this and the following, see Ranieri Sardo, *Cronaca di Pisa*, ed. Ottavio Banti, Rome: Istituto Palazzo Borromini, 1963, pp. 101, 161–63, as cited in Smith, *Baptistery of Pisa*, p. 31.

27 Sardo, *Cronaca di Pisa*, pp. 161–62.

28 Rolando the Deacon, *Liber de Ordine Officorum*, fols. 20 verso–21 recto; as cited in Thompson, *Cities of God*, p. 320.

29 The ceremony began to the accompaniment of antiphons and hymns, as the bishop convened a procession outside the city walls. After a reading from Matthew's account of Christ's entry, the procession approached the city gates, chanting "Gloria, Laus et Honor." Once inside, the bishop blessed olive branches and flowers in the center of the piazza. The procession then proceeded through the cemetery, around the Baptistery, and to the Duomo. As it reached the closed western doors of the cathedral, the choir sang the responsory "Ingrediente," the bishop knocked on the doors with his crozier and they were flung open. To the ringing of bells, the procession entered for Mass. The service entailed the chanting of the Passion from Matthew's gospel in dialogue form – a dramatic performance that was a culmination to the Entrance ceremony. See also Robert Ousterhout, "Flexible Geography and Transportable Topography," in Bianca Kühnel, ed., *The Real and Ideal Jerusalem in Jewish, Christian and Islamic Art*, Jerusalem: The Hebrew University, 1997–98, p. 394; Michele Bacci, "Performed Topographies and Topomimetic Piety: Imaginative Sacred Spaces in Medieval Italy," in Alexei Lidov, ed., *Spatial Icons: Performativity in Byzantium and Medieval Russia*, Moscow: Indrik, 2011, pp. 101–18; and Michele Bacci, "The Pisan Camposanto and the Staging of Sanctity: An Introductory Essay," in Bacci et al, eds., *Journeys of the Soul*, pp. 7–39.

30 On burial practices generally, see Philippe Ariès, *The Hour of Our Death*, New York: Alfred A. Knopf, 1981, pp. 29–92; Donald Bullough, "Burial, Community and Belief in the Early Medieval West," in Patrick Wormald, ed., *Ideal and Reality in Frankish and Anglo-Saxon Society*, Oxford: Basil Blackwell, 1983, pp. 177–201.

31 On the cult of the saints, see Peter Brown, *The Cult of the Saints: Its Rise and Function in Latin Christianity*, Chicago: University of Chicago Press, 1981, especially pp. 69–85.

32 Mauro Ronzani, "Il 'cimitero della chiesa maggiore pisana': Gli aspetti istituzionali prima e dopo la nascita del Camposanto," *Annali della Scuola normale superiore di Pisa, Classe di lettere e filosofia*, ser. 3, vol. 18, no. 4, 1988, pp. 1665–90; Mauro Ronzani, "Dal 'cimitero della chiesa maggiore di Santa Maria' al Camposanto," in Baracchini and Castelnuovo, eds., *Il Camposanto di Pisa*, pp. 49–56.

33 Guillelmus Durandus, *Rationale Divinorum Officiorum* [1284], ed. A. Davril and T. M. Thibodeau, 2 vols. Turnout: Brepols, 1995–98, bk. 1, ch. 5. English translations have been published by Timothy Thibodeau, book 1, New York: Columbia University Press, 2007; books 2–3, Scranton: University of Scranton Press, 2010; books 4 and 5, Turnhout: Brepols, 2013–15; and by Janet Gentles, 6 vols., Bedford: Paschal Light, 2019.

34 On the legal status of cemeteries, see Elsa Marantonio Sguerzo, *Evoluzione storico-giuridica del istituto della sepoltura ecclesiastica*, Milan: Giuffrè, 1976, pp. 150–76; Thompson, *Cities of God*, pp. 408–10.

35 Thompson, *Cities of God*, p. 408.

36 On the origins and development of this legend, see Bacci, "The Pisan Camposanto and the Staging of Sanctity," in Bacci et al, eds., *Journeys of the Soul*, pp. 10–31; David Ganz, "*Campo santo, campi dipinti*: The Legend of the Earth and the Spaces of the Camposanto's Early Fresco Decoration," in Bacci et al, eds., *Journeys of the Soul*, pp. 65–89.

37 Ronzani, "Dal 'cimitero della chiesa maggiore di Santa Maria' al Camposanto," p. 52. Ronzani, *Un'idea trecentesca di cimitero*, p. 87, also notes references in wills from around 1400 to a "tabernacle" of the Santissima Trinità in the uncovered space of the Camposanto.

38 Paul Binski, *Medieval Death: Ritual and Representation*, Ithaca: Cornell University Press, 1996, pp. 73–74.

39 Ronzani, *Un'idea trecentesca di cimitero*, p. 87.

40 The following is a summary of the account in Thompson, *Cities of God*, pp. 381–417; but see also Richard Rutherford, *The Death of a Christian: The Rite of Funerals*, New York: Pueblo, 1980, pp. 56–69. Thompson has identified the *Liber de Ordine Officiorum* by Rolando the Deacon, in Bologna, Biblioteca Universitaria, ms. 1785, from the late twelfth century, as by a Pisan deacon. Durandus's *Rationale Divinorum Officiorum* from 1284 presents a detailed description and allegorical interpretation of the Office of the Dead; see bk. 7, ch. 35; trans. Gentles, vol. 6, pp. 108–25. Battistoni, *L'Opera del Duomo di Pisa*, p. 48, publishes a summary of expenses for the funeral of Michele Morrocchi, a potter who made construction materials and left a substantial bequest to the Opera in 1363, illuminating some aspects of the funeral rite in the fourteenth century. Expenses were for candles, the rental of a canon's cape in which to clothe the body during the ceremony, seven clerics from the cathedral chapter to carry the body to the Camposanto, celebration of the funerary Mass and memorial Masses, bunting for his house, and refreshment for those assisting in the ceremonies.

41 Durandus, *Rationale*, bk. 7, ch. 35, pt. 35; trans. Gentles, vol. 6, pp. 108–25; Luigi Simoneschi, *Ordinamenti suntuari pisani per gli anni 1350, 1386*, Pisa: Mariotti, 1889, p. 23; Catherine Kovesi Killerby, *Sumptuary Law in Italy 1200–1500*, Oxford: Clarendon Press, 2002, p. 74.

42 Simoneschi, *Ordinamenti suntuari pisani*, p. 28; Killerby, *Sumptuary Law in Italy*, p. 72.

43 Durandus, *Rationale*, bk. 7, ch. 35, pt. 35; trans. Gentles, vol. 6, pp. 119–20, interpretes this practice as a reminder of mortals' passage "from dust to dust," as does the twelfth-century Sicardo of Cremona, *Mitrale; sive De Officiis Ecclesiasticis Summa*, in *Patrologiae Latinae Cursus Completus*, ed. J. P. Migne, vol. 213, Paris: 1855, ch. 49, col. 427, in which the liturgy for All Saints is described; as cited in Thompson, *Cities of God*, 392.

44 While knights, professors, lawyers, and clerics might be buried in rich robes, laypersons were usually sewn into shrouds, their clothes given to the church. Penitents and confraternity members were buried in the vestments of their respective sodalities; Thompson, *Cities of God*, pp. 396–97. Durandus, *Rationale*, bk. 7, ch. 35, pt. 40; trans. Gentles, p.122, deplored the Italian practice of burying the lay deceased in everyday clothes.

45 Durandus, *Rationale*, bk. 7, ch. 35, pt. 37; trans. Gentles, p. 121.

46 Bonaini, *Statuti inediti* vol. 2, p. 350; Killerby, *Sumptuary Law in Italy*, pp. 72–74, 106–7; Thompson, *Cities of God*, p. 403.

47 In Pisa, the procession was limited to the neighborhood, forbidding a citywide procession; Bonaini, *Statuti inediti*, vol. 2, p. 350; Thompson, *Cities of God*, p. 404.

48 Simoneschi, *Ordinamenti suntuari pisani*, p. 28; Killerby, *Sumptuary Law in Italy*, p. 72.

49 The Pisan statues of 1313 limited the number of accompanying priests to ten; Bonaini, *Statuti inediti*, vol. 2, p. 350; Thompson, *Cities of God*, p. 399.

50 Bonaini, *Statuti inediti*, vol. 2, pp. 519, 627; Thompson, *Cities of God*, p. 399. The 1350 sumptuary law prohibited the *Podestà*, *Capitano del Popolo*, and any member of their *famiglie* from attending funerals, except when the deceased was a foreigner, a communal official, or one of the *Anziani*; Simoneschi, *Ordinamenti suntuari pisani*, p. 29; Killerby, *Sumptuary Law in Italy*, p. 76.

51 On the history of the Office of the Dead and its variations, see Knud Ottosen, *The Responsories and Versicles of the Latin Office of the Dead*, Aarhus: Aarhus University Press, 1993, pp. 31–49.

52 Roger S. Wieck, "The Death Desired: Books of Hours and the Medieval Funeral," in Edelgard DuBruck and Barbara Gusick, eds., *Death and Dying in the Middle Ages*, New York: Peter Lang, 1999, pp. 431–77.

53 As described by Durandus, *Rationale*, bk. 7, ch. 35; trans. Gentles, vol. 6, pp. 108–25.

54 Simoneschi, *Ordinamenti suntuari pisani*, p. 26; Killerby, *Sumptuary Law in Italy*, p. 78.

55 Durandus, *Rationale*, bk. 7, ch. 35, pts. 2 and 20; trans. Gentles, pp. 108–9, 113.

56 Giuseppe Sainati, *Diario Sacro Pisano*, 2nd ed., Siena: Editrice S. Bernardino, 1886, pp. 196–97; see also Giuseppe Martini, *Theatrum Basilicae Pisanae*, 2nd ed., Rome: Antonii de Rubeis, 1728, p. 97.

57 Samuel K. Cohn Jr., *The Cult of Remembrance and the Black Death*, Baltimore: Johns Hopkins University Press, 1992; Eleonora Rava, *"Volens in testamento vivere": Testamenti a Pisa, 1240–1320*, Rome: Istituto storico italiano per il Medioevo, 2016.

58 Cohn, *The Cult of Remembrance*, pp. 13–14; for example, Bonaini, *Statuti inediti*, vol. 2, pp. 756–88; as cited in Thompson, *Cities of God*, p. 386.

59 For this and the following Thompson, *Cities of God*, pp. 123–27; and Cohn, *The Cult of Remembrance*, pp. 122–27. Cohn's survey of wills includes that of a certain Lazarus who in 1264 orchestrated each stage of his funeral and provided funds for the clergy performing the offices at altars on the day of death, for the shroud, for bread to be distributed to the poor, and for his burial. Seven and thirty days after his death, six lire were allotted for bread to be distributed to clerics and the poor for the health of his soul. On the anniversary of his death, a further two lire's worth of bread were to be given to the poor.

60 Thompson, *Cities of God*, p. 397.

61 Caleca, "Costruzione e decorazione," pp. 16–17, suggests sources in medieval domestic structures, as well as the arcaded tombs on the façade of Santa Maria Novella in Florence.

62 Neta B. Bodner, "Earth from Jerusalem in the Pisan Camposanto," in Renana Bartal et al., eds., *Between Jerusalem and Europe: Essays in Honour of Bianca Kühnel*, Leiden: Brill, 2015, pp. 74–93; Neta B. Bodner, "The Camposanto, Pisan Medieval Architecture, and Military Commemoration," in Bacci et al, eds., *Journeys of the Soul*, pp. 41–64.

63 Howard Colvin, *Architecture and the After-Life*, New Haven and London: Yale University Press, 1991, pp. 124–32, 364–66.

64 Fulvia Donati and M. Cecilia Parra, "Pisa e il reimpiego 'laico': La nobilità di sangue e d'ingegno, e la potenza economica," in Bernard Andreae and Salvatore Settis, eds., *Colloquio sul reimpiego dei sarcofagi romani nel medioevo*, Marburg: Verlag des Kunstgeschichtlichen Seminars, 1984, pp. 103–32. For the sarcophagus of Beatrice of Tuscany, see Paolo Enrico Arias, Emilio Cristiani, and Emilio Gabba, *Camposanto Monumentale di Pisa: Le Antichità*, Pisa: Pacini Editore, 1977, pp. 133–35; and Banti, *Le*

Iscrizioni delle tombe terragne, p. 272, no. 27. Tolaini has proposed that the sarcophagai were removed from the cathedral only in the early fifteenth century; see Emilio Tolaini, "Quando i sarcofagi entrarono in Camposanto," *Critica d'arte*, vol. 33/34, 2008, pp. 51–56. For the inscriptions generally, see Ottavio Bani, "Le iscrizioni della cattedrale," in Garzella et al., eds., *La Cattedrale di Pisa*, pp. 111–19.

65 Fulvia Donati, "Il reimpiego dei sarcofagi; profilo di una collezione," in Baracchini and Castelnuovo, eds., *Il Camposanto di Pisa*, pp. 69–96.

66 Donati, "Il reimpiego dei sarcofagi," pp. 93–96, for the inscriptions.

67 Roberto Paolo Ciardi, "'Quest'insigne dormentorio de' morti': Chiesa, cimitero, museo," in Baracchini and Castelnuovo, eds., *Il Camposanto di Pisa*, pp. 57–68.

68 Binski, *Medieval Death*, pp. 89–90.

69 Banti, *Le Iscrizioni delle tombe terragne*.

70 Ariès, *The Hour of Our Death*, p. 52.

71 Ronzani, *Un'idea trecentesca di cimitero*, pp. 25–29. Durandus's *Rationale* likened the practice of celebrating the Office of the Dead for three days to the Trinity: since the dead sinned in thought, word, and deed, the Trinity forgave their sins; Durandus, *Rationale*, bk. 7, ch. 35, pt. 5; trans. Gentles, vol. 6, p. 109.

72 Archivio di Stato, Pisa (ASPi), Opera del Duomo, 77, cc. 29 recto, 37 verso, 40 recto; Leopoldo Tanfani-Centofanti, *Notizie di artisti tratte dai documenti pisani*, Pisa, 1897, pp. 492–93; Caleca, "Costruzione e decorazione," pp. 16 and 41, note 37; Ronzani, *Un'idea trecentesca di cimitero*, p. 15. For a brief history of the Opera del Duomo, see Mauro Ronzani, "L'Opera del Duomo nel medioevo," in Garzella et al., eds., *La Cattedrale di Pisa*, pp. 37–44.

73 "Fecie Fare l'Eclesia di Chanpo Sancto da L'archoara in su."

74 "Cimiterii sive mortuarii et cappelle sive ecclesie dicti mortuarii sive cimiterii," ASP, Dipl. Opera della Primaziale, 9 March 1319; as cited in Ronzani, *Un'idea trecentesca di cimitero*, pp. 36–37.

75 For the history of tomb forms, see Erwin Panofsky, *Tomb Sculpture: Four Lectures on Its Changing Aspects from Ancient Egypt to Bernini*, H. W. Janson, ed., New York: Harry N. Abrams, n.d; on papal tombs, see Julian Gardner, *The Tomb and the Tiara: Curial Tomb Sculpture in Rome and Avignon in the Later Middle Ages*, Oxford: Clarendon Press, 1992.

76 The testament of the *operaio* Giovanni Rosso (d. 1333) refers to an altar dedicated to Ognissanti. In 1349, construction costs for an altar dedicated to the Trinity in fulfillment of testamentary bequests of the *operaio* Giovanni Scorcialupi (d. 1337) are also recorded. Supino, *Il Camposanto di Pisa*, p. 17; Caleca "Costruzione e decorazione," pp. 20–21; Ronzani, *Un'idea trecentesca di cimitero*, pp. 46–48. References to a common tomb for the *operai* del Duomo near the altar of Ognissanti occur in later testaments: in 1374 and 1379 in the testaments of Piero da Luciana e Piero del fu Iacopo Sampante; in 1390 in the testament of Parasone Grasso and in the 1450 will of Giuliano di Colino Scarsi; Ronzani, *Un'idea trecentesca di cimitero*, p. 48, nn. 118–19.

77 Payments and receipts for this purpose are recorded from 1299 to 1346 in ASPi, Opera del Duomo, 77, cc. 3 verso, 41 recto; 78,1 verso, 28 recto; 79, 2 recto; 81, c. 2 recto; 86, c. 9 verso; 89, c. 25 recto; 486, c. 4 recto; 487, c. 3 verso; Ronzani, *Un'idea trecentesca di cimitero*, pp. 29–30.

78 Ciardi, "Quest'insigne dormentorio de' morti," in Baracchini and Castelnuovo, eds., *Il Camposanto di Pisa*, p. 58; Ronzani, *Un'idea trecentesca di cimitero*, p. 64, note 169.

79 Sainati, *Diario Sacro Pisano*, pp. 195–97. On the evening of All Saints, the archbishop celebrated Vespers in the Camposanto, while the next day, after Mass in the Duomo, the archbishop, with other priests, processed to the cemetery, where they recited Nocturnes, blessed the tombs, chanted a requiem Mass, and performed Absolution.

80 Fulvia Donati, "Storia della Collezione; Raccolta delle opera antiche," in Salvatore Settis, ed., *Camposanto Monumentale di Pisa: Le Antichità*, vol. 2, Modena: Edizioni Panini, 1984, p. 12, estimates the number of sarcofagi at this time at thirty-six, thirty-seven with the

addition of that of Matilde of Canossa, removed to the Camposanto in 1303. See, however, Tolaini, "Quando i sarcofagi entrarono in Camposanto," pp. 51–56.

81 Fulvia Donati, "Il reimpiego dei sarcofagi," p. 79; Donati and Parra, "Pisa e il reimpiego 'laico,'" p. 112. One of the earliest of these burials is that of Giovanni Parghia degli Antelminelli, an exile from Lucca, whose testament of 1310 requested burial in the Camposanto "in lavello meo quod ibi haebo"; Ronzani, *Un'idea trecentesca di cimitero*, pp. 33–34. The ancient sarcophagus, oval in form, to which a coat of arms and contemporary inscription were added, still exists in the Camposanto; Arias et al., *Le Antichità*, p. 160, C7 int.

82 An example is the sarcophagus signed by Biduinus, or that of the noble Da Caprona family from the fourteenth century; Arias et al., *Le Antichità*, p. 112, A22 int; 172, D1 int; Donati and Parra, "Pisa e il reimpiego 'laico,'" p. 117, note 37.

83 Ronzani, *Un'idea trecentesca di cimitero*, p. 46; Rava, *"Volens in testamento vivere,"* pp. 107–8, found the Camposanto named as place of burial in only seven wills in her sample, all written by the same notary between 1309 and 1315.

84 Ciardi, "'Quest'insigne dormentorio de' morti," p. 63.

85 Banti, *Le Iscrizioni delle tombe terragne*, pp. 158–59, no. 366; Giovanni Rosso was *operaio* from 1319 to 1333.

86 Banti, *Le Iscrizioni delle tombe terragne*, p. 157, no. 363.

87 Banti, *Le Iscrizioni delle tombe terragne*, respectively p. 159, nos. 368–69; p. 160, no. 370. Ronzani, *Un'idea trecentesca di cimitero*, p. 48, note 120, suggests this arrangement of tombs may be the result of a later restoration.

88 Ronzani, *Un'idea trecentesca di cimitero*, p. 48.

89 Ronzani, *Un'idea trecentesca di cimitero*, pp. 46–47, 111–40. The flagellant company of San Giovanni Evangelista di Porta della Pace had its headquarters in Santa Caterina; the historical evidence for Frate Giovanni as founder of this sodality is lacking, even if it is probable; see Ronzani, *Un'idea trecentesca di cimitero*, p. 122.

90 Banti, *Le Iscrizioni delle tombe terragne*, p. 263, no. 1; see also Arias et al., *Le Antichità*, pp. 68–69, A17 est.

91 Banti, *Le Iscrizioni delle tombe terragne*, pp. 65–66, no. 54. The south corridor included tombs for the fourteenth-century *disciplinati* confraternities dedicated to Saint Rainerius, the Holy Cross, Saint Margaret, and Pope Gregory; Banti, *Le Iscrizioni delle tombe terragne*, p. 57, no. 17; p. 65, nos. 51, 52; p. 68, no. 63. Ronzani, *Un'idea trecentesca di cimitero*, p. 136, notes that the tombs for these confraternities cannot be documented before 1360–70; but the practice could have begun in the first half of the Trecento.

92 Ronzani, *Un'idea trecentesca di cimitero*, pp. 121–25, documents devotion to Frate Giovanni in several testaments of the early fourteenth century.

93 Chiara Frugoni, "Altri luoghi, cercandi il paradiso," *Annali della Scuola Normale Superiore di Pisa, Classe di Lettere e Filosofia*, 3. Ser. vol. 18, 1988, p. 1639. When the mural was detached from the wall, several layers of plaster indicated previous alterations. The original layer perhaps contained the painted effigy of the saint within the wooden baldacchino, while a second layer included the effigy flanked by two penitents dressed in white in the act of self-flagellation. The date of this middle layer is unknown. Ronzani, *Un'idea trecentesca di cimitero*, pp. 137–39, suggests that it was painted in the 1340s, when he sees a revival of the *disciplinati* companies. These figures were altered again about 1386, when the artist Antonio Veneziano repainted the lacuna resulting from the removal of the baldacchino and substituted for the two *flagellants* two angels with censers. In the process of detachment, the decorative border and figures, with the exception of the tips of the angels, were lost; Czarnecki, "Antonio Veneziano," pp. 70–71.

94 Caleca, "Costruzione e decorazione," pp. 25, 29; Ronzani, *Un'idea trecentesca di cimitero*, p. 115, note 19. The citation, dated 8 November 1343, is from ASPi, Opera del Duomo 87, c. 5 verso, in which the amount of one lira is paid to the *operaio* Giovanni Cocchi by "Leone maestro di legname e Otto di Cione da Righoli … pro moratura che

l'operai fe a l'uscio di Canposanto unde intravano li Batuti a lato a lo Canposanto soprascripto."

95 These include tombs of the noble Malcondime, Ripafratta, and Scorcialupi families, as well as of the sons of the non-noble Ser Leopardi del Fornario and of the heirs of the "civis pisani" Casini Benini; Banti, *Le Iscrizioni delle tombe terragne*, respectively p. 53, no. 2; p. 54, no. 8, no. 5, no. 6; p. 59, no. 28. See also Emilio Cristiani, *Nobilità e popolo nel comune di Pisa*, Naples: Istituto italiano per gli studi storici, 1962, pp. 416–17, 426, 432.

96 Frugoni, "Altri luoghi, cercandi il paradiso," p. 1564; Lina Bolzoni, "La predica dipinta: Gli affreschi del 'Trionfo della Morte' e la predicazione domenicana," in Baracchini and Castelnuovo, eds., *Il Camposanto di Pisa*, pp. 97–114. More generally, Gianfranco Fioravanti, "Il convento e lo studium domenicano di Santa Caterina," in Lucia Battaglia Ricci et al., eds., *Pisa crocevia di uomini, lingue e culture: L'età medievale*, Rome: ARACNE, 2009, pp. 81–95.

97 Salomone Morpurgo, "Le epigrafi volgari in rima del 'Trionfo della Morte' del 'Giudizio Universale e Inferno' e degli 'Anacoreti' nel Camposanto di Pisa," *L'arte*, vol. 2, 1899, pp. 51–87.

98 Domenico Cavalca, *Le Vite de' S.S. Padri*, ed. Carmelina Naselli, Turin: Unione Tipografico-Editrice Torinese, 1926.

99 Domenico Cavalca, *Volgarizzamento delle vite de' S.S. Padri*, Milan: Tipografia di Gio. Silvestri, 1853, vol. 6, p. 19 "Da ogni cosa sono fuori; solo speranza di Dio rimane. In loro è vera castità e umilità, e in loro non è altro pensiero nè altra battaglia, se non come possono digiunare e fare sacrificio a Dio."

100 For much of the following discussion, I am indebted to Alison Goddard Elliot, *Roads to Paradise: Reading the Lives of the Early Saints*, Hanover: University Press of New England, 1987, especially pp. 59–62, 104–80; in addition, Alessandra Malquori, "L'immagine della morte e l'edificazione attraverso l'immagine nelle *Storie degli anacoreti* del Camposanto di Pisa," in Bacci et al, eds., *Journeys of the Soul*, pp. 143–63.

101 Elliot, *Roads to Paradise*, pp. 90–91; Frugoni, "Altri luoghi, cercandi il paradiso," pp. 1618–24.

102 Cavalca, *Le Vite de' S.S. Padri*, pp. 175–77.

103 Cavalca, *Le Vite de' S.S. Padri*, pp. 7–11.

104 Cavalca, *Le Vite de' S.S. Padri*, pp. 280–81.

105 Cavalca, *Le Vite de' S.S. Padri*, pp. 105–7.

106 Cavalca, *Volgarizzamento delle vite de' S.S. Padri*, vol. 3, pp. 154–55.

107 Cavalca, *Le Vite de' S.S. Padri*, pp. 7, 18; Cavalca, *Volgarizzamento delle Vite de' S.S. Padri*, vol. 1, p. 16; vol. 6, p. 14.

108 Cavalca, *Le Vite de' S.S. Padri*, p. 283.

109 Cavalca, *Volgarizzamento delle Vite de' S.S. Padri*, vol. 3, p. 152.

110 Elliot, *Roads to Paradise*, p. 207; Cavalca, *Volgarizzamento delle Vite de' S.S. Padri*, p. 153.

111 Cavalca, *Le Vite de' S.S. Padri*, p. 6.

112 Elliot, *Roads to Paradise*, pp. 144–67.

113 Cavalca, *Volgarizzamento delle Vite de' S.S. Padri*, vol. 6, pp. 25–26.

114 Cavalca, *Vite de' S.S. Padri*, 17; Cavalca, *Volgarizzamento delle Vite de' S.S. Padri*, vol. 3, p. 186.

115 Cavalca, *Vite de' S.S. Padri*, p. 10.

116 Morpurgo, "Le epigrafi volgari in rima," p. 71; Cavalca, *Vite de' S.S. Padri*, p. 12.

117 Cavalca, *Vite de' S.S. Padri*, p. 15: "Ho veduto Elia, ho veduto Giovanni Battista nel diserto, e veramente ho veduto Paolo in paradise."

118 Cavalca, *Volgarizzamento delle Vite de' S.S. Padri*, vol. 6, p. 25.

119 Cavalca, *Volgarizzamento delle Vite de' S.S. Padri*, p. 153; Morpurgo, "Le epigrafi volgari in rima," p. 75: "Questo è Sancto Machario romano, il quale fece penitensia grandissimo tempo nel diserto, ch'è presso al Paradiso dilisiano a venti miglia [circon]dandolo senpre due leoni."

120 Morpurgo, "Le epigrafi volgari in rima," p. 75.
121 Cavalca, *Vite de' S.S. Padri*, p. 14.
122 See Saint Paphnuntius's life of Saint Onofrio in Cavalca, *Volgarizzamento delle Vite de' S.S. Padri*, vol. 6, pp. 13–30.
123 Cavalca, *Le Vite de' S.S. Padri*, pp. 289–93.
124 Cavalca, *Le Vite de' S.S. Padri*, p. 17.
125 Cavalca, *Volgarizzamento delle Vite de' S.S. Padri*, vol. 6, pp. 25–26.
126 Cavalca, *Le Vite de' S.S. Padri*, p. 18: "Paulo, sepulto vilmente in terra, risusciterà con gloria; voi coi sepolcri de' marmi ed esquisiti ed aurati risusciterete a pena."
127 Cavalca, *Volgarizzamento delle Vite de' S.S. Padri*, vol. 3, p. 159.
128 Morpurgo, "Le epigrafi volgari in rima," p. 75; Cavalca, *Le Vite de' S.S. Padri*, p. 139.
129 Morpurgo "Le epigrafi volgari," p. 78: "Seguite adunque la lor sancta vita/ Per far del campo una bella partita."
130 Antonio Caleca, "I Novissimi, le storie dei santi Padri e le storie evangeliche di Bonamico Buffalmacco," in Enzo Carli, ed., *Pisa – Museo delle sinopie del Camposanto Monumentale*, Pisa: Opera della Primaziale Pisana, 1979, p. 55; Frugoni, "Altri luoghi, cercandi il paradiso," pp. 1634–38; and Ronzani, *Un'idea trecentesca di cimitero*, pp. 122, 130–34. Frugoni and Ronzani have noted the efforts in 1331 on the part of Bonaggiunta da Calcinaia, the vicar of archbishop Poli, to formalize the status of the eremetic community of Giovanni "Soldato" vis-à-vis the church hierarchy by emphasizing their status as an eremetical group, not a flagellant sodality. This characterization of Giovanni and his adherents is more in keeping with the piety of the desert fathers of the *Vite de' Santi Padri* and depicted in the mural. It also conforms to widespread efforts to bring flagellant groups under the aegis of the established church, especially the mendicant orders; for which, see Giovanna Casagrande, *Religiosità penitenziale e città al tempo dei comuni*, Rome: Istituto Stoico dei Cappuccini, 1995, pp. 127–38.
131 See Frugoni, "Altri luoghi, cercandi il paradiso," pp. 1616–17, 1633, for the view that the Church played an instrumental role in the devout's attainment of salvation. The episode of Saint Macarius's conversation with the skull is not included in published editions of Cavalca, but it is found in manuscript copies and in Jacopo Passavanti, *Lo Specchio di Vera Penitenza*, Florence: P. Fraticelli, 1843, vol. 2, p. 43; and *The Golden Legend* of Jacobus de Voragine, trans. William Ryan, Princeton: Princeton University Press, 1993, vol. 1, p. 90.
132 Caleca, "Costruzione e decoratione," p. 25.
133 Frugoni, "Altri luoghi, cercandi il paradiso," p. 1616.
134 Morpurgo, "Le epigrafi volgari," pp. 54–56.
135 Durandus, *Rationale*, bk. 1, ch. 1, pts. 16, 28; trans. Thibodeau, pp. 16, 19–20.
136 Frugoni, "Altri luoghi, cercandi il paradiso," pp. 1614–15.
137 See Samuel K. Cohn, Jr., "Collective Amnesia: Family, Memory and the Mendicants," in Giovanni Ciappelli and Patricia Rubin, eds., *Art, Memory and Family in Renaissance Florence*, Cambridge: Cambridge University Press, 2000, pp. 277–80.
138 "The Temple represents the Church triumphant, while the cloister signifies the celestial paradise where there will be one heart in the love and will of God." Durandus, *Rationale*, bk. 1, ch. 1, pt. 42; trans. Thibodeau, p. 22. See also Paul Meyvaert, "The Medieval Monastic Claustrum," *Gesta*, vol. 12, 1973, pp. 53–59; and Christoph Auffarth, "Paradise Now – but for the Wall between: Some Remarks on Paradise in the Middle Ages," in Gerard Luttikhuizen, ed., *Paradise Interpreted; Representations of Biblical Paradise in Judaism and Christianity*, Boston: Brill, 1999, pp. 168–79.
139 Lawrence Besserman, *The Legend of Job in the Middle Ages*, Cambridge, MA: Harvard University Press, 1979, pp. 29–30.
140 Ottosen, *The Responsories and Versicles of the Latin Office of the Dead*, pp. 42–49; Besserman, *The Legend of Job*, pp. 73, 94, 101–3.
141 Besserman, *The Legend of Job* pp. 59–64. Selected passages from the first seven chapters of Job were also read in the lessons for Mass during the first two weeks of September.

142 Supino, *Il Camposanto*, pp. 168–76; Mario Bucci and Licia Bertolini, "Gli affreschi, le sinopie," in Piero Sanpaolesi et al., eds., *Camposanto Monumentale di Pisa*, Pisa: Opera della Primaziale Pisana, 1960, pp. 93–102; Ladis, *Taddeo Gaddi*, pp. 247–50; Edith Tomasberger, "Beobachtungen über die Fresken der Hiobsgeschichte im Camposanto," *Storia dell'arte*, vol. 62, 1988, pp. 25–27; Caleca, "Costruzione e decorazione," pp. 27–29; Burresi, ed., *Affreschi medievali a Pisa*, pp. 103–7.

143 See G. Von der Osten, "Job and Christ: The Development of a Devotional Image," *Journal of the Warburg and Courtauld Institutes*, vol. 16, 1953, pp. 153–58.

144 Supino, *Il Camposanto*, p. 175.

145 Ottosen, *The Responsories and Versicles of the Latin Office of the Dead*, pp. 53–54; Besserman, *The Legend of Job*, pp. 59–64.

146 Ottosen, *The Responsories and Versicles of the Latin Office of the Dead*, p. 53.

147 Besserman, *The Legend of Job*, p. 64.

148 Giovanni Boccaccio, *The Decameron*, trans. Richard Aldington, New York: Garden City, 1930, pp. 5–6.

149 Ronzani, *Un'idea trecentesca di cimitero*, pp. 75–76; Rava, *"Volens in testamento vivere,"* pp. 104–7, found 26 percent of testators in her sample wished to be buried in the cathedral.

150 Caleca, "Costruzione e decorazione," pp. 44–45, note 125, provides the transcription from ASPi, Opera del Duomo, 2, cc. 18 verso–19 recto; and Comune A, 197, cc. 118 recto–119 recto: "ne usus laudabilis locusque devotionis cimiterii seu mortuarii Campi Sancti in abusum seu desuetudinem valeat devenire salubriter provideant, quod nulla persona maschulus vel femina, cuiuscumque status vel (struck out; illegible) condiciojnis existat, sepeliri possit vel valeat in suprascripta pisana maiori ecclesia, in aliquo monumento quod fieret sub sacrato ipsius ecclesie vel super astracum supradictum vel in muris seu parietibus ipsius ecclesie intus vel extra ecclesiam, seu super gradibus ipsius eccelsie; et Operarius dicte ecclesie qui nunc est et pro tempore fuerit non possit nec ei liceat alicui concedere vel permictere directe vel per obliquum aliqua cadavera sepeliri seu poni in ecclesia supradicta vel super astracum marmoris sive in muris vel parietibus Campi Sancti." Ronzani, *Un'idea trecentesca di cimitero*, p. 59, note 152, suggests that the scribe mistakenly wrote *Campi Sancti* instead of *ecclesie* (cathedral); but there is no reason not to accept the passage as written. Both entries, in the Opera del Duomo and the Comune A ledgers, and the marginal gloss repeat the information, and there is no evidence of hesitation or correction in the writing. The language of the entries is confusing; but as discussed above, the Camposanto was frequently referred to as a church in the early documents. As we shall see, the prohibition against lavish burial was not enforced: Ronzani, *Un'idea trecentesca di cimitero*, p. 74, has signaled continued construction of altars and tombs in the Duomo in the late 1350s.

151 ASPi, Comune A 197, c. 119 recto; Caleca, "Costruzione e decorazione," p. 45, note 125. Battistoni, *L'Opera del Duomo di Pisa*, p. 64, note 4, cites payments in 1472 and 1480 for the restoration of murals that had been damaged by youths.

152 Caleca, "Costruzione e decorazione," p. 45, note 129; ASPi, Opera del Duomo, 90, cc. 60 recto, 111 verso.

153 Caleca, "Costruzione e decorazione," p. 45, note 132; Ronzani, *Un'idea trecentesca di cimitero*, pp. 64–67.

154 ASPi, Comune A, no. 197, c. 120 recto; Supino, *Il Camposanto*, p. 7; Ronzani, *Un'idea trecentesca di cimitero*, p. 64.

155 Ronzani, *Un'idea trecentesca di cimitero*, p. 71, from ASPi, Comune A, no. 121, cc. 89 recto–verso.

156 See Caleca's synopsis of the documentation, "Costruzione e decorazione," p. 46, note 144. The *Anziani* also in 1388 allowed Parasone Grasso, then *operaio* del Duomo, to secure a loan of 800 florins for the completion of work in the Camposanto; and in 1393, the *operaio* Giovanni Macigna a loan of up to 2,000 florins to complete the work on various buildings of the Opera; ASPi, Deliberzioni e Partiti del Comune riguardanti l'Opera, no. 1, as cited in Supino, *Il Camposanto*, pp. 7–8.

157 Caleca, "Costruzione e decorazione," p. 31.

158 Michele Luzzati, "Il sepolcro del maestro medico Ligio Ammannati nel Camposanto pisano," *Rassegna periodico culturale e di informazione*, vol. 5, 1969, nos. 6–8, pp. 31–38. The execution document is in Florence, ASF, Notarile Antecosimiano 12,208 (1359–60), unnumbered folios. A document recording the sale of property that was intended to endow the chapel is dated 17 August 1359 and provides further details. A large altarpiece for the chapel was commissioned 22 July 1359, in which fifteen figures were to be depicted, painted and ornamented with excellent colors and gold over the entire surface and of good ultramarine blue. The artist, Giovanni del Gese, was to have between thirty and thirty-five florins, depending on an appraisal. There is no indication that the painting was executed. The tomb, which survives and has been returned to its original location in the chapel, was commissioned 8 June 1359 from four Pisan stoneworkers employed in the Opera del workshops: Francesco di Lippo, Colo Mucido, Puccio di Landuccio, and Matteo di Tone; Puccio would be later *capomaestro* of the Opera del Duomo from 1369–89. It was to cost 200 florins, the last payment of which was made 17 May 1360.

159 Ronzani, *Un'idea trecentesca di cimitero*, p. 73, note 210.

160 Cohn, *The Cult of Remembrance and the Black Death*, pp. 112–14, 127, notes that Pisan testamentary practices list expenses for the funeral and burial but that they become less specific over time, especially after 1362. Yet testators increasingly specify the location of the bodily remains and memorialize them with tangible markers such as tombstones.

161 See the testaments cited by Cohn, *The Cult of Remembrance and the Black Death*, pp. 123–27; Mauro Ronzani, "Chiesa e clero nella Pisa del Trecento attraverso la biografia di un protagonista: attività ecclesiastica, affari finanziari e vita privata di Bonaggiunta da Calcinaia (1297–1362)," in *Mediterraneo, Mezzogiorno, Europa*, vol. 2, 2004, pp. 926–28, 956–58; and Battistoni, *L'Opera del Duomo di Pisa*, p. 64. Rava, *"Volens in testamento vivere,"* pp. 105, 176–78, found in the earlier period that while only between 2–6 percent of testators wished to be buried in the churches of the mendicant orders, of the monetary bequests, 27 percent went to San Francesco and 28 percent to Santa Caterina.

162 Anita Moskowitz, *The Sculpture of Andrea and Nino Pisano*, Cambridge: Cambridge University Press, 1986, pp. 80–90.

163 Ciardi, "'Quest'insigne dormentorio de' morti," p. 63; Banti, *Le Iscrizioni delle tombe terragne*, pp. 38–39. Examples are the tomb slab of Simone Trincalossi de Bocci, from the mid-fourteenth century, Banti, p. 60, no. 32; Ser Coli di Beneveni de Scorno, from the beginning of the fifteenth century, Banti, p. 91, no. 156, Piero di Gaetani, from 1362 to 1363, Banti, p. 78, no. 102, and Guelfo Gualterotti, from 1375, Banti, p. 156, no. 361. For burials in the church of Santa Caterina, see Joanna Cannon, *Religious Povety, Visual Riches: Art in the Dominican Churches of Central Italy in the Thirteenth and Fourteenth Centuries*, New Haven and London: Yale University Press, 2013, pp. 227–49. Mauro Ronzani and Elisabetta Salvadori note the burial in Santa Caterina in 1363 of the commander of the Pisan army in an elaborate funeral organized and financed by the commune; "I frati Domenicani in Santa Caterina dalle origini al 1406," in Marco Collareta, ed., *Santa Caterina d'Alessandria a Pisa*, Pisa: Pacini Editore, 2019, p. 37.

164 Banti, *Le Iscrizioni delle tombe terragne*, p. 96, no. 174: "Sepulcrum Presbiteri Tomasi Francisci Capellani Pisane Maioris Ecclesie et Suorum" (acquired 31 May 1374, cf. ASPi, Opera del Duomo 99, c. 33 verso).

165 Marco Paoli, "Un aspetto poco noto della scultura trecentesca pisana: La lapide sepolcrale con ritratto," *Antichità viva*, vol. 21, nos. 5–6, 1982, pp. 38–47. For the tomb slab of Magister Antonio di Santopietro, see Banti, *Le Iscrizioni delle tombe terragne*, p. 158, no. 364.

166 Cohn, "Collective Amnesia," p. 277.

167 Ronzani, *Un'idea trecentesca di cimitero*, pp. 74–75, note 213.

168 Vigo, *Una festa popolare a Pisa*, pp. 85–88; Ronzani, *Un'idea trecentesca di cimitero*, p. 75, notes 215–16.

169 Battistoni, *L'Opera del Duomo di Pisa*, pp. 64–66.

170 See also Ciardi, "Quest'insigne dormentorio de' morti," p. 64.
171 Banti, *Le Iscrizioni delle tombe terragne*, p. 90, no. 153: Sepulcrum Ser Pieri Notarii Condam Ser Iohannis Notarii de Ghessano" (acquired in 1377; ASPi, Opera del Duomo 102, 23 verso); see also the collective tomb of the tailors, p. 98, no. 183: "Sepulcrum Universitatis sutorum Pisane civitatis" dated 1377.
172 Banti, *Le Iscrizioni delle tombe terragne*, p. 85, no. 131: "Sepulcrum Antone di Mighele Tintore da Pedone et Rede Suorum," p. 96, no. 175: Sepolcro Ambrogio di Vanni Fornaio Herede Suorum (acquired 1 August 1374; ASPi, Opera del Duomo 101, c. 2 verso).
173 Banti, *Le Iscrizioni delle tombe terragne*, p. 73, no. 79.
174 Banti, *Le Iscrizioni delle tombe terragne*, p. 93, no. 165: "Hic Iacet Dominus bernardus Ladom Catalano de civitate maioricam" (acquired 3 May 1382; ASPi, Opera del Duomo 106, c. 20 recto).
175 Banti, *Le Iscrizioni delle tombe terragne*, respectively, p. 65, no. 51; no. 52 (acquired 15 November 1373; ASPi, Opera del Duomo, 99, c. 11 recto); p. 68, no. 63.
176 Ronzani, *Un'idea trecentesca di cimitero*, p. 74–76.
177 Supino, *Il Camposanto*, p. 37.
178 Supino, *Il Camposanto*, p. 39.
179 Tripps, *Tendencies of Gothic in Florence*, p. 46, note 155.
180 Francesco Bonaini, "Memorie inedite intorno alla vita e ai dipinti di Francesco Traini e ad altre opere di disegno dei secoli XI, XIV, e XV," in *Annali delle università toscane*, vol. 1, part 1, 1846, p. 569, first published the document, many times reprinted, as in Tripps, *Tendencies of Gothic in Florence*, p. 13; Patrizia Castelli, "Ranieri da cantore a santo taumaturgo: agiografia e immagini di propaganda civica e religiosa nella città di Pisa (secoli XII–XIV)," in Patrizia Castelli and Maria Luisa Ceccarelli Lemut, eds., *L'invenzione di Ranieri il taumaturgo tra XII e XIV secolo: agiografia ed immagini*, Pisa: Pacini Editore, 2013, p. 157, no. 4. Gambacorta's effort to promote the cult of additional civic saints is noted by Cecilia Iannella, "Pietro Gambacorta and the City of Pisa (1369–92)," in Daniel Bornstein et al., eds., *Languages of Power in Italy (1300–1600)*, Turnhout: Brepols, 2017, pp. 161–76.
181 Franca Rangone in *Dizionario Biografico degli italiani*, vol. 52, 1999, pp. 19–22.
182 Diane Cole Ahl, "Introduction," and Gail Solberg, "Pisa as a Center of Tuscan Painting in the 1390s: The Case of Tadddeo di Bartolo," *Le arti a Pisa nel primo Rinascimento, Predella Monografie*, vols. 13–14, 2016, pp. 7–16 and 17–35. See also Marco Collareta, "Art in Pisa in the Middle Ages," in Karen Rose Mathews et al., eds., *A Companion to Medieval Pisa*, Leiden: Brill, 2022, pp. 435–55.
183 Cecilia Iannella, "Il ciclo pittorico di San Ranieri in Camposanto nel contesto storico pisano," in Patrizia Castelli and Maria Luisa Ceccarelli Lemut, eds., *Intercessor Rainerius ad Patrem: Il santo di una città marinara del XII secolo*, Pisa: Pacini Editore, 2011, p. 177; Castelli, "Ranieri da cantore a santo taumatugo," pp. 74–78.
184 Tripps, *Tendencies of Gothic in Florence*, pp. 258–59.
185 Ann Roberrts, *Dominican Women and Renaissance Art: The Convent of San Domenico of Pisa*, Aldershot: Ashgate, 2008, pp. 9–13.
186 Castelli, "Ranieri da cantore a santo taumatugo," pp. 72–94.
187 Giorgio Vasari, *Le vite de' più eccellenti pittori scultori e architettori*, ed. Gaetano Milanesi, Florence: Sansoni, 1906, vol. 1, pp. 575–76; Ladis, *Taddeo Gaddi*, pp. 14, points out the difficulty connecting Vasari's assertion with works extant in the chapel; Serena Skerl del Conte, *Antonio Veneziano e Taddeo Gaddi nella toscana della seconda metà del Trecento*, Udine: Campanotto, 1995, p. 71; Castelli, "Ranieri da cantore a santo taumatugo," pp. 89–90.
188 Ronzani, "Arcivescovi, chiesa cittadina e comune," pp. 31–32.
189 Ronzani, "'Figli del comune' o fuorusciti?," pp. 816–18.
190 Ronzani, "Arcivescovi, chiesa cittadina e comune," pp. 6–37; Ronzani, "'Figli del comune' o fuorusciti?," pp. 819–22.
191 Luigina Carratori, "Il Capitolo della cattedrale nelle vicende pisane della fine dell Trecento e degli inizi del Quattrocento," *Bollettino storico pisano,* vol. 56, 1987, p. 8.

192 F. Ragone in *Dizionario biografico degli Italiani*, vol. 52, 1999, pp. 19–22.

193 Pietro Silva, *Il Governo di Pietro Gambacorta in Pisa e le sue relazioni col resto della Toscana e coi Visconti*, Pisa: F. F. Nistri, 1910, pp. 168–69. See also Ottavio Banti, *Jacopo D'Appiano. Economia, società e politica del Comune di Pisa al suo tramonto (1392–1399)*, Livorno: Il Telegrafo, 1971, pp. 83–89, on the previous 1369 treaty with Florence, in which privileges such as exemption from customs and tolls conferred on Florentine merchants caused hardship and resentment in Pisa. For a general view, see Giuseppe Petralia, "The Late Middle Ages and the Florentine Conquest," in Mathews et al., eds., *A Companion to Medieval Pisa*, pp. 163–83.

194 Silva, *Il Governo di Pietro Gambacorta in Pisa*, pp. 230–43.

195 For a view of this period from the perspective of Francesco Datini's business activity, see Marcello Berti, "The Pisa Company: A Difficult Political Context," in Giampiero. Nigro, ed., *Francesco di Marco Datini: The Man the Merchant*, Florence: Florence University Press, 2010, pp. 281–320.

196 Tripps, *Tendencies of Gothic in Florence*, p. 258.

197 The documents are published in Tripps, *Tendencies of Gothic in Florence*, p.13, from, respectively, ASPi, Opera del Duomo 107, c. 68 recto; and Florence, Archivio di Stato, Notarile Antecosimiano, Appendice 83 (241), vol. 1, c. 25 verso.

198 Tripps, *Tendencies of Gothic in Florence*, p. 14, from ASPi, Opera del Duomo 104, c. 100 recto.

199 Tanfani Centofanti, *Notizie di Artisti*, pp. 34–40.

200 Rainerius may never have been canonized, and he was only officially declared a principal patron of the city in 1633. In general, see Réginald Grégiore, *San Rainerius di Pisa (1117–1160) in un ritratto agiografico inedito del secolo XIII*, Pisa: Pacini Editore, 1990; Colin Morris, "San Ranieri of Pisa: The Power and Limitations of Sanctity in Twelfth-century Italy," *Journal of Ecclesiastical History* 45, no. 4, 1994, pp. 588–89; Lily Richards, "Saint Ranieri of Pisa: A Civic Cult and Its Expression in Text and Image," in Joanna Cannon and Beth Williamson, eds., *Art, Politics, and Civic Religion in Central Italy 1261–1352*, Aldershot: Ashgate, 2000, pp. 179–235; and the many useful essays in *Intercessor Rainerius ad Patrem: Il santo di una città marinara del XII secolo*, ed. Castelli and Ceccarelli Lemut. For the textual sources, see Silvano Burgalassi, *San Ranieri attraverso nove secoli di storia pisana*, Pisa: Edizioni ETS, 2004, pp. 25–45; Gabriele Zaccagnini, *La vita di San Ranieri: Analisi storica, agiografica e filologica del testo di Benincasa: Edizione critica dal codice C181 dell'Archivio Capitolare di Pisa*, Pisa: GISEM, 2011; Gabriele Zaccagnini, "San Ranieri: profilo storico e agiografico," in *Intercessor Rainerius ad Patrem*, pp. 53–71. Other representations of the saint are in George Kaftal, *The Iconography of the Saints in Tuscan Painting*, Florence: Sansoni, 1952, pp. 874–83.

201 Barbara Kathryn Dodge, "Tradition, Innovation, and Technique in Trecento Mural Painting: The Frescoes and Sinopie Attributed to Francesco Traini in the Camposanto in Pisa," PhD dissertation, Johns Hopkins University, 1977, pp. 144–46.

202 Guido Botticelli, *Metodologia di restauro delle pitture muali*, Florence: Centro Di, 1992, pp. 33–48.

203 Alessandro Da Morrona, *Pisa illustrata nelle arti del disegno*, Pisa: Francesco Pieraccini, vol. 1, 1787, pp. 291–93; see also Sanpaolesi et al., *Camposanto Monumentale di Pisa*, pp. 69–82; Tripps, *Tendencies of Gothic in Florence*, pp. 214–15, 222–23, 234–35 244–64; A. Andreotti et al., "The Wall Paintings of the Monumental Cemetery of Pisa: The War, the Restoration, the Conservation," in Antonio Sgamellotti et al., eds., *Science and Art: The Painted Surface*, Cambridge: Royal Society of Chemistry, 2014, pp. 193–209; G. Bentivoglio et al., "Una svolta tecnica e operative. Il nuovo restauro," in M. L. Testi Cristiani, ed., *La Umana Commedia nel Trionfo della Morte di Buffalmacco nel Camposanto di Pisa*, Pisa: 2017, pp. 250–55; G. Ranalli, "Hi-tech Restoration by Two-steps Biocleaning Process of *Triumph of Death* Fresco at the Camposanto Monumental Cemetery (Pisa, Italy)," *Journal of Applied Microbiology*, 13 May 2018; https://doi.org/10.1111/jam.13913;

Carlo Giantomassi, "Il ricollocamento dei dipinti del Camposanto Monumentale di Pisa," in *Kermes*, vol. 32, no. 116, 2019, pp. 55–58.

204 Pisa, Archivio Storico Diocesano, Archivio Capitolare, signature C93 95. Brown leather binding, with gold tooling; 32.6 x 22.9 cm. Red chalk and red wash on white paper, size of each page 32 x 48.8 cm; size of each drawing 29.2 x 43.8 cm; the drawings have been folded to fit the bound book. The drawings are labeled *1 di sopra*, *2 di sopra* etc. Each sheet bears an inscription in brown ink: "Trasferitomi Io notaio infrascritto e testimoni infranotati in Camposanto cimetieri della Primaziale di Pisa per fare il riscontro con l'originale delle sopradette pitture e memoria sotto di quelle esistente a man sinistra nella parte di muro interiore et alla porta di detto luogo, nel quale infra le altre pitture e descrizione furono da me e dagli medesimi testimoni viste e considerate e diligentemente riscontrate e benche la detta iscrizione fusse alta da terra non di meno rendendosi intelligibile il tutto in detta forma e le precise parole fu trovato concordare col medesimo originale. Riguardandi alle predette cose il Maestro Reverendissimo Stefano Morandini, ceremoniere di detta primaziale et Tommaso Gorini sacrestano della medesima e ambi due Cappellani di detta Primaziale testimoni, in questa firmarono, il 18 Ottobre 1663 – Pisano. Ego Mattheus Gian-Pietro Maffei, pisanus civis, Notaio publico ufficiale e . . . originali concordare inveni et infradicti subscritti signum apponi." His seal of a sunburst is drawn to the left of his signature. At the bottom of each page is a later inscription in a different hand. The drawings were reproduced in Burgalassi, *San Ranieri*, pp. 33–37, figs. 10–14.

205 Burgalassi, *San Ranieri*, p. 66.

206 Parallels between the *Lives of the Hermit Saints* and the Saint Rainerius cycle include the depiction of Rainerius being tortured by devils in the Holy Land, reminiscent of Saint Anthony's torments, or his taming of two leopards, much like the lions of Saint Marcarius or the miraculous multiplication of bread after Rainerius returns from Mount Tabor, seen at the far right of the top level, recalling the miraculous provisioning of several of the desert saints. See Grégiore, *San Rainerius di Pisa*, p. 53; Diana Webb, *Saints and Cities in Medieval Italy*, Manchester: Manchester University Press, 2007, pp. 1–45; and Maria Luisa Ceccarelli Lemut, "La città e i santi: Pisa tra XII e XIII secolo," in *Intercessor Rainerius ad Patrem*, pp. 50–52.

207 Castelli, "Ranieri da cantore a santo taumaturgo," pp. 100–4, suggests that the palace refers to the new palace of Pietro Gambacorta.

208 Chiara Frugoni, *A Distant City*, trans. W. McCuaig, Princeton: Princeton University Press, p. 97.

209 Cavalca, *Vite de' S.S. Padri*, p. 18.

210 The white cross on red ground is a symbol of the Pisan people. The cross is decorated with roundels. Pope Benedict VIII had granted the emblem to the Pisans when they conquered Sardinia from the Saracens in 1017, hence it recalled the city's maritime power. See Tripps, *Tendencies of Gothic in Florence*, p. 222; Castelli, "Ranieri da cantore a santo taumaturgo," pp. 104–5. See also Max Seidel, "Building a Cathedral at the Time of the Crusades: On the Iconography of the Architectural Complex of the Primaziale of Pisa," in *Italian Art of the Middle Ages and the Renaissance*, Venice: Marsilio Editore, 2003, pp. 49–70, especially 56–60, on the Pisan conquest of Sardinia.

211 Tripps, *Tendencies of Gothic in Florence*, p. 222. A third emblem on the ship's stern has been reconstructed by Tripps as a red damask banner that was the emblem of the city republic of Pisa; see 247–48. The eagle above the prow of the ship is clearly visible in the 1662 drawings but it is missing from later reproductions of the scene; see Tripps, p. 248.

212 In the fourth scene, when Rainerius returned home he dined with the cathedral canons in a loggia that perhaps recalled the new cloister of the canonry; Redi, *Pisa come'era*, p. 382.

213 Jaroslav Folda, "Jerusalem and the Holy Sepulchre through the Eyes of Crusader Pilgrims," in Kühnel, ed., *The Real and Ideal Jerusalem in Jewish, Christian and Islamic Art*, pp. 161–62.

214 Nicole Chareyron, *Pilgrims to Jerusalem in the Middle Ages*, trans. W. Donald Wilson, New York: Columbia University Press, 2005, pp. 3–4, 84–85.

215 John Wilkinson, *Jerusalem Pilgrimage 1099–1185*, London: Hakluyt Society, 1988, p. 36.

216 Burchard of Mount Sion, *A Description of the Holy Land*, trans. A. Stewart, London: Palestine Pilgrims' Text Society, 1896, pp. 75–77, as cited in Folda, "Jerusalem and the Holy Sepulchre," p. 163.
217 See the illustrations in Jonathan J. G. Alexander, "'Jerusalem the Golden': Image and Myth in the Middle Ages in Western Europe," in Kühnel, ed., *The Real and Ideal Jerusalem in Jewish, Christian and Islamic Art*, pp. 255–64; figs. 4, 6; and the small models of the Holy Sepulcher illustrated in *In Terrasanta: Dalla Crociata alla Custodia dei Luoghi Santi*, Florence-Milan: ArtificioSkira, 2000, pp. 110–11. See also the map of Jerusalem in *Geographie de Ptolémée*, trans. Jacopo d'Angiolo de Florence (late fifteenth century), ed. H. Omont, Paris: Catala frères, 1926, pl. 73.
218 Felicity Ratté, *Picturing the City in Medieval Italian Painting*, Jefferson: McFarland and Company, 2006, pp. 91–118; Sabine Frommel and Gerhard Wolf, *Architectura Picta nell'arte italiana da Giotto a Veronese*, Modena: Franco Cosimo Panini, 2016, pp. 16–19.
219 Goro Dati, *L'Istoria di Firenze dal 1380 al 1405*, Florence: Giuseppe Manni, 1735, p. 100.
220 Smith, *The Baptistery of Pisa*, pp. 40–41, 83–84.
221 Smith, *The Baptistery of Pisa*, 226–28; Neta Bodner, "The Baptistery of Pisa and the Rotunda of the Holy Sepulcher: A Reconsideration," in Bianca Kühnel et al., *Visual Constructs of Jerusalem*, Turnhout: Brepols, 2014, pp. 95–105.
222 Ratté, *Picturing the City*, pp. 142–44.
223 Lester Little, *Religious Poverty and the Profit Economy in Medieval Europe*, Ithaca, 1978, p. 217, as quoted in Frugoni, *A Distant City*, p. 96.
224 Sainati, *Diario Sacro Pisano*, p. 74; Burgalassi, *San Ranieri*, p. 85.
225 Bonaini, *Statuti inediti* vol. 1, p. 339; vol. 2, p. 245.
226 On Rainerius's status as a layman, see Zaccagnini, "San Ranieri: Profilo storico e agiografico," pp. 62–65; Iannella, "Il ciclo pittorico di San Ranieri in Camposanto nel contesto storico pisano," pp. 174–75.
227 Thompson, *Cities of God*, p. 299; see also Jonathan Sumption, *Pilgrimage: An Image of Mediaeval Religion*, Totowa: Rowman and Littlefield, 1975, pp. 98–104; Franco Cardini, "San Ranieri a Gerusalemme tra pelegrinaggio e crociata," in *Intercessor Rainerius ad Patrem*, pp. 95–99. For the importance of pilgrimage to the Camposanto, see Diane Cole Ahl, "Camposanto, Terra Santa: Picturing the Holy Land in Pisa," *Artibus et historiae*, vol. 24, 2003, pp. 95–122.
228 See Grégiore, *San Rainerius di Pisa*, pp. 120–21 paragraph 22; pp. 125–26, paragraph 28. It is also called the *schiavina* in the written sources; see the inscription formerly included on the mural: "e vestissi d'una schiavina"; Richards, "Saint Rainerius of Pisa," p. 216; Castelli, "Ranieri da cantore a santo taumaturgo," pp. 14–15.
229 Richards, "Saint Rainerius of Pisa," p. 206, note 68; p. 208, note 106.
230 Castelli, "Ranieri da cantore a santo taumaturgo," p. 47; for the idea of pilgrimage as a form of *imitatio Christi*, see Sumption, *Pilgrimage*, pp. 89–94.
231 Frugoni, "Altri luoghi, cercandi il paradiso," pp. 1615–16.
232 Frugoni, "Altri luoghi, cercandi il paradiso," p. 1585.
233 Hans Belting, "Remarks on Communal Paintings in Siena and Pisa," *Studia artium orientalis et occidentalis*, vol. 2, 1985, pp. 11–16.
234 On this theme, see especially Aviad Kleinberg, *Flesh Made Word: Saints' Stories and the Western Imagination*, trans. J. Todd, Cambridge, MA: Harvard University Press, 2008, pp. 181–205.
235 Kleinberg, *Flesh Made Word*, pp. 200–5.
236 Zaccagnini, "San Ranieri: Profilo storico e agiografico," p. 69; and Gabriella Garzella, "Gli interlocutori di San Ranieri: La società di una città di mare," in *Intercessor Rainerius ad Patrem*, pp. 101–13.
237 Tripps, *Tendencies of Gothic in Florence*, p. 47.
238 Hilary Anne Haakenson, "Casting the Continents: Sacred History and Spiritual Odyssey in the Camposanto of Pisa," in Maryanne Cline Horowitz and Louise Arizzoli, eds., *Bodies and Maps: Early Modern Personifications of the Continents*, Leiden: Brill, 2021, pp. 172–77.

239 Grégiore, *San Rainerius di Pisa*; Richards, "Saint Rainerius of Pisa," pp. 180–81. Maria Luisa Ceccarelli Lemut, "La città e i santi: Pisa tra XII e XIII Secolo," p. 41, and "Pisa e il mediterraneo nella Vita di San Ranieri," p. 119, in *Intercessor Rainerius ad Patrem*, has remarked on Raninerius's many connections to the cathedral canons and to the monastic clergy, in contrast to few relations with the secular clergy.

240 C. Romby, in *L'architettura di Lorenzo il Magnifico*, ed. G. Morolli et al., Milan: Silvana Editoriale, 1992, p. 215.

241 The inscription as recorded on the 1662 drawing reads: "Co [me essendo passato da] questa Vita il Beato Ranieri nel Campanile nella badia di S. Vito et essendo recato a Duomo dal Chericato con grande solennitade di Cittadini con infiniti lumi in mano fece di molti e vari Miracoli Sonando etiam Dio le Campane di Pisa miracolosamente p[er] loro stesse e' molti altri miracoli li quali appariscono nella sua leggenda Amen." See also Burgalassi, *San Ranieri*, p. 38.

242 The text of the inscription as recorded on the 1662 drawing is as follows: "Come il Beato Ranieri andando oltra mare con sue Mercansie e forte spussando conovve per Spirito che a' Dio piaceva che lassasse il Mondo onde dispensato il suo a' poveri, e vestitosi di una Schiavina da due Vecchi fu appresentato dinanti nostra Donna dicendoli tu ti [riposerai nel mio Grembo] nella Città di Pisa in sempiterno." The missing words can be supplied from the legend of Benincasa, Grégiore, *San Rainerius di Pisa*, 124, 27:575–76; see also Richards, "Saint Rainerius of Pisa," 194; and Burgalassi, *San Ranieri*, p. 35.

243 Although Benincasa says it was removed to the pulpit – perhaps the monumental pulpit of Giovanni Pisano in the cathedral.

244 The inscription as recorded on the 1662 drawing reads: "Come [essendo posto] il Beato Ranieri nella Chiesa maggiore di Pisa et alla Tomba sua venendo molti Infermi con diverse Infirmitade furono tutti liberati et un Fanciullo Morto essendo cascato da alto fu Resucitato et molto altri [e come una nave essendo assalita da terribil tempest fù liberata per esser stato implorato il Divino aiuto, e gettata nel mare da un Pisano un poco d'acqua benedetta del Santo mentre subito si fece il mare tranquillo]." See Burgalassi, *San Ranieri*, p. 39.

245 Grégiore, *San Rainerius di Pisa*, pp. 176–77, paragraph 127; Richards, "Saint Rainerius of Pisa," pp. 187–91; Max Seidel, "Studien zu Giovanni di Balduccio und Tino di Camaino," *Städel-Jahrbuch*, vol. 5, 1975, pp. 37–84.

246 That the mendicants of Santa Caterina embraced civic virtues as well, and that they played a role in the legitimization of the communal regime, has been discussed in Cecilia Iannella, "Civic Virtues in Dominican Homiletic Literature in Tuscany in the Thirteenth and Fourteenth Centuries," *Medieval Sermon Studies*, vol. 51, 2007, pp. 22–32.

247 Ronzani, "Arcivescovi, chiesa cittadina e comune," pp. 11–32; and Ronzani, "'Figli del comune' or fuorusciti?," pp. 773–827.

248 The stipends from the benefices held by the cathedral canons were paid on Saint Rainerius's feast day, 17 June; Carratori, "Il Capitolo della cattedrale," p. 10.

249 Frugoni: "Altri luoghi, cercandi il paradiso," pp. 1593–94, suggests the alteration of the image of Fra Giovanni from penitent to hermit harmonized better with the depiction of the hermit saints. See also Kleinberg, *Flesh Made Word*, pp. 198–99, on the relationship of the eremitic movement and the mendicant orders. Battistoni, *L'Opera del Duomo di Pisa*, p. 76, cites the decline of public flagellation in the late Trecento.

250 Richards, "Saint Rainerius of Pisa," p. 185. See also D. Lucciardi, "Federigo Visconti Arcivescovo di Pisa," *Bollettino storico pisano*, vol. 1, 1932, pp. 7–47; vol. 2, 1933, pp. 7–37.

251 Ronzani, *Un'idea trecentesca di cimitero*, pp. 139–40.

CHAPTER THREE

"MOST HOLY AND UNIQUE IN THE WORLD"

Filippo de' Medici, Benozzo Gozzoli, and the Completion of the Camposanto in the Fifteenth Century

Filippo de' Medici (1426–74), archbishop of Pisa from 1461, was buried in the Camposanto with great pomp on 10 October 1474. Town criers announced the ceremony to the populace; the great bell was covered in black buckram; Lancillotto Decio, a doctor from the university, of which Filippo was chancellor, gave the funeral oration; and the Pisan clergy were charged to celebrate 110 Masses in his memory. Filippo's testament, drawn up just five days before, left detailed instructions for his burial in the Camposanto, in a chapel dedicated to the Holy Cross to be built off the east corridor (Appendix III).[1] It was to include an altar, surmounted by a gilded and painted altarpiece depicting the cross, flanked by the Virgin and Saint Phillip. Furnishings were to include choir stalls and an inlaid wooden ceiling. Filippo entrusted his brother Tanai with building the chapel. Francione and his associate Baccio Pontelli, collaborators on the archepiscopal palace, were commissioned to build the chapel the same month as Filippo died. The terms of the contract make clear the structure was intended to harmonize with the ambience of the Camposanto.[2] Especially striking is the call for a prodigious amount of marble in the floor, windows, altar, and "the choir done in the form of the chapel of the Annunciation in Florence, which is at the side when you enter."[3] The chapel referred to is undoubtedly the tabernacle in the Santissima Annunziata in Florence, commissioned by Piero de' Medici; on the inside of the architrave is inscribed, "costo fiorini 4000 el marmo" (the marble cost 4,000 florins).[4] Doris Carl has recently argued for another prestigious model, the chapel in the

Medici palace.[5] The ground plan and furnishings in Filippo's chapel were to replicate those in the Florentine palace chapel. Surely, Filippo meant his chapel to rival in splendor those of his Medici cousins. Similarly, Pontelli and his younger brother Piero, perhaps with the prospect of this sumptuous commission and another for woodwork in the Duomo, for which they had made a demonstration piece delivered in Pisa on 2 March 1475, moved their residence to Pisa in November 1475. Scholars have assumed neither project was begun, as, after minor commissions in the Duomo and the Palazzo Arcivescovile in 1476 and 1477, Baccio and his brother left for Urbino in 1478.[6] Carl has recently discovered payments for the construction of the chapel, however, that prove work was ongoing until at least 1480 and that the chapel must have been finished or nearly so.[7]

It is perhaps surprising that Filippo, a Medici, would choose to be buried in Pisa rather than Florence. Yet, as this chapter argues, Filippo was a tireless advocate for his adopted city, in which he resided throughout his archbishopric. He was particularly devoted to the Camposanto, which he called, "Most Holy and Unique in the World." Through his efforts, the Camposanto, which as we have seen was begun in the late thirteenth century, was completed and decorated as part of his campaign to make Pisa the "jewel in the crown" of the Florentine territorial state.

In 1488, Michelagnolo di Cristofano da Volterra, a musician in the employ of the Pisan Capitano Virginio Orsino, signed a laudatory poem describing the Camposanto, with particular emphasis on the murals.[8] Entering through the same portal as our earlier visitor, he recounted the stories of the south and east walls and then retraced his steps to the northwest corner for a glowing account of the Old Testament murals, begun between 1389 and 1391 and completed by Benozzo Gozzoli in 1468–84:

> Then there begins a unique story / that the Florentine Benozzo painted/ from the Old Testament clearly taken / as are all such stories, never did he pretend / to just paint it with expertise/but in brush stroke and in style all did he surpass: / this is what can be achieved in painting / first in singular composition.[9]

Michelangelo ended with an account of the fifty-six marble windows filling the internal arcade, also completed in the mid-fifteenth century, the sculpted heads surmounting pilasters on the internal walls, and the central "sacred field," on which rested so many tombs he could not count them. As a climax to his paean, he wrote, "A temple such as this is so worthy and elegant, that in the world its equal I believe does not exist; should one look round everywhere in the West and the East, a more beautiful thing cannot be found." Almost as an afterthought, he mentioned the indulgences and other spiritual benefits accrued to visitors.[10] His emphasis on the fame, scale, and beauty of the

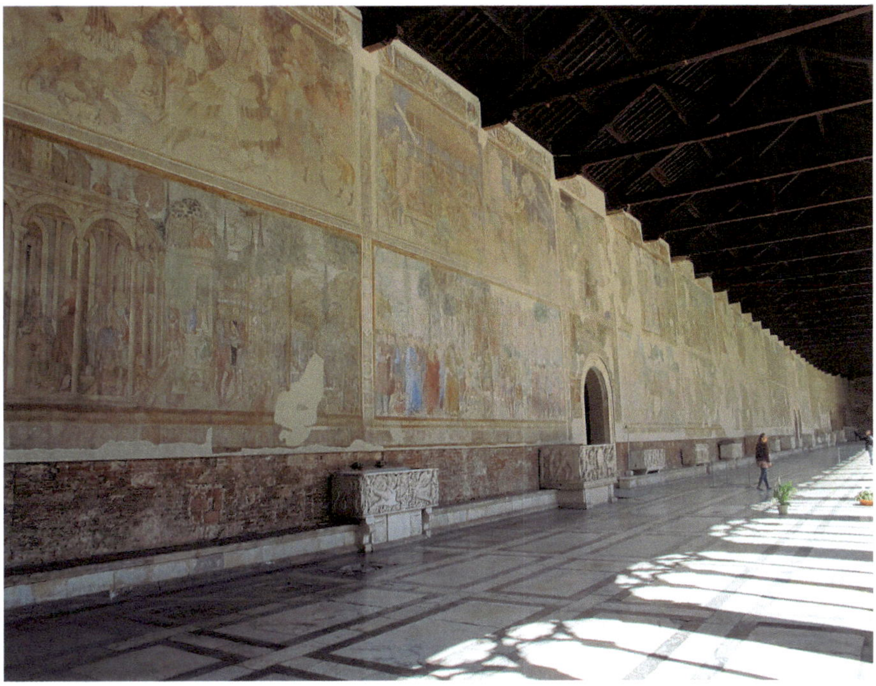

3.1. Scenes from the Old Testament, north wall, Camposanto, Pisa. Photo: Author.

Camposanto presaged the shift in perception from sacred space – Paradise, as we have seen – to tourist attraction that occurred in the sixteenth century.[11]

The Old Testament murals are noteworthy first for their physical expanse, extending over the entire north wall of the Camposanto, as well as their textual breadth (Figure 3.1). Thirty fields, twenty-six of which Gozzoli painted between 1468 and 1484, depict stories primarily from the Hebrew Bible: from Genesis, Exodus, Numbers, Deuteronomy, Kings, and Chronicles. As such, it is the most extensive Old Testament cycle in Tuscan painting. Previous Old Testament cycles executed in the late trecento and early quattrocento, such as in the Collegiata in San Gimignano, and in the Chiostro Verde in Santa Maria Novella in Florence, both of which Gozzoli would have known well, visualize a smaller number of scenes or textual range.[12]

The scenes are horizontal rectangles arranged in two levels. Adjacent to a giant *Theological Cosmos*, stories of Adam and Eve, Cain and Abel, Noah's Ark and the Flood painted by the Orvietan artist Piero di Puccio (active c. 1355–1400) between 1389 and 1391 occupy the top level.[13] Benozzo's first scenes of the *Drunkenness of Noah*, the *Curse of Ham*, and the *Tower of Babel* were painted below. The area between the Ammannati and Aulla chapels displays histories of Abraham, Isaac, and Jacob, while the vast area from the Aulla chapel to the northeast corner shows stories from Joseph, Moses, Joshua, David, and Solomon. Scenes from the history of the Virgin and the infancy of

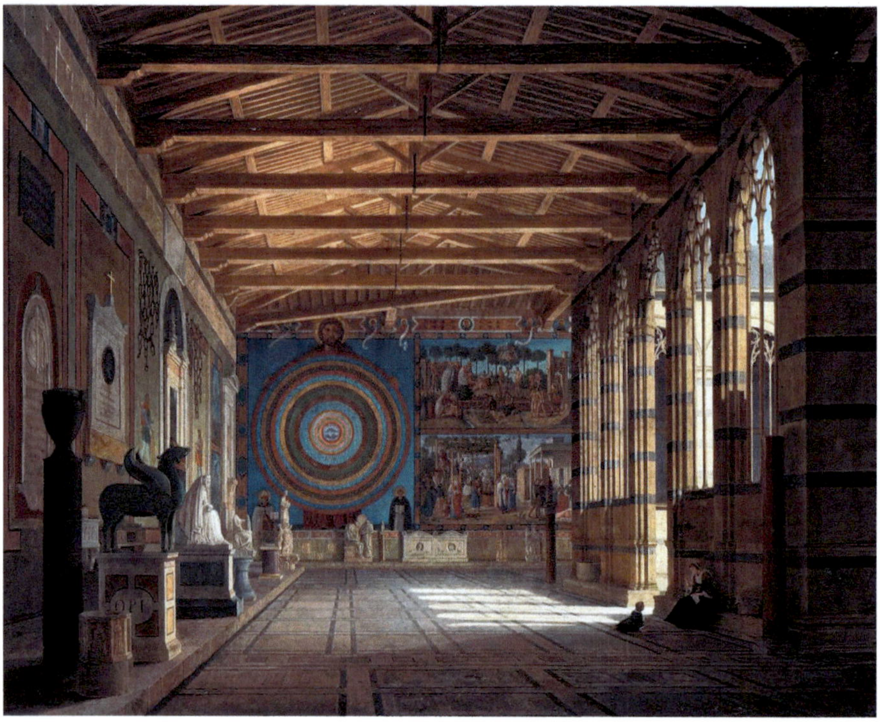

3.2. Leo von Klenze (1784–1864), *Camposanto in Pisa*, 1858, Munich, Neue Pinakothek, Photo: Bayerische Staatsgemäldesammlungen/ Creative Commons Attribution-Share Alike 4.0 International.

Christ, including the *Annunciation*, *Adoration of the Magi*, *Assumption*, and *Coronation of the Virgin* were situated over the entrances to the chapels opposite the main entrance portals.

While the murals today are ghosts of their former selves, victims to the dampness of the Pisan climate, defects in the original technique, and the disastrous fire following a bomb strike during the Second World War, visitors today can still see most of the original works thanks to the decades-long conservation campaign, now nearing completion.[14] The sheer scale of the murals, particularly when seen in the spaces for which they were designed, allows visitors to experience some of their original impact as recorded by nineteenth-century painters (Figure 3.2). Engravings by Carlo Lasinio in 1812, a set of which was hand-colored by his son Giovanni Paolo Lasinio (1796–1855) and is preserved in the Museo dell'Opera del Duomo in Pisa (Figures 3.3, 3.11, 3.15, and 3.16), also recapture some of their original detail and color.[15]

The murals of the north wall completed the vast sweep of universal history and the promise of eternal salvation begun in the Trecento scenes on the south, southeast, and southwest walls.[16] Typological links between the Old Testament and the New, implicit in the Mariological scenes, were reinforced

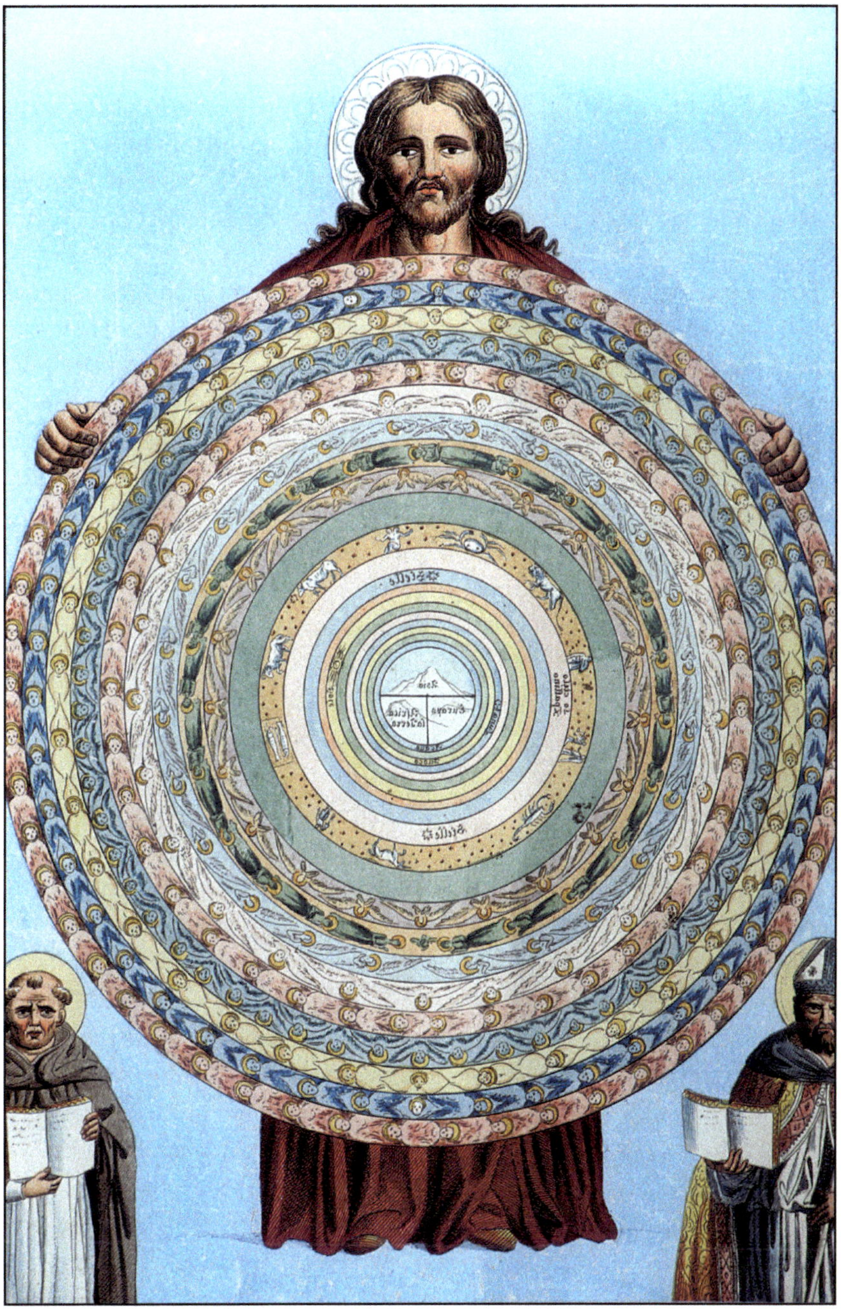

3.3. Carlo Lasinio, engraving (1812) after Piero di Puccio, *Theological Cosmos*, 1389–91, from *Pitture a fresco del Camposanto di Pisa*, Florence, 1812, hand-colored by Giovanni Paolo Lasinio, Pisa, Museo dell'Opera del Duomo, photo: Scala / Art Resource, NY.

by inscriptions, no longer extant, on banderoles held by prophets and saints depicted in the borders of the upper scenes. The Old Covenant and the New would have literally confronted each other, if the stained-glass windows filling the arcade arches, showing scenes from Christ's life on earth, including the Nativity, Christ and the Woman from Samaria, and the Expulsion of the Moneylenders from the Temple, had been completed.[17] Such iconographic schemes replicate prestigious examples from early Christianity in Roman basilicas, such as Old Saint Peter's.[18]

This chapter focuses on the imagery and production of the murals of the Old Testament celebrated by Michelagnolo di Cristofano.[19] They were painted during a period of difficult political and economic relationships between Pisa and Florence in the fifteenth century. This period traditionally had been neglected by historians, but it has been reexamined recently in the context of Florence's growing territorial state. In the late fifteenth century, Lorenzo de' Medici (1449–92) sought to make Pisa a site of Florentine cultural magnificence, second only to Florence itself. In this effort, the drive to complete the Camposanto loomed large.

The Medici campaign was spearheaded by Filippo de' Medici, a distant cousin of the Florentine family who was archbishop of Pisa from 1461 until his death in 1474. A reexamination of Filippo's biography and patronage reveals his role as pastor, diplomat, and ambassador. His activities as a patron of art and architecture shed new light on his role in Pisa and call into question the view, presented in the only in-depth study of him published over fifty years ago, of Filippo as a bumbling Medici toady whose only ambition was to be made a cardinal. We have no direct evidence of his intervention in the completion of the Camposanto; however, by examining his patronage of other monuments, his preserved letters and orations, his testament, and his portraits, a convincing case can be made for his role in the project. In their imagery and style, Gozzoli's murals were aptly suited to the site and Filippo's ambitions for the project. Gozzoli's invention of figural compositions, landscape, and architectural settings built on his previous works in San Gimignano. The Camposanto murals responded to the quantum leap of scale and historical scope that the Old Testament subjects presented. They were recognized then – and later – as an extraordinary accomplishment. A wider picture of Filippo's career as papal courtier and envoy enlarges the cultural context in which the later murals in the Camposanto must be understood and includes the Florentine territorial state, the papacy, north Italian courts, and European powers such as France. Through Filippo's efforts, Pisa established its preeminence among the subject towns of the Florentine dominion and its role as a vital link to the papacy in Rome. Filippo's ties to Rome, as well as to Italian and European allies, were central to the diplomacy of the Medici regime in the last decades of the fifteenth century and to Pisa's cultural revival as well.

Filippo de' Medici has long been seen as a key player in the project, but his contribution is difficult to isolate. Letters and payment records that clarify his role in the project amplify a broad view of Filippo's patronage of art and architecture in Pisa during these years. The imagery of the murals reflects his input in its grandiose sweep and its themes of military triumph and regal splendor. While, as discussed in Chapter 2, the southwest murals promote the lives of local Pisan saints, the north murals present a comprehensive account of the Old Testament stories. Just as the earlier murals reflect aspects of Pisan civic identity and they relate to the burial function of the Camposanto generally, their specific imagery responds to political and economic realities at the times when they were painted.[20] While the early fourteenth-century murals reflect the values of the cloister, the late Trecento murals visualize the ethos of the city-state. The north wall, by contrast, depicts the Hebrew patriarchs as princely rulers, reflecting a decisive shift to Florentine domination. Like the Prato murals in the chapel of the Holy Belt examined in Chapter 1, the Old Testament murals enhanced an impressive locus of local identity and pride, while signaling the political reality of Florentine control.

The copious documentation for the project that survives in the archives of the Opera del Duomo reveals Benozzo Gozzoli's role in the murals and the scale of his worksite, active for more than sixteen years.[21] Like those records discussed for Agnolo Gaddi's work in Prato, they shed light on Benozzo's relations with his patrons, the secular *operai*. Benozzo enjoyed enhanced status as a master from Florence with a distinguished history of papal and Medici patronage. His stature demonstrates the value of artisan skill in the context of high-profile civic projects, such as the completion of the Camposanto.

PISA IN THE FIFTEENTH CENTURY

Piero di Puccio's unfinished Old Testament cycle had been abandoned for more than seventy years when Benozzo Gozzoli arrived from Florence in January of 1468. By then, conditions in Pisa had irreparably changed. In 1406, the proud city had become subject to Florence in the wake of political upheaval, treachery, and siege.[22] Florence had long coveted the city as an outlet to the sea for its booming commercial trade. During the twelfth and thirteenth centuries, the period of Pisan maritime dominance, the Florentines depended on Pisan shipping and access to domestic and foreign ports. In the fourteenth century, with the decline of Pisan maritime power and the growth of Florentine economic might, the tables turned. By 1397, Florence faced the threat to her political and commercial autonomy by Gian Galeazzo Visconti, *Signore* of Pisa and Milan. After Gian Galeazzo's death in 1402, Florence determined to subjugate Pisa once and for all. The city and countryside were purchased from Gabriele Maria Visconti, Gian Galeazzo's successor, in August 1405 for 206,000 florins, as a fief under French rule. Six days after the French administrator Marshal Boucicaut ceded the citadel to the Florentines, the Pisans attacked, reoccupying the fort. The Florentines, determined to secure their possession, ravaged the countryside and besieged the city. After ten months, the starving Pisans surrendered, but the bitter memory of the siege tainted Pisan-Florentine relations for many years. Even Florentine observers expressed unease: Goro Dati, in his *History of Florence*, wrote,

> Never was there a city in the world that held out until death in order not to be overcome as much as the Pisans did, or that knew how to resist with so much determination and intelligence as they did .... [Once the bread was gone] they ate grass, cats, other animals, and the excrement of horses. Nor were they spared the ultimate misery of eating human flesh .... Adults and children fell dead from hunger every day, and the entire city was filled with grief. Speaking of it fills my heart with horror.[23]

The capitulation of Pisa on 9 October 1406, while marked by celebrations in Florence, was a humiliation for Pisans.

During the first period of Florentine domination, from 1406 until the Pisans revolted in 1494, local chroniclers dwelt on the ignominious subjection of the city to its historical enemy. Under the yoke of Florence, the once prosperous city experienced economic decline and depopulation, the result of the "cruelty and greed" of the Florentines.[24] Excluded from meaningful self-government and subject to onerous taxation, politically suspect citizens were deported to Florence or took refuge in the countryside. Pisan guilds were subject to those of the dominant city, and international trade, traditional lifeblood of the economy, was stifled.

Twentieth-century historians presented a more nuanced view, highlighting efforts by Florence to revive Pisa as a commercial center.[25] In the last decades of the twentieth century, historians produced many specialized studies on the politics, demographics, and economics of Pisa and its countryside in the fourteenth century. Broader studies of the Florentine territorial state renewed focus on the fifteenth century.[26] Viewed within a larger territorial context, many aspects of Florentine control seen as punitive by previous historians, were understood as measures taken by Florence with many of its subject towns.[27] Zorzi summarized the current view: Florence instituted in Pisa a direct dominion, without treaties or statutes, to control the subject city. The countryside was uncoupled from the city and annexed to the Florentine domain. Florence reorganized the administrative structure of the countryside under the exclusive control of Florentines, as elsewhere in its territory. In the city, the outward forms of self-rule were maintained, but the Anziani (the most important magistracy of the communal government), now renamed the Priors, were deprived of real power. Florentines also controlled all aspects of government, trade, taxation, and, increasingly, the church. Throughout the fifteenth century, Florence – more so than with other subject towns, such as Arezzo or Pistoia – ruled Pisa with no concessions to, or participation from, the commune, propelled by a profound suspicion of Pisan loyalty.[28]

Tax records show that the population declined by half in the first half of the fifteenth century.[29] Orlandini's analysis of the 1447 catasto confirms that many families of the old nobility or the mercantile elite had by then left Pisa and that taxes fell heaviest on the middle classes. In addition, baptisms and notarial acts reveal substantial numbers of foreigners in Pisa; scholars suggest an estimate of 35 percent non-Pisan population in the city in the second half of the fifteenth century.[30]

THE CAMPOSANTO IN THE FIFTEENTH CENTURY

Florentine conquest profoundly affected the urban fabric of Pisa. The city lauded by contemporaries for its wide streets, soaring churches, and magnificent palaces became victim to the occupation, depopulation, and abandonment that accompanied the economic decline of the city.[31] The traditional wealth of the Opera del Duomo and the flow of donations to it mitigated the effects of economic decline on the monuments of Piazza del Duomo, especially the Camposanto. Tax policies favored bequests of property, allowing donors to retain lifetime use.[32] Even so, burdened by expenses and debts, the Opera bemoaned its inability to maintain its properties, especially the Camposanto, "locus devotissimus." Repeated prohibitions of ballgames suggest depredations of the structure, tombs, and mural decoration.[33]

Ottavio Banti reckons the number of datable tomb slabs in the Camposanto reached a high of forty-four during 1350–1400. There were thirty-nine tombs from 1400 to 1450, and twenty-five from 1450 to 1500.[34] These numbers reflect an 11 percent decline in the first half of the fifteenth century and a 27 percent decline in the second half. Compared to the drastic population decline indicated in tax records, the fall in tomb slabs seems moderate. Foreigners, who were not recorded in the tax rolls, purchased many of the burial spots; immigration seems to have mitigated the effects of population decline on burial practices in the Camposanto.[35]

The social position of those who chose the Camposanto for burial in the first half of the fifteenth century seems to have been predominantly middle class, as it had been in the fourteenth century.[36] The old political elite, many of them having left the city, purchased fewer tombs.[37] Of the ancient sarcophagi used as tombs, few date to the fifteenth century. Nonresidents who do not occur in the tax rolls likely purchased those few.[38] Some newly prominent families, such as the Pone da Cascina, purchased tombs. Pone de Grandonibus de

Cascina was buried in the north corridor of the Camposanto in 1450, his tomb slab ornamented with his arms and a neo-Latin inscription.[39]

The catasto instituted by Florence in 1428–29 allows a closer look at the economic position of those buried in the Camposanto in the first half of the fifteenth century.[40] Of the twenty-five or so taxpayers in the 1428–29 catasto who were buried in the Camposanto, most were prosperous artisans and small businessmen.[41] Others possessed greater assets, such as Ser Bartolomeo and Antonio di ser Simone da Farneta, whose taxable gross assets totaled 2,676 soldi; they had an ironworks shop and must also have engaged in trade; they reported that in Tunis the Saracens had seized a ship and goods valued at more than 400 florins. Their tomb slab in the north corridor is dated 1445.[42] Yet of the richest taxpayers in the 1428 catasto discussed by Mallett, none was buried in the Camposanto.[43]

The communal cemetery continued to attract a middle-class clientele in the second half of the fifteenth century as well. Most taxpayers in the 1447 catasto who purchased graves paid less than one florin in tax.[44] The range of professions of the deceased is broad, including many tradesmen, such as *cuoiai* (leather worker),[45] *tavolai* (furniture maker),[46] *beccai* (butcher),[47] *barbieri* (barber),[48] *vinaioli* (vintner),[49] and *farsettai* (doublet maker),[50] among others. Their wealth also varied, from the 45th and 47th place to the 1,023rd place among the 1,170 taxpayers in the 1447 catasto, as calculated by Orlandini.

The Opera, facing reduced income while encountering increased costs, nonetheless continued work on the Camposanto in the fifteenth century. The pavement was completed in 1440, as the *operaio*, Giuliano di Colino degli Scarsi da San Giusto (1435–46), recorded in an inscription, now lost.[51] Construction of the tracery or "marble windows" in the courtyard arcade, begun in the fourteenth century, was taken up again in 1451, though it was not actively pursued until 1455.[52] It was then that the Florentine stained glass workshop of Leonardo and Bartolomeo Della Scarperia was commissioned to fill the arches with historiated stained glass, ultimately producing nine windows between 1455 and 1463.[53]

PISAN CULTURAL REVIVAL

While some Pisan artists found work in the Opera del Duomo workshops, foreign artists gravitated to Pisa to study its ancient artifacts, to profit from its expertise in marble carving, and to exploit its access to maritime trade. Recent studies underline the continued vitality of Pisa as a center of cultural exchange and production in the early fifteenth century.[54] The activity of Florentine artists such as Donatello, Michelozzo, Masaccio, and others is well known.[55] The construction of fortifications by Brunelleschi and Giuliano da Sangallo indicate the strategic importance to Florence of Pisa and, after 1421, Livorno and Porto Pisano.[56] The trade in marble from the quarries to the northeast of Pisa in Carrara, Pietrasanta, and other towns indicate continued activity of quarrying and carving.[57] Giovanni di Gante, a Pisan sculptor and former *capomaestro* of the Opera del Duomo in Pisa (1399–1406), finished the tomb of Ladislas of Durazzo, begun earlier, for the Neapolitan church of San Giovanni a Carbonara.[58] Nonetheless, artisans such as Giovanni, his brother Lupo, and son Pippo (Filippo), faced with decreased demand for their skills, expanded their activities to work in wood, to general managerial roles, and to other markets such as the neighboring town of Lucca.[59] Many artists sought work elsewhere. Pippo di Gante quickly detached himself from the family workshop and moved to the orbit of Donatello and Michelozzo during their sojourn in Pisa in 1426–28. He was working in the Vatican by 1431. His son Isaiah followed his father and made his entire career outside of Pisa, particularly in Rome in the employ of Pope Pius II.[60]

Cultural production increased in the second half of the fifteenth century; however, artisans from outside Pisa carried on much of the carving and building. They came from Lucca, from Settignano, and other towns near Florence, and from other centers of building and carving such as Piacenza and Como.[61] The major sculptors in Pisa in the second half of the century, such as Domenico di Giovanni da Milano, and the Florentine Andrea di Francesco Guardi, were from outside of Pisa.[62] Whether this shift was owing to earlier emigration of the artisan class from Pisa, or to policies allowing Florentine artisans to work in Pisa without having to join a Pisan guild, or to changing taste for style and materials is difficult to ascertain.

As the work force became regionalized, patronage expanded. Pisa benefited from Florentine cultural patronage which, as shown in Chapter 1, gained impetus in the fourteenth century with the growth of the territorial state. In the fifteenth century, this policy took on a decisive Medici cast. Cosimo de' Medici, patron of Donatello, was one of the executors of the estate of cardinal Brancacci (d. 1427) and partly financed his tomb that was shipped from Pisa to Naples.[63] Cosimo had economic interests in Pisa; in 1441, he acquired a palace and the next year opened a branch of the Medici bank.[64] His sons purchased land in the *contado*.[65] Giovanni di Cosimo (1421–63) was the first in the family to purchase large tracts to the west of Florence, in Fucecchio on the Arno, and in the Pisan Maremma, including pastures at Donoratico and Pasco de' Bolgheri.[66] Piero di Cosimo (1416–69) bought land at Collemezzano and Casalgiusto in the Maremma in 1468.[67] For the Medici, land purchases in and around Pisa signaled a reorientation of property investment away from their ancestral lands in the Mugello.[68] Lucrezia Tornabuoni de' Medici (1427–82), wife of Piero di Cosimo, also made substantial investments in and around Pisa.[69]

Lorenzo de' Medici bought land in and around Pisa beginning in 1471.[70] In the latter part of the 1480s, beset by financial problems, Lorenzo nonetheless continued to buy up large properties in the Pisan countryside, notably at Vicopisano and Agnano.[71]

While his landholdings were extensive, Lorenzo was hardly the only Florentine to amass large tracts of land in the Pisan *contado*. Florentines had been buying land in the former *contado* of Pisa since early in the century.[72] Many Florentine families, including the Martelli, Pucci, Capponi, Rucellai, Ridolfi, Salviati, and Tommaso Soderini owned property in the city and *contado*. They were often the same families that had commercial, political, or maritime interests in the city itself or were involved with the communal galley system.[73] They, too, would support a resurgent Pisa.

Lorenzo's agricultural schemes seemed to be a logical response to the declining fortunes of the Medici bank, yet they were on a scale that stands out. He fostered milling, livestock management, dairy production, mulberry cultivation, and horse breeding, activities that were as innovative as his real estate projects in Florence or his architectural plans for the villa at Poggio a Caiano.[74] He spent considerable time around Pisa on his many estates, and he enjoyed hunting the abundant wildlife for which the Pisan countryside was famous.[75] Lorenzo's Pisan holdings were the setting against which he participated in the cultivated *otium* of classically inspired villa life.[76] Although it was not until the 1470s that conditions in the countryside started to improve, to the extent that his wide-ranging activities affected official Florentine policy, they signal a new stage in the dominant city's management of the Pisan *contado*.

How much Lorenzo's activities in and around Pisa reflect economic self-interest, or Florence's generally more benign attitude to its subject city, has been debated. Scholars have argued that Florence pursued measures to improve conditions earlier in the fifteenth century, before the ascent of the Medici and certainly before the active career of Lorenzo. Historically Pisa's *contado* had long struggled against the conversion of arable land to pasturage.[77] Traditionally, local communes and landowners had maintained dykes and drainage ditches that made farming possible. When land was turned to pasturage, it reverted to swamp, a breeding ground for mosquitoes that were the source for malaria, the historical scourge of Pisa and its *contado*.[78] The Florentine signoria undertook measures to control the pasturage of wild beasts and manage the *contado* through various bodies, including the Ufficiali delle Torri (Officials of the Towers), who were responsible for maintaining fortifications, and the Ufficiali dei Danni Dati, who oversaw drainage and pasturage. In his attempts to improve and cultivate land in the *contado* and reclaim it from pasturage, Lorenzo at times opposed the interests of some of his compatriots, including his own mother, who wished to maintain the land for grazing.[79]

The Canal Officials, a group tasked with extending the navigability of the Arno from Pisa to Florence, included Cosimo de' Medici among its first members when it was set up in 1458. Lorenzo's first appointment as one of the Canal Officials in 1468 signaled the continuing strategic and economic importance of Pisa to Florence and to the Medici.[80] As Kent has argued, Lorenzo's service as a canal officer from the age of nineteen began his lifelong absorption in matters of military engineering and formed a basis of expertise for later projects. In 1475, the signoria also created the Opera della Riparazione del Contado di Pisa (Board for the Repair of the Countryside of Pisa), later called the Ufficio dei Fiumi e Fossi (Office of Rivers and Canals), which was charged with repair of ditches, bridges, and roads. That it drew Lorenzo's particular attention might be inferred from a letter to Lorenzo from Gasparre della Volta, the superintendent of drainage, in 1478.[81]

FLORENCE AND PISA IN THE FIFTEENTH CENTURY

A telling snapshot of Florentine attitudes toward Pisa in the middle of the fifteenth century emerges from the record of a debate, held in 1460, on the merits of moving the University of Florence to Pisa.[82] Founded in 1348, the university had a checkered history up until its reorganization in 1473, which was marked by periods of florescence, as well as decline and closure.[83] By 1460, the university had been struggling for years, closing in 1449, reopening in 1451, but still inadequately funded.

The debate, a *pratica*, was held at the Palazzo della Signoria on 19 January 1459/60. Economic concerns dominated the discussion. Yet traditional Florentine suspicions of Pisan loyalty were uppermost in the minds of participants. Manno Temperani worried, "If the Studio should become famous in Pisa, all kinds of men would go there to receive tuition, some of whom would be enemies of Florence. Having been paid to go there, they would be able with Pisans responsive to their stimulus to make the city hostile to Florence." Others, such as Bernardo Gherardi, countered, "I do not think any danger threatens from students since they are usually good young men and do not have minds capable of doing such things." The most compelling arguments urged the economic revival of the subject town. Francesco Neroni recounted, "I see in fact that the city of Pisa has for a long time been oppressed by many afflictions and has now finally been reduced to such a state that it is little more than a ruin. I also observe that for a long time now by their resolutions and laws the rulers of Florence have only concerned themselves with putting that city on a better footing. And thus honor would go to Florence when everyone saw Pisa had been preserved and rescued from destruction." More than honor was at stake. Neroni went on, "There would be an advantage as the taxes and gabelles would be increased. Among the many things which can be for the advantage and adornment of that city, I think nothing could be better or more honorable than to establish a studio of liberal arts there. As a result of this, many people will immediately go to live in the city. Consequently the revenue could be increased."

Otto Niccolini observed the city of Pisa offered fewer distractions than Florence to young scholars, and it was, by virtue of its location, a short journey. He foresaw a vibrant university reviving the population and economy of the subject town. Students' experiences would, in future, foster a positive view toward Pisa and Florence: "I have always loved those cities where I have studied, and I found in the Roman curia very worthy men who have protected those cities where they received their academic training."[84]

Acknowledging the long-standing Medici interests in the Studio, two participants thought Piero and Cosimo de' Medici should be consulted.[85] In the end, the studio remained in Florence until its reorganization in 1473, discussed below. Nonetheless, the debate reflects the old suspicions mingled with a new view in which economic interests prevailed. Florentines began to see that a thriving Pisa would benefit Florence too.

Lorenzo's reestablishment of the university in Pisa thirteen years later demonstrated his special fondness for the city and determination to revive its fortunes.[86] Lorenzo's support for the studio followed in the tradition of Medici patronage from the early fifteenth century.[87] Lorenzo de' Medici was central to the transfer of the Studio to Pisa in 1473, and he served as one of the Ufficiali dello Studio (Officers of the Studio) for the extraordinarily long period between 1473 and 1483.[88] The bill that authorized the relocation of the Studio to Pisa mixed revenue enhancements for Florence with provisions to revive the Pisan economy. The bill provided for the transfer of the Studio's faculties of law and medicine to Pisa for a trial period of five years, while the humanities faculty remained in Florence.

Apart from the economic aspects of the Studio, Lorenzo's involvement in the Studio had its greatest impact on Florentine intellectual life. Long considered backward and ineffectual, the Studio from the 1420s on elevated the *studia humanitatis* to primacy among the academic disciplines.[89] In particular, Lorenzo's study at the Studio was central to his intellectual formation and continued support for the Studio, which became, in James Hankins's words, "the centerpiece of [his] literary and philosophical patronage."[90]

Davies has underlined the novel aspects of Lorenzo's support for the Studio.[91] As with his land acquisitions in Pisa, his efforts were on an unprecedented scale. When in 1475 the duties of the Ufficiali dello Studio, of which Lorenzo was one, expanded to include oversight of tax collection, Lorenzo's influence grew. Davies has concluded that in this way Lorenzo transformed the Studio into yet another vehicle of his power. Nor would this be the only instance that Lorenzo exercised his influence through membership of standing committees. Kent's discovery of Lorenzo's role in the Opera del Duomo during these same years is only one example among many others.[92] Lorenzo thus fundamentally redefined the means and the ends of cultural patronage. While the reformed Studio furthered Lorenzo's intellectual interests and constituted a focus of cultural magnificence, it also expanded Lorenzo's web of supporters and clients both at home and abroad.

Yet scholars have challenged the idea of a "Pisa Laurenziana," extending from the 1470s to the 1490s. Petralia, citing Florence's obvious economic self-interest in a repopulated and productive city and its countryside, traced the change in the attitude of Florence to Pisa to the lifetime of Cosimo il Vecchio.[93] Petralia concluded that all of the measures promoted by Lorenzo derived, in fact, from a political necessity to build up Florentine support in the traditionally hostile Pisan territory to counter forces, such as those of Naples, that potentially threatened the Florentine state. And it may be, as Davies has suggested, that Lorenzo's political vulnerability in Florence in the 1470s led him to seek support outside the city. Connell's analysis of Medici correspondence with subject towns reveals a marked change in relations with them after Piero's death in 1469. Lorenzo's handling of territorial matters highlights the personalized nature of his patronage in the last decades of the fifteenth century.[94] Yet, as Petralia has outlined, Lorenzo's network of personal relationships in Pisa and its *contado* included none of the old Pisan elite but rather *nouveaux riches* and recent arrivals in the city. Political integration of the Pisan and Florentine ruling elite in Pisa proved elusive, primarily because, as Ciccaglioni has observed, with the emigration of the old elite, no new political class emerged during the fifteenth century to engage with Florentine authorities.[95] Lorenzo's strategy of personal diplomacy was not entirely successful as indicated by the dramatic events of the Pazzi conspiracy (1478), in which the Pisan archbishop Salviati was implicated – and executed – and the later Pisan revolt in 1494.[96]

ARCHBISHOP FILIPPO DE' VIERI DE' MEDICI

Apart from Lorenzo, Archbishop Filippo de' Vieri de' Medici, who took up his post in Pisa in 1461, played a pivotal role in Pisan cultural revival generally, and in the Camposanto during his tenure.[97] In the context of Florentine policy toward the subject city, Filippo's actions cast into sharp relief Medici ambitions to make Pisa a centerpiece of the territorial state. To his efforts to build and repair monuments of the Piazza del Duomo, hospitals, and the archiepiscopal palace, he brought a taste for magnificence and display formed at courts at the Vatican, in North Italy, and abroad. It is worth taking a fresh look at Filippo's activities as a courtier and diplomat in some detail to show how he was uniquely qualified to establish a Medici court in Pisa. At the same time, Filippo's career reveals Pisa's role in Florentine foreign policy, which sought a balance of power among the Italian states and support from European allies such as France. In this reframed context, Filippo's role in Benozzo's Old Testament murals in the Camposanto takes on new meaning.

Born in 1426 in either Florence or Avignon, Filippo was the son of a banker, Vieri di Nicola de' Medici (d. 1456).[98] Vieri's father, Nicola (1385–1454/5), and his uncle, Cambio (1391–1465), had been partners in a bank that opened around 1410.[99] Their father, Vieri di Cambio (1322–95), Filippo's great grandfather, had founded a bank in the second half of the fourteenth century that expanded into a lucrative and wide-ranging enterprise. He became one of the richest men in Florence before closing the operation at the beginning of the 1390s. In addition to his wealth, Vieri di Cambio had adroitly navigated the political turmoil of the late fourteenth century and emerged as an ally of the Albizzi regime, escaping for himself and his descendants the banishment and disqualification from political office suffered by most of the Medici clan between 1390 and 1400.

Vieri di Cambio was a distant relative of Giovanni di Bicci de' Medici (1360–1429), who began his banking career in the Rome office of Vieri's firm. Giovanni became the branch manager and partner in Vieri's bank, before beginning his own company in Rome in 1395, taking over assets and clients from Vieri's shuttered operation. From thenceforth Giovanni's bank prospered, primarily from its association with Baldassare Cossa (c. 1370–1419), the anti-Pope John XXIII (r. 1410–15), who appointed it as Depository of the Papal Chamber, the office that managed papal revenues and expenditures. Even after Cossa's expulsion from the papacy in 1415, Giovanni sheltered him in Florence and commissioned a magnificent tomb in the baptistery after his death in 1419. Medici bank associates retained the position until the 1440s, laying the foundation for the family's great wealth and political domination in the fifteenth century.

Cosimo and Lorenzo de' Medici, Giovanni's sons, took over the bank in 1420. Meanwhile the enterprise of Nicola and Cambio di Vieri went bankrupt in the late 1420s. Cosimo de' Medici was one of the creditors to the company who lost money. Nonetheless, he remained favorably disposed toward the family of his distant relatives, who through Vieri di Cambio's early support had begun its spectacular rise.

Fillipo de Medici spent his early career in Rome as an apostolic protonotary, probably in the early 1450s.[100] His career benefited from the close attention of Cosimo, whom he often referred to as "father" in his letters, 160 of which survive in the *fondo* Mediceo Avanti il Principato in the Archivio di Stato in Florence.[101] Filippo was nominated bishop of Arezzo in January of 1457, during the brief pontificate of Callixtus III (r. 1455–58), largely owing to Cosimo's advocacy.[102] In Arezzo, Filippo paid close attention to the needs of his parishioners and to the desire of his Medici relatives to gain influence, as attested to in his letters. Even after Filippo's departure for Pisa, the Aretines continued to seek his help in establishing an annual fair in Arezzo.[103]

During his tenure as bishop of Arezzo, Filippo became a *referendarius* in the Curia in 1458.[104] The position entailed managing petitions to the pope, and it was perhaps the reason he spent much of his time in Rome or traveling with the pope, leaving his diocese in the care of his vicars, Antonio da Cercina, and later Antonio Moroni da Borgo Sansepolcro.[105]

Pius II (r. 1458–64) named Filippo archbishop of Pisa on 9 January 1461 as part of the pope's attempt to enlist Cosimo's support for a new Crusade, a pressing issue in the aftermath of the fall of Constantinople in 1453.[106] Writing to Cosimo, Pius regretted only that he could not name Filippo a cardinal.[107] In fact, Medici ambitions for a cardinal in the family were realized only much later, owing more to changing papal-Florentine relations than to any action of Filippo's.

Filippo took up his post on 8 February 1461.[108] Riding a white horse, he approached the piazza Duomo from the southeast, along the borgo San Marco, flanked by members of the ancient noble Lanfranchi Chiccoli family, city officials, and citizens.[109] On reaching the cathedral, the archbishop dismounted and processed to the high altar. There, he celebrated Mass, then repaired to the archbishop's palace for a banquet. At the end of the meal, the new archbishop donated the silver gilt cup from which he had drunk wine to the noble family. Participating in the ceremony were his uncle Donato de' Medici, the bishop of Pistoia, and Leonardo di Francesco Salutati, bishop of Fiesole.[110] The pomp and spectacle of Filippo's entrance, and the participation of the cathedral chapter and communal authorities, visualize the *chiesa cittadina* which, as seen in Chapter 2, had first emerged in the late Trecento.[111] The Lanfranchi presence highlighted, as well, the continuing role of the old nobility in the Pisan church.[112] The appointment of Filippo, however, made plain the continual domination of Pisa by Florence.[113]

Unlike all previous archbishops, Filippo mostly resided in Pisa from then on.[114] His letters to Medici correspondents testify to his immediate concern to improve the "disorganized affairs" that he had discovered there.[115] The diocese was in more difficult financial straits than he had thought, as he revealed in a letter to Giovanni and Piero di Cosimo. "We have discovered that the house and possessions are the opposite of what we had expected,"[116] he wrote, and just eight days after his installation, he lamented the archbishopric's many creditors.[117] Filippo's letters reveal that much of his time as archbishop was spent attending to the needs of his parishioners. He furnished letters of recommendation for various posts,[118] and he mediated disputes.[119] He appealed for favors on behalf of others, including his brother Tanai.[120]

Other letters detail Filippo's efforts to facilitate actions of his Medici relations within areas of his control or influence. "Advise me in everything and I will follow you as much as you like," he wrote in an early letter to Giovanni di Cosimo, after pledging to help him resolve a dispute.[121]

Still others detail gifts sent by Filippo to his various correspondents.[122] He dispatched to Giovanni di Cosimo four marzipan tarts, advising, "If they not as your Magnificence deserves, you must be patient."[123] Acquainted with Lorenzo's love of hunting, in November of 1472 he presented him with a boar that had been killed in a hunt.[124] Such delicacies were highly valued in the gift-giving culture of the Medici circle.[125] He also helped Lorenzo secure some horses, although the one that Lorenzo wanted was "a crazy and dangerous horse." Instead, he sent two others.[126] Six days later Filippo wrote to follow up on the horses, of which one was pleasing, the other not.[127]

Filippo also alerted Giovanni di Cosimo to a cache of manuscripts in an abbey in Poppi, in the Casentino.

> There is a beautiful bible in three volumes, and Augustine on the Psalms, also very beautiful, in two volumes, and a beautiful Augustine on Genesis. And in another place, I have been told, there are more than twenty volumes of antique books, which, my friend says, are rather more beautiful than those in Poppi.[128]

Filippo's relationship with Giovanni di Cosimo seems to have been particularly close; more letters were written to him than to any of the Medici before Giovanni's death in 1463. Giovanni's refined taste and knowledge were manifest in his building projects, and Filippo may have found him the most congenial and closest to his own interests of any of his Medici cousins.[129]

For all the solicitation – formulaic or heartfelt – in his letters to his powerful Medici relations, Filippo's own responses to Medici requests were not uniformly obliging. He was protective of the possessions and income of his church, which he was struggling to organize. In a remarkable letter to Giovanni di Cosimo, he reasserted control over a fief held by the commune of Bibbona, against the recommendation of Giovanni. Supposing that Giovanni had been misinformed, he described the events, concluding, "but I cannot pay my debts if I cannot recover from those who owe me."[130] Similarly, Fillippo's response to Lorenzo, who supported (along with his mother Lucrezia) the petition of an abbot who sought refuge from a sanction from the archbishop over usurpation of a pasture:

> But I am very much amazed at the said abbot of Morrona, who complains about me, and I have cause to complain about him countless times, because he claims a pasture which the archbishopric of Pisa has already possessed peacefully and without any impediment for two hundred years.[131]

Estimates are that by his vigorous pursuit of church claims he doubled or even tripled the income of the Pisan church.[132]

Filippo's efforts to reorganize the city and provincial churches are also documented in the accounts of two pastoral visits made during his tenure, the first, from 3 June 1462 to 16 July 1463, and the second by Filippo's vicar, Mariano da Vecchiano, in 1469.[133] The sheer number of churches, monasteries, and hospitals surveyed, and the extensive participation of Fillipo himself in the exhausting rounds of visits, signal an unusually activist archbishop. The visits also allowed him to view at first hand the living conditions of the inhabitants of both city and country. He further organized a synod in his diocese in May 1461, to reform the leadership of the Pisan clergy.

Filippo summarized his efforts to reclaim church lands alienated by previous officials or usurped by private interests, to reorganize the provincial churches, and to repair the fabric of his diocese in an undated, autograph memorandum, presumably composed toward the end of his life, simply entitled "memorandum of the things I have done since becoming archbishop of Pisa" (Figure 3.4; Appendix II).[134] Efforts to increase the productivity of the church lands dominate the list. He planted olives and vines at the castles of Calci and Filettole, while he transformed pastures into cultivation at Santa Lucia and Barbaricina. He reclaimed mills at Vecchiano and Rosignano. He also recovered or expanded church possessions in Asciano, Collesalvetti, and many others.

At the papal court in the 1450s, Filippo served as an intermediary for the Medici regime in the delicate relations of Florence and the papacy. Many of the letters underscore Filippo's role as the "eyes and ears" of the Medici family in the Curia. An early letter to Giovanni, for example, includes some juicy gossip on future appointments to bishoprics of Terni and Volterra, as well as advice on future actions. Exchange of information and opinion, as well as an intimate tone, recur in many of Filippo's letters, especially to Giovanni di Cosimo.[135]

As the most highly placed clerical member of the Medici family,[136] Filippo was, by 1458, Cosimo's and Piero's candidate for the College of Cardinals, a post they eagerly sought for the prestige and power it would bring.[137] Pius's regret that he could not grant the request implies that it was requested by Cosimo in 1457.[138] The signoria's instructions of 28 September 1458 to the ambassadors sent to Rome to congratulate Pius II on his accession requested a cardinal's hat for Filippo, whom they characterized as "the respected bishop of Arezzo, who for honest life and highest wisdom is worthy of every great dignity, and for us there cannot be a more grateful thing than the said bishop assumes this honor, especially because of the honor and glory that would result to this city and to his deeply respected and beloved family."[156] Pius's response, despite their "very effective" request, as reported by the ambassadors, was noncommittal. He asked, amused, why, among the many recommendations, they had not included the saintly archbishop Antoninus (r. 1446–59), underscoring the overtly political nature of their request.[139] Pius reports in the *Commentaries* that in 1460, visiting Florence on his return from Mantua, Cosimo de' Medici again requested the honor for his relative.[140]

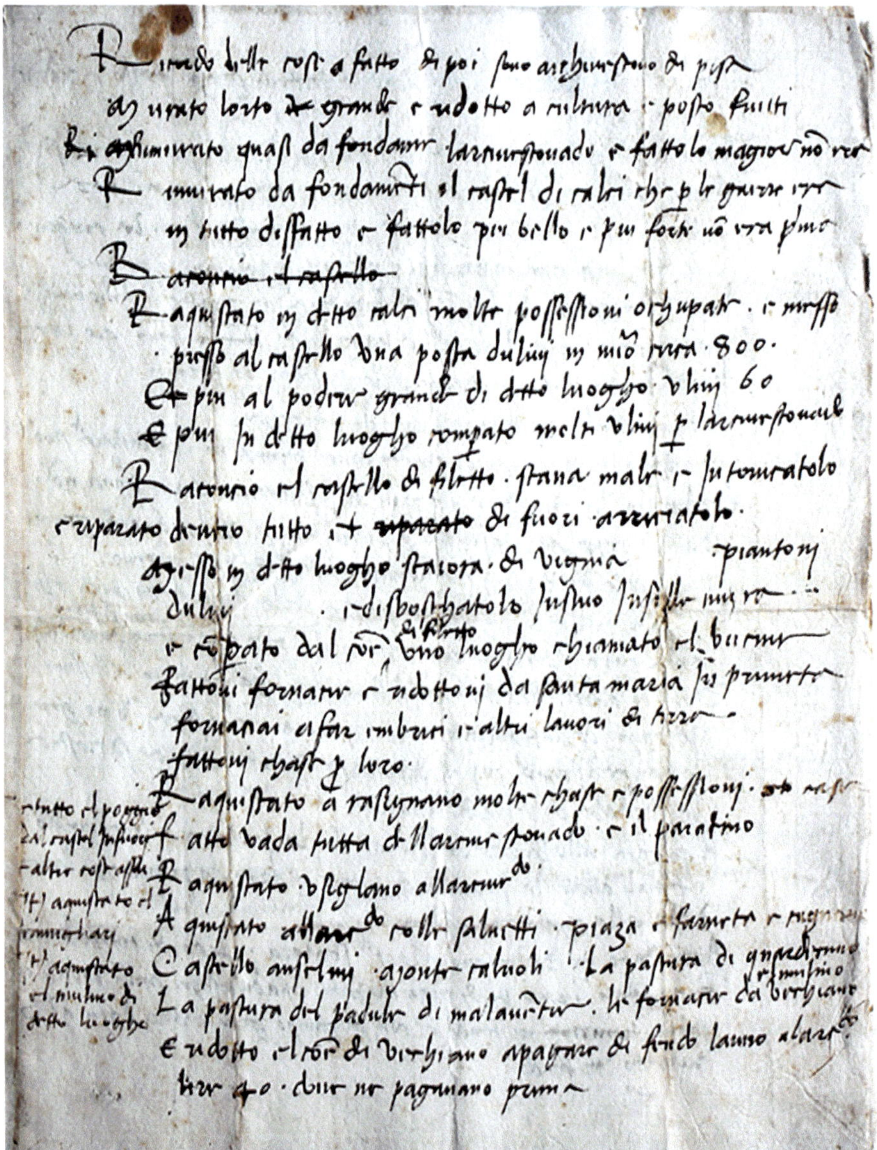

3.4. Filippo de' Medici, Memorandum, c. 1474, Archivio di Stato, Pisa. Photo: Archivio di Stato, Pisa.

Filippo seems to have sought the cardinalate eagerly as well. Several letters discuss in detail the timing, supporters, and rival candidates for the honor. Yet the survival of his letters almost exclusively to Medici correspondents has led to undue emphasis on this aspect of Filippo's career. Filippo pursued a long-standing goal of Medici policy, not simply personal prestige. For example, a letter from Rome to Cosimo, written 21 March 1457/8, while Filippo was bishop of Arezzo, already signals this theme. He reports a conversation with the pope, in which Filippo expresses "a great desire to exalt your house."[141] Another letter, written to Giovanni di Cosimo 18 February 1459/60 from Siena, where Filippo was with Pope Pius II, begins, "I do not doubt that we will achieve everything."[142] In a letter to Piero di Cosimo, from Rome, written in the last year of Piero's life, Filippo reported on upcoming appointments of cardinals, and he solicited written support for his candidacy. He also alludes to the long campaign to secure for the family this honor, concluding, "You have done so much work in the past, which this [request] adds to the other cares you had for this cause."[143]

Filippo continued to be the official candidate for the cardinal's hat, as shown in one of the mandates carried by Filippo, Ottone Niccolini, and Antonio Ridolfi as ambassadors for Florence to the emperor Frederick III in December 1468. It stated:

> And because the city has long lacked the dignity of the Cardinalate, as it appears to you a suitable thing and when an occasion arises, we pray your His Majesty . . . to make us equal to other cities of Italy . . . and if it were necessary to descend to particularities, you will recommend Messer Philippo de 'Medici, archbishop of Pisa, who through family nobility and virtues seems worthy of all honor.[144]

After Piero's death in 1469 and Lorenzo's consolidation of power in the early 1470s, Filippo's candidacy for the cardinalship was eclipsed.[145] His deteriorating health, alluded to in some letters, was one factor; perhaps his less cordial relations with Lorenzo may have been another.[146] In letters, some of which address Lorenzo in the familiar, others of which call him "brother," Filippo is deferent but not obsequious.[147] In one remarkable letter, Filippo chastised the young man for requesting a French-style doublet formerly in his possession; Filippo had given it away, adding, "in this land there are few youths who have anything, much less 'farsetti alla Francesa.'"[148]

By 1470, Lorenzo's ambitions for a Medici cardinal focused first on his brother Giuliano, and, after Giuliano's death in the Pazzi conspiracy in 1478, on his son Giovanni, who was created cardinal at the age of thirteen in 1489.[149] Lorenzo declared, "This is the greatest thing our house has ever done."[150] The deviation from the policy of his father and grandfather signaled an expansion of Lorenzo's ambition for his family – from one centered on Florence, to one that extended to the Italian peninsula and beyond to Europe.[151] At the election of Sixtus IV (r. 1471–84) in 1471, Filippo was excluded from the official Florentine delegation to honor the new pope. Nonetheless, he went to Rome and met with Sixtus, reporting to Lorenzo the pope's warm welcome to him, "He would help me and other things with time, which it was not necessary to say here: where the work is done words are not needed."[152]

After Filippo's death in October of 1474, Lorenzo wished to have Gentile Becchi, longtime tutor to the Medici children who had succeeded Filippo as bishop of Arezzo, named archbishop of Pisa. Pope Sixtus IV rebuked Lorenzo's strenuous efforts to promote a pro-Medicean candidate, appointing as archbishop Francesco Salviati, an ally of the pope's nephew Girolamo Riario and of the Pazzi family. Relations between Florence and the papacy reached a nadir with the Pazzi conspiracy and the subsequent Pazzi war.[153]

Despite Filippo's unsuccessful campaign for the cardinal's hat, his knowledge of the personalities and formalities of the papal court served the Medici well beginning in the 1450s. In 1459, he accompanied Pope Pius II to Mantua to rally forces for a new Crusade stopping in Siena, Florence, Bologna, and Ferrara, before arriving in Mantua.[154] Although he was not part of the official delegation, Filippo reported regularly to his Medici correspondents on the activities of the pope's retinue and its reception. In Florence, he presumably formed part of the visitors accommodated in the palazzo Medici, including the young son of Duke Francesco of Milan, whose reports of the lavishness of the new palazzo are well known.[155] From Ferrara he wrote to Giovanni di Cosimo, "Now we are here where his Holiness with all his court has been received very magnificently; . . . today His Holiness and all the cardinals have gone to Belfiore."[156] He also sojourned with the Pope in Siena in February 1460 on his return trip from Mantua.[157]

In a mark of exceptional status, Filippo led the Florentine delegation to Rome to honor the newly elected Venetian pope, Paul II (r. 1464–71), from October to December 1464. Filippo gave the official oration.[158] Four years later, he took part in the delegation to the emperor Frederick III, who had arrived in Rome in December of 1468. Filippo, once again, assumed the post of orator.[159] As Maxson has shown, designation as an ambassador and orator, as Filippo was three times, was a mark of highest honor, for a diplomat had to possess high social status as well as eloquence. Filippo was an archbishop, a Medici, and a scholar. He was thus superbly suited for the most important missions, which for Florence were those to the pope, the Holy Roman Emperor, the duke of Milan, and the kings of Naples and France. The missions Filippo headed were ceremonial affairs to welcome a new leader. By the second half of the fifteenth century, orations in humanist Latin were the centerpiece of the diplomatic ritual. As Maxson has argued, these orations not only signaled goodwill and sincerity, but they also implied reciprocal recognition, deference, or obedience from the host. The oration enhanced the reputation for learning, and in sending a distinguished orator, the city honored the host as well, for the implication was that the host could appreciate and reciprocate the gift. Filippo's oration in 1464 to the new pope makes liberal reference to classical and biblical sources embedded in humanist rhetoric.[160]

Filippo also performed more personal diplomatic service to the Medici, most notably when he represented the groom in Rome at the 10 December 1468 wedding of Lorenzo de' Medici and Clarice Orsini, of the old Roman baronial family.[161] His letters on this occasion to Piero de' Medici and to the young groom reveal his intimacy with the ruling family and the extraordinary loyalty and trust they shared. He later accompanied the bride to Florence, where the marriage was celebrated in great splendor on 4–6 June 1469.[162]

Filippo's diplomatic skills were also deployed internationally. A mere eight months after his appointment as archbishop of Pisa, in September of 1461, he was dispatched as Florentine ambassador to the new French king, Louis XI (r. 1461–83).[163] In the context of the Florentine alliance with Duke Francesco Sforza (r. 1450–66) of Milan, relations with the new French king were delicate, given renewed Angevin attempts to take Naples from the Crown of Aragon.[164] Milan had so far favored the Aragonese, as did Florence, while trying to maintain the appearance of neutrality. Filippo was accompanied by Buonaccorso di Luca Pitti and Piero de' Pazzi. Giovanni Cecchi, a notary who served as secretary, recorded the itinerary and expenses for this famous voyage, which is worth recounting in some detail for the light it sheds on Filippo's taste for art and architecture.[165] The ambassadors were determined to present an impression of magnificence equal to that of their royal hosts.

The party traveled first to Bologna, where they met with the principal citizens, including the papal legate Cardinal Bessarion, and then to Modena.[166] The *capitano* and *podestà* of Modena escorted them to the city, where they were lodged, "magnificently at the expense of the lord," in the castle of the duke. From Modena and Reggio they reached Parma, where they were met by the son of the duke of Milan and escorted to their lodgings "with many attendants, trumpeters and pipers." While in Parma, they toured the baptistery of San Giovanni, marveled at the large, granite baptismal font, and remarked on the beauty of the large piazza. In Piacenza, they viewed the cathedral and remarked on a beautiful cross, but they thought, "our new one in San Giovanni in Florence is much more beautiful," referring to the silver cross recently completed for the Baptistery by Antonio del Pollaiuolo. They reached Milan on 8 November, where city authorities and members of the ducal court welcomed them. Musicians and performers provided lavish entertainment. Two days later, they visited Duke Francesco Sforza of Milan, and the next day Pigello Portinari, head of the Milan branch of the Medici bank, treated them to a sumptuous dinner in the Medici palace. Touring the fortress of Milan, they judged it "the most beautiful fortress in the world." The following day, they visited Madonna Bianca Maria Visconti, wife of Duke Francesco, with her sons and daughter Ippolita, promised bride of Alfonso of Calabria and a noted diplomat herself.[167] The castle of the duke was judged one of the largest and most beautiful in the world, "and there were three internal courtyards, one of the duke, one of count Galeazzo, and one of Madonna Bianca, and beyond that there was the lodging of the ambassador of the Duke of Burgundy." The party also visited the principal churches, including Sant'Eustorgio, where they saw the tomb of Saint Peter Martyr; Sant'Ambrogio, where they saw the relic of one of the Holy Innocents and the golden altar frontal; and the incomplete cathedral, where they heard Mass. Behind the scenes of this decorous visit, however, Piero de' Pazzi was maneuvering to promote French interests in the Angevin cause and recruit Duke Francesco to the French side.[168]

The party left Milan on 14 November. As they progressed toward the mountains, their pace slowed. They arrived at the foot of the Saint Bernard mountain on 23 November, then made the difficult crossing, encountering wind and snow and arriving "more dead than alive." In Geneva, they met Florentine merchants and dined at the seats of the Medici and Pazzi banks. By 8 December they had reached Lyon, and by the 19th they entered Bourges.

The cathedral of Bourges impressed them with its double aisles, its length equal to that of the cathedral in Pisa, and its high windows. Noteworthy were the reliquaries of gold and silver, covered with gems and pearls. The chapel built by Duke John of Berry (r. 1360–1416), in which he was buried in a splendid tomb, was a marvel, "and all around [arches] of more than six *braccia* filled with stained glass with figures, which are very bright, and so dense, that the sun does not penetrate them." The sacristy was furnished with embroidered and damasked liturgical vestments from Paris and Florence "and [paintings] from all parts of the world where they have the greatest masters," including eighteen altar panels with scenes from the life of Christ and many other relics that they venerated by kissing.

They also saw in Bourges the house of Jacques Coeur (c. 1395–1456), the fabulously wealthy banker of King Charles VII who was later banished. They remarked that the house was "very beautiful, and in a form different from our customs," and it contained portraits of the banker from life, one of the late king, one of Duke René of Anjou, and many other lords, as well as an altarpiece in the chapel and a seven *braccia*-long crocodile.

On the 23 December, they reached Tours and were greeted, without warning, by King Louis XI of France, who was en route to celebrate the Christmas holiday in Amboise. In a gesture of extraordinary regard, the royal party, consisting of thirty or forty mounted courtiers, rode out six miles beyond the walls of the city to greet them.[169] The king welcomed them with great courtesy, taking off his hat, and, preventing the archbishop from dismounting, embraced him. Speaking in French, the king vowed friendship with Florence, while Filippo responded, presumably in Italian, which the king understood. The delegation then met with others of the king's retinue, including ambassadors and the archbishops of Tours and Bourges. After the king left, Filippo's delegation remained "stupefied" by the unscripted encounter, not least because they had not had time to change into suitable clothing.

On the 30 December, the Florentine ambassadors had an audience with the king, in which Filippo delivered the Latin oration to an audience of lords, gentlemen, and others.[170] The oration celebrated the historic links between Florence and France, traced back to Charlemagne, and placed the king in a long line of heroic leaders from ancient and biblical history, including David, Solomon, Vespasian, Trajan, Theodosius, and Heraclius.[171] The Florentines met a second time with the king on 2 January when Donato Acciaiuoli, traveling in the retinue of Piero de' Pazzi, presented him a copy of his *History of Charlemagne.*

The party attended Mass in the cathedral of Tours the next day and then went to dine with the king, where, Cecchi proudly reported, "the place at the head of the table was given to Monsignor the archbishop of Pisa." On 6 January, in the company of many ambassadors, Piero de' Pazzi was unexpectedly made a knight by the king in a grand ceremony. Piero delivered his extemporaneous oration of thanks in Italian, instead of the expected Latin, which he had no time to prepare.[172] On 11 January, the ambassadors were presented with lavish gifts and granted various offices by the king.

The king departed Tours on 12 January, while the party visited the church of Saint-Martin, of which the king was the abbot, and which held the body of the saint. Piero remained in Tours, preparing his return to Florence, while Filippo and Bonaccorso left for Amboise, Blois, Orleans, and Étampes on 14 January, finally arriving in Paris on 22 January.

In Paris, the party visited Notre Dame, noting its great length and the richness of the sculpture, reliquaries, and treasures. They also saw the hospital; the royal palace of the Parliament, in which the chapel of the king (the Sainte Chapelle) held many relics; the church of Sainte-Geneviève; the university; the Bastille; the four bridges across the Seine; and the prison (Châtelet). At Saint-Denis, they marveled at the beauty of the choir, the richness of the sculpture and altars, and especially the great gemmed cross and tabernacle with the head of Saint Denis. In the treasury, they admired the head and arm of Saint Benedict, the crowns of the kings and queens of France, the lily of precious stones, and the scepter used in the coronation ceremony. Other relics included the hand of Saint Thomas, the sword of Charlemagne, a nail and the crown of thorns, and a piece of the True Cross.

The party left Paris on 25 January, visiting the park and castle at Vincennes, describing the complex of towers (*donjons*) in detail. From there they traveled eastward to Troyes, and eventually Dijon, and continuing to Chalons-sur-Saône; remarking on the beautiful countryside planted with vines. On 8 February, they boarded a barge and went down the Rhône to Tornus and

Mâcon, arriving eventually at Lyon on 11 February. From there they traveled through Savoy and finally to Milan, Pavia, Piacenza, Parma, Reggio, Modena, and Bologna. Finally, on 14 March, they reentered Florence, greeted by the "the banners of the people and the Guelf party." The voyage showcased Filippo's extensive connections, his wide diplomatic experience, and his participation in the ceremonies and spectacle of foreign courts. His experience positioned him perfectly to serve as the central figure in a Medici presence at Pisa and linchpin of Florentine relations with the papacy, Milan, and France.

Filippo also revealed himself in his letters to be a tireless advocate for Pisa. In addition to his efforts on behalf of parishioners and associates, he took advantage of access to his Medici relations in Florence to bring conditions in the city and countryside to their attention. In a letter to Lorenzo in 1471, as Lorenzo was still securing control of Florence in the aftermath of Piero's death, Filippo wrote,

> After I left Florence, I never wrote to your Magnificence to recommend this city, knowing well your affection and disposition towards it, and not needing either my persuasions or anyone else's; and because I am sure you understand and know this city to be the principal member and of usefulness and honor that our republic could have, and being well judged and governed it will be honorable and useful to Your Magnificence and to our entire republic.[173]

He also advocated for the rights of some Pisan guilds against the encroachment of Florentine counterparts, justifying his intervention, "wishing to do every good and lend every help that I honestly can for the city and citizens and dwellers, I pen these few lines to Your Magnificence."[174] He concluded, saying, "This will please Your Magnificence, and not only them and me, but universally the whole city, to which help is highly laudable and of very great merit before God." On another occasion, Filippo alerted Lorenzo to policies that were driving people from the land, resulting in "considerable expense and inconvenience to this countryside, which would have no need if it did not have need of men."[175]

Even toward the end of his life, when Filippo's candidacy as a cardinal had been unofficially abandoned by Lorenzo, Filippo labored for Medici interests in Pisa. He was the point person for building galleys for the pope at Pisa in early 1472, after the end of the Florentine galley program.[176] He also supported Lorenzo in his drive to relocate the Studio to Pisa, where, by virtue of his position as Archbishop, he was chancellor, and he presided over its inauguration on 1 November 1473.[177] Writing just two days after the inauguration to prepare Lorenzo for a delegation from the Studio, he expressed pride:

> The University is sending ambassadors to the signoria for their needs. It is not necessary to recommend them to you, as you are the leader, guide,

> and protector of this family of which everyone marvels, being led as it is in such good terms; although I do not think there is a Studio in Italy that has as many worthy men as there are here. Of which you are very well pleased to be the leader of such an honored work.[178]

FILIPPO DE' MEDICI AS A PATRON OF ART

The account of the French voyage affords a glimpse of Filippo's interest in works of art and architecture. While no letters of Filippo survive from the voyage, Cecchi's record likely reflects Filippo's and his companions' experiences. They were impressed by the scale of certain structures – reporting precise dimensions – and they admired precious materials. Some of their comments suggest sophisticated awareness of regional style. For example, they noted the choir of Bourges cathedral, with its piers of eight faces, elevated main chapel, and tall windows.[179] Their attention to the house of Jacques Coeur, "in a form different from our custom," as well as the portraits and an altarpiece "from the hand of a great master," reveals openness to northern European architectural styles and pictorial genres. Filippo's earlier letters to Giovanni di Cosimo about potential manuscript acquisitions, in which he freely offers opinions on their quality, come to mind and reinforce a view of an acute artistic sensibility.

Filippo's archbishopric in Pisa marked an intensified revival of cultural activity in the city. In the 1460s, major projects were undertaken, many of which can be traced to the archbishop's initiatives.[180] In expense records of the Mensa Arcivescovile and as noted in his memorandum, Filippo's efforts to rebuild institutions within his control as archbishop of Pisa are clear.[181] He improved the archiepiscopal residences at Calci and Fillettole, where he often entertained his Medici relations.[182] At Calci, he rebuilt the castle and planted vines and olives. Similarly, he recorded repairs to the castle at Filettole and vast plantings.[183] Later alterations make it difficult to isolate what might have been done during Filippo's time. However, his emphasis in his memorandum on plantings and cultivation, as much as on building, seems to echo Lorenzo's own passion for agriculture, and the classically inspired life of *villeggiatura*. In addition to plantings, Fillippo also showed concern for productive infrastructure, reclaiming for the archbishopric the mills at Vecchiano and Rosignano. He also constructed kilns for making brick at Vecchiano and Filettole and houses for the workers there. Evidently Filippo took a broad economic and social view of his duties as archbishop.

At the top of the list in the memorandum Filippo noted that he rebuilt the archiepiscopal palace "practically from the foundations and made it larger than it was before," after having "walled in the large garden, subjected it to cultivation and planted fruit trees." Begun in 1461, construction largely took

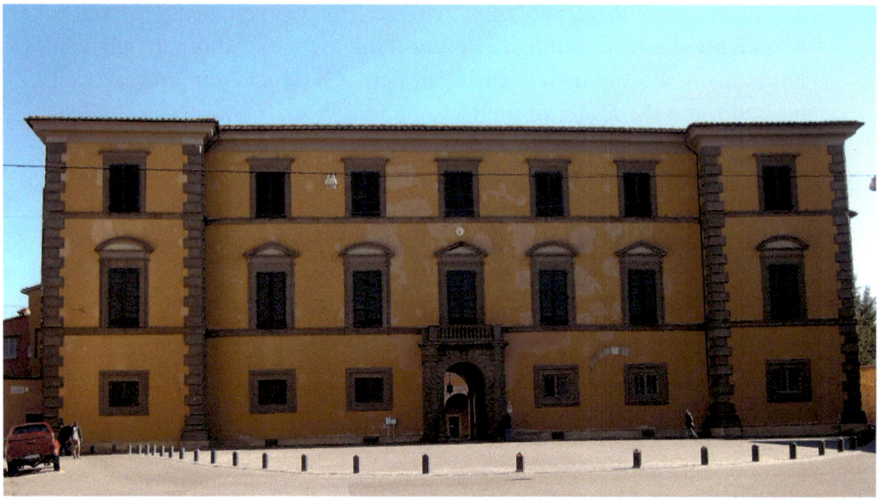

3.5. Palazzo Arcivescovile, 1464–76, Pisa. Photo Author.

place between 1465 and 1472. While Filippo did not live to see the completed palace, substantial portions built during and just after his tenure allow a view of Filippo as a patron of architecture. Recent analyses have placed the palazzo in the context of fifteenth-century princely palaces, highlighting its innovative and distinctive features.[184] Filippo has emerged as a patron of ambition and sophistication previously unknown. He conceived the palace as the centerpiece of a brilliant archiepiscopal court and center of Medici splendor second only to the Palazzo Medici in Florence.

Filippo inherited an archiepiscopal palace that dated from the eleventh century (Figure 3.5). The Florentine archbishop Simone Saltarelli renovated the palace during his tenure (1323–42).[185] A large structure with a courtyard and garden, its brick façade faced the piazza and created the impression of a "buon castello."[186] Filippo's rebuilding of the palace as reconstructed by Morolli included an enormous north wing built *ex novo* and renovation of the existing wings, including a large peristyle courtyard, the only part that remains essentially intact today (Figure 3.6). The archbishop expanded and replanted the encircling gardens and orchards, no trace of which survives. The western façade, with projecting corner towers and central portal, faced the long rectangular Piazza del Arcivescovado. It was last renovated in the nineteenth and twentieth centuries, but in Filippo's time it probably retained its fourteenth-century appearance.

Filippo's renovations reflected his expansive ambitions for his archbishopric. The palace provided a magnificent setting for gatherings of the cultivated elite, public officials, his clerical *famiglia*, and supplicating parishioners – all activities that his letters document in vivid detail. In the area between the north wing and the city walls, Filippo planned a large walled garden with vines and a

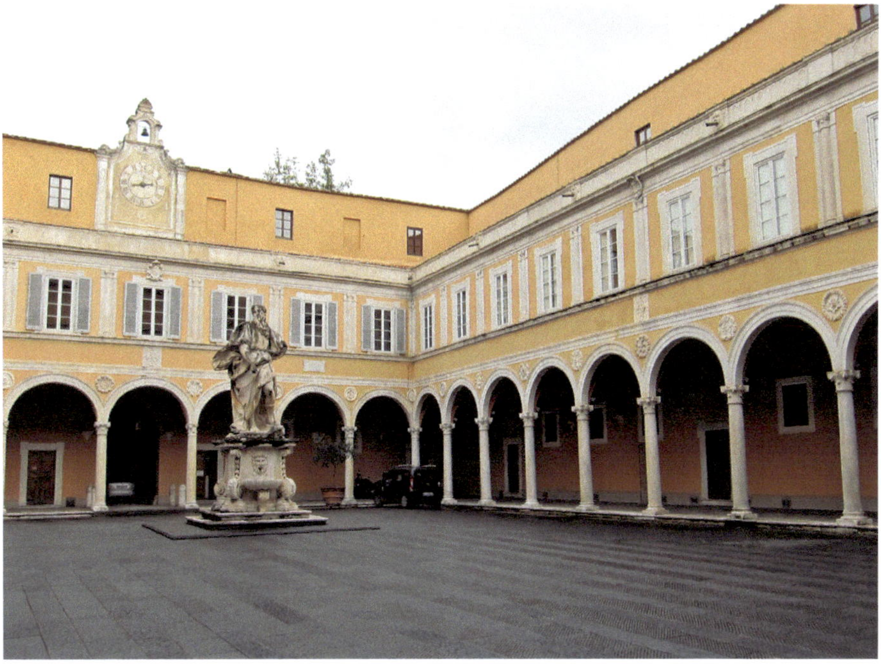

3.6. Palazzo Arcivescovile, courtyard, Pisa. Photo: Author.

trellis, again establishing links between the city and the countryside, and the spiritual and material needs of the archbishopric.

In the central courtyard of the palace, Filippo embraced progressive architectural styles. Usually compared to the courtyard of the Palazzo Medici in Florence, constructed by Michelozzo in the 1440s, its sheer scale – a large rectangular volume of space with open logge on the second floor – marks a departure. The capitals and columns reveal a Brunelleschian architectural vocabulary and the tradition of north Italian carving that prevailed in Pisan sculptural workshops from the mid-fifteenth century.[187] The rosettes in the spandrels of the arches are particularly distinctive in their varying naturalistic motifs and high relief carving (Figure 3.7). These architectural details alluded to the grand tradition of marble carving exemplified in the monuments of the Piazza del Duomo and its link to antiquity. Even Filippo's coat of arms, which graces every façade of the courtyard, displays the Medici *palle* in the language of florid neo-Romanesque naturalism.

In its site and design, the Palazzo Arcivescovile recalled the Palazzo Piccolomini in Pienza, which Filippo may have visited with Pius in 1459 or 1460.[188] Pienza's monuments could have been in an advanced enough state to serve as models for Filippo's structures. In addition, Filippo presumably knew of, or participated in, the discussions of architecture with Leon Battista Alberti at the Gonzaga court in early 1460, during the Mantuan Diet, and he was generally familiar with new architectural ideas from his years in Florence. In his

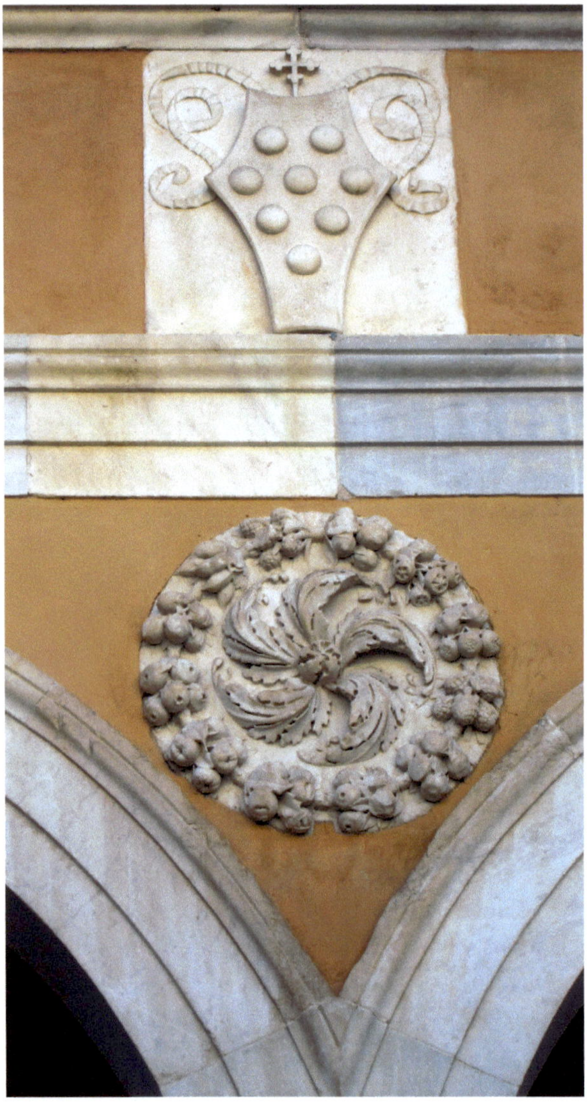

3.7. Palazzo Arcivescovile, courtyard, detail, c.1475, Pisa. Photo: Author.

Commentaries, Pius emphasized the convenience and comfort of the palace's layout, and the experience of the countryside – of views, sunlight, and breezes – from various points inside.[189] Pius's remarkable celebration of the practicality of the palace, how inhabitants experienced it, and the way the palace functioned – instead of its abstract design principles or magnificent materials – might all have shaped Filippo's vision for his new palace.

Papal building in Rome that Filippo had come to know during his residence there in the 1450s also shaped his architectural taste.[190] The vast wing of the Palazzo Venezia, constructed by the Cardinal of San Marco, later Pope Paul II, was begun in 1455 and resumed from 1466 to 1471. The courtyard of the *palazzetto*, in its scale and open logge, echoed the archiepiscopal palace in Pisa. The Pisan palace can also be compared in its scale, materials, and elegant architectural details to the later ducal palace in Urbino, aspects of which the Pisa palace may have anticipated. The palace thus takes its place as one of the great princely palaces that were built in the second half of the fifteenth century and served ecclesiastical and lay patrons of courtly and humanist ambitions. The new palace was a sumptuous theater for a Medici court presence in Pisa, presided over by the archbishop.

The archbishop's accounts reveal that he employed Pisan and Florentine artisans in the project.[191] The building site of the new palace constituted a miniature public works project, bolstering the artisan economy of Pisa.[192] The well-established Domenico di Giovanni da Milano was the primary director of the works from 1464 to 1476. A payment of 3 March 1466 noted his close relationship with Filippo.[193] He may have carved several of the *stemma* and rosettes of the courtyard. The primary supplier of the marble was Bartolomeo d'Andreuccio da Carrara, in collaboration with other stone workers from Carrara. Other names in the documents include the sculptors Guasparre d'Antonio, active in Pisa from the 1440s to the 1470s in the Camposanto and elsewhere, and Banco d'Andrea, documented as working on the marble windows of the Camposanto between 1457 and 1467.

Artists and architects from Florence played an increasingly larger role. The woodworker Francesco di Giovanni, called Francione (1428–95), was a key contributor. Filippo likely made his acquaintance at the papal court in Rome in the mid-1450s. Francione appeared in Pisa soon after Filippo's arrival as archbishop, entrusted with a new coffered wooden ceiling in the tribune and transepts of the Duomo, executed between 1462 and 1465.[194] He further worked in the Duomo on ceilings for the chapels of the Annunziata and dell'Incoronata in the transept (1467–70).[195] Six seats or benches with spalliere for the *operai* of the Duomo and the Baptistery were commissioned in 1466 and finished in 1468. New inlaid stalls for the priors were commissioned in 1470 but left incomplete when Francione left Pisa in 1470; they were manufactured in Florence and sent to Pisa in 1474, valued at delivery at 1,000 lire, the costliest objects in wood commissioned by the Opera during the fifteenth century.[196] Unfortunately, they, like most of the woodwork in the Duomo, survive only in fragments. The Florentine architect Giuliano da Maiano executed between 1470 and 1475 a bench with "*figure in prospettiva*" for the celebrants at the high altar in the Duomo and another smaller work that was installed in 1476. He signed the contract, with the stipulation that the figures would be "like those he made in the sacristy of Santa Liberata [that is, the Florentine cathedral], or better," on 9 February 1470, in the presence of the archbishop.[197] Francione's student, Baccio Pontelli, and his younger brother Piero, first appeared in Pisa in 1469 during the work on the Duomo ceiling, and they reappear sporadically in the accounts of the Opera and the Mensa Arcivescovile up until their transfer to Urbino in 1478.[198] The author of a wooden model, sent to Pisa from Florence in 1466, is often speculated to be Francione, though both the attribution and the function of the model, either of the Palazzo Medici or of the new Palazzo Arcivescovile, is unknown.[199] Members of the équipe assembled in Pisa, including Francione and Giuliano da Maiano, took part in the siege of Volterra in 1472 (directed by Federigo da Montefeltro of Urbino) and the construction of its fortress. Later, several worked on grandiose princely projects in Urbino and Rome, Pontelli prominently among them. They also took part in the various building projects of Lorenzo de' Medici in the 1480s, including his villa at Agnano. It may have been Filippo who introduced Lorenzo to Francione, who went on to become the center of a cluster of engineers, architects, and builders to whom Lorenzo turned for expertise and advice throughout his career. Giuliano da Maiano perhaps entered this circle through his work in Pisa for Filippo.[200]

In the monuments of the Piazza del Duomo, Filippo's influence is often assumed but is seldom documented. As we have seen, Francione's commissions in the Duomo follow closely on Filippo's arrival as archbishop. In the Camposanto, Filippo is often credited with the completion of the marble tracery in the arcade and with the resumption of the mural decoration. In fact, however, the archbishop had no legal role in the administration of the Duomo or the Camposanto. That power rested firmly with the Opera del Duomo, the secular body reporting to the Pisan priors and ultimately to the signoria of Florence.[201] The *operaio* of the Opera del Duomo, appointed by the Priors, was the active manager of the building campaigns in the Duomo and Camposanto. In the copious documentation that survives in the Opera del Duomo archive relating to the Quattrocento projects during Filippo's tenure, there is no mention of an active role for the archbishop. Only on a few occasions the Opera and the Archbisopric exchanged materials, including timber, marble, and a column, most likely for the archiepiscopal palace.[202]

The *operaio* during Filippo's tenure as archbishop was Antonio di Jacopo dalle Mura (1415–88), a goldsmith whose family had emigrated from Siena.[203] Antonio seems to have won the favor of the Pisan priors and the Florentine signoria through his promises to reorganize and reform the Opera, which officials charged with mismanagement. In this, and other areas, Antonio seems to have been an effective manager and was charged multiple times with ambassadorships to Florence to argue for various measures on behalf of the Opera.

Antonio assumed his post on 5 February 1461, just three days before Filippo took possession of the archbishopric, and although there is no documented previous contact, there is evidence of good relations between them. Both held offices of considerable prestige and pursued their duties assiduously; Antonio, as well as the archbishop, sought to reclaim alienated properties and to increase income, and both were in some measure successful.[204] In their parallel roles, the *operaio* and the archbishop perhaps felt a certain comradery. Antonio, too, was politically attuned and well connected. He corresponded with Lorenzo de' Medici on several occasions; in one he thanks him for his support, "If I did not have the support of you Magnificence, I would not know how to run this office."[205] In another letter he acknowledges, "as always I am governed by the counsel of this magnificent house." Presumably this *consiglio* extended to the ideas and opinions offered by the archbishop who was, of course a Medici.[206] We have scant evidence for interaction between the two men, but it makes sense that they communicated, perhaps in person on site.

Antonio's profession of goldsmith also must have played a role in the exercise of his duties as *operaio*. Known for their work with precious materials and their expertise in design, goldsmiths were also praised for versatility of skill.[207] Artisan knowledge would be helpful in the management of the many craftsmen and workers that made up the Opera's work force. Filippo's sensitivity to works of art, from architecture to book illumination, made him appreciate the skills that Antonio brought to his position and perhaps facilitated collaboration between them.

As the foremost religious authority in Pisa, Filippo de' Medici surely had some influence over the management of the most sacred spaces in the city, if only through the prestige of his position and his personal relationship with the *operaio*. A plaque in the Camposanto commemorates the completion of the tracery in 1464 (Figure 3.8). It reads: "At the time of Archbishop of Pisa Filippo de' Medici, Antonio di Jacopo *operaio* with three years of diligent work, brought to completion four great arches and twenty-eight tripartite marble windows."[208] The inscription implies the archbishop's support, if not active role. In fact, the project to complete the marble windows began in 1451, before either the *operaio* or the archbishop assumed office.[209] The wording of the plaque conforms to that on the inscription from 1278 on the façade of the Camposanto.[210] Both inscriptions are strategically placed to confront the visitor, the earlier one to the left of the main entrance of the Camposanto; the later to the right, on the path through the sacred field that leads from the main entrance to the north corridor. Their formulaic and ceremonial content was as significant as their historical message.

Even if Filippo de' Medici had no formal authority over construction and decoration projects in the Camposanto, his influence can be detected in aspects of the decoration itself. Apart from his role in the religious ceremonies of the Camposanto – during Easter and the vigil to All Souls' Day, at funerals and memorial Masses – Filippo's veneration for the Camposanto was manifest. As we have seen, Filippo chose to be buried in the Camposanto in a

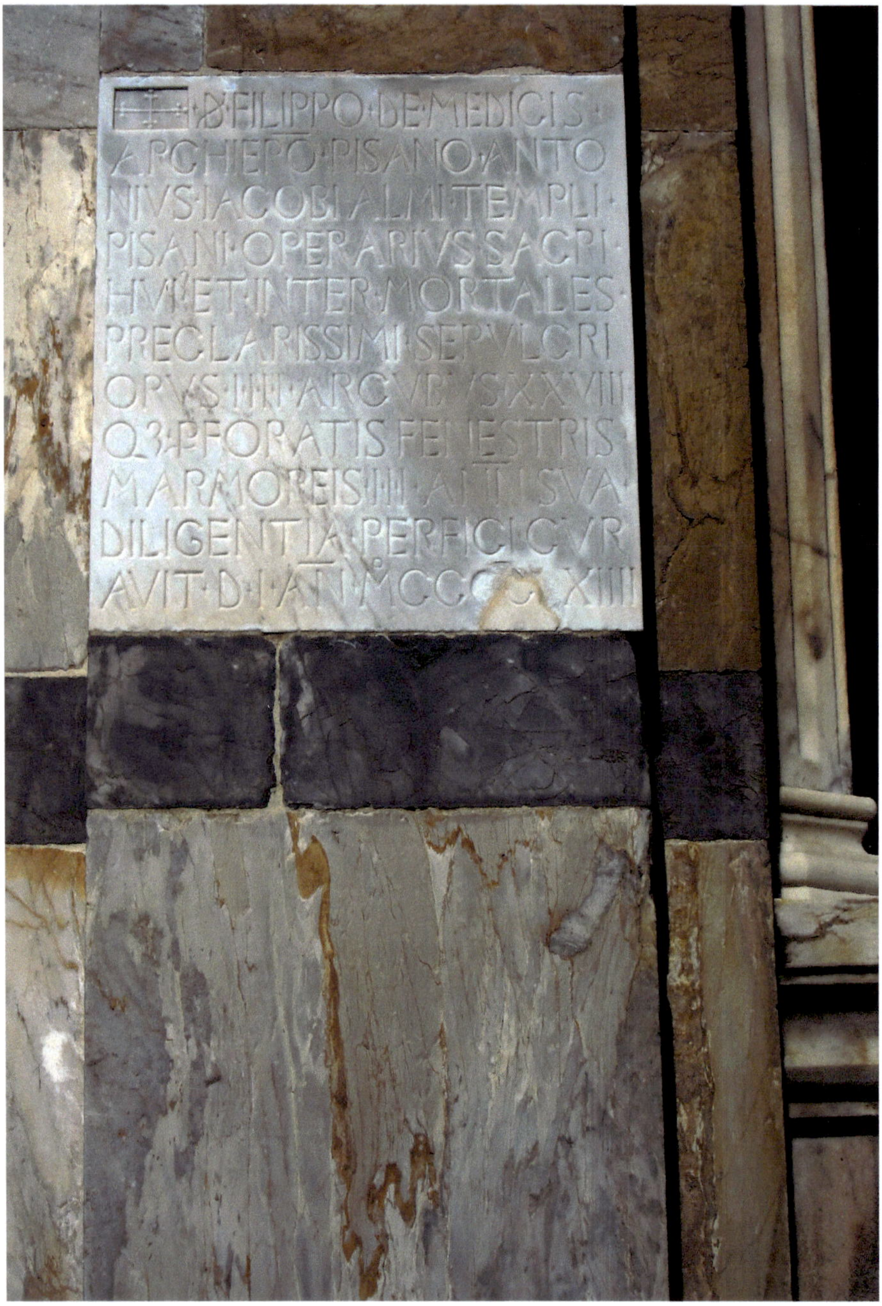

3.8. Inscription, 1474, Camposanto, Pisa. Photo: Author.

magnificent, purpose-built chapel. Even from the beginning of his tenure as archbishop, the accounts of the Mensa Arcivescovile – over which, unlike the Opera del Duomo accounts, he did have control – recorded payments for Masses to be said in the cemetery.[211] A medal showing Filippo's profile on the

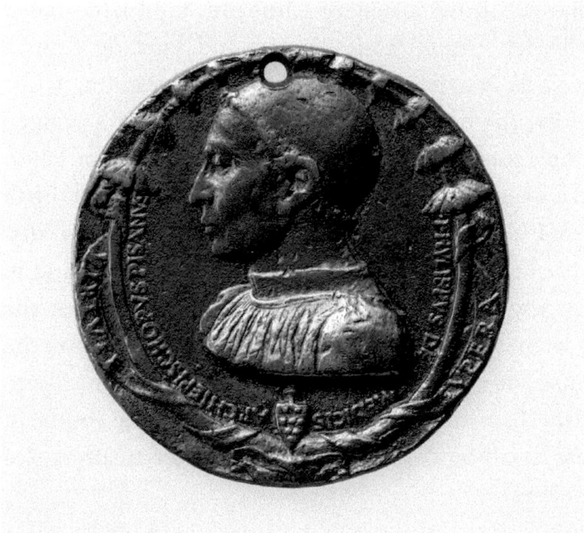

3.9. Bertoldo di Giovanni, medal of Filippo de' Medici, obverse, c. 1468–69, bronze, New York, The Metropolitan Museum of Art, Rogers Fund 1974.166. Photo: The Metropolitan Museum of Art.

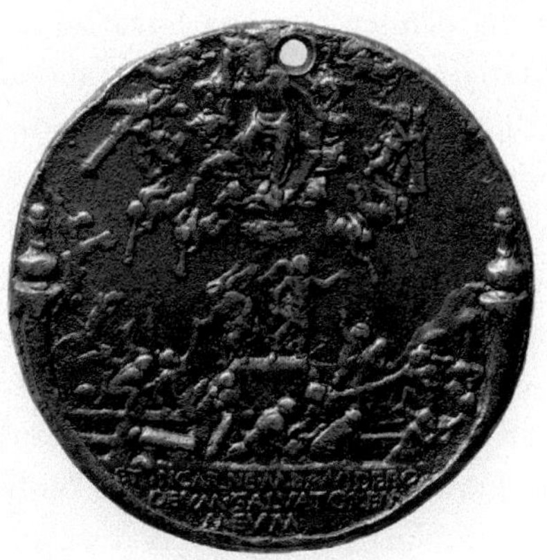

3.10. Bertoldo di Giovanni, medal of Filippo de' Medici, reverse, c. 1468–69, bronze, New York, The Metropolitan Museum of Art, Rogers Fund, 1974.166. Photo: The Metropolitan Museum of Art.

obverse was probably designed by Bertoldo di Giovanni and cast in Pisa or Rome around 1470 (Figures 3.9–3.10).[212] It shows the prelate facing left, his shoulders foreshortened, wearing a surplice and *zuchetto*. The inscription, PHYLIPPUS DE MEDICIS ARCHIEPISCHOPVS PISANVS, flanks a *stemma* of eight balls crowned by a cross, like those seen on the archiepiscopal palace. The reverse makes references to the Camposanto, and, as far as it shows highly personalized imagery, it indicates Filippo's devotion to the space.[213]

The image of the Last Judgment shows a solitary Christ, his right hand raised and his torso twisted to his left, rising from his seat and bursting from a mandorla flanked by angels. Angels hold the cross and the column, while others sound trumpets. Below, the dead climb from opened tombs; a winged putto to the left helps a rising soul, while another holding a sword or baton gestures toward the damned. The inscription, ET INCARNE MEA VIDEBO DEUM SALVATOREM MEUM is from the lament of Job ("I believe that my redeemer liveth, and that in the last day I shall rise from the earth: and in my flesh shall see God my savior"), and formed part of the Office for the Dead.[214] The story of Job, we may recall from Chapter 2, was depicted on the southwest wall of the Camposanto. The vengeful God raising his arm calls to mind the searing image of the Last Judgment by Buffalmacco in the southeast corridor of the Camposanto and points to Michelangelo's later treatment of the theme in the Sistine Chapel.

THE OLD TESTAMENT MURALS IN THE CAMPOSANTO

Five years after Filippo's appointment as archbishop, the mural decoration of the north corridor remained unfinished. The Opera's search for a painter began energetically in 1466, when the painter "Andrea Squarcione," better known as Andrea Mantegna, was entertained at a meal on 3 July and identified in payments as the artist "who is to finish the painting in the Camposanto."[215] Nothing came of this encounter, and the painter returned to Mantua where he resumed his post as court painter to the Gonzaga. Perhaps thinking an artist of Mantegna's stature was beyond their reach, the Opera next engaged a local artist, Michele Ciampanti, called Michele da Lucca, to paint an *Incredulity of Saint Thomas* in the Opera offices as a trial piece, for which he was paid on 18 April 1467.[216] The artist disappears from the records, and this work is lost, and we presume that the painting did not satisfy the authorities. Nonetheless, the search for a painter continued as scaffolding was erected in the Camposanto in July and August.[217] On 9 January 1468, the first evidence of Benozzo Gozzoli's employment was noted in the records, when he received an advance of forty-five lire for "the painting he is to do in the Camposanto."[218] Subsequent payments were made on 3 May, when he returned to Florence for his *brigata* and on the 14th, for rent on the house he occupied in Pisa. Benozzo painted a trial piece, "next to the World, which is the history of Noah," for which he received payments early in the next year."[219] A payment on 14 May 1468 suggests that Benozzo's mural pleased the authorities and the many citizens who were consulted, as he was awarded a deposit to demonstrate the good faith of the Opera.[220]

Although the contract between Benozzo and the Opera has not survived, we can deduce from subsequent payments its approximate date and terms.

Payments recorded in the *debitori e creditori* ledger beginning on 1 January 1469 summarize payments through 17 May 1473.[221] In these payments, it is clear that Benozzo was allocated the commission on 17 January 1469, in a legal contract drawn up by the Opera's notary, and that it called for him to paint three murals each year, for a price of 66 2/3 florins each, excluding the cost of scaffolding and lime. The first mural, already completed, described as "when Noah collected the grapes and became intoxicated," was paid for on 1 January 1469. The next group included the *Curse of Ham* below Piero di Puccio's scenes and the *Adoration of the Magi* and *Annunciation* above the entrance to the Ammannati chapel, for which Benozzo was paid 200 florins on 8 November 1470. Approximately seven months later, on 31 May 1471, payment is recorded for the *Tower of Babel* and the first mural to the right of the chapel, *Abraham and the Adoration of Baal*, the first scene in the Abraham series.[222] The payments track the steady progress of the work year after year, culminating in the final payment, on 1 May 1484, permitting us to follow Benozzo's chronology in the Camposanto with great precision.[223] They also provide insights into workshop structure and technique that could not otherwise be known, owing to the reduced condition of the murals themselves. They reveal Benozzo's relationship with the Opera, which seems to have been throughout this long process a mutually congenial one.[224]

Benozzo, fresh from his work in the choir of Sant'Agostino in San Gimignano, completed in 1467, likely came to the attention of the Pisan officials through Piero de' Medici, with whom he had worked closely in the murals for the chapel in the Medici palace ten years before. As we have seen, Filippo de'Medici maintained close relations with Piero, and he was conceivably the instigator of Benozzo's commission. Filippo was often in Florence and visited the city with Pius II on the way to Mantua in the spring of 1459. Possibly he toured the newly completed chapel with the young Galeazzo Maria Sforza in 1459.[225] Benozzo's work in the late 1440s in Rome, with Fra Angelico in the Vatican palace and basilica (among which only the chapel of Nicholas V survives) and other independent works, such as manuscript illuminations attributed to Benozzo and made for Nicholas V, predate Filippo's arrival in Rome.[226]

However, Filippo would certainly have known the painter's Roman works from the 1450s, when Gozzoli was in and out of Rome, working there and in Umbria and Lazio.[227] Gozzoli was one of the artists charged with preparations for the coronation of the new Pope Pius II in 1458. He also decorated a funerary chapel (c. 1453–57) for Angelo di Piermatteo degli Albertoni in the Aracoeli with scenes from the life of Saint Anthony of Padua, of which only the image of Saint Anthony with two kneeling donors survives.[228] Gozzoli's narrative style in the 1450s had roots in the Roman works of Fra Angelico, and featured portraits of contemporaries and prominent architectural and landscape settings. In the surviving chapel for Nicholas V, pointed references to structures and settings in the Eternal City – the basilica of old Saint Peter's, the Roman walls – create a setting for narrative action that informs Benozzo's work in Montefalco, datable to 1450–52, and the lost cycle in Viterbo, documented to 1453.

In Rome itself, whose artistic scene was slowly coming to life with the patronage of successive Popes Martin V, Eugenius IV, and Nicholas V, a distinctive narrative idiom emerged in the work of artists such as Antoniazzo Romano;[229] seen, for example, in the Bessarion chapel in Santissimi Apostoli, commissioned in 1464 and painted in 1467–68, just before Benozzo's move to Pisa.[230] This work, a funerary chapel for the Greek-born cardinal Bessarion (c. 1403–72), originally depicted stories of Saint John the Baptist and the Archangel Michael, crowned with a Triumphant Christ encircled by an angelic choir. Surviving fragments show scenes of the apparitions of the Archangel Michael. Identifiable settings of undulating hills and distant castles connect the Roman chapel to an extended topography linked to the archangel. (see Figure 4.17). Portraits of contemporaries populate the *Dream of Saint Aubert*; the saint, clad in a sumptuous cope, bears the features of the French King Louis XI, in whom Bessarion's hopes (mistakenly) for a Crusade against the Turks rested. Two prelates follow closely behind, the one in red recognizable as Francesco Maria della Rovere, the future Sixtus IV, and, to his right, in purple, his nephew Giuliano della Rovere, who would become Julius II. The della Rovere were intensely involved in Santissimi Apostoli, and family members would be buried there.[231] The expansive landscape, recognizable sites, and prominent portraits of contemporary figures were aspects of contemporary Roman painting that Benozzo's works in Rome and Lazio had helped to form.[232] The grand narratives of Gozzoli's murals in San Gimignano further developed this Roman mural style and provide a more immediate precedent for the murals in the Camposanto than those in the intimate, opulent setting of the Palazzo Medici chapel.[233]

Piero di Puccio's scenes from Genesis that initiated the Old Testament cycle are conventional, but the giant mural the *Theological Cosmos* (Figure 3.3) perhaps set the tone for what followed. The pairing of a cosmography with scenes from Genesis occurred in the fourteenth century in several Old Testament cycles, among them Bartolo di Fredi's murals in San Gimignano, which, as we saw in Chapter 2, show several links to Camposanto murals. The cosmological map, held by God the Father, shows the earth in the center divided by a T-shape into Asia, Africa, and Europe.[234] Concentric bands denoting the elements, planets, sky and nine angelic spheres surround the earth. A tiny sun is located below Aries. The arrangement of the planets and sun indicates that the moment depicted is the creation of the universe. Figures of Saints Augustine and Thomas Aquinas at the bottom left and right hold open books, whose inscriptions allude to the status of angels and their creation at the same moment as the material world.[235] Further verses beckon the viewer to "raise the eyes of your intellect," to "consider how the universe is ordered," to "praise him who has created it", and to "hope to enter the happy state of the beatified angels." The exhortations to engage the intellect seem to reflect continuing Dominican influence on the imagery in Trecento murals in the Camposanto.[236]

Learned input in the program is evident in Gozzoli's murals as well, though the inscriptions on banderoles held by prophets in the frames have disappeared. The influence of the Dominican convent of Santa Caterina, so pronounced in the fourteenth century, seems to have waned in the fifteenth. Renaissance theology emanating from the papal court more likely shaped the imagery of the Old Testament murals, and Filippo de' Medici may have been instrumental.

Nonetheless, Gozzoli's murals bear the distinct imprint of Pisan culture at the time they were painted. The rich presentation of the Old Testament histories reflects the revival of patristic studies that began in Florence in the 1430s and continued in the papal courts, beginning with Nicholas V, and notably under Pius II and Sixtus IV. Humanists extended their interest in the Latin Church fathers – Augustine, Ambrose, Gregory, and Jerome – to the Greek fathers such as Basil, John Chrysostom, and Gregory of Nazianzus. Study of the Hebrew Bible and early Christianity – "Christian antiquity" – in addition to the pagan past, shaped humanist history and was actively encouraged by the popes.[237] Filippo's oration before Pope Paul II, given in 1464, sounds similar themes.[238] His references to the Church Fathers, such as Gregory, and his support for a Crusade to retake the Holy Land from the Turks resonate in the murals, in which heroic protagonists such as Abraham, Isaac, Jacob, and Moses lead their people, triumph in battle, and obey God. Filippo's oration had also cited Moses as precedent for the popes. The Pisan history of Moses, begun in 1477, represented in six large, multi-episodic scenes the most comprehensive presentation of his life before the Sistine chapel decoration in 1481–82. Moreover, the final scene in Pisa, the *Meeting of King Solomon and the Queen of Sheba*, recalled the attempt by Pope Eugenius IV at the council of Florence in 1439 to unite the eastern and western churches.[239] Filippo's oration before Paul II described the council and predicted that Paul would fulfill the mission begun by his uncle Eugenius. These same themes had been sounded by Saint Antoninus in his oration in honor of Pius II's election to the papal throne in 1458. Antoninus equated the new pope to the biblical King Solomon. He cast the history of the papacy as a struggle of Christianity, united by the pope, against forces of the Antichrist. The militant, heroic tone of the Pisa murals finds a counterpart in the dramatic rhetoric of the papal court, with which Filippo would have been well acquainted.

Additional incidents in the murals, such as Abraham's trial by fire in the mural of the *Adoration of Baal*, finished by 1471, which do not have a source in the biblical text, suggest a program shaped by learned input that Filippo might also have provided.[240] The incident is the first of Abraham's ten trials, in which God tests the patriarch's faith. Nimrod, on the left of the scene, commands his subjects to worship the god Baal, seated in the central temple. Abraham refuses to worship the god, and he is thrown into the furnace. He escapes with God's help, while his brother Haran, who followed Abraham, was burnt to death. We see Haran engulfed by flames, while Abraham, marked by a halo, rushes to leave the city as God commanded. This incident, which takes many forms, is from rabbinic legend and appears in commentaries of the Hebrew Bible.[241] Several fourteenth- and fifteenth-century Haggadot, liturgical books for the Passover seder, from northeast Spain and Germany illustrate the scene.[242] Christian writers such as Jerome and Augustine discussed the incident.[243] Its inclusion in the Camposanto underscores the expansive Old Testament imagery of the cycle, spurred by the early Christian revival of the church fathers that is its distinctive characteristic. The rich narratives of illustrated Haggadot might have been sources for the incident in the murals. The Abraham story also reflects the study of Hebrew Bible and its commentary literature by Florentine humanists such as Poggio Bracciolini, Ambrogio Traversari, and Giannozzo Manetti during the fifteenth century.[244] And it may point to the presence in Pisa of a significant Jewish population of bankers and traders who contributed to the economic and cultural life of the city.[245]

That Filippo de' Medici was instrumental in the program and the larger message of the murals is likely. Although he was not a theologian – being probably schooled in law, at least from what we can judge of his library – his experience of the papal court in the 1450s shaped his outlook. Nicholas V's well-known campaign of *renovatio*, including urban projects and refurbishment of the Vatican palace, and Pius II's attempts to mount a new Crusade to the Holy Land, cast a revived Rome as the New Jerusalem, and the church as the recreation of the celestial city of Revelation. Pisa's traditional association with Rome may have reinforced Filippo's Roman experience in recalling these themes. Similarly, Benozzo's long activity in Rome was at least as significant a qualification as his activity in Florence in awarding him the commission in Pisa.

The mural depicting the tower of Babel was one of the first of the scenes Benozzo painted after the trial piece of the *Drunkenness of Noah*, with the *Curse of Ham* completing the three scenes below Piero di Puccio's stories of Adam and Eve (Figures 3.11–3.12).[246] It was completed by November of 1470.[247] At the center, workers mix mortar, haul stones, and lay bricks while the giant Nimrod gestures toward the rising structure. Interestingly, in the accounts the scene is identified as "*A history of Nimrod king of Babylonia.*" Nimrod was the mythical founder of Babylon.[248]

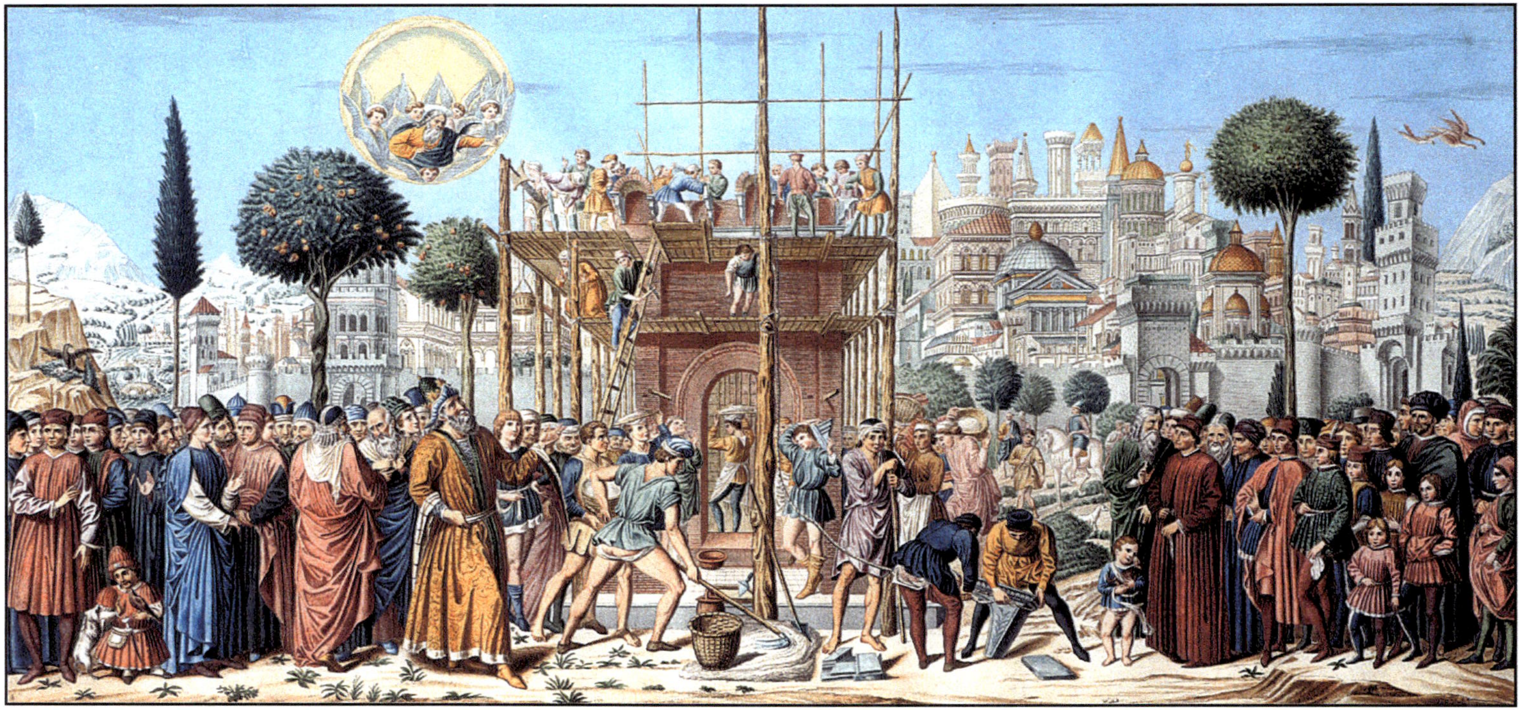

3.11. Carlo Lasinio, engraving (1812) after Benozzo Gozzoli, *The Tower of Babel*, 1470, from *Pitture a fresco del Camposanto di Pisa*, hand-colored by Giovanni Paolo Lasinio, Museo dell'Opera del Duomo, Pisa. Photo: Scala / Art Resource, NY.

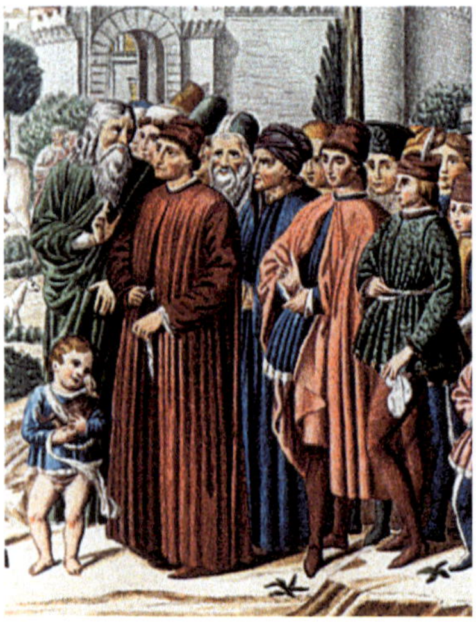

3.12. Carlo Lasinio, engraving (1812) after Benozzo Gozzoli, *The Tower of Babel*, detail, 1470, from *Pitture a fresco del Camposanto di Pisa*, hand-colored by Giovanni Paolo Lasinio, Museo dell'Opera del Duomo, Pisa. Photo Scala / Art Resource, NY.

As Luzzati has shown, Fillippo de' Medici is portrayed at the right, leading a group of figures in contemporary dress who calmly view the building site.[249] At first it would seem strange for the archbishop to be associated with this scene. The biblical text describes building the tower as an act of overarching ambition, which brought the wrath of God on man.[250] God caused the workers to speak in many tongues, so that the workings of the building site, here seen humming with activity, foundered in confusion. The descendants of Noah scattered. Nimrod's city of Babylon, conflated with the tower of Babel in medieval exegesis, is an emblem for chaos.[251] Saint Augustine, in *The City of God*, identifies Babel with Babylon, the earthly city of man, in contrast the heavenly city of the just.[252] Gozzoli shows the mythical city to the right, cinched by walls and pierced by a towered gate above which is written *Babilonia*. Tall buildings rise, among which can be recognized a mix of old and new from Rome: the Pantheon, Trajan's column, the pyramid of Cestius, and Florence: the Palazzo Vecchio, the tower of the Badia, and the Palazzo Medici. The traditional association of Babylon with Rome is here extended to Florence. Yet the structures are jumbled together, showing a chaotic mix of scale, type, and style. And as God appears at the upper left, the tower of Babel and the city of Babylon will fall.

Filippo stands at the front of a crowd of onlookers, occupying a position roughly opposite Nimrod on the left side of the rising tower. None of the buildings, new or old, in the walled city of Babylon are Pisan, and yet Filippo is associated with both the construction of the tower and the magnificent cityscape behind.[253] But the traditional negative connotations of the Babel/Babylon story have been muted. The destruction of the city, with which this scene is often paired – as, for example, in the stained-glass window installed in the Duomo in 1453–54 – is notably absent.[254] Instead, Filippo views with interest the construction site, much as he might have done in the Camposanto during projects directed by the *operaio* Antonio di Jacopo dalle Mura. Similarly, the city of Babylon, explicitly linked with Rome and Florence, draws admiration rather than reproach. The ceremonial aspect of the scene, with dignitaries grouped to the left and right has been likened to *Sagra* paintings – depictions of the consecration of churches, with their echoes of commemoration and celebration.[255]

The changed meaning of this scene from traditional depictions of Babel reflects a fundamental change in attitudes toward cities and toward building.

Rather than an act of hubris, building was seen as the performance of civic duty; princes, wealthy merchants, and city officials justified the expense with reference to the concept of magnificence, derived from ancient and modern authors.[256] In this idea, opulent expenditures on building, in accordance with a patron's social stature, brought prestige to the city and the state, as well as to the individual. Giovanni Rucellai, the Florentine merchant, memorably expressed this ideal in his memoirs, when he said that a man's principal goals were "to procreate and to build."[257] Filippo's appearance in this scene implicates him in this view, reinforced by his many visits to the Medici palace. In Rome, he would have witnessed the building projects of popes Nicholas V and Pius II firsthand and observed the future Paul II's new palace rising at San Marco. As we have seen, Filippo also visited princely courts in Italy: he would have seen construction in Milan and elsewhere. During his ambassadorship to the French royal court, he sought out and reacted sensitively to Northern European architectural monuments. He intended the new Palazzo Arcivescovile, the most direct expression of his preferences in architecture, to be a reflection of magnificence as he had experienced it.

In the Babel scene, the tower itself indicates aspects that signal classically inspired magnificence in architecture. It is a brick structure with a round arched entrance, defined by a foliate molding. Above, workers at the right corner of the scaffolding are setting in place a marble bracket, while others prepare to hoist another carved with classically inspired ornament. Just above the scaffolding platform, we can glimpse a marble molding below the row of brackets. The combination of stone and brick immediately recalled Rome to Renaissance viewers – and perhaps Suetonius's assertion that Augustus found Rome a city of brick and left it a city of marble.[258] Marble, too, as we have seen, recalls Pisa's historical link with Rome, evident in the gleaming Piazza del Duomo monuments and more personally in the plans for Filippo's funerary chapel in the Camposanto. Filippo's presence in the scene with other figures likely to have been members of his court signaled approval and sanction of the actions before them.[259]

Other buildings in the murals reflect architectural and urbanistic ideals of humanist thinkers such as Alberti.[260] Filippo likely encountered Alberti in Rome in the 1450s, where his treatise *On Architecture* was presented to Nicholas V in 1452.[261] In Mantua in 1459, Alberti was present, and on the return journey to Rome, Filippo may have visited Pienza, Pius's rebuilt hometown (1459–64), with the pope. There, he would have seen the rising structures on the central square – the impressive cathedral, Palazzo Piccolomini, bishop's palace, canon's palace, and communal palace.[262] As noted by Christine Smith and others, the mixture of medieval and classicizing structures in Pienza visualizes the concept of *varietas* – a pleasing contrast of materials, textures, colors, and architectural forms – in the buildings of the

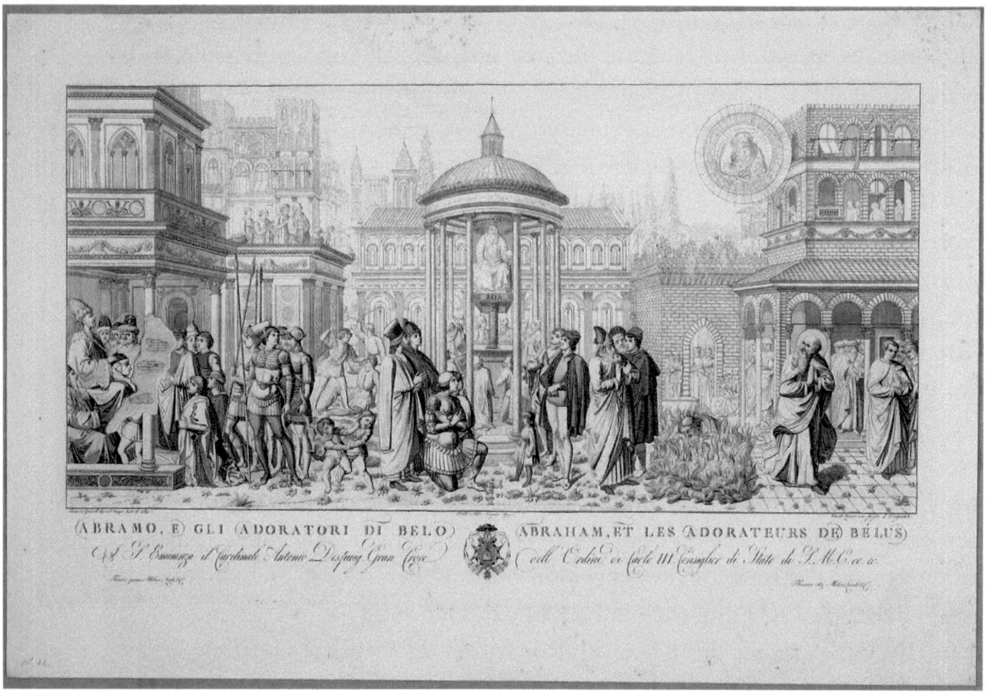

3.13. Carlo Lasinio, engraving (1812) after Benozzo Gozzoli, *Abraham and Baal*, 1471–72, Harvard Art Museums/Fogg Museum, gift of William Gray from the collection of Francis Calley Gray, G2160. Photo: © President and Fellows of Harvard College.

square.[263] *Varietas* is the key to interpreting the vast, imaginary cityscapes that unfold in Benozzo's murals in the Camposanto. Similarly, different materials, marble, brick, and colored stone, betray a taste for variety that characterizes Benozzo's vision of the cities of the Holy Land.

For example, in the mural *Abraham and Baal*, in which King Nimrod commands the worship of the god Baal, a circular baldacchino where the idol is enshrined is flanked by classicizing palaces to the left and right (Figure 3.13). The palace of the rich merchant that we saw in the Rainerius cycle here gives way to a regal setting. These structures are imaginary. In the imperial palace of Nimrod on the left, we see the emperor seated in a loggia with columns and composite capitals; fluted pilasters articulate the wall behind. The entablature features classical moldings, a frieze sculpted with swags, and portrait busts. Yet, on the floor above, the bifores show pointed arches, reminiscent of the windows in the Florentine Palazzo Vecchio. Fluted pilasters and roundels that probably denote inlaid colored marble, the *opus sectile* of Roman use, articulate the façade of the building behind and to the right. Similarly, the vast structure in the center behind the idol recalls a classical basilica, but its lower story features fluted pilasters that flank round arches centered on gothic bifores. In the upper story, the round arched windows, with simple moldings, recall those in the Florentine baptistery. Drafted masonry with marble columns supporting a loggia, and what might be a terracotta frieze above, ornament the palace to the right. Behind it to the left is a machicolated and crenelated structure with a pointed arched portal. A mix of building types – sacred, domestic, and civic – fills the scene.

These structures epitomize the profusion of materials, forms, styles, and colors that are encompassed by the concept of *varietas*, but they are hardly a demonstration of architectural "rules" deduced from contemporary writers, or implemented by contemporary architects, in their real architecture.[264] In their mix of historical styles, colors, and materials, they approach the excessive or chaotic; humanist writers urged tempering *varietas* with what was appropriate, so as not to venture into *luxuria* – extravagance.[265] In keeping with their fictive status, they instead contribute to the air of splendor and exoticism that these scenes, set in the distant past and far away, recall.[266]

Yet the architecture varies from scene to scene, keyed to the subjects. For example, those in the flaming city of Sodom seem to be constructed of roughhewn blocks with little of the classicizing forms or materials seen in the scenes from Nimrod's palace (Figure 3.14). The glimpses of a distant city in the scene of *Abraham's Victory* are devoid of what seem to be classically inspired structures (Figure 3.15). And the tents seen in the scenes of *Moses and the Tablets of the Law* or of the *Brazen Serpent* signify the lack of permanent architecture as the Israelites wandered in the desert. While Benozzo does not seem to confine classical architecture styles to particular times or places, he does use it to depict dwellings of rulers, conquerors, and patriarchs who are the heroes of the Old Testament, in contrast to structures in morally compromised cities.

The mural with the stories of Jacob and Esau links Pisa with this imagined sacred land (Figures 3.16–3.17). Diane Cole Ahl has eloquently described the Camposanto's evocation of the Holy Land.[267] The "sacred field" recreated the terrestrial and celestial Holy Land by virtue of the *terra santa* brought during Crusade, by the ceremonies of Holy Week, and by funerals performed there. The magnificent triumphal arch in the center of the mural, with its drafted masonry, coffered arch, and profuse sculpted detail, forms the backdrop of Esau selling his birthright; the birth of the twins takes place in a sumptuous palace at the left. To the right is a building with an arcade and trabeated second floor loggia that would recall to viewers the courtyard elevation of the archbishop's palace, newly built on Filippo's initiative.[268] The prominent rosettes in the spandrels of the arches recall those of the palace arcade, a striking feature of the courtyard that directly recalls the decorative motifs of the Piazza del Duomo. Filippo's efforts to rebuild the urban fabric of Pisa, especially the monuments of the Piazza del Duomo, would be fresh in viewer's minds. The mural was completed sometime between 1473 and 1477, and it may be that this architectural "portrait" is a posthumous tribute – he died in 1474.

Filippo's wide-ranging efforts to rebuild Pisa – economically, institutionally, and physically – did not end with his death. In his campaign, he enlisted the young

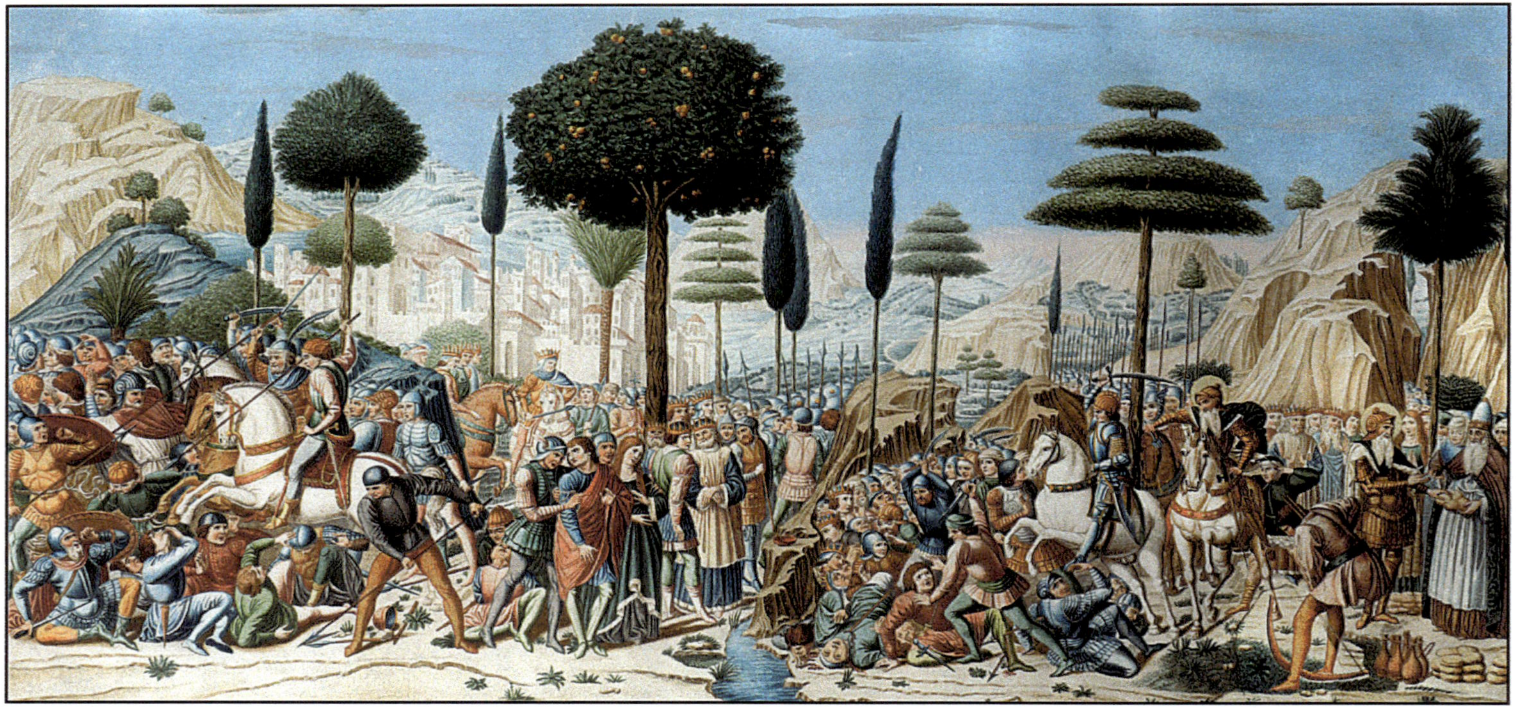

3.14. Carlo Lasinio, engraving (1812) after Benozzo Gozzoli, *Abraham's Victory over the Assyrian Kings*, 1472, from *Pitture a fresco del Camposanto di Pisa*, hand-colored by Giovanni Paolo Lasinio, Museo dell'Opera del Duomo, Pisa. Photo Scala / Art Resource, NY.

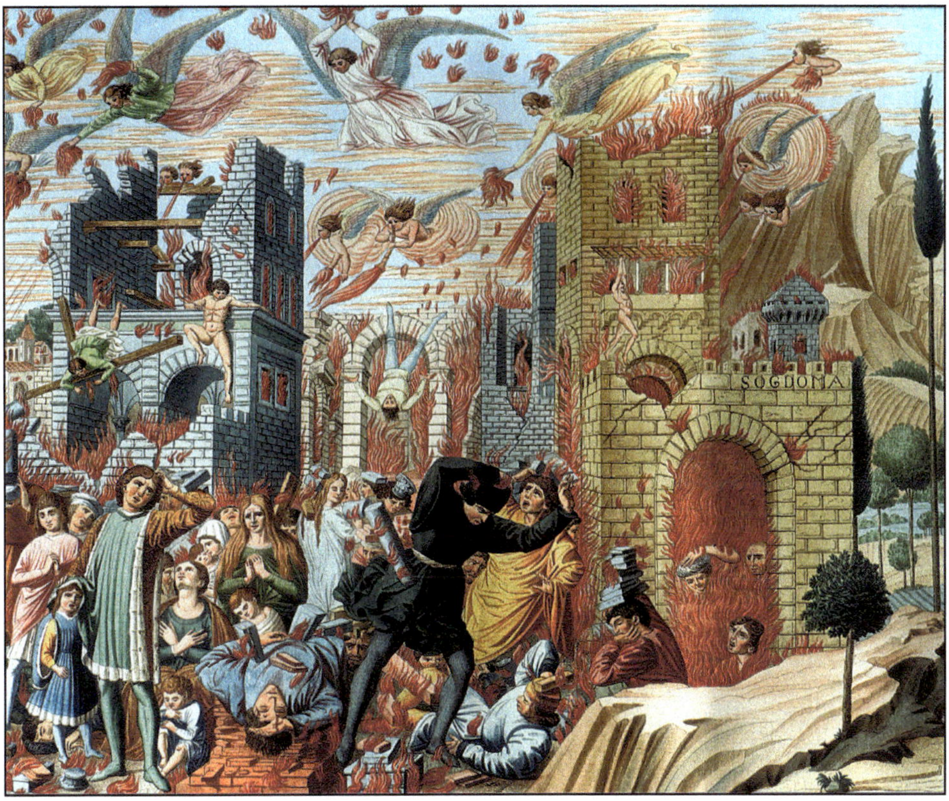

3.15. Carlo Lasinio, engraving (1812) after Benozzo Gozzoli, *The Fire of Sodom*, detail, c.1473–77, from *Pitture a fresco del Camposanto di Pisa*, hand-colored by Giovanni Paolo Lasinio, Museo dell'Opera del Duomo, Pisa. Photo: Scala / Art Resource, NY.

Lorenzo de' Medici, who appears as one of his regular correspondents starting in 1464, when Lorenzo was a teenager, and who became Filippo's principal Medici correspondent with the deaths of Giovanni, Cosimo, and finally, Piero in 1469. As we have seen, Lorenzo's love of Pisa for hunting, and his expansive land holdings in the countryside, explain his support of Pisa's revival – most notably in Lorenzo's reestablishment of the university in Pisa in 1472. In these efforts, Filippo de' Medici was Lorenzo's role model and right-hand man.

Filippo's death in 1474 meant the loss of his vital presence as archbishop to Medici interests. Filippo's successor, Archbishop Francesco Salviati, was executed in the Pazzi conspiracy.[269] Raffaele Riario, the nephew of Girolamo Riario, was appointed to fill Salviati's place. He had studied in Pisa, but as archbishop he never lived there. The diocese was administered by the bishop of Calcedonia, the Pisan Zaccaria Palmieri, assisted by several vicars. Lorenzo's projects for Pisa, notably his plans to construct a grand palace for the university, initiated in 1489, were delayed or never begun.[270]

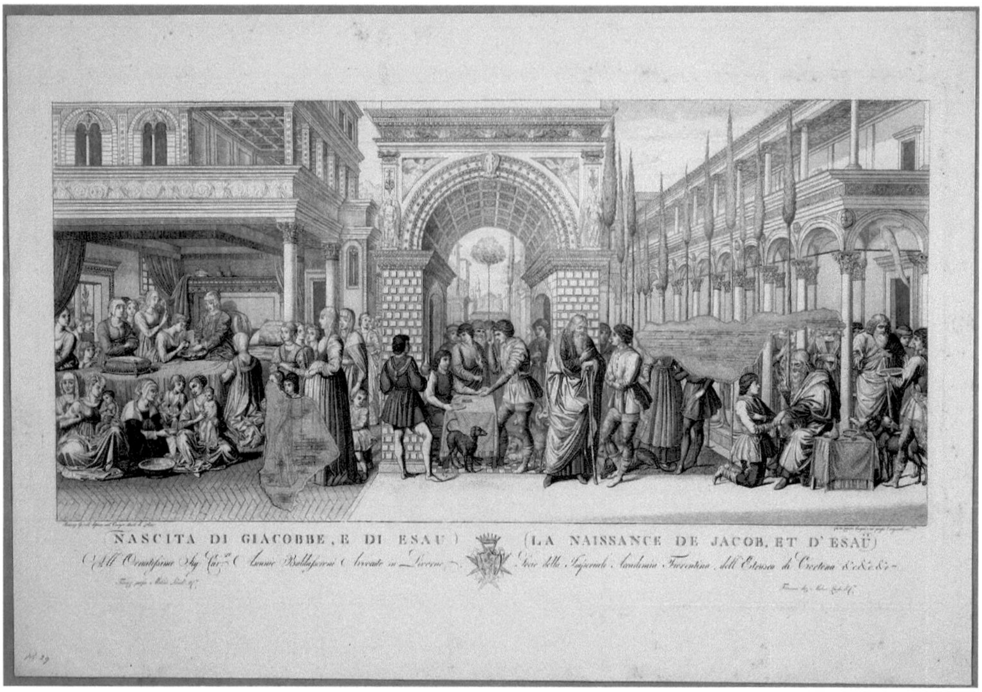

3.16. Carlo Lasinio engraving (1812) after Benozzo Gozzoli, *The Birth of Jacob and Esau*, c.1473–77, Harvard Art Museums/Fogg Museum, gift of William Gray from the collection of Francis Calley Gray, G2168. Photo: © President and Fellows of Harvard College.

Through the turmoil of the 1470s, Gozzoli steadily covered the walls of the Camposanto with murals, a testament to the administrative continuity of Antonio di Jacopo's role as *operaio*, documented in the payments in the ledgers. By 29 October 1472, *Abraham and Lot in Egypt*, *Abraham's Victory over the Assyrian Kings*, and the *Story of Abraham and Hagar* were finished. An entry summarizing undated payments tell us that by 31 October 1477 Benozzo had painted eighteen murals and was about to begin the nineteenth, the first of the Moses cycle.[271] A payment for 266 2/3 ducats was for the *Destruction of Sodom*, the *Youth and Sacrifice of Isaac*, the *Marriage of Isaac and Rebecca*, and the *Birth of Jacob and Esau*, datable to perhaps May of 1473 and 1475. A second, for 216 2/3 florins, was for the *Marriage of Jacob and Rachel*, the *Meeting of Jacob and Esau*, the *Rape of Dinah*, and the Apostles and saints above the Aulla chapel, datable to between 1475 and October of 1477.[272] That day Benozzo was paid for the two stories of Joseph, *The Youth of Joseph* and *Joseph and His Brothers in Egypt*. A payment of 17 March 1480 summarizes Benozzo's most recent activity. It records completion of four more stories from the Moses cycle.[273] We know from payments that the *Infancy and Miracles of Moses* was completed by 15 April 1478 and the *Crossing of the Red Sea* on 15 September 1478. On 20 March 1479, *Moses and the Tablets of the Law* had been completed and the *Punishment of Korah, Dathan, and Abiram* by March of 1480.[274] Another payment on 29 March 1480 notes the increased size of the later murals.[275] The

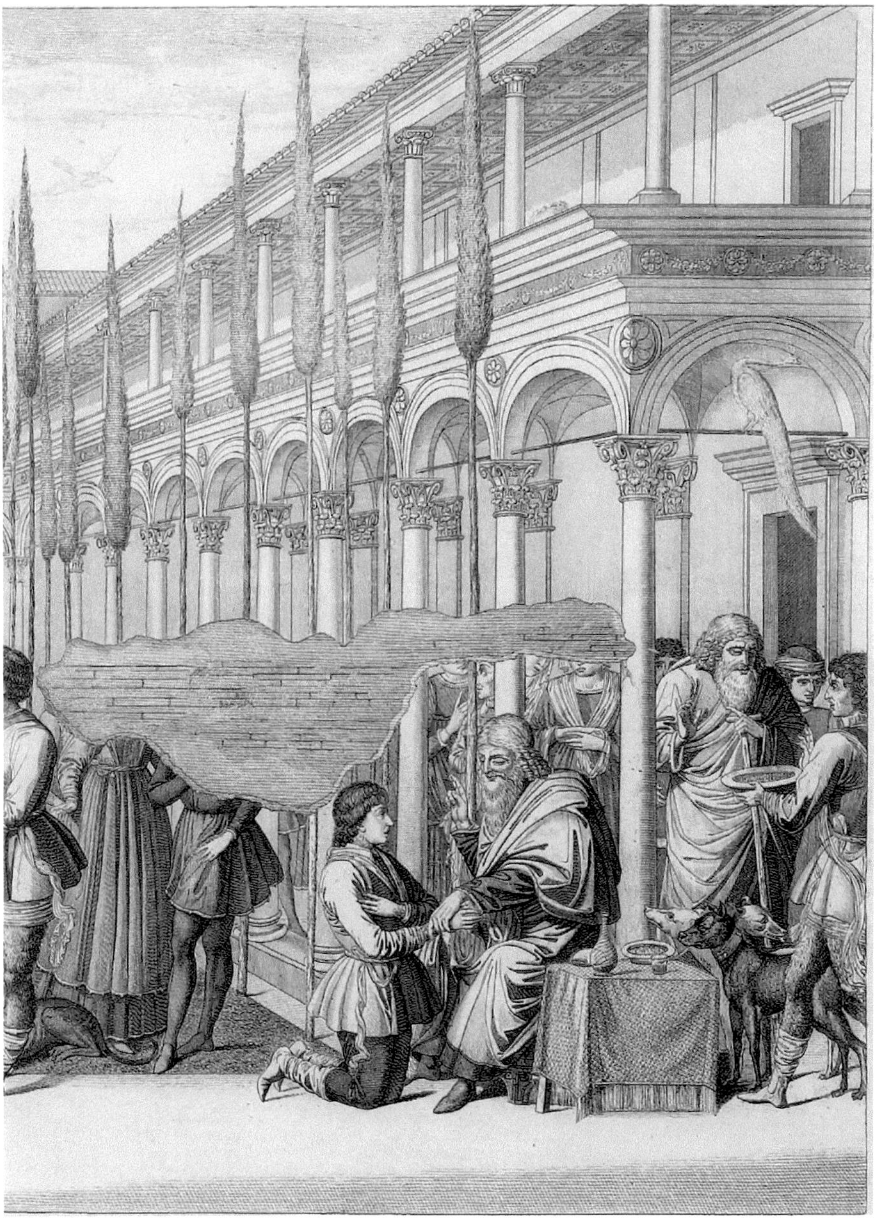

3.17. Carlo Lasinio engraving (1812) after Benozzo Gozzoli, *The Birth of Jacob and Esau*, detail, c.1473–77, Harvard Art Museums/Fogg Museum, gift of William Gray from the collection of Francis Calley Gray, G2168. photo: © President and Fellows of Harvard College.

payment of 1 July 1481 records the completion of the mural of the *Rod of Aaron* and the *Miracle of the Brazen Serpent.* On 1 May 1484 Benozzo was paid for the last three murals, the *Story of Balaam* and the *Death of Moses* (begun 14 July 1481),[276] *Joshua at the Battle of Jericho* and *David and Goliath*, and the last the *Meeting of King Solomon and the Queen of Sheba.* This was for 1,466 lire, the equivalent of 183 1/3 florins, more than the agreed upon rate because, as the payment records, "there are two [stories] at the end that count for three."[277] Another payment on 22 March 1483 to Benozzo for wood and charcoal was for four lire rather than the customary six, because, as the payment reads, "he has not worked continuously," perhaps reflecting the many other commissions Benozzo received even while working in the Camposanto.[278]

Benozzo responded to the larger fields of the last murals with even more expansive and monumental designs.[279] Starting with the *Marriage of Jacob and Rachel*, the scale of figures, architecture, and landscape features diminished, as the multi-episodic stories unfold in even more vast landscape settings that recede infinitely. Benozzo choreographed throngs of figures in groups, keyed to architecture and landscape elements that allow a reading of the complex stories. His narrative style, evolved through his career, adapted to the heroic scale and content of the Old Testament scenes. In the *Youth of Joseph*, for example, stately palaces enclose an expansive view of rolling hills and distant mountains. The figures rise to a third of the buildings' heights, rather than half as in earlier episodes. The episodes of Joseph's betrayal by his brothers and his exploits in Egypt are divided into three in the foreground; two more episodes occupy the middle ground.

At the same time, Florentine presence in the imagery of the Pisa murals becomes more insistent and reflects Florentine efforts to assert its control of Pisa culturally, politically, and economically. As an example, we might look at the mural *Joseph and his Brothers in Egypt*, completed by October 1477 (Figures 3.18–3.19). Visitors

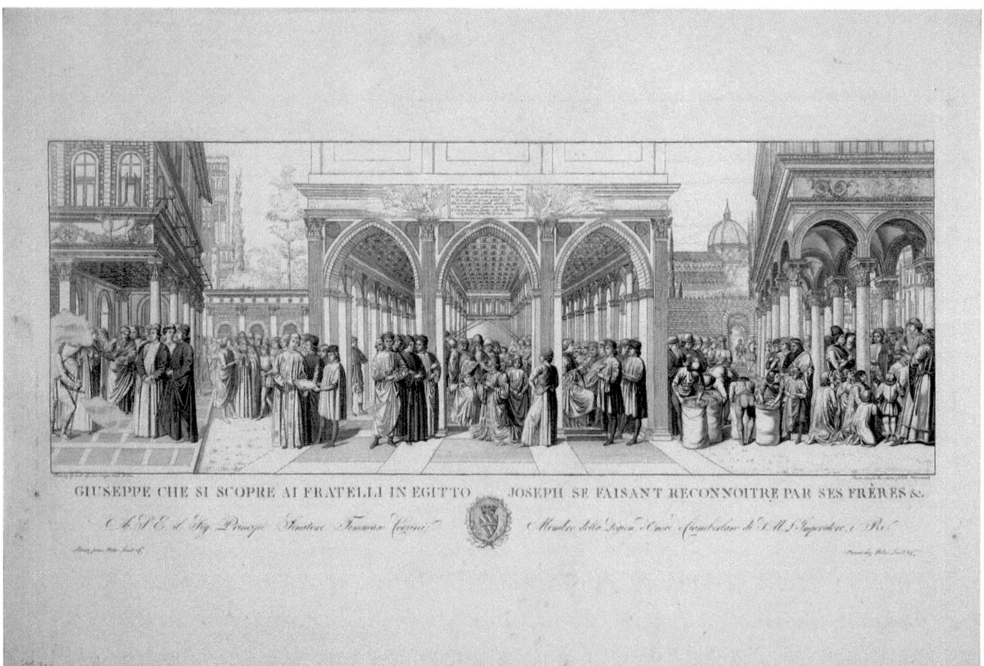

3.18. Carlo Lasinio engraving (1812) after Benozzo Gozzoli, *Joseph and His Brothers in Egypt*, 1477, Harvard Art Museums/Fogg Museum, gift of William Gray from the collection of Francis Calley Gray, G2173. photo: © President and Fellows of Harvard College.

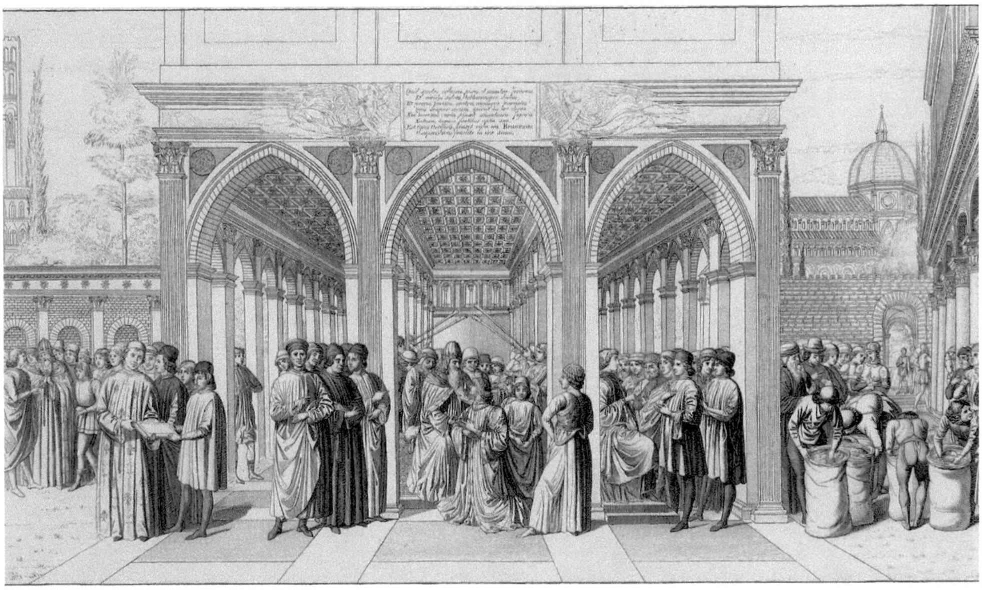

3.19. Carlo Lasinio engraving (1812) after Benozzo Gozzoli, *Joseph and His Brothers in Egypt*, detail, 1477, Harvard Art Museums/Fogg Museum, gift of William Gray from the collection of Francis Calley Gray, G2173. Photo: © President and Fellows of Harvard College.

approached this mural directly on axis from the main door, across the central sacred field; the plaque commemorating the completion of the marble windows is located on the right. A central loggia with three pointed-arched bays and a coffered ceiling dominates the narrative action. While the architecture fits in with the imaginary character of the painted architecture throughout the cycle, it may also refer to the interior of the Pisa Duomo, distinguished by its pointed triumphal arch (Figure 3.20). The coffered ceiling also recalls the new ceiling in the choir and transept arms, one of the first projects begun during Filippo de' Medici's term, work on which continued during the 1470s.[280] Yet, looming in the background, to the right of this structure, is an unmistakable image of the Florentine cathedral. By transposing the Florentine image into the imaginary scenes from pharaoh court, the mural draws together Pisa, Florence, and the legendary court of ancient Egypt.

An inscription inserted into the central loggia of the Joseph mural celebrates the painter, Benozzo, in terms that reflect humanist discourse on creativity and fame:

> How beholdest thou birds, fish, and monsters prodigious, Sylvan greenery or heavenly habitations? / Children, youths, mothers, and hoary-headed elders, / Their countenances live with decorous charm? / Who fashioned these images of such varied form / Was not Nature, her genius engendering that brood. / This is the work of Benozzo: by his art their visages live: / O gods above, endow them with voice as in life![281]

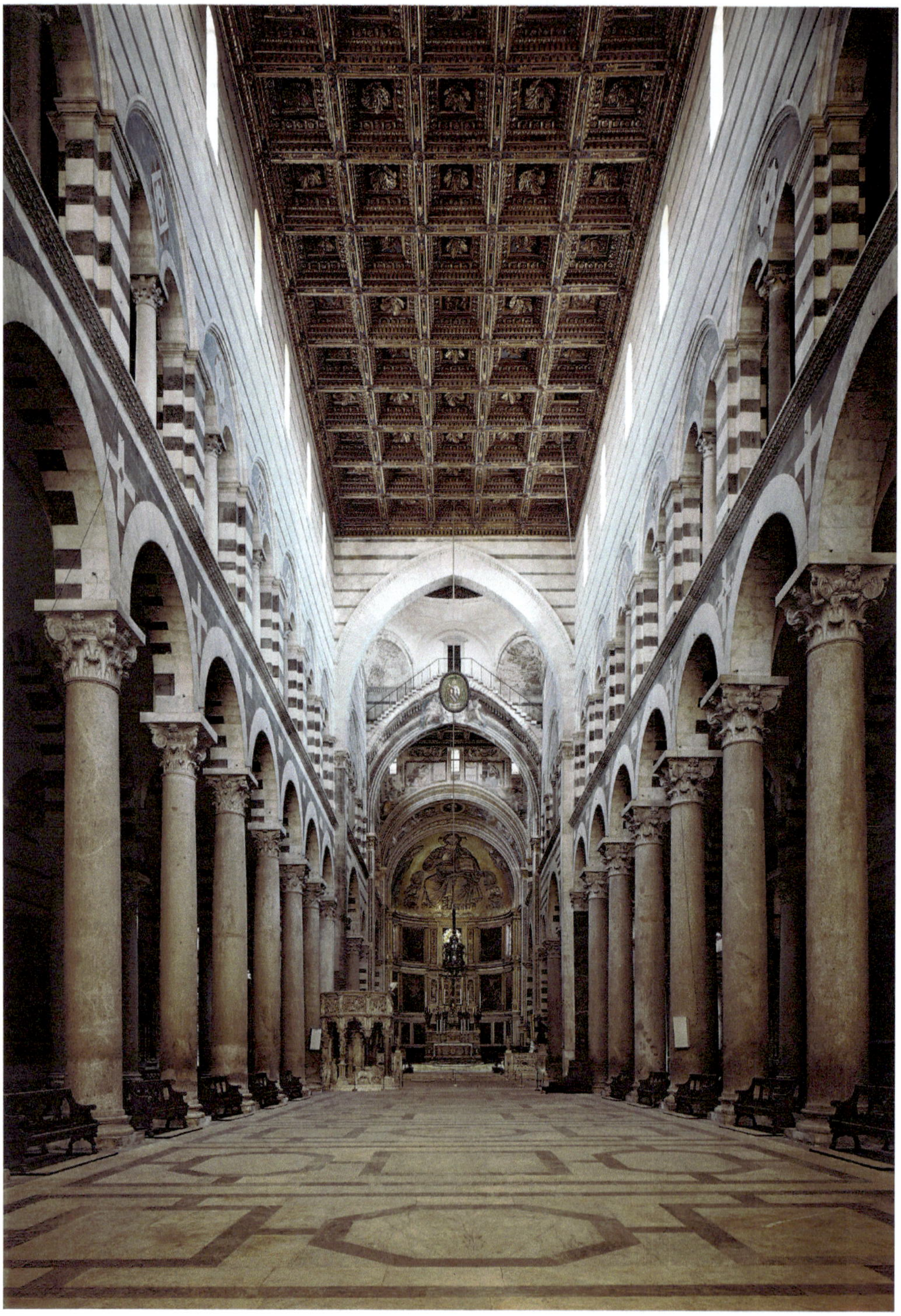

3.20. View of nave facing apse, Duomo, Pisa. Photo: Scala / Art Resource, NY.

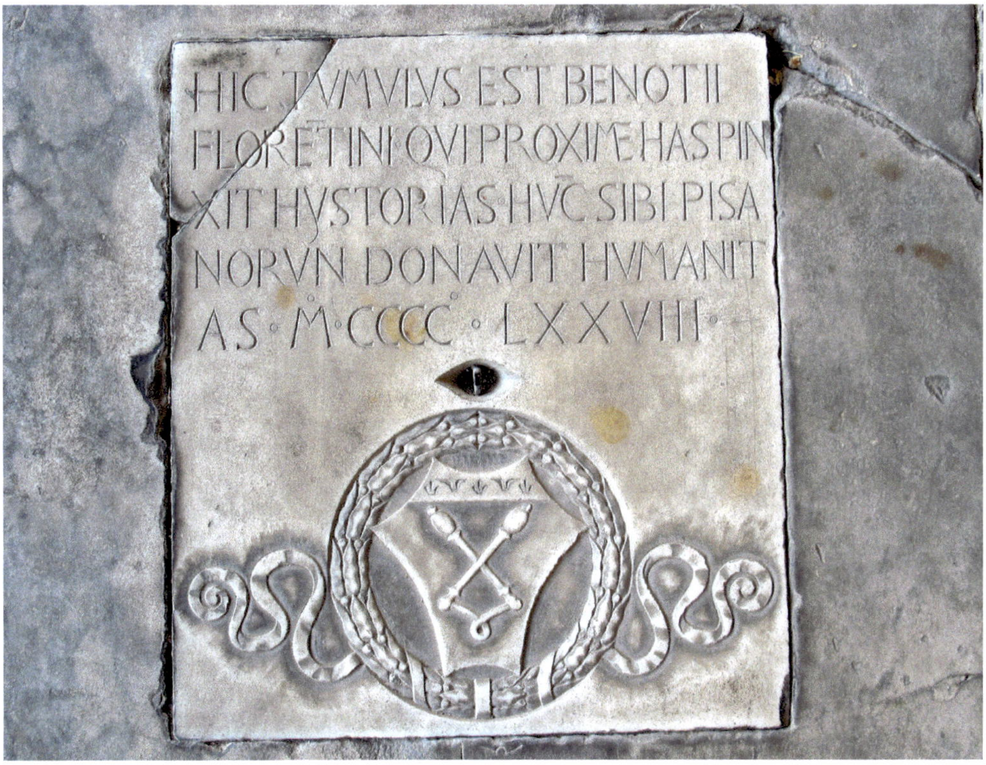

3.21. Cenotaph of Benozzo Gozzoli, 1478, Camposanto, Pisa. Photo Author.

Possibly composed by Lorenzo's confidant, Agnolo Poliziano, it signals a new status for artists.[282] Benozzo enjoyed favored treatment during his long sojourn in Pisa. When he first arrived, the Opera rented and renovated a house; it purchased another house for the artist in 1473. The accounts record generous in-kind payments as well.[283] When his father died in 1469, the Opera provided an *avello* in the Camposanto; Benozzo himself was given a tomb at the foot of the Joseph mural (Figure 3.21).[284] Ultimately, it was not used; Benozzo was forced to leave Pisa, as were all Florentines, two years before his death in 1497.[285]

The final payment to Benozzo on 1 May 1484 contains a telling detail. The records show that the painter was given a little more than twenty-four soldi, a not inconsiderable sum, for no particular reason, except that "he could have asked more, as messer Antonio the *operaio* and Antonio di Duccio know."[286] The suggestion that Benozzo was working for more than just salary implies that his skill was "without price" – that is, that his relationship with the Opera was more than simply a commercial one, but it entailed ties of honor and obligation, such as those that bound artists to princes in the courts of northern Italy.[287] While hardly enjoying the status of the "republican court artist" Bertoldo di Giovanni, who resided in the Medici palace and traveled in Lorenzo's entourage, these accommodations of the Pisan Opera to Benozzo

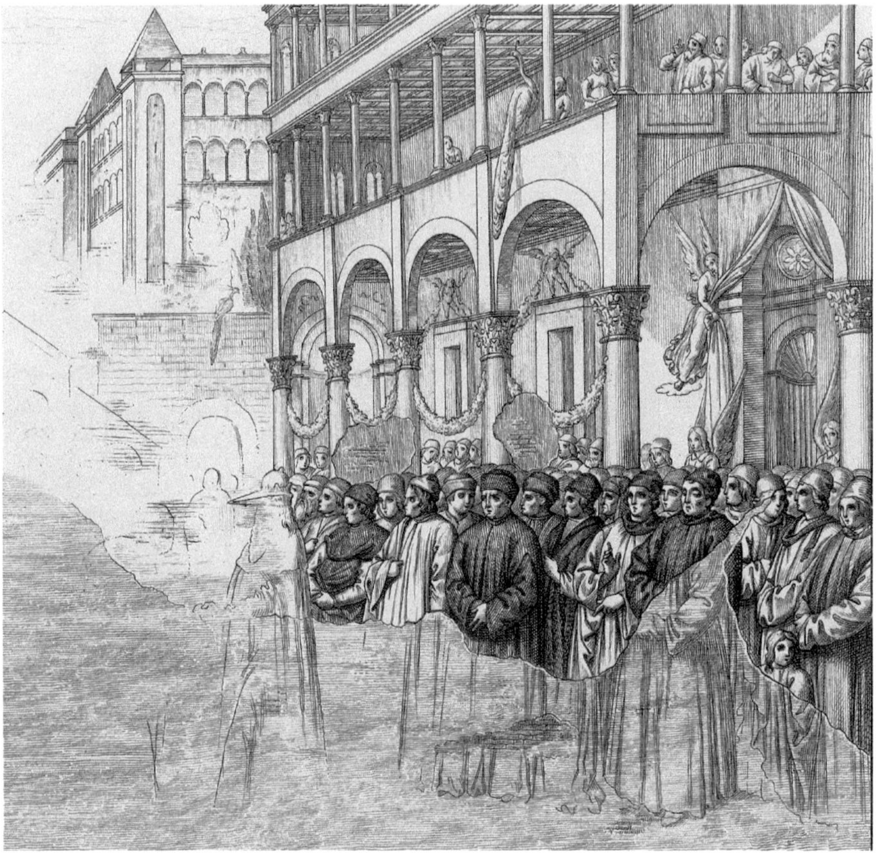

3.22. Giovanni Paolo Lasinio and Giuseppe Rossi engraving (1833) after Benozzo Gozzoli, *The Meeting of King Solomon and the Queen of Sheba* (fragment), 1484, from *Peintures à fresque du Camposanto de Pise*, Florence: Dante, 1833, Collection National Library of Poland. Photo: Polona Digital Library.

indicate enhanced status.[288] Fittingly, Benozzo's full-length portrait was inserted into the scene at the right, among the many portraits of contemporaries that are unidentifiable today.[289] More broadly, Benozzo's style and imagery in the Camposanto murals visualize the cultural patronage pursued by Lorenzo de' Medici during these years of the fifteenth century

The last mural of the cycle, the *Meeting of King Solomon and the Queen of Sheba*, completed before May of 1484, reinforces the idea of a Pisa "Laurenziana" (Figures 3.22–3.23). Known only in fragments and copies, the mural depicts the meeting against a magnificent backdrop of Solomon's temple – an evocation of Old Saint Peter's in Rome – and to the right his palace, depicted as a Renaissance loggia, ornamented by sculpture and draped with garlands.[290] Unlike the multi-episodic scenes of the previous murals, this last mural focuses on the arrival of the queen and her vast entourage at the palace of Solomon. The wise Hebrew leader and the proud

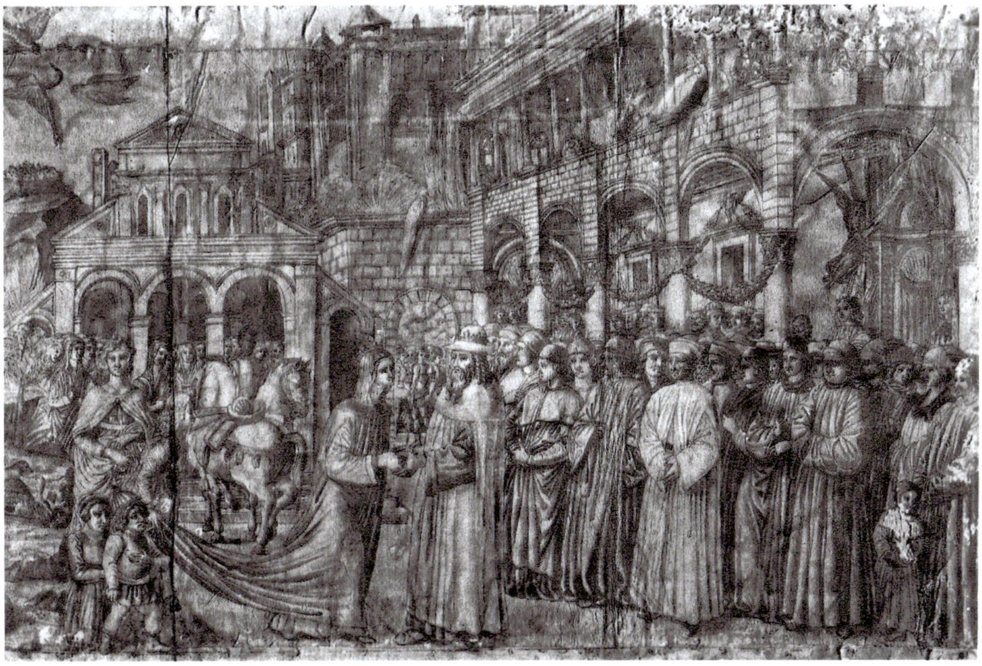

3.23. Anonymous copy after Benozzo Gozzoli, *The Meeting of King Solomon and the Queen of Sheba*, detail, 1484, Museo dell'Opera del Duomo, Pisa. photo: Soprintendenza ai Beni Artistici, Architettonici, Ambientali, e Storici per le Provincie di Pisa, Lucca, Livorno, Massa Carrara.

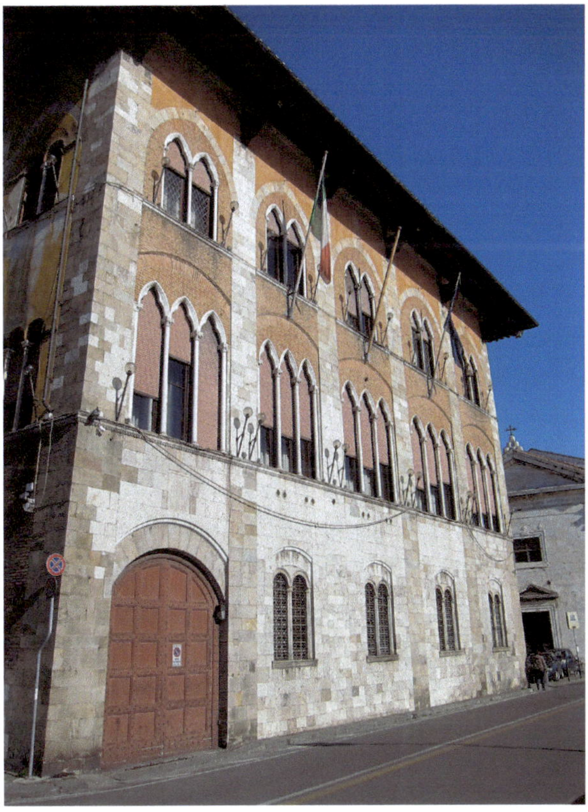

3.24. Palazzo Medici, Pisa. Photo: Author.

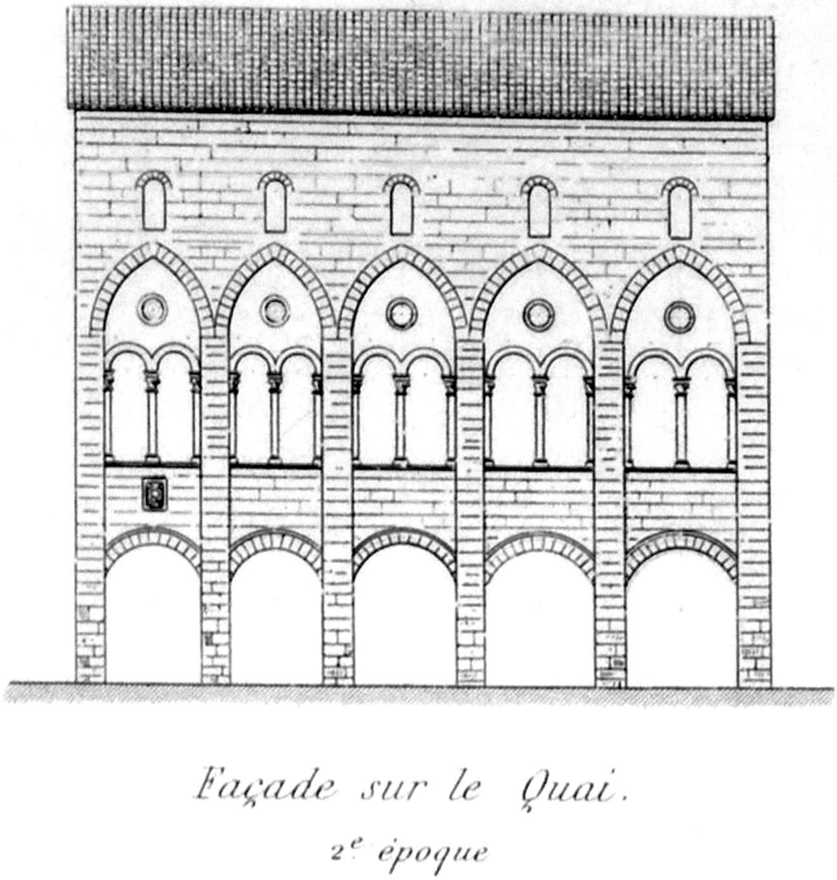

3.25. *Palazzo Medici in Pisa*, façade, from Georges Rohault de Fleury, *Les monuments de Pise au moyen âge*, Paris: A. Morel, 1866, plate I.

queen of Egypt embrace, as crowds of dignitaries look on. In the drawing after the mural, the design of Solomon's palace might allude to another Pisan building, the Palazzo Vecchio de' Medici on the Lungarno (Figure 3.24). This palace, drastically renovated in the nineteenth century, was originally built in the fourteenth century and purchased by Cosimo de' Medici in 1441. It was renovated between 1539 and 1545 for Eleanora di Toledo by the architect Giovan Battista del Tasso; the façade was reconstructed starting in 1550.[291] While evidence is scant, Rohault de Fleury published in 1866 a reconstruction of the façade, with its use of the local building stone, *verruca*, and prominent buttresses flanking the slightly depressed arches on the ground floor (Figure 3.25). His reconstruction of the courtyard elevation shows classicizing columns.[292] In the copy of the

Pisa mural, the indication of masonry – drafted or ashlar is hard to tell – and articulation of the ground floor might recall aspects of the Palazzo Medici in Pisa that signal Pisan building traditions.[293] The equivalence of the palace of the magnificent King Solomon, with that of Lorenzo "il Magnifico" in the city of Pisa, underlines the Medici reshaping of Pisa as the foremost city of the Florentine state.

Ultimately, Florentine efforts to absorb Pisa into its territory, its politics, and its culture failed. In the wake of Lorenzo's death, the expulsion of the Medici from Florence, and the invasion of the French King Charles VIII, Pisa regained independence until 1509. The effort to make Pisa truly Florentine would be taken up again by the Medici Grand Dukes in the sixteenth century, with different results.[294]

NOTES

1 Florence, Archivio di Stato (hereafter ASF), Mediceo Avanti il Principato (hereafter MAP) F. 81, doc. 22, cc. 123 recto–26 verso. The document text was copied into the MAP from the original, in ASF, Notarile Antecosimiano 8180 [Gaspare Franchi], cc 170 recto–71 verso; cc.192r–99r. The copyist eliminated references to bequests to individuals referred to in separate entries. Maria Ausilio Pisano has pointed out that the legal form of the document is a *charta concessionis*, but it is actually a *volontà testamentarie*. In addition to the testament, three notarial acts detail bequests. In one, cc. 127 recto–28 recto, Filippo gave his books of civil and canon law to his nephews, the sons of his brother Tanai: Vieri, Roberto and Gerolamo. In another, cc. 128 verso–29 verso, Filippo left all his other books and belongings to the sacristy of the Duomo, including a brevary that Filippo had made by the nuns of Santa Maria Maddalena di Siena. In the fourth document, cc. 129v–32v, Filippo made bequests to Tanai and his family, Pandolfo de' Medici, Alamanno and Giovanni his *cappellani*, Simone de Lupi "notaio della sua corte," Giovanni Stefano "suo scudiero," and six "servitors suos dilectos." These bequests were copied into the accounts of the Mensa Arcivescovile; Pisa, Archivio Storico Diocesano, Archivio Capitolare (hereafter ASD, ACP), Debitori e creditori, no. 1, 1462–76, c. 76 recto–77 recto. In addition, the Mensa accounts record gifts of cloth from the archbishop to his family and associates worth over 500 florins, including 6 3/4 braccia "di monachino per una cioppetta per thanai nostro fratello," worth almost 8 florins; 22 braccia "di moschino per una cioppa e un mantello per monna chaterina donna di Thanai," worth more than 26 florins, 4 braccia of V [... ?] "per Vierai et ruberto figliuoli di thanai nostro fratello," worth 4 florins; and 12 braccia "di vinaii per li fanciulli cioè le fanculle feminine di thanai," worth 12 florins.

2 Expenses for Filippo's funeral on 10 October 1475/74 were also recorded in the accounts of the Mensa Arcivescovile, ASD, ACP, Debitori e creditori, no. 1, 1462–76, cc. 77 verso–79 recto, written by Nicolo d'Urbano by order of Antonio Moretto, Gerardo da Vivaia, Leonardo d'Antonio Vernagalli, "fidecomissi alla buona memoria di Messer Phylippo de' Medici arcivescovo di Pisa." They included 110 memorial Masses said by the Pisan clerics, the bell to be covered in black buckram, and the sermon delivered by Lancillotto Decio, a doctor at the Studio. See also Michele Luzzati, "Filippo de' Medici Arcivescovo di Pisa e la visita pastorale del 1462–1463," *Bollettino storico pisano*, vols. 33–35, 1964–66, p. 379, note 35. For the chapel, the contract with Francione and Baccio Pontelli was published in I. B. Supino, "I maestri d'intaglio e di tarsia in legno nella Primaziale di Pisa," *Archivio storico dell'arte*, vol 6, 1893, pp. 162–63; see Roberto Paolo Novello, "Baccio Pontelli a Pisa: Una rilettura," in Gabriele Donati and Valeria Genovese, eds., *Forme del legno: Intaglio e tarsie fra*

gotico e rinascimento, Pisa: Edizioni della Normale, 2013, p. 81. Doris Carl, "Zu Francione und den Brüdern da Sangallo. Ihre Partnerschaft im Licht neuer Dokumente," in A. Belluzzi et al., eds., *Giuliano da Sangallo*, Milan: Officina Libraria, 2017, p. pp. 183–84, doc. no. 5, has published a new transcription. Tanai's return in the 1480 catasto is in ASF Catasto [1480], 1017, fol. 560 recto–61 recto. His large family possessed considerable assets, including real estate in Pisa and its *contado*; see Michael Mallett, "Pisa and Florence in the Fifteenth Century: Aspects of the Period of the First Florentine Domination," in *Florentine Studies: Politics and Society in Renaissance Florence*, London: Faber and Faber, 1968, p. 433.

3 "Il coro lavorato a modo che quello della cappella della Nonsiata di Firenza, quando l'omo entra dentro."

4 Francis Ames-Lewis, "Art in the Service of the Family: The Taste and Patronage of Piero di Cosimo de' Medici," in Andreas Beyer and Bruce Boucher, eds., *Piero de' Medici "il Gottoso" (1416–1469)*, Berlin: Akademie Verlag, 1993, pp. 207–8. Alina Payne discusses such structures and their rich materials in "Style and the Aesthetic of Surface in Architecture from Alberti to Michelangelo," in Dario Gamboni et al., eds., *The Aesthetics of Marble from Late Antiquity to the Present*, Munich: Hirmer, 2021, pp. 114–31.

5 Carl, "Zu Francione und den Brüdern da Sangallo," pp. 169–85.

6 Novello, "Baccio Pontelli a Pisa," pp. 82–86.

7 Carl, "Zu Francione und den Brüdern da Sangallo." Carl, pp. 183–85, doc. nos. 4–6, publishes newly discovered payments for the chapel, a new transcription for the contract, and excerpts from Filippo's testament.

8 Michelagnolo di Cristofano da Volterra, "Le Mirabili et inaldite beleze e adornamenti del Camposanto di Pisa," in I. B. Supino, ed., *Il Camposanto di Pisa*, Florence: Alinari, 1896, pp. 301–17.

9 "Poi comicia a seguir la storia nuova, / la qual Benozzo fiorentin dipinse: / del Testamento Vechio chiar si trova / tutte tal storie, e già mai non se finse / di farla sufficiente a tutta pruova, / e tutti colpi e modi costui vinse: / ciò della pittura si può fare/ prima d'inponimento singular"; Supino, *Il Camposanto di Pisa,* p. 310.

10 "Questo tal tempio è sì degno e galante / ch' al mondo el pari non credo che sia; / cercando tutto el ponente e levante / più bella cosa non se troveria"; Supino, *Il Camposanto di Pisa*, pp. 316–17.

11 See, for example, the account of Michel de Montaigne, whose visit to Pisa in 1581 included the Camposanto. He expressed nostalgia but evinces little sense of the Camposanto as a sacred space. See Marina Bailo et al., *Viaggiatori stranieri a Pisa dal '500 al '900*, Pisa: Nistri Lichi, 2003, pp. 4–5. See also Roberto P. Ciardi, "'Quest'insigne dormentorio de' morti': Chiesa, cimitero, museo," and "Da cimitero a famedio: L'età moderna," in Clara Baracchini and Enrico Castelnuovo, eds., *Il Camposanto di Pisa*, Turin: Einaudi, 1996, pp. 57–68, 133–46; and Michele Bacci, The Pisan Camposanto and the Staging of Sanctity: An Introductory Essay," in Michele Bacci et al, eds., *Journeys of the Soul: Multiple Topographies in the Camposanto of Pisa*, Pisa: Edizioni della Normale, 2020, pp. 36–39.

12 For the San Gimignano frescoes, see Christie Knapp Fengler, "Bartolo di Fredi's Frescoes in San Gimignano," *Art Bulletin*, vol. 63, 1981, pp. 374–84; C. Griffith Mann, "From Creation to the End of Time: The Nave Frescoes of San Gimignano's Collegiata and the Structure of Civic Devotion," PhD. dissertation, Johns Hopkins University, 2002; Gaudenz Freuler, *Bartolo dei Fredi Cini*, Disentis: Desertina Verlag, 1994. For the Santa Maria Novella frescoes, which survive only in part, see Amber McAllister, "Narrative and Allegory in the Genesis Fresco Cycle in the Chiostro Verde, Santa Maria Novella, Florence," PhD dissertation, University of Georgia, 2003.

13 Antonio Caleca, "Costruzione e decorazione dale origini al secolo xv," in Baracchini and Castelnuovo, eds., *Il Camposanto di Pisa*, pp. 34–35.

14 Alessia Andreotti et al., "The Wall Paintings of the Monumental Cemetery of Pisa: The War, the Restoration, the Conservation," in Antonio Sgamellotti et al., eds., *Science and Art: The Painted Surface*, Cambridge: Royal Society of Chemistry, 2014, pp. 193–209.

15 Carlo Lasinio, *Pitture a fresco del Camposanto a Pisa intagliate da Carlo Lasinio*, Florence: Molini, 1812; Giovanni Paolo Lasinio and Giuseppe Rossi, *Pitture a fresco del Camposanto a Pisa disegnate da Giuseppe Rossi ed incise dal Prof. Cav. G. P. Lasinio*, 2nd ed., Florence: Tipografia all'Insegna di Dante, 1832. The hand-colored set is from the 1812 edition.

16 Diane Cole Ahl, *Benozzo Gozzoli*, New Haven and London: Yale University Press, 1997, pp. 158–59.

17 Renée K. Burnam, "Le vetrate del Duomo di Pisa," *Annali della Scuola Normale Superiore di Pisa*, serie iv, quaderno no. 13, 2002, pp. 245–50. The windows, all for the southeast corridor, included subjects of the Nativity, the Temptation of Christ, Christ and the Samaritan Woman, the Calling of Matthew, Saint Peter Walks on Water, Christ Chasing the Moneylenders from the Temple, and Christ heals a Paralytic.

18 Ahl, *Benozzo Gozzoli*, p. 158; see also William Tronzo, "The Prestige of St. Peter's: Observations on the Function of Monumental Narrative Cycles in Italy," *Studies in the History of Art*, vol. 16, 1985, pp. 93–112; Herbert Kessler, "Caput e speculum omnium ecclesiarum: Old St. Peter's and Church Decoration in Medieval Latium," in William Tronzo, ed., *Italian Church Decoration in the Middle Ages and Early Renaissance*, Bologna, 1989, pp. 119–46.

19 A preliminary version of this chapter was presented in Jean Cadogan, "Benozzo Gozzoli, Filippo de' Medici and the Old Testament Murals in the Campo Santo in Pisa (1468–1484)," *Predella Monografie*, nos. 13–14, 2016 [2018], pp. 217–29.

20 The existence of a coherent program established in the early fourteenth century is unlikely; but see Patrizia Castelli, "Ranieri da cantore a santo taumaturgo: Agiografia e immagini di propaganda civica e religiosa nella città di Pisa (secoli XII–XIV)," in Patrizia Castelli and Maria Luisa Ceccarelli Lemut, eds., *L'"invenzione" di Ranieri il taumaturgo tra XII e XIV secolo: Agiografia ed immagini*, Pisa: Pacini Editore, 2013, pp. 72–73; and Hilary Ane Haakenson, "Casting the Continents: Sacred History and Spiritual Odyssey in the Camposanto of Pisa," in Maryanne Cline Horowitz and Louise Arizzoli, eds., *Bodies and Maps: Early Modern Personifications of the Continents*, Leiden: Brill, 2021, pp. 159–90.

21 These have been published in Maria Luigia Orlandi, *Benozzo Gozzoli a Pisa; I documenti (1468–1495)*, Pisa: Pacini Editore, 1997.

22 Sergio Tognetti, ed., *Firenze e Pisa dopo il 1406: La creazione di un nuovo spazio regionale*, Florence: Olschki, 2010.

23 Goro Dati, *Istoria di Firenze dal 1380 al 1405*, Florence: Giuseppe Manni, 1735, pp. 123–24; cited in John Najemy, *A History of Florence 1200–1575*, Chichester: John Wiley & Sons, 2008, pp. 196–97.

24 Francesco Guicciardini, *Storia d'Italia*, [book I, 1494], ed Silvana Seidel Menchi, Turin: Einaudi, 1971, vol. 1, pp. 103–5. For a historiographic overview, see Giovanni Ciccaglioni, "Patrimonio culturale e formazione territoriale nella Toscana fiorentina: Il caso pisano," in Denise La Monica et al., eds., *Municipalia. Storia della Tutela: Patrimonio artistico e identità cittadina: Pisa e Forlì (sec. XIV–XVIII)*, Pisa: Edizioni ETS, 2010, vol. 1, pp. 91–100.

25 Pietro Silva, *Pisa sotto Firenze dal 1406 al 1433*, Pisa: A. Valenti, 1909, pp. 11. Silva highlighted, however, growing awareness in Florence of the deplorable conditions in Pisa as a "danger and shame to the commune," and he pointed to changes in policy following 1433. Maria Luisa Mori, *La dominazione fiorentina a Pisa dal 1451 al 1469*, Pisa: Orsolini-Prosperi, 1936, continued the lament of Pisan decline. She asserts that Florentine benevolence after 1433 did not last. By 1451, Mori related, the city had fallen into misery again for the same reasons as before. Michael Mallett examined maritime trade, concluding that depopulation, rather than repressive Florentine policies, led to general impoverishment; Michael Mallet, "The Sea Consuls of Florence in the Fifteenth Century," *Papers of the British School at Rome*, vol. 27, 1959, pp. 156–69; Michael Mallett, "Pisa and Florence in the Fifteenth Century: Aspects of the Period of the First Florentine Domination," pp. 403–41. Mallett outlined Florence's continued efforts throughout the fifteenth century to regulate pasturage and repair the drainage system in the countryside, instituting various

governing bodies, especially the Sea Consuls, established in 1421. The Opera della Riparazione del Contado di Pisa (Board for the repair of the Pisan countryside) was founded in 1475 and over the century undertook measures to drain marshes and repair the banks of the Arno.

26 This interest culminated with the conference "1406: Firenze e Pisa. La creazione di un nuovo spazio regionale" held in 2008, the acts from which were published in Tognetti, ed., *Firenze e Pisa dopo il 1406.*

27 Andrea Zorzi, "L'inquadramento di Pisa e del suo territorio nel dominio fiorentino," in Tognetti, ed., *Firenze e Pisa dopo il 1406*, pp. 85–107. See also Elena Fasano Guarini, "Città soggette e contadi nel dominio fiorentino tra Quattro e Cinquecento: Il caso pisano," in Mario Mirri, ed., *Ricerche di storia moderna*, vol. 1, Pisa: Pacini Editore, 1976, pp. 1–94; Giorgio Chittolini, "Ricerche sull'ordinamento territoriale del dominio fiorentino agli inizi del secolo XV," in *La formazione dello stato regionale e le istituzioni del contado*, Turin: Einaudi, 1979, pp. 292–352; Mario Mirri, ed., *La città e il contado di Pisa nello stato dei Medici (XV–XVII secoli)*, Pisa: Pacini Editore, 2000; Patrizia Salvadore, "Florentines and the Communities of the Territorial State, in William Connell, ed., *Florentine Tuscany*, Cambridge: Cambridge University Press, 2000, pp. 207–24; Alessandro Potenti, *Uomini, villaggi, terreni: Aspetti economici e demografici delle campagne pisane del Quattrocento*, Pisa: Pacini Editore, 2002; Roberto Castiglione, "Pisa e l'Opera di Santa Maria del Fiore di Firenze: I rapport fiscali dal 1416 al 1430," *Bollettino Storico Pisano*, vol. 81, 2012, pp. 1–25.

28 Zorzi, "L'inquadramento di Pisa," pp. 90–93.

29 Bruno Casini, "I fuochi di Pisa e la prestanza del 1407," *Bollettino storico pisano*, ser. 3, vol. 27, 1958, pp. 156–272; Bruno Casini, "Contribuenti pisani alle taglie del 1402 e 1412," *Bollettino storico pisano*, ser. 3, vols. 28–29, 1959–60, pp. 90–318; Bruno Casini, *Il Catasto di Pisa nel 1428–29*, Pisa: Giardini, 1964; Nicoletta Orlandini, "Economia e società a Pisa alla metà del XV secolo," 2 vols., Tesi di laurea, University of Pisa, 1984–85; Miria Fanucci, Michele Luzzati, and Lionel Lovitch, *L'estimo di Pisa nell'anno del Concilio (1409)*, Pisa: Pacini Editore, 1986. Giuseppe Petralia, "1406: Il dissolversi di una società tardocomunale come premessa alla costruzione di uno stato toscano," in Tognetti, ed., *Firenze e Pisa dopo il 1406*, pp. 123–35. There is a decline of almost half of taxpayers over the period from 1409 to 1447: from 2,254 contributors in 1409, to 1,729 in 1428, to 1,171 in 1447. Even if the average number of persons making up each household increased (a parallel development is traceable in Florence) from 3.5 in 1402, to 4.28 in 1428, to 5 in 1447, a sharp decline is still visible, from an estimated population of 12,250 in 1402, to 7,331 in 1428, to 5,855 in 1447. There were 2,660 taxpaying households in 1402, but only 1,272 of the surveyed 1,729 households were taxed in 1428. Of the 1,171 households taxed in 1447, only 917 actually paid any tax; the others were written off by the officials as *fogne*. Effectively, the contributing households to the tax declined 34.5 percent from 1402 to 1447. Orlandini, "Economia e società a Pisa alla metà del XV secolo," pp. 31–33.

30 Bruno Casini, *Aspetti della vita economica e sociale di Pisa dal catasto del 1428–29*, Pisa: S.E.I.T., 1965, p. 7; Luigina Carratori, Michele Luzzati, "'Forestieri' a Pisa nella second metà del Quattrocento," in Rinaldo Comba et al., eds., *Strutture familiari, epidemie, migrazione*, Pisa: Edizioni scientifiche italiane, 1984, pp. 389–400; Petralia, 1406: "Il dissolversi di una società tardocomunale," p. 126.

31 Property was subject to requisition by Florentines; this situation likely led to the destruction of derelict houses and decay of the urban fabric; Orlandini, "Economia e società a Pisa alla metà del XV secolo," p. 33.

32 Marta Battistoni, *L'Opera del Duomo di Pisa: Il patrimonio e la sua gestione nei secoli xii–xvi*, Pisa: Pacini Editore, 2013, p. 80. Battistoni traces this trend to the difficult years of the late fourteenth century; she says such assets, once exempted from tax, were no longer exempt, thus fueling donations to pious institutions while the donors retained usufruct. As Battistoni recounts, in 1393, the Anziani, on behalf of the Opera del Duomo, sent an appeal to Pope

Boniface IX requesting indulgences for testators who left property to the Opera, signaling the increasing importance of this source of revenue.

33 Supino, *Il Camposanto di Pisa*, pp. 37–39.

34 Ottavio Banti, *Le iscrizioni delle tombe terragne del Camposanto di Pisa*, Pontedera: Bandecchi & Vivaldi, 1998. If we include the tombs that are approximately datable, according to Banti, the numbers rise to 134 for the period 1350–98; 92 for 1401–48, and 34 for 1450–1500. Of these, 13 were tombs for confraternities and 12 for clergy connected to the cathedral or *operai* during 1350–98; 1 for confraternities and 4 for clergy or *operai* during 1401–48; and 2 for confraternities and 0 for *operai* etc. during 1450–1500. These gross numbers correspond to a 31 percent decline for the period 1401 to 1448 and a 63 percent decline during 1450–1500. Although approximate, they reflect a general picture of decreasing use of the floor tombs in the Camposanto that accelerated in the second half of the fifteenth century.

35 See Luigina Carratori and Michele Luzzati, "'Forestieri' di Pisa nella seconda metà del Quattrocento"; Ciardi, "'Quest'insigne dormentorio de' morti,'" p. 60; Banti, *Le iscrizioni delle tombe terragne*, pp. 39–40. Among the foreigners buried in the fifteenth century in the Camposanto are those in service to military captains (Banti nos. 73, 272, 279), to the pope (nos. 129, 142) or other sovereigns (no. 303); residents of Pisa from foreign lands (nos. 309, 299) or other Italian cities (no. 150 from Parma; no. 238 from Volterra; no. 276 from Lucca, nos. 130, 195, 287, 289, 300, 328a from Florence).

36 For example, Simone Matrasarium, a merchant from the Ponte neighborhood, who was buried in the southwest corridor probably in the early fifteenth century is a typical example. He paid four florins in tax and was the 66th highest taxpayer in the 1409 estimo; Banti, *Le iscrizioni delle tombe terragne*, no. 155; Fanucci, Luzzati, and Lovitch, *L'estimo di Pisa*, p. 49, no. 228. Other examples: The tomb slab of Martinus Amadoris Amador *vinarius*, from the Sancta Lucia del Rifuccho parish in the Ponte quartiere, is also in the southwest corridor. His heirs paid tax in the 1409 estimo of one florin, seven soldi, the 333rd highest levy out of a total of 2,250 taxpayers; Banti, *Le iscrizioni delle tombe terragne*, no. 141; Fanucci, Luzzati, and Lovitch, *L'estimo di Pisa*, p. 41, no. 55. Stefano di Cione *orafo*, also from Sancta Lucia del Rifuccho, also buried in the southwest corridor in the early fifteenth century, paid 5 soldi, 1,321 of 2,250 taxpayers in 1409; Banti, *Le iscrizioni delle tombe terragne*, no. 144; Fanucci, Luzzati, and Lovitch, *L'estimo di Pisa*, p. 40, no. 38. Nuccio di Parente, *coriarius*, from the San Casciano parish in the Kinzica quartiere, buried in the southwest corridor in 1427, is listed in the 1409 estimo as paying four soldi, the 1,559th highest tax; Banti, *Le iscrizioni delle tombe terragne*, no. 120; Fanucci, Luzzati, Lovitch, *L'estimo di Pisa*, p. 146, no. 2042.

37 Ser Matteo d'Appiano, nephew of ser Andrea d'Apiano, buried in the southwest corridor in 1412, paid only 10 soldi tax in 1409, the 820th highest taxpayer of 2,250 in 1409; Banti, *Le iscrizioni delle tombe terragne*, no. 199; Fanucci, Luzzati, and Lovitch, *L'estimo di Pisa*, p. 128, no. 164. Ser Matteo di Fanuccio d'Appiano and Lancillotto suo figlio at the time of the 1447 catasto lived in the district of Sant' Andrea in Kinzica and paid s.14 d. 2 in tax; Orlandini, "Economia e società a Pisa alla metà del XV secolo," no. 724, 124th place. Nicolaus de Franciscus de Roselminis, from a prominent family who died in the second half of the fifteenth century, was buried in the north corridor, but in 1489 the tomb, purchased by his father, had not yet been paid for; Banti, *Le iscrizioni delle tombe terragne*, no. 217. For this originally merchant family, see Emilio Cristiani, *Nobiltà e popolo nel comune di Pisa*, Naples: Istituto italiano per gli studi storici in Napoli, 1962, pp. 469–70. His tax return from the 1428–29 catasto lists his gross taxable income as 339 soldi, though with deductions he paid only 13 soldi in tax. He noted the family had lived in the countryside for twenty years; Casini, *Il catasto di Pisa del 1428–29*, no. 1539. Several family members appeared in the 1447 catasto, some of them as exiles who had not paid tax in many years (listed as *fogna*) including Giovanni di Gherardo Rosselmini, Orlandini no. 471, 64th place; Francsco and Adovardo di Niccolo Rosselmini, Orlandini no. 472, 176th place; and

Lodovico di Niccolo Rosselmini, Orlandini no. 1055, listed as *fogna* paid just six denari, placed 1143/1170 in Orlandini's records.

38 See, for example, Aldobrando del Bondo, Banti, *Le iscrizioni delle tombe terragne*, appendix nos. 25, 33: Michele de Scorno e fratelli, Banti appendix no. 4; Gherardi quondam Petri del Canfera, Banti appendix no. 6; Giovanni Baccareto and Bontura his son, Banti appendix no. 24.

39 Banti, *Le iscrizioni delle tombe terragne*, no. 243. His prosperous family paid the 32nd highest tax in the 1447 catasto, 1 florin, 15 soldi and 6 denari, out of 1,170 returns; Orlandini, "Economia e società a Pisa alla metà del XV secolo," no. 184.

40 For this and the following, see Casini, *Il catasto di Pisa*, pp. ix–xii; and Casini, *Aspetti della vita economica e sociale di Pisa*, pp. 3–8. The catasto valued assets in ways that resulted in more consistent assessments in contrast to the earlier estimi, which taxpayers considered arbitrary. Heads of households filed returns, including information on the names and ages of the family members, servants, and slaves. Returns often specified occupations and included locations and employees of offices or workshops. Immovable possessions and mobile goods were described in detail, including animals, slaves, merchandise, credits, and cash. Net taxable income was calculated after deductions for dependents, debts, and other obligations, and the amount payable reckoned according to a fixed formula.

41 Piero di Bartolomeo, goldsmith, had taxable gross assets of 535 soldi; Banti, *Le iscrizioni delle tombe terragne*, no. 138, buried in the south corridor between the east and west entrances in the early fifteenth century; Casini, *Il catasto di Pisa,* no. 829. In between were the 455 soldi of Andrea di Piero *chascaiulo* and his brothers; Banti, *Le iscrizioni delle tombe terragne*, no. 252. The tomb was that of his father Petro di Simone and his sons, Andrea, Jacopo, Bartolomeo, and Simone, dated 1426, just before the catasto was instituted. The return, Casini, *Il catasto di Pisa*, no. 1050, filed by Andrea and his brothers, also lists several botteghe, one in which Andrea sold cheese, and another in which Jacopo and Simone repaired and sold leather, employing one garzone at a salary of 9 florins. Nocchus Bartoli *speziale*, sostanza valued 443 soldi; Banti, *Le iscrizioni delle tombe terragne*, no. 241, was buried in the north corridor in 1436; Casini, *Il catasto di Pisa,* no. 1194. His son Piero and his family lived with him in the Santa Cecilia parish in the quartiere di Mezzo. Those of more modest wealth include: Batista di Giovanni da Buti *pattiere*, valued at 272 soldi; Banti, *Le iscrizioni delle tombe terragne*, no. 214, Casini, *Il catasto di Pisa,* no. 1199. Battista di Giovanni rented a workshop in the cappella San Martino alla Pietra for 42 lire, where he had a garzone he paid a salary of 16 lire per year and listed inventory valued at 125 florins. Gaspare di Tomaso *calzolaio*, valued 243 soldi; Banti, no. 255, Casini no. 728. Gaspare also owned a house he rented to another *calzolaio*, Pasquino di Ghino, Casini no. 717. Piero di Giovanni Marti *vinaiuolo*, valued 209 soldi; Banti no. 277, Casini no. 420. Piero di Giovanni rented a workshop for 24 florins and 2 lire, where he paid his garzone 10 florins in salary. Pacino di Pace *calzolaio* of Arezzo valued 187 soldi; Banti no. 129, Casini no. 1263. The inventory in his bottega was valued at 40 florins. Benedetto di Piero *pattiere* valued 181 soldi; Banti no. 113, Casini no. 1047. He shared a workshop with another *pattiere*, Simone di Tinuccio. Gherardo di Tomeo *barbiere*, valued 73 soldi, Banti no. 208, Casini no. 584. He had half of a bottega where the inventory was valued at 20 florins. Domenico di Michele da Cisanello *chascaiulo*, valued 65 soldi; Banti, no. 292, Casini no. 1027. He rented a workshop in the cappella of San Jacopo del Mercato for 14 florins. Antonio di Giovanni da Cascina, valued 20 soldi; Banti no 278, Casini no. 1298. Simone di Cione da Cascina *pontonaio*, valued 10 soldi; Banti no. 250, Casini 821. Stefano di Cione *orafo* da Piombino possessed 109 soldi of gross taxable assets; he was nonetheless listed as *miserabile* and paid no tax; Banti no. 144, Casini no. 722. Stefano rented his house in the cappella of Santa Lucia di Ricucco from the archbishop of Pisa for 16 soldi; he also rented two pieces of land in Macerata from the archbishop, and he owed 80 florins to the Opera del Duomo.

42 Casini, *Il catasto di Pisa*, no. 489, Banti, *Le iscrizioni delle tombe terragne*, no. 210. Ser Giovanni di Matteo da Forcoli was a notary whose assets totaled 782 soldi. His *avello*, also in the north corridor, is from the mid-fifteenth century; Casini no. 428; Banti, no. 283.

43 Mallett, "Pisa and Florence in the Fifteenth Century," pp. 415–18, listed Giovanni Maggiolini, Jacopo di Corbino, Guglielmo and Piero de' Paganelli, Buonacorso Buonconti, Piero di Stefano Gaetani, Bartolomeo di Neri detto Maschiano, Lupardo da Vecchiano, Antonio da Settimo, Jacopo Vernagalli, Gaspare di Ser Venvenuto da Lavaiano, and Piero di Ser Colo Galletti among the sixty Pisan families with gross wealth of more than 2,000 florins.

44 Coordinating the inscriptions from Banti, *Le iscrizioni delle tombe terragne*, with the tax data compiled by Orlandini, "Economia e società a Pisa alla metà del XV secolo," we see that tax payments ranged from the 32nd, 41st and 64th highest payments to the 1,023rd (paying one soldo) out of 1,170 returns, as follows: Rede di Ser Bartolomeo da Farneta e nipote, Banti no. 210, Orlandini 808, 41st place; Antonio Giovanni and Jacopo di Guido da Castello *vinaiuolo*, Banti no. 359, Orlandini no. 185, 45th place; Nanni d'Agostino *barbiere*, Banti no. 317, Orlandini no. 432, 82nd place; Giovanni di Jacopo del Ciarpa *beccaio* da Vico, Banti no. 249, Orlandini no. 80, 156th place; Paulo di Giovanni Dondasso, Banti no. 306, Orlandini 727, 298th place; Battista di Giovanni da Buti *pattiere*, Banti no 214, Orlandini no. 275, 349th place; Gherardo di Tommaso *barbiere*, Banti no. 208, Orlandini 851, 374th place; Benedetto and Lorenzo di Antonio di Falcone, Banti 224, Orlandini 135, 386th place; Benedetto di Piero *pattiere*, Banti no. 113, Orlandini 181, 636th place; Paolo di Jacopo Morovelli, Banti no. 215, Orlandini 261, 832nd place.

45 Antoniotto di Giovanni di Peretto da Chamaiore, *cuoiaio*, Banti, no. 218, 1440; Orlandini as 1,023/1,170 taxpayers, paying just one soldo.

46 Ghirigorio di Migele, *tavolaio*, Banti, no. 149, 1444; Orlandini 1,023/1,170 taxpayers, paying also one soldo.

47 Antonio di Urbani *beccaio* e fratelli, Banti, no. 244, 1451; Orlandini 47/1,170 taxpayers, paying one florin, six soldi.

48 Gherardo di Tomeo *barbieri*, Banti, no. 208, 1452; Orlandini, 374/1,170, paying five soldi and ten denari.

49 Antonio Giovanni and Jacopo di Guido da Castello *vinaiuoli*, Banti, no. 359, 1465; Orlandini, 45/1,170, paying one florin, six soldi and three denari.

50 Iohannis et Michaelis Antoni Berti, Banti, no. 245, 1456, possibly related to the taxpayer in Orlandini Jacopo d'Antonio di Berto *farsettaio* e fratelli, 117/1,170, paid fourteen soldi eight denari.

51 "COMPLETUM EST HOC PAVIMENTUM TEMPORE OPERAIATUS EGREGII MILITIS IULIANI OPERARII, DIE XXIV MARTII MCCCCXL"; Banti, *Le iscrizioni delle tombe terragne*, p. 25, note 28.

52 Caleca, "Costruzione e decorazione," pp. 30–31.

53 Caleca, "Costruzione e decorazione," pp. 36–37; Burnam, "Le vetrate del Duomo di Pisa," pp. 16–17; Takuma Ito, *La vetrata nella Toscana del Quattorcento*, Florence: Olschki, 2011, pp. 82–84, 116–22; Battistoni, *L'Opera del Duomo di Pisa*, pp. 105–38; Marco Collareta, "Le vetrate," in Gabriella Garzella et al., eds., *La Cattedrale di Pisa*, Pisa: Pacini Editore, 2014, pp. 211–17; Renée K. Burnam, "The Lost Stained-Glass Windows of the Camposanto of Pisa and Fifteenth-Century Florentine Politics," in Molly Bourne and A. Victor Coonin, eds., *Encountering the Renaissance*, Ramsey, NJ: WAPACC Organization, 2016, pp. 327–38.

54 *Le arti a Pisa nel primo Rinascimento / The Arts in Pisa during the Early Renaissance*, ed. Diane Cole Ahl and Gerardo de Simone, *Predella Monografie*, no. 13–14, Pisa: Edizioni ETS, 2016 [2018]; in particular Gabriele Fattorini, "Giovanni di Pietro da Napoli e Martino di Bartolomeo 'in compagnia' nella Pisa di primo Quattrocento (con un accenno alle tele che fingevano affreschi), pp. 37–66; and Gerardo de Simone, "Tra decadenza e Rinascenza: Spigolature sul Quattrocento a Pisa," pp. 287–305. See also Diane Cole Ahl, *Painting in Fifteenth-Century Italy*, New Haven and London: Yale University Press, 2023, pp. 182–84.

55 Donatello's and Michelozzo's work on the tomb for Brancacci, carved in and shipped from Pisa, and Masaccio's polyptych painted for Giuliano di Colino degli Scarsi for the Pisan church of the Carmine, are well known; see Ronald Lightbrown, *Donatello and Michelozzo:*

An Artistic Partnership and Its Patrons in the Early Renaissance, London: Miller, 1980, vol. 1, pp. 86–89; for Masaccio's Pisa altarpiece, see Paul Joannides, *Masaccio and Masolino: A Complete Catalogue*, London: Phaidon, 1993, pp. 382–98, cat. no. 21.

56 Emilio Tolaini, *Pisa: La città e la storia*, Pisa: ETS, 2007, pp. 115–28.

57 Christiane Klapisch-Zuber, *Carrara e i maestri del marmo*, trans. Bruno Cherubini, Massa: Palazzo di St. Elisabetta, 1973; Roberto Paolo Ciardi, "Il Quattrocento," *Scultura a Pisa tra Quattro e Seicento*, ed. Claudio Casini et al., Pisa: Cantini, 1987, pp. 12–110; Roberto Paolo Ciardi, "'Ars marmoris': Aspetti dell'organizzazione del lavoro nella Toscana ocidentale durante il Quattrocento," in Enrico Castelnuovo, ed., *Niveo de marmore*, Genoa: Colombo, 1992, pp. 341–49. See Ciccaglioni, "Patrimonio culturale e formazione territoriale," pp. 120–22, on the continuity – or discontinuity – of marble carving traditions in the fifteenth century.

58 Francesco Abbate, "Il monument a Ladislao di Durazzo," in Roberto Paolo Ciardi et al., eds., *Le vie del marmo: Aspetti della produzione e della diffusione dei manufatti marmorei tra quattrocento e cinquecento*, Florence: Giunti, 1992, pp. 17–22.

59 Ciardi, "'Ars marmoris,'" pp. 342–43.

60 Stefano Borsi, Francesco Quinterio, and Corinna Vasic Vatovec, *Maestri fiorentini nei cantieri romani del quattrocento*, Rome: Officina Edizioni, 1989, pp. 115–28.

61 For example, Bartolomeo delle Cime, *lombardo*, was named "master of the arches in the Camposanto" in 1457–64, at just the time of the final campaign to finish the marble windows and fill them with stained glass. All his assistants came from Como. Many artisans from Florence and its environs such as Signa, Settignano, and Rovezzano who were attached to the Opere of Santa Maria del Fiore or of Orsanmichele established themselves at Pisa to manage the transfer of marble from the quarries to Florence by way of the Arno.

62 Ciardi, "Il Quattrocento," pp. 19–85; Ciardi, "'Ars marmoris,'" pp. 344–46; Claudio Casini, "Il caso di Domenico di Giovanni da Milano: Un 'lombardo' tra i magistri lapidum a Pisa nella metà del XV secolo," *Arte e storia*, vol. 14, 2014, pp. 60–65.

63 Ciardi, "Il Quattrocento," p. 16.

64 Mallett, "Pisa and Florence in the Fifteenth Century," pp. 433–35; on the palazzo Medici in Pisa, see Alberto Niccolai, *Palazzi, ville e scene medicee in Pisa e nei dintorni*, Pisa: Editrice Mariotti, 1914, pp. 45–47; Maria Adriana Giusti, "Il 'palazzo vecchio' di Pisa," in Gabriele Morolli, Cristina Acidini Luchinat, and Luciano Marchetti, eds., *L'architettura di Lorenzo il Magnifico*, Milan: Silvana Editoriale, 1992, pp. 208–9; Vittorio di Feliciantonio, "Palazzo Vecchio de' Medici," in Ewa Karwacka Codini, ed., *Architettura a Pisa nel primo periodo mediceo*, Pisa: Gangemi Editore, 2010, pp. 162–65. For the Medici bank in Pisa, see Raymond de Roover, *The Rise and Decline of the Medici Bank*, New York: W.W. Norton, 1966, pp. 275–78. Its activities are uncertain owing to sporadic documentation; see Philip Foster, "A Study of Lorenzo de' Medici's Villa at Poggio a Caiano," PhD dissertation, Yale University, 1974, p. 578, note 892.

65 At the death of Lorenzo de' Medici in April of 1492, an inventory of Medici possessions was made by the office of the Magistrati dei Pupilli, which oversaw estates in which the owners died intestate or the heirs were minors. The original inventory made in 1492 does not survive. A copy of the 1492 inventory of all Medici possessions was made in 1512 by Simone di Stagio delle Pozze, commissioned by Lorenzo di Piero de' Medici (born 1492), the grandson of Lorenzo il Magnifico, to aid in the restitution of property confiscated in 1494, is preserved in ASF, MAP, F. 165 and published by Marco Spallanzani and Giovanna Gaeta Bertelà, *Libro d'inventario dei beni di Lorenzo il Magnifico*, Florence: Associazione Amici del Bargello, 1992. The Pisan possessions are listed on cc. 106 verso–10 verso; Spallanzani, pp. 217–28; the Pisa palace is described c. 115 recto; Spallanzani, p. 236. A copy of the 1492 inventory of Medici possessions in Pisa and its *contado* made in 1509 exists in ASF, MAP, F. 104, doc. 42, cc. 418 recto–24 verso.

66 These possessions are listed separately in the catasto of 1458; see ASF, MAP, F. 82, doc. 182, c. 591 recto–verso; and the catasto of 1469, ASF, Catasto 924/1, cc. 308 verso–9 recto; cited

in Foster, "A Study of Lorenzo de' Medici's Villa at Poggio a Caiano," p. 580, note 895; and Amanda Lillie, "Lorenzo de' Medici's Rural Investments and Territorial Expansion," in *Rinascimento: Rivista dell'Istituto Nazionale di Studi sul Rinascimento*, 2nd ser., vol. 33, 1993, pp. 58–59, notes 16, 18.

67 ASF, Catasto, 924/1, 1469, c. 310 recto, as cited in Foster, "A Study of Lorenzo de' Medici's Villa at Poggio a Caiano," p. 580, note 895; and Lillie, "Lorenzo de' Medici's Rural Investments," p. 59, note 20.

68 Lillie, "Lorenzo de' Medici's Rural Investments," p. 59.

69 See Lucrezia Tornabuoni de' Medici, *Lettere*, ed. Patrizia Salvadori, Florence: Olschki, 1993, pp. 23–26; and Francis W. Kent, "Sainted Mother, Magnificent Son: Lucrezia Tornabuoni and Lorenzo de' Medici," in Francis W. Kent, *Princely Citizen: Lorenzo de' Medici and Renaissance Florence*, ed. Carolyn James, Turnhout: Brepols, 2013, pp. 74, 86.

70 In 1471, Lorenzo rented land at Peccioli and, in 1473, at Monte Nero and Santo Luce. In 1474 and 1477, he purchased properties adjacent to the city palace to be used as storage and for falcons, as well as a house in the parish of Santa Viviana for stables. He expanded the family properties in the Maremma at Belora and Paretino, mostly for pasturage, and, from 1473, he participated in an ingenious scheme, called the *magona*, to rent out farm animals to local small landholders; Berta Costa, "Amministrazione di Pisa e aspetti della vita pisana al tempo di Lorenzo il Magnifico," PhD dissertation, University of Pisa, 1950–51, pp. 78–80; Mallett, "Pisa and Florence in the 15th century," p. 434; but see also Giuseppe Petralia, "Pisa Laurenziana; Una città e un territorio per la conservazione dello 'stato,'" in Riccardo Fubini, ed., *La Toscana al tempo di Lorenzo il Magnifico* Pisa: Pacini Editore, 1996, pp. 970–71. The enterprise encouraged the draining of the swamps around Pisa and the maintenance of arable land, a concerted effort that intensified in 1476. Lorenzo purchased two large estates at Colle Salvetti and Vicarello in 1476. They were enlarged over the years so that by 1490 they numbered 27,000 *staiora* of mixed pasturage and cultivation and included a house, tower, two taverns, workers' houses, stables, and other buildings; ASF, Catasto, 1016/2, 1480, cc. 472 recto–73 recto; as cited in Lillie, "Lorenzo de' Medici's Rural Investments," p. 61, note 28. Lorenzo expanded his holdings to the north of Pisa in 1477 when he bought a mill for the grinding of grain at Ripafatta, on the river Serchio. He developed a fishery there in 1479 and, in 1489, another mill that manufactured paper, as well as a canal. The holdings by 1492 included a house, tower, millers' dwellings, furnace, and an inn. Further purchases of land in the Val di Serchio were made before 1492, so that his holdings there were valued approximately 6,000 florins with an estimated income of 600 florins. To the west of Pisa, at Castagnuolo and Poggiuoli, near San Piero a Grado, Lorenzo owned property from 1478 where he stabled his racehorses. He added adjacent properties in 1489, near San Giusto, which he rented to the *magona*, although in 1492 the value and income of these properties were modest. For the above, see Foster, "A Study of Lorenzo de' Medici's Villa at Poggio a Caiano," pp. 295–304, 578–604, notes 895–960; Spallanzani, *Libro d'inventario*, pp. 228–42.

71 Foster, "A Study of Lorenzo de' Medici's Villa at Poggio a Caiano," p. 295; Lillie, "Lorenzo de' Medici's Rural Investments," pp. 63–64. Vicopisano was the site of a large dairy operation; Foster, "A Study of Lorenzo de' Medici's Villa at Poggio a Caiano," pp. 302, 593–96, nos. 934–39; Spallanzani, *Libro d'inventario*, pp. 241–42. Lorenzo acquired an estate at Agnano, just to the east of the city at the foot of Monte Pisano, in 1486 and 1490, that included trees, olive groves, vines, and grain. An oil press, kilns for tiles, jars, bricks and lime, a rabbit hutch, and workers' quarters were located on the property, which amounted to 3,200 *staiora*, of which 1,500 were cultivated. The income in 1492 was about 600 florins and the value of the estate 10,000 florins; Foster, "A Study of Lorenzo de' Medici's Villa at Poggio a Caiano," pp. 302–4, 596–604, nos. 940–60, including a proposed reconstruction of the villa at Agnano. See also Spallanzani, *Libro d'inventario*, pp. 228–32, 241.

72 Mallett "Pisa and Florence in the Fifteenth Century," pp. 427–39; Battistoni, *L'Opera del Duomo di Pisa*, pp. 156–57. Families such as the Rucellai, Capponi, and Pitti owned estates,

and families such as the Soderini continued Florentine investment in this area; Paula Clarke, *The Soderini and the Medici: Power and Patronage in Fifteenth Century Florence*, Oxford: Oxford University Press, 1991, pp. 117–18; Patrizia Salvadori, "Lorenzo de' Medici e le communità soggette tra pressioni e resistenze," in Fubini, ed., *La toscana al tempo di Lorenzo il Magnifico*, vol. 3, pp. 891–906; and Salvadori, "Florentines and the Communities of the Territorial State," pp. 207–24.

73 Mallett, "Pisa and Florence in the 15th century," pp. 435–41. See also Luigi Lazzerini, "Benozzo Gozzoli e la Fraternita dei fiorentini di Pisa," *Predella Monografie*, nos. 13–14, 2016 [2018], pp. 234–37, for membership in the confraternity of Florentines in the second half of the fifteenth century in Pisa.

74 Foster, "A Study of Lorenzo de' Medici's Villa at Poggio a Caiano," p. 304; Lillie, "Lorenzo de' Medici's Rural Investments," pp. 65–66.

75 Mallett, "Pisa and Florence in the 15th century," p. 435, note 4.

76 Francis W. Kent, *Lorenzo de' Medici and the Art of Magnificence*, Baltimore: Johns Hopkins University Press, 2004, pp. 112–51; Mario Martelli, "Nelle stalle di Lorenzo," *Archivio storico italiano*, vol. 150, no. 552, 1992, pp. 267–302.

77 Mallett, "Pisa and Florence in the 15th century," pp. 428–31; Potenti, *Uomini, villaggi, terreni.*

78 David Herlihy, *Pisa in the Early Renaissance: A Study of Urban Growth*, New Haven and London: Yale University Press, 1958; for an account of the twentieth-century history, see Frank Snowden, *The Conquest of Malaria; Italy, 1900–1962*, New Haven and London: Yale University Press, 2006.

79 Potenti, *Uomini, villaggi, terreni*, pp. 246–50. Patrizia Salvadori, *Dominio e patronato: Lorenzo dei Medici e la Toscana nel Quattrocento*, Rome: Edizioni di storia e letteratura, 2000, pp. 219–21, argues that Lorenzo's activities in the Pisan *contado* built on preexisting practices of the Florentine patriciate.

80 Michael Mallett, *The Florentine Galleys* in the Fifteenth Century, Oxford: Clarendon Press, 1967, pp. 16–17; Mallett, "Pisa and Florence in the 15th century," pp. 427–32; Francis W. Kent, *Lorenzo de' Medici and the Art of Magnificence*, pp. 24–28.

81 Costa, "Amministrazione di Pisa," pp. 60, 79; the letter is in ASF, MAP, F. 22, doc. 304, 20 October 1478.

82 Gene Brucker, "A Civic Debate on Florentine Higher Education (1460)," *Renaissance Quarterly*, vol. 34, no. 4, 1981, pp. 517–33.

83 For what follows, see Jonathan Davies, *Florence and Its University during the Early Renaissance*, Leiden: Brill, 1998, pp. 2–3.

84 Brucker, "A Civic Debate," p. 524.

85 Brucker, "A Civic Debate," p. 528; Davies, *Florence and Its University*, p. 87.

86 For this and what follows, see Davies, *Florence and Its University*.

87 Lorenzo, brother of Cosimo, served several times up to his death in 1440, while Piero di Cosimo served from 1445–46, 1455–56, and 1458–61, and Giovanni di Cosimo from 1447–48; Davies, *Florence and Its University*, pp. 150, 151, 153. Cosimo de' Medici studied at the Studio in 1402, while his son Piero possibly studied there with Francesco Filelfo, and son Giovanni with Carlo Marsuppini. Lorenzo di Piero studied under Cristoforo Landino and Argyropoulos. For Cosimo's study, see Robert Black, ed., *Studio and scuola in Arezzo durante il medioevo e il rinascimento*, Arezzo: Accademia Petrarca di lettere, arti e scienze, 1996, pp. 120, 354, 364–65, 387–88, 393–94, 396–408. For Piero, see Ingeborg Walter in *Dizionario biografico degli italiani*, vol. 73, 2009 pp. 151–58; and for Giovanni, see Ingeborg Walter in *Dizionario biografico degli italiani*, vol. 73, 2009, pp. 63–67. On Lorenzo, see André Rochon, *La jeunesse de Laurent de' Médicis*, Paris: Les Belles Lettres, 1963, pp. 35–39; and generally Davies, *Florence and Its University*, pp. 49–64.

88 Davies, *Florence and Its University*, p. 87.

89 After the return of Cosimo from exile in 1434, the Medici were involved in the selection of teachers of the humanities at the Studio, among them Carlo Marsuppini, Giovanni Argyropoulos, and Cristoforo Landino. Generations of Medici were interested in humanist

study; Davies, *Florence and Its University*, pp. 106–24; James Hankins, "Cosimo de' Medici as a Patron of Humanistic Literature," in Francis Ames-Lewis, ed., *Cosimo 'il Vecchio' de' Medici, 1389–1464*, Oxford: Clarendon Press, 1992, pp. 69–94; Francis Ames-Lewis, *The Library and Manuscripts of Piero de' Medici*, New York, 1984, pp. 3–12.

90 James Hankins, "Lorenzo de' Medici as a Patron of Philosophy," *Rinascimento: Rivista dell'Istituto Nazionale di Studi sul Rinascimento,* vol. 34, 1994, p. 16.

91 Davies, *Florence and Its University*, pp. 125–42; Francis W. Kent, *Lorenzo de' Medici and the Art of Magnificence*, pp. 67–72.

92 Francis W. Kent, "Lorenzo de' Medici at the Duomo," in Timothy Verdon et al., eds., *La Cattedrale e la città. Atti del VII centenario del Duomo di Firenze*, Florence: Edifir, 2001, vol. 1, pp. 341–68.

93 Petralia, "Pisa Laurenziana," pp. 959–61; and Petralia, "1406: Il dissolversi di una società tardocomunale, "in Tognetti, ed., *Firenze e Pisa dopo il 1406*, pp. 128–35. Petralia cites the Cinque Riformatori e governatori della citta e contado di Pisa, active from 1458 until 1461.

94 Najemy, *A History of Florence*, pp. 361–69; William Connell, "Changing Patterns of Medici Patronage: The Florentine Dominion during the Fifteenth Century," in Gian Carlo Garfagnini, ed., *Lorenzo de' Medici e il suo mondo*, Florence: Olschki, 1994, pp. 88–107.

95 Ciccaglioni, "Patrimonio culturale e formazione territoriale," pp. 99–100. He has also noted, pp. 124–25, that the Studio had few Pisan supporters and that it played no role in Pisan cultural identity.

96 Petralia, "Pisa laurenziana," pp. 977–80. See also Lauro Martines, *April Blood: Florence and the Plot against the Medici*, Oxford: Oxford University Press, 2003; Najemy, *A History of Florence*, pp. 356–61.

97 The monographic study of Luzzati is fundamental: "Filippo de' Medici Arcivescovo di Pisa," pp. 361–408.

98 For this and what follows, see Giovanni Ciccaglioni, "Filippo de' Medici," in *Dizionario Biografico italiano*, vol. 73, 2009, pp. 47–50; Gene Brucker, "The Medici in the Fourteenth Century," *Speculum*, vol. 32, 1, 1957, pp. 1–26; and Najemy, *A History of Florence*, pp. 262–63.

99 Raffaella Zaccaria, "Cambio di Vieri di Cambio de' Medici," and "Vieri di Cambio de' Medici," in *Dizionario biografico degli italiani*, vol. 73, 2009, pp. 29–31, 175–78; Francis W. Kent, "Cosimo de' Medici," pp. 36–43; and generally, Pompeo Litta, *Famiglie celebri italiane*, Milan: Tipografia delle famiglie italiane, 1 ser., vol. 4, 1827–30, pl. VII. For Nicola di Vieri's literary interests and contacts, see Lauro Martines, *The Social World of the Florentine Humanists, 1390–1460*, Princeton: Princeton University Press, 1963, p. 323. Kurt Weissen, "I banchieri fiorentini ai concili di Costanza e Basilea," in Lorenzo Tanzini and Sergio Tognetti, eds., *"Mercature è arte": Uomini d'affari toscani in Europa e nel Mediterraneo tardomedievale*, Rome: Viella libreria editrice, 2012, p. 86, reports Vieri di Nicola's presence with other Florentine bankers at the Council of Basel in 1437.

100 The earliest of Filippo's letters surviving in ASF, MAP are undated but are signed *protonotarius*. Three were written from Rome: F. 14, doc. 509, to Piero di Cosimo; F. 6, doc. 787, and F. 7, doc. 248, to Giovanni di Cosimo. Two were written from Florence to Giovanni di Cosimo: F. 6, doc. 784 and F. 6, doc. 773. Another without indication of place or date was sent to Piero di Cosimo, F. 137, doc. 947. Luzzati, "Filippo de' Medici Arcivescovo di Pisa," p. 364, note 6. The MAP is available online at www.archiviodistato.firenze.it/map/. For transcriptions of some of Filippo's letters, see M. G. Rossi, "Lettere dell'arcivescovo Filippo dei Medici," tesi di laurea, Università di Pisa, 1973.

101 For example, ASF, MAP, F. 6, doc. 784 to Giovanni di Cosimo, undated; F. 12, doc. 402, from Rome to Cosimo di Giovanni, 21 March 1457/8.

102 Robert Black, "Cosimo de' Medici and Arezzo," in Ames-Lewis, ed., *Cosimo 'il Vecchio' de' Medici*, pp. 41–42.

103 Black, "Cosimo de' Medici and Arezzo," pp. 39, note 50; 42.

104 Ciccaglioni, "Filippo de' Medici," p. 48. From this time, he signed his letters *Sanctitatis Domini nostri referendarius*, for example, ASF, MAP, F. 9, doc. 435, to Giovanni di Cosimo, 20 May 1459, from Ferrara, where he was with the papal court.

105 For the pope's journey to Mantua, see Ludwig von Pastor, *Storia dei papi*, vol. 2, trans. Angelo Mercati, reprint of the 4th ed., revised, Rome: Desclée & Co., 1961, pp. 37–47; Luzzati, "Filippo de' Medici Arcivescovo di Pisa," pp. 366–68; Waldo Dolfi, *Vescovi e Arcivescovi di Pisa: I loro stemmi e il palazzo*, Pisa: Opera della Primaziale Pisana, 2000, vol. 1, pt. 1, p. 199.

106 George Holmes, "Cosimo and the Popes," in Ames-Lewis, ed., *Cosimo 'il Vecchio' de' Medici*, pp. 26–27.

107 Pius's letter is published in Ludwig von Pastor, *Ungedruckte Akten zur Geschichte der Päpste*, Freiburg im Breisgau: Herder, 1904, I, p. 120. On Medici efforts to secure a cardinalship, see D. S. Chambers, "A Cardinal in Rome. Florentine and Medici Ambitions," in Robert Black and John Law, eds., *The Medici: Citizens and Masters*, Cambridge: Villa I Tatti, Harvard University Center for Italian Renaissance Studies, 2015, pp. 205–17.

108 Dolfi, *Vescovi e Arcivescovi di Pisa*, vol. 1, pt. 1, p. 199, publishes the memorial for the entrance, from Pisa, Archivio Arcivescovile Pisano, Atti Strordinari dall' anno 1461 al 1574, no. 10.

109 For this family, see Cristiani, *Nobiltà e popolo nel comune di Pisa*, pp. 410–11.

110 Antonio Mattei, *Ecclesiae Pisane Historia*, Lucca: Typographia Leonardi Venturini, 1772, pp. 144–47; Luzzati, "Filippo de' Medici Arcivescovo di Pisa," p. 368.

111 Mauro Ronzani, "Arcivescovi, chiesa cittadina e comune," *Bollettino storico pisano*, vol. 57, 1988, pp. 31–32.

112 Luigina Carratori, "Il Capitolo della cattedrale nelle vicende pisane della fine dell Trecento e degli inizi del Quattrocento," *Bollettino storico pisano* vol. 56, 1987, p. 8.

113 Roberto Bizzocchi, "Vescovi e potere politico nello stato regionale fiorentino fra quattrocento e primo cinquecento," in Giuseppina de Sandre Gasparini et al., eds., *Vescovi e diocese in Italia dal xiv alla metà del xvi secolo*, Rome: Herder, 1990, vol. 2, pp. 957–64.

114 Dolfi, *Vescovi e Arcivescovi di Pisa*, vol. 1, pt. 1, p. 200.

115 ASF, MAP, F. 16, doc. 98, to Piero di Cosimo, from Pisa, 30 September 1461. He expresses worry about the short time he has to prepare for his trip to France, "considerato l'occupationi et le cose disordinate ò nelle mani."

116 "Habiamo trovato la casa e le possessini, che è il contrario di quello stimava la M.V. et io"; ASF, Carte Strozziane, I, f. III, c. 71, to Giovani di Cosimo, from Pisa, 20 February 1461; Luzzati, "Filippo de' Medici Arcivescovo di Pisa," p. 369. (Filippo generally used Florentine dating in his letters, beginning the year on 25 March; but this letter must be using Pisan dating, which also began the year on 25 March, but was one year ahead of Florentine dating.)

117 "Di poi sono stati da me tanti creditori de l'arcivescovado, che credo non vi resterà quello stimavamo a uno gran pezo"; ASF, MAP F. 16, doc. 116, to Piero di Cosimo, in Pisa 14 February 1461.

118 He wrote to Lorenzo in support of Fra Giordano da Bergamo's candidacy for a position on the faculty of the newly formed Studio; ASF, MAP, F. 26, doc. 90, to Lorenzo di Piero, from Pisa, 16 February 1472/3: "Et avendo io per le mani uno solemnissimo huomo chiamato maestro Jordano da Bergamo dell' ordine de' frati di Sancto Domenico, al quale quello ordine oggi non ha pari, che volentieri verrebbe a legger qua in philosophia, piacesse alla Magnificentia Vostra ordinar con chi supra ciò fusse deputato, che a decto maestro Jordano fussi riservato il luogo suo a legger in decta facultà et che li fussi facto el salario conveniente." See also for the same request, ASF, MAP, F. 24, doc.79, to Lorenzo di Piero, from Pisa, 31 January 1472/3; and Armando Verde, *Lo studio fiorentino 1473–1505; ricerche e docomenti*, Florence: Istituto Nazionale di Studio sul Rinascimento, vol. 4, 1985, p. 22.

119 He appealed to Giovanni di Cosimo to intercede with the Florentine authorities in a disagreement between two families from Cascina: ASF, MAP, F. 10, doc. 218 to Giovanni

di Cosimo from Pisa, 1 August 1461: "Hora sentendo la valitudine vostra, ho auto charo m'achagia casone di dovervi scrivere; e questo è che Simone di Berrigo da Cascina, el quale sia aportatore di questa, ha una certa differentia con un'altra buona famiglia da Cascina la quale sa cognoscere costì dinanzi agl'Otto. E perchè detto Simone è persona dabbene et volentieri vorebbe stare in pace, et anche perchè mi pare mio initeresse a oviare agli scandoli che potrebbene seguire, racomando strectissimamente questa facenda alla Magnificentia Vestra che vogla operare con gl'Otto che, inanzi che le dette parti partino di costì, restino d'acordo e faccino buona pace, maxime perchè l'una parte et l'altra è potente et, non s'aconciando, ne seguiria qualche gran male."

120 For example, when he sought Giovanni di Cosimo's support in helping two men from Filletole reduce their taxes: ASF, MAP, F. 10, doc. 378, to Giovanni di Cosimo, from Pisa, 21 July 1462: "L'aportatore di questa sia Sigismondo nostro el quale sarà colla Magnificentia Vestra insieme con uno de' miei huomini da Filetto per alcune loro facende le quali da loro intenderete. Priego la vostra Magnificentia gli sia favorevole et haverli per racomandati per mio amore et anche chè sono poverissimi, et, fra le graveze del Comune et le mie, hanno più noie non gli bisognarebbe. Preterea Sigismondo haverà sua facenda dinanzi alla Signoria, prego la Magnificentia Vestra gli presti el suo favore in modo cognosca lui essere servidore vostro et di tutta la chasa. Gli giovi assai ne' suoi bisogni, di che mi farete singularissimo piacere, et resteronne obligato alla Vestra Magnificentia, alla quale sempre mi racomando." He asked Giovanni di Cosimo's help in moving his brother Tanai to Pisa; ASF, MAP F. 6, doc. 670, to Giovanni di Cosimo from Pisa, 3 June 1462: "Thanai mio fratello sarà aportatore della presente el quale viene costì per ordinare e' fatti suoi, intendendo ripatriare come da lui intenderà la Magnificentia Vestra, la quale priegio lo prenda per ricomandato, chè sempre lo troverete obediente et riverente a ogni comandamento della prefata Vestra Magnificentia, all quale iterum et lui et me racomando." See also ASF, MAP F. 27, doc. 241 to Lorenzo di Piero from Pisa, 21 April 1471; in the same letter he asked Lorenzo for his aid in helping his cousin Pandolfo de' Medici receive a canonry at the Florentine cathedral.

121 "Sichè di tutto m'avisiate et seguirò quanto vi piacerà"; ASF, MAP, F. 7, doc. 334, to Giovanni di Cosimo from Rome, 28 January 1457/8.

122 Other gifts not noted in letters are traceable in the expenses of the Mensa Archivescovile; for example, in May of 1464, Filippo had some stockings made for Piero di Cosimo: ASD, ACP, Mensa Archivescovile, Entrata e Uscita, no. 9 (formerly no. 10), c. 34 verso: "A dì 2 di Maggio [1465/64] lire quattro per uno paio di calze per Messer Piero de' Medici." On 29 September, Filippo spent 16 soldi and 6 denari for a pair of shoes for Piero; and on 7 October he spent 5 lire 12 soldi on a pair of shoes, and on the 10 October 5 lire on "una berretta paronazza," also for Piero (c. 35 verso). Other gifts furnished to Piero were for 1 lire, 4 soldi, "uno paio di pianelli" on 6 November 1465/64 and "uno giubbbanello" on 21 November for 8 lire (c. 36 recto).

123 "Si non sono come merita la Magnificentia Vostra, habiate pazienza"; ASF, MAP F. 6, doc. 465, to Giovanni di Cosimo from Siena, 13 March 1460.

124 "Abbiamo preso uno porco molto bello all'iudicie nostro, il quale mando alla Magnificentia Vostra"; ASF, MAP, F. 28, doc. 684, to Lorenzo di Piero from Rasignano, 19 November 1472.

125 See Alison Brown, "Lorenzo de' Medici's New Men and their Mores: The Changing Lifestyle of Quattrocento Florence," *Renaissance Studies*, vol. 16, no. 2, 2002, pp. 120–21.

126 "Uno chavallo pazo e pericoloso .... Di quello v'abiamo mandato n'arete perfecto servitio et di questo vi mandiamo anche stimiamo el simile. Et quando si scortichassino non ve ne date pensiere nessuno, chè metteremmo altro che 2 chavalli per voi." ASF, MAP, F. 22, doc. 24, to Lorenzo di Piero from Pisa, 3 April 1465.

127 ASF, MAP, F. 22, doc. 27, to Lorenzo di Piero from Pisa, 9 April 1465.

128 "Anchora mi dite d'alcuni libri sono in Poppi, e' quali in vero sono bellissimi, e avevovene scritte due versi. Ben è vero che io vi dissi che io credevo che non si potrebbono avere; non

ebbi risposta da voi e in questo mezo venne el prete di Piero nostro con una sua lettera a me, dove detto Piero mi priegha che io facci avere lo inventario di detti libri e glieli mandi; e essì ò fatto. Ben è vero che io credo non si potranno avere. Chome ò detto e' libri sono belli et evene alcuno bellissimo, ma la magior parte sono comuni. 'Evi una Bibia bellissima in tre volumi e uno Agostino sopra il Saltero, anche molto bello, in due volumi, e uno Agostino sopra il Genesi, bello. 'Ecci un altro luogo dove io sono informato v'è più di venti volume di libri antichi, e' quali, mi dice l'amicho mio, sono assai più belli di questi di Poppi, e anche facilmente gli arete se verrete. E questo è che voi scriviate una lettera al conte Princivalle da Monteughi, chome voi avete inteste che nella badia a Socastello, la quale è stata nobilissima e magna badia, v'è alcuni libri antichi, e' quali voi desideresti avere e che sia contento di compaicervene ricompensando etc., chome saprete dire. E mandatemi subito la lettera et io darò ordine al bisognio, ché intendo sono sanza comparatione più belli che quelli di Poppi. Fate presto risposta aciò che io vi possa servire innanzi che lo sapressi altri. E non ne dite a persona cosa alcuna perchè non ci venissi altri che cie lo levassi dinanzi. A Piero nostro ... et avendole sarete forniti e l'uno e l'altro, avisandovi che io intendo che in questo vescovado se ne truova assai di questi libri antichi; e se così è, ne sarete fornito abbastanza e di questo non dubitate." ASF, MAP F. 7, doc. 208, to Giovanni do Cosimo, from Soci, 4 October [1457 or 1458].

129 Vittorio Rossi, "L'Indole e gli studi di Giovanni di Cosimo de' Medici. Notizie e documenti," *Atti della Accademia nazionale dei Lincei. Rendiconti, classe di scienze morali, storiche e filologiche*, ser. 5, vol. 2, 1893, pp. 38–60; Lillie, "Lorenzo's Rural Investments," and Lillie, "Giovanni di Cosimo and the Villa Medici at Fiesole," in Beyer and Boucher, eds., *Piero de' Medici 'il Gottoso,'* pp. 189–205.

130 "Ma io non posso pagare e' miei debiti si io non rischuoto da chi io ho havere." ASF, MAP, F. 10, doc. 402, to Giovanni di Cosimo from Pisa, 13 August 1462.

131 "Ma io mi posso assai meravigliare del detto abbate di Morrona, il quale si lamenta di me, et io ho cagione di lamentarmi infinite volte di lui, perchè à allogato una pastura la quale à posseduto pacificamente et sensa alcuno impedimento l'arcivescovado di Pisa già anni dugento. Unde mi pare abbi usato una grandissima presunctione et temerità; et nientedimeno io ne feci remissione a sua petitione dell'abbate di Sancto Michele, il quale si chiamò arbitro d'accordio sopra questa differentia, benchè fusse con detrimento dello arcivescovado, il quale era stato tanto tempo pacifico possessore." ASF, MAP, F. 27, doc. 226, to Lorenzo di Piero, from Pisa 2 April 1471.

132 Michele Luzzati, "Un arcivescovo Mediceo del quattrocento pisano," *Comune di Pisa: Rassegna periodica di informazioni*, vol. 3, no. 4, 1967, pp. 22–29.

133 For what follows, see Luzzati, "Filippo de' Medici Arcivescovo di Pisa," pp. 393–408. See also in general Luigina Carratori Scolaro, *Le visite pastorali della diocese di Pisa*, Pisa: Pacini Editore, 1996, especially pp. 44–46, 70–73.

134 "Ricordo delle cose a fato di poi sono archivescovo di Pisa." ASPi, Miscellanea Manoscritti, no. 84, ins. 50; Luzzati, "Filippo de' Medici Arcivescovo di Pisa," p. 408; Luzzati, "Un arcivescovo Mediceo del quattrocento pisano, pp. 22–29; Michele Luzzati, "Su due ritratti di Filippo de' Medici arcivescovo di Pisa (1461–1474)," *Bollettino storico pisano*, 3rd ser, no. 71, 2002, pp. 193–98. The document is transcribed in Appendix II.

135 "Messer Francesco Coppini domatina sarà facto Veschovo di Terni, con reservatione della sua pieve, et el chanonichato ha messer Lionardo Dati .... Credo che io farò tanto, che la differenza del cardinale di San Marco con frate Santi sia rimessa in voi, perchè già n'ò favellato e dato le vostre lettere. Per lo primo v'aviserò di quello arò fatto, chome per altra ò detto alla Magnificentia Vostra, e non si può torre posta de' fatti de' cardinali. Bisognia che il compagnio stia sempre aparechiate. Parrémi che fusse utile che il ducha ne scrivesse al suo imbasciadore qui in questo effetto che, trattandosi di fare cardniali, facesse ogni sforzo, e facesse lettere al papa e a che gli paresse necessarie. E questo credo seadendo il bisognio sarebbe molto utile." ASF, MAP, F. 7, doc. 334, to Giovanni di Cosimo from Rome, 28 January 1457/8.

136 Donato di Nicola di Vieri (1402–74) was a canon of the Florentine cathedral in 1432 and bishop of Pistoia from 1436 until his death. He was the Medici candidate for archbishop of Florence in 1444, when Saint Antoninus was named instead. Filippo was close to Donato, as revealed by letters, for example, an undated letter from Soci to Giovanni di Cosimo, which reports on his upcoming visit to Pistoia in which he says "cerchare insieme col vescovo di fare qualche buono acordo nelle vostre facende e così ò dilibirato di fare a ciò che non paya che per me manchi di venire a ogni ragionevole conclusione." ASF, MAP, F. 6, doc. 792. Filippo was also in touch with Carlo de' Medici, the illegitimate son of Cosimo, who was apostolic protonotary and later provost of Prato cathedral, as also signaled in letters. For example, he writes in a letter, "Messer Carlo nostro, come havete intese, è sute fatto conlettore di Toschana che, sicondo comprendo, è di pocho utile, nientedimeno è d'onore, el quale l'uomo debba assai stimare." ASF, MAP, F. 7, doc. 334, to Giovanni di Cosimo from Rome, 28 January 1457/8. In a slightly later letter, he reports to Cosimo that he and Carlo are about to depart from Rome; ASF, MAP, F. 12, doc. 412, to Cosimo di Giovanni, from Rome, 26 March 1458.

137 Melissa Bullard, "In Pursuit of Honore et Utile: Lorenzo de' Medici and Rome," in Gian Carlo Garfagnini, ed., *Lorenzo il Magnifico e il suo mondo*, Florence: Olschki, 1994, pp. 123–42; and Chambers, "A Cardinal in Rome," pp. 209–11.

138 Letter of Pope Pius II to Cosimo de'Medici, Siena, 7 March 1460, in Pastor, *Ungedruckte Akten zur Geschichte der Päpste*, p. 120. The election of cardinals in early 1460 is related in Pius's *Commentarii*, see Pius II, *Commentaries*, ed. and trans. Margaret Meserve and Marcello Simonetta, Cambridge, MA: Harvard University Press, vol. 2, 2007, bk. 4, ch. 9, pp. 225–35.

139 Cesare Guasti, *Due legazioni al Sommo Pontefice per il Comune di Firenze presedute da Sant'Antonino Arcivescovo*, Florence: Bianchi E. C. Barbera, 1857, pp. 52, 56, publishes the correspondence. The ambassadors' report is dated 12 October 1458.

140 Pius II, *Commentaries*, ed. and trans. Meserve et al., vol. 2, bk. 4, ch. 7, pp. 218–19.

141 "Magnifice vir, pater et benefactor honorande, post officiosam commendationem etc. Avendo avuto a questi dì una lettera da Giovanni nostro, e con essa una del duca al suo imbasciadore in mio favore, e cercando molti per diverse vie d'esser promossi alla dignità del cappello, non ò voluto per negligentia essere lasciato adrieto, venendo caso d'alcuna promotione .... Onde, avendo ieri sera exposto alla Santità sua tutto il bisognio, e in buono modo, ebbe gratissima risposta in questo effetto, che la Santità sua desiderava assai di fare cossa grata al duca et a voi, et che avrà gran desiderio d'exaltare la casa vostra. Et poi sugiunse che la comunità avea scritto caldamente in favore del vescovo di Perugia, ma nietedimeno che sopra ogni altra cosa desiderava exaltare la casa vostra; avendo avuto lettere della signoria, non arebbono altro che giovato. Nietedimeno io non dubito che se era si fa nulla, ché credo di no, noi ci aremo assai migliore parte che alcuno altro. Ma credo s'indugerà allo Spirito Santo e in questo mezo si potrà avere de' favori assai. E perchè il tempo è buono, io farò una lettera honesta e in buon modo da vostra parte alla Santità sua, la quale anchora gioverà assai, et di tutto quello seguirà aviserò la Magnificentia Vostra, quam Deus diu feliciter conservet." ASF, MAP F. 12, doc. 402, to Cosimo di Giovanni from Rome, 21 March 1457/8.

142 "Io non dubito che noi abbiamo a ottenere ogni cosa, essendoci fatti tanti buoni provedimenti. Ora, perchè la Magnificentia Vostra mi dà sicurtà, dirò quello resta per compimento della materia etc. Oltra quello s'è fatto, che la signoria scriva tre lettere caldissime, in diversa data, aciò paia vogli in ogni modo per me, non per altro, chome già è prevedute, e che la Magnificientia Vostra il primo dì di quaresima sia qui, che questo in ogni modo pare a messer. E se Ruberto [Martelli] non è partito all'avuta di questa, si parta aciò che in questo mezo possa sollecitare, perchè a llui starà bene dire cosa che a me sarebbe notata, o ch'egli abbi possanza di fare ogni cosa. E questo è necessario insieme cogli altri prevedimenti; e non dubitato che otterremo ogni cosa coll'aiuto di messer di Roano [Cardinal

d'Estouteville], il quale à diliberato di mettersi la coraza per ottenere questa posta."ASF, MAP, F. 6, doc. 347, to Giovanni di Cosimo from Siena, 18 February 1459/60.

143 "In questo punto Monsignore delli Visini [Latino Orsini] à mandate per me e dettomi, chome m'avisava, che certamente si faranno in questo Natale cardinali, e che io ve ne avisassi, e che si pervedesse d'avere lettere di buono inchiostro di costì e d'altrove, se vi paresse, perchè egli stimava che giovirebbono assai .... Avisandovi che farà [Pope Paul II] due sue nipoti e forse il vescovo di Terangi, che è veniziano e suo parente, e credo el castellano di Santo Angelo, che è spagnolo, e l'arcivescovo di Lione. D'altri non si dice, ma sento andrà insino al numero d'otto et, essendovi tanti veniziani, vi doverebbe pure ragionevolmente capere uno fiorentino; e questa è quella volta chiarirà ogniuno. E perchè non possa dire non li sia suto scritto nulla di costì e che non se ne facci conto, priegho la Magnificentia Vostra che vogli adoperassi ch'io abbi lettere in buona forma. Tanta faticha v'avete durato per lo passato, che questa si porta mettere coll'altre noye avute per questa cagione; et io ò ordinate al bancho costì sia pagato le spese necessarie per dette lettere." ASF, MAP, F. 16, doc. 354, to Piero di Cosimo, from Rome, 19 November 1468.

144 "Et perchè la città nostra lungo tempo ha mancato della dignità del Cardinalato, parendovi cosa conveniente et accadendovi occasione, pregherete la Sua Maestà che vogli pregare il Santo Padre che si degni qualche volta in questa parte farci pari alle altre città d'Italia ... et se occorressi discendere alle particularità raccomanderete Messer Philippo de' Medici arcivescovo pisano, il quale per nobilità di famiglia et per le sue virtù ci pare degno d'ogni honore." ASF, Signori, Missive, Legazioni, Commissarie, etc, no. 16, cc. 192–93 verso; Luzzati, "Filippo de' Medici Arcivescovo di Pisa," pp. 373–74, note. 25. Bertoldo di Giovanni's medal of Emperor Frederick III has been linked to this visit. The medal, with a portrait of the emperor on the obverse, shows on the reverse a scene from 1 January 1469 when he knighted 122 men on the Ponte Sant' Angelo. James David Draper, *Bertoldo di Giovanni, Sculptor of the Medici Household*, Columbia: University of Missouri Press, 1992, pp. 80–81; and Graham Pollard, *The Collections of the National Gallery of Art: Renaissance Medals*, Washington, DC, 2007, vol. 1, p. 301, have suggested that Filippo de' Medici commissioned the medal as a gift to the emperor, and that Bertoldo, whose medal of Filippo was made at about the same time, may have accompanied Filippo to Rome.

145 Luzzati, "Filippo de' Medici Arcivescovo di Pisa," pp. 375–76, quotes letters from Gentile Becchi to Lorenzo in which Filippo's candidacy is discussed and alludes to Lorenzo's weakening support of the traditional nomination, ASF, MAP, F. 61 (not 66 as in Fubini and Chambers), doc. 35, to Lorenzo di Piero from Rome, 3 December 1470; and F. 61, doc. 39, from Rome, received in Florence 5 January 1471; see also Rochon, *La Jeunesse*, p. 58, note 149; Lorenzo de' Medici, *Lettere*, vol. 1, ed. Riccardo Fubini, Florence: Giunti, 1977, pp. 228–29, note 2; Chambers, "A Cardinal in Rome," p. 212. See also Jacopo Ammannati's letter to Lorenzo in Jacopo Ammannati Piccolomini, *Lettere (1444–1479)*, ed. Paolo Cherubini, Pubblicazioni degli Archivi di Stato, no. 25, Rome: Ministero per i beni culturali e ambientali, Ufficio centrale per i beni archivistici, 1997, vol. 3, pp. 1699–1700, no. 653, 25 April 1473.

146 Luzzati, "Filippo de' Medici Arcivescovo di Pisa," p. 374. Filippo was unable to attend Piero di Cosimo's funeral in December 1469, sending his chaplain Antonio de' Boni instead.

147 Filippo's first letter to the sixteen-year-old Lorenzo, written from Pisa on 31 January 1464/5, recommending a certain Paolo notaio, begins: "Lorenzo carissimo. Io non posso fare che per li amici non ti dia continuamente noya. Abbi pacienza et quando vedi che io ti possa servire fa el simile a me." ASF, MAP, F. 20, doc. 112. Other letters assume a different tone, for example in the letter concerning the horses he had requested: "Magnifice vir et frater noster honorande etc. Ier mattina per Ciesare nostro familiar vi mandammo el baio." ASF, MAP, F. 22, doc. 24, to Lorenzo from Pisa, 3 April 1465.

148 ASF, MAP, F. 22, doc. 512, to Lorenzo from Pisa, 13 February [1472–74]: "Lorenzo mio carissimo. Io ò assai dispiacere che in questo tuo bisognio non t'abbi potuto servire di quelli

giubirelli franzesi che altra volta vedesti, chome dì, ne' miei armari, perchè più tempo fa gli donai, ché ad altri servirono e a me nulla allora facane né arei stimato m'avessino potuto mai servire in cosa alcuna. Hora à permessa la fortuna che quando a me sarebbono suti carissimi e di magior contento avarli avuti che per la principale chagione furono fatti, ne sono private onde non posso satisfare né a te né a me medesimo, di che assai mi duole. E se per altra via si potesse suplire rimarrei paciente, ma in questa terra si è sì pochi giovani che abbino chosa alcuna, che, nonché abbino farsetti alla francesa, ma non li ánno alla taliana et nonché di seta, ma n'ànno charestia di guarnello. Nientedimeno n'abbiamo avuti dieci che sono assai belli e volontieri ne siamo suti serviti. E nonchè gubirelli, ma se anchora bisognassono le persone, le aresti sempre a farne quello ti piacesse. Per questa non altro. L'Altissimo felicemente ti conservi."

149 Luzzati, "Filippo de' Medici Arcivescovo di Pisa," pp. 377–78; Rochon, *La Jeunesse*, pp. 28–29; letter from Ammannati to Lorenzo published in Lorenzo de' Medici, *Lettere*, vol. 2, pp. 58–59, from ASF, MAP F. 61, doc. 4, to Lorenzo from Rome, 25 April 1473.

150 Lorenzo to Giovanni Lanfredini, 11 March 1489; in Lorenzo de' Medici, *Scritti scelti*, ed. Emilio Bigi, 2nd ed., Turin: UTET, 1965 (reprinted 1977), p. 663; cited in Francis W. Kent, "'Lorenzo ... amico degli uomini da bene': Lorenzo de' Medici and Oligarchy," in Kent, *Princely Citizen*, p. 228.

151 G. B. Picotti, *La Giovinezza del Leone X*, Milan: Hoepli, 1928, pp. 160–234; Bullard, "In Pursuit of *Honore et Utile*," pp. 139–40. See also Lorenzo Tanzini, "Tuscan States: Florence and Siena," in Andrea Gamberini and Isabella Lazzarini, eds., *The Italian Renaissance State*, Cambridge: Cambridge University Press, 2012, pp. 99–101.

152 "Fecemi asistente e dell'altre cose sarebbe col tempo le quali non bisignava dire quia ubi opus est facto verba non sufficient."ASF, MAP, F. 27, doc. 513, to Lorenzo from Rome, 15 November 1471; see Rochon, *La Jeunesse*, pp. 28–29; Luzzati, "Filippo de' Medici Arcivescovo di Pisa," pp. 376–77. On Acciaiuoli's oration, see Brian Maxson, *The Humanist World of Renaissance Florence*, Cambridge: Cambridge University Press, 2014, pp. 171–72.

153 Lauro Martines, *April Blood*; see also Scott Nethersole, *Art and Violence in Early Renaissance Florence*, New Haven and London: Yale University Press, 2018, pp. 39–63.

154 For the trip to Mantua in 1459, see G. B. Picotti, *La Dieta di Mantova e la politica dei veneziani*, Trento: Università degli studi di Trento, 1996, pp. 89–135; Pastor, *Storia dei papi*, vol. 2, pp. 37–46; Pius II, *Commentaries*, ed. and trans. Meserve et al., vol. 1, bk. 2, chs. 10–44, pp. 245–377. For Renaissance diplomacy generally, see Isabella Lazzarini, *Communication and Conflict: Italian Diplomacy in the Early Renaissance, 1350–1520*, Oxford: Oxford University Press, 2015, especially pp. 133–35, on the role of clerics as occasional diplomats.

155 Rab Hatfield, "Some Unknown Descriptions of the Palazzo Medici in 1459," *Art Bulletin*, vol. 52, 1970, pp. 232–49; Alessandro Taidelli Palmizi, "Galeazzo Maria Sforza a Firenze: L'ospite d'onore," *Art e dossier*, vol. 27, no. 285, 2012, pp. 60–63. See also Pius II's account in the *Commentaries*, ed. and trans. Meserve et al., vol. 1, bk. 2, ch. 26, pp. 309–13.

156 "Magnifice vir et benefactor honorande, post commendationem etc. Da Bologna scripsi alla Magnificentia Vostra. Di poi siamo venuti qui dove Nostra Santità con tutta la sua corte è ssuta riceuta molto magnificamente et staracci insino al dì del Corpo di Cristo et la matina seguente si partirà per esser a Mantova, dove sarà sabbato in ogni modo. Questo dì ha desinato Nostra Santità con tucti e' cardinali a Bellofiore. Non ci è altro di nuovo. Visitai el Signor Marchese et presentali lettere di Cosimo et per rispecto della sua Magnificentia mi fece molte chareze. Delle cose che subcederanno dì per dì n'aviserò la Magnificentia Vestra, quam Deus diu feliciter conservet." ASF, MAP F. 9, doc. 435, to Giovanni di Cosimo from Ferrara, 20 May 1459.

157 See letters written from Siena to Giovanni di Cosimo, ASF, MAP F. 6, doc. 347, 18 February 1459/60, and F. 6, doc. 465, 13 March 1459/60.

158 Instructions for the delegation are in ASF, Signori, Legazioni e Commissarie, no. 15, cc. 125 verso–28 recto; Luzzati, "Filippo de' Medici Arcivescovo di Pisa," pp. 371–72; Maxson, *Humanist World*, p. 104.

159 ASF, Signori, Legazioni e Commissarie, no. 16, cc. 192–93 verso; see also ASF, MAP F. 17, doc. 604, to Piero di Cosimo 4 January 1468/9 from Rome, where Filippo reports to Piero on affairs in Rome; Luzzati, "Filippo de' Medici Arcivescovo di Pisa," p. 373–74.

160 The oration is preserved in the Biblioteca Universitaria di Padova, ms. 537, cc. 28 recto–31 verso; see also Maxson, *Humanist World*, p. 171.

161 For the marriage, see Rochon, *La jeunesse*, pp. 98–99; Luzzati, "Filippo de' Medici Arcivescovo di Pisa," pp. 373–74; Filippo's letter of 27 November 1468 is published in Cesare Guasti, *Tre lettere di Lucrezia Tornabuoni a Piero de' Medici ed altre lettere di varii concernenti al matrimonio di Lorenzo il Magnifico con Clarice Orsini*, Florence: per le nozze Gherardi – Baldelli, 1859, pp. 12–14. See D. S. Chambers, "Cardinal Francesco Gonzaga in Florence," in Peter Denley et al., eds., *Florence and Italy: Renaissance Studies in Honour of Nicolai Rubinstein*, London: Committee for Medieval Studies, 1988, p. 260; and Martines, *April Blood*, pp. 26–28.

162 Filippo's letters concerning the marriage are in ASF, MAP F. 106, doc. 20, to Piero di Cosimo from Rome 27 November 1468; and F. 20, doc. 671, to Lorenzo di Piero from Rome 10 December 1468. An eyewitness account of the festivities was recorded by Piero Parenti, published by Gaetano Milanesi as *Delle nozze di Lorenzo dei Medici con Clarice Orsini nel 1469, informazione di Piero Parenti Fiorentino*, Florence: Bencini, 1870.

163 The appointment was made 26 September 1461, the official instructions to the delegation were given on 20 October, and the party departed 27 October, returning 14 March 1462. The instructions to the ambassadors, their reports to the signoria, Filippo's oration, and Louis's letter of thanks are published in A. Desjardins and G. Canestrini, *Négociations diplomatiques de la France avec la Toscane*, vol. I, Paris, 1859, pp. 109–35. The final report of the ambassadors to the signoria is transcribed and translated in *Italian Renaissance Diplomacy: A Sourcebook*, ed. Monica Azzolini and Isabella Lazzarini, Durham: Institute of Medieval and Early Modern Studies, 2017, pp. 63–68.

164 Abel Desjardins, "Mémoire sur la politique extérieure de Louis XI et sur ses rapports avec l'Italie," *Mémoires présentés par divers savants à l'Académie des inscriptions et belles-lettres de L'Institut de France*, 1 series, vol. 8, part 2, 1874, pp. 1–36. The actions of Piero de' Pazzi on the diplomatic mission are examined in Oren Margolis and Brian Maxson, "The 'Schemes' of Piero de' Pazzi and the Conflict with the Medici (1461–2)," *Journal of Medieval History*, vol. 41, 2015, pp. 484–503.

165 The register is found in ASF, Legazioni e Commissarie, 52; published by Gaetano Milanesi, "Il viaggio degli ambasciatori fiorentini al re di Francia nel MCCCCLXI descritto da Giovanni di Francesco di Neri Cecchi loro cancelliere," in *Archivio storico italiano*, ser. 3, vol. 1, 1865, pt. 1, pp. 4–62.

166 For what follows, see Milanesi, "Il viaggio," pp. 4–62.

167 On Ippolita Maria Sforza (1445–84) wife of Alfonso of Aragon (1448–95), duke of Calabria, see Lazzarini, *Communication and Conflict*, p. 141.

168 Margolis and Maxson, "The 'Schemes' of Piero de' Pazzi," pp. 492–94.

169 Maxson, *Humanist World*, p. 90. The meeting of the king and the Florentine ambassadors is recounted in Milanesi, "Il viaggio," pp. 23–24.

170 Desjardins, "Mémoire sur la politique extérieure," pp. 117–24.

171 Although Luzzati suggested that Filippo was not the author of the oration, his reputation for scholarship and subsequent orations to the papal court and the emperor cast doubt on this assertion; Luzzati, "Filippo de' Medici Arcivescovo di Pisa," p. 370, note 19; Maxson, *Humanist World*, p. 171.

172 See Lazzarini, *Communication and Conflict*, pp. 245–46; and Owen Margolis, *The Politics of Culture in Quattrocento Europe: René of Anjou in Italy*, Oxford: Oxford University Press, 2016, p. 166. The account of the incident is translated in Azzolini and Lazzarini, *Italian Renaissance Diplomacy*, pp. 155–58.

173 "Magnifice vir tanquam frater honorande sanutem. Poi che io partì da Firenze non ho mai scripto alla Magnificentia Vostra in commendatione et favore di questa città, vedendo maxime et conoscendo Vostra Magnificentia esser verso di quella affectionata et benissimo disposta, et non avere a ciò bisogno né di mie persuasioni né d'alcuno altro, et perché io sono certo lei intende et conosce questa città esser il principal membro et d'utile et di honore che abbi la nostra republica, et essendo bene recta et guvernata, ne conseguita et honore et utile principalmente alla Magnificentia Vostra et successive a tucta la nostra republica. Al presente ritornando costà ser Simone, per le medesime cagioni per le quali v'è stato tanto tempo, non ho voluto pretermettere in alcuno modo di non scriver questi pochi versi alla Magnificentia Vostra sì per satisfare a me medesimo et al mio debito, sì et all'onore della nostra città per le quali priego quella quanto più et meglo posso, ché non essendo seguito insino a qui alcuno effecto delle cose tractate in favore di questa città, lei di nuovo vi vogli mettere l'animo et il pensiero in modo che si prevegga non solamente in particulare ma in universali a' bisogni à d'essa et che ella resti consolata; certificando la Magnificentia Vostra che essa si ritruova in tanto disordine che dir non si potrebbe maggiore. Unde di nuovo benché sono certo non bisogni, conforto la Magnificentia Vostra all'aiuto, favore et mantenimento di questa città et che si facci qualche provisione a llei utile et salutare. Della qual cosa Vostra Magnificentia im primis et tucta la nostra republica ne conseguiterà commendation et laude grandissima. Bene valeat Magnificentia Vostra, quam Deus diu felicam servet." ASF, MAP, F. 27, doc. 180, to Lorenzo di Piero from Pisa, 18 March 1471/2.

174 "Unde io, desiderando per mio il debito et alla città et a' cittadini et habitatori di quella fare ogni bene et prestar ogni aiuto che honestamente posso, ho facto questi pochi versi alla Magnificentia Vostra ... per li quali li significo chome questa arte delli spetiali di qua mai fu sottoposta all'arte di Firenze, secondo m'ànno riferito costoro, ma sempre si sono governati da per loro colli capitoli et brievi, i quali fanno di tempo in tempo confermare da cotesta ex[ ]sa Signoria, né alcuna comunione né sogettione ànno mai avuto con decta arte di Firenze. Il perché questa innovation, che vide esser lor facta dà detrimento et scandolo assai, non solamente alli spetiali ma a tucta questa città, perché sono io de' miglor membri ci sia, et pertanto io li raccomando alla Magnificentia Vostra strectissimamente pregandola li vogli favorir sì et in tal modo che siano conservati nelle loro ragioni et che questa novità mescolata con danno et scandolo non sia lor facta .... Della qual cosa Vostra Magnificientia ne compiacerà, non solamente a llor et a me, ma universalmente a tucta questa città, alla qual prestare aiuto è sommamente laudabile et di merito grandissimo appresso di Dio." ASF, MAP F. 26, doc. 75, to Lorenzo di Piero from Pisa, 2 February 1472/3. This request was repeated in another letter, ASF, MAP, F. 29, doc. 184, to Lorenzo di Piero from Pisa, 17 March 1472/3.

175 "E' pare ch'e' rectori del contado di Pisa abbino facto commandamente a tucti e' sottoposti che debbino portare per scripto tucte le teste sono ne' luoghi a llor sottoposti, et dicesi esser per cagione di voler mectere più pregio al sale et levar loro alcune alter spese. Unde è nato tra loro grandissimo sospecto et molti a me sono venuti per simil materia et ancor assai di questi forestieri ci sono stantiali perché, essendo vera simil cosa, ce n'è assai, sicondo dicono, che si partirebbeno et andrebbene altrove. Unde nascerebbe dispendio et inconveniente assai a questo contado il quale non ha bisogna se non di huomini et faccendo legge nuove, le quali avesseno a comprehenderli, non dubito puncto ce n'è assai s'andrebbono con Dio et così il paese n'arebbe detrimento." ASF, MAP F. 29, doc. 130, to Lorenzo di Piero from Pisa, 1 March 1472/3.

176 For the galleys, see Mallett, *The Florentine Galleys in the Fifteenth Century*, Oxford: Clarendon Press, 1967; see also ASF, MAP, F. 27, doc. 73, 3 February 1471/2, and F. 27, doc. 87, 12 February 1471/2 to Lorenzo di Piero from Pisa. Pastor, *Storia dei papi*, vol. 2, p. 450, note 3.

177 Luzzati, "Filippo de' Medici Arcivescovo di Pisa," p. 378; for the oration at the opening ceremony, see Lorenzo Lippi, "L'orazione di Lorenzo Lippi per l'apertura dell'Università di Pisa," ed. Vito Giustiniani, *Rinascimento*, 2nd ser., no. 4, 1964, pp. 265–84. See also

Verde, *Lo Studio Fiorentino*, vol. 4, 1987, pp. 22, 39, 40, 51, 54, 56, 59, 72; Davies, *Florence and Its University*, pp. 125–26.

178 "L'Università manda costì imbasciadori alla signoria per loro bisogni. Non è bisognio ve li racomandi essendo voi capo e guida et protectore di questa famiglia della quale si maraviglia ognuno, essendo condotta in sì buoni termini chome è, benché non credo sia Studio in Italia abbia tanti huomini dabbene quanti n'è qui. Di che ò piacere assai, per Vostro rispetto, che siate conduttore di tal e sì honorevole opera." ASF, MAP, F. 29, doc. 971, to Lorenzo di Piero from Pisa, 3 November 1473.

179 Milanesi, "Il viaggio," p. 20.

180 One of the first initiatives credited to Filippo, rebuilding the Hospital for Foundlings, the Ospedale dei Trovatelli on the southeast perimeter of the Piazza del Duomo, is documented in the accounts of the hospital. Begun on 28 April 1461, its construction lasted until 1473. The hospital has been renovated extensively, but remnants of the internal courtyard and façade provide evidence of the plan and architectural character; Ewa Karwacka Codini, "Ospedale dei Trovatelli," in Karwacka Codini, ed., *Architettura a Pisa nel primo periodo mediceo*, pp. 36–47.

181 Miria Fanucci Lovitch, *Artisti attivi a Pisa fra XIII e XVIII secolo*, vol. 1, Pisa: Pacini Editore, 1991, p. 6: payments 1462–66 to Adamo di Domenico da Como working in Calci; p. 10: payments to Andrea scalpellatore 1462–63 for a chimney in the palace at Filettole. See also Dolfi, *Vescovi e arcivescovi di Pisa*, vol. 2, p. 55; Ewa Karwacka Codini, "Prima dominazione fiorentina a Pisa: Avvio verso una nuova stagione architettonica tra il gusto di antiche magnificenze, l'eredità brunelleschiana e gli echi albertiani," in Karwacka Codini, ed., *Architettura a Pisa nel primo periodo mediceo*, pp. 12–13.

182 For example, writing to Cosimo 30 September 1461 from Pisa, ASF, MAP, F. 16, doc. 98: "Alla venuta vostra qua, priegho la Magnificentia Vostra vegniate a riposare a Filetto, ché vi trovarete assai commodamente proveduto per uno castelletto, non però come meriterebbe la Magnificentia Vostra, ma l'agio o disagio vi patisse anche in casa sua che credo vi verrà vegla di starvi più d'uno dì."

183 "Rimurato quasi da fondamente l'arcivescovado e fatto lo magior non era"; "Rimurato da fondamenti il castel di calci che per le guerre era in tutto disfatto e fattolo più bello e più forte non era prima"; "Raconcio el castello di filetto. Stava male e intonacatolo e riparato dentro tutto [crossed out: riparato] et di fuori arriciatolo." ASPi, Miscellanea Manoscritti, no. 84, ins. 50; see Appendix II.

184 Dolfi, *Vescovi e arcivescovi di Pisa*, vol. 2, pp. 48–78; Ewa Karwacka Codini, "Dimore nobiliari a Pisa e metamorfosi del volto urbano nel period mediceo," and Gabriele Morolli, "La *domus cardinalis* di Filippo de' Medici, arcivescovo di Pisa. Una 'prova generale' del nuovo palazzo umanistico all'antica di metà quattrocento: Tra Vitruvio e Alberti," in Emilia Daniele, ed., *Le dimore di Pisa: L'arte di abitare; i palazzi di una antica repubblica marinara dal medioevo all'unità d'Italia*, Pisa: Alinea Editrice, 2010, pp. 43–54 and pp. 55–82.

185 For this and what follows, see Morolli, "La *domus cardinalis*," pp. 57–82; Francesca Bardotti, "Il Palazzo Arcivescovile: architetettura, arte, storia nel contest religioso e civile," in *Il Palazzo dell'Arcivescovado*, Cristina Cagianelli, ed, Pisa; Edizioni ETS, 2021, pp. 17–38.

186 Emilio Tolaini, *Forma Pisarum, Storia urbanstica della città di Pisa*, Pisa: Nistri-Lischi, 1979, p. 103, citing an anonymous description of Pisa from c. 1430: "Grande edifizio spiccato dattorno et è bello et magnio et in quello chortile è di begli aranci et molti cedri et ha un orto bellissimo chon molti fructi di più ragioni e è l'arciveschovado chon tutto il territorio chom uno buono chastello." See also Morolli, "La *domus cardinalis*," p. 55.

187 Claudio Casini, "La scultura," in Cagianelli, ed, *Il Palazzo dell'Arcivescovado*, pp. 47–49.

188 For this and following, see Karwacka Codini, *Architettura a Pisa nel primo periodo mediceo*, pp. 7–14; Morolli, "La *domus cardinalis*," pp. 55–82; and, more generally Georgia Clarke, *Roman House – Renaissance Palaces: Inventing Antiquity in Fifteenth-Century Italy*, Cambridge: Cambridge University Press, 2003, pp. 162–273.

189 Pius II, *Commentaries*, bk. 9, trans. Florence Alden Gragg, *Smith College Studies in History*, vol. 35, 1951, pp. 597–604.

190 For description and documentation on the construction, see Dolfi, *Vescovi e arcivescovi di Pisa*, vol. 2, pp. 50–79. For the Palazzo Piccolomini, see Jan Pieper, *Pienza; Il progetto di una visione umanistica del mondo*, London: A. Menges, 2002, pp. 144–69. For the Palazzo di San Marco, see Christoph Luitpold Frommel, *Architettura e committenza da Alberti a Bramante*, Florence: Olschki, 2006, pp. 158–80.

191 Dolfi, *Vescovi e arcivescovi di Pisa*, vol. 2, p. 55; Karwacka Codini, *Archtettura a Pisa nel primo periodo mediceo*, pp. 12–13.

192 Luzzati, "Un arcivescovo Mediceo del quattrocento pisano," pp. 25–26.

193 ASD, ACP, Mensa Arcivescovile, Entrate e uscite, no. 9, dal 5 Augusto 1464–70, c. 46 verso: "A dì 3 detto M[aestr]o Domenico di Giovanni da Milano scarpellatore di pietra el quale lavora con monsignore L. ventidue in qattro due larghi larghi [*sic*] per parte di suo debito di lavoro fa L. 22"; Karwacka Codini, *Archtettura a Pisa nel primo periodo mediceo*, p. 12, note 49.

194 See I. B. Supino, *L'arte del rinascimento nella primaziale di Pisa: I maestri d'intaglio e di tarsia in legno, i pittori e gli scultori*, Rome: Tipologia dell'Unione Cooperativa Editrice, 1893, pp. 160–63; L. Tanfani-Centofanti, *Notizie di artisti tratte dai documenti pisani*, Pisa: Enrico Spoerri Editore, 1897, pp. 198–200; Borsi et al., *Maestri fiorentini nei cantieri romani del quattrocento*, pp. 177–78. Gaetano Milanesi published the contract with the Primaziale, dated 10 March 1462 (Milanesi reported the date erroneously as 1461), in *Nuovi documenti per la storia dell'arte Toscana dal XII al XV secolo*, Florence: Dotti, 1901, p. 111, doc. 131. It was pointed out by Roberto Paolo Novello, "Le tarsie lignee," in A. Peroni, ed., *Il Duomo di Pisa*, Modena: Panini, 1995, vol. 3, p. 302, that the appraisal of the finished work was to be done by Piero de' Medici.

195 Borsi et al., *Maestri fiorentini nei cantieri romani*, pp. 176 97.

196 Roberto Paolo Novello, "Tarsie di Guido da Seravallino per il Duomo di Pisa," *Bollettino storico pisano*, vol. 55, 1986, pp. 129–47; and Novello, "Le tarsie lignee," pp. 301–12. For a general view of woodwork in the Duomo, see Gabrielle Donati, "L'arte del legno. Intagli e tarsie," in Garzella et al., eds., *La Cattedrale di Pisa*, pp. 219–31.

197 These works were executed in Giuliano's Florentine bottega and shipped to Pisa. The contract is in ASPi, Opera del Duomo, 564, c. 166. See Supino, *I maestri d'intaglio e di tarsia in legno*, p. 156; Novello, "Le tarsie lignee," p. 311, note 5; Francesco Quinterio, *Giuliano da Maiano, "grandissimo domestico,"* Rome: Officina Edizioni, 1996, p. 62.

198 Novello, "Baccio Pontelli a Pisa," pp. 81–92.

199 For the model, see ASD, ACP, Mensa Archivescovile, Entrata e Uscita, no. 9, c. 46 verso: "E a dì detto [4 March 1466] a Francesco da carchali vetturale grossi dieci per vettura duno modello de legname venne da Firenze . . . l. 2 s. 15"; and Giusti, "Architetture a Pisa nella seconda metà del Quattrocento," in Morolli et al., eds., *L'Architettura di Lorenzo*, pp. 199–202.

200 Francis W. Kent, *Lorenzo de' Medici and the Art of Magnificence*, pp. 25–28, 50–53.

201 Pio Pecchai, *L'Opera della Primaziale Pisana*, Pisa: F. Mariotti, 1905; Giuseppe Fusco, *L'Opera della Primaziale attraverso i tempi*, Pisa: F. F. Nistri, 1908, pp. 15–20; R. Martino, "Gli atti di elezione e investitura degli Operai dell'Opera del Duomo di Pisa nei secoli XIII e XIV," tesi di laurea University of Pisa, 2001–2, pp. 3–4. For a brief history of the Opera del Duomo, see Mauro Ronzani, "L'Opera del Duomo nel medioevo," in Garzella et al., eds., *La Cattedrale di Pisa*, pp. 37–44; and Battistoni, *L'Opera del Duomo di Pisa,* pp. 72–73.

202 ASPi, Opera del Duomo, Ricordanze, no. 443, c. 26 recto–verso: 25 February 1468 and 12 May 1469/68; c. 33 recto: 9 June 1469/68 and 10 October 1470; cited in Marta Battistoni, "Antonio di Jacopo dalle Mura, orafo e operaio del Duomo di Pisa, 1461–1488," *Bollettino storico pisano*, vol. 63, 1994, p. 148, note 54.

203 For what follows, see Battistoni, "Antonio di Jacopo dalle Mura," pp. 131–48.

204 For the financial situation of the Opera in the second half of the fifteenth century, see Battistoni, *L'Opera del Duomo di Pisa*, pp. 188–89, 193–95.

205 "E per me non avendo il favore della Magnificentia Vostra come altra volta v'o detto non saprei governare tale opera." ASF, MAP, F. 29, doc. 669, to Lorenzo di Piero, from Pisa, 25 August 1474; quoted in Battistoni, "Antonio di Jacopo dalle Mura," p. 144, note 44.

206 "Perche sempre mi sono governato col consiglio di cotesta magnificha chasa"; ASF, MAP, f. 27, doc. 83 (not 127 as in Battistoni), to Lorenzo di Piero from Pisa 11 February 1472; quoted in Battistoni, "Antonio di Jacopo dalle Mura," p. 144, note 44.

207 Antonella Capitanio, "Scultura preziosa; il Quattrocento orafo a Firenze," in Franco Franceschi and Gloria Fossi, eds., *Il Grande Libro di artigianato*, vol. 2, Florence: Giunti, 1999, pp. 251–75.

208 "+DOMINO FILIPPO DE MEDICIS / ARCHIEPISCOPO PISANO ANTO / NIUS JACOBI ALMI TEMPLI / PISANI OPERARIUS SACRI / HUIUS ET INTERMORTALES / PRECLARISSIMI SEPULCRI / OPUS IIII ARCUBUS XXVIII / Q[UAM] P[ER]FORATUI FENESTRIS / MARMOREIS III ANNIS SUA / DILIGENTIA PERFICICUR / AVIT D[EI] I[NCARNATIONIS] AN[NO] MCCCCLXIII"

209 Caleca, "Costruzione e decoration," p. 36; see also for payments to Gaspare di maestro Antonio picchiapietre, Simone di Domenicho da Firenze and Salvi d'Andrea da Firenze, for "tutte le finestre mancavano al fornimento in ca[m]posanto," in Tanfani Centofanti, *Notizie*, pp. 286–87.

210 "+ A(nno) D(domini) MCCLXXVIII T(em)P(o)R(e) D(omiNI FEDIERIGI ARCHI / EP(iscopi) PIS(ani) / ET D(omi)NI TERLLATI POTESTATIS OP(er)ARIO ORLLANDO / SARDELLA (et) IOHANNE MAG(ist)RO AEDIFICA(n)TE." Ottavio Banti, "A proposito del 'Iohanne magistro edificante' 'architetto' del Campo Santo di Pisa," *Critica d'arte*, 8th ser, vol. 75, nos. 53–54, 2013 [2015], pp. 101–8, has, however, dated this inscription later.

211 ASD, ACP, Mensa Arcivescovile, Entrata e Uscita no. 9, dal 1464/63, c. 35 recto: A dì 30 detto [June 1465/64] soldi vinti a prete Luca per le messe di campo Sancto. E a dì detto [11 September 1465/64] a prete lucha di Piombino lire uno grossi quattro per limosine delle messe di campo sancto." Similar payments are made 29 September 1465/64 (c. 35 verso), 3 November and 22 December 1465/64 (c. 36 recto–36 verso), 20 February 1465 (c. 37 verso), 15 March 1465 (c. 38 recto), 25 May 1466/65 (c. 39 recto) 13 June and 13 August 1466/65 (c. 39 verso), 3 October 1466/65 (c. 42 recto), 29 November 1466/65 (c. 44 recto), 29 March 1467/66 (c. 47 verso), 29 April 1467/66 (c. 48 recto), 4 June 1467/66 (c. 49 recto), 21 October 1468/67 (c. 140 recto).

212 Draper, *Bertoldo di Giovanni*, pp. 82–86, no. 2; Aimee Ng, Alexander Noelle, et al., *Bertoldo di Giovanni: The Renaissance of Sculpture in Medici Florence*, New York: The Frick Collection, 2019, pp. 397–400, no. 13. At the circumference is a cord with five tassels at each side, diminishing in size toward the top, which perhaps refers to the *fimbriae* (fringes) of an archbishop's hat, the *galero*. It is intertwined with a scroll at the bottom bearing the inscription VIRTVTE SVPERA (By higher virtue). The coat of arms below shows the Medici balls (*palle*) with a cross above.

213 The testament consists of four legal documents dated 5 October 1474, found in ASF, MAP, F. 81, doc. 22, cc. 122–32; the first is transcribed in Appendix III.

214 Job 19:26–27.

215 For this well-known sequence of events, see Supino, *Il Camposanto*, pp. 22–28; Caleca, "Costruzione e decoration," pp. 36–37; Ahl, *Benozzo Gozzoli*, pp. 159–60.

216 Tanfani Centofanti, *Notizie*, p. 385. See also Maurizia Tazartes, "Anagrafe Lucchese II: Michele Ciampanti, Il maestro Stratonice," *Richerche di storia dell'arte*, vol. 26, 1985, pp. 18–26.

217 Supino, *Il Camposanto di Pisa*, p. 195; Ahl, *Benozzo Gozzoli,* p.160.

218 For an assemblage of all the documents relative to the commission, see Orlandi, *Benozzo Gozzoli*.

219 The payment is from ASPi, Opera del Duomo, Entrata e Uscita, no. 144, 18 January 1469, c. 84 recto: "per resto della prima storia fatta in Chaposanto, a lato al mondo, ed è la storia di Noè." Orlandi, *Benozzo Gozzoli*, p. 11, doc. no. 3.

220 "Per caparra di dipingniere certe storie in Camposanto, àsene a pigliare parere di citadini." ASPi, Opera del Duomo, Debitori e Creditori, no. 564, c. 159; Orlandi, *Benozzo Gozzoli*, p. 12, doc. no. 3

221 ASPi, Opera del Duomo, Debitori e Creditori, no. 564, c. 159; Orlandi, *Benozzo Gozzoli*, pp. 17–19, doc. no. 6.

222 These scenes are described as "una storia di Nino re di Babbilonia e d'Abran quando fu misso nel fuocho"; Orlandi, *Benozzo Gozzoli*, pp. 17–19, doc. no. 6.

223 For a detailed analysis of the works, see Ahl, *Benozzo Gozzoli*, pp. 161–62.

224 Ahl, *Benozzo Gozzoli*. Benozzo was one of the witnesses when Antonio di Jacopo dalle Mura, the *operaio*, drew up his will on 9 December 1472; ASF, Notrarile Anticosimiano, no. 19492, cc. 257 verso–260 verso; Orlandi, *Benozzo Gozzoli*, pp. 40–41, doc. No. 22.

225 Palmizi, "Galeazzo Maria Sforza a Firenze, l'ospite d'onore", pp. 60–63. Rab Hatfield, "Cosimo de'Medici and the Chapel of His Palace," in Francis Ames-Lewis, ed., *Cosimo de'Medici*, Oxford, 1992, pp. 221–44. Hatfield suggests, p. 226, that the murals of the chapel had not been finished by the time of the ducal visit.

226 See Miklós Boskovits, "La bottega del Beato Angelico tra Firenze e Roma, e la formazione di Benozzo Gozzoli"; and Diane Cole Ahl, "Da Roma a Montefalco," in Bruno Toscano and Giovanna Capitelli, eds., *Benozzo Gozzoli, Allievo a Roma, maestro in Umbria*, Milan: Silvana Editoriale, 2002, pp. 133–218.

227 Giovanni Capitelli and Graziano Alfredo Vergani, *Benozzo Gozzoli: A Growing Workshop*, Milan: Silvana Editoriale, 2003, pp. 15, 43–46.

228 Beatrice Cirulli, "Note sulla cappella Albertoni all'Aracoeli a Roma e la *Vergine in Gloria* della Collegiata dell'Assunta a Sermoneta (1456–58)," in Toscano et al., eds, *Benozzo Gozzoli, allievo a Roma, maestro in Umbria*, pp. 230–37.

229 Anna Cavallaro, "Benozzo Gozzoli e Antoniazzo Romano nel Lazio Meridionale," in Anna Cavallaro and Stefano Petrocchi, eds., *La pittura del quattrocento nei feudi caetani*, Rome: Edizioni di Storia e Letteratura, 2013, pp. 269–90.

230 For a discussion of Roman painting in the mid-fifteenth century, see Meredith Gill, "The Fourteenth and Fifteenth Centuries," in Marcia Hall, ed., *Artistic Centers of the Italian Renaissance: Rome*, Cambridge: Cambridge University Press, 2005, pp. 27–46; Claudia Tempesta, "Arte a Tor de' Specchi," in Alessandra Bartolomei Romagnoli, ed., *Francesca Romana; La santa, il monastero e la città alla fine del medioevo*, Florence; Edizioni del Galuzzo, 2009, pp. 214–45; Anna Cavallaro, "Antoniazzo Romano, pittore 'dei migliori che fussero allora in Roma,'" in Anna Cavallaro and Stefano Petrocchi, eds., *Antoniazzo Romano Pictor Urbis*, Milan: Silvana Editoriale, 2013, pp. 23–24; and Stephen Campbell, *The Endless Periphery: Towards a Geopolitics of Art in Lorenzo Lotto's Italy*, Chicago: University of Chicago Press, 2019, pp. 30–31.

231 These include tombs of Cardinal Pietro Riario (d. 1474) and Cardinal Raffaele Riario (d. 1521) in the choir and the cenotaph of Raffaele della Rovere, brother of Sixtus IV and father of Julius II (d. 1477) in the crypt.

232 A precedent for the murals may have been the decoration of the chapel of Saints Michael Archangel and Peter in Santa Maria Maggiore, which the powerful Cardinal Guillaume d'Estouteville had commissioned from Piero della Francesca or one of his close followers c. 1458–59. As only fragments from this decoration survive, it is impossible to surmise. See Meredith Gill, "Where the Danger Was the Greatest: A Gallic Legacy in Santa Maria Maggiore, Rome," *Zeitschrift für Kunstgeschichte*, vol. 59, 1996, pp. 506–10.

233 For Gozzoli's work in San Gimignano, see Gerardo de Simone and Cristina Borgioli, eds., *Benozzo Gozzoli a San Gimignano*, Florence: Giunti, 2016.

234 Kristen Lippincott, "Giovanni di Paolo's 'Creation of the World' and the 'thema mundi,'" *Burlington Magazine*, vol. 132, 1990, pp. 467–69. Vasari's description, in his *vita* of

Buffalmacco, Giorgio Vasari, *Le vite de' più eccellenti pittori scultori e architettori*, ed. Gaetano Milanesi, Florence: Sansoni, 1906, vol. 1, pp. 513–14, included the verses once visible.

235 Lippincott, "Giovanni di Paolo's 'Creation of the World,'" p. 468; see also Meredith Gill, *Angels and the Order of Heaven in Medieval and Renaissance Italy*, Cambridge: Cambridge University Press, 2014.

236 The reinforcement of Augustine's and Thomas's view of the angels might reflect a Dominican context, as noted by Lippincott, "Giovanni di Paolo's 'Creation of the World,'" p. 468, note 52.

237 Charles Stinger, *The Renaissance in Rome*, Bloomington: Indiana University Press, 1985, pp. 166–234; Charles Stinger, "Italian Renaissance Learning and the Church Fathers," in Irena Backus, ed., *The Reception of the Church Fathers in the West*, Leiden and New York: Brill, 1992, vol. 2, pp. 473–510; and generally, John O'Malley, *Praise and Blame in Renaissance Rome*, Durham: Duke University Press, 1979.

238 For this and what follows, see Maxson, *Humanist World*, pp. 148–51, 170–71. Filippo's oration is found in Padua, Biblioteca Universitaria, ms. 537, cc. 28 recto–32 verso. I am grateful to Brian Maxson for digital images of this document. Saint Antoninus's oration of 1455 is published in *Divi Antonini Archiepiscopi Florentini ... Chronicorum opushis*, Lugduni: Juntae, 1586, vol. 3, pp. 585–89; his oration of 1458 in vol. 3, pp. 593–98.

239 Richard Krautheimer, *Lorenzo Ghiberti*, 2nd ed., Princeton: Princeton University Press, 1970, I, pp. 182–88; Amy Bloch, *Lorenzo Ghiberti's Gates of Paradise: Humanism, History and Artistic Philosophy in the Italian Renaissance*, Cambridge: Cambridge University Press, 2016, pp. 269–71.

240 Rachel Wischnitzer-Bernstein, "Jüdische Legendenstoffe bei Benozzo Gozzoli," in *Feschrift zum 70. Geburtstage von Moritz Schaefer*, Berlin, 1927, pp. 271–74, for references to Hebrew sources for this scene. See also Joseph Gutmann, "Abraham in the Fire of the Chaldeans: A Jewish Legend in Jewish, Christian and Islamic Art," *Frühmittelalterliche Studien*, vol. 7, 1973, pp. 342–52. It was also included in the Chiostro Verde cycle in Santa Maria Novella, designs of which were most likely used by the stained-glass workers in the Duomo; Burnam, "Le vetrate," pp, 76, 81–83.

241 See Katrin Kogman-Appel, *Illuminated Haggadot from Medieval Spain: Biblical Imagery and the Passover Holiday*, University Park: Pennsylvania State University Press, 2006, pp. 152–54. She discusses further cultural issues in the production of these manuscripts in Katrin Kogman-Appel, "Coping with Christian Pictorial Sources: What Did Jewish Miniaturists *Not* Paint?," *Speculum*, vol. 745, 2000, pp. 816–58; and "Hebrew Manuscript Painting in Late Medieval Spain: Signs of a Culture in Transition," *Art Bulletin*, vol. 84, 2002, pp. 246–72.

242 These include the Golden Haggadah, London, British Library Ms. Add. 27210, from Spain, c. 1320; and the so-called Sister Haggadah, London, British Library, Or. 2884, from Spain, second or third quarter of the fourteenth century; see see B. Narkiss, *The Golden Haggadah, a Fourteenth Century Illuminated Manuscript in the British Museum*, 2 vols., London: Eugrammia Press, 1970; Kogman-Appel, *Illuminated Haggadot from Medieval Spain*, p. 74. It is also found in the Second Nuremberg Haggadah, fol. 30 verso; Katrin Kogman-Appel, "The Second Nuremberg Haggadah, a Stylistic and Iconographic Analysis," PhD thesis, Hebrew University, Jerusalem, 1993, p. 178.

243 Sources include Jerome, *Questiones in Genesis*, II, 28, in J. P. Migne, *Patrologiae Latinae*, vol. 23, col. 956; Augustine, *De civitate Dei*, in *Patrologiae Latinae*, vol. 41, bk. 16, ch. 15, cols. 494–96; and Peter Comestor, *Historia scholastica*, in *Patrologiae Latinae*, vol. 198, col. 1091.

244 Umbeto Cassuto, *Gli ebrei a Firenze nell'età del Rinascimento*, Florence: Galletti and Cocci, 1918, pp. 274–75; Bloch, *Lorenzo Ghiberti*, p. 276.

245 Michele Luzzati, *La casa dell'ebreo: Saggi sugli ebrei a Pisa e in Toscana nel medioevo e nel rinascimento*, Pisa: Nistri-Lischi, 1985; Michele Luzzati, "Caratteri dell'insediamento ebraico medievale," in Michele Luzzati, ed., *Gli ebrei di Pisa (secoli IX–XX)*, Pisa: Pacini Editore,

1998, pp. 1–44. While Pisa was not known to be a production center for Hebrew manuscripts, Florence was; Giannozzo Manetti's library of a dozen Hebrew books stands out; see Nurit Pasternak, "Together and Apart: Hebrew Manuscripts as Testimonies to Encounters of Jews and Christians in Fifteenth Century Florence," PhD thesis, Hebrew University, Jerusalem, 2009, pp. xvi–xvii.

246 Silvia Maddalo, "Babele," in *Enciclopedia dell'arte medioevale*, Rome: Istituto della Enciclopedia italiana, vol. 2, 1991, pp. 820–26, lists several examples when the story of Babel follows narratives of the story of Noah; including the fresco of Giusto de' Menabuoi in the baptistery of Padua from c. 1376.

247 Orlandi, *Benozzo Gozzoli*, p. 18, doc. 6.

248 Genesis 10:8–10.

249 Luzzati, "Un arcivescovo mediceo del quattrocento pisano," pp. 22–29; Luzzati, "Su due ritratti di Filippo de' Medici arcivescovo di Pisa," pp. 193–98.

250 Genesis 11:1–9.

251 For what follows, see Maddalo, "Babele," pp. 820–27.

252 Saint Augustine, *De Civitate Dei*, in *Patrologiae Latinae*, vol. 41, coll. 483: "est nomen illius Confusio."

253 Gabrielle Morolli, "'Aethereasque domus ... pinxit': Benozzo Primo illustratore delle istituzioni albertiane di architettura," p. 37, identifies the cathedral of Pisa in the scene; but Francesco Quinterio, "La costruzione della torre di Babele," p. 59, sees no Pisan monument, except for perhaps an allusion to the campanile. Both essays are in Emanuela Andreatta et al., eds., *Benozzo Gozzoli e l'architettura*, Florence: Edam, 2002.

254 Burnam, "Le vetrate," pp. 112–13, no. XVs, fig. IX.

255 Ahl, *Benozzo Gozzoli*, p. 308, note 63.

256 For a summary of the arguments and sources, see Clarke, *Roman House – Renaissance Palaces*, pp. 55–65.

257 Francis W. Kent, "The Making of a Renaissance Patron of the Arts," in Alessandro Perosa, ed., *Giovanni Rucellai ed il suo zibaldone*, London: Warburg Institute, 1960, vol. 2, p. 13.

258 Clarke, *Roman House – Renaissance Palaces*, pp. 180–84.

259 In the 1488 poem cited at the beginning of the chapter (Supino, *Il Camposanto*, p. 311), Michelagnolo di Cristofano da Volterra identifies among the portraits the mercenary soldier Giovanni Francesco da Sanseverino and his brothers, including the captain Roberto da Sanseverino (1418–87), the latter of whom built a magnificent palace in Naples in just these years; see Clarke, *Roman House – Renaissance Palaces*, pp. 59, 245. In the current state of the mural, it is not possible to identify these portraits.

260 Morolli, "Aethereasque domus ... pinxit," pp. 23–40.

261 Filippo de' Medici's grandfather, Nicola di Vieri di Cambio de'Medici (1385–1455), an immensely learned humanist and bibliophile, was a friend of Poggio Bracciolini, Ambrogio Traversari, Niccolo Niccoli, Leonardo Bruni, and Alberti, as Luzzati, "Fillippo de' Medici Arcivescovo di Pisa," p. 362, points out. See also Martines, *The Social World of the Florentine Humanists*, pp. 323–24; Raffaella Maria Zaccaria, "Nicola di Vieri de' Medici," in Roberto Cardini et al., eds., *Alberti e la cultura del quattrocento*, Florence: Edizioni Polistampa, 1997, vol. 1, pp. 418–23; and Brian Maxson, *The Humanist World*, p. 55.

262 Pius visited Pienza (then Corsignano) 22 February 1459 and on the return trip from Mantua 11–23 September 1460; see the accounts in the *Commentaries*, ed. and trans. Meserve et al., vol. 1, bk. 2, ch. 20, pp. 281–83; and vol. 2, bk. 4, chs. 34–36, pp. 329–33. Surviving letters to Giovanni di Cosimo from Filippo indicate he was in Arezzo on 4 August and 20 October 1460; ASF, MAP, F. 6, doc. 507, and F. 6, doc. 530, allowing time for Filippo to rejoin the pope at Pienza in September. By all accounts, Pienza was built quickly; when the pope visited in August–September 1462, the cathedral and Palazzo Piccolomini were close to completion; see the famous account of Pienza in the *Commentaries*, bk. 9, trans. Gragg, vol. 35, pp. 597–606. On the chronology of Pienza, see Charles Mack, "Studies in the Architectural Careeer of Bernardo di Matteo Ghamberelli

called Rossellino," PhD dissertation, University of North Carolina at Chapel Hill, 1972, pp. 243–49.

263 Christine Smith, *Architecture in the Culture of Early Humanism*, Oxford: Oxford University Press, 1992, pp. 98–129; Clarke, *Roman House – Renaissance Palaces*, pp. 42–54.

264 Cammy Brothers, *Giuliano da Sangallo and the Ruins of Rome*, Princeton: Princeton University Press, 2022, points out Giuliano's expansive understanding of ancient architecture, before its codification in later theory and practice. It is this view that I believe is visualized in Benozzo's fictive architecture.

265 Clarke, *Roman House – Renaissance Palaces*, p. 62.

266 Pietro Ruschi, "Antico e moderno nell'architettura dipinta di Benozzo Gozzoli," in Andreatta, et al., eds., *Benozzo Gozzoli e l'architettura*, pp. 45–47, emphasizes the aspect of fantasy in Benozzo's painted architecture.

267 Diane Cole Ahl, "Camposanto, Terra Santa: Picturing the Holy Land in Pisa," *Artibus et historiae*, vol. 24, 2003, pp. 95–122.

268 Luzzati, "Un arcivescovo mediceo," p. 27.

269 Najemy, *History of Florence*, pp. 354–57.

270 Dolfi, *Vescovi e arcivescovi di Pisa*, vol. 1, pp. 209–19. For the palazzo della Sapienza, see Ewa Karwacka Codini, "Il palazzo della Sapienza a Pisa: Della sua edificazione rinascimentale," in B. Azzaro, ed., *L'Università di Roma 'La Sapienza' e le università italiane*, Rome, 2008, pp. 235–46; Ewa Karwacka Codini, "La Sapienza," in Karwacka Codini, ed., *Architettura a Pisa nel primo periodo mediceo*, pp. 48–61; Ferruccio Canali, "La'domus sapientiae' di Pisa e Lorenzo il Magnifico: Novità tipologiche e stratificazioni d'ornato tra Leon Batista Alberti e Giuliano da Sangallo (1471–92)," in Daniele, ed., *Le dimore di Pisa*, pp. 83–90.

271 ASPi, Opera del Duomo, Debitori e Creditori, no. 564, c. 178; Orlandi, *Benozzo Gozzoli*, pp. 55–58, doc. no. 31. A curious payment on 20 September 1475 to Botticelli for a trial piece of the Assumption in the chapel of the Incoronata in the cathedral, that he was to paint in the Camposanto, perhaps suggests an attempt to supplant Benozzo there; Battistoni, *L'Opera del Duomo di Pisa*, p. 193, note 7.

272 Ahl, *Benozzo Gozzoli*, pp. 161–62.

273 ASPi, Opera del Duomo, Entrata e Uscita, no. 146, c. 82 recto; Orlandi, *Benozzo Gozzoli*, pp. 68–70, doc. no. 45.

274 Ahl, *Benozzo Gozzoli*, p. 162. See also Tanfani-Centofanti, *Notizie di artisti tratte dai documenti pisani*, pp. 83–93; Fanucci Lovitch, *Artisti attivi a Pisa*, vol. 1, pp. 49–51.

275 ASPi, Opera del Duomo, Debitori e creditori, no. 564, c. 200; Orlandi, *Benozzo Gozzoli*, p. 83, doc. no. 58.

276 ASPi, Opera del Duomo, Ricordanze, no. 444, c. 27 recto; Orlandi, *Benozzo Gozzoli*, p. 93, doc. no. 63.

277 "Misse quattro a misura perchè ve n'è storie due a l'ultimo che sono per tre storie"; ASPi, Opera del Duomo, Debitori e creditori, no. 564, c. 207, Orlandi, *Benozzo Gozzoli*, pp 87–89, doc. no. 60.

278 "Perchè non à lavorato chontinuo"; ASPi, Opera del Duomo, Ricordanze, no. 444, c. 61 verso; Orlandi, *Benozzo Gozzoli*, p. 118, doc. no. 78.

279 Ahl, *Benozzo Gozzoli*, pp. 175–85.

280 Borsi et al., *Maestri fiorentini nei cantieri romani del quattrocento*, pp. 177, 180–84. It might also reference the new coffered ceilings planned in Rome for Santa Maria Maggiore by Callixtus III, realized much later (1498) under his nephew Alexander VI and for San Marco projected by Paul II. For the ceiling of San Marco, begun c. 1466 and finished 1468, see Frommel, *Architettura e committenza da Alberti a Bramante*, pp. 181–82. For the Santa Maria Maggiore ceiling, see Fabrizio Mancinelli, "La basilica nel quattrocento," in Carlo Pietrangeli, ed., *Santa Maria Maggiore a Roma*, Florence: Nardini Editore, 1988, pp. 202–4.

281 "QUID SPECTAS VOLUCRES, PISCES, ET MONSTRA FERARUM, / ET VIRIDES SILVAS AETHEREASQUE DOMOS? / ET PUEROS, IUVENES,

MATRES, CANOSQUE PARENTES? / QUEIS SEMPER VIVUM SPIRAT IN ORE DECUS? / NON HAEC TAM VARIIS, FINXIT SIMULACRA FIGURIS/ NATURA INGENIO FOETIBUS APTA SUO: / EST OPUS ARTIFICIS: PINXIT VIVA ORA BENOZZUS: / O SUPERI, VIVOS PUNDITE IN ORA SONOS." Ahl, *Benozzo Gozzoli*, p. 194.

282 Martin Warnke, *The Court Artist: On the Ancestry of the Modern Artist*, trans. David McLintock, Cambridge: Cambridge University Press, 1993, pp. 34–45.

283 See the documents in Orlandi, *Benozzo Gozzoli*, for example, pp. 15–16, doc. 4, ASPi, Opera del Duomo, Ricordanze, no. 443, c. 33 recto.

284 On 6 October 1469, the Opera sent three florins to Benozzo's house, "quando Lese suo padre morì"; ASPi, Opera del Duomo, Ricordanze, no. 443, c. 54 recto; Orlandi, *Benozzo Gozzoli,* p. 24, doc. no. 9. The payment for the tomb slab is recorded in ASPi, Opera del Duomo, Ricordanze, no. 443, c. 58 recto; Orlandi, *Benozzo Gozzoli*, pp. 26–27, doc. no. 11.

285 The cenotaph's inscription reads, "HIC TUMULUS EST BENOTII FLORENTINI QUI PROXIME HAS PINXIT HISTORIAS. HUNC SIBI PISANORUM DONAVIT HUMANITAS. MCCCCLXXVIII"; Ahl, p. 309, note 98. Benozzo was granted safe conducts for himself and his family on 5 June and 6 July 1495; ASPi, Comune C, no. 11, c. 74 verso, 121 verso; Orlandi, *Benozzo Gozzoli,* p. 147, docs. nos. 108–9. He sold his house on 24 August 1495; it was later seized by the Pisan government and then restituted to his heirs after the end of the Pisan revolt in 1509. It was later the subject of litigation, resolved only in 1538; Orlandi, *Benozzo Gozzoli*, pp. 149–50, doc. no. 111.

286 "Perchè potea domandare magiore, come sa messer Antonio Operaio e Antonio di Duccio"; ASPi, Opera del Duomo, Debitri e Creditori no. 564, c. 207; Orlandi, *Benozzo Gozzoli*, p. 88, doc. no. 60.

287 Warnke, *The Court Artist*, pp. 143–55.

288 Luke Syson, "Bertoldo di Giovanni, Republican Court Artist," in Stephen Campbell et al., eds., *Artistic Exchange and Cultural Translation in the Italian Renaissance City*, Cambridge: Cambridge University Press, 2004, pp. 96–133; and Alexander Noelle, "Reframing Bertoldo and His Legacy," in Ng, Noelle, et al., *Bertoldo di Giovanni*, pp. 43–45.

289 Vasari, *Le vite,* ed. Milanesi, vol. 3, p. 49, also mentions "infiniti ritratti di naturale" in the cycle, few of which he could identify even then. The Museo Nazionale di San Matteo has a painted copy from the second half of the nineteenth century by Alessandro Lanfredini of several figures taken from the scene of the *Meeting of King Solomon and the Queen of Sheba*; Inv. 2197. Vasari identified portraits of Marsilio Ficino, Giovanni Argyropoulos, and Bartolomeo Platina in this scene.

290 The description of Solomon's temple and palace is in 1 Kings 6:1–37 and 7:1–12. The tradition that the palace of Solomon featured a three-story loggia was derived from biblical text as well as pilgrim accounts; see Pieper, *Pienza*, pp. 120–22.

291 On the palace, see Niccolai, *Palazzi*, p. 33; Giusti, "Il 'palazzo vecchio' di Pisa," pp. 208–9; Feliciantonio, "Palazzo Vecchio de' Medici," pp. 162–65; Karwacka Codini, "Dimore Nobiliari a Pisa," pp. 45–46.

292 Georges Rohault de Fleury, *Les monuments de Pise au moyen âge*, Paris: A. Morel, 1866, pp. 5–8, plates I–III.

293 Fabio Redi, "I palazzi pisani nel medioevo. Una lettura archeologica e tipologica delle strutture superstiti," in Daniele, ed., *Le dimore di Pisa*, pp. 33–42.

294 Elena Fasano Guarini, ed., *Storia della civiltà toscana*, vol. 3: *Il principato mediceo*, Florence: Le Monnier, 2003.

CHAPTER FOUR

ROME IN SPOLETO

Bishop Berardo Eroli, Fra Filippo Lippi, and the Coronation of the Virgin *Murals in the Duomo of Spoleto*

At vespers on the evening of 14 August 1668, the translation of the *Madonna Avvocata*, the holy icon of Spoleto cathedral, to a new chapel, where it is still to be seen, began with solemn ceremony (Figures 4.1–4.2). After the evening office, the prior, assisted by the canons and other clergy, carried the icon from the old chapel to the main altar, where it was displayed amid blazing candles, silver vases, and angel figurines. The church was sumptuously decorated with tapestries, yellow and red taffeta bunting, and red velvet hangings. Twelve roundels, each showing one of the mysteries of the Virgin, hung from the arches of the nave arcade, and great vases filled with citrus boughs, alternating with silver candelabra, surmounted the cornice. Candles and silver lamps blazed from every altar. The Archbishop Cesare Facchinetti (r. 1655–72) celebrated Mass, along with clergy and civic officials, and the bishop delivered a sermon extolling the meaning of translation. The icon remained on the altar through the night for the veneration of the public.

After vespers the next day, the feast of the Assumption of the Virgin, the procession began. The prior, accompanied by ranks of clergy, magistrates, confraternity members, and worshippers, carried the icon, sheltered by a canopy of crimson brocade. The cortege through the city followed the route taken on the early summer feast of Corpus Christi, passing by palaces decorated with tapestries, taffeta hangings, paintings, flowers, and torches.[1] Temporary arches erected of freshly cut boughs and fruits marked the way, and wine flowed from fountains. In the Piazza Pubblica, arches formed an octagon; over one segment

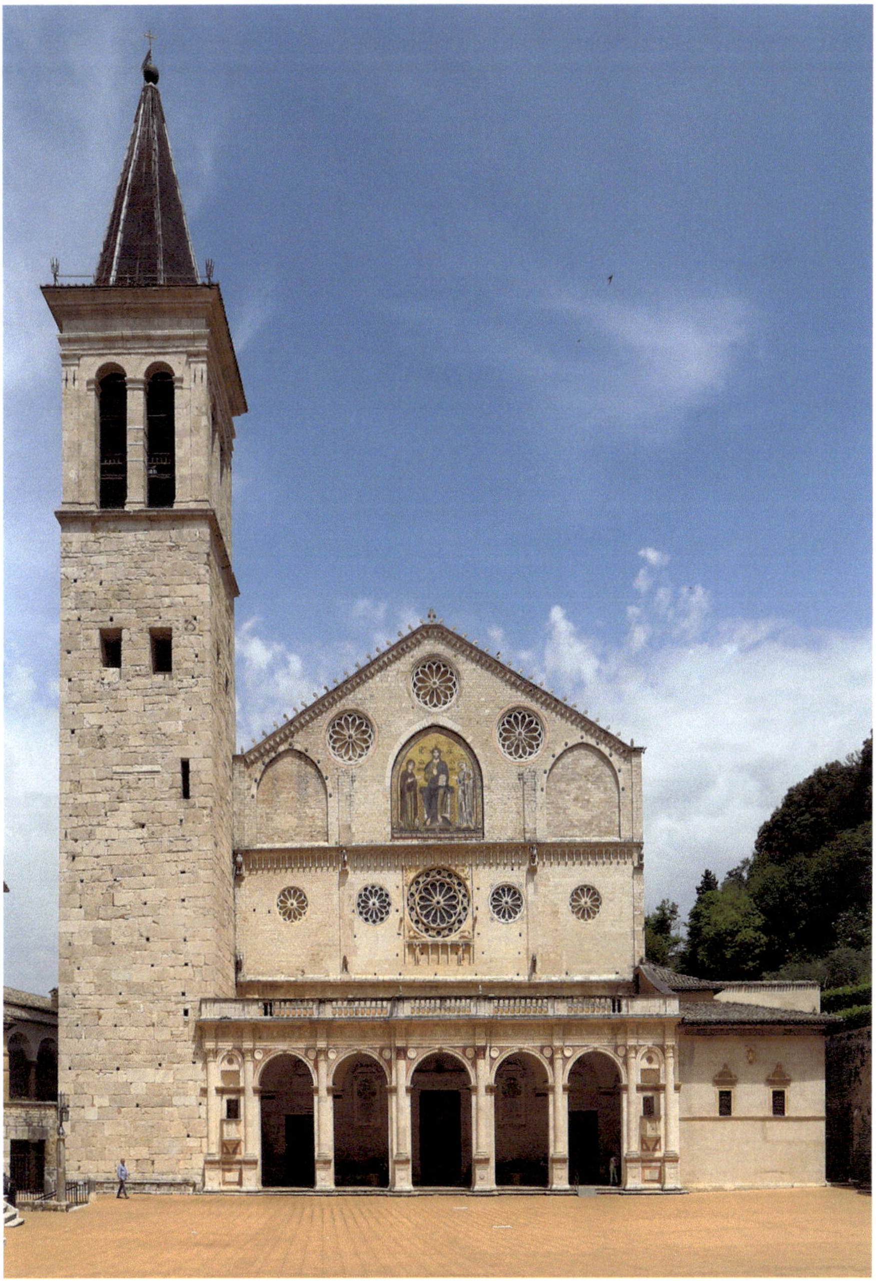

4.1. Duomo, Spoleto. Photo: Sailko / Creative Commons Attribution 3.0 Unported.

loomed a statue of Emperor Frederick Barbarossa (r. 1155–90), the legendary donor, holding the icon. As the bishop returned to the church, he received the sacred icon from the prior and displayed it from the portico of the church to worshippers in the piazza and surrounding streets. He then processed to the new chapel and installed the icon in its new home.[2] The procession and display of the

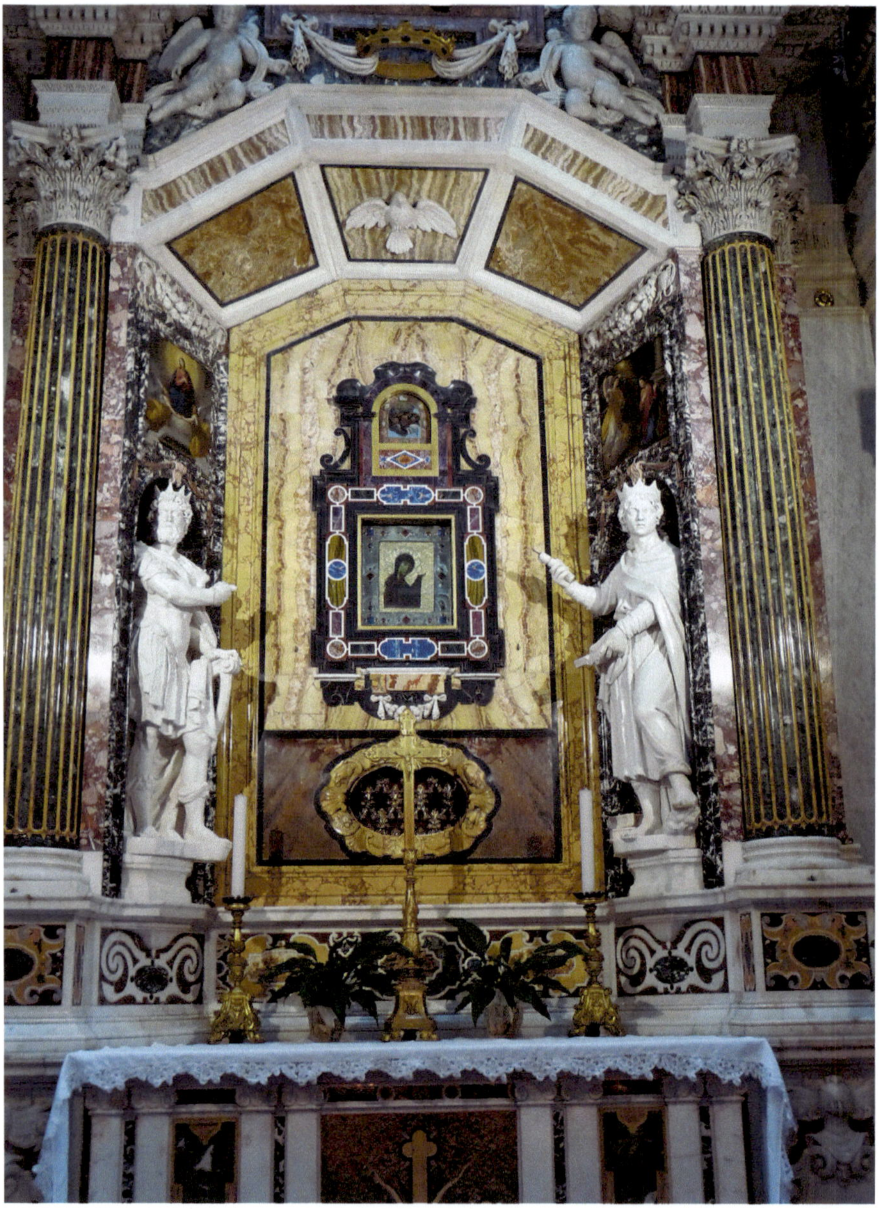

4.2. Chapel of the Santissima Icone, 1668, Duomo, Spoleto Photo: Author.

icon dates from earlier times, as discussed below; but the translation ceremony of 1668 is the first detailed description we have of it.

The new chapel of the icon was at least the fourth one to house Spoleto's sacred image. The panel of the Madonna was, according to local legend, given to the city by Emperor Frederick in 1185 in recompense for having sacked the city in 1155 (Figure 4.3). No document connected to the donation survives, and the first mention of it in Spoleto dates to 1291, when indulgences were

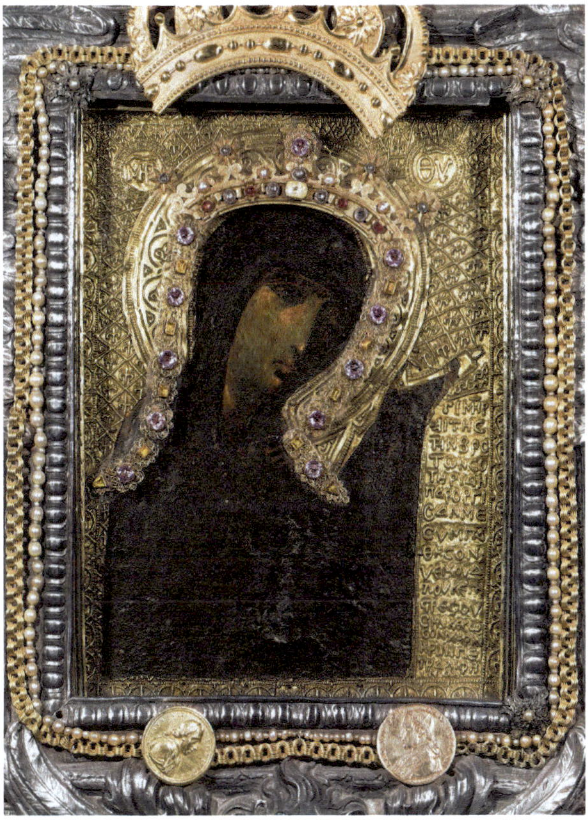

4.3. *Santissima Icone*, first half of the twelfth century, Duomo, Spoleto. Photo: Scala / Art Resource, NY.

granted.[3] Scholars suggest the icon was painted in Constantinople between 1100 and 1150.[4] It is a replica of the fifth-century icon, the so-called *Haghiosoritissa*, now lost, from the church of the Virgin in the Chalcoprateia neighborhood of Constantinople. As a holy icon originating from the East, not a Western replica, the image had extraordinary prestige, at least in the territory of the old duchy of Spoleto.[5]

The Madonna, facing right, bends her head slightly while holding up a scroll with her left hand. Posed without the Christ Child, she presents a petition for the salvation of mankind. The scroll is inscribed with the dialogue she has with Christ. As Belting pointed out, the scroll, in its dual role as a petition and transcript of the dialogue, has the status of a legal document. She acts then, as both intercessor and lawyer (*avvocata*) for the people. In the original location in Constantinople, the Son was represented by another icon, also lost, of Christ who answered.[6] The image of the Virgin who makes this moving appeal to her Son came to be known as the Madonna as Advocate, or *Madonna Avvocata*, while the Christ "who gave answer" was known as the *Antiphonites*.[7] The Spoleto image seems never to have had a pendant icon of Christ. However, gilded rays at the upper right signify the presence of the Savior, as is seen in other versions of the image, although She does not directly address Him.[8]

Recent technical analysis and conservation has revealed aspects of the work that were previously difficult to see or to interpret.[9] A silver plate, dating most likely to shortly after the image was produced, covers the surface of the panel except for the figure.[10] The cover reproduces the inscription on the unfurled scroll of the panel in embossed letters, in addition to two lines of dialogue and the name of the donor of the cover. The differences in the two inscriptions suggest the original panel has been cut down on all sides. The image was for centuries encased in a now-lost reliquary dated 1396. It was replaced by the actual one in 1674. The image, painted in tempera on a wood panel overlaid with fine linen, has suffered losses to the paint film, in the Virgin's face and her right hand. Her mantle, originally a rich purple, is now a dark blue-black, and the gilded background is heavily abraded. The letters of the scroll have been reinforced.

THE ASSUMPTION CEREMONY IN SPOLETO

From earliest times, the icon became a centerpiece of Spoleto's ceremonial life. The papal bull of indulgence dated to the feast of the Assumption in 1291 referred to a procession to the altar – presumably the high altar – with "a painting of wondrous beauty . . . which contains the image of the Mother of God painted with the highest skill by Saint Luke evangelist."[11] A further bull of indulgence for one hundred days, issued on 23 May 1295, described the icon in the same terms and specified that it was brought to the altar during the celebration of Mass.[12] A reduced indulgence of forty days was granted for the veneration of the icon on less solemn occasions, when it was viewed in its usual place. From this we learn that from at least 1295 the icon was housed in a dedicated space.

Whether a procession of the *Madonna Avvocata* through the city on the Assumption, as happened in other cities, was part of the festivities in Spoleto is, however, not known.[13] The translation ceremony related above was an infrequent event, celebrated on the feast of the Assumption. Yet the procession followed the route of another feast, Corpus Christi; hence, it would seem that there was not an established processional route through the town for the feast of the Assumption.[14] We know that in the nineteenth century on the eve of the Assumption a procession took place, but it was limited to the ostentation of the sacred icon on the portico of the cathedral, a ceremony that continues today.[15] For earlier times, however, we have no evidence of the precise nature of the celebration for the Assumption.

This chapter describes renovations to the cathedral in the late fifteenth century for which the ceremonial context provides the interpretative key.

These included a new chapel for the holy icon, new chapels off the north and south aisles, and reconstruction of the tribune and apse. The apse decoration, murals of the life of the Virgin and her coronation in heaven, which were painted by the Florentine artist Fra Filippo Lippi between 1466 and 1469, is a particular focus (Figure 4.4).[16] Payments for the work in the accounts of the Opera del Duomo of Spoleto, which have been known in part, reveal details of the chronology, materiality, and execution of the murals.[17] A close rereading of the documents, published in the Appendix in full for the first time, sets Lippi's work in the context of the cathedral restoration campaign. They also reveal the role the bishop of Spoleto, Berardo Eroli (r. 1448–74), played in its genesis. A broad picture of Eroli's patronage in Spoleto and in Rome shows that Eroli conceived the new apse decoration as a magnificent setting for the Madonna icon of the cathedral and its display on feast days, especially the Assumption. In this way, Eroli also sought to link the Spoleto Duomo – visually and liturgically – with the venerable Marian Basilica Santa Maria Maggiore in Rome.

Lippi's apse murals present an impressive vision of the Virgin's last days to the visitor who approaches down the nave from the entrance portal. In the late fifteenth century, this effect must have been even more striking. Chapels added to the north and south aisles in the late fifteenth century were screened somewhat from view by the twelve Romanesque piers, which were not aligned with the chapels. Hence, the nave must have preserved its tunneling, Romanesque austerity.[18] Lippi also took care to foreshorten the architecture in the frame and narratives of the apse murals according to geometric perspective, thus emphasizing the illusion of depth and continuity with the actual space of the church.[19]

The Virgin kneels before a white bearded God the Father, who blesses her with His right hand while placing a crown on her head with His left (Figure 4.5). Behind them, a giant aureole with snaking flames radiates light, while concentric bands studded with gilded wax bosses trace the celestial spheres. Crowds of angels blowing trumpets and offering flowers surround the central figures. At the lower left and right, Old Testament prophets and heroines and pagan sibyls resting on clouds regard the holy figures with amazement. Directly beneath the *Coronation*, the *Dormition of the Virgin* takes place, while her *Assumption* and donation of her girdle to Saint Thomas are barely visible, having been nearly obliterated by previous restorations (Figure 4.6). The program was likely devised by Eroli himself, who, as we will see, took an active hand in this and other projects under his aegis.[20]

Lippi had painted the *Coronation of the Virgin* before, in two large altarpieces during the 1440s (Figure 4.7).[21] As we have seen in Chapter 1, it was a subject dear to the pictorial tradition of Tuscany – and to all Italy.[22] Lippi's treatment of the subject in the Spoleto mural is distinguished from most Florentine

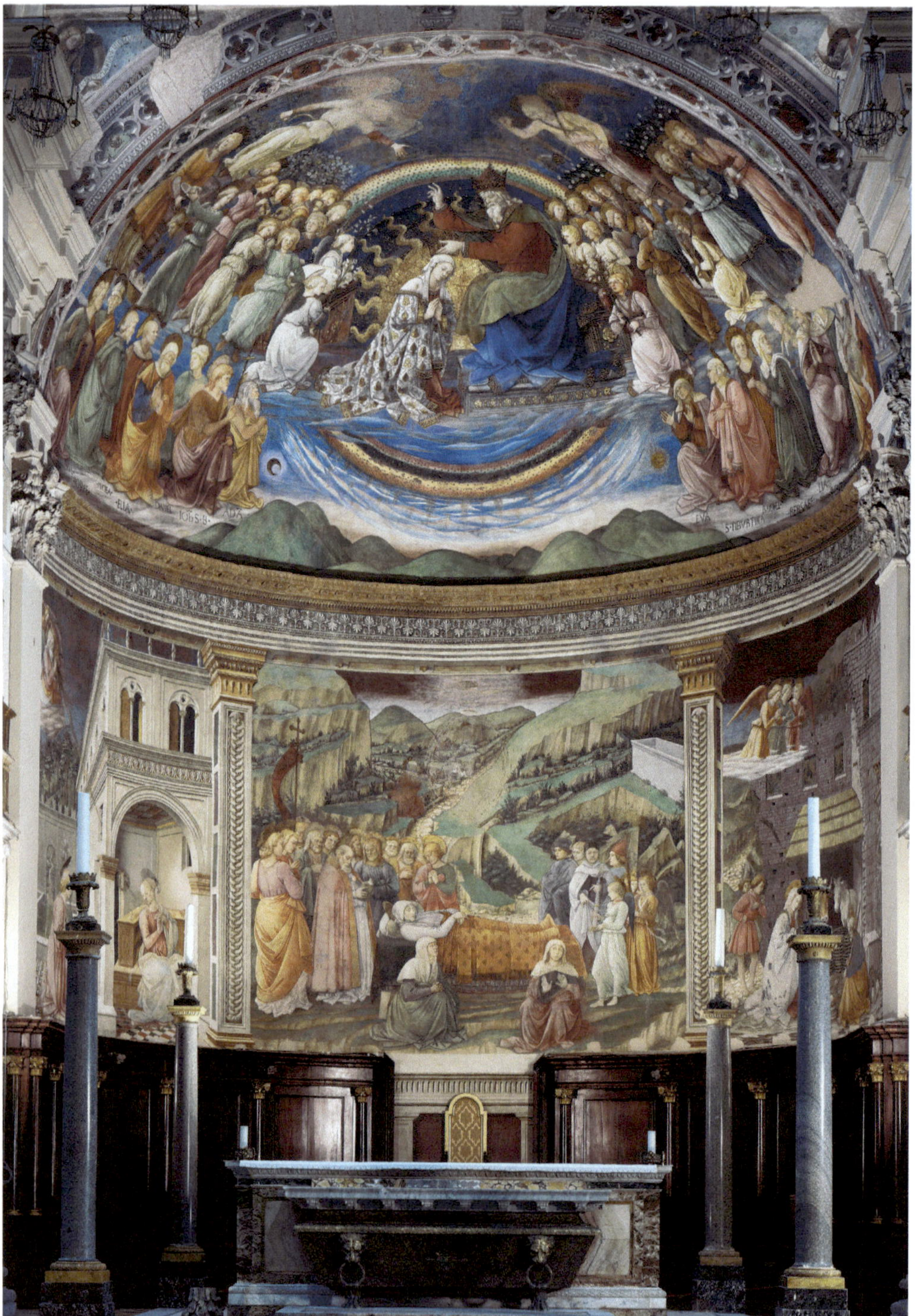

4.4. Fra Filippo Lippi, Apse Murals, 1466–69, Duomo, Spoleto. Photo: Scala / Art Resource, NY.

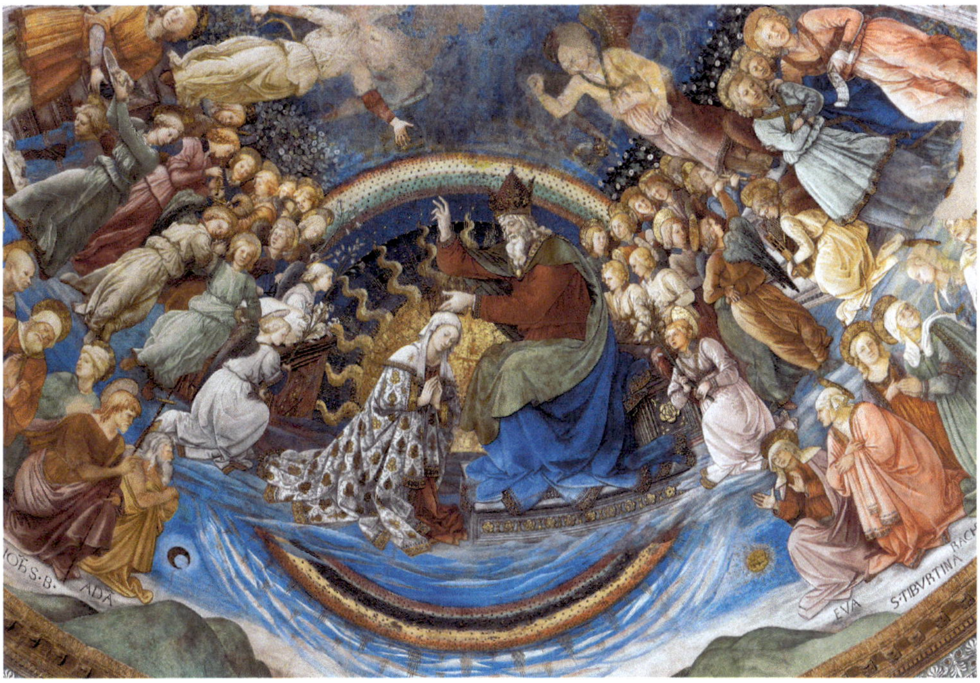

4.5. Fra Filippo Lippi, Apse Murals with *Coronation of the Virgin*, 1466–69. Photo: Scala / Art Resource, NY.

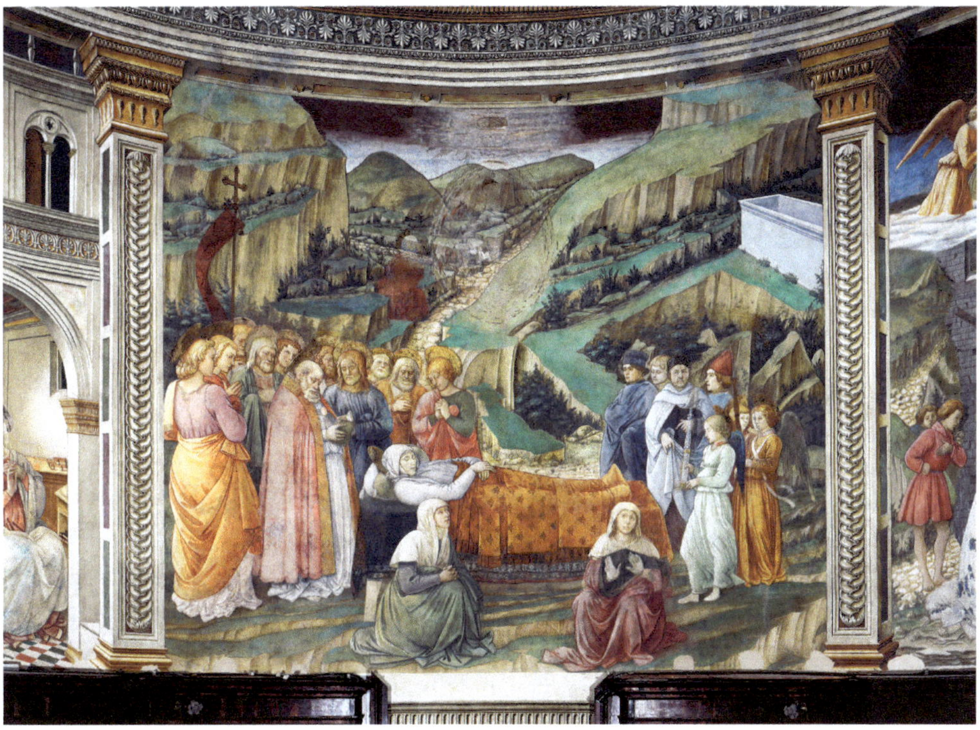

4.6. Fra Filippo Lippi, *Dormition and Assumption of the Virgin*, 1466–69, Duomo, Spoleto. Photo: Scala / Art Resource, NY.

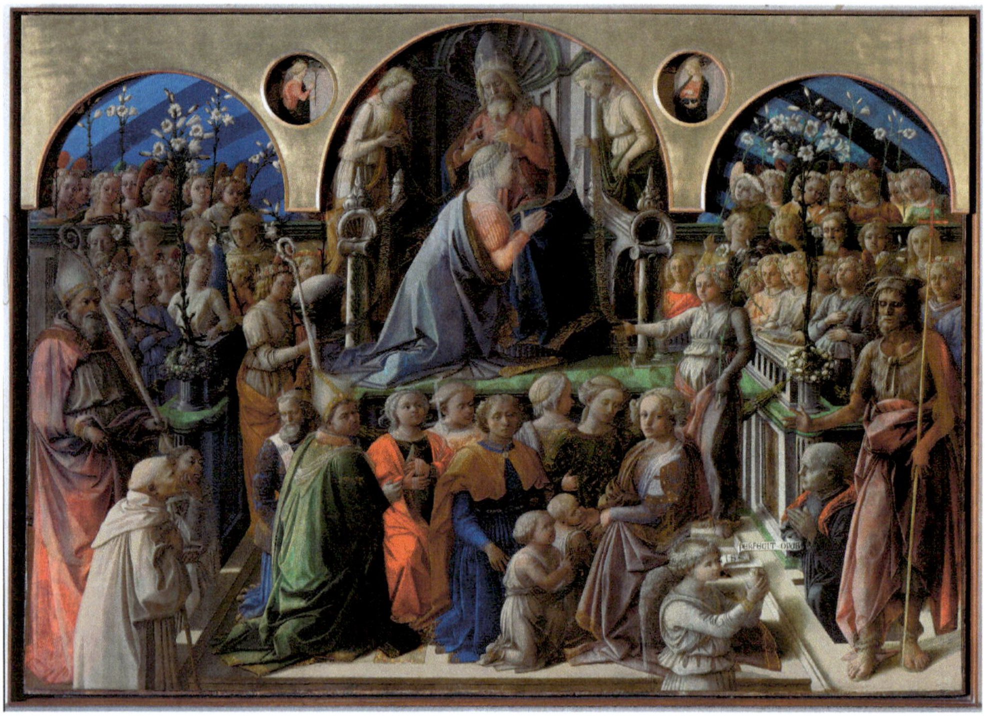

4.7. Fra Filippo Lippi, *Coronation of the Virgin*, 1439–47, Gallerie degli Uffizi. Photo: Scala / Art Resource, NY.

precedents by showing the Virgin kneeling. This motif had appeared before in Tuscan art, for example, in a panel by Taddeo di Bartolo, now part of the Kress Collection, and in the altarpiece by Fra Angelico, originally in Fiesole and now in the Louvre. It had also appeared in North Italian works; in fact, during Lippi's youthful visit to Padua in c. 1434–36, he was said by an early source to have painted a *Coronation of the Virgin*.[23] Lippi's preference for the kneeling pose for vastly different settings and patrons and at different times suggests a conscious choice on the part of artist or patron, or both.

BISHOP BERARDO EROLI

Eroli, whose role in the cathedral renovations was key, was a powerful figure in the Roman church and a decades-long force in the spiritual life of Spoleto. He was born in Narni in 1409.[24] His father was Ludovico Eroli di Narni, but of his mother, nothing is known.[25] The origins and social stature of his family are obscure.[26] Pius II (r. 1458–64), who appointed him a cardinal, seemed to address anticipated criticism when, in his address 8 March 1460 in Siena, he said, Eroli "comes from a noble family from Narni." Pius adds that, under his predecessor Pope Callixtus III (r. 1455–58), "the only barrier to his promotion was the jealousy of a few people."[27] The latter remark refers to the argument, reportedly advanced by the Cardinals Domenico Capranica and Prospero Colonna, that Eroli's modest income disqualified him from the high office of cardinal.[28]

Contemporaries praised Eroli during his lifetime and later for his learning, but where and what he studied and any academic positions he might have held are not known.[29] Pius's oration asserted, "He has held many chairs at Italian universities and has lectured there to the delight and benefit of his audiences."[30] Vespasiano da Bisticci lauded him as a great jurist and expert in canon law, and Gaspare da Verona praised his "amazing knowledge of civil and canon law."[31]

All contemporary accounts praise the modesty, to the point of austerity, of Eroli's person. Gaspare da Verona described him as severe, stern, and uncompromising.[32] Vespasiano characterized him as "most gentle and foreign to any ostentation, either at home or outside the house."[33] In his own testament, he asked that his funeral be conducted without sumptuousness by only cardinals and prelates.[34] Yet contemporaries also noted his obstinacy; Jacopo Ammannati Piccolomini, the cardinal of Pavia, relates that when Frederick of Aragon, the younger son of King Ferdinand of Naples, passed by Rome in November of 1474, the cardinals advised the pope to receive him with the honors normally reserved for royalty. Eroli, by contrast, refused to acknowledge him.[35]

In Rome, Eroli's long career at the papal court, during which he served five popes in varying capacities, began probably in the late 1440s. Nicholas V (r. 1447–55) appointed him referendary, the office whose duty it was to review petitions directed to the pope and to advise on the actions to be taken. Nicholas also appointed him to the position of auditor, or judge, of the Roman Rota, the apostolic tribunal. On 13 November 1448, Nicholas appointed Eroli bishop of Spoleto, the diocese of which included his natal city. After less than a year, in 1449, he returned to the Eternal City to serve as papal vicar for the city of Rome, residing there for the rest of his life. As papal vicar, Eroli assumed vast responsibilities for the spiritual administration of the city and its surrounding district.[36] The appointment supports Eroli's reputation for probity and justice voiced by later sources. He held the position under the next pope, Callixtus, until at least 1457.[37]

Pius II raised him to the cardinalate on 5 March 1460 as cardinal-priest of Santa Sabina.[38] In the pope's address to the new cardinals, he declared of Eroli, "we took him into Our own household because of his exceptional reputation, and he has richly deserved Our favor and the goodwill of the courtiers. He always had Our high regard since We admired and loved his prudence, loyalty and learning."[39] Contemporaries attest to Eroli's intimacy with the humanist pope. Writing to Duke Francesco Sforza in 1458, the diplomat Ottone del Carretto observed that Pius consulted Eroli "in matters of state and in those of the court . . . and he did almost nothing without him."[40] Two days after his election as pope, on 20 August 1458, Pius named Eroli the lieutenant to the chamberlain of the Holy Roman Church, a post he held at least until 24 February 1460. The chamberlain administered the property of the Holy See.[41]

Pius praised Eroli in his Commentaries as "a distinguished lawyer, highly esteemed for his probity and his reputation for justice,"[42] and he turned to him to solve troubling disputes.[43] Eroli often traveled with Pius.[44] Platina describes the pope's habits: "He could not eat willingly alone, and therefore invited either the Cardinal of Spoleto, of Trani or of Pavia commonly to sup with him. At supper he used to discourse on learning."[45]

Under subsequent Popes Paul II (r. 1464–71) and Sixtus IV (r. 1471–84), Eroli assumed numerous offices. He served as the chamberlain of the Sacred College of Cardinals in 1466 and 1474. After resigning the bishopric of Spoleto in 1474 in favor of his nephew Costantino Eroli, he became cardinal bishop of Sabina, the suburban district. Sixtus also charged Eroli, by now cardinal protector of the Cistercian order, with the reform of the abbey of Chiaravalle, outside Milan, the oldest Cistercian foundation in Italy, then involved in a dispute with Duke Galeazzo Maria Sforza of Milan. During this dispute, which involved the distribution of the abbey's assets, the duke's envoy described Eroli as rigid and severe but of great authority in the College of Cardinals.[46]

Despite modest means, Eroli received numerous benefices from the popes he served.[47] Pius, perhaps to remedy the charge of Eroli's insufficient wealth, awarded him the rich benefice of the Cistercian Abbey of Saints Vincent and Anastasius at the Three Fountains just outside the Roman walls, according to legend on the spot Saint Paul was martyred.[48] In addition, Paul II assigned him a pension of 100 ducats a month.[49]

In Rome, Eroli's palace was on the via dell'Arco della Ciambella, incorporated into the remains of the baths of Agrippa, which abutted the Pantheon complex to the north.[50] It was in the parish of Santa Maria in Monterone and stood next to the houses of the della Valle family. Pasquale Adinolfi, in the *Via sacra o del papa*, described the palace as on the via Papale, traveling east just past the small Piazza de'Quatracci, at the angle of the complex of the della Valle family.[51] Eroli's palace, as we learn from an extract of his testament, consisted of two parts: a *domus antiqua* and a *domus nove*.[52] The old part included a hall with a solarium above and another solarium where the rooms of his household were located. These rooms faced the courtyard of the rear house of the late Lelio della Valle. The antique house was also where the cardinal's bedroom was located, and a small room next to the bedroom, located in the lower part of a tower, served as a chapel. This part of the antique house also had a kitchen and an open-air courtyard and was accessed by a stair. The *domus nove* included a *camera paramenti*, which served as a dining room, two large rooms, as well as a stair, a main entry, a *cameris ligneis* for his household and other rooms. The references to furnishings – fabric hangings and paneled rooms – suggest a comfortable, if not sumptuous abode, with a few exceptions: the silver candelabra that were in the chapel were bequeathed to the Lateran baptistery. Eroli left his books to his nephew Costantino, whom, he stipulated in his testament, was to have the use of his houses for as long as he lived. Eroli's justification for this generosity was that Costantino had been responsible for the "great labors in building the houses I live in in Rome," thus establishing a precedent for Costantino's later patronage in Spoleto.[53]

The house was visible from the via Papalis, the processional route traveled by newly elected popes to the Lateran Basilica, the cathedral of Rome, and on other occasions.[54] The procession that transferred the relic of Saint Andrew's head to the Vatican on Palm Sunday in 1462, a highlight of Pius's papacy, passed by Eroli's palace, as related in Pius's *Commentaries*:

> The route followed the Tiber till they reached the closely built districts on the right. Then the procession turned left and through narrow streets between high buildings came to the Pantheon, which the heathen consecrated to all the gods, that is demons, and our ancestors to the glorious Virgin, Mother of our Lord, and to all the saints. There after crossing the great square before the church it turned to the right till it passed the chapel of Sant' Eustachio, where it turned left again till it reached the house of Berardo, Cardinal of Santa Sabina, a most virtuous man and an authority on law. Here, bearing a third time to the right, it followed the street called the Pope's to the newly erected church of Maximo, where it again turned left to the Campo dei Fiori. Crossing this on the right it reached the square of San Lorenzo in Damaso, where it took a street to the left which brought it to the Tiber bank, and finally a road to the right which brought it to Hadrian's tomb. Here it crossed the bridge and proceeded to Saint Peter's by the Via Sacra, which was everywhere strewn with flowers and fragrant herbs.[55]

Along the route, residences of cardinals were decorated, as Pius noted:

> All the cardinals who lived along the route had decorated their houses magnificently (There was one exception whom I forbear to mention out of respect, for fear he might be thought irreligious.) The Cardinal of Spoleto, though not present himself (for he had gone to his own church to minister to his people and his sheep during Holy Week), had left stewards at his house who had covered the adjacent square with carpets and decorated the house walls most beautifully.... But all were far outstripped in expense and effort and ingenuity by Rodrigo [Borgia], the vice-chancellor. His huge, towering house which he built on the site of the ancient mint was covered with rich and wonderful tapestries, and besides this he had raised a lofty canopy from which were suspended

> many and various marvels. He had decorated not only his own house but those nearby, so that the square all about them seemed a kind of park full of sweet songs and sounds, or a great palace gleaming with gold such as they say Nero's palace was. Furthermore, on the walls were hung many poems recently composed by great geniuses which set forth in large letters praises of the Divine Apostle and eulogies of Pope Pius.[56]

This vivid description reveals what passed for magnificence in mid-fifteenth century Rome. First, the Borgia palace was large and occupied a prestigious ancient site. The display of tapestries – presumably figurative tapestries woven in Northern Europe, not the carpets Eroli hung – reveals what inventories tell us – that tapestries were among the most luxurious possessions of collectors.[57] That they spilled over to the adjacent structures shows the impressiveness of sheer scale. The tall canopy, which Borgia built, framed and focused viewing; what marvels were suspended from it we can only guess: perhaps ornaments of gold and silver. While precious materials such as gold were expected, the display of poems and orations extended the ornament to include humanist learning. Pius recorded the multisensory dimension of the experience, which delighted not only the eye but also the ear. Even though, as Pius noted, Eroli was not among the participants during the procession, nor were his efforts as lavish as those of Borgia, he knew well enough the display that was expected of his clerical rank.

Eroli's Roman palace does not survive; we glean from his fragmentary testament only its location and general layout. Eroli received from Callixtus in 1455, confirmed by Sixtus IV in 1472, the right to leave his houses in Rome, his books, and other personal property to his relatives, rather than having them revert to the church, as was customary.[58] Beneficiaries of his Roman property were the Basilica of Saint Peter's and the hospital of Santissimo Salvatore, whose confraternity he joined after 1476. His nephew, Costantino, retained the use of the palace during his lifetime.[59]

Eroli's alertness to decorum and display was evident in his care for sacred sites in his control. From Pius, Eroli obtained by1461 permission to install the observant Franciscans in the convent of San Paolo inter Vineos in Spoleto, outside the city walls to the southwest, "among the vines."[60] The church, which dates to at least the sixth century, became a Benedictine convent in the eleventh century, and it was renovated in 1230 by Gregory IX (r. 1227–41). Gregory installed the Clarissan order there, endowed it with precious relics and granted indulgences. In 1396, the nuns abandoned it in favor of the more secure site of Sant'Agata inside the walls. Eroli restored and decorated the church, reportedly at his own expense.[61] Of the original decor, only fragments remain after further baroque alterations in 1771 and a drastic restoration concluding in 1965, which restored the interior to its early thirteenth-century state.[62] Eroli's only possible extant contribution is the lunette above the portal of the *Virgin and Child with Saints Peter and Paul*, which appears to date from the mid-fifteenth century.

Particularly dear to Cardinal Eroli was the monastery of San Girolamo on the via Flaminia, just southeast of his natal city of Narni.[63] Dominican nuns had abandoned the monastery in the early fifteenth century.[64] Eroli appealed to Pius in 1461, and then to Paul II, for the installation of the observant Franciscans in 1463.[65] He undertook the complete renovation of San Girolamo, which, in addition to the church, included a convent with a cloister, a library, and a pharmacy to serve the nearby hospital of Santissima Trinità. Cardinal Ammannati, in a letter of 7 August 1472, praised Eroli for the magnificence of the complex.[66] It was so sumptuous, however, that when the construction was finished in 1471, the friars refused to move in, citing vows of poverty. After Eroli sought the support of Sixtus IV and threatened the friars with eviction from San Paolo in Spoleto, they succumbed to his wish.[67]

The convent at the time included a central cloister, with the church along the south side. The church was remodeled to include ribbed groin vaults with pointed arches in the fourteenth century. The façade included a single portal with a small portico, beneath a tympanum and rose window. The church comprised a single nave; the walls were frescoed, the ceiling decorated with stars on a blue ground. Eroli seems not to have altered the architectural form of the church, but he may have restored the campanile. The complex has suffered extensive renovations since the suppression of the monastery in 1860, including its acquisition by the Istituto Diocesano Sostentamento del Clero in 2010, which continues renovations.

Eroli furnished the church with works of art, among them the lunette above the façade portico, a *Madonna and Child with two Angels between Saint Francis and Saint Jerome*, which was detached in 1880 and is now in the Museo Civico. In poor condition, it has been attributed to Pierantonio Mezzastris (c. 1430–c. 1506), whom, as discussed below, Eroli employed on other occasions.[68] The imagery commemorated the new dedication of the church to the Franciscans, and it echoes in design the lunette in San Paolo inter Vineos. Both are indebted to the lunette in San Fortunato in Montefalco by Benozzo Gozzoli, who greatly influenced Mezzastris's style.[69] Mezzastris may have executed murals on the interior of the church, again following the example of Benozzo in San Fortunato, but these would have perished in the repainting of the late nineteenth century.[70]

For the high altar of the church, Eroli commissioned Domenico Ghirlandaio to paint the *Coronation of the Virgin* (Figure 4.8), now on view in the Pinacoteca in Narni.[71] A document of 3 June 1486 recorded the agreement between the artist and Fra Giovanni Galeotti, the *procuratore* of the observants of San Girolamo, to appoint as an appraiser for the picture completed by Ghirlandaio Pietro di Ser Lorenzo de' Paoli, in place of the miniaturist

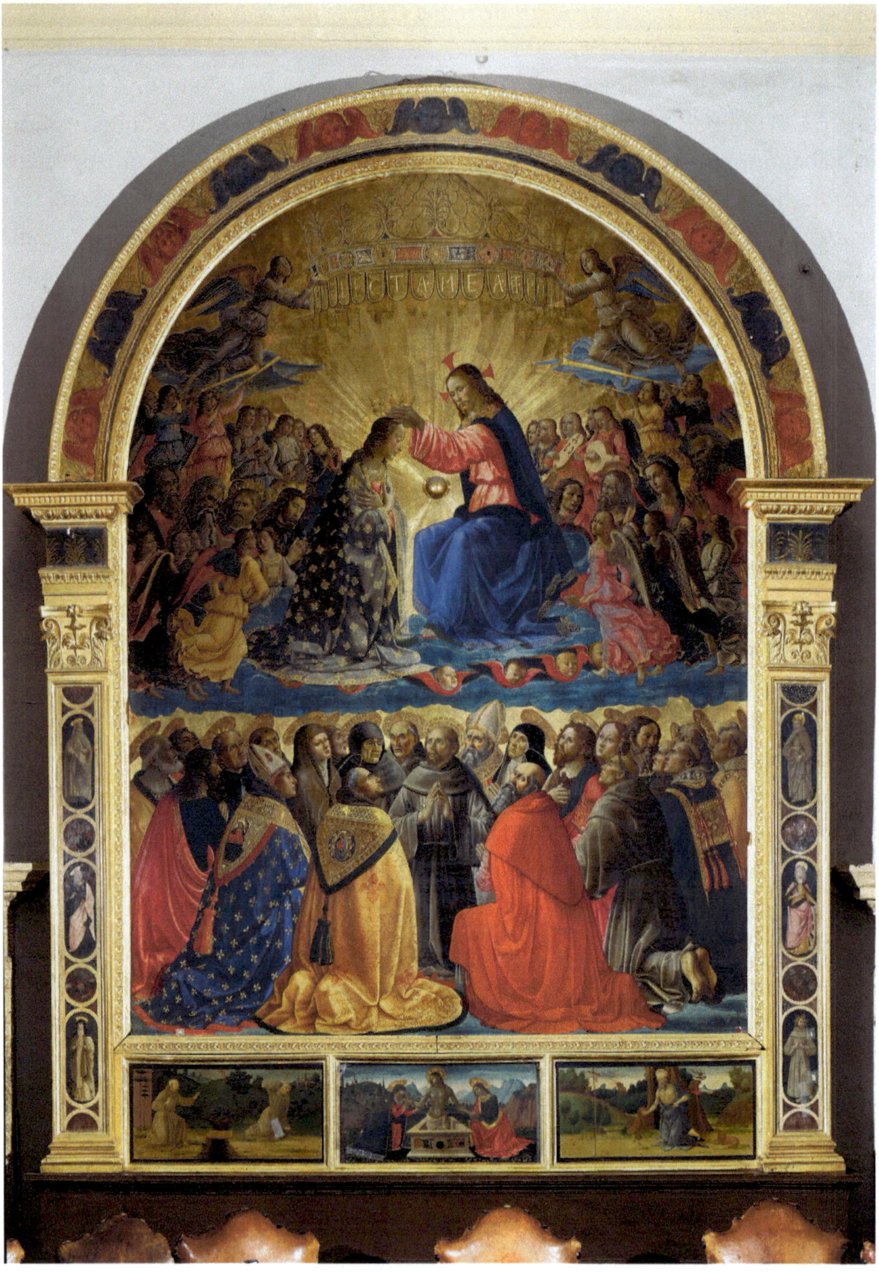

4.8. Domenico Ghirlandaio, *Coronation of the Virgin*, before 1486, Pinacoteca Comunale, Narni. Photo: Scala / Art Resource, NY.

Francesco d'Antonio, who had died 27 October 1484. While Eroli is not named in the document, and indeed, he had died seven years before, it is likely that the impetus for this commission, as for the entire refurbishment of the church, came from the cardinal. Certainly, the altarpiece had been commissioned before 1484, the date of Francesco d'Antonio's death; but Eroli, or possibly his nephew Costantino, who succeeded him as bishop of Spoleto and resided in Rome in his palace, is most likely responsible for it.

The altarpiece alone, with its shimmering gold background, luminous colors, and luxurious tooling detail, gives some idea of the splendor of San Girolamo's refurbishment described by the Cardinal of Pavia. Giovanni Eroli, who saw it in the apse of the church, before the panel was moved to the Palazzo Comunale in Narni in 1871, remarked on the striking sight, even though the light conditions in the apse were not as favorable as they would have been in its original location on the high altar.[72] It also provides guidance into Eroli's taste for magnificence, as hinted in Pius's account of the decor of his palace along the processional route for the relic of Saint Andrew's head. That Eroli, personally austere, understood the contemporary culture of opulence that had come to define the papal court is clear. He is portrayed in the altarpiece in guise of Saint Berard, one of five Franciscan protomartyrs killed in 1120 in Morocco for their faith. His head, wrapped in a dark brown Franciscan cowl, his expression withdrawn, is to the left at the side of Saint Francis and above the kneeling figure of Saint Bonaventure.[73] Sixtus IV canonized the protomartyrs in 1481, hence a halo encircles his rapt countenance.

Of Eroli's other building projects we have little surviving evidence.[74] He has been identified as the patron of the so-called Eroli chapel in the church of San Francesco in Narni. The chapel, from 1458 the seat of a confraternity dedicated to San Bernardino of Siena and attached to the church of San Francesco, was originally an oratorio with a separate entrance on the wall opposite the current portal, which opens onto the south aisle and is a later addition.[75] Adjacent to the Palazzo Eroli on the current via Saffi (formerly via San Francesco), the chapel was only acquired by the Eroli family at the beginning of the nineteenth century. Nonetheless, Berardo Eroli has been convincingly linked to the murals, and it is likely he commissioned the painter and devised the imagery.[76] A bull of Pius II from 13 June 1464 granted indulgences for visiting the chapel on the feast of Saint Bernardino, a grant reaffirmed by Sixtus IV in 1476. In his bull, Pius referred to the chapel as newly built and to the sculpture of Saint Bernardino within.[77]

Pierantonio Mezzastris, as reported by Gnoli, signed the murals of the scenes from the lives of Saint Francis and Saint Bernardino of Siena.[78] The murals repeat selective works from the church of San Francesco in Montefalco: the six scenes depicting the life of Saint Francis from the main chapel, painted by Benozzo Gozzoli in 1452, and the pair from the life of Saint Bernardino from the chapel of San Bernardino, painted in 1461, attributed to a follower of Gozzoli.[79] Mezzastris had faithfully imitated Gozzoli's work from San Fortunato in Montefalco at San Girolamo, also under Eroli's patronage, so it is not surprising that he would turn to the artist for this commission as well. The imagery, which seems to record a moment of reconciliation between the

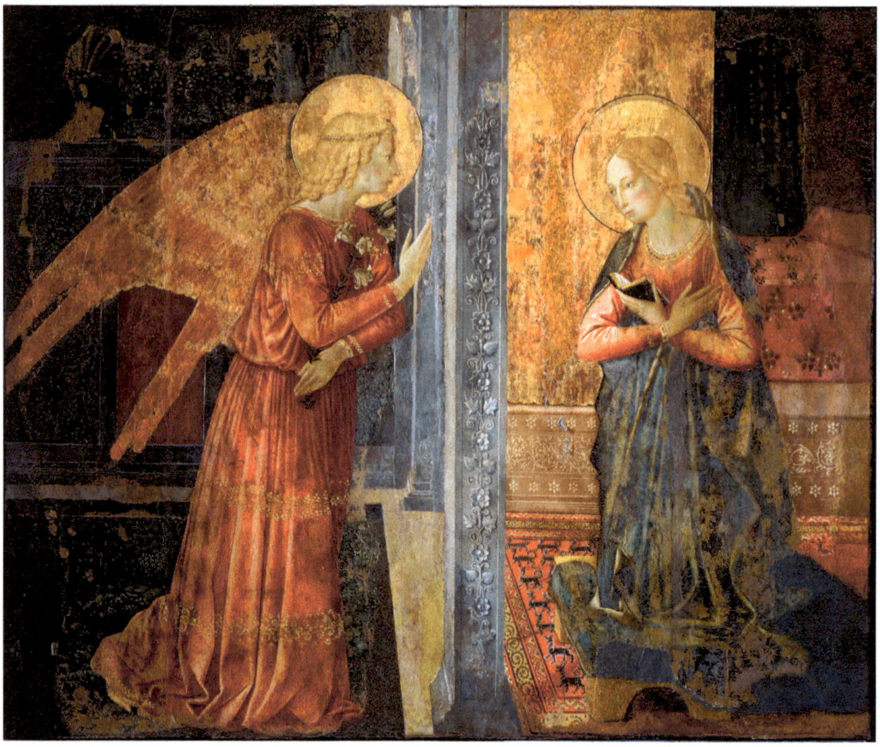

4.9. Benozzo Gozzoli, *Annunciation*, c. 1449, Pinacoteca Comunale, Narni. Photo: Scala / Art Resource, NY.

conventual and spiritual Franciscans, was most likely devised by Eroli and reflects his concerns in the mid-1460s, when the murals were probably painted. The sculpture of Saint Bernardino signed by the Sienese sculptor and painter Vecchietta, now in the Bargello in Florence, originally stood on the altar of the chapel and was probably part of the original program for the chapel as devised by Eroli.[80]

It may also be that Eroli was responsible for the earliest employment of Benozzo Gozzoli in Umbria. As we have seen, Gozzoli worked extensively in Rome – in the Vatican with Fra Angelico (1448) and in the mother church of the Franciscan observants in the Aracoeli (1447–49).[81] Eroli knew his work, most likely from the time he arrived in Rome in the late 1440s. An *Annunciation* in Narni is signed by the artist, and based on visual evidence, it has been dated to about 1449, that is, just before the artist's work in San Fortunato in Montefalco (Figure 4.9).[82] The panel is in very poor condition, but an inscription, OPV[S] BENOTI[I[DE FLORENT[IA], is tooled in gold along the border of the brocaded curtain to the left of the Virgin. The altarpiece was originally painted for the Dominican church of Santa Maria Maggiore in Narni, although Guardabassi saw it at the end of the nineteenth century in San Domenico.[83] Perhaps Eroli's link to the panel is indicated in the foliate decoration of the central pier in the composition, which clearly depicts pointed leaves of ivy, similar to those featured on Eroli's coat of arms.[84] Eroli may have facilitated Gozzoli's work from 1450 in Montefalco, which was part of his diocese, although the connection cannot be documented.[85]

In Narni, Eroli's patronage extended to the cathedral of San Giovanale, where the choir stalls (1474) bear his coat of arms. In his testament, he provided for the chapel of San Leonardo (no longer extant) in the cathedral, where his parents were buried. Eroli's nephew, Costantino, buried the cardinal in a decorous tomb by Giovanni Dalmata in Old Saint Peter's, fragments of which survive in the Vatican Grotte.[86] Eroli's employment of artists from Siena and Florence, such as Vecchietta and Ghirlandaio, as well as local artisans such as Mezzastris, points to a wide-ranging network of contacts forged in Rome and elsewhere.

THE APSE IN SPOLETO CATHEDRAL

We do not know how Eroli came to enlist Fra Filippo Lippi for his projects in the cathedral of Spoleto. Vasari says he had been advised to employ Lippi by Cosimo de' Medici.[87] Surviving letters from Eroli in the archive of the Medici Avanti il Principato in Florence, however, were mostly from the 1470s and written to Lorenzo di Piero, not his grandfather, and none of them addressed cultural matters.[88] The earliest, from 1462, was sent to Giovanni di Cosimo, the brother of Piero, not to their father.[89] Giovanni di Cosimo, as we have seen in Chapter 3, was a patron actively engaged with artists. His 1456 commission to Lippi of an altarpiece for King Alfonso of Naples is well known, as is Lippi's letter to Giovanni from 1457, complete with a sketch of the altarpiece with its elaborate frame.[90] The tone of Lippi's letter, familiar yet deferent, suggests an ongoing relationship.

Eroli could also have encountered Lippi in Perugia during one of his visits to the city; Lippi evaluated Bonfigli's work in the Palazzo dei Priori in September 1461, but he was known in the city by the 1450s.[91] We know from a letter of 1438 from Domenico Veneziano, then in Perugia, to Piero de' Medici, in which he refers to Fra Filippo, that Lippi's reputation had reached a certain audience in Perugia by then.[92] According to Vasari, Lippi painted an altarpiece of the *Virgin and Child with Saints* for the church of San Domenico Vecchio in Perugia.[93] This work may be the one commissioned by Antonio del Branca, a Perugian citizen resident in Florence, who noted in the contract "the fame of the said Fra Filippo as a singular and worthy man in the field of painting."[94] Lippi filed a suit against Branca with the merchants' court in 1451 for nonpayment. The suit was decided in Lippi's favor, and he received final payment on 25 September 1451.

Another point of contact between Eroli and Lippi may have been Saint Antoninus, archbishop of Florence. Some of Eroli's letters to Antoninus survive, although they do not mention artists.[95] Antoninus knew Lippi but perhaps not in the way that would result in a favorable recommendation. In 1455, the archbishop rejected Lippi's appeal to retain his position as rector at San Quirico at Legnaia, a position he had held since 1442 but from which he was removed for neglect of his duties.[96]

However it was that Lippi came to be employed in the cathedral of Spoleto, Eroli's involvement is attested to in the surviving expense records, which reveal in considerable detail the progress of the work.[97] While known since their publication in 1915 by Luigi Fausti, they are transcribed in full for the first time in Appendix IV. It is worth rereading these records because they reveal contemporaneous projects in several areas of the cathedral and the furious pace of activity. The payments, like those from Prato examined in Chapter 1, reveal relationships between workers and patrons and among artisans, and they offer insights into the context and motives for their actions. The payments are recorded in a volume called an *Entrata e Uscita* that begins 29 January 1465 for the *entrata* (income) and 11 January for the *uscita* (expenses) and ends 26 July and 30 August 1505, respectively.[98] The chamberlain and the *operai* are named at the beginning of each year, which in the papal states began on 1 January. The account book seems to have been dedicated to projects undertaken in the cathedral; entries in the existing volume refer to a *libro di cottimo* and a *libro di debitori* that no longer survive. The chamberlain also refers to his *libro di memorie* at one point, also unknown.[99] In the surviving ledger, payments related to construction and repairs to the fabric of the church and adjacent structures included materials and labor, as well as objects such as clappers for bells to ring on Good Friday.[100] Interspersed are payments for a wide range of services, such as for notaries in conjunction with bequests to the Opera, or for crushing olives. Workers were paid regular salaries for playing the organ and maintaining the roof.[101] The Opera del Duomo, as in the case of Prato and Pisa, was a lay board governing the management of the cathedral fabric.[102] At the time of Lippi's employment, the board included the chamberlain Giordano di Tommaso and the *operai* Cesari d'Angelo and Vanni di Girolamo. In 1467, Vanni was replaced by Tommaso di Giacomo di Pietro Paulo. As we will see, however, the bishop of Spoleto, referred to as *Monsignore* either personally, or through his vicar, was the real impetus for most of the activity in the church.[103]

Lippi first arrived in Spoleto on 1 May 1466 accompanied by Tommaso di Giacomo da Spoleto, who had been sent to Prato by the Opera to fetch him. That day Lippi received nine florins for coming to Spoleto and for the expense of his return.[104] The advance payment for his return suggests he was meant to stay only a short time. He seems to have left Spoleto to return to Florence sometime after 2 July, at which time he was paid more than 77 florins, the equivalent of 50 papal ducats "as part of the 700 ducats he will have for painting the tribune."[105] This payment is revealing; the artist's total compensation was to be 700 ducats, which, when converted to florins amounted to the substantial payment of about 1,100 florins.[106] In his recently completed murals for the main chapel in the cathedral of Prato, a much larger project that took more than fourteen years, Lippi was paid 1,962 florins, although exact comparisons are difficult because the expenses, especially for precious materials such as gold leaf and pigments, were structured differently. In Spoleto, the purchases of materials were made by designated agents of the Opera, sometimes venturing as far as Venice, and by the artist; while in Prato, Lippi secured materials directly from suppliers.

Another curious aspect of these payments is that, while all the other payments listed in the ledger are in Florentine florins, the payments to Lippi are cited in papal ducats, though they were converted, and the actual payouts were made in florins. The reason for this arrangement may be the original terms of Lippi's agreement with the Opera. While the original contract for the project does not survive, we may have a reference to it in the final payment for the work. After Lippi's death, a payment of 210 florins was made on 23 February 1470 to his longtime collaborator Fra Diamante.[107] The payment was made by the Opera officials "at the command . . . of the vicar of *Monsignore* of Spoleto." The entry refers to a written document "by the hand of Golino di Govanni, the notary of the Episcopal Camera." This wording suggests that the notarial document was not simply a payment order but was more likely a contract that specified the total compensation. If so, it may be that Eroli had commissioned Lippi through a contract drawn up by the bishop's notary – not by the notary of the Opera del Duomo, or any of the other notaries that the Opera employed, as would seem normal if the Opera had been the patron. The Opera del Duomo was responsible for the disbursement of the payments, but not, it would seem, for the expenses.[108] It is telling that the Opera del Duomo played a minor role in the commission, unlike the projects discussed in previous chapters in Prato and Pisa. Spoleto's communal government, as part of the papal states, was subject to church control that was more intrusive than in the Tuscan cities discussed above. The accounts reveal Eroli as the prime patron for the apse redecoration, and the civic themes of the Tuscan projects are muted. The *chiesa cittadina* that we saw emerge in fourteenth-century Pisa and Prato, in which secular and clerical concerns were balanced, seems absent in Spoleto. If Eroli were the true patron, as seems likely, it is understandable that the payments are quoted in papal ducats, the currency of the papal states. However, most of the payments in the ledger are listed in florins, perhaps used as money of account. That Lippi's payments were made in florins, converted at a stated rate from ducats, is shown by the occasional mention of expenses for currency exchange.

It seems, also, that Eroli provided a large part of the funds. The very first payment to Lippi, on 2 July 1466, for seventy-seven florins, the equivalent of fifty papal ducats, was made on the same day that Pier Nicola di Manzolo da Spoleto, another artisan, was paid by the vicar of *Monsignore*, that is, the bishop, for making a door for the chapel of the icon.[109] Lippi's payment followed immediately, and these two payments were the only ones recorded that day. An entry on the same day in the records of the *entrata* that recorded the donation of fifty ducats to the opera by the bishop confirms Eroli's role.[110]

A payment made on the previous 8 February for more than 105 florins for gold, ultramarine, and other things was likely made in anticipation of the mural project.[111] If so, the payments suggest that an agreement with the painter may have already been in the works months in advance of Lippi's arrival in Spoleto. While these first expenses for materials were not charged against Lippi's compensation, later payments for these materials were counted as part of the total expense of 700 ducats specified in the contract, as was frequently the case.[112] In fact, according to Fausti's calculation, with expenses for his household, pigments, and materials, Lippi paid 246 florins, 86 soldi, and 3 denari, an equivalent of over 161 ducats, or not quite a quarter of the total sum of 700 ducats.[113] The expenses charged against the 700 ducat total are generally flagged *frate Filippo* written in the margins of the account book, perhaps helping the bookkeeper tally. On 8 October 1468, about eighteen months after Lippi began work and fourteen months before the murals were finished, a mid-way summation indicated Filippo had been paid more than 444 florins, equivalent to just over 290 ducats of the promised 700. By Fausti's calculation, subsequent payments up to 30 September 1469 total over 338 florins, bringing his payment just before his death close to 511 ducats. Between then and the final payment to Fra Diamante on 23 February 1470, his son Filippino collected 48 ducats, bringing the total payments to Lippi of 696 ducats, close to the 700 figure cited in references to the contract. Fausti reckoned that little of this amount could be counted as profit except perhaps the more than 76 florins that he sent to Prato to buy a house in early 1468.[114] The Opera seems to have been responsible for Lippi's housing, renting several abodes for him during his stay. They also bore the cost of repair to the cathedral roof, materials and construction of the wall, the scaffolding, and plastering of the apse that preceded the painting.

The chronology of the work can be summarized based on these payments. Lippi spent two months in Spoleto during his initial visit between May and July 1466. During this time, payments were made to two innkeepers for food and lodging for the painter. In addition, on 21 June, the Opera purchased a saddle for Lippi's return trip.[115] There is no indication of what Lippi did during this time, but it can be imagined he made preliminary measurements and drawings for the mural. He also likely traveled to sites in and near Spoleto, perhaps making drawings of some of the distinctive monuments of the city, such as the cathedral itself, local churches, and the surrounding countryside.[116] References to these monuments appear in the architectural details of the murals.

In September, perhaps to incentivize him to return, the Opera sent Piermatteo di Caracosa to Florence to deliver the equivalent of fifty ducats to Lippi, received by him on 1 October.[117] Piermatteo must have been a kind of sacristan, as he was paid a salary of over fifteen florins as caretaker of the sacred icon for two years, 1465 and 1466. Two more times Piermatteo traveled to Florence, for which he was paid on 12 November and on 21 December. On the second occasion, he waited three days for Lippi before journeying to Prato to find him.[118] These visits did not result in Filippo's move to Spoleto, perhaps because he was involved in other projects, or because mid-winter is not the best time to work in fresco.

The artist finally arrived in Spoleto on 26 April 1467, when he was paid the equivalent of fifteen ducats, which he sent back to Florence to his assistants.[119] From this point on, the payments were frequent and record expenses for Lippi's personal needs, for his workshop, and household, which included his assistant Fra Diamante and young son Filippino.[120] Characteristically precise, they reveal with great immediacy quotidian details of the celebrated artist's life. The Opera rented him a house and they paid for services such as sweeping it out or digging the ground in the "garden of friar Filippo."[121] Gifts such as a pair of capons, a kid, pigeons, melons, and other fruit indicate the Opera's regard for the artist.[122] Lippi himself paid for food and wine, rent for beds and kitchen utensils, and occasionally for clothing, such as *Perpignano* fabric (a woolen jersey fabric originally made by weavers in Perpignan, France) to make stockings for Filippino.[123]

The payments also indicate that Lippi worked steadily on the mural from then until his death more than two years later, on 10 October 1469. He traveled back to Florence at least once, where on 1 September 1468 he requested a favor from Lorenzo di Piero de'Medici; of other travel we have no indication in the records.[124] Often Lippi sent his assistant on the road; Fra Diamante went to Florence in June 1467 and in May and June 1468, to Rome in May 1468, and again in May of 1469.[125] Bouts of illness, recorded in purchases of medicine and visits from doctors in April and November 1468 and in 1469, might indicate some interruption in the work, but these seem not to have been protracted.[126]

Scaffolding construction began soon after Lippi's arrival in Spoleto, with frequent expenses for materials and labor from 5 May 1467 through August. In September, payments for sand, specifically *rena sottile* – fine sand perhaps for the upper layer of plaster (the *intonaco*) – lime and *crocioli da mettere colori* – small saucers for pigments – indicate painting had finally begun. The scaffolding was taken down and reconstructed in November 1468, indicating that perhaps the first phase of painting, probably of the *Coronation*, had been completed and that the lower level containing the narrative scenes had begun.[127] *Certi garzoni* were paid to carry away wood from the dismembered scaffolding, and workers were paid to make holes for iron curtain rods on 24 of December; Fra Diamante was paid for its disassembly on 31 December 1469.[128]

The scaffolding must have been carefully designed for the project, undoubtedly at Lippi's direction.[129] It made use of an existing stairway from the chapel of the icon to the organ loft to access the structure by way of a small bridge (*pontecello*) constructed from the organ.[130] Cloth was purchased to encase the scaffolding, and a door with a lock was installed.[131] In addition, it allowed the painter access to the full width of the wall surface to be painted in its two configurations, one for painting the *Coronation* and the other for the narrative scenes on the lower level.

Analysis of the *giornate* that were mapped during the last restoration confirm these assumptions and offer insights into how Lippi organized the work.[132] These unpublished maps suggest a procedure that encouraged the participation of assistants during execution. The artist started the *Coronation of the Virgin* in the center at the top, including the apex of the architectural frame and the tall, gesturing angel at the left; he then proceeded to paint the head and upper garment of the standing angel holding a basin below at the left and the two lower left framing elements. A second sequence began with the lower part of the standing angel and proceeded down through the head and body of the seated Jonah. Meanwhile, he began the throng of angels in the middle left, starting with heads and torsos, moving in a zigzag pattern from left to right. While the diagram makes it seem that this was done in linear sequence, it is not hard to imagine that these figures could have been painted in tandem; that is, one artist completing the lower part of a figure, while on the scaffolding next to him his collaborator was beginning the head or heads of the next sequence to the right.

In general, the *giornate* reveal that Lippi worked from the peripheral areas toward the center, where what Virilli calls "hinge" *giornate* united the two sides. This reading suggests that painters were working concurrently in two or three zones, occupying a single scaffolding – a work organization that has been discovered in other projects.[133] For the smaller murals on the walls of the apse below the semi-dome – probably painted after restructuring of the scaffolding in November 1468 – the *giornate* suggest that they, too, were executed in zones.

No holes from the scaffolding that might offer clues to how this was constructed were discovered during the restoration, likely due to later alterations to the apse. We have a general idea of its structure from technical and visual evidence. Depictions of builders' scaffolds attached to the wall show that wooden supports sunk at right angles into the wall were commonly used.[134] Scaffoldings could be crowded with workers performing various tasks, such as grinding pigments on a stone slab with a muller – the dome-shaped, flat-bottomed stone. Furthermore, subdivisions in level of the scaffolding were erected with ladders and stepstools, thereby minimizing the considerable effort to reposition the entire scaffolding. Payment for one such *scaletta* was recorded in the accounts.[135]

The payment records indicate the murals were painted quickly. Starting in 1468, expenses for medical treatment are mentioned. When Filippo died in October 1469, the work must have been almost complete, because it required only until the end of December for his main assistant, Fra Diamante, to finish the job.

The last restoration has also revealed the exceptional variety of Lippi's technique. Except for the decorative borders, Lippi avoided the use of detailed cartoons – a practice widely in use by the 1460s by Tuscan painters to ensure precise transfer of figural designs worked out in small scale. Instead, he freely drew his designs on the wet plaster. He must have prepared at least a general design in small scale of the whole composition beforehand and perhaps also for individual figures. Application of the *intonaco* followed a freely sketched *sinopia* design on the *arriccio*, visible now only at the lower right of the *Coronation* where the *intonaco* has fallen away. For architecture, however, multiple incisions indicate careful preparation. Widespread use of painting *a secco*, after the plaster had dried, has been discovered and with it a rich surface more like paintings on panel than on a wall. That this *a secco* treatment was not merely a finishing layer, but planned from the outset, is suggested by the application of gold, which is exceptionally lavish and nuanced. Gilding was applied both in liquid form, with a brush, or in sheets, often over wax bosses that were graduated in size and placement to produce dazzling light effects, especially in the haloes and angel wings.

While the *giornate* maps indicate rapid execution, the repeated return of the painter to the wall to work *a secco* must therefore modify our view of the work's progress and might also give us pause in the search for individual assistant's "hands" in the execution. In addition, as Benazzi pointed out, Lippi's extemporaneous manner required the constant presence of the master on the scaffolding and implied continuous interaction with his assistants.[136] His forgoing of cartoons might suggest he conceived the act of painting as virtuoso performance rather than simply rote transfer of the design and execution. In showcasing an intuitive process, he underscored the mastery of his skill and the imaginative scope of his creativity. The immediate audience would only have been Lippi's coworkers, but his previous work in Prato and his panel paintings followed this procedure. It may have contributed to the exceptional fame that brought him to Spoleto in the first place. The extensive work *a secco* has also had severe consequences for the legibility of the murals. The most dramatic example – the figure group of the Virgin being assumed into heaven while handing her girdle to Saint Thomas – has almost entirely disappeared. The analysis of the pigments done during restoration has also revealed an exceptional range, many of them, azurite, ultramarine (made from lapis lazuli), and *verderame* (verdigris or copper acetate), generally restricted to application *a secco*.[137] Again, the surviving payments corroborate the restoration findings: payments for gold and ultramarine are frequently cited.

The apse murals were finished under the direction of Fra Diamante, as is borne out by the payments made slightly more than two months after Lippi's death. It seems likely that little remained to be done. The last purchases for materials included a small amount of ultramarine on 10 September and gold leaf on 11 October.[138] Fra Diamante was still in Spoleto on 23 February 1470, but by 24 May 1470 he had returned to Prato. Filippino, who as Lippi's heir was named in the payments for the remainder of the project, returned to Florence shortly after the mural was finished.[139]

While the accounts provide a keyhole view of the chronology and the organization of the worksite for the apse murals, they also reveal contemporaneous projects in the cathedral. From the dense detail of the payments emerges a frenetic campaign of renewal; the apse mural was not the only, or even the most ambitious project undertaken at this time in the Duomo of Spoleto. For the entire second half of the fifteenth century, construction projects were ongoing: efforts to erect a retaining wall against the slope to the southeast of the cathedral, toward the Rocca, to dig ditches for better drainage, and to build a wall and erect a new roof over the apse.[140] The east end of the cathedral was a particular focus in the years before Lippi's appearance on the scene. The master, Battista da Campello, was paid regularly for work on the roof of the tribuna, the sacristy, and the organ loft.

The modifications to the cathedral were contemporaneous with urban renewal projects: renovations to the Palazzo del Podestà and Palazzo dei Priori. The city walls were repaired, four towers were added, and the porta San Pietro and porta San Gregorio were reinforced, among other projects.[141] Joint projects of the commune and the church were instigated by Eroli, to whom Sansi ascribes rebuilding of the archbishop's palace and the decoration of the piazza del Duomo with a fountain.[142]

Inside the church, in 1469, also at Eroli's initiative, artisans began reconstruction of the chapels on either side of the nave; the left, north chapels *verso la canonica* were completed in 1470, but those off the right aisle *verso la rocca* were begun in 1473 and only finished in 1488.[143] The placement and semicircular plan of the chapels are reminiscent of Brunelleschi's design for Santo Spirito in Florence, which seems to have been widely influential, also in Rome in the rebuilding of San Marco and Sant'Agostino.[144] In the cathedral of Spoleto, they may have been intended to systematize the array of chapels, altars, and funerary monuments that are mentioned in documents and must have crowded the nave and aisles.[145] The accounts also identify many of the chief artisans involved in these projects, and, like Lippi, some of them were Tuscan and had links to projects underway in Rome at the time. Master Giacomo da Pietrasanta had worked in Rome for Popes Pius II and Paul II – including, just before he appeared in Spoleto, renovations to the church of San Marco. [146] He was paid on 18 January 1469, having been sent by *Monsignore* to construct the chapel or chapels in the cathedral.[147] He and his assistant, Francesco da Bologna, were cited frequently in the payments for the chapels off the north aisle between 1469 and 1470.[148] Giacomo returned in 1473 with assistants Matteo di Francesco da Settignano, called Rosso, and Leonardo di Cristoforo da Pietrasanta, brother of Giacomo, to construct the chapels off the south aisle from 1473 to 1485.[149] Hence, Eroli's guiding hand in the renovation of the Romanesque church seems clear and suggests a taste for sophisticated, up-to-date design practiced by Tuscan artists in Rome.

Perhaps the most important of the projects Eroli spearheaded in the cathedral was the construction of a new chapel to house the *Santissima Icone*. Cecco di Luca da Spoleto had been employed by the cathedral authorities since 1456 for various projects in the church and the piazza.[150] In May of 1458, the *operai* engaged him to repair the roof of the tribune, "to improve the repair of the roof and covering so that it does not rain in the church." The new chapel project began in 1463 with an agreement between the *operai* and Cecco to construct a large wall.[151] On 21 October 1466, he also received payment for a door in the chapel of the icon that "leads to the organs." Other artisans were involved; on 2 July 1466, Pier Nicola di Manzolo da Spoleto was paid more than 22 florins, which he had "from the vicar of *Monsignore*," that is, the bishop; and on 2 September 1466, a laborer was paid to transport marble for the doorway to the chapel of the icon from the bishop's palace to the church.[152] Eroli's impetus behind this project is confirmed by the heretofore unpublished payment on 26 December 1466, again to master Pier Nicola di Manzolo, for "a crowning (*frontone*) above the door [to the chapel of the icon] with the arms of *Monsignore*."[153] The chapel was perhaps not in use right away, for almost two years later the floor was paved and hardware, including a lock, was purchased for the door.[154] Nonetheless, Piermatteo di Caracosa was paid a salary as a guardian or sacristan in the chapel, starting in 1465.[155]

While we lack precise evidence, this new chapel was likely located next to the tribune to the south, where the sacristy and the organ were located. Bozzoni and Carbonara posit that this chapel may be the space that was referred to later as the old sacristy.[156] Work on the chapel was done in tandem with repairs to the roofs of the chancel and sacristy, for the relocation of the organ, and renovation of the sacristy including a new chimney, implying that they were in close proximity.[157] As mentioned, Lippi's scaffolding for the apse was accessed by a little bridge from the organ loft, reached through a stairway, probably from the new chapel.

In addition to the more than 192 florins paid to Cecco di Luca for construction of the chapel, other artisans were named in the ledgers in connection with its construction, for example, to measure the wall built by Cecco, build the roof, pave the floor, and supply hardware for the doors. A sum of approximately 200 florins was paid to these artisans, thus marking the chapel of the icon, at almost 400 florins total cost, as one of the most expensive endeavors in the cathedral during this time.

Much of what is recorded in the payments was destroyed by subsequent alterations to the church, most notably in the seventeenth-century renovations under Pope Urban VIII (r. 1623–44), who as Maffeo Barberini had been bishop of Spoleto between 1608 and 1617.[158] After Maffeo's elevation to the papacy in 1623, the work was carried on by his nephew, Francesco Barberini, and finished only in 1668. Giuseppe Valadier constructed new altars and portals between 1785 and 1792.[159] Valadier's plans foresaw demolishing the apse and reconstructing an enlarged choir and apse with rich stucco decoration and dramatic lighting. Opposition to this part of Valadier's project assured that Lippi's murals escaped destruction.[160]

As we see it today, Lippi's mural cycle in Spoleto is a fragment. While the apse was preserved, much of the decorative and figurative elements of the triumphal arch was destroyed, as was the architectural framing of the apse itself (see reconstruction, Figure 4.10). Fragmentary angels holding scrolls on the triumphal arch indicate the loss of pictorial surface; the painted piers framing the narrative scenes have disappeared. The transepts and presbytery, originally elevated above the floor level of the nave, were lowered in the baroque refurbishment. The nineteenth-century choir stalls further obscure the original wainscoting and reduce the architectural context of the murals. Vast areas of *a secco* painting have fallen away, resulting in a loss of detail and color. A restoration undertaken from 1987 to 1990 has revealed the vibrant colors of Lippi's work, but it could not put back the rich surface effects that must have characterized his original painting.[161]

THE *CORONATION OF THE VIRGIN* IN SPOLETO AND ROME

It has often been noted by scholars that the Spoleto apse murals recall in their subject and general design the mosaic in the apse of Santa Maria Maggiore in Rome (Figure 4.11).[162] The Roman mosaic was undertaken by Pope Nicholas IV (r. 1288–92), signed by the artist Jacopo Torriti, and was formerly dated by inscription to 1296.[163] It was part of a much larger project in the church, which included a Last Judgment on the interior façade and mural decoration of the

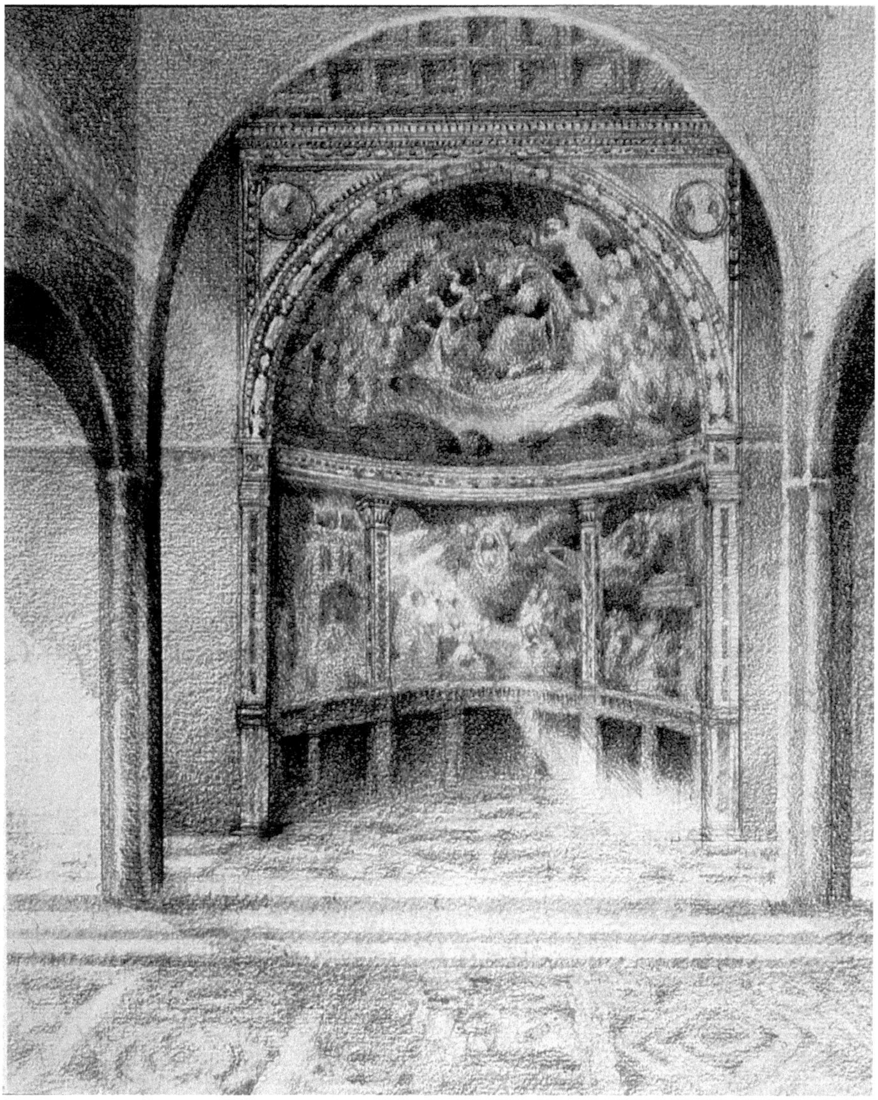

4.10. Reconstruction of the Apse, Duomo, Spoleto, by Mario Brunetti, from Giordana Benazzi and Paolo Virilli, *Filippo Lippi nel Duomo di Spoleto 1467–1469; Notizie dopo il restauro*, Spoleto: Panetto & Petrelli, 1992, p. 6, fig. 2.

transepts, including a Genesis cycle and large roundels, perhaps to be filled with prophets. Much of this decoration was either destroyed or never completed.[164]

The two designs share many features. The Roman *Coronation of the Virgin* occupies the center of the semi dome encircled by the cosmic spheres, studded with stars, with the sun and moon below. To each side, throngs of angels press toward the center. Further to the sides of the conch, saints and other holy figures turn to observe the heavenly sight. The alignment on the vertical axis of the *Dormition*, out of chronological order in the narrative scenes of the Virgin's

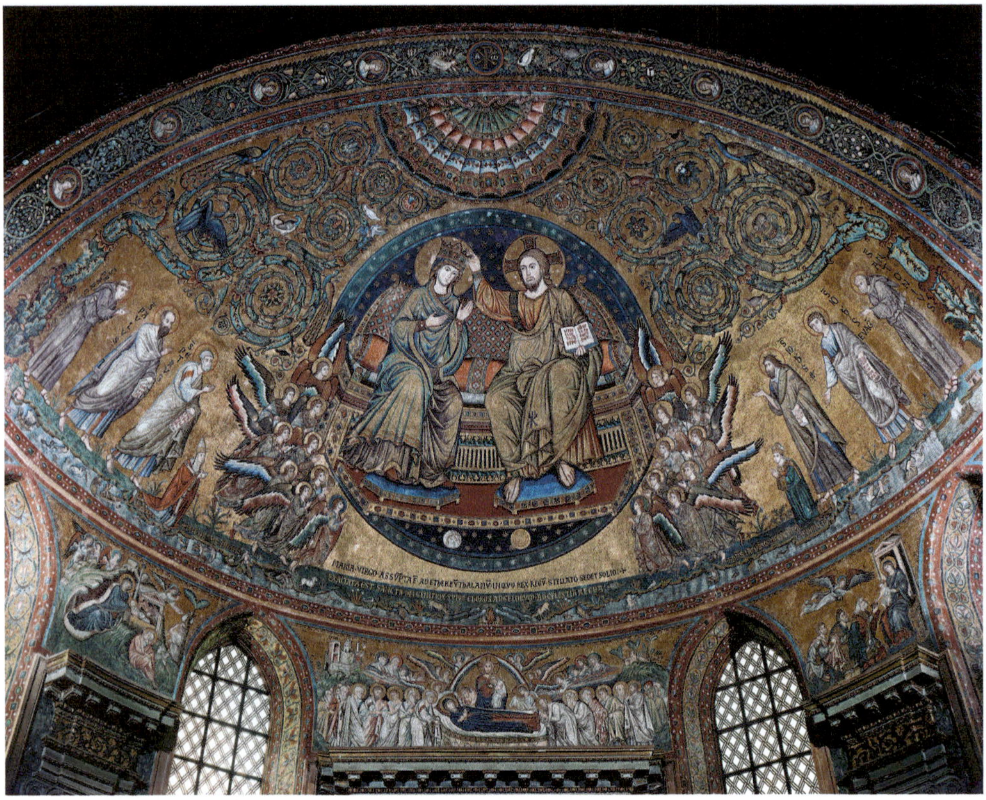

4.11. Jacopo Torriti, *Coronation of the Virgin*, 1296, Santa Maria Maggiore, Rome. Photo: Scala / Art Resource, NY.

life below the *Coronation*, is a distinctive aspect of the Roman work that is repeated in Spoleto.

As has been noted, the cathedral of Spoleto was referred to contemporaneously as "Santa Maria Maggiore," although its official dedication to the Assumption appears to date only to the seventeenth century.[165] Spoleto, the ancient duchy under Lombard rule from the sixth century, was incorporated into the Carolingian empire in the eighth century and ceded to the Papal States in 1198.[166] From 1213, it was under direct control of the papacy, ruled by a governor, usually a cardinal, although communal institutions emerged in the course of the twelfth century to exercise some temporal power. Egidio Albornoz, as cardinal legate between 1353 and his death in 1367, reinforced papal authority by, among other things, building fortresses such as the Rocca of Spoleto (Figure 4.12).[167] Strategically placed high above the city, between the Nera river valley and the ancient via Flaminia, the Rocca controlled the traffic to and from Rome and was a powerful symbol of church authority. Very often, the papal-appointed governor of Spoleto and the *castellano* were one in the same person, usually a member of the pope's family, much against

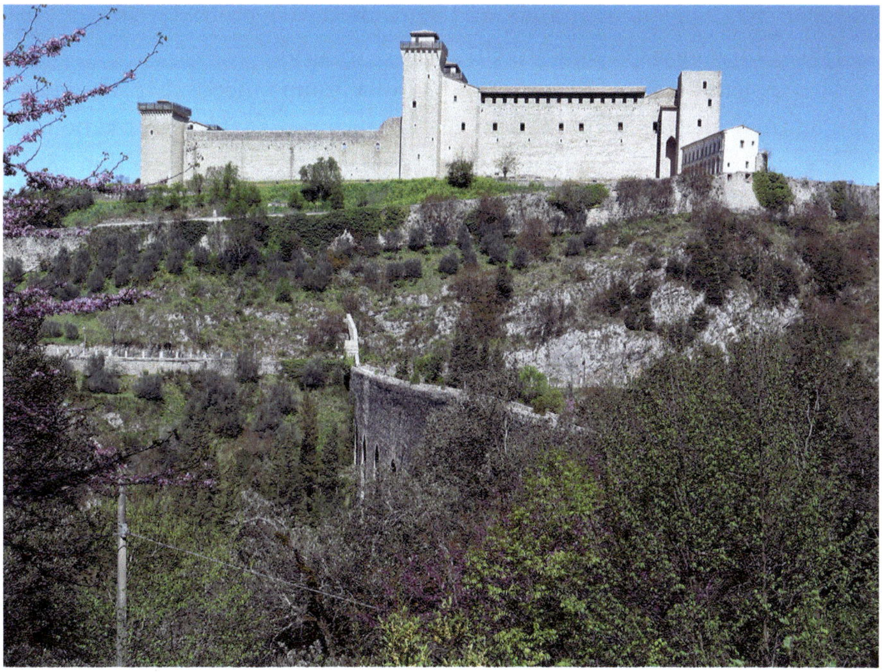

4.12. Rocca, begun 1359, Spoleto. Photo: Author.

the wishes of the city officials.[168] Hence, the link between Spoleto and Rome, while often contested, was well established. The pairing of Santa Maria in Spoleto with the papal basilica of Santa Maria Maggiore in Rome may have been only natural and widely understood. Eroli might also have been personally motivated to replicate the Roman *Coronation of the Virgin* in Spoleto. The rich abbey of the Three Fountains, of which he was commendatory abbot, was ornamented with an ancient mural of the Coronation, itself perhaps a predecessor of the mural in Santa Maria Maggiore.[169] Hence, bishop Eroli, deeply enmeshed in the papal court, may have sought to underscore the connection of his diocese with the Eternal City.

The relationship between the images in Rome and Spoleto extends to their ceremonial context. As related above, we know that a new chapel for the holy icon of Spoleto was being built at the same time as Lippi's murals were underway. Although nothing of this chapel remains today, the bishop's coat of arms crowning the chapel entrance suggests that it was likely commissioned by Bishop Eroli. An indication of the significance of the icon and its chapel is that, already by 1519, a new, lavish central plan chapel for the icon was planned that was never executed.[170] Yet again, between 1540 and 1545, another chapel was built on the site of the current chapel of the reliquaries, at the east end of the north aisle, to which the icon was transferred in 1561. In the seventeenth century, as we have seen, the ornate chapel was built where the icon was translated in 1668 and remains today, probably close to the location of the fifteenth-century chapel built by Eroli.[171]

The Spoleto *Madonna Avvocata* was part of a group of icons that was widely disseminated in Rome and the surrounding territory.[172] The most famous in Rome was from Santa Maria in Tempore, known as the San Sisto Madonna.[173] Painted in Byzantium, it is the oldest of a related group. The prestige of the San Sisto icon derived from its reputation as having been painted by Saint Luke. More than seven versions exist in Rome, including one in Santa Maria in Aracoeli. The proliferation of images reflects the belief that the power and authority of the original icon are replicated in its close copies. These images became powerful identifiers of the institutions in which they resided and of the congregations that worshiped there.

Like the Spoleto icon, the San Sisto icon shows the Madonna without the Child, but it differs in that the Virgin faces left rather than right, addresses the viewer directly, and, although she raises her hands, she does not hold a scroll. The San Sisto icon may have played a role in the well-known procession in Rome on the eve of the feast of the Assumption of the Virgin, celebrated on 15 August. In that procession, the sacred icon of Christ from the Sancta Sanctorum at the Lateran was taken to meet the icon at Santa Maria Maggiore, known as the *Salus Populi Romani*. The procession has been described as "a visit of Christ to his mother on her great Feast day, a palpable demonstration of the honor in which he held her," or, more explicitly, "the visit of Christ, who was fetching his mother up to heaven."[174] Themes of honor and triumph, and intercession and salvation reverberate in the accounts of the Assumption procession.[175] The procession also served as the prologue to her assumption into heaven where she sits enthroned aside her Son. Accounts of the processional route differ and undoubtedly changed over time; all include the starting point at the Lateran, a route through the ancient forum, to the church of Saint Hadrian, formerly the ancient curia of the Roman Senate, and then to Santa Maria Maggiore. One version, dated to c. 1000, suggests that the procession passed by Santa Maria in Tempore, where the San Sisto icon was united with the Lateran Christ and may have been taken with it to Santa Maria Maggiore.[176] In another version, from about 1143, the Lateran icon stopped at Santa Maria Nova (renamed Santa Francesca Romana) in the Roman forum, site of another venerated icon of the *Madonna Avvocata*, where its feet were washed.[177] In a version of the procession in 1462, the people assembled in Santa Maria in Aracoeli, next to the Capitol, where they prayed before another version of the San Sisto Madonna before proceeding to the Sancta Sanctorum.[178]

The Assumption processions influenced the imagery of the *Coronation of the Virgin*.[179] The Coronation mosaic in Santa Maria in Trastevere from the early 1140s was the earliest example of the subject in the apse of a Roman church.[180]

The mosaic of the *Coronation of the Virgin* in Santa Maria Maggiore was made at the behest of Pope Nicholas IV and Cardinal Giacomo Colonna between 1292 and 1295.[181] The apse image in Santa Maria Maggiore generally imitates that in Santa Maria in Trastevere, but with significant innovations. In the newer image, Christ places a crown on the Virgin's head, a motif is derived from the liturgy.[182] Christ's gesture, referred to in Canticles 4:8, had appeared earlier in the twelfth century, especially in French portal sculpture.[183] The inscription beneath the Virgin's feet also presents the Virgin as the bride of Christ.[184] The scene of her Coronation represents the union of divinity and humanity as an indivisible marriage bond.

The Virgin in Santa Maria Maggiore extends her left hand outward in a gesture of advocacy, resembling images of the *Madonna Avvocata*. Scholars have pointed out that the Virgin's face in Santa Maria in Trastevere was modeled on the San Sisto icon or one of its variants.[185] The quotation of the icon, and its juxtaposition to the face of Christ, recalls the meeting of the two icons during the Assumption procession. The ceremony, as reconstructed from the various accounts, included carrying the Lateran icon to the apse of Santa Maria Maggiore and installing it on the pulpit used to read the gospels during Mass, inside the *schola cantorum*. Meanwhile, the sacred image of the Virgin and Child, the *Salus Populi Romani*, was brought from its shrine in the nave and installed on the pulpit at the right used to read from the Epistles of Saint Paul. Hence, the two icons resided in the *schola cantorum* side by side. As Kessler describes: "Escorting Christ and Mary into a sanctified chamber, the procession realizes the language of love from the Song of Songs and other texts underlying the liturgy of today's feast. Christ takes his mother to heaven, as a groom leads his bride into the wedding chamber. Enacted by two of Rome's principal icons, moreover, and under the auspices of the pope, the ceremony also symbolized the marriage with the Ecclesia Romana, the Church of Rome."[186] The Coronation mosaics in Santa Maria in Trastevere and Santa Maria Maggiore, by explicitly evoking these holy images and their encounter during the Assumption ceremony, recalled the event as experienced by worshippers. In adding references to the Virgin's role as advocate of humanity to the traditional themes of triumph, honor, and marital love in the Coronation scenes, the Roman mosaics iniated a distinctive iconographic tradition shaped by the Roman ceremony.

The apse in Santa Maria Maggiore depicts below the *Coronation* the earthly history of the Virgin: *Annunciation*, *Nativity*, *Dormition*, *Adoration of the Magi*, and *Presentation in the Temple*. As has been pointed out, these scenes firmly anchor the events of the last days of the Virgin in historical time. Moreover, in Santa Maria Maggiore, the alignment on the vertical axis of the *Dormition*, with Christ holding the soul of the Virgin, and *Coronation* creates an upward movement from earth, through the celestial spheres, to heaven, as the events took place in historical time and point to the end of time. In this sense, the procession as the event just preceding the Assumption – the approach of Christ who will bring his mother up to heaven – while not depicted, takes its place in the temporal sequence the narrative scenes depict.

Eroli's participation in the Assumption Day procession is undocumented, but it is likely. The 1462 description of the procession noted that the participants included clergy as well as the populace.[187] It is also noteworthy that he joined the confraternity of the Santissimo Salvatore, the sodality charged with carrying the Savior icon from the Sancta Sanctorum to Santa Maria Maggiore, among other duties, sometime after 1476.[188] The excerpt from his testament preserved in the archives of the hospital of the Santissimo Salvatore, a dependent of the confraternity, records his bequest of half of his Roman houses to the hospital; hence, he must have been involved before his death in 1479.

As mentioned above, whether a procession on the Assumption through the city with the *Madonna Avvocata* was performed in Spoleto in the fifteenth century is not known.[189] The records of the Duomo renovations perhaps provide a clue. A project carried out after Berardo Eroli's death but under the aegis of his nephew Costantino was the building of a new portico abutting the Duomo façade (Figure 4.13). The portico, called a vestibule or *trasanna* in the contract, was commissioned by the Opera del Duomo on 1 December 1491 to Antonio da Milano and Pippo di Antonio da Firenze.[190] At the time, Antonio was working in Urbino, while Pippo was resident in Rome. In elegant *all'antica* style, ornamented with colored marbles and relief carvings – all specified in great detail in the contract – the portico extended the interior refurbishment of the Duomo to the exterior, where the piazza had recently been repaved and a fountain erected.[191]

The portico created a new, updated public face of the cathedral, but it also had a liturgical function. Two pulpits flanked the five arched openings and were evidently used for public services, likely for readings of the gospels and epistles during Masses or for sermons. It might also have been used by civic leaders; Sansi found a reference to a pulpit in the old porch of the cathedral from which speakers addressed the assembled people.[192] Referring to a model supplied by Master Pippo, the contract called for a parapet with a balustrade above the entablature of the portico, furnished with candelabra and ornamented with narrative reliefs, and a balcony of some kind.[193] Perhaps the need to accent the central space also led to the slight widening of the central arch and projection forward of the flanking columns and entablature, with dark red capitals and the *stemma* of the commune carved in the oculi of the spandrels that we see today.

This ornamented and well-lighted space was where, as the documents reveal, the sacred icon of the Madonna was to be shown. The year before the contract for the new portico, work had begun to repair the old portico.

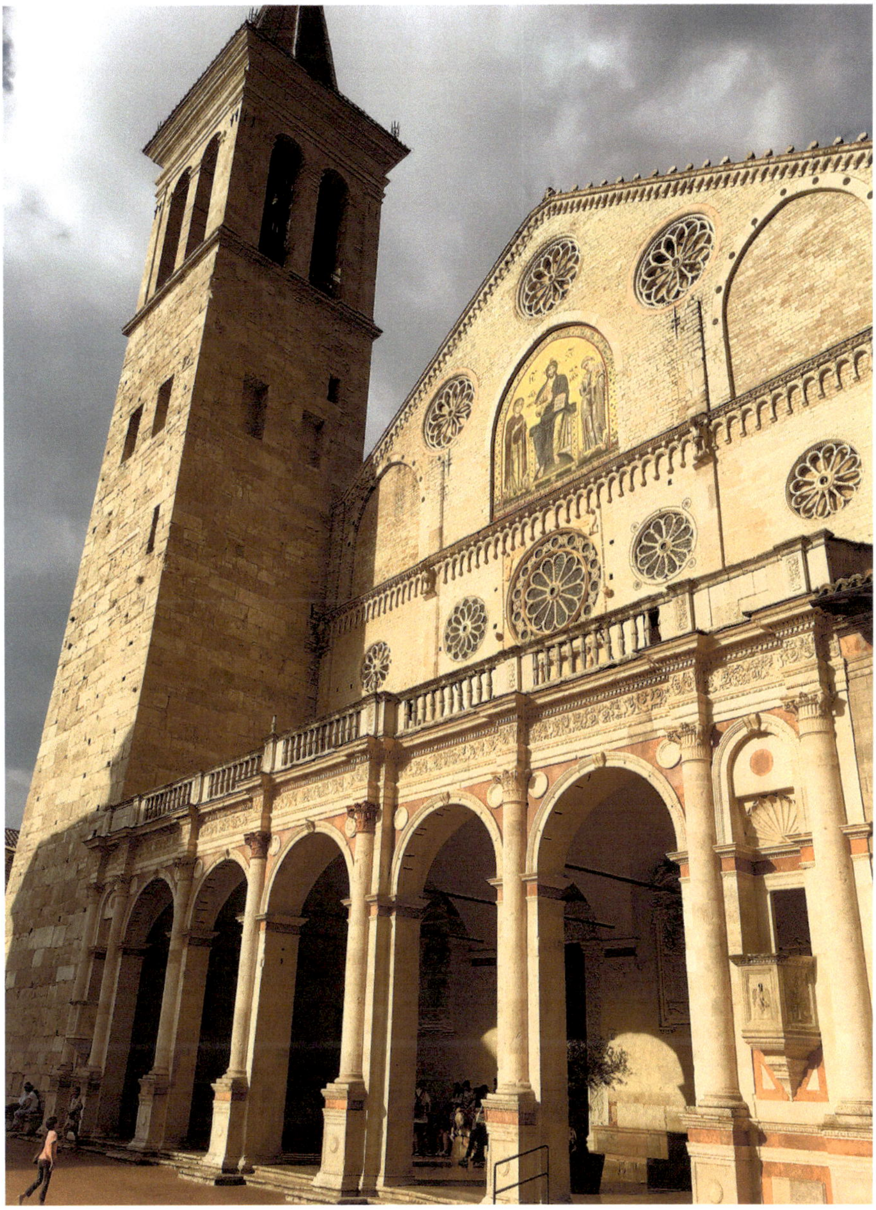

4.13. Portico, begun 1491, Duomo, Spoleto. Photo: Manuelarosi / Creative Commons Attribution-Share Alike 3.0 Unported.

A new wall adjacent to the old portico was built, and the roof of the old portico was repaired.[194] Payment of was made 15 September 1489 to master Giovanni Antonio da Como for building a wall "above the portico next to where the icon is shown."[195] At some point, Ceriana posits, a decision was made to rebuild the portico entirely, perhaps as a reflection of the importance the ostentation ceremony had assumed in the religious life of the town.[196] The sumptuous materials, architectural details, and figurative decor in an up-to-date classical style, executed by masters with experience of the most innovative structures in Rome and Urbino, would seem to be a fitting ambience for the ostentation ceremony.[197]

The contract for the portico also called for the master to construct a stairway, whose location was to be specified, from which the elevated space was reached.[198] That the portico served continuously as an podium from which the icon was displayed was confirmed by the account of Maffeo Barberini's pastoral visit in 1610, which stated that the icon was displayed from this spot on the feasts of the Annunciation and the Assumption.[199]

Hence, we might imagine that on these feast days, the *Madonna Avvocata* was taken from its chapel and displayed on the high altar during Mass. Probably after the service, it was processed at least as far as the portico of the façade for ostentation to the assembled worshippers in the piazza. Whether the procession ranged further into the city, before or after the ostentation, as in Prato with the Holy Belt, or like the Roman procession of the Savior icon, seems unlikely. However, since the habit of displaying the icon is referred to in the payments before the new portico was begun, and since an earlier portico is referred to in the contract as needing to be disassembled, we can infer that the display of the icon had gone on for some time before the construction of the new portico.

The display of the holy icon from the balcony above the portico might suggest another analogy of the Spoleto ceremony with that in Santa Maria Maggiore in Rome. The most prominent part of the Spoleto façade, centered beneath the gable on the upper level, is the mosaic of Christ flanked by the Virgin and Saint John the Evangelist, an image derived from Byzantine art called the *Deesis* (Figure 4.14).[200] Christ is seated on a backless throne, His right hand blessing, His left holding a book inscribed "I am the light of the world," from the gospel of Saint John (8:21). To his right stands the Virgin, who inclines her head toward Christ while her raised hands gesture toward Him. Saint John the Evangelist stands to his left, holding his gospel and gesturing toward Christ. The figures are clad in blues and purples, while the background is formed of gilded tesserae. The mosaic is dated by inscription to 1207.[201] When the icon was displayed from the balcony, it would have appeared below the rose window and the mosaic, inevitably bringing the two holy images together in view of the assembled populace. Nessi has stressed the unified effect of the façade – portico, tower, and mosaic – even in the twelfth century.[202]

As discussed above, we know that in Rome and in many surrounding small towns, the Assumption eve processions involved two images: of the Madonna and of Christ, imitating the Roman ceremony. In Tivoli, the climax of the procession was the ceremony of the *Inchinata*, when the images of Christ and the Virgin face each other in the piazza outside the church of Santa Maria Maggiore and bow. Taken inside, the icons were installed facing each other on either side of the nave, where they remained for the night.[203] In another

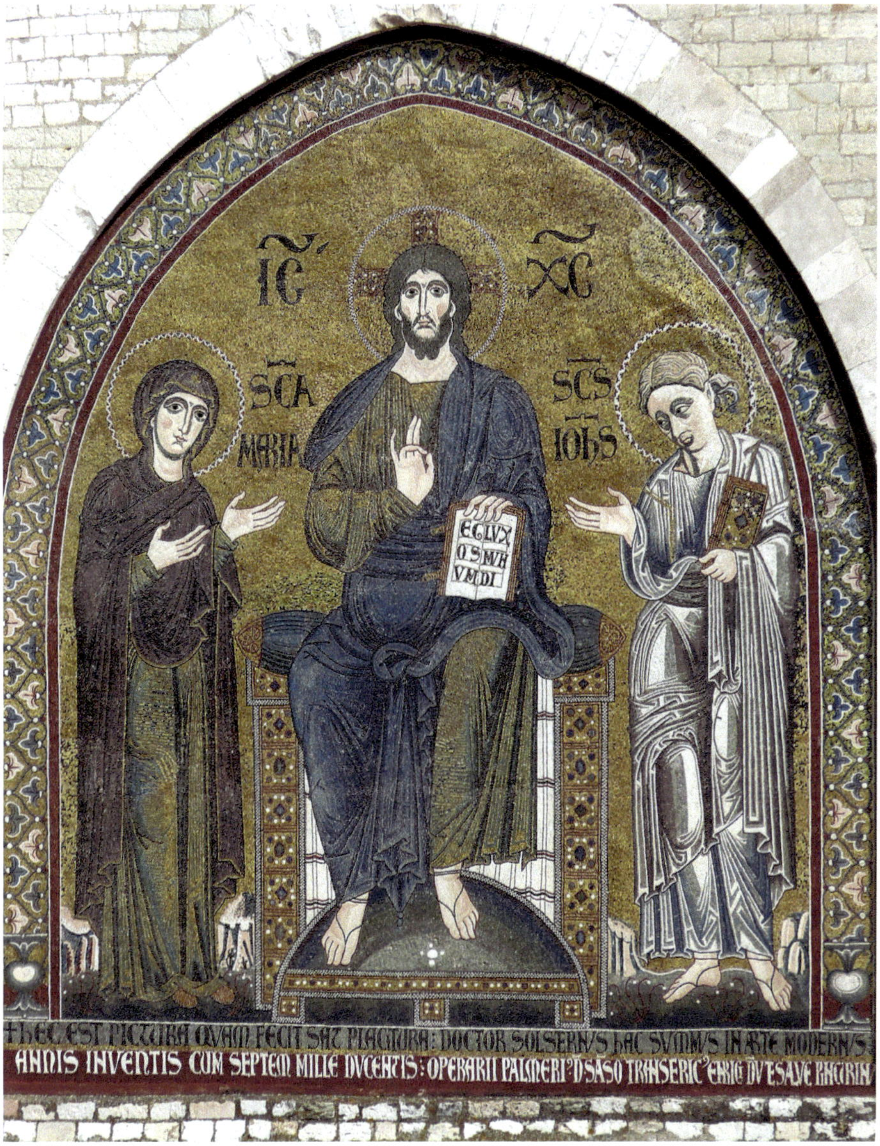

4.14. Solsterno (signed), *Christ, the Virgin, and St. John the Evangelist (Deesis)*, façade detail, 1207, Duomo, Spoleto. Photo: Sailko / Creative Commons Attribution 3.0 Unported.

regional variation in Orte, the Madonna icon was displayed at the right side of the high altar in the Cathedral, paired with an image of the Blessing Redeemer to the left.[204] In the Assumption procession, the Madonna icon traveled through the town, returning to the piazza in front of the cathedral, where it met the Redeemer icon. The ritual bowing of the images occurred at this moment, after which the Madonna image turned to face the populace, at the right of the Christ icon. The images then were taken again inside the church and installed at the sides of the altar, while Mass was celebrated.

We know from inventories of the sacristy that the Spoleto cathedral possessed no image of Christ comparable to those in Rome, Orte, or Tivoli.[205] Might the façade mosaic have served as the companion to the sacred image in the Spoleto ceremony? When the icon was displayed above the portico, brought into proximity with the mosaic of the façade, the ritual meeting of Christ and Madonna images that is the essence of the ceremonies in Rome and elsewhere might have been evoked in the Spoleto ceremony. The Roman icon, showing Christ seated on a throne, holding a scroll, and blessing with his right hand, was encased in a silver gilt covering at the end of the twelfth century.[206] The Savior's face, replicating the original, was added in the tenth century and is the only visible painted surface. Yet the image of the seated savior would be known to worshippers through its many replicas, as in the Tivoli image. The Tivoli icon depicts a seated Christ flanked by the Virgin and Saint John the Evangelist, as in the Spoleto mosaic. In the absence of any account of the ceremony, however, this question remains unanswered.

Yet the meaning of these ceremonies, in which the Madonna as Advocate for humankind comes together with her son as a prelude to her Assumption and Coronation, would undoubtedly have been understood in Spoleto. The façade mosaic would reinforce that meaning. The *Deesis*, called "the standard figuration of intercessory prayer in the Middle Ages," shows the Virgin with hands outstretched toward the enthroned Christ.[207] The Assumption feast was imbued with associations of intercession, and the Assumption itself was understood as the confirmation of Mary's special relationship with Christ and her central role in the salvation of humankind. Hence, the coming together of the *Deesis* and the *Madonna Avvocata* icon on the portico of the Duomo of Spoleto might be seen as a variation on the meeting of mother and son, performed during the Assumption procession in Rome. The subsequent removal of the icon to its place inside the cathedral, either on the altar or in the chapel adjacent to the apse, would then link the icon – physically and conceptually – to the apse murals depicting her triumphant Coronation.

The association, both liturgically and historically, of the icon of the *Madonna Avvocata* and the apse narrative of her last days in Lippi's new mural in Spoleto is therefore very likely, and it may have been the motivation for Bishop Eroli's concurrent projects in the cathedral to renovate the chapel of the icon and the apse mural. At the same time, repairs were made to the façade and portico. A new *telaro impannato* – that is, a frame with oiled cloth or paper covering – was erected on the rose window of the façade and a roof above the mosaic of the Savior constructed; the mosaic was also restored.[208] Hence, contemporaneously with the work in the tribune, and the chapels in the north aisle, improvements were made to the façade.

Similarly, the relationship of icon and apse would make the parallels between the cathedral and Santa Maria Maggiore in Rome even more explicit.

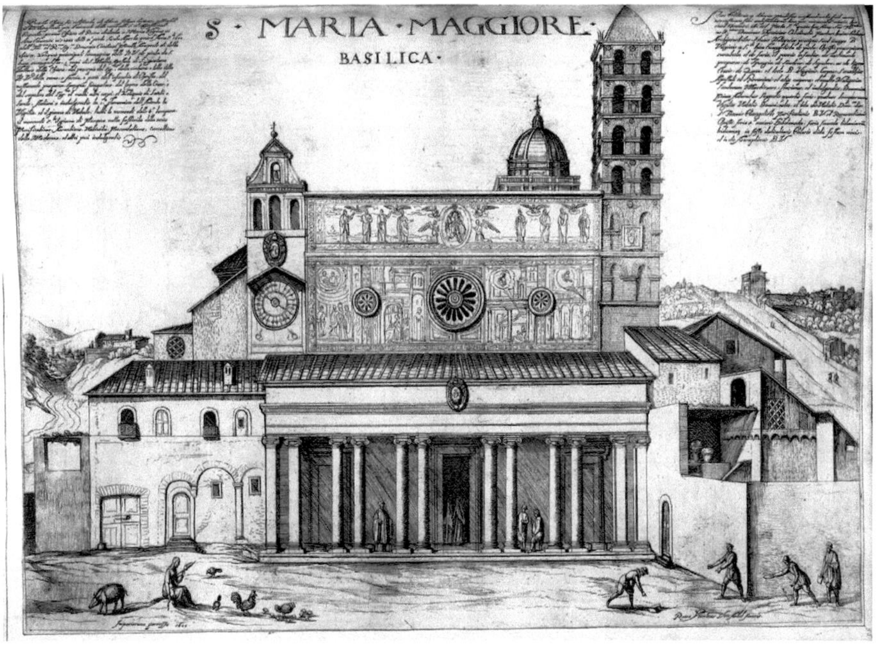

4.15. *Santa Maria Maggiore*, Rome, engraving. From Cassiano Dal Pozzo, *[Templa Diversa]*, 1541–1632, British Library, shelfmark: Maps 3 TAB.34. Photo: British Library.

Apart from their dedication to the Virgin, both church façades featured central rose windows with mosaics (Figure 4.15). In the fifteenth century, mosaics at Santa Maria Maggiore, completed in the 1290s, were clearly visible, before the alterations of the later centuries, including Ferdinando Fuga's loggia (1743), engulfed them. In the upper level, gracing a façade curving gently outward, Christ in Majesty was depicted, seated on a throne, right hand raised in blessing and holding a book. As Kessler remarked, the mosaic may have been patterned on the icon from the Sancta Sanctorum, and it shares its subject, design, and inscription with the Spoleto mosaic, if not the exact form of the throne or its setting.[209] In the Roman façade, foundation narratives were clearly visible below the *Christ in Majesty* and above the medieval portico, with its paired ionic columns and straight entablature.[210] We know that in Spoleto, a portico of some sort preceded the one begun in 1490; but of its exact form, we know little.[211]

In its interior decoration, too, Santa Maria Maggiore provided a model for the Spoleto Duomo. Then, as now, in the Roman church, Old Testament narrative mosaics decorated the nave above the nave arcade, while on the triumphal arch some of the earliest Mariological scenes survive. On the interior, west façade, scenes of the Last Judgment, no longer extant, were shown.[212] While little of the original fifteenth-century wall decoration survives in Spoleto, descriptions and evidence from restoration suggest that Old and New Testament murals covered the nave walls and a Last Judgment the interior façade.[213] We have no indication of the preexistent decoration in the apse, which, based on the efforts to repair the roof from the 1450s on, may have been in an advanced state of disrepair.[214]

We can also see the explicit links between the great Roman church and the Spoleto Duomo, forged by Eroli's renovations, as evidence for a renewed focus on early Christian sites. Nicholas IV's renovations to Santa Maria Maggiore were, themselves, an early manifestation, and Gozzoli's Old Testament murals in the Camposanto, discussed in Chapter 3, were a near contemporaneous expression.[215] Eroli had, of course, firsthand knowledge of the papal urban renewal projects from the1450s, including Nicholas V's radical restructuring of the choir of Saint Peter's, construction in the Vatican palace, and surrounding Borgo Leonino; Pius's benediction loggia and piazza; Paul II's refurbishment of San Marco; and Sixtus's extensive work in the Vatican palace and throughout the city.[216] The themes of papal primacy and the centrality of Rome in Christendom, declaimed in orations at the papal court, might also have influenced his thinking and his architectural patronage. We have mentioned the projects he sponsored in his diocese, in Spoleto and Narni, and that in Rome, the sacristy in the venerable Abbey of the Three Fountains of which he was abbot, possessed an early image of the *Coronation of the Virgin*.[217]

LIPPI'S UMBRIAN MURALS

Lippi's Coronation murals, while they refer directly to Roman prototypes, differ substantially in detail. They are unlike Umbrian examples, such as the early fourteenth-century altarpiece of the Cesi Master, from the convent of the Stella in Spoleto, where the central motif of the Assumption of the Virgin shows Mary and Christ seated in a mandorla is modeled on Cimabue's image in Assisi.[218] A Coronation from the church of San Giuliano in Monteluco outside of Spoleto, from the 1440s, also shows another variation.[219] Lippi's mural shows the Virgin kneeling before a seated God the Father, who wears an elaborate, conical crown, the *triregnum*, alluding to papal authority.[220] The kneeling pose has been thought to derive from depictions of Queen Esther before King Ahasuerus, an image that was often paired with the Coronation of the Virgin in *Biblia Paupernum,* "poor man's bibles" – more likely preachers' handbooks – which were widely circulated in the fifteenth century, both north and south of the Alps. Their illustrations were arranged typologically, that is, a New Testament subject was flanked by two scenes of Old Testament figures, whom they were understood to prefigure. A monumental example is the tapestry of the *Three Coronations* in the treasury of the cathedral of Sens, commissioned by Charles of Bourbon, cardinal and archbishop of Lyon sometime after 1476. In it, the central scene of the *Coronation* shows a kneeling Virgin; at the left, King Solomon crowns Bathsheba, his mother (Kings 2:19), while at the right Ahasuerus, King of Persia, grants Esther's petitions. The scene of Ahasuerus crowning Esther is described in Esther 2:17.[221] Both Esther and Bathsheba, who are depicted at the far right of Lippi's mural, among the Old Testament heroines, were commonly thought to be types or prefigurations of the Virgin as the Church. The Sant'Ambrogio altarpiece also depicts God the Father as at Spoleto, but this imagery was rarely used for the Coronation in Florentine or Umbrian artists in the fifteenth century. It may be related to the doctrine of the Immaculate Conception, the belief that Mary was born without the stain of original sin, that was promoted by the Franciscans and others at this time.[222]

In addition, Lippi included the scene of the Assumption of the Virgin and the gift of her belt to the apostle Thomas, neither of which appeared in the Santa Maria Maggiore apse. The scene, now a ghostly motif but once clearly visible, was painted *a secco* over a completed landscape. Was it part of the original design or a last-minute addition? Both innovations in the imagery of the Assumption and Coronation of the Virgin emphasized the Virgin's mercy and her humanity. Especially in Tuscany, as we have seen, where the relic of the Holy Belt was kept in the *pieve* of Prato, her gift was tangible evidence that she was assumed, body and soul, into heaven and confirmed the Virgin's special role as Mother of God and Queen of Heaven.[223] The emphasis on the Virgin's corporeal assumption assumed particular force in the area in which the cult of the Holy Belt was most widely recognized. Lippi's long residence in Prato, where the relic was preserved only steps from his workplace in the apse, seems a likely explanation for this aspect of his mural in Spoleto.[224] Eroli must have agreed; we know that Eroli was close to the observant Franciscans, whom he installed in his churches in Narni, and the Franciscans were especially devoted to the corporeal Assumption as well as the Immaculate Conception.[225]

Agnolo Gaddi's murals in the chapel of the Holy Belt in Prato may also have inspired the panorama of hills that frame the Lippi's *Coronation* below and the rocky landscape unfolding in the *Dormition* and *Assumption*. Again, the Roman mosaic shows a sliver of Nilotic landscape, a survival of classical imagery.[226] These details evoked the topography of the Holy Land, where these events unfolded: the disciples buried the Virgin in the rocky Val of Josaphat; Thomas received the gift of the Belt from the Mount of Olives.

Yet Lippi's murals also respond to the culture of Spoleto. It has been noted that architectural details of the framing replicate classical *spoglia* in local monuments, such as in the Basilica of the Savior in Spoleto (Figure 4.16). Here the distinctive square capital of the Basilica, reused from an ancient building, is repeated in the design of Lippi's framing piers. This correspondence was likely not by chance; in the 1519 contract for a new icon chapel in the Duomo, the

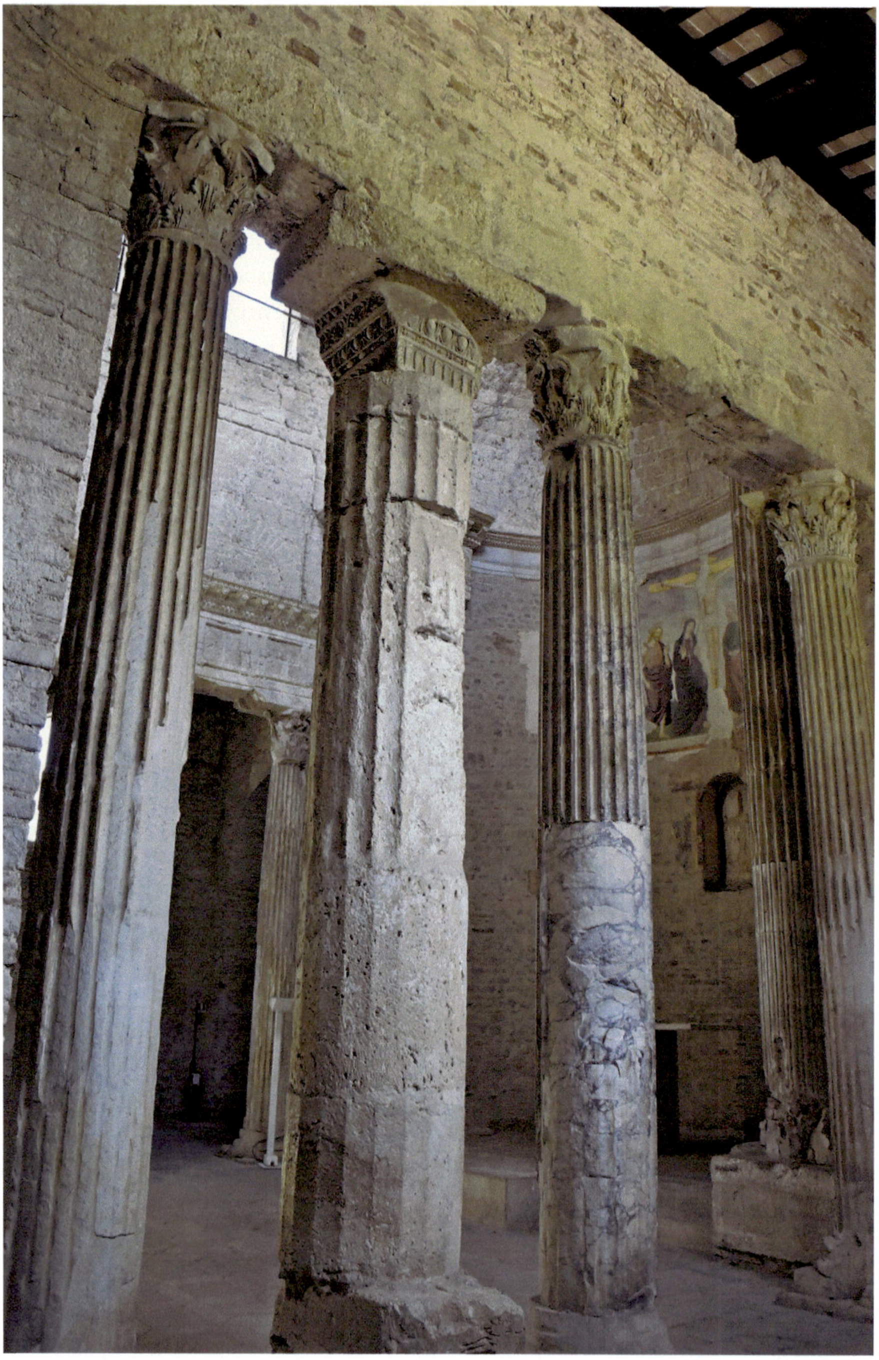

4.16. Basilica of the Savior, interior, detail of pier, late fourth century or early fifth century, Spoleto. Photo: Author.

architect was required to furnish "capitals carved in antique form" specifically modeled on those of the church of the Savior.[227] The landscape, deeper and more sweeping than the landscapes in the Prato murals, has been thought to evoke the hilly terrain of Spoleto itself.

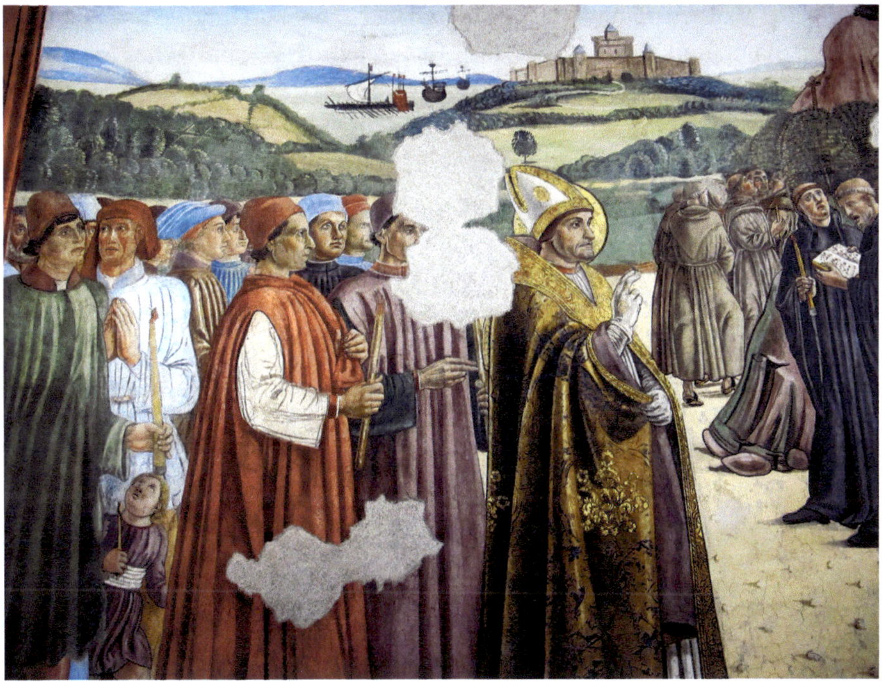

4.17. Antoniazzo Romano, *Stories of Saint Michael the Arcangel*, detail, 1464–67, Santissimi Apostoli, Rome. Photo: Author.

The striking illusionism of the Spoleto murals might also respond to contemporary trends in Rome, such as the fragmentary murals in the chapel of Cardinal Bessarion in Santissimi Apostoli, painted between 1464 and 1467 by Antoniazzo Romano, discussed in Chapter 3 (Figure 4.17).[228] It is noteworthy that the Bessarion chapel was similarly an apse, and the scheme of the murals, as it has been reconstructed, conforms very closely to Lippi's design. It is not known how Lippi would be familiar with these, as he never went to Rome, as far as we know. Certainly, Cardinal Eroli would have known them, as he and Bessarion had served as judges in a trial for heresy of the King of Bohemia at just this time (1464).[229]

In addition, if the Spoleto murals were modeled on those in Santa Maria Maggiore, there must have been some communication of basic design information to the artist, either verbally or by means of a drawing, according to which Lippi could compose his design. In this connection, it is noteworthy that during the time the Spoleto murals were being executed, Lippi sent Fra Diamante, his right-hand man, to Rome on two occasions. The first was in May 1468; on 18 May, Lippi was reimbursed more than three florins for sending Fra Diamante, when he was sought by the Monsignore of Vicenza.[230] Almost a year later, on 15 May 1469, Lippi was again paid three florins that he gave to Fra Diamante when he went to Rome.[231] The dates of his trip are too late to have influenced the design of the Spoleto murals, for by then, as we know from the payments, they were well advanced. However, the travel to Rome might suggest a broader context for Lippi's activity. Unremarked until now is that the *Monsignore* of Vicenza who called Fra Diamante to Rome, was none other than Marco Barbo (1420–91), the cousin of Pietro Barbo, the current Pope Paul II, whom Marco served in many capacities at the papal court, beginning in the spring of 1465. These included paymaster for Paul's various construction projects.[232] In just these years, 1468–69, Paul was directing the completion of the complex at San Marco, which included the palace, which he had begun as a cardinal, the palazzetto – the block to the southeast of the palace proper and its garden – and renovations to the church, which had been his titulus, including a new portico.[233] Upon his election as pope, Paul continued to live at San Marco, in spite of the construction, rather than move to the Vatican palace. Paul himself revealed that this unusual living arrangement was a result of his desire to see the construction continue apace. [234] Paul made Marco a cardinal in 1467 and gave him his titulus San Marco. Marco's personal apartments were in the triangular east wing of the palazzetto, where he continued to live until 1489; after Paul's death in 1471, Marco supervised the building of the complex.[235] Marco's visit to Donatello's workshop, as related by Pomponius Gauricus, might indicate that he was an active patron of art.[236] Was the papal nephew considering Lippi for one of his Roman projects? In 1468–69, construction was nearing completion at the Palazzo San Marco, while at the church, major renovations were concluding in the spring of 1468. Perhaps Lippi's work in the Spoleto Duomo suggested the possibility of his decorating some aspect of San Marco's interior. What this might have been is unknown; there is no indication in the documents that work was planned in the apse, and indeed, the ninth-century mosaic in the apse survives to this day. We are left to wonder at a possible career for Lippi in Rome had he lived longer.

It is also possible that Marco Barbo summoned Lippi's primary assistant on the recommendation of Cardinal Eroli. At Eroli's instigation, it may be recalled, Jacopo da Pietrasanta and an associate were sent to Spoleto to build the new chapels in the cathedral. Jacopo was among the sculptors employed at this time at San Marco, carving architectural elements for the side chapels off the aisles, the same work he would do in Spoleto.[237] Certainly, Eroli was aware of contemporary building projects in Rome, and most certainly he was intimate with the pope, and perhaps Cardinal Marco Barbo, as well.

We also know that Eroli – or his nephew – supplied a drawing of a fountain for the piazza facing the cathedral, which was renovated in 1490. A fountain had been part of the renovations to the piazza in 1468 that had been spearheaded by Eroli.[238] In 1490, the commune decided to repave the piazza and restore the fountain. In the contract, Francesco di Bartolomeo da Pietrasanta was charged "to remake the fountain of the piazza according to the form and design given to them previously by the said bishop."[239] While Nessi suggests that Berardo Eroli supplied the drawing, by 1490 he had long been dead. Was the drawing supplied by Eroli for the fountain constructed in 1468, or was it a new design supplied by the current bishop, Costantino Eroli? Without further evidence, it is impossible to answer these questions, yet in the context of his patronage, it is not impossible that Berardo Eroli sent the drawing. Eroli, himself, may have been the conduit of design information from Rome to Spoleto, conforming to his hands-on role in the project, as attested to in the documents.

CONCLUSION

Lippi's murals in Spoleto, then, show the artist's response to Umbrian traditions of patronage, ceremony, and imagery. They form a fitting conclusion to his long career, for he died in Spoleto on 10 October 1469 and was buried in the cathedral.[240] As we have seen, the artist was treated with considerable regard as a visiting artist, invited at the instigation of the cosmopolitan cardinal Eroli. His stature is visualized by his self-portrait, just to the right of the Virgin's bier, in the Dormition scene (Figure 4.18). The artist stands facing forward, flanked by younger figures, including Filippino, jauntily clothed in a red cap (we have seen Lippi lavished care on Filippino's wardrobe). With his left hand, he points toward his right hand. From Lippi's pen drawings, with parallel diagonal hatching from upper right to lower left, we can assume Lippi was right-handed, and that the portrait is a visual signature. The arrangement of Lippi's fingers as he grasps his drapery forms what is called the *mano cornuta*, popularly understood as protecting against the evil eye.[241] However, this gesture also appears in other contexts, such as the hand of God descending from clouds in the sixth-century mosaics in the scene of the *Sacrifice of Abel and Melchizedek* in San Vitale in Ravenna, where it denotes divine sanction. Lippi's gesture perhaps alludes to the metaphor of God as artisan or creator of the universe, widely known in the Middle Ages. Lippi's pose directs the viewer's attention to his hand and his claim of authorship for the murals.

While Lippi had included self-portraits in previous works, none is on a monumental scale, nor as prominently placed. Here, it assumes the place occupied by donor figures in his mural at Prato, the *Celebration of the Relics of Saint Stephen*.[242] Lippi seems to claim that his gift is the imagination and skill viewers saw before them. While Agnolo Gaddi's portrait was not included in the Prato cycle (nor, *pace* Vasari, in the Alberti chapel in Santa Croce), and Gozzoli's image was reported, but no longer identifiable in Pisa, neither, we can assume, would have made as powerful a claim to authorship as Lippi's.[243]

Lippi's reputation, and the prestige he lent the town of Spoleto, endured after his death. Twenty years later, according to Vasari, Lorenzo de'Medici

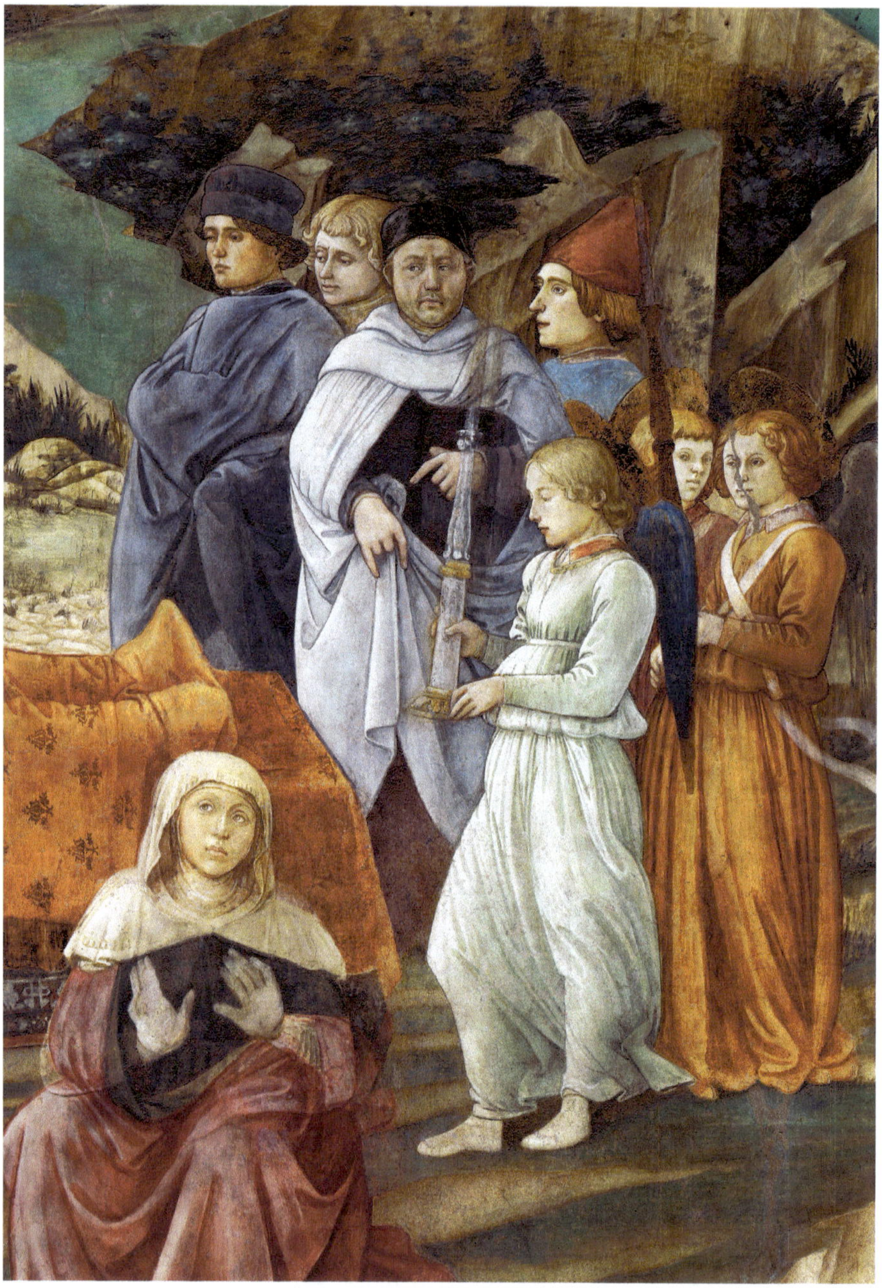

4.18. Fra Filippo Lippi, *Dormition and Assumption of the Virgin*, 1466–69, detail, Duomo, Spoleto. Photo: Scala / Art Resource, NY.

desired to erect a monument to Lippi to commemorate his close ties to the Medici family. He visited Spoleto on his way to Rome in 1480 to ask that the painter's remains be removed to Florence. The Spoleto fathers refused, and in the end, Lorenzo paid 100 florins for a tomb monument to Lippi in Spoleto

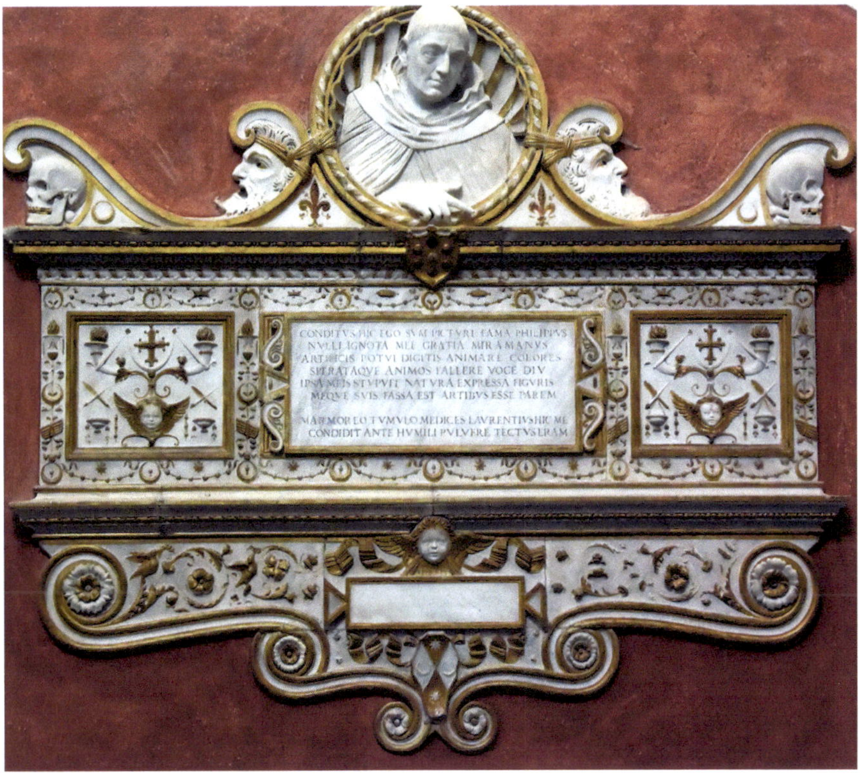

4.19. Cenotaph of Fra Filippo Lippi, c. 1490, Duomo, Spoleto. Photo: Author.

Cathedral, complete with portrait bust of the painter and an inscription (reportedly composed by the poet Poliziano, to whom Gozzoli's encomium is also attributed) celebrating his skill and crediting Lorenzo with the monument:

> Here am I brought, Filippo, painting's fame,
> To nought unknown my wondrous grace of hand.
> With craftsman's fingers I gave color life
> And fooled the living with its long-awaited voice.
> Nature herself by my expressive figures stilled
> Confesses me the equal of her arts.
> Lorenzo de Medici placed me here in this marble tomb,
> Who before was covered with common dust. (Figure 4.19)[244]

This monument to Lippi was only one of several that Lorenzo commissioned, including those to Giotto and the famous organist Squarcialupi, following the pattern of Brunelleschi's cenotaph in Florence cathedral, which lends tangible form to the Florentine canon of artists.[245]

The inscription also calls to mind that celebrating Benozzo in the Camposanto, and indeed aspects of their experience working in Pisa and Spoleto were, as we have seen, similar. Both artists carried the prestige of

Florentine painting to distant cities. Since Spoleto was not – as Pisa was – part of the Florentine territorial state, it would not have the political resonances of Gozzoli's murals. And yet, the Spoleto murals, guided by Bishop Eroli and created by the "wondrous grace" of Lippi's hand, shaped Spoleto's identity as a foremost city in the papal states, intimately linked to Rome through history, culture, and faith.

NOTES

1 For the feast of Corpus Christi, see Miri Rubin, *Corpus Christi: The Eucharist in Late Medieval Culture*, Cambridge: Cambridge University Press, 1991.

2 Gaetano Lironi, *Notizie storiche sul culto della B. Vergine che si venera nella Chiesa metropolitan di Spoleto*, 1877, pp. 19–30. See also Achille Sansi, *Storia del comune di Spoleto dal secolo XII al XVII*, Foligno: P. Sgarogoa, 1879, vol. 2, p. 275.

3 Mara Bonfioli, "Un importante restauro: L'icone del Duomo di Spoleto," *Spoletium*, vol. 24, no. 27, 1982, pp. 35–38; Mara Bonfioli and Elisabetta Ermini, "Premesse ad un riesame critico dell' 'icone' del Duomo di Spoleto," in *Atti del IX congresso internazionale di studi sull'alto medioevo*, Spoleto, 1983, pp. 821–36; Mara Bonfioli, "L'Icona del Duomo di Spoleto: Nuovi contribute alla sua storia," *Spoletium*, vol. 33, 1988, pp. 17–25; Mara Bonfioli, "Per la storia dell'icona di Spoleto. Documenti," in V. Casale et al., eds., *Scritti di archeologia e storia dell'arte in onore di Carlo Pietrangeli*, Rome: Edizioni Quasar, 1996, pp. 237–42; Mara Bonfioli, "La 'santissima icone,'" in Giordana Benazzi and Giovanni Carbonara, eds., *La cattedrale di Spoleto*, Milan: Federico Motta Editore, 2002, pp. 185–87.

4 Pietro Toesca, *Storia dell'arte italiana: Il medioevo*, vol. 2, Turin: Unione Tipografico-Editrice Torinese, 1927, p. 1025, note 10; Edward Garrison, *Italian Romanesque Panel Painting*, Florence, 1949, p. 70, no. 147; Silvio Mercati, "Sulla santissima icone del Duomo di Spoleto," *Spoletium*, vol. 3, no. 1, 1956, pp. 3–6; Silvio Mercati, *Collectanea Byzantina*, vol. 2, Bari: Dedalo Libri, 1970, pp. 509–13; Kurt Weitzmann, *The Monastery of St. Catherine at Mount Sinai: The Icons*, vol. 1, Princeton: Princeton University Press, 1976, pp. 21–23; Bonfioli and Ermini, "Premesse ad un riesame critico dell' 'icone' del Duomo di Spoleto," p. 829; Hans Belting, *Likeness and Presence; A History of the Image before the Era of Art*, trans. Edmund Jephcott, Chicago: University of Chicago Press, 1994, p. 241; Bonfioli, "La 'santissima icone,'" p. 186.

5 Belting, *Likeness and Presence*, pp. 241–44. 323.

6 The dialogue, in Greek, has been transcribed into Italian as follows:

MADONNA:	Accogli la preghiera di tua madre o compassionevole.
CHRIST:	che domandi o Madre
MADONNA:	a salvezza dei mortali
CHRIST:	mi irritarono
MADONNA:	compatisci Figlio mio
CHRIST:	Ma non si convertono
MADONNA:	E salvali gratis
CHRIST:	Avranno il riscatto
MADONNA:	ti ringrazio o Verbo.

The last two lines are missing but can be supplied from copies of the original; Mercati, "Sulla santissima icone del Duomo do Spoleto," p. 5; Bonfioli, "La 'santissima icone,'" p. 186.

7 Belting, *Likeness and Presence*, p. 241.

8 For example, the twelfth-century icon from San Gregorio Nazianzeno in Rome, formerly in the Cini Foundation, Venice, now Rome, Palazzo Barberini; the *Madonna Avvocata* by Taddeo di Bartolo at Orte, and the so-called Leo Madonna by Antoniazzo Romano

painted in 1490, originally in Santa Maria Maggiore and now in Dublin; Belting, *Likeness and Presence*, pp. 320, 442.

9 Bonfioli, "Un importante restauro," pp. 35–38; Bonfioli, "La 'santissima icone,'" p. 186.

10 This cover is inscribed, as the last line of the dialogue, with the name Irene Petralifina, who was most likely the donor but of whom nothing is known.

11 Bonfioli and Ermini, "Premesse ad un riesame critico dell' 'icone' del Duomo di Spoleto," p. 832. They transcribe the excerpt from the bull, found in the Archivio del Duomo, perg. no. 496.

12 Bonfioli and Ermini, "Premesse ad un riesame critico dell'Icone," p. 833, quoting from perg. no. 508 from the Archivio del Duomo. See also Lironi, *Notizie storiche*, p. 11.

13 As Silvestro Nessi, "La cattedrale nella storia diocesana e civile di Spoleto," in Benazzi and Carbonara, eds., *La cattedrale di Spoleto*, p. 68, notes, the 1296 statutes confirm an earlier practice of the lords of subject castles processing through the city to the cathedral to present tributes of wax candles on the vigil of the Assumption.

14 The feast of Corpus Christi, instituted in the thirteenth century, was celebrated at Spoleto; see Rubin, *Corpus Christi*, pp. 243–71, on the processions associated with the feast. Sansi, *Storia del comune di Spoleto*, vol. 2, p. 34, notes that, during Nicholas V's visit to the city in 1449, the feast was celebrated with extraordinary pomp at the request of the newly appointed Bishop Eroli. He requested that, in addition to the usual decorations, the streets be covered for the procession.

15 Lironi, *Notizie storiche*, p. 12; Matteo Ceriana, "Il portico rinascimentale e l'opera di Ambrogio Barocci a Spoleto," in Benazzi and Carbonara, eds., *La cattedrale di Spoleto*, p. 291.

16 For Lippi's biography, see the entry by Luca Bortolotti in *Dizionario biografico italiano*, Rome: Istituto della Enciclopedia italiana, 2005, vol. 65, pp.198–207. The most recent discussion of the murals in Spoleto is Giordana Benazzi, "Le storie della Vergine di Filippo Lippi," in Benazzi and Carbonara, eds., *La cattedrale di Spoleto*, pp. 261–77. See also Jeffrey Ruda, *Fra Filippo Lippi: Life and Work*, London: Phaidon, 1993, pp. 292–305 and 473–77, cat. no. 66.

17 The payments are found in Spoleto, Archivio di Stato, Archivio di Opera del Duomo di Spoleto (hereafter ASS, AODS), registro no. 4 (formerly no. 1), dal 1455 al 1505, cc. 105 recto–24 verso (new pagination; formerly cc. 116 recto–35 verso). They were selectively published by Luigi Fausti, "Le pitture di Fra Filipo Lippi nel Duomo di Spoleto," *Archivio per la storia ecclesiastica dell'Umbria*, vol. 3, 1915, pp. 1–36 (reprinted as a book by the Ente Roca di Spoleto in 1970); by Ruda, *Fra Filippo Lippi*, 1993, pp. 542–44, doc. no. 27; and in digest form by Laura Andreani, "Regesti," in Benazzi and Carbonara, eds., *La cattedrale di Spoleto*, pp. 465–67, doc. nos. 85–174. The entries in this document are transcribed in Appendix IV.

18 Corrado Bozzoni and Giovanni Carbonara, "Il quattrocento e il cinquecento: Ulteriori sviluppi," in Benazzi and Carbonara, eds., *La cattedrale di Spoleto*, p. 105.

19 Benazzi, "Fra Filippo Lippi a Spoleto," p. 81.

20 Benazzi, "Le storie della Vergine di Filippo Lippi," p. 277, note 4; Maria Laura Moroni, "Itinerari a Spoleto," in Saverio Ricci, ed., *Piermatteo d'Amelia e il rinascimento; itinerari in Umbria*, Milan: Silvana Editoriale, 2009, p. 17.

21 Ruda, *Fra Filippo Lippi*, pp. 137–52, 418–21, cat. no. 34; 422–26, cat. no. 36.

22 The literature on the iconography of Coronation of the Virgin includes Émile Mâle, *L'art religieux du xiiie siècle en France*, Paris: Armand Colin, 1923, pp. 248–59; Louis Réau, *L'Iconographie de l'art chrétien*, vol. 2, Paris: Presses Universitaires de France, 1957, pp. 597–635; Penelope Dunford, "Iconografia della dormizione e dell'Assunzione della Vergine Maria nell'arte rinascimentale italiana," *Arte Cristiana*, vol. 63, 1975, pp. 284–98; Philippe Verdier, *Le Couronnement de la Vierge*, Montréal: Institut d'études médiévales Albert-le-Grand, 1980, pp. 153–62; Daniel Russo, "Les représentations mariale dans l'art d'occident: Essai sur la formation d'une tradition iconographique," in *Marie: Le culte de la Vierge dans la société Médiévale*, Paris: Beauchesne, 1996, pp. 173–291. On the Coronation in

the fifteenth century, see Mary Echols, "The Coronation of the Virgin in Fifteenth-Century Italian Art," PhD dissertation, University of Virginia, 1976, pp. 123–74 and the useful appendices pp. 245–84; Eliot Rowlands, "Filippo Lippi and His Experience of Painting in the Veneto Region," *Artibus et Historiae*, vol. 19, 1989, pp. 43–52.

23 Rowlands, "Filippo Lippi and His Experience of Painting in the Veneto Region," p. 53. Ruda, *Fra Filippo Lippi*, p. 515, doc. no. 3, publishes the documentation for Lippi in Padua. The early source is the notebook assembled by the Venetian Marcantonio Michiel between c. 1521 and 1534.

24 For Eroli's biography, see the entry by Anna Esposito in *Dizionario biografico degli italiani*, vol. 43, 1993, pp. 228–32.

25 Giovanni Eroli (1813–1904), a descendent (G. Fagioli Vercellone in *Dizionario biografico degli italiani*, vol. 43, 1993, pp. 236–38) gives further family history in *Notizie de' vescovi Eroli estratte dalle vite de' Narnesi illustri*, Terni: Polsenli, 1852, pp. v–xxix. He states that in the family archive there is no mention of Berardo, nor of his clerical relatives, Costantino (b. first half of the fifteenth century, named bishop of Spoleto in 1474, died c. 1500) and Francesco (bishop of Spoleto1500, died 1540).

26 Gaetano Moroni, *Dizionario di erudizione storico-ecclesiastica*, Venice: Tipografia Emiliana, 1843, vol. 22, p. 69, cites Alphonso Ciaconius [Alphonso Chacón], *Vitae et res gestae pontificum Romanorum et S.R.E. cardinalium ab initio nascentis Ecclesiæ usque ad Urbanum VIII. Pont. Max*, vol. 2, Rome, 1677, coll. 1036–37 and 1273; and F. Ughelli-N. Coleti, *Italia sacra*, Venice: Sebastianum Coleti, 1717, vol. 1, col. 1268, in favor of a modest origins; and Francesco Sperandio, *Sabina sagra e profana antica e moderna*, Rome: Zempel, 1790, p. 234; Giorgio Viviano Marchesi, *La galeriadell'onore ove sono descritte le segnalate memorie del'sagr'ordine militare di S. Stefano p. e m.'e de' suoi cavalieri colle glorie antiche e moderne'del-l'illustri loro patrie e famiglie dentro e fu'ri d'Italia*, Forlì: Fratelli Marozzi, 1735, vol. 1, p. 100; for a more elevated lineage. Further bibliography includes Lorenzo Cardella, *Memorie storiche de' cardinali della Santa Romana Chiesa*, Rome: Stamperia Pagliarini, 1793, vol. 3, pp. 137–40; "Essai de liste générale des cardinaux. VIII. Les cardinaux du XVIe siècle," *Annuaire Pontifical Catholique 1933*, Paris: Maison de la Bonne Presse, 1933, p. 132; Conradus Eubel, *Hierarchia Catholica Medii Aevi*, vol. 2 (1431–1503), Monasterii: Sumptibus et Typis Librariae Regensbergianae, 1950, pp. 13, 36, 38, 43, 47.

27 Pius II, *Orations "Messis quidem," "Quamvis non dubitamus." "Vocati estis," and "Maxima" of Pope Pius II (5 and 8 March, 1460, Siena)*, Michael von Cotta-Schønberg, ed. and trans., Copenhagen, 2015, pp. 20–21.

28 Esposito, p. 229.

29 The *Biographical Dictionary of the Cardinals of the Holy Roman Church* says that he studied in Rome but without providing a specific source for this information, www2.fiu.edu/~mirandas/bios1460.htm.

30 Pius II, *"Quamvis non dubitamus,"* p. 19.

31 Vespasiano da Bisticci, *Le vite*, ed. Aulo Greco, Florence: Istituto Nazionale di studi sul rinascimento, 1970, vol. 1, p. 201; Gasparis Veronensis, *De gestis tempore Pontificis Maximi Pauli secundi*, ed. G. Zippel in *Rerum Italicarum Scriptores*, 2nd ed., ed. Giosù Carducci and Vittorio Fiorini, vol. 3, part 16, Città di Castello: Casa Editrice Lapi, 1904, p. 35. *Il diario romano di Jacopo Gherardi da Volterra*, ed. E. Carusi in *Rerum Italicarum Scriptores*, 2nd ed., ed. Giosù Carducci and Vittorio Fiorini, vol. 23, part 3, Città di Castello: Casa Editrice Lapi, 1904, p. 146, also records his opinion on the subject of the election of bishops.

32 Gasparis Veronensis, *De gestis tempore Pontificis Maximi Pauli secundi*, p. 35.

33 Vespasiano, *Le vite*, p. 201.

34 "Sine aliqua pompa fieri solita cardinalibus aut prelatis"; Rome, Archivio di Stato (hereafter ASR), Ospedale del Santissimo Salvatore ad Sancta Sanctorum, 450, no. 45.

35 Jacopo Ammannati Piccolomini, *Lettere(1444–1479)*, ed. Paolo Cherubini, Rome: Ministero per i beni culturali e ambientali, Ufficio centrale per I beni archivistici, 1997, vol. 3, p. 1886, no. 765.

36 For these positions, consult *Catholic Encyclopedia*, ed. Charles Herbermann, New York: Robert Appleton, 1913, www.catholic.org/encyclopedia/view.php?id=2552.

37 Esposito, p. 229. Callixtus entrusted Eroli, among others, with the enormous task of reforming the churches and monasteries of Rome and its surrounding district. Among other duties, he presided over the final proceedings in the examination of Francesca Romana for sainthood in 1451; Arnold Esch, "I processi medioevali per la canonizzazione di santa Francesca Romana (1440–1451)," in Alessandra Bartolomei Romagnoli and Giorgio Picasso, eds., *La Canonizzazione di Santa Francesca Romana: Santità, cultura e istituzioni a Roma tra medioevo ed età moderna*, Florenze: Edizioni del Galluzzo per la Fondazione Ezio Franceschini, 2013, p. 41. In 1457, he adjudicated a dispute over inheritance among members of the noble Roman Boccapaduli family; Marco-Ubaldo Bicci, *Notizia della famiglia Boccapaduli*, Rome: Stamparia di Appollo, 1762, pp. 617–21.

38 A cardinal priest is the middle of the three orders of cardinals, below the cardinal bishops but above the cardinal deacons. Cardinal priests are assigned one of the titular churches of Rome, www.catholic.org/encyclopedia/view.php?id=2550. Santa Sabina, one of the oldest Roman basilicas located on the Aventine hill, is the mother church of the Dominican order.

39 Pius II, *"Quamvis non dubitamus,"* pp. 20–21. Pius describes the ceremony in his *Commentaries*, ed. and trans. Margaret Meserve and Marcello Simonetta, Cambridge, MA: Harvard University Press, 2007, vol. 2, bk. 4, ch. 11, pp. 239–41.

40 Esposito, p. 229. Ottone della Carretto (d. 1465) was a diplomat in service to the Sforza court. See Franca Petrucci, in *Dizionario Biografico degli Italiani*, vol. 36, 1988, pp. 436–39.

41 Esposito, p. 229; see also www.catholic.org/encyclopedia/view.php?id=2433. In addition, he assumed the direction of the Ufficio delle Suppliche as coordinator of the work of the referendaries; Esposito, p. 229.

42 Pius II, *Commentaries*, ed. Meserve et. al, vol. 1, bks. 1–2, and vol. 2, bk. 3, ch. 6, p. 233. He also named Eroli among his cardinals as, "Berardo, bishop of Spoleto, a man of distinguished character and learning, with a reputation as a champion of justice. A native of Narni, he was serving at the time as papal Referendary and a member of Pius's private household"; vol. 2, bk. 4, ch. 9, pp. 232–33.

43 See Esposito, pp. 229–30 for what follows. Eroli handled negotiations with Ferdinand I of Naples for the restitution of Benevento and Terracina to the Holy See. Eugenius IV had ceded these lands to Alfonso of Aragon in 1443 for his help in ridding the Papal States of Francesco Sforza's control; Peter Partner, *The Lands of St. Peter: The Papal State in the Middle Ages and the Early Renaissance*, Berkeley: University of California Press, 1972, pp. 391, 417. He also brokered solutions to minor territorial disputes. Eroli acted in 1464 as a judge in the examination of Giorgio Podiebrad, the king of Bohemia, for heresy, serving with Nicolas of Cusa and later Cardinals Carvajal and Bessarione; Ludwig von Pastor, *Storia dei papi*, 4th ed., trans. Angelo Mercato, reprint, Rome: Desclée, 1961, vol. 2, pp. 156–74. Eroli served numerous times as papal legate to Perugia, Todi, and Civitacastellana, residing in Perugia for eleven months from July 1462 to June 1463. The city authorities of Perugia thanked him for his fairness and sagacity by giving him a silver sword with the arms of the commune. At that time, he founded the Monte di Pietà of Perugia. Opposing the forced loan of 2,000 florins from Jews to fund the Monte, he negotiated directly with Pius to restore their rights to moneylending; Stanislao Majarelli and Ugolino Nicolini, *Il Monte dei poveri di Perugia*, Perugia: Banco del Monte di Credito, 1962, pp. 38, 127, 152, 192, 231–34, 279–80. Further legations to Perugia took place in 1471, 1474, and 1477; see also Ammannati, *Lettere*, vol. 3, pp. 1505–6, no. 524.

44 He was with the pope in Siena in March of 1460 where he received his cardinal's hat, and he stayed afterward for two weeks at the observant Franciscan convent of La Capriola, near Siena; Pius II, *Commentaries*, ed. Meserve et al., vol. 2, bk. 4, ch. 14, pp. 250–51. He accompanied Pius to the consistory in Piacenza in August 1462 and joined him in Todi in December 1462; he was in Tivoli with the pope on 9 July 1463; *Biographical*

Dictionary of the Cardinals of the Holy Roman Church, http://webdept.fiu.edu/~mirandas/bios1460.htm#Eroli. Eroli rejoined the pope in Terni in June 1464, accompanying him to Spoleto, where he was ill with fever, and finally to Ancona to embark on a Crusade against the Turks, where the pontiff died; von Pastor, *Storia dei papi*, vol. 2, p. 262. See also Ammannati, *Lettere*, vol. 2, p. 509, no. 74, for an account of Pius's last days.

45 Platina (Bartolomeo Sacchi), *The Lives of the Popes*, ed. and trans. William Benham, vol. 2, London: Griffith, Farran, Okeden and Welch, 1888, p. 271.

46 Esposito, p. 230; Marco Pellegrini, "Ascanio Maria Sforza: La creazione di un cardinale 'di famiglia,'" in Giorgio Chittolini, ed., *Gli Sforza, la chiesa lombarda, la corte di Roma*, Naples: Liguori, 1992, pp. 231–33.

47 Nicholas named him commendatory abbot of the monastery of Colleantico near Spoleto in 1451 and of San Cassiano outside Narni in 1453; Esposito, pp. 229–30. On San Cassiano, see Giovanni Eroli, *Descrizione delle chiese di Narni e suoi dintorni*, Narni: Petrignani, 1898, pp. 399–407; Guerriero Bolli, *L'abbazia di San Cassiano nel monastero narnese di Belisario*, Terni: Diocesi di Terni-Narni-Amelia, 2010; Giustino Fernedi and Nadia Togni, *Monasteri Benedettini in Umbria*, Cesena: Centro Storico Benedettino Italiano, 2014, pp. 313–15, no. 83.

48 Joan Barclay Lloyd, *SS. Vincenzo e Anastasio at Tre Fontane near Rome: History and Architecture of a Medieval Cistercian Abbey*, Kalmazoo: Cistercian, 2006, pp. 3–35. Eroli was involved in a long dispute with Siena over the possessions of the abbey; see Ammannati, *Lettere*, vol. 2, pp. 620–21, note 23, no. 104; p. 766, note 6, no. 169; p. 882, note 3, no. 211.

49 Gasparis Veronensis, *De gestis tempore Pontificis Maximi Pauli secundi*, p. 35, note 4.

50 Fra Mariano da Firenze, *Itinerarium Urbis Romae*, ed. Enrico Bulletti, Rome: Pontificio istituto di archeologia cristiana, 1931, p. 236; Charles Burroughs, *From Signs to Design: Environmental Process and Reform in Early Renaissance Rome*, Cambridge, MA: MIT Press, 1990, pp. 110–11, 263, note 25; Simona Sperindei, "Repertorio delle residenze cardinalizie," in Giorgio Simoncini, ed., *Roma: Le trasformazioni urbane nel quattrocento*, Florence: Olschki, 2004, vol. 2, p. 148; Carol Richardson, *Reclaiming Rome: Cardinals in the Fifteenth Century*, Leiden: Brill, 2009, p. 312.

51 Pasquale Adinolfi, *La via sacra o del papa*, Rome: Monaldi, 1865, pp. 19–20, 73–74.

52 The particula of the testament is preserved ASR, Ospedale del Santissimo Salvatore ad Sancta Sanctorum, 450, no. 45, *Legati di case a favore della nostra compagnia*. The particula is a parchment document by the hand of the notary Benincasa de Benincasis and dated 17 March 1479, the date of the testament. Also preserved is a seventeenth-century copy on paper of the provisions bequeathing a part of Eroli's palace to the hospital of the Santissimo Salvatore; this document is transcribed in Adionolfi, *La via sacra o del papa*, pp. 145–47.

53 Stefania Magliani, "Il fregio decorativo della cappella Eroli nella cattedrale di Spoleto," *Spoletium*, vols. 31/32, nos. 34/35, 1990, pp. 191–97; Giordana Benazzi, "La cappella di San Leonardo e la committenza di Costantino Eroli," in Benazzi and Carbonara, eds., *La cattedrale di Spoleto*," pp. 279–87.

54 For the route of the via Papalis, see Simoncini, *Roma: Le trasformazioni urbane nel quattrocento*, vol. 1, pl. 5.

55 Pius II, *Commentaries*, trans. Florence Alden Gragg, *Smith College Studies in History*, vol. 35, 1951, bk. 8, pp. 551–56.

56 Pius II, *Commentaries*, trans. Florence Alden Gragg, pp. 535–36. The identity of the delinquent cardinal is unknown, but possibilities include Bessarion or Prospero Colonna at Santissimi Apostoli, Filippo Calandrini at San Lorenzo in Lucina, or Angelo Capranica at the Palazzo Capranica; Richardson, *Reclaiming Rome*, p. 311, note 162.

57 Paula Nuttall, *From Flanders to Florence*, New Haven and London: Yale University Press, 2004, pp. 114–15.

58 Esposito, p. 230.

59 Esposito, p. 230; Eroli's will, recorded in Rome 17 March 1479, just a few weeks before his death on 2 April, has not been located. A summary of some of the provisions is in ASR, Ospedale del Santissimo Salvatore ad Sancta Sanctorum, 450, no. 45.

60 For the history of the church, see Ludovico Iacobilli, *Vite de'santi e beati dell'Umbria e di quelli, i corpi de'quali riposano in essa provincia*, vol. 3, Foligno: Agostino Alterii, 1661, pp. 300–301, 319–20; Eroli, *Notizie*, pp. xii, xvii–xix, note 19; Achille Sansi, *Degli edifici e dei frammenti storici delle antiche età di Spoleto*, Foligno: P. Sgariglia, 1869, repr. 1993, pp. 250–51; Mariano Guardabassi, *Indice-guida dei monumenti pagani e cristiani riguardanti l'istoria e l'arte esistenti nella provincia dell'Umbria*, Perugia: Boncompagni, 1872, pp. 301–2; Michele Faloci Pulignani, "Le Clarisse di San Paolo presso Spoleto in documenti inediti del XIII secolo," *Miscellanea di storia, lettere ed arti*, vol. 11, Fasc. iii, 1909, pp. 65–82; Michele Faloci Pulignani, "Ancora del monastero di S. Paolo presso la città di Spoleto," *Miscellanea di storia, lettere ed arti*, vol. 11, Fasc. iii, 1910, pp. 57–59; Bruno Toscano, "Sul San Paolo 'inter vineas,'" *Spoletium*, vol. 4, no. 3, 1957, pp. 20–26; Bruno Toscano, *Spoleto in pietre: Guida artistica della città*, Spoleto: Azienda del turismo, 1963, pp. 102–3; Gisberto Martelli, "Spoleto (Perugia), Chiesa di S. Paolo 'inter vineos,'" *Bollettino d'arte*, vol. 50, 1965, pp. 139–40; Lamberto Gentili et al., *L'Umbria: Manuali per il territorio; Spoleto*, Rome: Edindustria, 1978, pp. 244–45; Renzo Pardi, *Architettura religiosa medievale in Umbria*, Spoleto: CISAM, 2000, p. 205; Bernardino Sperandio, *Chiese romaniche in Umbria*, Perugia: Quattroemme, 2001, pp. 108–9; Francesco Guarino et al., *Abbazie benedettine in Umbria*, Perugia: Quattroemme, 2008, pp. 150–51; Fabio Coden, "Sgurardo d'insieme all'architettura umbra del Duecento," in Enrico Menestò, ed., *L'Umbria nel XIII secolo*, Spoleto: CISAM, 2011, pp. 354–55; Simona Moretti, "Spoleto. Chiesa di San Paolo inter vineas," in Mara Bonfioli, ed., *Corpus della pittura monumentale bizantina in Italia*, vol 1: Umbria, Rome: Edizioni Quasar, 2012, pp. 99–108; Giustino Farnedi, et al., *Monasteri benedettini in Umbria: Alle radici del paesaggio umbro*, Cesena: Centro Storico Benedettino Italiano, 2014, pp. 232–34.

61 Eroli, *Notizie*, p. xix, note 19.

62 An inventory of 1723 reveals that the monastery comprised a large cloister, four dormitories, an infirmary, a pharmacy, and a library; *L'Archivio storico della Provincia Serafica di San Francesco d'Assisi dei Frati Minori in Umbria. Inventario della Sezione Conventi chiusi (1230–2004)*, a cura di A. Maiarelli, Santa Maria degli Angeli di Assisi: Edizioni Porziuncola, 2005, pp. 31–32. See also, Bisberto Martelli, "Il restauro della Chiesa di San Paolo 'inter vineas,'" *Spoletium*, vol. 12, 1966, pp. 3–13.

63 He included a bequest to the Santissima Trinità hospital attached to the monastery in his testament; ASR, Ospedale del Santissimo Salvatore ad Sancta Sanctorum, 450, no. 45 (see note 34).

64 For the history of the monastery, see Eroli, *Notizie*, pp. xix–xx, note 19; Eroli, *Le chiese di Narni*, pp. 385–95; Guardabassi, *Indice-guida*, pp. 135; L. Wadding, *Annales minorum*, vol. 13, 1932, pp. 224–25; Francesco Russo, "S. Girolamo di Narni," *Miscellanea francescana*, n.s. vol. 37, no. 1, 1937, pp. 167–81.

65 The request was published in Carlo Stefano Bucciarelli, *Cathedralis Narniensis ecclesiae ejusque capituli et canonicorum antiquitas, nobilitas, indulta et praerogativae*, Narni, 1720, pp. 130–31. The directive included the condition that the friars offer to the bishop and to the canons of the cathedral of San Giovanale each year in perpetuity a pound of wax; Eroli, *Notizie*, p. xix, note 19.

66 Esposito, p. 231; *Il diario romano di Jacopo Gherardi da Volterra*, in Giosu Carducci and Vittorio Fiorini, eds., *Rerum Italicarum Scriptores*, 2nd ed. vol. 23, part 3, Città di Castello: Casa Editrice Lapi, 1904, p. 41; Ammannati, *Lettere*, vol. 3, pp. 1585–86, no. 576: "Proximo Februario, cum iter Narnia agerem, comtemplatus sum opus coenobii vestra cura erectum, fratrum frequentia et structura ipsa insigne."

67 Eroli, *Notizie*, p. xix, note 19; Russo, "S. Girolamo di Narni," p. 171.

68 Guardabassi, *Indice-guida*, p. 135; Alessandro Novelli and Lucilla Vignoli, *L'arte a Narni tra medioevo e illuminismo*, Perugia: Era Nuova, 2004, pp. 73–78, cat. no. 6; Lucilla Vignoli, *Pierantonio Mezzastris: Pittore a Foligno nella seconda metà del Quattrocento*, ed. G. Benazzi and E. Lunghi, Foligno: Edizioni Orfini Numeister, 2006, pp. 155–56, cat. no. 35.

69 Diane Cole Ahl, *Benozzo Gozzoli*, New Haven and London: Yale University Press, 1997, pp. 41–47; Diane Cole Ahl, "Frescante a San Fortunato," in Bruno Toscano et al., eds., *Benozzo Gozzoli, Allievo a Roma, maestro in Umbria*, Milan: Silvana Editoriale, 2002, pp. 93–94.

70 Vignoli, *Pierantonio Mezzastris*, p. 156.

71 Guardabassi, *Indice-guida*, p. 135; Eroli, *Notizie*, pp. xviii–xx, note 19 (attributed to Lo Spagna); Giovanni Eroli, *La Coronazione di Maria Vergine del Ghirlandaio e la Madonna del Libro di Raffaello*, Narni, 1880, pp. 29–30; Russo, "S. Girolamo di Narni," pp. 174–76; Jean K. Cadogan, *Domenico Ghirlandaio: Artist and Artisan*, New Haven and London: Yale University Press, 2000, pp. 255–57, cat. no. 31, p. 357, doc. no. 27; Novelli and Vignoli, *L'arte a Narni*, pp. 79–88.

72 Eroli, *Descrizione delle chiese di Narni*, pp. 388–90.

73 Novelli and Vignoli, *L'arte a Narni*, pp. 85–88.

74 Ammannati describes a hospice for the poor and an adjacent chapel Eroli built "from the foundations" in Monterosi, in the diocese of Nepi, to the north of Rome toward Viterbo. Paul II had sold him the dilapidated castle, surrounding town and dependent territories of Monterosi in 1469; Esposito p. 230; see also Ciaconius, *Vitae et res gestae pontificum Romanorum*, vol. 2, col. 1036; Gasparis Veronensis, *De gestis tempore Pontificis Maximi Pauli secundi*, p. 35, note 4. Ammannati described passing by Monterosi: *Lettere*, vol. 3, pp. 1585–86, no. 576. In 1474, he rebuilt the bridge in Narni over the river Nera that formerly displayed his coat of arms; Esposito, p. 231. Of the other abbeys in his control, such as San Cassiano, just across the Nera River outside Narni, nothing survives from the period of his stewardship. The Abbey of the Three Fountains was said to have been restored by Eroli; Ughello reported that the choir was rebuilt and ornamented with sacred pictures, of which today little remains; Ughelli-Coleti, *Italia sacra*, vol. 1, col. 1268; see Barclay Lloyd, *SS. Vincenzio e Anastasio*, p. 30; this activity is not documented and nothing survives that might have been done at this time.

75 Vignoli, *Pierantonio Mezzastris*, pp. 49–76, cat. no. 34.

76 Vignoli, *Pierantonio Mezzastris*, pp. 193–217.

77 Vignoli, *Pierantonio Mezzastris*, pp. 194–95, 213, note 25.

78 U. Gnoli, *Pittori e miniatori nell'Umbria*, Spoleto: C. Argentieri, 1923, p. 239–41; Vignoli, *Pierantonio Mezzastris*, pp. 76, 153.

79 M. R. Silvestrelli, "Dal maestro di Cesi a Piermatteo d'Amelia: Aspetti della cultura figurativa nell'Umbria meridionale tra XIV e XV secolo," in Bruno Toscano, *La pittura nell'Umbria meridionale dal Trecento al Novecento*, Terni: Provincia di Terni, 1993, pp. 27–43; Vignoli, *Pierantonio Mezzastris*, pp. 152–53.

80 Vignoli, *Pierantonio Mezzastris*, pp. 152–53, 195–96.

81 See most recently, Gerardo de Simone, *Il Beato Angelico a Roma 1445–1455*, Florence: Olschki, 2017.

82 Ahl, *Benozzo Gozzoli*, pp. 232–33, cat. no. 42; Ahl, "Frescante a San Fortunato," pp. 198–99, cat. no. 18; Novelli and Vignoli, *L'arte a Narni*, pp. 61–69, cat. no. 5.

83 Guardabassi, *Indice-guida*, p. 134.

84 Novelli and Vignoli, *L'arte a Narni*, p. 68.

85 Novelli and Vignoli, "Il cardinal Berardo e Benozzo di Lese: Ipotesi di un rapport di committenza," in *L'arte a Narni*, pp. 70–72. Ahl, *Benozzo Gozzoli*, pp. 41–43, suggests that Fra Antonio da Montefalco, from 1442 Provincial General of the Franciscan observants and rebuilder of San Fortunato as an observant monastery, was the patron that first brought Gozzoli to Montefalco in 1450, after his work in the Aracoeli in 1447–49. See also Adede Breda, "Benozzo Gozzoli a Montefalco," in Adele Breda, ed., *Benozzo Gozzoli; La Madonna della Cintola*, Milan: Silvana Editoriale, 2015, pp. 46–48.

86 Giovanni Dalmata (c. 1440–after 1509) from Traù, came to Rome in the late 1460s and resided there until 1485. He collaborated with masters Andrea Bregno and Mino da Fiesole, notably with the latter on the altar of San Marco (now in the sacristy) and the tomb of Paul

II (fragments in the Vatican grotte). It is not surprising that Costantino would turn to Dalmata for his uncle's tomb, for Berardo himself seems to have employed artisans from the worksite of San Marco (for which see below). R. Cordelli, "Un'opera inedita di Giovanni Dalmata a Norcia (Umbria): L'altare della *Madonna della Palla*," *Acta historiae artium Academiae scientiarum Hungaricae*, vol. 27, 1981, pp. 233–46 especially p. 245, note 3; and Francesco Negri Arnoldi, "L'attività romana di Giovanni Dalmata," in Maria Grazia Bernardini and Marco Bussagli, eds., *Il '400 a Roma: La rinascita delle arti da Donatello a Perugino*, Milan: Skira, vol. 1, pp. 41–47, 145, note 10, suggest a prior relationship between Berardo and Dalmata, for the patron of the sculptor's work in San Giovanni in Norcia was the prior Don Andrea di maestro Pietro, who was in 1462 the vicar of Bishop Eroli. In 1465, as prior of San Giovanni, he received Sante Lalli da Norcia, Eroli's vicar, in Norcia. For Dalmata, see also Johannes Roll, "Un'opera ignota di Giovanni Dalmata: Il monument Fusconi a Norcia," *Spoletium*, vols. 36–37, 1992, pp. 72–75; Dusko Keckemet in *Dizionario Biografico degli Italiani*, vol. 42, 1993, pp. 152–54; Johannes Roll, *Giovanni Dalmata*, Worms: Werner, 1994, pp. 43–47 and 102–8.

87 Giorgio Vasari, *Le vite de' più eccellenti pittori scultori e architettori* (1568), ed. Gaetano Milanesi, Florence: Sansoni, 1906, vol. 2, p. 628.

88 Archivio di Stato, Florence (hereafter ASF), Archivio Mediceo avanti il Principato (hereafter MAP); the letters to Lorenzo di Piero in Florence are the following: F. 46, doc. 261, from Spoleto, 27 July 1473; doc. 348, from Narni, 3 August 1474; doc. 363, from Rome, 30 September 1474; doc. 372, from Rome, 14 October 1474; doc. 376, from Rome, 29 October 1474; doc. 381, from Rome, 7 January 1475; doc. 452, from Rome, 31 May 1477; doc. 466, from Rome, 19 July 1477; doc. 484, from Rome, 29 November 1477; F. 34, doc. 30, from Rome, 10 February 1476. See also Lorenzo de' Medici, *Lettere*, vol. 1, ed. Riccardo Fubini, Florence: Giunti, 1977, pp. 411, 415; vol. 3, ed. Nicolai Rubinstein, 1977, p. 42; vol. 4, ed. Nicolai Rubinstein, 1981, p. 17.

89 ASF, MAP, F. 46, doc. 37, from Rome, 25 March 1462.

90 Ruda, *Fra Filippo Lippi*, pp. 36–40, 194–99, 536–37, doc. no. 21.

91 Ruda, *Fra Filippo Lippi*, pp. 540–41, doc. no. 25; Francesco Federico Mancini, *Benedetto Bonfigli*, Perugia: Electa, 1992, p. 152, doc. no. 13; pp. 157–58, doc. nos. 34–38.

92 Ruda, *Fra Filippo Lippi*, pp. 29–30; see also Hellmut Wohl, *Domenico Veneziano*, New York, 1980, pp. 339–40, doc. no. 1.

93 Vasari, *Le vite*, ed. Milanesi, vol. 2, p. 626.

94 Ruda, *Fra Filippo Lippi*, pp. 524–26, doc. no. 11.

95 Esposito, p. 231; Francesco da Castiglione, *Epistula super vita beati Antonini*, Venice: Iohannes Emericus de Spira, 1495.

96 Ruda, *Fra Filippo Lippi*, p. 34; p. 519, doc. 5.

97 See note 17. A recent discussion is Giordana Benazzi, "Filippo Lipi a Spoleto. Tempi, costi, materiali e collaboratori," in Paolo Benassi et al., eds., *Officina Pratese: Tecnica, Stile, Storia*, Florence: Edifir, 2014, pp. 77–92.

98 ASS, AODS, registro 4. The officials beginning in January 1465 are listed on c. 104 recto; in 1467, Vanni di Girolamo was replaced by Tommaso di Giacomo di Pietro Paulo; c. 111 recto, and these officials remained in place until 1470.

99 ASS, AODS, registro 4, c. 106 recto, 27 June 1466; c. 124 recto, 23 March 1470.

100 "Battici da sonare el Venerdì Sancto"; ASS, AODS, registro 4, c. 105 recto, 19 March 1466.

101 ASS, AODS, registro 4, c. 105 recto, 5 March 1466: "Pagose di volontà di ditti ad Micchiorre di Beneditto da Spoliti f. V, sonno per li fatti della heredità di Iohannolo pertenente a ditta Opera e ad lui, f. 5 s. _ d. _." The olives are paid for on c. 107 verso, 28 August 1466; the organ player c. 114 recto, 17 August 1467 and c. 117 recto, 19 May 1468.

102 The history of the Opera del Duomo in Spoleto has not been written. It is referred to in the statutes of 1296, with *operai* and a notary, and a procedure for election; so it must have existed

sometime before that date. See *Statuti di Spoleto del 1296*, ed. Giovanni Antonelli, Florence: Olschki, 1962, pp. 30, 53, 86, 121. A reference to the Opera c. 1190 was published by Silvestro Nessi, "Il Duomo di Spoleto nel secolo XII," *Spoletium*, vol. 10, 1966, no. 12, p. 33.

103 The *vicario generale* from at least 1463 through 1466 was Sante da Norcia, *priest* of Santa Maria Argentea in Norcia; see P. de Angelis, "Un frammento di sacra visita della diocese spoletina del 1465," *Archivio per la storia ecclesiastica dell'Umbria*, vol. 3, no. 1, 1916, pp. 440–50. In 1469, a document names Don Andrea de' maestro Pietro da Norcia, priest of San Giovanni Evangelista in Norcia; he had been Eroli's vicar in 1462; see Romano Cordella, "Un opera inedita di Giovanni Dalmata a Norcia," *Acta Historiae Artium Academiae Scientiarum Hungaricae*, vol. 27, 1981, pp. 233–46; Romano Cordella, "Aggiunta all'articolo "Un opera inedita di Giovanni Dalmata," *Acta Historiae Artium Academiae Scientiarum Hungaricae*, vol. 28, 1982, pp. 265–66.

104 "Per chortesia fattali venenda a Spoliti e per spese per la sua retornata"; ASS, AODS, registro 4, c. 105 verso, 1 May 1466.

105 "Sono per parte et arra di ducati 700 doverà havere per depegnere la tribuna"; ASS, AODS, registro 4, c. 106 verso, 2 July 1466.

106 Fausti, *Le pitture*, pp. 11–12, 16, 20; Ruda, *Fra Filippo Lippi*, p. 475.

107 ASS, AODS, registro 4, c. 124 recto, 23 February 1470.

108 Fausti, *Le pitture*, p. 6, notes the lack of any reference to the project in the legislative records of the commune of Spoleto, on whom the Opera depended. He also notes that the payments would have come from the chamberlain of the commune rather than the administration of the Opera if the commune had commissioned and paid for the murals.

109 ASS, AODS, registro 4, c. 106 verso, 2 July 1466.

110 Fausti, *Le pitture*, p. 7; Ruda, *Fra Filippo Lippi*, p. 473; Benazzi, "Le storie della Vergine di Filippo Lippi," p. 261. Yumi Watanabe, "Filippo Lippi's Frescoes at Spoleto, Cardinal Eroli, and the Immaculate Conception," *Mitteilungen des kunsthistorischen Instituts in Florenz*, vol. 64, 2023, p. 221, note 4, transcribes the entry: "Da messer Santi vicario di Monsignore di Spoliti fiorini cento, quali sonno per commissione di Monsignore, quale vole se paghino parte per la depintore della tribuna et per uno uscio da farse nella cappella della Ymagine, delli quali se ne pagano fiorini 77 soldi 95 ad frate Filippo dipintore di Firenze per dipignere detta tribuna et fiorini 22 soldi 5 ad Piernichola per fattura de detto uscio, como appare a uscita c. 2," from ASS, AODS, registro 4, c. 4.

111 "Oro battuto, azurri oltramarini et altre cose"; ASS, AODS, registro 4, c. 105 recto 8 February 1466; see also Fausti, *Le pitture*, p. 7; Benazzi, "Filippo Lippi a Spoleto," pp. 78–79.

112 Michele O'Malley, *The Business of Art: Contracts and the Commissioning Process in Renaissance Italy*, New Haven and London: Yale University Press, 2005, pp. 1–46.

113 Fausti, *Le pitture*, p. 12. Fausti's calculation is based on the sum of payments on 7 July and 2 September 1467; 12 April, 30 September, 12 October, 26 November 1468; and 10 August, 10 September, and 11 October 1469.

114 Fausti, *Le pitture*, pp. 11–12, 20.

115 ASS, AODS, registro 4, c. 105 verso, 106 recto, 2, 21, and 26 June 1466. The word used, *scotti*, in two of the entries is defined in John Florio, in *Queen Anna's World of Words*, London, Printed by Melch. Bradwood, 1611, as a payment for meat and drink.

116 Benazzi, "Filippo Lippi a Spoleto," p. 81.

117 ASS, AODS, registro 4, c. 107 verso, 108 recto and verso, 2 and 21 September and 1 October 1466.

118 ASS, AODS, registro 4, c. 108 verso and 109 verso, 12 November and 21 December 1466.

119 "Ad suo' garzoni"; ASS, AODS, registro 4, c. 111 verso, 26 April 1467.

120 Fausti, *Le pitture*, pp. 10–13; Ruda, *Fra Filippo Lippi*, pp. 475–76; Benazzi, "Filippo Lippi a Spoleto," pp. 82–84.

121 "Orto di frate Filippo"; ASS, AODS, registro 4, c. 111 verso, 24 April 1467; c. 112 verso, 30 May 1467.

122 "Un paio di capponi," "un capretto," "piccioni," "popuni." See, for example, ASS, AODS, registro 4, c. 112 recto, 16 May and 23 May 1467; c. 113 verso, 4 July 1467; c. 114 recto, 2 September 1467.
123 "Calze per Filippino"; ASS, AODS, registro 4, c. 112 recto, 13 May 1467.
124 Ruda, *Fra Filippo Lippi*, p. 545, doc. no. 29.
125 ASS, AODS, registro 4, c.113 recto, 17 June 1467; c. 117 recto, 23 June 1468; the Roman trips are recorded c. 117 recto, 18 May 1468; and c. 119 recto, 15 May 1469.
126 Payments to doctors and for medicines are on ASS, AODS, registro 4, c. 116 verso, 26 April 1468; c. 117 verso, 2 December 1468; c. 119 verso, 22 and 26 July 1469; c. 121 recto, 21 October; c. 121 verso, 29 November; c. 123, 31 December 1469.
127 ASS, AODS, registro 4, c. 117 verso, 12 November and 16 December 1468.
128 ASS, AODS, registro 4, c. 123 recto, 31 December 1469.
129 Benazzi, "Filippo Lippi a Spoleto," pp. 83–84. On mural painting worksites, see most recently Monciatti, "With Much Mastery of Handling but Not with Much Design"; Alberto Felici, "The Scaffolding for the Frescoes of the Cappella Maggiore"; Cecilia Frosinini, "Design, Planning and Drawing in the Legend of the True Cross," in Cecilia Frosinini, ed., *Agnolo Gaddi and the Cappella Maggiore in Santa Croce in Florence: Studies after Its Restoration*, Milan: Silvana Editoriale, 2014, pp. 85–111, 203–15, 217–33. The pioneering work of Bruno Zanardi, *Il cantiere di Giotto*, Milan: Skira, 1996, is also relevant.
130 ASS, AODS, registro 4, c. 112 verso, 30 May 1467.
131 ASS, AODS, registro 4, c. 114 recto, 20 August 1467; c. 116 recto, 4 February 1468; c. 118 verso, 1 April 1469.
132 Giordana Benazzi, "Le storie della Vergine," *Art e dossier*, no. 51, 1990, pp. 16–23; Giordana Benazzi and Paolo Virilli, *Filippo Lippi nel Duomo di Spoleto 1467–1469; Notizie dopo il restauro*, Spoleto: Panetto & Petrelli, 1992; Giordana Benazzi, "Le 'storie della Vergine' di Filippo Lippi nel Duomo di Spoleto. Alcune considerazioni dopo il restauro," in C. Acidini Luchinat et al., eds., *Scritti per l'Istituto Germanico di Storia dell'Arte di Firenze*, Florence: Casa editrice Le lettere, 1997, pp. 125–32; Paolo Virilli, "I dipinti di Filippo Lippi nell'abside del Duomo di Spoleto," in S. Rinaldi, ed., *Tecniche della pittura murale dall'alto medioevo al quattrocento*, Viterbo: 1998, pp. 32–37; Benazzi, "Filippo Lippi a Spoleto," pp. 85–90; Giordana Benazzi, Sergio Fusetti, and Paolo Virilli, "Filippo Lippi e aiuti; Storie della Vergine," in Barbara Fabjan, et al., eds., *Materiali e techniche nella pittura murale del quattrocento*, Atti del Convegno Internazionale Sapienza Università di Roma, 20–22 February 2002, vol. 2., Rome: ENEA, 2010, pp. 207–19.
133 Zanardi, *Il cantiere di Giotto*; Felici, "The Scaffolding for the Frescoes of the Cappella Maggiore", pp. 209–13, for a hypothesis of execution by teams of painters.
134 Felici, "The Scaffolding for the Frescoes of the Cappella Maggiore," pp. 203–6, for further discussion of scaffoldings.
135 ASS, AODS, registro 4, c. 113 recto, 16 June 1467.
136 Benazzi, "Filippo Lippi a Spoleto," p. 86.
137 For a glossary of pigments, see Cennino Cennini, *Il libro dell'arte*, ed. Fabio Frezzato, Vicenza: Neri Pozza Editore, 2003, pp. 235–77.
138 ASS, AODS, registro 4, c. 120 verso, 10 September and 11 October.
139 ASS, AODS, registro 4, c. 123, 31 December 1469; Fausti, *Le pitture*, p. 20, notes 62, 63.
140 Benazzi, "Le storie della Vergine," p. 261. The payments for these projects are also summarized in Andreani, "Regesti," pp. 464–69.
141 Sansi, *Storia del comune di Spoleto*, vol. 2, pp. 36–37; Silvestro Nessi, "Restauri antichi e recenti alle mura e alle porte di Spoleto," *Spoletium*, vol. 22, 1977, pp.19–36.
142 Sansi, *Storia del comune di Spoleto*, vol. 2, p. 62.
143 Bozzoni and Carbonara, "Il quattrocento e il cinquecento:," pp. 103–9; Nessi, "La cattedrale nella storia diocesana," p. 69.
144 Bozzoni and Carbonara, "Il quattrocento e il cinquecento," p. 104.
145 These fifteenth-century alterations are seen in a drawing in the Vatican library made in 1614; Bozzoni and Carbonara, "Il quattrocento e il cinquecento," pp. 104–5, 109, note 7,

note that the plan is lacking in detail and somewhat inaccurate. See also the letter from Parenzio to cardinal Maffeo Barberini accompanying the plan, 20 December 1614; Andreani, "Regesti," p. 493, no. 23, in which he states it is a design for the tribune, including the Cappella del Sacramento. This focus may explain the inaccuracies in the disposition of the side chapels to the west.

146 Giacomo (or Jacopo) is documented as a marble sculptor, primarily of architectural elements, in Rome from the early 1450s, employed on Nicholas V's improvements to the Campidoglio; Eugène Müntz, *Les arts à la cour des papes pendant le XVe et le XVIe siècle*, part I, Paris: Ernest Thorin Editeur, 1878, p. 84. Perhaps through an association with Bernardo Rossellino, Giacomo entered the service of Pius II, for whom in 1463–64 he worked with Isaia da Pisa, Paolo Romano, and Mino da Fiesole, responsible for the benediction loggia and the systemization of the Piazza San Pietro. Under Paul II, Giacomo is documented in 1466–68 working on the piazza, church, and palace of San Marco (see Müntz, part II, 1879, p. 95, note 2; p. 96, note 2; Christoph Luitpold Frommel, "Francesco del Borgo," *Romisches Jahrbuch für Kunstgeschichte*, vol. 21, 1984, pp. 71–164). His contribution in the church was marble and stucco embellishments of the side chapels and the *tribunette*, including a large cornice for the tribune, Müntz, part II, p. 15, note 3. In 1468, he was named "praesidenti fabricate palatii apostolici" (Müntz, part II, p. 16, note 1, 53). The palace in question either the Palazzo San Marco or the Palazzo Vaticano, or both, where Paul II also planned improvements (Müntz, p. 37). Shortly after Giacomo's first appearance in Spoleto (18 January 1469), on 27 February 1469, he received in Rome the large sum of more than 283 florins for work in marble (Müntz, 1879, p. 16). He also worked for Sixtus IV and in the church of Sant'Agostino for Cardinal d'Estouteville (Müntz, part III, pp. 208, 156). Later projects for Sixtus included the construction of the port of Civitavecchia; Eugène Müntz, "L'architettura a Roma durante il pontificato di Innocenzo VIII," *Archivio storico dell'arte*, IV, 1891, pp. 6–63, 363–70, 456–70. For Innocent VIII, Giacomo participated in restoration at the Lateran palace (1484–85) and the Villa del Belvedere (from 1485); Eugène Müntz, *Les arts à la cour des papes; Innocent VIII, Alexandre VI, Pie III*, Paris: Ernest Leroux, 1898, pp. 46, 94, 135, 166, note 2. The date of his death is unknown but c. 1495. See Stefano Borsi, Francesco Quinterio, and Corinna Vasic Vatovec, *Maestri fiorentini nei cantieri romani del quattrocento*, Rome: Officina Edizioni, 1989, pp. 226–36; Christoph Luitpold Frommel, *Architettura e committenza da Alberti a Bramante*, Florence: Olschki, 2006, p. 184.

147 ASS, AODS, registro 4, c. 118 recto, 18 January 1469; c. 118 verso, 8 April 1469 and 29 April 1469; c. 119 recto, 10 may 1469 and 8 June 1469; c. 119 verso 8 July 1469; c. 120 recto, 19, 23, 26 August and 2, 5, 6 September 1469; c. 120 verso, 30 September, 4, 6, 10 October; c. 121 recto, 14, 18, 20, 27, 28, October; c. 121 verso 2, 7, 11, 21, November; c. 122 recto, 29 November, 2, 5, 11, December; c. 122 verso, 18 December; c. 124 verso, 13 and 26 April 1470. On 5 November 1470, Giacomo received a last payment of 75 florins 55 soldi of the 1,200 florins promised for the construction of the chapels, according to a contract drawn up by ser Giovanni di Luca de Spoleto; c. 128 verso. Giacomo is cited in payments beginning again in March 1473 and continuing until 1478 for the chapels "verso la canonica," i.e., the north aisle; but payments for work on the pavement and the roof continued until 1486; see Andreani, "Regestri," pp. 467–68, doc. nos. 198–235.

148 ASS, AODS, registro 4, c. 121 verso, 2 November 1469, where Francesco is named "da Bologna." Francesco left the partnership at this date and Giacomo assumed full responsibility for the work.

149 Silvestro Nessi, *Nuovi documenti sulle arti a Spoleto: Architettura e scultura tra romanico e barocco*, Spoleto: Banca popolare di Spoleto, 1992, p. 20; Bozzoni and Carbonara, "Il quattrocento e il cinquecento," p. 103.

150 "Indigere meliori reparatione maxime circha tectum et coperimentum ne pluat in dicta ecclesia"; Nessi, *Nuovi documenti*, pp. 24–28; Andreani, "Regesti," pp. 464–65, doc. nos. 80–84.

151 At completion, the wall measured 27 *pertiche* and 50 *piedi*; he received different rates of payment in 1465 and 1466 that totaled 192 florins and 50 soldi. A *pertica* was in Roman usage a measuring rod that was about 10 feet (3 meters) long. A Roman *piede* in the

fifteenth century was approximately 11.73 inches. Cecco received final payment for the construction on 21 October 1466; ASS, AODS, registro 4, c. 108 verso, 21 October 1466.

152 ASS, AODS, registro 4, c. 106 verso, 2 July 1466.

153 ASS, AODS, registro 4, c. 110 recto, 26 December 1466: "Pagose di volontà di ditti ad maestro Pier Nicchola di Manzolo f. 23 s. 35, sonno per l'ultimo pagamento di quello monta lo posto dell'organi per lo refarlo, cioè per ralugarlo, per l'uscio fatto nella cappella della imagine et per uno frontone fatto sopra ditto uscio con l'arme di monsignore."

154 ASS, AODS, registro 4, c. 120 verso, 27 September, 4 October and c. 122 verso, 18 December 1469.

155 "Dello stare alla imagine"; ASS, AODS, registro 4, c. 109 verso, 21 December 1466; c. 115 verso, 31 December 1467; c. 117 verso, 31 December 1468; he is called "Pier Mattio dalle ymagine" in a payment on c. 124 verso, 10 May 1470.

156 Bozzoni and Carbonara, "Il quattrocento e il cinquecento," pp. 105–7.

157 ASS, AODS, registro 4, c. 109 verso, 14 December 1466; c. 110 recto, 26 December 1466.

158 Claudio Varagnoli, "Il Seicento: la cattedrale barberiniana," in Benazzi and Carbonara, eds., *La cattedrale di Spoleto*, pp. 111–21.

159 Varagnoli, "Il Seicento," pp. 111, 114. On the original altar, see Bruno Toscano, "L'antico altare del Duomo di Spoleto," *Spoletium*, vols. 50/51, new series nos. 6/7, 2013–14, pp. 99–111.

160 Gentili et al., *L'Umbria; Manuali per il territorio: Spoleto*, p. 344.

161 Benazzi, "Le storie della Vergine," pp. 16–23; Virilli, "I dipinti di Filippo Lippi nell'abside del Duomo di Spoleto," pp. 32–37; Benazzi, "Le 'storie della Vergine' di Filippo Lippi nel Duomo di Spoleto. Alcune considerazioni dopo il restauro," pp. 125–32; Benazzi, "Filippo Lippi a Spoleto," pp. 85–90.

162 Ruda, *Fra Filippo Lippi*, p. 477; Verdier, *Le Couronnement de la Vierge*, p. 162.

163 *Santa Maria Maggiore a Roma*, ed. Carlo Pietrangeli, Florence: Nardini, 1988, especially for the apse mosaics Marina Righetti Tosti-Croce, "La Basilica tra due e trecento," pp. 129–69; and Fabrizio Mancinelli, "La basilica nel quattrocento," pp. 191–213; Julian Gardner, "Pope Nicholas IV and the Decoration of Santa Maria Maggiore," *Zeitschrift für Kunstgeschichte*, vol. 36, 1973, pp. 1–50; Julian Gardner, *The Roman Crucible: The Artistic Patronage of the Papacy 1198–1304*, Munich: Hirmer Verlag, 2013, pp. 260–67.

164 Gardner, *The Roman Crucible*, pp. 267–68.

165 Ruda, *Fra Filippo Lippi*, p. 293; Emore Paoli, "I santi titolari della cattedrale: L'Assunta e san Primiano," in Benazzi and Carbonara, eds., *La cattedrale di Spoleto*, pp. 61–62.

166 Daniel Waley, *The Papal State in the Thirteenth Century*, London: Macmillan, 1961; Partner, *The Lands of St. Peter*; Sandro Carocci, *Vassalli del papa: Potere pontificio, aristocrazie e città nello stato della chiesa (XII–XV secolo)*; Rome: Viella, 2010; Sandro Carocci, "The Papal State," in Andrea Gamberini and Isabella Lazzarini, eds., *The Italian Renaissance State*, Cambridge: Cambridge University Press, 2012, pp. 69–89. Sansi, *Storia del comune di Spoleto*, remains a valuable source.

167 On Albornoz, see Eugenio Duprè Theseider, "Egidio de Albornoz," in *Dizionario Biografico degli Italiani*, vol. 2, Rome: 1960, pp. 45–53; for the rocca di Spoleto, see Claudio Regni, "La rocca di Spoleto tra impegni finanziari e rappresentazione del potere," pp. 213–33 ; and Giordana Benazzi, "Dalla reconquista dell'Albornoz alla renovatio di Nicolò V: Le trasformazioni quattrocentesche della rocca di Spoleto," in M. Grazia Nico Ottaviani, ed., *Rocche e fortificazioni nello stato della chiesa*, Naples: Edizioni Scientifiche Italiane, 2004, pp. 235–54.

168 Bruno Bruni, "Fortezza, residenza, carcere. Contributi per la storia dell'usa della Rocca," in *La Rocca di Spoleto: Studi per la storia e la rinascita*, Milan: Silvana Editoriale, 1983, pp. 103–11; Regni, "La rocca di Spoleto," pp. 226–33.

169 On the Cistercian abbey of Saints Vincent and Anastasius at the Three Fountains, see Angiola Maria Romanini, "La storia architettonica dell'abbazia delle Tre Fontane a Roma. La Fondazione cistercense," *Melanges Anselme Dimier*, vol. 3, 1982, pp. 653–95; Barclay Lloyd,

SS. Vincenzo e Anastasio; Fabrizio Alessio Angeli and Elisabetta Berti, *Abbazia delle Tre Fontane*, Rome: Associazione Culturale Sesto Acuto, 2007; and specifically on the pictorial decoration Carlo Berrtelli, "L'Enciclopedia delle Tre Fontane," *Paragone*, vol. 20, no. 235, 1969, pp. 24–49; Anna Menichella, "Il maestro delle Tre Fontane," in Angiola Maria Romanini, ed., *Atti della IV settimana di studi di storia medioevale dell'università di Roma*, 1983, pp. 477–85.

170 Bozzoni and Carbonara, "Il quattrocento e il cinquecento," p. 107–8; the contract for the construction is published in A. Rossi, "Di una cappella fabbricata a Spoleto nel Cinquecento per la santa Icone," *Giornale di erudizione artistica*, vol. 2, 1873, pp. 218–22.

171 C. Metelli, "Vicende decorative prima e dopo il rifacimento barberiniano," in Benazzi and Carbonara, eds., *La cattedrale di Spoleto*, pp. 335–39.

172 Belting, *Likeness and Presence*, pp. 314–29; Gail Solberg, "The Madonna Avvocata Icon at Orte and Geography," in Andrew Ladis and Shelley Zuraw, eds., *Visions of Holiness: Art and Devotion in Renaissance Italy*, Athens: Georgia Museum of Art, University of Georgia, 2001, pp. 123–35; Rebekah Perry, "The Medieval Inchinata Procession at Tivoli: Ritual Construction of Civic Identity in the Age of the Commune," *Journal of the Society of Architectural Historians*, vol. 76, no. 1, 2017, pp. 36–62.

173 Pietro Amato, *De vera Effigie Mariae; Antiche Icone Romane*, Milan: Mondadori, 1988, pp. 42–49; Hans Belting, "Icons and Roman Society in the Twelfth Century," in William Tronzo, ed., *Italian Church Decoration of the Middle Ages and the Early Renaissance*, Bologna: Nuova Alfa, 1989, pp. 27–41; Belting, *Likeness and Presence*, pp. 72, 314. The San Sisto icon was moved in 1221 to the convent of San Sisto Vecchio, then to Santi Domenico e Sisto in 1575, and then to the convent of Santa Maria del Rosario at Monte Mario in 1931.

174 Ernst Kitzinger, "A Virgin's Face: Antiquarianism in Twelfth-Century Art," *Art Bulletin*, vol. 62, 1980, p. 11; Belting, *Likeness and Presence*, p. 498.

175 William Tronzo, "Apse Decoration, the Liturgy and the Perception of Art in Medieval Rome: S. Maria in Trastevere and S. Maria Maggiore," in Tronzo, ed, *Italian Church Decoration*, pp. 180–82. See Gerhard Wolf, *Salus Populi romani: Die Geschichte römischer Kultbilder im Mittelalter*, Weinheim: VCH Verlagsgesellschaft, 1990, pp. 184–89, for another view.

176 Belting, *Likeness and Presence*, pp. 499–500, no. 4.D. On the August procession, see Filippo Caraffa, "La processione del SS. Salvatore a Roma e nel Lazio nella notte dell'Assunta," *Lunario romano*, vol. 5, 1976, pp. 127–51; Belting, *Likeness and Presence*, pp. 323–29; Herbert Kessler and Joanna Zacharias, *Rome 1300: On the Path of the Pilgrim*, New Haven and London: Yale University Press, 2000, pp. 65–125; Enrico Parlato, "Le icone in processione," in Maria Andaloro and Serena Romano, eds., *Arte e iconografia a Rome: Da Costantino a Cola di Rienzo*, Milan: Jaca Book, 2000, pp. 74–78. Belting, *Likeness and Presence,* pp. 498–502, no. 4, publishes excerpts from texts from the seventh to the eighteenth century that describe the procession over time. Included is a description from the archive from the confraternity Compagnia de Raccomandati del Santissimo Salvatore dated 1462 (G). The procession was banned in 1566 by Pope Pius V. There was also during the procession a reunion of the Lateran icon with an image of the Virgin from Santa Maria Nova (now Santa Francesca Romana) on the Via Sacra in the Roman forum, according to Belting, p. 72. Tronzo posits that the earliest route of the procession c. 1100 may have stopped by Santa Maria in Tempore and that the use of the Avvocata icon there fell out of use, perhaps to be replaced by a copy or by the icon at Santa Maria Maggiore; "Apse Decoration, the Liturgy and the Perception of Art in Medieval Rome," pp. 178–80.

177 Belting, *Likeness and Presence*, pp. 500, 4.E.

178 Belting, *Likeness and Presence*, pp. 501, 4.G.

179 Kitzinger, "A Virgin's Face," pp. 6–19; Tronzo, "Apse Decoration, the Liturgy and the Perception of Art in Medieval Rome," pp. 167–93.

180 Dale Kinney, *S. Maria in Trastevere from its Founding to 1215*, New York: New York University, 1975, pp. 325–30; and Echols, "The Coronation of the Virgin," pp. 23–27, 44–54, from which the following is drawn.

181 Julian Gardner, "Pope Nicholas IV and the Decoration of Santa Maria Maggiore," pp. 4–6; Serena Romano, "I Colonna a Roma: 1288–1297," in Sandro Carocci, ed., *La nobilità romana nel medioevo*, Rome: École française de Rome, 2006, pp. 291–312; Donal Cooper and Janet Robson, *The Making of Assisi*, New Haven and London: Yale University Press, 2013, pp. 27–33; Gardner, *The Roman Crucible*, pp. 261–67.

182 Antiphons for the Assumption declare the Virgin as queen of heaven: "Beata mater et innupta virgo gloriosa regina mundi ... regina coelorum ... exaltata es super choros angelorum, intercede pro nobis ad Dominum Deum nostris ... cum Christo regnat in aeternum"; J.P. Migne, *Patrologiae Latinae*, vol. 78, cols. 798–99. See Rachel Fulton, "Quae est ista quae ascendit sicut aurora consurgens? The Song of Songs as the Historia for the Office of the Assumption," *Mediaeval Studies*, vol. 60, 1998, pp. 82–85.

183 Echols, "The Coronation of the Virgin," p. 4; Kitzinger, "A Virgin's Face," p. 11; Verdier, *Le couronnement de la Vierge*, pp. 9–10, 15.

184 "Maria virgo assumpta est ad aetherem thalamum in quo Rex Regnum stellate sedet solio" (The Virgin Mary has been carried up to the celestial bridal chamber where the King of Kings is seated on a starry throne).

185 Kitzinger, "A Virgin's Face," p. 13; Hellmut Hager, *Die Anfänge des italienischen Altarbildes*, Munich: Schroll, 1962, p. 179, note 169.

186 Kessler and Zacharias, *Rome 1300*, p. 142.

187 Belting, *Likeness and Presence*, pp. 501, 4.G.

188 ASR, Ospedale Santissimo Salvatore ad Sancta Sanctorum, 450, no. 45; Esposito p. 230. Eroli and his nephew Costantino Eroli were members of the confraternity; see *Necrologi e libri affini della provincial romana*, ed. Pietro Egidi, vol. 1, Rome: Forzani, 1908, p. 480; vol. 2, 1914, pp. 13, 139, 457; for Costantino Eroli vol. 2, 1914, p. 505. On the confraternity generally, see Matizia Lumbroso and Antonio Martini, *Le confraternite romane nelle loro chiese*, Rome: Fondazione Marco Besso, 1963, pp. 394–97; Paola Pavan, "Gli statuti della società dei Raccomandati del Salvatore ad Sancta Sanctorum 1331–1496," *Archivio della Società Romana di Storia Patria*, vol. 101, 1978 [1980], pp. 35–96; Paola Pavan, "La confraternita del Salvatore nella società romana del Tre-Quattrocento," *Ricerche di storia religiosa di Roma*, vol. 5, 1984, pp. 81–90; and the various essays in *Tra Campidoglio e curia: L'ospedale del SS. Salvatore ad Sancta Sanctorum tra medioevo ed età moderna*, ed. Philine Helas and Patrizia Tosini, Milan: Silvana Editoriale, 2017.

189 As Nessi, "La cattedrale nella storia diocesana," p. 68, notes, the 1296 statutes confirm an earlier practice of the lords of subject castles processing through the city to the cathedral to present tributes of wax candles on the vigil of the Assumption.

190 The contract was published by Adamo Rossi, "Documenti per la storia della scultura ornamentale in pietra," *Giornale di Erudizione artistica*, vol. 3, 1874, pp. 153–55, no. 18. See also Luigi Fausti, "Il portico del Duomo di Spoleto; nuovi documenti," *Bollettino della regia deputazione di storia patria per l'Umbria*, vol. 22, 1917, pp. 339–44; Ceriana, "Il portico rinascimentale," pp. 289–303. The payment records are summarized in Andreani, "Regesti," pp. 468–69. On the earlier portico that was dismantled see Nessi, "Il Duomo di Spoleto nel secolo XII," pp. 31–36.

191 Fausti, "Il portico del Duomo di Spoleto," pp. 343–44; Nessi, *Nuovi documenti*, pp. 31–32, publishes the contract, dated 30 October 1490, for the repaving of the piazza and the reconstruction of the fountain. Nessi, pp. 19, 24–27, publishes further documentation of 1456 commissioning the reconstruction of the retaining wall along the southeastern wall of the piazza. This contract requires the workers to set aside columns and capitals dismantled from a portico there, suggesting that the piazza in the mid-fifteenth century was considerably more monumental than has been assumed. Sansi, *Storia del comune di Spoleto*, vol. 2, p. 62, relates the construction of the first fountain on the initiative of Cardinal Eroli in 1468. The contract specified the use of a local stone, pietra di Faubello, travertine, and "lapidibus rubeis" (red stones). There were also to be letters placed where indicated by the

operai: "cum illis litteris missis que videbuntur operariis." As Rossi, p. 154, note 1, notes, there is no trace of lettering.

192 Sansi, *Storia del Comune di Spoleto*, vol. 2, p. 104, note 1; he cites documents from the Riformazi from 1444, fol. 60. Bruno Toscano, *Il Duomo di Spoleto. La piazza vicende e guida artistica del monumento*, Spoleto: Ente Rocca di Spoleto, 1969, p. 10.

193 Rossi, "Documenti per la storia della scultura," p. 153; as Rossi notes, note 5, only two candelabra above the two middle piers remain. As Ceriana notes, it is not clear exactly what this "sporto de mezzo tundo" would look like; he proposes it was a feature of the model – a balcony protruding over the central arch with a baldachin on four columns – that was then modified to a rounded platform with two columns; Ceriana, "Il portico rinascimentale," p. 292.

194 "Pagose a volontà alli operali e riformatori . . . e di maestro iovanni Antonio da como per facitura allo muro novo che sta accanto della trasanna." ASS, AODS, registro 4, c. 189 recto, 5 September 1489. Further payments are made 7 November, 22 November, and 21, 30, and 31 December 1489; see Andreani, "Regesti," p. 468.

195 "Sopra la trasenna accanto allo muro dove se mostrar l'icone nella piazza"; ASS, AODS, registro 4, c. 189 recto, 15 September 1489.

196 Ceriana, "Il portico rinascimentale," p. 289.

197 Ceriana, "Il portico rinascimentale," pp. 289–90, for the building history of the portico, which was not finished until 1504.

198 Rossi, "Documenti per la soria della scultura," p. 155.

199 Archivio Storico Diocesano di Spoleto, Visite Pastorali, Maffeo Barberini, vol. 1, 1 July 1610, c. 56 recto; published in Andreani, "Regesti," p. 493.

200 See Maria Andaloro, "Il mosaico di Solsterno," in Benazzi and Carbonara, eds., *La cattedrale di Spoleto*, pp. 213–19.

201 M. Bonfioli, "Qualche appunto sull'iscrizione metrica latina sotto il mosaico della facciata del Duomo di Spoleto," in *Temi e Metodi. Arte d'Occidente. Studi in onore di Angiola Maria Romanini*, Rome: 1999, pp. 1001–11.

202 Nessi, "Il Duomo di Spoleto nel secolo XII," p. 36.

203 Perry, "The Medieval Inchinata Procession at Tivoli," p. 40; Solberg, "The Madonna Avvocata Icon at Orte and Geography," pp. 123–24; and more generally Kirstin Noreen, "Shaping the Sacred: Icons, Processions and the Presence of the Holy," in Nicholas Denusenko, ed., *Icons and the Liturgy, East and West*, South Bend, IN: University of Notre Dame Press, 2017, pp. 77–103.

204 Solberg, "The Madonna Avvocata Icon at Orte and Geography."

205 The inventory of 18 May 1425 is published by Andreani "Regesti," p. 464, doc. no. 78. Another inventory from the same year is doc. no. 79. For the True Cross relic, see Mara Bonfioli, "La reliquia della croce del duomo di Spoleto," *Spoletium*, vols. 31/32, 1990, nos. 34–35, pp. 55–60.

206 Giorgio Leone, *Icone di Roma e del Lazio*, Rome: "L'Erma" di Bretschneider, 2012, vol. 1, pp. 54–55, no. 1, for the Lateran icon, and pp. 67–68, no. 15, for the Tivoli image.

207 On the *Deesis*, see Cristopher Walter, "Two Notes on the Deesis," *Revue des études byzantines*, vol. 26, 1968, pp. 311–36; Cristopher Walter, "Further Notes on the Deesis," *Revue des études byzantines*, vol. 28, 1970, pp. 161–87; Doula Mouridi, "A Deesis Icon in the Art Museum," *Record of the Art Museum, Princeton University*, vol. 28, 1968, pp. 13–28; Tronzo, "Apse Decoration, the Liturgy and the Perception of Art in Medieval Rome," pp. 180–83. For the Byzantine source, see Bissera Pentcheva, *Icons and Power: The Mother of God in Byzantium*, University Park: Pennsylvania State University Press, 2006, pp. 111–12.

208 On 25 April 1466, the *operai* paid two florins to Dominicho d'Antonio Schiavo "per telari fece da ponersi nello rose del frontespizio per impannarele"; ASS, AODS, registro 4, c. 105 verso. Further payments for this purpose are recorded on the 21 June 1466, c. 106 verso; 26 February 1467, c. 111 recto; on 2 March 1467, c. 111 recto. In 1470, there are payments for wood to make a roof above the mosaic of the Savior on the façade: "A die 9 del dicto

[May 1470] Pagose de volontà de dicti, f. 1 ad Redolfino magistro di legname, per tavole comparate da lui per lu ticto da farse sopra al Salvatore nel frontespizio de dicta chiesia, lavora Mariano d'Antonio; A di 10 del dicto Pagose de volontà de dicti f. 1 ad Boccio, per tavole comparate da lui per lo ticto et trasanna da farsi sopra al Salvatore del frontispizio." ASS, AODS, registro 4, c.124 verso, 9–10 May 1470; c. 125 recto, 4 June 1470; c. 126 recto, 28 July 1470; c. 133 vero, 28 March 1472; c. 134 recto, 11 May 1472; cc 134 recto–verso, 7 July and 4 August 1472; c. 135 verso, 9 December 1472.

209 Kessler and Zacharias, *Rome 1300*, p. 130.

210 Kessler and Zacharias, *Rome 1300*, pp. 131–32.

211 Nessi, "Il Duomo di Spoleto nel secolo XII."

212 Gardner, *The Roman Crucible*, pp. 260–68.

213 Elvio Lunghi, "I cicli pittorici, le opere d'arte medievali e la cappella di Sant'Anna," in Benazzi and Carbonara, eds., *La cattedrale di Spoleto*, pp. 241–45.

214 Nessi, *Nuovi documenti*, p. 27.

215 Gardner, *The Roman Crucible*, p. 23; Otto Demus, *The Mosaics of San Marco in Venice*, Chicago: University of Chicago Press, 1984, vol. 2, p. 220.

216 Included in the very copious literature on Roman renewal in the fifteenth century are Torgil Magnuson, *Studies in Roman Quattrocento Architecture*, Stockholm: Almquist and Wiksell, 1958; Caroll William Westfall, *In This Most Perfect Paradise: Alberti, Nicholas V, and the Invention of Conscious Urban Planning in Rome, 1447–55*, University Park: Pennsylvania State University Press, 1974; Charles Stinger, *The Renaissance in Rome*, Bloomington: Indiana University Press, 1985, pp. 235–91; Frommel, *Architettura e committenza da Alberti a Bramante*; Gerardo de Simone, *Il Beato Angelico a Roma 1445–1455*, Florence: Olschki, 2017, pp. 19–36.

217 On this mural, see Carlo Bertelli, "L'enciclopedia delle Tre Fontane," *Paragone*, vol. 20, no. 235, 1969, pp. 24–49; Anna Menichella, "Il maestro delle Tre Fontane," pp. 477–85; Joan Barclay Lloyd, "The Medieval Murals in the Cistercian Abbey of Santi Vincenzo e Anastasio ad Aquas Salvias at Tre Fontane, Rome, in Their Architectural Settings," *Papers of the British School at Rome*, vol. 65, 1997, pp. 334–36.

218 Marilyn Aronberg Lavin, "The Stella Altrpiece: Magnum Opus of the Cesi Master," *Artibus et historiae*, vol. 22, 2001, no. 44, pp. 9–22; and more generally, Maria Rita Silvestrelli, "Dal Maestro di Cesi a Pier Matteo da Amelia: Aspetti della cultura figurative nell'Umbria meridionale tra XIV e XV secolo," *in La pittura nell'Umbria meridionale dal Trecento al Novecento*, ed. Liliana Barroero et al., Terni: Provincia di Terni, 1993, pp. 27–47.

219 Gentili, et al., *L'Umbria, Manuali per il territorio: Spoleto*, pp. 472–76.

220 Braun, Joseph, "Tiara," in *The Catholic Encyclopedia*, vol. 14, New York: Robert Appleton Company, 1912, www.newadvent.org/cathen/14714c.htm.

221 Martha Wolff, ed., *Kings, Queens and Courtiers: Art in Early Renaissance France*, Chicago: Art Institute of Chicago, 2011, pp. 70–71, no. 17.

222 Watanabe, "Filippo Lippi's Frescoes at Spoleto, Cardinal Eroli, and the Immaculate Conception," pp. 221–22.

223 Gardner, *The Roman Crucible*, pp. 263–67, notes earlier examples of the Coronation paired with the Assumption, such as the stained-glass window in Siena cathedral and the cope at Anagni, a gift to the church by Boniface VIII; see Julian Gardner, "Papal Exactions, Royal Gifts and Fashionable Cardinals: The Curial Clientele for Opus Anglicanum c. 1300–1370," in M. A. Michael, ed., *The Age of Opus Anglicanum*, New York: Brepols, 2016, pp. 22–35; for the Sienese window, see Diana Norman, *Siena and the Virgin*, New Haven and London: Yale University Press, 1999, pp. 35–37.

224 Lippi had designed the stained-glass window, executed by Lorenzo da Pelago, with the *Assumption and Gift of the Belt to Thomas* in the main chapel of the *pieve* in Prato; see Eve Borsook, "Fra Filippo Lippi and the Murals for Prato Cathedral," *Mitteilungen des kunsthistorischen Institutes in Florenz*, vol. 19, no. 1, 1975, pp. 54–55.

225 Gardner, "Pope Nicholas IV and the Decoration of Santa Maria Maggiore," p. 10.

226 Gardner, *The Roman Crucible*, p. 263; Alessandro Tomei, *Jacobus Torriti Pictor*, Rome: Argos, 1990, p. 110; Beat Brenk, *The Apse, the Image and the Icon*, Wiesbaden: Reichert Verlag, 2010, pp. 15–24.

227 "Capitelli intagliati in forma antiqua"; A. Rossi, "Di una cappella fabbricata a Spoleto nel cinquecento per la santa icone," *Giornale di Erudizione Artistica*, vol. 2, 1873, pp. 218–22. The contract includes the following condition: "Item quod capitelli debeant fieri et incidi ut apparet in ecclesia sancti Concordii extra muros spoleti videlicet ad exemplum et instar pulchriorum capitellorum dicte ecclesie sancti Concordii." Saint Concordia was the name in the fifteenth century for San Salvatore.

228 Meredith Gill, *Angels and the Order of Heaven in Medieval and Renaissance Italy*, Cambridge: Cambridge University Press, 2014, pp. 79–83; see also Meredith Gill, "Where the Danger Was the Greatest: A Gallic Legacy in Santa Maria Maggiore, Rome," *Zeitschrift für Kunstgeschichte*, vol. 59, 1996, pp. 506–10; Richardson, *Reclaiming Rome*, pp. 220–32.

229 Esposito, p. 229.

230 "Quando fo mandato cerchando da Monsignore di Vicenza"; ASS, AODS, registro 4, c. 117 recto, 18 May 1468. This trip must have been taken at some point previously, because on 23 June Lippi was paid two florins seventy soldi for hiring a horse to take Fra Diamante to Florence, where he stayed for twenty-seven days; c. 117 recto, 23 June 1468.

231 ASS, AODS, registro 4, c. 119 recto, 15 May 1469.

232 Marco Barbo was appointed bishop of Treviso in 1455 and bishop of Vicenza in 1464, a post he held until his death. He was elevated to cardinal on 18 September 1467 and installed as Cardinal-priest of San Marco on 4 October 1467. Platina claimed Paul's close relationship to Marco, "whose advice he [Paul] always took in great affairs"; *Lives of the Popes*, trans. Benham, p. 284. In 1470, he became Patriarch of Aquileia, and on 6 November 1478, Cardinal Bishop of Palestrina. He was also chamberlain of the Sacred College from 1478 to 1479; Germano Gualdo, in *Dizionario Biografico degli Italiani*, vol. 6, 1964, pp. 249–52. Marco was referred to as "Monsignor Vicenza" in an epigraph dated September 1466; see Frommel, *Architettura e committenza da Alberti a Bramante*, p. 176; cf. also Giuseppe. Zippel, "Paolo II e l'arte," *L'arte*, vol. 13, 1919, pp. 241–58. For his activity as paymaster for the construction at San Marco, see Frommel, p. 227 and Gualdo, p. 249.

233 For a detailed account, see Frommel, *Architettura e committenza da Alberti a Bramanti*, pp. 157–313.

234 Frommel, *Architettura e committenza da Alberti a Bramanti*, p. 202.

235 Frommel, *Architettura e committenza da Alberti a Bramanti*, pp. 219–27.

236 Pomponius Gauricus, *De sculptura* (1504), ed. André Chastel and Robert Klein, Geneva: Droz, 1969, pp. 64–65. According to Gauricus, Marco Barbo asked to see Donatello's abacus, but when the cardinal arrived the artist had no such instrument. The artist was brought paper and pen and drew some figures, so that Barbo might see his tools were only his imagination and skill.

237 Frommel, *Architettura e committenza da Alberti a Bramanti*, p. 184; cf. also Müntz, *Les arts à la cour des papes*, part 2, p. 75.

238 Sansi, *Storia del comune di Spoleto*, vol. 2, p. 62; Nessi, "La cattedrale nella storia diocesana," p. 69.

239 Nessi, *Nuovi Documenti*, p. 31.

240 Vasari, *Le vite*, ed. Milanesi, vol. 2, pp. 629–30; vol. 3, pp. 467–68. The tomb was moved several times, during which at one point Lippi's remains were lost; see Fausti, *Le pitture*, pp. 22–26. For the cenotaph, designed by Filippino, see most recently Paola Mercurelli Salari, "I lavori in pietra e legname e le opere d'arte del quattrocento," in Benazzi and Carbonara, eds., *La cattedrale di Spoleto*, p. 267.

241 Frederick Thomas Elworthy, *The Evil Eye: An Account of This Ancient and Widespread Superstition*, London: John Murray, 1895, pp. 260–61, 265.

242 Ruda, *Fra Filippo Lippi*, p. 295.

243 Carl Brandon Strelhlke, "Agnolo Gaddi and Trecento Florentine Portraiture," in Frosinini, ed., *Agnolo Gaddi and the Cappella Maggiore in Santa Croce in Florence*, pp.155–63. See also Joanna Woods-Marsden, *Renaissance Self-Portraiture*, New Haven and London: Yale University Press, 1998, pp. 57–60.

244 The inscription reads, "CONDITVS HIC EGO SVM PICTVRE FAMA PHILIPPVS/ NVLLI IGNOTA MEE GRATIA MIRA MANVS/ ARTIFICIS POTVI DIGITIS ANIMARE COLORES/ SPERATAQUE ANIMOS FALLERE VOCE DIV/ IPSA MEIS STVPVIT NATVRA EXPRESSA FIGVRIS/ MEQVE SVIS FASSA EST ARTIBVS ESSE PAREM/ MARMOREO TVMVLO MEDICES LAVRENTIVS HIC ME/ CONDIDIT ANTE HVMILI PVLERE TECTVS ERAM." For the transcription and translation, see Ruda, *Fra Filippo Lippi*, p. 43.

245 Doris Carl, "Il ritratto commemorativo di Giotto di Benedetto da Maiano nel Duomo di Firenze," in Margaret Haines, ed., *Santa Maria del Fiore. The Cathedral and Its Sculpture*, Florence: Villa I Tatti, 2001, pp. 129–47; Doris Carl, *Benedetto da Maiano: A Florentine Sculptor at the Threshold of the High Renaissance*, Turnhout: Brepols, 2006, vol. 1, pp. 146–50.

CONCLUSION

"Marvelous Grace of Hand"

WHAT MAKES AN ARTIST'S REPUTATION?

Giorgio Vasari, the sixteenth-century artists' biographer, explained why the painter Pietro Perugino (1446–1523) came to Florence, and why he left:

> It is true, indeed, that when a man has learnt there [Florence] as much as suffices him, he must, if he wishes to do more than live from day to day like an animal, and desires to become rich, take his departure from that place and find a sale abroad for the excellence of his works and for the repute conferred on him by that city.[1]

Florence was known in the Renaissance for its cutthroat competition and hypercritical environment, which sustained the city's reputation for superb craftsmanship and innovative design. Yet many of its most successful artists worked for long periods outside the city. Vasari states that, to make a reputation at home, an artist had to travel abroad, to execute highly visible and well-compensated projects commissioned by prestigious patrons. Ambrogio Lorenzetti was "called outside his homeland to honor another; and if by chance [that other place] is more noble in customs, mind and ability, he, once unhappy, is filled with joy in seeing himself awarded, embraced and largely honored."[2]

Artists traveled for many reasons.[3] Giotto, as the prototypically "modern" artist, traversed the Italian peninsula from Florence, to Rome, to Padua, Milan,

Assisi, Naples, and elsewhere, working for clerics, kings, bankers, and magistrates. Toward the end of his career, he worked for King Robert of Anjou in Naples, where he was awarded a lifetime annuity and privileges as a *familiaris* of the court.[4] Upon his return to Florence, he was appointed as *magister et gubernator* for life, not charged with a specific task, but, as has been speculated, available for various roles, which may have included cultural ambassador.[5] Warnke's thesis, that artists made their reputations in courts and were able to leverage the prestige attained there when they returned home, seems less persuasive in Giotto's case. Surely Giotto's reputation was the reason for his call to Naples, not its effect.

Vasari acknowledged the appeal of works by prestigious artists to patrons, when he writes again, about Ambrogio, "much greater should that [debt] be that is due from us to them [great artists], seeing that they, with great solicitude, fill the cities with noble and useful buildings and with lovely historical compositions."[6] Vasari wrote almost a century after most of the works discussed in this book were created, and his view enfolds an agenda to promote Florentine art and the ideal of the "modern manner," the classicizing style formed in Rome in the first decades of the sixteenth century. As we have seen in the previous chapters, however, Agnolo Gaddi, Andrea Bonaiuti, Benozzo Gozzoli, and Filippo Lippi enjoyed privileged status as visiting artists engaged on prestigious projects in Prato, Pisa, and Spoleto. We know that Pietro Gambacorta, the *Signore* of Pisa, personally drew up the agreement between Andrea Bonaiuti and the *operaio* of the Primiziale di Pisa in 1377. Documents reveal the courtesies beyond compensation that Agnolo, Benozzo, and Filippo enjoyed. The works examined here were all undertaken at advanced stages in the artists' careers. In fact, their reputations were well established and were the primary reasons city authorities sought their employment. The public, highly visible nature of wall painting is one reason that it emerged as one of the most prestigious art forms of the late Medieval and early Renaissance period. Wall paintings were also socially useful. In urban centers and in princely courts, figurative art, architecture, and decorative arts visualized the power of elites and authenticated their rule. Patrons valued the visual arts and their practitioners for their visibility and their ability to transmit ideas. Artists' relations with patrons and associates revealed their rising social status.

The previous chapters describe the social role of monumental wall painting in the cities of Prato, Pisa, and Spoleto during the fourteenth and fifteenth centuries. The institutional histories of the sites in which the murals were painted – the chapel of the Holy Belt in the *pieve* of Prato, the Camposanto in Pisa, and the cathedral of Spoleto – shed light on their imagery and form. Primary sources help reconstruct the ceremonies that took place within these sites, ceremonies that celebrated precious relics or images associated with the cities' civic and religious identities: the Virgin's Holy Belt in Prato, the hallowed ground of Pisa's monumental cemetery, and the sacred image of the *Madonna Avvocata* in Spoleto. The centrality of these artifacts to the historical, institutional, and religious identities of the host cities is the reason that patrons sought artists from outside their usual stable of local artisans. The impulse to seek artists from abroad for enterprises of exceptional stature and importance was long standing. The case of Taddeo Gaddi in San Giovanni Fuorcivitas in Pistoia in 1353 discussed in the Introduction, was one of the first of many instances in which the prestige attached to artists from Florence in the eyes of provincial patrons was revealed. As Stephen Campbell has noted, in such enterprises, distance conveyed value.[7]

In Prato, Agnolo was valued as a longtime employee of the Florentine Opera del Duomo, for whom he supplied decorative paintings and designs for sculpture for the Duomo and the Loggia della Signoria. In addition, he had worked for patrons from powerful families in Florence on highly visible family chapel complexes in Santa Croce and elsewhere. His collaboration with the Florentine architect Lorenzo di Filippo, *capomaestro* of the Florentine Duomo and overseer of the new chapel construction, most likely brought Agnolo to the attention of the Pratese patrons. He might have been further recommended to the Pratese Opera della Sacra Cintola by the merchants who served on the Florentine Opera del Duomo, many of whom had links to Prato through the wool trade. Agnolo's association with the Pratese merchant Francesco Datini, for whom he had worked on minor decorative painting in his palace, was not decisive, since Datini's influence was modest, and he did not become an *operaio* in Prato until well after Agnolo had begun work.

Most importantly, Agnolo's reputation derived from his highly visible narrative murals in the Alberti and Castellani chapels in Santa Croce, one of which was surveyed to establish Agnolo's compensation for the Prato work. The Castellani chapel resembled the plan of the new chapel of the Sacra Cintola; while the Alberti chapel was adorned with narratives of the True Cross, like the murals of the Virgin's Belt, a translation legend centered on a holy relic. The Florentine chapels attested to Agnolo's technical and organizational competencies. He was able to collaborate with Florentine assistants as well as local workers and to exploit a network of specialist suppliers in Florence, demonstrating command of a far-flung network of artisans, as well as adaptability to local conditions. Agnolo was a proven professional, whose skill had been honed in the intensely competitive arena of late Trecento Florence. At the same time, Agnolo reimagined the translation of the Holy Belt from the Holy Land to Prato, a subject heretofore treated only in small scale. In this feat, he replicated his triumph in Santa Croce in Florence, where he similarly conceived the first monumental narratives of the legend of the Holy Cross. The city fathers' faith in Agnolo's skill was well placed.

Benozzo Gozzoli's long sojourn in Pisa was the culmination of a prolific career. An artist with close ties to the Medici, he famously painted the sumptuous *Adoration of the Magi* in the chapel of their new palace in 1459. Benozzo worked in Fra Angelico's workshop at San Marco from the late 1430s and continued his collaboration with the older master in Orvieto and Rome up to 1447. Independent commissions in the 1450s took Benozzo from Rome to Lazio and Umbria, working in Viterbo (1453) and Montefalco (1450–52), for a variety of papal, civic, and monastic patrons. In the 1460s, Benozzo undertook the decoration of the apse in Sant'Agostino in San Gimignano with scenes from Saint Augustine's life, just before his move to Pisa in 1468. Benozzo's *curriculum vitae*, with its impressive sequence of monumental narrative cycles and range of eminent patrons, most likely brought him to the attention of Pisan patrons. Above all, his connections to Rome and to the papal court recommended him to Archbishop Filippo de' Medici, whose role as a mediator between his Medici relatives in Florence and his contacts in Rome would alert him to Benozzo's unique suitability to his project, to create in Pisa a center of cultural magnificence second only to Florence in the territorial state. Gozzoli's narrative style, with its roots in Angelico's Roman murals, its panoramic architectural and landscape settings, its dynamic figural compositions, and its portraiture, was perfectly tailored to complete the vast mural decoration of the Camposanto in an impressive and up-to-date figural idiom. Gozzoli was the most important Florentine artist painting murals in the 1460s and 1470s, and he worked primarily outside of Florence.

The apse decoration in the cathedral of Spoleto was to be Fra Filippo Lippi's final work; he died in October 1469, just before it was completed. His profuse output was capped by the completion, in 1465, of the scenes from the life of Saint John the Baptist and Saint Stephen, in the apse of Prato's main church, just prior to his work in Spoleto. How Lippi came to the attention of the Opera del Duomo officials in Spoleto, or to Cardinal Berardo Eroli, who likely spearheaded the commission, is not known, but by the 1460s, Lippi's reputation throughout Italy was well established. Already in 1438, Domenico Veneziano, writing from Perugia to Piero de' Medici, had praised the artist, who was patronized by the Medici over many decades. Most notable was Lippi's commission from Giovanni di Cosimo de' Medici for an altarpiece for king Alfonso of Naples in 1456–58. The painting was a diplomatic gift whose rich finishing was tailored to the courtly taste of its recipient. Unfortunately, the central panel and the elaborate frame are now lost; however, its design was recorded in a 1457 letter from the artist to Giovanni. About 1460, Filarete, in his architectural treatise dedicated to Duke of Milan, envisioned Lippi as part of his international team of artists, including Piero della Francesca, Vincenzo Foppa, Andrea Mantegna, and Cosmè Tura, who would build and decorate the palace in Sforzinda, his utopian city.[8] And, as we have seen, Lippi may have been on the verge of employment in Rome after completion of the Spoleto project. He was called to Rome in 1468 by Cardinal Marco Barbo, the nephew to Pope Paul II, when work on the refurbishment of the cardinal's titulus church, San Marco, was ongoing, as was the construction of the Palazzo Venezia.

Of what did an artist's reputation consist? What drew these various patrons to the artists they employed? If we turn to Cennino Cennini's *Libro dell'arte* of c. 1400, we find he used several words that refer to an artist's reputation or prestige, primarily honor (*onore*) and fame (*fama*). From the context, we can surmise that Cennino was alert to the value of highly visible works, such as an altarpiece made with expensive materials, in shaping the artist's reputation.[9] Quality of materials and their skillful deployment in refined techniques brought renown among knowledgeable patrons.[10] Versatility of skill in the mastery of a wide range of materials and techniques contributed to the artist's fame.[11] Expertise in *l'operazione di mano* (manual skill) was Cennino's focus. In spite of his precocious celebration of artistic fantasy, this quality was not uppermost in patrons' minds during this period.[12] The citations to Giotto at the court of Naples conferring on him the title of *familiaris* mention his "honest acts and fruitful services," but they do not celebrate his creativity.[13] The document announcing Giotto's appointment in Florence call him "experienced and famous" (*expertus et famosus*), "qualified" (*sufficientior*), and celebrates his "science and knowledge" (*scientia et doctrina*).[14] Giovanni Villani's *Chronicle* cited his "virtue and goodness" as reason for his salary.[15] The artist's social, intellectual, and moral qualifications seem of greater interest than the specific attributes of his style. Visual delight in colors and design were secondary to the morally improving impact of images, and their role in fostering devotion, respect, or awe in viewers.[16]

Cennino notably shows the way for the artist to develop an individual style.[17] From Cennino's prescriptions this would seem to consist of technical mastery and visual distinction from other artists. In Florence's competitive field, artists needed to find a way to stand out, yet remain within expected norms of form and imagery. Innovation was not prized for its own sake.[18] The extent to which patrons in the fourteenth century were alert to stylistic distinctions is difficult to gauge, as they rarely articulated the reasons for their choices, and the vocabulary they used was imprecise in expressing visual or aesthetic qualities. And yet, as we know from deliberations recorded in documents from the Opera del Duomo in Florence, they made distinctions and rendered quality judgments.[19] While Giotto, celebrated for his naturalistic figural language, dominated Florentine painting during the first half of the fourteenth century, Florentine artists deviated from this mode in the second half of the century. Later trecento Florentine painters produced a vast body of works, but their paintings display a numbing conformity in style and imagery.[20] Agnolo Gaddi, as we have seen, was firmly linked to Giotto through professional and familial ties, but both his style and technique show profound differences. The reasons the Pratese Opera employed him, as suggested above, were likely factors secondary to individual artistic style.

In locales besides Florence, plurality of styles was the norm, often practiced by visiting artists from far afield. As Campbell and Ahl have described, prior to the sixteenth century, mobile artists linked smaller centers, such as the princely states of Ferrara or Padua to larger centers such as Milan or Naples.[21] Recent studies reveal Naples as a center where artists from elsewhere contributed to a princely culture marked by diversity of manner.[22] The Angevin rulers of Naples from the late thirteenth through the mid-fifteenth centuries cultivated an image of cosmopolitan sophistication, employing artists from Florence, Rome, and Siena, such as Giotto and Tino di Camaino. The series of tombs sculpted by Tino between 1324 and 1337 for the royal family evoked ecclesiastical, imperial, and French royal models. From the mid-fifteenth century, the Aragonese kings drew from a far-flung Mediterranean empire, employing craftsmen from Florence and Central Italy, but also from Lombardy, Provence, Dalmatia, and Catalonia. The role of place in art historical accounts has been shown to be a powerful idea since Vasari. Rethinking notions such as "the Florentine school" and analyzing works of art in the context of cultural exchange among places animates recent scholarly work.[23] Campbell asserts, "styles belonged to artists, not to places."[24] Elite artisans built and sustained their reputations by traveling to distant places and producing highly visible works for prestigious patrons.

If we examine literary tributes from the second half of the fifteenth century to Benozzo and Lippi, we encounter terms of praise informed by humanist ideas, marking a shift from the fourteenth century in the perception of artistic reputation, or at least as voiced by patrons and critics. As we have seen, the inscription in Benozzo's mural of *Joseph and his Brothers in Egypt*, finished in 1477, celebrates Benozzo's fidelity to the variety of nature in his landscapes, buildings and figures, and his ability to bring them to life.[25] In this passage, the values of mimesis, variety, and invention, celebrated by Alberti in *De Pictura*, mark the shift in the components of artistic reputation, from technical mastery to mimetic and creative invention.

Similarly, an inscription dated 1486, two years after the Camposanto frescoes were finished, was formerly affixed to the wall next to the *Meeting of Solomon and Sheba*.[26] Here Benozzo was compared to the Greek painters Apelles and Parrhasius, whose fame and skill were related in Pliny's anecdotes.[27] The tale that painting began with the outline of a shadow was also related by Pliny. The terms and criteria of excellence that humanists derived from ancient sources transformed the way in which artists were celebrated.

The epitaph celebrating Fillippo Lippi on his cenotaph, datable to 1488–89, also sounds these themes.[28] The inscription, by Poliziano, employs the topos of naturalistic art lacking only voice.[29] It goes beyond even Benozzo's enconium in its mention of his hand, and even his "craftsman's fingers," which calls vividly to mind the physical manipulation of materials that breathes color, and even voice, into his "expressive figures." This inscription recalls Cristoforo Landino's 1480 preface to his commentary on Dante's *Divine Comedy*, in which he characterized Lippi's style as "grazioso" and "ornato."[30] Lippi himself, in his self-portrait in the *Dormition* mural, emphatically points to his right hand, calling attention to his skill and visualizing the artist's pride in his expertise and mastery (Figure 4.28). In the cenotaph, designed by Filippino Lippi, the artist, shown bust length in the robes of the Carmelite order, emerges from a shell-backed tondo. His right hand extends over the frame, the index finger pointing downward toward the inscription but also calling attention to the plaques on either side of the central one, where overlapped pens and brushes, the painter's instruments, flank a cross, signifying his status as a cleric. Both epitaph and image make explicit references to physical activity and signal new appreciation of artisanship and manual work and their practitioners. They also signal alertness to individual style, the artist's "handwriting" or signature, visualized in Lippi's self-portrait, that contemporary critical writing on the arts, such as Landino's commentary, highlight. As Michelle O'Malley has remarked, by this time, "works of art stood as much for their creators as for their purchasers."[31]

Campbell's hypothesis that patrons did not associate individual artists' styles with a particular place might be tested in the cases we have studied above for Pisa and Prato, particularly when seen in the context of Florentine state building starting in the mid-fourteenth century. In the projects for the chapel of the Holy Belt in Prato from the 1390s and the murals in the Camposanto from 1468–84, both cities of the Florentine state, the Florentine artists Agnolo Gaddi and Benozzo Gozzoli incorporated into their imagery pointed references to their home city. As we have noted, Agnolo included a replica of the Florentine sacred image the *Santissima Annunziata* into the narrative cycle of the Virgin's life in the new chapel of the Holy Belt. While thereby linking the Florentine image to the prestige of the Holy Belt, the most widely venerated relic at that time, he triggered the memory of a network of Tuscan Marian shrines, including the tabernacle of Orsanmichele and the altarpiece at the Collegiata at Impruneta, which housed the famous miracle working image of the *Madonna and Child*. The image of the *Annunciation* in Prato was also a way of drawing the cult of the Holy Belt into a Florentine orbit of Marian shrines, and thus lending it a Florentine identity. In the narrative, he embedded referents to Florentine tradition by way of figurative and landscape style. In particular, he employed the stylistic idiom of his father, Taddeo Gaddi, himself Giotto's most faithful student, seen, for example, in the *Marriage of the Virgin*. As we have seen, the primary agents in the building and furnishing of the chapel were from Florence, such as the *capomaestro* Lorenzo di Filippo. These artisans were experienced and prestigious, and there is no evidence that the *operai* in Prato sought expertise from anywhere else. Indeed, their employment followed a long-standing tradition, dating back to the early fourteenth century, of importing artisans from Florence.

In the case of Benozzo in Pisa, we have seen the image of the Florentine cathedral looming over the scene of *Joseph and his Brothers in Egypt*, an unmistakable marker of Florentine cultural identity. This image joins other references to contemporary monuments in Pisa, such as to the Archepiscopal palace, the Pisan Duomo, and the Medici palace. Benozzo's narrative style, formed primarily in Florence and Rome and perfected in San Gimignano just prior to his move to Pisa, excelled in the choreography of multiple figures, including portraits, in vast fields featuring topographically specific views. The richness of Benozzo's style, featuring the copiousness and variety celebrated by humanist writers such as Poliziano, as well as his prior employment in the Medici palace in Florence, surely recommended him to the Pisan authorities such as the *operaio*, Antonio di Jacopo della Mura, who was, ultimately answerable to Florentine authorities. The somewhat desultory search for an artist to complete the Camposanto decorations in 1466–68, in which artists as diverse as Mantegna, working in Mantua, the Lombard Vincenzo Foppa (these two also named by Filarete about 1460 as part of the team to decorate Sforzinda), and the local artist Michele Ciampanti were considered, suggests a search guided by reputation but not any artistic style. It was at this point in 1467, when Benozzo was just finishing the Sant'Agostino murals, that Filippo de'Medici intervened and proposed Benozzo for the job, given Filippo's long-standing acquaintance with the artist, Benozzo's impressive list of clients, and the archbishop's larger project to make Pisa a dazzling center of culture in the Florentine territorial state. Benozzo's willingness to be guided by patronal wishes is also documented in his letters to Piero de'Medici during the execution of the Medici chapel.[32] That Filippo's ideas shaped the imagery as well accords with the general picture of a knowledgeable and hands-on patron of art and architecture. Benozzo's identity as a Florentine artist was part and parcel of his appeal to his patrons in Pisa. Both he and Agnolo benefited from the reputation and prestige of Florentine craftsmanship that patrons from Robert of Naples to the *operai* in Prato sought to engage for their most important civic projects.

The employment of Agnolo in Prato and Benozzo in Pisa carried added meaning from their identities as Florentine artists beyond associations with professional expertise. As Florence began to build its territorial state beginning in the mid- fourteenth century, Prato was one of the first Tuscan city states to come under its control in 1351. Agnolo's decoration of the chapel of the Holy Belt, where the precious relic was preserved and displayed, incorporated references to the Florentine Marian shrine of the Santissima Annunziata, thereby putting a Florentine stamp on the ensemble. This is an early instance of Florentine cultural patronage, a kind of "soft power," in which works of art and architecture create ties of mutual regard among groups but also potentially signal cultural superiority and control.[33] Giovanni de' Medici's gift of an altarpiece by Fra Filippo Lippi to the king of Naples is an example.[34] The actions of Lorenzo de' Medici in the later fifteenth century are well known and took on an insistently political cast.[35] He sponsored Florentine artists in Rome, Naples, and Milan, as well as smaller centers such as Mantua. Filippo de' Medici strategically deployed Florentine artists in his many projects in the cathedral complex, the archepiscopal palace, and other sites. In these instances, Florentine artists acted as cultural ambassadors, and their skills had value beyond individual reputation and renown. How effective cultural patronage was in the broader campaign to build the Florentine territorial state is difficult to assess. It is one thing to dominate a city militarily and politically and another to change the allegiances of its citizens. Certainly, in the cases of Prato and Pisa, civic identities endured, and Florentine dominance was challenged in the later fifteenth and early sixteenth centuries. Duke Cosimo I de' Medici, ruler of what became the Grand Duchy of Tuscany, has been shown to have skillfully deployed cultural patronage in Florence and the cities of his domain.[36] His success perhaps profited from the experience of his predecessors.

In the period between 1377 and 1484 – just slightly more than a century – when the murals examined in this book were painted, patrons and artists collaborated and negotiated to produce some of the most impressive and important narrative cycles of the early Renaissance. The patrons, for their part, sought famous artists to decorate spaces in which precious images and relics were housed and in which ceremonies that reenacted core civic histories and memories were performed. The artists, all Florentine, responded with visual narratives that both shaped and reflected the foundational legends and identities of their host cities. The newly transcribed documents have revealed the inner workings of patronal motivation and artistic production with greater detail than previous accounts.

During this time, artists' reputations evolved from one based on the material richness and technical skill of their products, to one that celebrated artists themselves for ingenuity and inventiveness; in Baxandall's formulation, a shift of value "from gold to 'brush.'"[37] For artists such as Agnolo Gaddi, Andrea Bonaiuti, Benozzo Gozzoli, and Filippo Lippi, employment outside Florence sustained reputations built up over careers. We have seen evidence of the exceptional regard with which their employers treated them, including gifts of food and clothing beyond subsistence support. Particularly in the fifteenth century, literary sources celebrated these artists' mimetic and expressive skills in neo-Latin terms. The stage is set for the emergence of the "modern" artist in the sixteenth century.

NOTES

1 Giorgio Vasari, *Le vite de' più eccellenti pittori scultori ed architettori scritte da Giorgio Vasari pittore Aretino* (1568), ed. Gaetano Milanesi, Florence: Sansoni, 1906, vol. 3, p. 568; trans. Gaston de Vere, New York: Knopf, 1996, vol. 1, p. 585.

2 David Kim, *The Traveling Artist in the Italian Renaissance*, New Haven and London: Yale University Press, 2014, p. 74; quoted from Vasari, *Le vite* (1550), ed. Luciano Bellosi, Turin: Einaudi, 1986, p. 136.

3 Claudia Caesar, *Der 'Wanderkünstler' Ein kunsthistorischer Mythos*, Berlin: Lit Verlage, 2012; Kim, *The Traveling Artist in the Italian Renaissance.*

4 Cathleen Fleck, "The Rise of the Court Artist: Cavallini and Giotto in Fourteenth-Century Naples," *Art History*, vol. 31, 2008, pp. 467–70; repr. in Cordelia Warr and Janis Elliott, eds., *Art and Architecture in Naples 1266–1713: New Approaches*, Oxford: Basil Blackwell, 2010, pp. 38–61.

5 Martin Warnke, *The Court Artist: On the Ancestry of the Modern Artist*, trans. David McLintock, Cambridge: Cambridge University Press, 1993, p. 12.

6 Vasari, *Le vite*, ed. Milanesi, vol. 1, p. 521; trans. Gaston de Vere, New York: Knopf, 1996, vol. 1, p. 585.

7 Stephen Campbell, *The Endless Periphery: Towards a Geopolitics of Art in Lorenzo Lotto's Italy*, Chicago: University of Chicago Press, 2019, p. 17.

8 Filarete, *Treatise on Architecture: Being the Treatise by Antonio di Piero Averlino, Known as Filarete*, trans. John R. Spencer, New Haven and London: Yale University Press, 1965, vol. 1, p. 116.

9 Cennino Cennini, *Il libro dell'arte*, ed. and trans. Lara Broecke, London: Archetype, 2015, p. 158, ch. 122.

10 Ed. Broecke, pp. 131–32, ch. 96.

11 Ed. Broecke, p. 238, ch. 217.

12 Wolf-Dietrich Löhr, "'Disegnia Sechondo che Huoi': Cennino Cennini e la Fantasia Artistica," in Marzia Faietti e Gerhard Wolf, eds., *Linea I: Grafie di immagini tra Quattrocento e Cinquecento*, Venice: Marsilio, 2008, pp. 163–90; and the essays in Wolf-Dietrich Löhr and Stefan Weppelmann, eds., *"Fantasie und Handwerk": Cennino Cennini und die Tradition der toskanischen Malerie von Giotto bis Lorenzo Monaco*, Berlin, Gemäldegalerie, 2008.

13 Fleck, "The Rise of the Court Artist," p. 470.

14 Giuseppe Guasti, *Santa Maria del Fiore. La costruzione della chiesa e del campanile*, Florence: M. Ricci, 1887, pp. 43–44, doc. 44.

15 Giovanni Villani, *Istorie fiorentine di Giovanni Villani*, Milan: Nicolò Bettoni, 1834, bk. 11, ch. 12, p. 404.

16 Michelle O'Malley, *Painting under Pressure: Fame, Reputation and Demand in Renaissance Florence*, New Haven and London: Yale University Presse, 2013, pp. 64–65.

17 Ed. Broecke, p. 47, ch. 27.

18 Roberto Bellucci and Cecilia Frosinini, "'Di greco in latino.' Considerazioni sull'under-drawing di Giotto, come modello mentale," in Marco Ciatti, ed., *L'officina di Giotto. Il restauro della Croce di Ognissanti*, Florence; Edifir, 2010, pp. 167–77.

19 Jean K. Cadogan, "Agnolo Gaddi's Career and the Opera del Duomo in Florence," in Cecilia Frosinini, ed., *Agnolo Gaddi and the Cappella Maggiore in Santa Croce in Florence: Studies after Its Restoration*, Milan: Silvana Editoriale, 2014, pp. 55–71.

20 Stefan Weppelmann, "Florentine Painting around 1400: A Question of Standard?," in Francesca Pasut and Johannes Tripps, eds., *Da Giotto a Botticelli: Pittura fiorentina tra Gotico e Rinascimento*, Florence: Giunti, 2008, pp. 127–43; and more generally Miklós Boskovits, *Pittura fiorentina alla viglia del rinascimento*, Florence: Edam, 1975.

21 Campbell, *The Endless Periphery*, p. 15; Diane Cole Ahl, *Painting in Fifteenth-Century Italy: "This Splendid and Noble Art,"* New Haven and London: Yale University Press, 2023, pp. 7–9.

22 Ferdinando Bologna, *I Pittori alla corte angoioina di Napoli 1266–1414*, Rome: U. Bozzi, 1969; Ferdinando Bologna, *Napoli e le rotte mediterranee della pittura: Da Alfonso il magnanimo a Ferdinando il Cattolico*, Naples: Societa napoletana di storia patria, 1977; Samantha Kelly, *The New Solomon: Robert of Naples (1309–1343) and Fourteenth Century Kingship*, Leiden and Boston: Brill, 2003; Nicholas Bock, "Center or Periphery? Artistic Migration, Models Taste and Standards," in Livio Pestilli and Ingrid Rowland, et al., eds., *"Napoli è tutto il mondo." Neapolitan Art and Culture from Humanism to the Enlightenment*, Pisa: Serra, 2008, pp. 11–36; Cordelia Warr and Janis Elliott, "Introduction: Reassessing Naples 1266–1713," and Nicholas Bock, "Patronage, Standards and Transfert Culturel: Naples between Art History and Social Science Theory," *Art History*, vol. 31, 2008, pp. 423–37 and 574–97; repr. in Cordelia Warr and Janis Elliott, eds., *Art and Architecture in Naples 1266–1713: New Approaches*, Oxford: Basil Blackwell, 2010, pp. 1–15 and 152–75; Diana Norman, *Siena and the Angevins 1300–1350: Art Diplomacy, and Dynastic Ambition*, Turnhout: Brepols, 2018; Ahl, *Painting in Fifteenth-Century Italy*, pp. 239–55.

23 In the rapidly burgeoning literature on this subject, see most importantly, Enrico Castelnuovo and Carlo Ginzburg, "Centro e periferia," in *Storia dell'arte italiana*, vol. 1, Turin: 1979, pp. 283–352; Thomas DaCosta Kaufmann, *Toward a Geography of Art*, Chicago and London; University of Chicago Press, 2004, with an extensive historiography, pp. 17–104.

24 Campbell, *The Endless Periphery*, p. 17.

25 See Chapter 3, note 281; Ahl, *Benozzo Gozzoli*, p. 194.

26 SIT LAUS PRISCA VIRO PRIMUM QUI PINXIT AB UMBRA;
POST HOMINUM SENSUS NON TULIT ESSE RUDES.
SIC CYPRIS COAS ILLUSTREM TUNC FECIT APELLEM:
PARRASII TABULAE NOMEN IN ASTRA FERUNT.
GLORIA QUANTA TIBI, BENOTI, FULMINIS INSTAR,
HAEC NUNC TAM CELEBRI COMPOSUISSE MANU!
LAUDE QUIDEM TOTO DIGNUS CELEBRANDUS IN ORBE;
NAM TU PINXISTI QUIDQUID IN ARTE FUIT.
KAL. MAII. MCCCCLXXXVI; Supino, *Il Camposanto di Pisa*, p. 295.

27 Sarah Blake McHam, *Pliny and the Artistic Culture of the Italian Renaissance*, New Haven and London: Yale University Press, 2013, pp. 316–17, 319.

28 For the transcription and translation, see Ruda, Fra Filippo Lippi, p. 43.

29 The idea of a likeness lacking only voice has been traced to Ovid's *Letters from Heroines*, in which Laodamia addresses her absent husband Protesilaus, of whom she has made a wax portrait; (*Heroides* 13.149–54); see Harry Vredeveld, "'Lend a Voice': The Humanistic Portrait Epigraph in the Age of Erasmus and Dürer," *Renaissance Quarterly*, vol. 66, 2013, p. 519. Petrarch praises a polychrome stucco relief of Saint Ambrose in Milan by saying that "only the lack of a voice prevents one seeing the living Ambrose"; Michael Baxandall, *Giotto and the Orators*, Oxford: Clarendon Press, 1971, p. 51. In another example, Petrarch, in *Remedies for fortune Fair and Foul*, ed. and trans. Conrad Rawski, Bloomington: Indiana University Press, 1991, bk. 1, dialogue 40, Reason, countering Joy, says, "You take delight in the pencil strokes and colors which please because of price and skillfulness –their variety and artistic compositions. And you are fascinated by the likelike gestures, the movement in these inanimate and immobile pictures . . . and the portraits that seem about to breathe and make you think that they might utter words."

30 Michael Baxandall, *Painting and Experience in Fifteenth Century Italy*, 2nd ed., Oxford: Oxford University Press, 1988, pp. 128–33.

31 Michelle O'Malley, "Finding Fame: Painting and the Making of Careers in Renaissance Italy," *Renaissance Studies*, vol. 24, 2010, p. 9.

32 Ahl, *Benozzo Gozzoli*, pp. 276–77, docs. 10 a–d.

33 Brendan Cassidy, "Artists and Diplomacy in Late Medieval Tuscany: The Case of Giotto, Simone Martini, Andrea Pisano, and Others," *Gesta*, vol. 51, 2012, pp. 91–110, sets the itinerant activity of these artists in a political context, suggesting that political alliances led to cultural exchange. For a more general account of cultural diplomacy, see Oren Margolis, *The Politics of Culture in Quattrocento Europe: René of Anjou in Italy*, Oxford: Oxford University Press, 2016.

34 Ruda, *Fra Filippo Lippi*, pp. 194–99, 442–44, cat. no. 49.

35 Caroline Elam, "Art and Diplomacy in Renaissance Florence," *RSA Journal*, vol. 136, 1988, pp. 813–26.

36 See the various essays in *The Medici; Portraits and Politics, 1512–1570*, ed. Keith Christiansen, New York; Metropolitan Museum of Art, 2021.

37 Baxandall, *Painting and Experience*, p. 17.

APPENDIX I

DOCUMENTS FOR THE CHAPEL OF THE HOLY BELT IN PRATO

I.1 PRATO, ARCHIVIO DI STATO, PATRIMONIO ECCLESIASTICO 45 (ENTRATA E USCITA DELLA CAPPPELLA DELLA CINTOLA, 1393–1394)

C. 16 RECTO

Al nome di di Dio amen Anno MCCCLXXXXII, a dì primo di maggio Uscita de' denari e pecunia dell'opera e cappella della cintola della della [*sic*] pieve a Prato, dati e pagati per me Stefano d'Arigho nell'anno e dì detti e finito come seguie e come camarlingho della detta cappella e opera, e di licenzia overo dicreto delli infrascritti operai e capitani overo d'uno di loro in cui comettessino, la quale commissione fue fatta in Ridolfo di Nicholao operaio di sopra nominato colli altri, cioè

Messer Piero di Pavolo	tutti operai e capitani della detta	
Antonio di Marcho	cappella e opera,	e prima
Ser Tomaso di Ser Arighetto		
Ridolfo di Nicholao		

Biagio del Campana per due quaderna di folgli mezzane per fare uno libro dell'entrata e uscita e uno mezzo quaderno di folgli reali per fare uno bastardello, in tuto ebe adì 8 magio [1392] s. dicenove L.__ s. xviiii

Manno di Gianni Bartolini, cartaio, per le coverte de' detti libri e quadernelli ebbe adì 10 di maggio L.__ s. x

Zuchetta del ponte Ponzalglio per rechatura colli buoi viii lengni chessi comperarono da Jacopo da San Donn[in]o per per ii lengni che rechò da casa Cristofano per fare il ponte alla cappella lire una L. i

C. 16 VERSO

Anno MCCCLXXXXIIII [*sic*]

Cristofano di ser Francia adì x di magio [1392], per iii dì che stete a filare lengniame e per segare e inporre il balcho della cappella lire tre

L. iii

Niccholò da Lucina per due dì [struck out: e mezzo] ch'aiutò a Cristofano segare e imporre il detto balcho, lire una soldi sei detto dì
L. i s. vi

Panezzo e il figliu[o]lo adì detto per ii dì e mezo per uno a segare tramelli e tavole del dettto lengniame, per soldi xii il dì per uno l tre
L. iii

Bochalite trechone, per xviiii pani per le dette opere soldi dicenove
L.__ s. xviiii

Piero di Gue[l]fo adì detto per iiii dì che stette e a[e]ntò a'detti maestri, per soldi v il dì, in tutto lire una L. i

Lorenzo di Stefano per barile mezo di vino per li decti maestri, adì detto, lire una soldi cinque L. i s. v

Algomento Peratti, vetturale, adì xiiii di magio, perche comprò a Pistoia pezzi lxxvii di tavole d'abeti per lo balcho della chappella, per soldi v denari vii in Pistoia, lire xxi soldi viiii denari xi, e per la gabella a Pistoia lire una, e per sua vettura v some lire iii soldi–,

lire venticinque soldi nove denari xi L. xxv s. viiii d. xi

Galelucco Galelucci, dì detto per gabella delle dette tavole á Prato, lire tre soldi due L. iii s. ii

Pantuzzo e il figl[i]ulo adì xv di magio, per uno dì e terzo per uno a segare uno abete grosso per travicelli per lo decto ponte, lire una soldi dodici
L. i s. xii

Cristofano e Nicholò adì decto per II terzi per uno a compire il detto balcho, in tutto

lire una soldi uno denari otto L. i s. i d. viii

Piero di Gufo per ii dì che aiutò a' detti segatori adì detto e tras[s]e pietre di . . .
L.__ s. x

C. 17 RECTO

Anno MCCCLXXXXII

Antonio vetturale per ii terzi dì di cun II asini per regare le pietre che diede Mon[a] Giana di ser Piero . . . soldi sedici L.__ s. xvi

Michele Bechalite per xiii panni per le dette opere a' segatori, soldi tredici
L.__ s. xiii

[in margin: dì xv di magio]
Jacopo da Sancto Domino maestro, per viiii pezzi di legni d'abete per fare travi e puntone e mezzane e travicelli per lo balcho della cappella, in tutto lire quarantaquattro L. xliiii

Cristoforo di ser Francia per ii lengni per fare travi al decto balcho adì detto
L. xv

Zachetta dal ponte Ponzaglio adì detto, per recare i decti ii legni di Cristoforo e I di quelli di Jacopo alla pi[e]ve s. otto L.__ s. viii

[in margin: per lo soponte]
Antonio Michechi, adì xxv di magio, per xi correnti grossi di castangno per fare cavaletti per lo soponte della cappella, lire quatro soldi quatro
L. iiii s. iiii

Antonio detto [struck out: detto dì] xxviii di magio per iiii correnti grossi per fare cavaletti sopra il ponte, lire una s. dieci
L. i s. x

Antonio detto detto dì per xxiiii correntelli per fare piedi a detti cavaletti e catene
[struck out: lire viii s. due] per s. ii d. x del'uno lire tre s. otto
L. iii s. viii

Antonio detto, adì detto, per xxx mazzichetti per fare piedi a detti cavaletti l. una s. diece L. i s. x

Cristofano di ser Francia, adì xxviiii di magio per I lengno d'albero, che comperò per fare travicelli per lo balcho della cappella, l. una s. diece
L. i s. x

C. 17 VERSO

Anno MCCCLXXXXII

Cristofano di ser Francia, adì xxviiii di magio, per ii dì a fare il soponte sopra il balcho
lire due L. ii

Algomento Peratti, adì detto, per xxv pezi di tavole d'abeti comprò [struck out: affirenze] a Pistoia per lo decto soponte, per s. vi d. vi l'una colla gabella a Pistoia e sua vettura,
l. otto s. due d. vi
L. vii s. ii d. vi

Gabelletto, gabelliari per lo comune di Firenze, per la gabella delle decte tavole decto dì,
s. diecenove L.__ s. xviiii

Niccholò d'Agliana, adì detto, per II dì e terzo ch'autò a Cristofano affare il decto suponte alla cappella l. i s. dieci d. quatro
L. i s. x d. iiii

Benedetto Manetti fabro, a dì xxxi di magio, per sua ragione d'auti di più fatte, dati a Piero per le dette supponte della della [*sic*] decta cappella, levata da'libro del detto Benedetto a foglio xxxviiii, l. tre s. undici
L. iii s. xi

Rosso portatore, adì detto, per recare xi correnti da Antonio Michechi alla pieve
L.__ s. iii d. viii

Michele Bechalite, adì detto, per xii pan[n]i per le decti opere
L.__ s. xii

[in margin: per li fondamenti]
Guadagno del Mazza, xxx di magio, per uno dì a tramutare [struck out: la] pietre e rapianare la piaza per fare spengnere galcina per li fondamenti, s. undici
L.__ s. xi

Piero di Guido per iii dì ch'autò alle dette opere infino a dì detto s. quindici
L.__ s. xv

Piero detto per vi folgli doppi, che cumperò per li ragionieri di Stefano di ser Tingho, vecchio operario s. due
L.__ s. ii

Piero detto, adì detto, per uno mezo barile di vino per le dette opere, l. una s. cinque
L.i s. v

C. 18 RECTO

MCCCLXXXXII

[in margin: casso perchè fue . . .?]
[Struck out: Piero di Guefo adì xxxi di maggio per barile mezo di vino che comprò per le dette opere Lire una s. cinque
l. i s. v]

Guadangno del Mazza adì viii di giugno, per ii dì a spegnere chalcina per s. xi il dì [struck out: a spegnere chalcina mogia vii detto dì, di chalcina] lire una s. due
L. i s. ii

Giorgio di Fran[ce]scho adì detto per ii dì a ffare il detto lavorio della chalcina, per s. xi il dì l. una s. due L. i s. ii

Piero di Gu[e]fo per iii dì e ii terzi a a[i]utare alle decte opere e a Guadagno quando apianò la piaza sei dì l. s. dic[i]otto
L.__ s. xviii

Bochalite, adì detto, per xiiii pani per le dette opere s. quatordici
L.__ s. xiiii

Piero detto, adì detto, per bacelli e alli e insalata per le dette opere s. uno
L.__ s. i

Giovanni di Neri per raconciare la bigongia da rechare l'aqua s. dieci
L.__ s. x

Guadangno del Mazza e 1 compangno, per uno dì per uno a spengnere chalcina chassiele[?] da Bartolomeo di Nardo, l.una s. due
L.. i s. ii

Piero di Gufo per uno dì aiutare l'altro s. cinque
L.__ s. v

Piero detto, per v panni per le dette opere, s. cinque
L.__ s. v

Bartolomeo di Nando fornaciaio, adì xii di giungno, per moggia iiii di chalcina, ebe i danari adì xiiii di giugno, spesi son nel chiostro, per soldi xlvii mogio, l. nove s. otto
L. viiii s. viii

Piero Dati, fornaciaio, adì xiiii di giungno, per mogia ii di chalcina che ssi spense con quella di Meo di Stefano anto satto[?] lire quattro s. dieci
L. iiii s. x

C. 18 VERSO

Anno MCCCXXXXII

Piero di Gufo, adì xvi di giungno, che comprò una barcha da Fran[ce]scho del Garba, s. quatrodici L.__ s. xiiii

Lorenzo di Stefano, adì detto, per barile mezzo di vino per le dette opere, lire una s. dieci
L. i s. x

Antonio di Jacopo, vetturale, adì xxii di giungno, per ii dì a portare terra de' fondamenti, con ii asini, l. due
L. ii

Antonio decto per rechare mille mattoni e iiii cento mezane da Meo di Stefano, fornaciaio, per li decti fondamenti s. diecenove

L.__ s. xviiii

Domenico Santini [?], maestro, adì xxii di giugno, per iiii dì e ii terzi a detti fondamenti, per s. xv al dì, l. tre s. dieci

L. iii s. x

Milgli[o]re maestro, adì detto, per iii dì a fare i mulimenti, per s. quindici il dì l. due

L. ii

Cialdo manovale, per iiii dì e ii terzi, per s. xii il dì l. due s. sedici

L. ii s. xvi

Guadangno del Mazza, adì detto, per v dì e I terzo, per s. xii il dì a radere la galcina l. tre

L. iii s.iii

Lorenzo Cardati adì detto, per v dì e I terzo al detto lavorio l. tre s. Quattro

L. iii s. iv

Lorenzo detto, adì detto, per una trave a cavare cierti corpi di cierti mulimenti e metterli ne' mulimenti nuovi, l. una s. cinque

L. i s. v

Piero da Figline, adì detto, per iii dì e ii terzi per s. xii il dì al detto lavorio, l. due s. quattro

L. ii s. iiii

Salvestro di Fredino per ii [struck out: dì] terzi, adì detto, al detto lavoro per s. xii il dì s. otto

L.__ s. viii

Nanni manovale per iiii dì e ii terzi, per s. xii il dì l. due s. sedici

L. ii s. xvi

Nani della Rossa, con tre bestie a portare terra per I dì e ii terzi, l. due s. dieci

L. ii s. x

Piero di Guelfo per v dì e ii terzi aiutare a detti maestri ne' detti dì, l. una s. otto

L. i s. viii

C. 19 RECTO

Anno MCCCCLXXXXII

Piero di Gue[l]fo adì detto dinnanzi, i quale spese in corda rinforzata per li maestri, s. otto

L.__ s. viii

Piero detto, detto dì, per iiii manichi per fare due barelle per la chalcina s. tre
L.__ s. iii

Piero detto, detto dì, per alli e icascio per li decti maestri, s. nove d. sei
L.__ s. viiii d. vi

Piero detto, per detto dì, per xx pani per li decti maestri l. una
L. i

Piero detto, adì detto, che comprò da Antonio biadaiolo staia 1 di farina per fare pane per li detti maestri l. due s. dicesette
L. ii s. xvii

Piero detto, che comprò per li detti maestri e manovali dì ne' dì, per barili 1 e mezzo di vino, per lire tre barile, l. quattro s. dieci
L. iiii s. x

Antonio Michieli, adì detto, per vii pezi di correnti per mettere ne' mulimenti l. una L. i

Antonio detto, adì detto, per lxxxii pali per coprire i detti mulimenti l. quatro s. nove L. iiii s. viiii

Pavolo della Stufa, per vii fastella di stoppa per coprire i detti mulimenti detto dì, s. diciotto, denari otto
L. __ s. xviii d. viii

Meo di Stefano fornaciaio, adi xxvi di giungno, per mogia viii di calcina che ssi spense da [?] . . . Guadangio per li fondamenti, per l. ii s. iiii mogio, l. dicesette s. dodici
L. xvii s. xii

Meo detto, adì detto, per moggia 6 di mattoni per fare mulimenti adì detto, l. nove s. dic[i]otto
L. viiii s. xviii

Meo detto, adì detto per iii mezane per lo detto lavorio, l. due s. due
L. ii s. ii

Lorenzo di Pinzidimonte, adi xxviiii di giungno, per iiii dì a ffare i fondamenti alla pieve, per s. xv il dì l. tre
L. iii

Lorenzo detto, adì detto, perchè votò l'avello di ser Giovanni Serpieri e di Tucio e di Cristofano, e messe l'assa nelli loro avelli, l. due
L. ii

C. 19 VERSO

Anno MCCCLXXXXII

Nanni di Giovanni da fFirenze, adì xxviiii di giungno per iii dì a cavar fondamenti, per s. xii il dì, l. due s. otto

L. ii s. viii

Cialdo manovale, adì detto, per iiii dì al detto lavorio, per s. xi il dì lire due s. quattro

L. ii s. iiii

Giovanni da Feghine di Valdarno, adì detto, per iiii dì per s. xiiii il dì lire due s. quindici

L. ii s. xv

Domenicho Santini, per iii dì e mezzo a murare i detti fondamenti per s. xviii il dì, l. tre s. tre

L. iii s. iii

Milgliore Pucci, per iiii dì al detto lavorio adì detto, per s. xviii il dì, l. tre s. dodici

L. iii s. xii

Malfante, manovale, per iiii dì adì detto, per s. xiiii il dì, l. due s. quindici

L. ii s. xv

Nanni da Capalle, per ii dì adì detto, per s. xii al dì, l. una s. quattro

L. i s. iiii

Giovanni di Giovanni da Mezana, adì detto, per I dì, s. quattordici

L. __ s. xiv

Michele di Bonaco[r]so, a dì detto per I dì e I terzo s. dodici

L. __ s. xii

Antonio di Jacopo, renaiuolo, per ii dì a portare terra ne' due dì, lire due

L. ii

Piero di Gufo lavorò per iiii dì a servire i detti maestri, l. una

L. i

Piero detto, adì detto, che spese in cascio alli e lattugha s. dieci

L. __ s. x

Checcho Bandi adì detto, per staia I di farina per fare pane l. tre

L. iii

Piero detto, detto dì, per barile I di vino per lire iiii barile l. quattro s. dieci.

L.iiii s. x

Jacopo da Lasso, detto dì, per sottigliare matoni e pachini [?] per li maestri, s. cinque

L. __ s. v

Malfante, manovale, adì detto, che autò a Lorenzo una notte votare mulimenti,
s. dieci

L. __ s. x

Meo di Stefano, fornaciaio, adì detto, per C mattoni che mancharono, s. dic[i]otto

L. __ s. xviii

C. 20 RECTO

Anno MDCCCLXXXXII

Piero di Gufo, adì xxviiii di giungno, per uno fastello di schope per la notte che ssi cavarono i mulimenti, s. due d. otto

L. __ s. ii d. viii

Piero detto per adì ii di luglio, per mogia iiii di calcina rechò Antonio adì 1 del detto mese, per s. xlv mogio, l. nove

L. viiii

Milgliore di Piero, maestro, adì v di luglio, per iiii dì a detti fondamenti per s. xviii il dì, l. tre s. dodici

L. iii s. xii

Domenicho di Guiducio, adì detto, per iiii dì al detto lavorio per lo detto pregio,
l. tre s. dodici

L. iii s. xii

Domenico Santini, adì detto per 1 dì al detto lavorio, s. dic[i]otto

L. __ s. xviii

Cialdo Simoni, adì detto, al detto lavorio per s. xi il dì, l. due s. quattro

L. ii s. iiii

Lorenzo da Pinzidimonto, adì detto, per iiii dì al detto lavorio, per s. xv il dì l. tre

L. iii

Nanni da Volterra, adì detto, per iiii dì al detti fondamenti, per s. xii il dì l. due s. viii

L. ii s. viii

Nanni da Capalle adì detto, per iiii dì a detto laviorio, per s. xii il dì, l. due s. viii

L. ii s. viii

Lorenzo da Pinzidimonto, per uno dì al detto lavorio, s. quindici

L. __ s. xv

Giovanni di [?], adì detto, per uno dì e mezzo, l una s. uno

L. i s. i

Piero di Giovanni, a dì detto, per ii dì per s. xiii il dì l. una s. sei

L. i s. vi

Franceschо da [?], adì detto, per 1 dì, s. tredici

L. __ s. xiii

Giovanni di Stefano, adì detto, per ii dì , l. una s. sei

L. i s. vi

Giovanni di Piero, adì detto, per iiii dì per s. quindici il dì l. tre

L.iii

Piero di Guefo, adì detto, per v dì per s. v il dì l. una s. cinque

L. i s. v

Michele di Bernardo[?], adì detto, per iii dì per s. viiii il dì l. una s. sette

L. i s. vii

C. 20 VERSO

Anno MCCCLXXXXII

Checho Bandi, adì v di luglio, per staia uno di farina per li detti manovali

e maestri, per fare pane, l. due s. dic[i]otto

L. ii s. xviii

Piero di Gufo, detto dì, per barili i di vino che comprò per li detti maestri e manovali l. quatro s. dieci

L. iiii s. x

Piero di Gufo, detto dì, che comprò per li detti maestri e manovali cascio, cipolle, insalata, lire una

L. i

Piero di Gufo, adì detto, per viii pani, s. otto

L. __ s. viii

Giovanni di Neri, 1 cierchio e uno fondo a una turcha e mastelo, s. sei

L. __ s. vi

Antonio Michechi, per ii correnti di castangno per fare piedi a una capra per lo dipintore [struck out: per xx p] l. una s. sei d. otto

L. i s. vi d. viii

Piero dati, adì detto, per cento mattoni per cumpire di chiudere mulimenti, rechò Anton[i]o, s. dicotto

L. __ s. xviii

Domenicho Santini, adì detto, per ii terzi e mezo di dì s. quincdici

L. __ s. xv

Cieldo Simoni, adì detto, per ii terzi e mezzo, s. dieci

L. __ s. x

Piero di Gufo, per iii pani e alli e cipole, s. otto

L. __ s. viii

Piero detto per ii terzi e mezo, s. [struck out : tre] quatro

L. __ s. iiii

Barella ch'autò sabato portare pietre, s. due

L. __ s. ii

Lorenzo da Pinonte perchè vet__[?] l'anelo delli . . . [?] s. due

L. __ s. ii

Antonio vetturale, adì xiii di luglio, per ii dì a portare terra per s. xxv il dì l. due s. dieci

L. ii s. x

Antonio detto, adì detto, per rechatura mogia xviii di chalcina per li fondamenti,
e la rena, per s. xviii mogio, l. sedici s. quatro

L. xvi s. iiii

C. 21 RECTO

Anno MCCCLXXXXII

Antonio di Jacopo, renaiuolo, adì xvii di luglio, per iii dì che stette a portare terra da dì detto insino adì xx del detto mese, per s. xxv il dì, l. tre s. quindici

L. iii s. xv

Piero di Gufo, detto dì, per ii righe di noce per lo dipintore, s. quattro

L. __ s. iiii

Bartolomeo di Nardo, fornaciaio, adì xviiii di luglio, per ii misure di galena per lo dipintore, s. dodici

L. __ s. xii

Magio adì detto, per spengnere la detta galena, s. quattro
L. __ s. iiii

Piero di Gufo per uno dì a valgliare la rena e galena dello detto, per s. cinque
L. __ s. v

Antonio di Jacopo, rena[i]uolo, adì detto, per rechatura la detta galena s. uno
L. __ s. i

Ciecho tornaio, per uno bosulo, s. cinque
L. __ s. v

Piero di Guefo e	sagrestani, adì xviiii [struck out: d'agosto] di luglio per loro
Pardo d'Andrea	salario di tre mesi passati, cioè magio giugno e luglio, per l. iii al mese per uno a servire all'antare della cappella l. dic[i]otto

L. xviii

Mona Margherita che vende le candele, adì detto, per suo salario de' detti tre mesi a vendere le candele per l'Opera, per s. xxx il mese l. quattro s. dieci
L. iiii s. x

Monte di Lancio, che suona gli organi, adi detto, per suo salario di detti tre mesi, a ragione di f. xx per anno a suonare li organi, f. Cinque
f. v

Benedetto Maretti, fabro, adì detto, per libbre ii d'a[g]uti per fare bassoreli [?] per li fondamenti e raconciare 1 bechastrino e rinferratura ii marrine [?], fatti da dì xvii di giugno infino adì iiii di luglio, l. una s. uno, come appare a libro suo, a foglio xliiii

L. i s. ii

C. 21 VERSO

Anno MCCCLXXXXII

Antonio di Jacopo renaiu[o]llo, adì xx di luglio, per bracia 1 meno some L di pietre di Bisenzo, che reghina alla pieve, per lire xiiii braccio, netti di mistura e misture, per Domenicho di Guiducio e Domenicho Santini, tarate il detto L, sane per li detti maestri, lire dodici s. sei d.__
L. xii s. v

Algomento Peretti, vetturale, adì detto, per barili i di pietre bisenzane, che rechò alla pieve per li fondamenti, a Bernardo per Domenicho di Guiducio, per lire xiiii il l., netti di misura, lire quatordici
L. xiiii

Domenicho di Guiducio detto, detto dì, che misurò le decte pietre per ii dì che mi stette a mosuralle tra due volte, cioè quelli dal gimento e parte di quelle di Antonio decto, lire una s. dieci

L. i s. x

Milgliorato di messer Guido, adì detto, per some lxxx di pietre grosse e cantone per murare per facia a' fondamenti super terra, a ragione di lire xxiiii bracio, posti alla pieve, rechò Carlone vetturale

L. iiii s. viiii

Tarato per li maestri lire quarto soldi nove
[struck out: Matteo di Guerzone, danilo, adì v di aprile, per legato fatto alla cappella per Monna Chiaiana, sua madre carta per ser Varzo Bandini, di cera di libre ii once x, ebe Piero di Gefo, sagrestano, per la detta cappella, rechò Matteo decto.]

C. 22 RECTO

Anno MCCCLXXXXII

Io Ridolfo di Nicholao, operaio della pieve di Prato dell'anno che inchominciò dì primo d'aghosto dell'anno MCCCLXXXXI e finio nel'anno MCCCLXXXXII, dì ultimo di luglio, chome chommessario di messer Piero Rivaldeschi o degli altri miei chompagni, operai della detta pieve, le sopradette spese fatte nel detto tempo del nostro uficio per lo detto Stefano chamarlingho, dicho e apruovo esser fatte di volontà de' chompagni e mia, nonestante altri dicreti per me fatti, e chosì m'ò soscritto.

C. 22 VERSO

Uscita dell'opera e cappella della pieve a Prato nell'anno MCCCCLXXXXII, da dì primo d'agosto anno detto insino a calen di maggio prossimo che viene, al tempo delli iii infrascritti operai cioè

Paolo di Vanni Tachagnini	nuovi operai per uno anno incominciati dì
Francescho di Piero Camboni	primo d'agosto e finiti dì ultimo di luglio anno MCCCLXXXXIII
Messer Piero di Pavolo	Vecchi operai che ànno a stare insino a dì
Antonio di Marcho	ultimo di gennaio anno MCCCLXXXXII

Piero Dati, adì x d'agosto, per ii misure di calcina per le dipinture s. dodici

L. __ s. xii

Magio manovale, adì detto, per spnegnere la detto calcina s. sei
L. __ s. vi

Antonio renaulo per staia iiii di rena per la detta calcina s. quattro
L. __ s. iiii

Piero di Guefo per valgliatura e colatura la detta calcina s. cinque
L. __ s. v

Matteo di Cunveneuola adì xiiii d'agosto, per libbre dugento cinque di candele date per vendere al descho dell porta della cappella, reghò Piero di Guefo da dì xi di magio prosimo che passò in fino adì x d'agosto, per s. x d. vi libbra, lire ciento cinque s. due d. sei
L. cv s. ii d. vi

Matteo detto adì detto, per facitura di libbre xiiii di machili che portamo cum Messer Rancio di quelli della Pasqua del Risuresso, i quail avea auti di magio, per s. ii libbra, l. una s. otto
L. i s. viii

Guadangno del Mazza, adì xvi d'agosto, per uno dì a spengnere mogia iii di galena che ssi ebe da Meo fornaciario per li fondamenti, s. undici
L. __ s. xi

Martino di Giovanni, adì detto, che lli à 'uto al detto lavorio s. dieci s. x
L. __ s. x

Piero di Guefo, per iiii pani comprò [per dette] opere e companàticho s. tre d. quattro
L. __ s. iii d. iiii

Piero detto, adì detto, per suo salario a colare la detta chalcina s. cinque
L. __ s. v

C. 23 RECTO

Anno MCCCLXXXXII

Cialdo manovale, adì detto, che li menò la detta chalcina, s. quarto
L. __s. iiii

Giovanni di Vieri, adì decto, per ii fondi per li sabielli [?] della chalcina s. sette
L. __ s. vii

Michele delli Abati, adì detto, per una tavola di pero d'uno bracio e per piallatura ii altre tavole ch'erano dell'opera e per le dipinture s. sette
L. __ s. vii

Piero Tatteri, maestro di pietra, adì xxiii d'agosto, per vii dì che cei aiutò a conciare pietre vecchie per la barela [?] de' fondamenti, per s. xxi il dì, l. sette s. sette

L. vii s. vii

Michele di Giovanni, maestro adì detto e al detto lavorio per vii dì per li detti salari, lire sette s. sette

L. vii s. vii

Cichino di Tura, maestro di pietra, per iiii dì al detto lavorio per lo detto prezzo,
l. quarto s. dic[i]otto

L. iiii s. xviii

Jacopo da Lasso, fabro, adì xxiii d'agosto, per sottilgliatura scharpelli, marteline, pichoni, a detti maestri, che fue di patto, s. quattordici

L. __ s. xiiii

Lucha di Nardo, maestro di lengniame, adì detto d'agosto, per uno dì e ii terzi a raconciare e impiallaciare la porta diverso piazza, e chancheralla e bandellarlla di nu[o]vo, per s. xviii il dì , l. i s. dodici

L. i s. xii

Bartolomeo Gini, per vii pezzi di tavole di castangno per impiallaciare la detta porta in tutto, l. due s. sedici

L. ii s. xvi

Benedetto Manetti, fabro, adì detto, per libbre xxxi 1/2 di cancheri e bandelle per la detta porta, e per vii anelli che si imbiombarono alle colonne delle cappelle per porvi le croci di . . . per s. iii libbra lire quattro s. quattordici e d. sei

L. iiii s. xiiii d. vi

C. 23 VERSO

Anno MCCCLXXXXII

Benedetto Manetti anzi detto, adì xxiii d'agosto, per libbre viii once tre d'auti di xxxvi e di xxiiii per la decta porta, per s. iii d. viii libbra, come appare allibro suo a f. xliii, l. una s. cinque

L. i s. v

Giovanni di Bartolomeo speziale, adì detto, per libbre xxxvii oncie vi di piombo per impiomabare li cancheri della detta porta e anelli delle colonne, per s. ii libbra, l. tre s. tredici

L. iii s. xiii

Piero di Guefo, adì detto, per ii dì a[i]utare a detti maestri, s. quindici

L. __ s. xv

Piero detto, adì detto, per iiii panni e cascio per sè e per Lucha detto, s. tre d. otto

L. __ s. iii d. viii

Meo fornaciaio, adì detto, per mogia iii e misure iii di calcina per cumpire i fondamenti della pieve, per s. xlv mogio, l. sette s. dodici

L. vii s. xii

Milgliore Pucci, maestro, adì vii di settembre, per iiii dì ch'era stato a compire i fondamenti della pieve, per s. xvii il dì, l. tre s. otto

L. iii s. viii

Chimenti di Ghino, detto dì, per iii dì al detto lavorio per lo detto prezo, l.due s. undici

L. ii s. xi

Nanni di Guiduccio, adì detto, per iiii dì al detto lavorio, per lo detto prezo, l. tre s. otto

L. iii s. viii

Cialdo Simoni, detto dì, per iiii dì per manovale al detto lavorio, per s. xi al dì, l. due s. quattro

L. ii s. iiii

Materassa manovale, adi detto, e al detto lavorio, per s. xi il dì, l. due s. quattro

L. ii s. iiii

Malfante di Galeoto, adì detto, per ii dì, per s. xi il dì, l. una s. due

L. i s. ii

Filippo di Meo, adì detto, per iiii dì al detto lavorio, l. due s. quattro

L. ii s. iiii

Piero manovale, adì detto, per iii dì, l. una s. tredici

L. i s. xiii

Andrea di Pucio, adì detto, per iiii dì, l. due s. quatro

L. ii s. iiii

Materassa e uno compangno che spensero le dette mogia iii e misevi iii di galcina l. una

L. i

C. 24 RECTO

Anno MCCCCLXXXXII

Piero di Guefo, a dì [struck out: xxiii] vii di settembre, per iiii dì ch' a[i]utò al detto lavorio l. una

L. i

Piero di Guefo, adì detto, per fare pane per la detta opera fue del grano che li dì elo da . . . [?] da Domenicho, staio 1 di grano, staia 1

Meo di Stefano, fornaciaio, adì detto, per mogia 1 e misure 1 di galcina che manchò al detto lavorio, l. due s. quattrodici

L. ii s. xiiii

Meo detto, detto dì, per ii battitoi che si erano auti al detto lavorio l. una s. otto

L. i s. viii

Antonio vetturale, adì detto, per rechatura la rena e mogia iiii e mezo di calcina, per s. xviii mogio, l. iiii s. i, e per recatura i detti batitoi, l. quattro s. quattro

L. iiii s. iiii

Piero detto, adì detto, per cascio, cipolle, inslate e iiii pani che mancharono a detti maestri, s. quattordici d. otto

L. __ s. xiiii d. viii

Pavolo di Vanni, adì detto, per barili 1 1/2 di vino per li detti maestri, l. quattro s. dieci

L. iiii s. x

Bartolomeo pianellaio	adì x di setttembre che stetono a guardare la porta della
Antonio lastraio	pieve per la fiera, cum altri, che pagò il comune s. dieci

L. __ s. x

Nieri del Gatto, per ii dì e i notte che stette a spegnere . . . [?] la fiera, l. una s. dieci

L. i s. x

Matteo di Gore e il compangno, che tolsono a sonare la canpana per la fiera e poi la comandarono a' filglioli di Gianni Martini, l. quattro s. dieci

L. iiii s. x

Basalla 1 cumpangno, che regàrono i cieri della fiera da casa Matteo di Cunvenevole alla piazza, s. quattro

L. __ s. iiii

Piero di Guefo e cumpangni, che ricevono i ceri della fiera e per una metà delo dì uno,
soldi quattro

L. __ s. iiii

C. 24 VERSO

Anno MCCCLXXXXII

Meo di Stefano, fornaciaio, adì xxii di settembre, per misure iii di galcina per lo dipintori
s. dic[i]otto

L. __ s. xviii

Marco manovale, adì detto, perchè spense la detta galcina e pane, in tutto
s. [struck out: due] cinque

L. __ s. v

Piero di Gufo, adì detto, per valgliatura . . . [?] della detta galcina e colatura la decta galcina perchè fosse più delichata, s. [struck out: dodici] diece

L. __ s. x

Giovanni di bartolomeo casciau[o]llo, adì detto, per uno vaglio per colare la galcina,
s. dodici

L. __ s. xii

Antonio renaiu[o]llo, adì detto, per portatura la puza della piazza della pieve per la fiera, l. una s. quindici

L. __ s. xv

Bechalite, adì detto, che spazzò la detta piazza per la detta fiera l. una s. dieci

L. i s. x

Castrucio di Bartolino, fabro, adì detto, per raconciare i serrami della cassa de'mòcholi,
s. quattro

L. __ s. iiii

Matteo di Carnèvole, adì xxii di ottobre, per libbre lxiiii di chandele nuove per vendere al descho dell'Opera, diede a Piero di Gufo per dare a Monna Margherita che vendè al detto di Piero, dato per lui da dì xxiiii d'agosto infino adì vii di settembre, come appare al libro suo e al figlio di Piero, per s. x d. vi libbra, l. trentatre s. dodici

L. xxxiii s. xii

Matteo detto, adì detto, per facitura di libbre duecento iiii di cieri che riebe arsici per la fiera, di quantità di libre cclxxx in tutto e l'avanzo, sono stati nell-a[l]tra faccia, della quale quantità ebe lire sei

L. vi

C. 25 RECTO

Anno MCCCLXXXXII

Matteo di Convenevole, speziale, adì xxii d'ottobre per libbre lxxvi di cieri ch'avanzarono per la fiera, interi, computatovi entro libbre xvi ch'ebono di calo, sichè resta essere rimaso abia per libber lx ebe, per s. x libbra in tutto, lire trenta otto

L. xxxviii

Piero di Guefo e Pardo d'Andrea — sagrestani della cappella, adì vi di novembre, per iii mesi passati, cioè agosto settembre ottobre, che sono stati alla cappella per l. iii al
mese per uno, in tutto l. dic[i]otto

L. xviii

Monte di Lencio, a dì detto, per iii mesi passati, cioè agosto settembre ottobre, a ragione di fi.xx per anno a sonare gli organi, fi cinque

f. v

Monna Margherita, che vende le candele per l'Opera, per li detti iii mesi, per s. xxx il mese, a vendere le dette candele, in tutto l. quattro s. dieci

L. iiii s. x

Meo di Stefano, fornaciaio, adì detto, per misure iii di galcina per lo dipintore, s. dic[i]otto

L. __ s. xviii

Magio manovale, adì detto, per spengnere la detta galcina e per pane, s. cinque

L. __ s. v

Piero di Guefo detto, adì detto, per valgliatura e colatura la detta galcina s. dieci

L. __ s. x

Matteo di Convenevole, adì xiiii di dicembre, per facitura di libbre clxxi di candele fatte di anechili[?] che ssi partirono cum messer Raneri per la sua e per la nostra parte, per s. ii libbra l. quatordici s. due

L. xiiii s. ii

Ser Simone di Ser Raniero, il quale fue notaio della Camera, per scrittura il registro ch'è all'Opera levato da quello del . . . [?] dal MCCCLXVI infino anni MCCCLXXXXI, tassato per Paolo Operaio lire sette

L. vii

C. 25 VERSO

Anno MCCCLXXXXII

Io Pavolo di Vanni Operaio della pieve a Prato per chomessione di messer Piero di Pavolo e chonpagni Operari della detta pieve, vedute le dette spese, l'aproviamo essere fattte per lo detto Stefano legittimanente e di nostro volere, e chosì di mia mano mi soscrivo.

[. . .]

C. 26 VERSO

Uscita del Opera e cappella della pieve a Prato, nel anno che incominciò, anno MCCCLXXXXII, dì primo di magio, al tempo di

Lodovicho di ser Jacopo	nuovi operai incominciati anno detto e dì 1 di febraio
Piero di Gieri	per uno anno
Pavolo di Vanni	vecchi Operai e vi mesi prossimi che vengono, cioè
Francescho di Piero Cabioni	febraio, marzo, aprile, maggio, giugno, e luglio

Matteo di Convenevole, adi xviii di febraio [1393 modern style] per libbre lxxiiii di candele, avute da lui per vendere al descho dell'Opera, per s. xi libbra, date per lui da dì xvii di gennaio in fino adì xvi di febraio, rechò Piero di Gufo, lire quaranta soldi quartordici

L. xl s. xiiii

Castruccio toppaio, adì xxvii di febraio, per ii chiavi e ii toppe, l'una alla cassetta apichata alla cappella, l'altra al campanile, cum dua ferretti attraverso alla detta chassetta,
in tutto l. una s. otto

L. i s. viii

Piero detto, adì xxvii di febraio, per misture 1 di galena per lo dipintore e a Piero per chalcha[?] e a Magio per spengnerla, in tutto s. undici

L. __ s. xi

Matteo di Convenevole, adì xv di marzo, per libber xxiiii di candele date all'Opera per vendere al descho dell'Opera infino al detto dì, per s. xi libbra, lire tredici, s. quarto

L. xiii s. iiii

Cristofano di ser Francia, adì detto [xvi di marzo] per racconciatura la schala del balcho, s. tre

L. __ s. iii

Cristofano di ser Francia, a dì viiii d'aprile, per sonare le campane della pieve per la Pasqua che passò anno detto, e per la Pasque del Resurresso, anno MCCCLXXXXII, lire due soldi dieci

L. ii s. x

C. 27 RECTO

Anno MCCCLXXXXII [*sic*]

Canenevole speziale, adì xiii d'aprile, per uno quaderno di carte banbagine e iiii folgli de p_[?], ebono gli Operai, s. nove d. quattro

L. __ s. viiii d. iiii

Cialdo manovale e Piero di Gufo, adì xx di aprile, per ... [?] di mistura iiii di galcina per la finestra della cappela s. sei

L. __ s. vi

Meo di Stefano, fornaciaio, adì detto, per misure iiii di galcina l. una s. quattro per la detta finestra

L. i s. iiii

Meo detto, adì detto, per duecento mattoni per la detta finestra, l. una s. sedici

L. i s. xvi

Antonio Ranonculo per rigatura la terra alla [?] e la detta galcina e rigatura i mattoni, in tutto s. dodici

L. __ s. xii

Galatto di Canbione, adì xx d'aprile, per i dì ... [?] quando andamo a fFirenze messer Giovanni di Gherardo, ser Tomaso e io per li fatti della cappella mia [?] a tassalla volta, s. dieci

L. __ s. x

Franceschо albergatore de'Leoni, detti dì, per 2 sachetti [?] per me e uno m__ [?] propenda [?] tra lla matina e la sera, per me Stefano, lire una s. dodici

L.i s. xii

Francescho detto, per ii sachuci di messer Giovanni e 1 mezo quarto di spelda, lire una, soldi otto, e per 1 sachetto a ser Tomaso s. xii

L. ii

Monna Margherita di Cialdo, che vende le candele al descho, per tre mesi passati, cioè febraio, marzo, aprile, per s. xxx il mese, ebe adì xxx d'aprile, portò Cialdo

L. iiii s. x

Piero di Guefo Pardo d'Andrea	sagrestani della cappella, adì xxx d'aprile, per iii mesi passati, cioè febraio, marzo, aprile, per l. iii il mese, in tutto l. dic[i]otto
	L. xviii

C. 27 VERSO

Anno MCCCLXXXXIII

[. . .]

C. 28 RECTO:

Anno MCCCLXXXXII [*sic*]

[. . .]
Antonio di Jacopo Renaiu[o]lo, adì xxx d'aprile, per regatura viii misure di galcina levate
vii da Meo di Stefano come appare alla vegna del detto Meo a f. x, e per misure I di galcina da Piero Dati, come apare a f.xii, s. quindici d. sei

L. __ s. xv d. vi

Baldo di Vestro, adì detto, per una parte del testamento di monna Sapia di ser Bartolo, la quale lasciò al'Opera, la quale gli p__(?), lire I

L. i

C. 28 VERSO

Anno MCCCLXXXXIII

Maestro Angnolo di Tadeo, dipintore da fFirenze, il quale dipingne la cappella [struck out: del] nuova, dove de[v]e stare la cintola della Nostra Donna Vergine Maria, per sua faticha di oro, azurro, stangno e in funi, come appare al libro lungho, a f. ii, ebe dal'anno MCCCLXXXXII, a dì xviiii di giungno infino anno MCCCLXXXXIII, dì xxv d'aprile, in più partite, ed è scritta di sua mano:
f. novanta di sugello e montano per l. iii s. xvi l. cccxlii
f. sessanta due gravi, per s. xviii d. vi fi l. ccxlii l. [struck out: xxxv s. x] venti in moneta, soma in tutto l. se[i]centocinque s. sette

L. cccccv s. vii

Maestro Angnolo detto, da anno MCCCLXXXXII, dì xxx di luglio infino anno MCCCLXXXXIII, dì xiiii di settembre, per libre ii once vii 1/2 d'azuro oltramarino per f. x libra, per l. iii s. xv f., l. lxxxxviiii s. viii d. xviiii, e per stangno in iii partite l. viii s. vii; soma in tutto l. cientosei s. quindici d. nove, come appare a libro lu[n]gho a f. vii

L. cvi s. xv d. viiii

Donato di Bonifazio da Firenze, speziale, anno MCCCLXXXXII, adì iii di setembre infino anno MCCCLXXXXIII adì xx di novembre, per libbre 1 e mezzo d azur[r]o oltramarino finisso, per l. lxxx libbre l. cxx per M/II pezi d'oro l. lxv s. ii, e per i peso di stangno s. dic[i]otto, somma in tutto, come appare a libro lungho a f. viii ch'àne scritta di sua mano l. ciento ottanta sei

L. clxxxvi

C. 29 RECTO

Anno MCCCLXXXXII

Messer Bonacorso di messer Niccholao e	e altri, per spese fatte per li operai
Bertoldo di Charino Guazaloti	nella zufa che ssi fece nella pieve a Prato, quando volle esser preso il maestro Angnolo dipintore dal notaio dello asecutore di Firenze e fue battuto il decto notaio e il cavaliere dello Podesà di Prato, come appare al libro lungho a f. x in più partite e scritte nel decto anno da dì xxviiii di gennaio infino a dì xxx di marzo anno decto [1393 modern style], l. cinquanta otto s. diece d. otto

L. lviii s. x d. viii

Ser Giovanni della Camera, adì detto, per la terza parte d'uno libro che compro di comandamento delli Otto, per scrivere le ragioni rendute delli spedale, cieppo, opera e cappella, l. due s. otto d. otto

L. ii s. viii d.viii

Ser Lodovicho di Tartarino, adì xxx d'aprile, per parte del testamento di messer Manetto, il quale lasciò alla cappella e opera l. xv e due torchi, l. tre

L. iii

Io Piero di Geri di Ghetto, Operaio della pieve di Prato, per chomesione di Francescho di Francescho Chanbioni e chompagni operaio della deta pieve, vedute le dete spese, l'aproviamo esere fat[t]e per lo deto Stefano legitime e necesar[i]e e di nostro volere, che chosì per memoria di questo mi sono soscrito

C. 29 VERSO

Anno MCCCLXXXXII fino nel MCCCLXXXXIII

Stefano d'Arigho, nuovo camarlingho per l'anno che comincia anno MCCCLXXXXIII, dì primo di magio, il quali gli erano avanzati nel suo camarlinghatico del detto anno MCCCLXXXXII, messi a entrata del nuovo mio chamarlinghatico del MCCCLXXXXIIII, al mio libro dell'entrata del detto anno a f. xiiii, lire dugentoquarantaquatro s. undici d. sette

L. ccxliiii s. xi d. vii

I.2. PRATO, ARCHIVIO DI STATO, PATRIMONIO ECCLESIASTICO 46 (ENTRATA E USCITA DELLA CAPPELLA DELLA CINTOLA, 1393–1394)

[Cover]: Entrata e uscita della cappella della Cintola della Nostra Donna e Opera della pieve a Prato, nel tempo di Stefano d'Arrigho, camerlengho della detta Opera e cappella nell'anno del MCCCLXXXXIII di primo di giugno

C. 1 RECTO

Uscita dell'Opera e cappella della pieve a Prato nell'anno mccclxxxxiii, incominciato anno detto e dì primo di magio, al tempo di Stefano d'Arigho, camerlengho della detta Opera e cappella per uno anno incominciato anno e dì detto, al del tempo degli infrascritti operai, cioè:

Pavolo di Vanni Francescho di Piero	per dì qui a calendi agosto prossimo
Lodovicho di ser Jacopo Piero di Geri	per di qui a calendi febraio prossimo e . . . [?]

Gheraldo vetturale, adì xviiii di magio, per regatura da fFirenze il concio delle pietre della finestra della cappella nuova che fece Giovanni d'Anbruogio lastraiolo l. una s. cinque

L. i s. v

Giovanni detto, adì x di giungno, per lo detto concio e per ii dì elli e uno suo compagno a murallo e comettello nella finestra cum Domenicho Santini maestro, ebe per diliberazione
de' detti operai, in tutto f. sette

f. vii

Domenicho Santini, maestro, adì xvi di giungno, per iii dì amurare la detta finestra l'uno dì co' loro e i due soli, per s. xviii il dì, l. due s. quattrodici

L. ii s. xiiii

Marcho di Pino, a[l]bergatore, adì xii di giungno, per una sera ch'a[l]-bergarono e cenarono il detto Giovanni e compagno s. dic[i]otto

L. __ s. xviii

Antonio di Giovanni Martini, adì detto, per I mezzo dì a ffare uno ponte alla decta finestra, di fuori della cappella s. otto

L. __ s. viii

Michele bechalite, dì detto, per xx pani per li presenti maestri e manovali s. quatordici d. quattro

L. __ s. xiii d. iiii

Antonio vetturale, adì detto, per regatura mattoni da Bartolomeo fornaciaio s. tre

L. __ s. iii

Piero di Betto di Gascia, e Piero di Guefo, adì detto, per castrone, v__[?], cascio, per li detti maestri l. una s. quattro

L. i s. iiii

C. I VERSO

Anno MCCCLXXXXIII

Ciuto trecchone adì xvi di giungno, per xx pani e una coppia di cascio per Domenicho Santini e suoi manovali poi sse andarono i detti maestri e il p__[?] Ravilio,
s. tredici d. quatro

L. __ s. xiii d. iiii

Piero di Guefo, dì detto, per libbre i di piombo s. uno d. sei

L. __ s. i d. vi

Michele Bechalite, adì detto, per iii a[i]utare al detto lavorio a dì detto l. una s. sette

L. i s. vii

P__[?] manovale, per uno dì, a dì detto, s. nove

L. __ s. viiii

Nanni manovale per I dì, adì detto, che non furono altro, s. tredici

L. __ s. xiii

Giovanni di Neri, adì detto, per uno cerchio grande per la finestra e raconciare I mastello, s. cinque

L. __ s. v

Jacopo d'Alesso, detto dì, per auguzatura pichoni e scharpelli, s. cinque

L. __ s. v

Benedetto Manetti, fabro, per ii ferri, detto dì, per comettere la detta finestra s. cinque

L. __ s. v

Bartolomeo Nardi, adì detto, per C /II mattoni l. i s. dic[i]otto e per clx mezane l. i s. ii e per some vii di chalcina, l. i s. xv, somma in tutto l. quattro s. quindici

L. iiii s. xv

Gramignia vetturale, adì detto, per regatura il detto lavorio e L mattoni da Piero Dati, in tutto s. dieci d. sei

L. __ s. x d. vi

Lorenzo di Stefano, adì detto, per xxvi metadele di vino per le dette opere, a ragione di s. L barile, auto licenzia da Biagio di Lapo, l. una s. sei

L. i s. vi

Piero di Guefo per iiii dì, adì detto, aiutare a detti maestri e manovali, l. una

L. i

Manno di Giovanni, detto dì, per uno libro che mi rimase con fogli di carte, in suso il quale ci copiai questo, s. undici e d. otto

L. __ s. xi d. viii

Piero dete, adì detto, per L mattoni, s. nove

L. __ s. viiii

C. 2 RECTO

Anno MCCCLXXXXIII

Cristofano di ser Francia, adì viiii d'agosto, per iiii dì a disfare e rifare il ponte della cappella e fare uno ponte fuori dell'archo, l. quattro

L. iiii

Nicholò d'Algliana, adì detto, per iii dì e ii terzi aiutare al detto Cristofano, per s. xv il dì l. due s. quindici L. ii s. xv

Jacopo di Neri batrato, detto dì, per ii terzi di dì aiutare al detto Cristofano al detto lavorio,

s. sei s. vi

Piero di Gufo, adì detto, per iiii dì e mezo ch'a[i]utò alli maestri, l. una s. due d. sei

L. i s. ii d. vi

Chello Pucci e Resa, segatori, adì decto, per segare travicelli per lo detto ponte, in tutto s. dicesette L. __ s. xvii

C. 2 VERSO

Anno MCCCLXXXXIII

Bartolomeo di Gino lengnaiuolo, adì viiii d'agosto, per v lengni d'albero per fare travicelli e il ponte di fuori della cappella, in tutto l. sette

L. vii

Lorenzo di Stefano, adì detto, per barile mezzo di vino per li detti maestri, l. una s. dodici

L. i s. xii

Michele bechalite, adì detto, per viii pani per li detti maestri s. nove

L. __ s. viiii

Piero di Guefo, adì detto, per conpanacho di detti maestri, s. sette

L. __ s. vii

Benedetto Manetti fabro, adì detto, per libbre ii, oncie viiii d'auti, per lo detto ponte, s. sette d. tre

L. __ s. vii d. iii

Maestro Angnolo di Tadeo, dipintore da fFirenze, il quale dipingne la cappella della pieve, ebe in tre partite per horo, stangno, azuro, come appare a' libro lungho, a foglio xi, e spesi da dì xvii di magio infino a dì xxiii di luglio, messi a uscita adì xi d'agosto, in tutto lire quarantaquatro s. sedici d. otto

L. xliiii s. xvi d. viii

Donato di Bonifazio, speziale da fFirenze, ebe in tre partite per oro, azuro, dato per lui da dì vi di giungno infino a dì xxviiii di luglio, levati da'libro lungho in tre partite, a f. xii, l. settanta tre, ène scritta di sua mano

L. lxxiii

Maestro Angnolo detto, ebe da me Stefano camarlingho decto, da dì iiii magio infino a dì iii d'agosto, in x partite levate da libro lungho, a carte iii, f. xxxvi d'oro gravi, per [l. iii] s. xviii d. iiii l'uno, l. cxli e in moneta l. cxxxiii s. v, somma l. dugento settanta quatro s. cinque, messi a uscita adì xi d'agosto

L. cclxxiiii s. v

C. 3 RECTO

Anno MCCCLXXXXIII a dì xii d'agosto, si cavarono gli infrascritti nuovi operai, cioè

Ridolfo di Lanfrancho per di qui adì 1 d'agosto per fino . . [?]
Francescho di Marcho

Lodovicho di ser Jacopo per di qui a calendi febraio prossimo
Piero di Geri

Maestro Angnolo che dipingne alla cappella, come appare a' libro lungho a f. iiii, ebe adì xxi d'agosto f. xii d'oro gravi, per l. iii s. xviii l'uno, l. quarantasette s. due

L. xlvii s. ii

Maestro Angnolo che dipingne la cappella, adì vii di settembre, diedi per lui al discepolo suo, levati dal libro lungho a carta a f. iiii l. tre

L. iii

C. 3 VERSO

Anno MCCCCLXXXXIII

Don Marcho da fFirenze dell' ordine di Valunbrosa, adì xi di settembre, per parte di pagamento della finestra del vetro della cappella, diede Francesco di Marcho per me, infino adì x d'agosto, come appare a'libro lungho, a f. xiii, ebe f. x d'oro gravi, per l. iii s. xviii luno, rechato a moneta l. trenta nove

L. xxxviiii

C. 4 RECTO

Anno MCCCLXXXXIII

Maestro Angnolo che dipingne la cappella, adì xv d'ottobre, diede per me ser Gherardo, notaio della camera, come appare allo libro lungho, ala sua ragione, messi a entrata di ser Gherardo, l. ciento cinquanta

L. cl

Giovanni tenducci da Figline, adì xviii di novembre, per rechatura e gabella della finestra del vetro da Firenze, l. una d. sei

L. i s. __ d. vi

Antonio di Giovanni Martini, adì detto, per fare uno ponte alla finestra della cappella, per fare i buchi per li ferri s. dodici s. xii

Piero di Guefo, adì detto, e per pane, s. tre d. quattro

L. __ s. iii d. iiii

C. 4 VERSO

Anno MCCCLXXXXIII

Matteo di Convenevole, speziale, adì vii di novembre, per rifacitura di libbre xxxi di candele minute di cieri rotti, che furono di detto Stefano che passò, i quale erano nella sagrestia, per tutto l. due s. due d. quattro

L. ii s.ii d. iiii

Bartolo da Manghone, adì detto, per mochia ii di chalcina per la cappella e a palgliaio, e per rena e aqua per spengnerla, in tutto s. undici

L. __ s. xi

Maestro Angnolo adì vii di dicembre, portò Vettorio suo discepolo, disselo Ridolfo [di Lanfrancho, operaio], posti a sua ragione a libro lungho, l. dodici

L. xii

Maestro Giovanni lastraiu[o]lo da fFirenze, adì viiii di dicembre, per due dì che venne e stette a Prato a petizione delli Operai, per avere consilglio con lui del pillastro di verso la porta se fusse da condurre [rifondare or stondare] e colgliere le misure del capitello per farlo di nuovo, diedi di volere di Ridolfo l. tre s. dic[i]otto

L. iii s. xviii

Maestro Angnolo, adì xiiii di dicembre, per comperare stangno per la cappella, disseloRido[l]fo, l. una s. tre

L.i s. iiii

C. 5 RECTO

Anno MCCCLXXXXIII

Don Marcho che fece la finestra della cappella del vetro, adì xxi di dicembre, dissolo gli Operai, f. due per l. iii s. xviii fiorino, per tutti l. sette s. sedici

L. vii s. xvi

Maestro Angnolo di Tadeo da fFirenze, adì xxiiii di dicembre, porto elli, messo a sua ragione, l. sei

L. vi

Palgliaio vetturale, adì xxiiii di dicembre, per some xx di rena che rechò alla cappella, s. tredici d. quattro

L. __ s. xiii d. iiii

Bartolomeo fornaciaio, adì iii di gennaio [1394 modern style], per mogia i di chalcina per rimbochare l'archo della cappella l. due s. sei

L. ii s. vi

Cialdo manovale, adi detto, per spengnere la detta chalcina con Piero che lli a [i]uò, s. dieci L. __ s. x

Gramingma vetturale, per rechare la detta calcina s. tre

L. __ s. iii

Piero di Guefo, adì detto, perchè aiutò al detto Cialdo, s. cinque

L. __ s. v

C. 5 VERSO

Anno MCCCLXXXXIII

Ser Pavolo, prete della cappella, adì xxiiii di gennaio [1394 modern style], per cierti nastri di seta cum nappe per porre al messale della decta cappella, disselo Ridolfo di Lanfrancho, l. una s. diece L. i s. x

Stefano manovale, adì detto [iii febbraio], per uno dì che spense mogia i di chalcina per la cappella e pichono [?] di fuori della cappella cierto mancho che v'era a ffare, s. nove L. __ s. viiii

Palgliaio vetturale, adì detto, per rechatura il detto mogio della calcina da Meo da Caleano, s. tre, e per rechtura C mattoni s. ii, e per rechatura some xii di rena s. viii, somma s. tredici L. __ s. xiii

Jacopo da Lasso, adì detto, per sottilgliatura 1 pichone, s. uno

L. __ s. i

Piero di Guefo, adì detto, per ii dì che aiuto a Achelni, che spense la chalcina, e a' maestri che rimbocharo largho, s diece

L. __ s. x

C. 6 RECTO

Anno MCCCLXXXXIII

Maestro Angnolo, dipintore della cappella, adì xiii di febraio [1394 modern style], i quali ebe in due partite, cioè adì xx di gennaio e detto dì, come appare a libro lungho a sua ragione

L. vi

Chimenti del maestro Ghino e cumpagni, adì xiiii di febraio, per rimbochatura il muro e l'archo della cappella, f. iii doro . . . [?] l'uno, in tutto l. undici s. dicesette

L. xi s. xvii

Chimenti e cumpangni, adì detto, per muratura gli scudi che sono sopra l'archo della cappella per i di tre per . . . [?] l. una s. diece

L. i s. x

Piero di Guefo, che comprò a detti maestri malio [?] e e altre cose, e per suo salario d'uno dì, per tutto s. sette

L. __ s. vii

Meo di Stefano, adì xvi di febraio, per mogia i di chalcina l. iii s. v e per C mattoni per lo detto lavorio, s. xviii, in tutto l. tre s. tre

L. iii s. iii

Maestro Angnolo adì xvii di febraio, i quali diedi per lui a Vettorio, suo discepolo, come appare a libro lungho, l. due

L. ii

Cristofano di ser Francia	per disfare certi ponti e levare due atenne di ponti
Nicholo del Liana	che davano noia per la fiera che passò e ebeli adì detto s. dieci

L. __ s. x

C. 6 VERSO

Anno MCCCLXXXXIII

Maestro Angnolo che dipingne alla cappella, come appare a' libro lungho a f. iiii, ebe Vettorio, l. due

L. ii

Don Marcho dell'ordine di Vallombrosa, il quale àe fatto la finestra del vetro della cappella, i quali denari diede per me Francescho di Marcho adì xviiii di sett[em]bre prossimo passato, diedi al decto Francescho adì vii d'aprile [1394 modern style] f. vi d'oro gravi per l. iii s. xviiii d. iiii del'uno, montano l. ventitrè s. sedici

L. xxiii s. xvi

Giovanni Martini, adì xiii d'aprile, perchè raconciò le campane della pieve e il perbio, s. quindici L. __ s. xv

Piero di Guefo che lli à uto per uno dì, s. cinque

L. __ s. v

Benedetto Manetti, fabro, per libbra i d'auti di xxx e fare cie[r]te biette, s. otto

L. __ s. viii

C. 7 RECTO

Anno MCCCLXXXXIII

Piero di Guelfo, per pane e macho [?] per le detti maestri detto dì s. uno d. quattro

L. __ s. i d. iiii

Ferante manovale per uno dì a radere la galcina della cappella, che si guastava, e per e per ii [sic] pani, a dì detto, s. dieci

L. __ s. x

Ser Gherardo, notaio della Camera, adì xv d'aprile [1494 modern style], il quale ci prestò per dare al maestro Angnolo adì xvi di novembre prossimo passato l. ciento cinquanta

L. cl

Ser Gherardo detto a dì detto per porzione di detti denari diliberati per Ridolfo di Lanfrancho, l. nove

L. viiii

Lorenzo horafo, adì xvii d'aprile, per xii uncinelli per le lampane della cappella s. quattro

L. __ s. iiii

Piero di Guelfo, adì detto, per uno dì che li a[i]utò e per companaticho s. sei

L. __ s. vi

Benedetto Manetti adì detto per libbre C/ II d'auti di xxvi e di xlviii s. nove

L. __ s. viiii

C. 7 VERSO

Anno MCCCLXXXXIII

Romolo da Firenze, che cava il marmo a Feghine, adì xxx d'aprile [1394] per una cholonna di marmo novo conda, per por[r]e alla finestra del campanile della pieve dove cade lantra chavera, l. cinque

L. v

Maestro Angnolo che dipingne alla cappella, adì detto, come appare alla sua ragione al libro lungho, da dì xviii infino a dì xxiii d'aprile, l. sei

L. vi

C. 8 RECTO

Anno MCCCLXXXXIII

Bartolo da Mangone, adì detto [xxx aprile 1394], per una misura di galcina s. vi e per aqua e rena per la detta galcina, s. ii soma s. viii otto

L. __ s. viii

Francescho da Cappalle, adì detto, per cierto chiasso che'l detto Francescho avea comperato dal comune di Prato, del quale fue piato cum meser lo proposis per cierto benificio che 'l detto proposto àe aquistato alla cappella della Quitaia, Messer Ranieri comprò dal detto Francescho per la propositeria il detto chiasso, e io Stefano di volere delli Operai pagai al detto Francescho per lo detto messer Ranieri f. sei d'oro e lire due s. quatro

f. vi L. ii s. iiii

Ridolfo di Lanfrancho, adì decto, per ii dì ch'andò a fFirenze, in servigio dell'Opera a informarsi di cierti lavorii ch'avea fatto il maestro Angnolo in Firenze, e d'altri per fare la stima di quello della pieve, l. tre

L. iii

Bartolomeo di Meo, adì detto, per ii dì il ronzino suo che llo menò Messer Giovanni di Gherardo a fFirenze per la detta cagione, l. una

L. i

C. 8 VERSO

Anno MCCCLXXXXIII

Maestro Angnolo, adì xxx d'aprile [1494], levati dal libro lungho a f. iiii, dalla sua ragione e dì e dì viiii di magio l. due

L. ii

Maestro Giovanni d'Ambruogio, lastraiuolo da Firenze, adì detto, per parte di facitura di certo bechatello del pillastro della cappella nuova della pieve, f. due

f. ii

Lorenzo di Stefano, adì detto, per barile mezzo di vino ch'àe auto Piero di Guefo, per li maestri e manovali, messo alla cappella e campanile, s. dodici

L. __ s. xii

I.3. PRATO, ARCHIVIO DI STATO, PATRIMONIO ECCLESIASTICO 47 (ENTRATA E USCITA DELL'OPERA DELLA CAPPELLA DI NOSTRA DONNA, 1394–1395)

C. 17 RECTO

Qui scriverrò tutta l'uscita de'denari per me si daranno ad Agnolo di Taddeo, il quale dipigne la chapella di Nostra Donna

Ad Agnolo di Taddeo Ghaddi, dipintore, dì xi di lugl[i]o [1394], per parte di paghamento di suo lavoro, f. quaranta d'oro gravi, ebbe in sua mano

f. xl

A lui detto, dì vii di novembre, lire quaranta, di quello ebbe per me da Nicholao di Bernardo, e chosì schontai co' lui

L. xl

A lui detto dì xxvi di gennaio [1395 modern style] f. cinquanta d'oro ebbe in sua mano, furono gravi e di punto, achattai i detti denari da Nicholao di Bernardo

f. l

A lui detto, dì viii di febraio, l. centocinque s. otto, auti in sua mano e per lui a Vettorio e a Neri, suoi gharzoni a lavorare, chome apare al mio quaderno

L. cv s. viii

A lui detto, dì detto, f. tre d'oro e s. quindici, i quali diedi per lui a Gherardo di ser Bartolo f. iii L. __ s. xv

A lui detto, dì xi di febraio, l. trentatre s. tredici, per lui a Nicholao di Bernardo per panno tolse da lui

L. xxxiii s. xiii

A lui detto, dì xiii di febraio, f. sei d'oro il dì ch'andò a Firenze

f. vi

A lui detto, dì vi di marzo l. sesanta ebbe per me da Stefano d'Arigho e dal maestro Matteo L. lx

[Struck out: A lui detto dì detto f.l, per lui a me Ridolfo di pigione e vino auto da me in più partite fattone ragione co'lui

f. 1 L.]

A lui detto, dì vii di marzo, l. trentaquattro s. dodici d. sei, per lui a Nicholao di Bernardo lanaiuolo

L. xxxiiii s. xii d. vi

A lui detto, dì xxviiii di marzo, l. quaranta chavai della chas[s]etta

L. xl

A lui detto, dì detto, f. diece d'oro e per lui a Neri d'Antonio, suo compagno, chome disse gli si dessero f. x

A lui detto, l. quatordici s. quatordici d. sei, chome apare al quaderno, dati per lui a Neri e al Conte, suoi gharzoni, da dì xiii di febraio fine dì primo d'aprile

L. xiiii s. xiiii d. vi

A lui detto, dì viiii di maggio, l. quaranta, portò Meo di Fruosino suo discepolo

L. xl

A lui detto, dì xxv di maggio, per compimento del paghamento del lavoro della chapella, che fu lodato avesse f. cinquecento trentacinque, ebbe f. 200 l. 300 s. 5 da Stefano d'Arigho e da me in tutto f. 109 l. 369 s. 3, reghata la moneta a fiorini a s. 77 per fiorino ebbe in tutto f. quarantuno l. due s. cinque

f. xli L. ii s. v

C. 17 VERSO

Qui scriverrò tutti i denari dell'uscita in azurro, oro batuto, stagno il quale d'adoperà nella chapella e prima:

A Vettorio di . . . dì xxi di lugl[i]o [1394], l. trentatre s. undici, per uno lavoro d'oro battuto, sono pezzi 1100, tolselo da Maffio battiloro

L. xxxiii s. xi

A Vettorio detto, dì xxvii di lug[i]o, per uno peso di stagno s. dicessette

L. __ s. xvii

A Vettorio, detto dì, per libre una d'azurro da macinare rechò da Firenze, l. due s. otto

L. ii s. viii

A Vettorio detto, dì xxvi d'agosto, per uno peso d'oro, pezzi 1100 tolse da Maffio l. trentatre s. undici

L. xxxiii s. xi

A Donato di Bonifatio spetiale in Firenze, dì xxvii d'ottobre, per oncie sei g. tre d'azuro oltramarino, per l. ottanta libra, l. quarantacinque

L. xlv

A lui detto, detto [dì], per oncie sei d'azurro oltramarino, per f. xiiii libbra, f. sette di sugello, per s. 77 d. iiii fiorino

L. xxvii s. i d. i

A lui detto, per libbra una oncie sei d'azurro, per f. cinque s. due libra f. viii s. uno
di suggello, al detto pregio montano

L. xxxi s. xviii

A lui detto, dì vi di novembre, per cinquecento pezzi d'oro fine, l. sedici

L. xvi

A Piero di ser Vanozzo di [blank] . . . per sei fogli di stagno s. dodici

L. __ s. xii

A Francesco spetiale, dì xx di novembre, per tre fogli di stagno s. nove

L. __ s. viiii

A Nicholao di Bernardo, dì xxiii di gennaio [1395 modern style], per uno peso d'oro chomperò da Maffio, pezi 1100, l. trenta tre

L. xxxiii

A Piero di ser Vanozzo, dì xxvi di gennaio, per nove fogli di stagno s. diciotto

L. __ s. xviii

Al Massaio, discepolo d'Agnolo, dì iiii febraio, per uno lavoro d'oro tolse da Maffio, pezzi 1100, l. trentatrè, e di ghabella s. sedici, rechò il Massaio

L. xxxiii s. xvi

Item ebbe il Massaio detto [struck out; di ghabella], che andò per esso a Firenze s. dieci

L. __ s. x

A Nicolao di Bernardo, dì xviiii di febraio l. quarantacinque per 1500 pezzi d'oro tolse per la chapella da Maffio battiloro

L. xlv

Al maestro Matteo, dì xv di marzo, per uno fogl[i]o di stagno tolse Arigho, s. due

L. __ s. ii

A Vettorio, discepolo d'Agnolo, l. trentatre s. undici, per uno peso d'oro comperò da Maffio, diede i denari ser Naldo di Nicholozzo di volontà degli Operai e io gli missi a entrata. Regollo per fino dì iiii d'agosto 1394

L. xxxiii s. xi

A Donato di Bonifatio, dì xx d'aprile, per oncie viii d'azur[r]o fine per f. xiiii libra, f. nove s. nove d. otto a fiorino; e per oncie sei d'azurro di f. cinque ½ libra, a fiorino f. ii l. i s. i d. viiii a fiorino; e per oncie quatro del detto azurro f. 1 l. i s. iiii d. ii a fiorino; e per oncie due del detto azurro fine di f. 14 libra, f. ii s. viiii d. viii a fiorino; som[m]a in tutto f. xvi s. vii d. iii a fiorino, che sono di p[iocioli] a s. settantasei d. x per fiorino

L. lxii s. viii d. vi

A lui detto per libre 30 di gesso da munire, per d. 3 libra

L. __ s. vii d. vi

A Neri d'Antonio, dì detto, per uno fogl[i]o di stagno, s. uno d. otto

L. __ s. i d. viii

A Nicholaio di Bernardo, dì xxiii d'aprile, l. dodici per 400 pezzi d'oro, il quale paghò a Maffio battiloro, tolsesi per la storia di fuori e avanzonne 200 pezzi. Rechossi dì xv di marzo L. xii

C. 18 RECTO

Qui scriverrò tutti e denari e l'uscita de' marmi e chapitello della cholonna e altare si farà alla detta chapella.

A Giovanni d'Ambruogio, lastraiuolo, dì xxvi di lugl[i]o [1394], f. tre d'oro per parte di paghamento del chapitello del macigno si fece al pilastro della nuova chapella

f. iii

A lui detto, dì xxii d'aghosto, f. tre d'oro per residuo e chompimento del detto chapitello

f. iii

A lui detto, dì xxi di settembre, f. venti d'oro per parte di paghamento d'una lapida di marmo di braccia 4 per porre sopra l'altare

f. xx

A lui detto, dì xxviiii d'ottobre, l. ottanta di questo [?] i quali ebbe per manifatura di parte de' marmi de' gradi dell'altare e delle cornici a rosette commesse

L. lxxx

A lui detto, dì xxvi di gennaio [1395 modern style], l. sesanta per la detta chagione di sopra, diede per me Nicholao di Bernardo e Nicholao per me dal maestro Matteo

L lx

A Romolo di Benozzo, che chava il marmo, dì xi di febraio, per parte di paghamento de' marmi dati per la chapella, per lui a Nicholao di Bernardo l. ventisei

L. xxvi

A Giovanni d'Ambruogio, dì xviiii di febraio, f. iiii diede per me Nicholao di Bernardo, per lo detto lavorio, per s. 77 d. 4 f.

L. xv s. viiii

A lui detto, dì iiii di marzo, f. tre d'oro, per lui al Chofaccia vetturale da Fiesole

f. iii

A lui detto, dì vi di marzo, l. cinquanta contai in sua mano

L. l

A Romolo di Benozzo, dì ii di maggio, per lavoro fatto di marmi per l'altare, per resto di suo paghamento, l. quatordici s. sei

L. xiiii s. vi

C. 20 RECTO

Qui scriverrò universamente ogni altro denaro per me si pagherà per utile della chapella, excepte l'uscite scritte dinanzi.

A Bartolo da Manghone, di xvi di lugl[i]o per ii misure di ghalcina s. dodici

L. __ s. xii

Al Gramigna vetturale, per some otto di rena, per d. x soma, e per reghatura la ghalcina d. 8, s. sette d. quattro

L. __ s. vii d. iiii

A Piero di Guelfo, dì detto, per spegnere la detta ghalcina e cholarla e vagl[i]are la rena s. sette d. quarto

L. __ s. vii d. iiii

A Giovanni bighongiaro, dì xi di lugl[i]o, per rachonciatura uno mastello

L. __ s. iii d. vi

Ad Agostino di Giovanni Martini, dì detto [xxi di luglio], per rischiarare e ripulire i bechatelli e capitelli della volta della cappella per coprirgli d'oro, per un opera s. quatordici L. __ s. xiiii

A Giovanni d'Ambruogio, lastraiuolo da Firenze, che venne col maestro Lorenzo, chapomaestro di Sancta Liperata, quando si prese il consigl[i]o dell'altare e dell'uscio della chapella, l. una s. tredici

L. i s. xiii

A Lorenzo, maestro predetto, per simile chagione f. uno d'oro

f. i

C. 20 VERSO

A Piero Dati, dì detto [vii agosto], per una misura di chalcina per la chapella s. sei

L. __ s. vi

Al Rosso portatore, per spegniatura, e 'l Gramignia per rechatura la detta ghalcina

L. __ s. ii d. viii

A Pero di Guelfo, dì detto, per vino e poponi per lui,

L. __ s. ii d. viii

A Piero di Guelfo detto, per le spese fatte a Giovanni lastraiuolo e compagni, quando missono il chapitello nel pilastro e prima in uno venire per desinare mercholedi mattina s. iiii, e per carne per la sera s. iiii d. iiii, e in ispezi[e] e segholato s. uno, in tutto

L. __ s. viiii d. iiii

A lui, per la mattina, uno ventre s. quatro e per la sera carne s. quatro per uno, per merenda d. x e per libre sei di piombo s. x, in tutto

L. __ s. xviii d. x

A lui, venerdì, in xii uova s. tre, in fichi e uve s. ii, in libre v di gesso s. uno d. iiii, pani xxi s. vii, in tutto

L. __ s. xiii d. iiii

A Berto del Sera, dì xxii d'agosto, per chocitura, a detti maestro

L. __ s. iii

A Jacopo d'Alexo, dì detto, per soitigliatura gli scharpelli e pichoni di Giovanni, L. __ s. iiii

A Bonosino, dì detto, per chavatura il marmo pe' gradi,
L. __ s. v

A Nicholao per richopritura la fossa de marmi
L. __ s. ii

A Piero di Guelfo per iiii dì che stette a servire Giovanni detto l. una con Cristofano al ponte L. i

Al Chosaccia vetturale da Fiesole, per vettura di some iiii di pietre concie per la chapitello detto, l. due
L. ii

Al Bodda vetturale, dì xxvi d'agosto, per vettura d'una balla di cera, pesò libre 6 col sacho, s. dieci
L. __ s. x

A lui detto, per ghabella della detta cera, l. due s. dodici
L. ii s. xii

A Biagio da via Chava, carradore, dì v di settembre, per vettura e ghabella di marmi portò a Giovanni lastraiuolo a Firenze, l. due s. quindici
L. ii s. xv

C. 21 RECTO

A Piero di Guelfo, di xiiii di settembre, per una misura di chalcina s. vi e per spegnitura s. due e per fare portare il chalcinaccio era nella pieve s. undici d. 4 e per some iiii di rena s. tre L. __ s. xiiii d. iiii

A Francescho di Marcho, dì xviiii di settembre, per l. ventidue s. quatordici d. sei, i quali diede a don Lionardo per la finestra del vetro che fece per la chapella, per f. sei
L. xxii s. xiiii d. vi

A Michele di Toringho, dì detto, l. una s. due, per vino diede quando il maestro Giovanni aconciò il chapitello del pilastro
L. i s. ii

A Cristofano di ser Francia, dì xxii di settembre, per fare il ponte al pilastro e disfare e acconciarne un altro sotto, largho, l. una per 1 dì
L. i

A Piero di Guelfo, a dì xx di novembre, il quale diede alle infrascritte persone le infrscritture quantità: a Bartolo fornaciaio, per due misure di chalcina e 40 mattoni
L. i s. i

Al Gramigna, per rechatura i mattoni e la ghalcina s. tre
L. __ s. iii

A Biagio di Fatalbuio, per 2/3 d'opera e col manovale per rimurare la finestra della chapella L. __ s. xv

A un'opera per cavare il marmo della fossa per lo sportello dell'altare,
L. __ s. v

A Piero detto, per pane e chacio per Biagio e 'l compagno
L. __ s. v

A lui detto, per carbone di cerro, per bisogno della chapella,
L. __ s. i d. iiii

A Giovanni di Neri, per racconciatura il subiello della galchina e due doghe
L. __ s. v

A Piero di Guelfo per ii opere servite nella sopradette cose
L. __ s. x

A Cristofano di ser Francia, per diporre il ponte della volta e porlo più basso nel terzo valicho, per tre opere l. tre
L. iii

A Piero detto, per due opere con Cristofano s. diece
L. __ s. x

A Piero detto, per pane e chamangiare per le dette opere
L. __ s. iiii d. vii

A lui detto, per una funicella per lo batagl[i]o dello squillone, l. una s. sei
L. i s. vi

A Dormanno tedescho, per spegnere le due moggia della ghalcina e per riportare le tavole avanzarono del ponte
L. __ s. viiii

A Piero detto, per un'opera [struck out: per lui] co'llui
L. __ s. v

A Bettino Bettini per due opere fu con Cristofano al ponte, l. una s. quarto
L. i s. iiii

Al Gramigia vetturale, per rechatura le due misure di chalcina e some 8 di rena
L. __ s. vi d. viii

C. 21 VERSO

A Bartolo da Manghone, per due misure di chalcina, dì xx di novembre,
L. __ s. xii

A Dormano tedescho, per spegnere la detta ghalcina detto dì,

L. __ s. ii d. 8

A Biagio di [blank] da via Chava, carratore che portò a Firenze una lapide di marmo a Giovanni lastraiuolo per fare uno lato dell'altare dov'è lo sportello, l. due s. cinque

L. ii s. v

A Piero di Guelfo, dì detto [2 gennaio 1395 modern style], i quali diede alle infrascritte persone: a Bernardo di Bartolino che m'aconciò le sparghe [?] del tavolino s. tre, a Guasparre di ser Bartolo per iiii stuoie per chiudere il palco al dipintore, l. una, e per spagho per chuscire le stuoie [?]

A Nicholaio di Bernardo, dì xxvi di gennaio, l. una, per uno dì ch'andò a Firenze a rechare la misura della chapella di Santa Croce, che dipinse il maestro Agnolo

L. i

Al maestro Matteo di Giovanni l. sei, dì detto, ricevute pe' frati di Santo Franchescho per uno fitto da pahgare ogni anno la chappella al loro convento di l. iii per due anni passati, cioè 1393 e 1394

L. vi

Ad Antonio di Giovanni Martini, dì primo di febraio, s. dodici per facitura di porre il ponte di fuori per dipignere il compasso della chapella

L. __ s. xii

A Piero di Guelfo, dì ii di febraio, per salario di mesi sei passati, cioè agosto, settembre, ottobre, novembre, dicembre, e genaio, per l. tre al mese, l. diciotto

de' quali n'ebbe per staia xii di grano l. vi s. xii e l. iii s. viiii d. vi il maestro Matteo e l. vii s. xviii d. vi Giovanni di Pavolo Marcovaldi: in tutto

L. xviii

A Pavolo di Guelfo, di xi di febraio, per spese fatte per la chapella per una misura di chalcina s. vi e per spegnatura s. i d. iiii e per foglie e penne per ser Lodovico notaio della chap[p]ella, s. iii d. 8 in tutto

L. __ s. xi

A Domenico Santini, dì detto, per la taglia, el canope e tavole prestò all'opera, per la galcina si collò per lo [i]ntonico del dipintore, lire una, paghò per me Stefano d'Arigho

L. i

A Pardo d'Andrea, sagrestano dell'opera di cappella, dì xiii di febraio, l. nove per parte di salario del tempo servite per lui, cio[è] sono mesi nove e prima per li mesi di giugno, lugl[i]o, agosto L. viiii

C. 22 RECTO

A Pavolo di Guelfo, dì xiii di febraio, per vi misure di chalcina comperò per murare l'altare, s. trentasei

L. i s. xvi

A uno che lla spense, dì detto

L. __ s. v

A Biagio da via Chava, dì primo di marzo, per vettura e ghabella d'una lapida di marmo da Firenze per l'altare, l. tre

L. iii

A Cristofano di ser Francia, dì ii d'aprile, per otto opere altornitoio [?], doversi mostra la cintola l. otto

L. viii

A Guadagno del Mazza, dì detto, che stette al detto lavorio dì sette, l. due s. sediici

L. ii s. xvi

A Nicholao del Badia, dì detto, per cinque dì 1/3 stette al detto servigio, l. tre s. tre

L. iii s. iii

Ad Antonio di Fatalbano, dì detto, che stette al detto lavorio quatro dì, l. tre

L. iii

A lui detto, detto dì, per compitura uno pezzo di muro dove si fece la finestra tondo sopra la chapella vechia, l. sei

L. vi

C. 22 VERSO

A Piero da Chomo, dì ii d'aprile, il quale ruppe l'usciale che entra di fuori dalla faccia della chiesa in sul coritoio dove si mostra la cintola, l. dieci soldi dieci

L. x s. x

A Nanni di Duti, vetturale di Colle, per vettura d'uno sportello di marmo reghò da Firenze, dalla boteghа di Giovanni d'Ambruogio, per vettura e ghabella l. due s. otto d. quatro

L. ii s. viii d.iiii

A Bartolomeo fornaciaio, dì v d'aprile, per ghalcina auta per mura[re] l'altare e gradi, l. una s. dieci

L. i s. x

A Zacheri maestro, dì detto, per salario di cinque dì che stette a murare l'altare, l. quatro s. dieci

L. iiii s. x

A Naldo di Simone, per salar[i]o di due dì al detto lavorio, dì detto, s. sedici
L. __ s. xvi

A Bartolomeo da Firenze, maestro di scarpello, dì detto, per cinque dì serviti al detto lavoro, l. tre s. quindici
L. iii s. xv

A Jacopo da Sandonino, dì detto, per uno legno d'abete per lo corriolore, dove si mostra la cintola, l. sei
L. vi

A Chambio di Ferre, dì detto, per sei schotti diede a Giovanni lastraiuolo e 'l compagno, prima gli fosse aconcio la stanza nella pieve l. due
L. ii

A ser Andrea di Guiduccio, fattore degl'Operai, dì detto, per spese minutamente fatte nel detto lavorio, l. cinque
L. v

A ser Andrea detto, detto dì, per spese per lui fatte e da fare per simile chagione, l. cinque L. v

A Domenicho di Bartolo, manovale, dì detto, per salario d'uno dì, s. diece
L. __ s. x

A Nicholaio di Bernardo, dì ii di maggio, f. cinquanta d'oro, i quali rendè che s'erano achattati per bisogno dell'opera, chome apare alla mia entrata, e per tre mesi di providigione de' detti denari, f. uno d'oro, in tutto
f. li

A Pavolo di Guelfo, sagrestano della chapella, dì iii di maggio, perchè stette a servire i maestri stettero alla mutatione della chapella e all'altare uno mese intero, per tutto l. dieci, e stete 'iù notti co'lloro e a guardare la chapella
L. x

C. 23 RECTO

A Giovanni d'Andrea, mugnaio, dì iii di maggio, l. quattro il quale sonò le ca[m]pane la notte e 'l dì della pasqua del Perdono,

L. iiii

A Cristofano di ser Francia, dì detto, l. diciotto s. dieci, per xviii dì 1/2 stette al lavoro della chapella

L. xviii s. x

A Guadagno del Mazza, dì detto, l. cinque s. dicesette, per xiii dì stette per manovale alla detta chapella

L. v s. xvii

A Nencio di Nofri maestro, dì detto, l. una s. dodici per due dì e 2/3 stette al detto lavoro

L. i s. xii

A Pavolo di Bruno e uno compagno, seghatori, per due dì stettero a seghare legname per la chapella, l. due s. otto, dì detto

L. ii s. viii

Ad Antonio di Giovanni Martini e al fratello, dì detto, l. tre, per due dì stettero alla detta chapella a lavorare di legname

L. iii

A Franchescho di Vanni, spetiale, dì detto, per più cose tolte dalla sua bottegha, di bisogno al detto lavoro, l. tre s. diece

L. iii s. x

A Pietro Dati fornaciaio, per 400 quadrucci e 400 mattoni e 1/2 moggio di ghalcina per lo detto lavoro, l. otto s. quatordici, dì detto

L. viii s. xiiii

A Giovanni di Neri, bottaio, per raconciatura una bighoncia s. sei

L. __ s. vi

Al Gramigna, renaiuolo, per 40 some di rena e per vettura di mattoni e ghalcina, l. una s. undici, dì iii di maggio

L. i s. xi

A Bartolomeo fornaciaio, dì iiii di maggio, per 1/2 moggio di ghalcina e per sei fastelle di fraschoni, ch'arsono la notte del perdono in sulla piazza della pieve, l. una s. sedici L. i s. xvi

A Matteo di Fatalbuio, dì detto, per tre dì stette al detto lavoro l. due s. due

L. ii s. ii

A Bartolomeo di Jacopo, legnaiuolo, dì detto, per viii panchoncelli d'abete e per una tavola d'abete l. quatro s. dieci

L. iiii s. x

Ad Agostino di Giovanni Martini, per uno ponte fece di fuori dove si dipinse l'Asumpta s. dieci L. __ s. x

Al Nero battilana, dì detto, che stette iiii notti a guardare alla chapella

L. __ s. x

A Lorenzo spetiale, dì v di maggio, per libre 9 di funi per lo lampanaio

L. i s. vii

A Stefano chiamato Burro, dì xxv di maggio, l. una s. diece, per tre opere stette alo smalto L. i s. x

Al Gramigna renaiuolo, dì detto, per ghiaia e rena per lo detto smalto, l. due, e per vettura di chalcina s. due, in tutto
L. ii s. ii

A Piero da Chomo, dì detto, per una opera stette alla finestra del vetro a fare fare i ferri
L. __ s. xv

C. 23 VERSO

A Pavolo di Guelfo, dì xxv di maggio, per spese fatte per lui a' maestri in pane e altre cose da vivere quand'era fattore, l. cinque s. dodici d. sette
L. v s. xii d. vii

Al detto Pavolo, detto dì, per residuo di suo salar[i]o, che servette i detti maestri alla chapella nuova, l. una s. dieci L. i s. x

A lui detto, detto dì, l. una s. diece per stette co' maestri quando si fece lo smalto
L. i s. x

A ser Andrea di Ghiuccio, fattore degl'operai, l. dodici s. quatro d. sette, per spese fatte per lui ne' maestri da Firenze e di Prato in mangiare e in altre cose
L. xii s. iiii d. vii

A Luparella di Verzone, procuratore di Doffo Bernardini da Firenze, per uno lascio fece Lenzo cieriai lire cento, sì chome aparisce per suo testamento ebbe per me da Alberto di Giovanni Tavolini e fece fare carta per ser Lodovicho Tarterini, notaio della chapella, di
L. c

Stefano di Michele chiamato Chaterna, per due dì per manovale l. una
L. i

A Biagio Fei, dì detto, per rechatura some 12 di ghiaia, s. sette
L. __ s. vii

A Matteo di Jacopo da Settignano, dì xxv di maggio, per parte di paghamento di sue opere state alla chapella e altare, l. ventiquatro
L. xxiiii

A Giovanni d'Ambruogio, lastraiuolo da Firenze, dì detto l. ventiquatro, per parte d'opere stato a lavorare alla detta chapella
L. xxiiii

A Lodovicho Tarterini, dì detto, per uno dì ch'andò a Firenze al Veschovo, in compagnia del predichatore della pieve, perchè ssi predicasse il perdono,

L. i s. xiii

Al detto predichatore, detto dì, per la detta chagione, l. due

L. ii

A Lorenzo di Donato, orafo, dì detto, per rischiaratura i chandellieri dell'altare l. una s. dieci L. i s. x

A Bernardo Bartolini, dì detto, per due serrami fece all'usciouolo dell'altare, dov'è la cintura di nostra Donna, l. una s. diciotto

L. i s. xviii

A Lapo di Toringho, dì detto, per libre 13 oncie 8 di montoni per fare la chopertura dell'altare, per s. 9 d. 7 2/5 libbra, l. sei s. dieci d. sette

L. vi s. x d. vii

Al figliuolo di Fino chalzolaio, dì detto, per menatura il detto chorame s. otto

L. __ s. viii

Ad Antonio linaiuolo, dì detto, per due pelli rosse per la stampatura del detto chuoio, l. una s. otto

L. i s. viii

A Stefano pianellaio, per stampatura il detto chuoio negl'orli s. otto

L. __ s. viii

Al Gharzonaccio chalzolaio, per ristituire [?] il detto chuoio, dì detto, l una s. dieci

L. i s. x

A Lorenzo di Giovanni, lastraiuolo, dì detto, per uno dì ½ lavoro in ultimo a l'altare, l. una s. dieci

L. i s. x

A Vettorio, dipintore adì detto, per parte di suo lavoro all'altare e al lampanaio, l. dodici

L. xii

A Lorenzo manovale, per uno dì stette a spegnere ghalcina e mutare pietre, s. otto

L. __ s. viii

C. 24 RECTO

A Ridolfo di Lanfrancho, dì xxx di maggio, per barili x di vino e metadelle 39 tra biancho e vermiglio, dato a Piero e Pavolo di Guelfo nell'opere tenute alla chapella e altare, in tutto L. x s. [?]

A lui detto, per uno dì ch'andò a Firenze mandato dagl'operai a comperare azzurro e vedere la chapella di Messer Vanni e fare che'l Maestro Agnolo venisse a dipignere fu fine dì 27 di settembre, l. una

L. i

C. 25 RECTO

Questi sono i denari paghati per me Ridolfo di Lanfrancho chamarlingho dell'Opera e chapella della pieve de' quali non à stantiamento al tempo di messer Michele di messer Lapo e del maestro Giovanni del maestro Iacopo e di Biagio di Lapo e di Nicholò di Bernardo, Operai, 1394 [1395 modern style] di primo marzo

Ad Antonio di Giovanni Martini, dì primo di febraio, s. dodici, per fare il ponte dove si dipinse il compasso nella faccia della chapella di fuori

L. __ s. xii

A Pavolo di Guelfo, dì xi di febraio, per una misura di ghalcina s. 6 e per spegnitura s. i d. 2 e per fogli e penne per s Lodovicho s. 3 d. 8

L. __ s. xi

A Pavolo di Guelfo 13 dì febraro per 6 misure di ghalcina per murare l'altare l. una s. dieci L. 1 s. x

A Biagio churatore da via [?], per vettura e ghabella d'una lapida di marmo da Firenze, l. tre, dì primo di marzo

L. iii

C. 25 VERSO

A Matteo di Jacopo da Settignano, dì 25 di maggio, l. ventiquatro, per parte di paghamento di sue opere di scharpello, serviti all'altare

L. xxiiii

A Giovanni d'Ambruogio, lastraiuolo da Firenze, dì detto, l. ventiquatro, per parte dì serviti al detto lavore chollo scharpello e murare

L. xxiiii

A ser Lodovicho Tartorini, dì detto, per uno dì ch'andò al veschovo di Firenze in compagnia del predichare della pieve per predichare il perdono

L. i s. 13

A Lorenzo di Donato, orafo, dì detto, per rischiaratura i chandellieri dell'altare della chapella, l. una s. dieci

L. i s. x

A Bernardo Bartolini, chiavaiuolo, dì detto, per due serrami per l'usciuolo dell' altare, dove si ripone la cintola, l. una s. diciotto

L. i s. xviii

A Lapo di Toringho, dì detto, per libre 13 oncie 8 di montoni per fare la chopritura dell'altare, per s. 9 d. 7 2/5 libra, l. sei s. dieci d. sette

L. vi s. x d. vii

Al figliuolo di Fino chalzolaio, che menò il detto choiame

L. __ s. viii

Ad Antonio linaiuolo, dì detto, per due pelli rosse per fare gli orli alla detta chopritura, che ssi stamparono, l. una s. otto

L. i s. viii

A Stefano pianellaio, per la stampatura

L. __ s. viii

Al Gharzonaccio chalzolaio, per chuscitura il detto chuoio, l. una s. dieci

L. i s. x

A Vettorio, dipintore da Firenze, per parte di lavoro fatte alla chapella e all'altare, l. dodici, dì detto

L. xii

A Lorenzo manovale, dì detto, per una opera stette a spegnere ghalcina e mutare pietre, s. otto L. __ s. viii

A Ridolfo di Lanfrancho, dì xxx di maggio, per barili dieci e metadelle 39 di vino dato a Pavolo di Guelfo, per l'opere stettero a lavorare ala chapella

L. x s. xviiii

A lui detto, per uno dì che ando a Firenze per lo maestro Agnolo, al tempo del maestro Matteo e compagni, per sue spese l. uno

L. i

A Lorenzo di Giovanni lastraiuolo, per fine di 24 di maggio, l. venti ebbe per me dal detto ser Andrea di Guiduccio

L. xx

C. 26 RECTO

Questo soni i denari dati per me Ridolfo al maestro Agnolo di Taddeo, al tempo de' sopredetti uficiali [1 marzo 1395 modern style]

Al maestro Agnolo sopradetto, dì viii di febraio, per parte di suo lavoro l. centocinque s. otto L. cv

A lui, detto dì, f. tre s. quindici

f. iii L. __ s. xv

A lui, dì xi di febraio, l. trentatrè s. tredici

L. xxxiii s. xiii

A lui, dì xiii di febraio, fi. sei

f. vi

A lui, dì vi di marzo, l. sessanta

L. lx

A lui, dì vii di marzo, l. trentaquatro s. dodici d. sei

L. xxxiiii s. xii d. vi

A lui, dì xxviiii di marzo, l. quaranta

L. xl

A lui, dì primo d'aprile, l. quatordici s. quatordici d. sei

L. xiiiii s. xiiii d. vi

A lui, dì viii di maggio, l. quaranta

L. xl

A lui, dì xxv di maggio, per resto di suo paghamento, f. quarantuno l. due s. cinque

f. xli L. ii s. v

In tutto, se volete fare uno stanziamento, f. __ L.__ s.__ d. __

Questi sono i denari paghati ne'cholori e oro

Al Massaio, discepolo d'Agnolo, dì iiii febraio [1395], per uno lavoro d'oro, pezzi 1100 d'oro tolse da Maffio, l. trentatre, e di ghabella s. sedici, e per sua spese x. dieci

L. xxxiiii s. vi

A Nicholaio di Bernardo, dì xviiii di febraio, l. quarantacinque, per 1500 pezzi d'oro tolse dal detto Maffio battiloro

L. xlv

Al Maestro Matteo, dì xv marzo, per uno foglio di stagno s. due

L. __ s. ii

A Vettorio, discepolo d'Agnolo, l. trentatrè s. undici, per uno lavoro d'oro tolte dal detto Maffio, diede i denari ser Naldo Nicholozzi di quegli messi a entrata, alla ragione de' denari riscossi per lui, chome apare in questo

L. xxxiiii s. xi

A Donato di Bonifazio, dì xx d'aprile, per oncie 8 d'azurro fine per f. 13 libra, f. 9 s. 9 d. 8 a fiorino; e per oncie 6 d'azuro di f. 5 1/2 libra, f. 2 l. 1 s. 1 d. 8 a fiorino; e per oncie 3 del detto azurro f. 1 l. 1 s. 2 d. 2 a fiorino; e per oncie 2 del detto azurro fine f. 2 s. 9 d. 8 a fiorino; somma in tutto f. 16 s. 7 d. 3 che sono di piccioli a s. 76 d. 10 per fiorino

L. lxii s. viii d.__
s. vii d. vi

A lui detto, per libre 30 di gesso, per d. 3 libra

L. __ s. i

A Neri d'Antonio, dì detto, per uno fogl[i]o di stagno, s. uno d. 8

L. __ s. i d. viii

A Nicholaio di Bernardo, dì xxiiii d'aprile, l. dodici per 400 pezzi d'oro tolse da Maffio detto, del quale n'avanzò pezi 200, il quale si loghorò nell'altare

L. xii

Som[m]a L. 142 s. 16 d. 8

Questo sono i denari pagha a Giovanni lastraiuolo, resto de' suoi marmi

A Giovanni d'Ambruogio, lastraiuolo, dì xviiii di febraio, l. quindici s. otto d. quarto

L. xv s. viii d. iiii

A lui, dì iiii di marzo, f. tre d'oro

f. iii

A lui, dì vi di marzo, l. cinquanta

L. l

Somma f. 3 L. 65 s. 9 d. 6

I.4. PRATO, ARCHIVIO DI STATO, PATRIMONIO ECCELSIASTICO 48 (ENTRATA E USCITA DELL'OPERA DELLA CAPPELLA DI NOSTRA DONNA VERGINE MARIA, POSTA NELLA PIEVE DI PRATO, 1395–1396)

C. 20 RECTO:

Uscita dell'Opera e Cappella della Cintola della pieve a Prato per uno anno, incominciato anno Domini MCCCLXXXXV dì primo di giugno e finito come segue. È scritto da me Stefano d'Arigho, camarlingho della detta Opera per lo detto anno, al tempo degli infrascritti Operai cioè:

Messer Michele di Messer Lapo
Giovanni del Maestro Jacopo

E prima diedi io Stefano sopradetto, alle infrascritte persone per le infrascritte

Biagio di Lapo Niccholaio di Bernardo	cagioni e per stanziamenti fatti per li detti Operai, scritto per piùvicho notaio, e prima: a

Giovanni d'Ambruogio, dì xi di giugno, per resto e compimento di cio che avesse avere dall'Opera fino al detto anno e dì, l. settantasei s. dieci, stanziati detto dì

L. lxxvi s. x

C. 20 VERSO

Anno MCCCLXXXXV

Pavolo di Guelfo, sagrestano della Cappella, adì xxviii di giungno, per suo salario di v mesi, cioè febraio, marzo, aprile, magio e giungno, per l. iii al mese, parte al tempo di Ridolfo e parte mia, l. quindici stanzianti per Ser Vanozo decto adì xxiii

L. xv

Lippo di Lapo, sagrestano della detta cappella, adì xxviii di giungno, per suo salario di ii mesi, cioè magio e giugno, per l. tre il mese, l. sei stanziati per ser Vanozo detto, adì xxiii di giungno L. vi

Maestro Angnolo di Tadeo, dipintore da fFirenze, adì xxviii di giungno, per dipingnitura la storia della Assunta ch'è dipinta in su la piazza della della [*sic*] pieve, f. xiiii, ebe moneta per s. xviiii d. iiii l'uno, lire cinquanta cinque s. diece d. otto

Stanziati per ser Vanozzo dì xxiii di giungno

L. lv s. x d. viii

Pavolo di Guefo, adì detto, per compimento di pagamento di ii dì che stette a servire il maestro Angnolo quando compiè di dipingnere la cappella, s. sei

Stanziati per lo detto ser Vanozzo detto dì

L. vi

Manno di Giovanni Bartoli, per ii libri per l'entra[ta] e uscita del'Opera e per uno bastardello e xii folgli, l. una s. dodici

L. i s.xii

C. 21 RECTO

Anno MCCCLXXXXV

Don Marcho dell'ordine di Vallimbrosa, adì xx di luglio, per compimento della finestra del vetro della cappella f. iiii d'oro regato a quattrini per s. xviiii l'uno l. quindici s. sedici

L. xv s. xvi

C. 21 VERSO

Anno MCCCLXXXXV

Nicholaio di Bartolo, c[i]ai adì xxvii d'agosto, per iiii lampane grandi per la cappella, s. quindici

L. __ s. xv

Gherardo Consilgli, adì x di settembre, perchè venne in servigio dell'opera e stimò il lavorio del concio dell'altare, per resto di suo salario diedi per lui a Nicholaio di Bernardo l. una
Stanziamento per ser Vanozzo adì xv di giungno

L. i

C. 22 RECTO

Anno MCCCLXXXXV

Cristofano di ser Francia, adì x di settembre, per resto d'opere per lui date in servigio della cappella per infino al detto dì di sopra, l. quatro s. diece

L. iiii s. x

Vettorio dipintore, adì detto [xxv ottobre], per horo e dipintura la figura della Vergine Maria, e basa e piedistallio, la quale stae in suso l'antare, l. quatordici
Stanziati per ser Vanozo adì xv d'ottobre

L. xiiii

C. 22 VERSO

Anno MCCCLXXXXV

Vettorio dipintore, per residuo di l. xviii che dovea avere per dipignitura i lampanai travi della cappella, delle quali l. xviii ebe da Ridolfo di Lamfranco per arieto camarlingho, l. xii, ebe da me Stefano adì vi di dicembre l. sei

L. vi

Stanziati per s Vanozzo Bandini, dì ultimo di novembre

C. 23 VERSO

Anno MCCCLXXXXV

Giovanni Caribettoli, adi detto [6 dicembre], per libre lxxx di vitella che ssi comprò da lui per donare al veschovo quando sagrò l'antare della cappella l. dieci

L. x

Stanziati per ser Vanozzo, adì detto

Giovanni bustaio, per braccia viiii di panno lino per inincerallo e po[r]llo in suso l'antare quando si sagrò, l. quatro s. uno

L. iiii s. i

Stanziati per ser Vanozzo dì ultimo di novembre

Maestro Matteo, adì detto, per libre vi di candela moze per donare al detto veschovo quando sagrò la decta altare e per libre iiii oncie viiii di nigra tinta e per la schatola in
l. dieci s. due, stanziati per ser Vanozo dì ultimo di novembre

L. x s. ii

Maestro Matteo detto, per libre v once viiii di ciera posto in suso il decto panno lino che ssi puose in suso l'antare quando si sagrò l. tre
Stanziati per ser Vanozzo dì ultimo di novembre

L. iii

C. 29

Anno MCCCLXXXXVI

Piero Dati, fornaciaio, adì detto [xvii d'aprile 1496], per vi misure di galcina, la quale diede all'Opera al tempo di Ridolfo di Lanfrancho, per lo issmalto dove fue la cappella, l. una s. quatordici L. i s. xiiii

Bartolomeo di Stefano, fornaciaio, adì detto, per misure vi di chalcina, date per lui al tempo di Ridolfo di Lanfrancho e per la detta cagione, l. una s. quatordici

L. i s. xiiii

Nicholao di Bartolo c[i]ai, adì detto, per ii lampare ferrate per la detta cappella, s. quindici L. __ s. xv

C. 29 VERSO

Anno MCCCLXXXXVI

Algamento Peratti adì detto [xvii d'aprile], che rechò da fFirenze some xvii di [struck out: mattoni] marmo lavorato dell'antare della cappella e per gabella d'esso marmo, al tempo di Ridolfo di Lanfrancho, camarlingho, l. nove

L. viiii

Giovanni Martini, adì detto, perchè fece il il piedestallo ch'è sotto la figura della Nostra Donna, ch'è in suso s'antare, l. una s. dieci

L. I s. x

APPENDIX II

FILIPPO DE' MEDICI, *RICORDO*

Pisa, Archivio di Stato, Miscellanea manoscritti 39, inserto 50
Ricordo di mano propria dell'archivescovo Philippo

C.1 RECTO

Ricordo delle cose ò fatto di poi sono archivescovo di Pisa
Murato l'orto grande e ridotto a cultura [e] posto frutti
Rimurato quasi da fondame [fondamenti] l'arcivescovado e fattolo magior non era
Rimurato da fondamenti il castel di Calci che per le guerre era in tutto disfatto e fattolo più bello e

più forte non era prima [On the next line, struck out: Raconcio el castello].

Racquistato in detto Calci molte possessioni ochupate e messo presso al castello una posta d'ulivi in numero circa 800
E più al podere grande di detto luogho ulivi 60
E più in detto luogho comperato molti ulivi per l'arcivescovado
Raconcio el castello di Filetto [Filettole]. Stava male e intonacatolo e riparato dentro tutto [Struck out: riparato] et di fuori acconciatolo.
Messo in detto luogho staiora di vignia **** e piantoni d' ulivi **** e disboschatolo insino in sulle mura e comperato dal comune [between lines: di Filetto] uno luogho chiamato *el Bucine*

Fattovi fornacie e ridottovi da Santa Maria Impruneta fornaciai a far embrici e altri lavori di terra. Fattovi chase per loro
Raquistato a Rosignano molte chase e possessioni [. . .] case
[In the left margin: e tutto el poggio dal castel in fuori e altre cose assai. Item, aquistato el . . . gliari.

Item, aquistato el mulino di detto luogho]

Fatto vada tutta dell'arcivescovado e il paratino
Raquistato Usigl[i]ano all'arcivescovado
Aquistato all'arcivescovado Colle Salvetti, Piaza e Farneta e Cugniano
Castello Anselmi, Monte Calvoli, la pastura di Quarde[. . .]
La pastura del padule di Malaventre. Le fornacie da Vechiano [Vecchiano]

E ridotto el comune di Vechiano a pagare di feudo l'anno al'arcivescovado lire 40, due ne pagavano prima

C. 1 VERSO

Ispadalato el padule di Santa Lucie e fattovi grandissime fosse e ridotto a coltura
Acquistato la magior parte del padule di Calci da' Capionesi
Aquistato la possessione di Barbaricina che prima non era colla chiesa staiora 800, ora è più di [struck out: mille] dumilacinquecento e dove prima erea tutta padulescha l'ò ridotta a colture
Acquista tutta la iuresditione di Bientina e ridotto li huomini a ricognioscerla dall'arcivescovado e pagare di feudo [written above, struck out: livello] l'anno 40 lire
Raquistata la terza parte della pastura di Forcoli
Aquistata la pastura di Val di Perga
Aquistato tutto il pasto di Cimento dove prima non era dell'arcivescovado stava la metà
Ordinata la chiesa e fattovi le constitutioni dove prima non era;
dato a' capellani entrata per distributioni sacha 600 di grano e fiorini cento di denari e ordinato tutte l'ore vi si cantino
Visitato tutte le chiese exempte della diocesi di Pisa che ànno cura d'anima dove prima non erano mai state visitate [between lines: che si trovi].
Donato alla sacrestia Agostino, *Super Johanem*, libro bellissimo; Iosepho, *De antiquitate*; la *Historia ecclesiastica*, uno grande evangelistario coperto d'ariento; unito a detta sacrestia la spedale di Chasa I[. . .]lia
Aquistata allo spedale de' trovatelli la pastura di Vicherello e fattoli avere la heredità di mona Maria da Piano che l'avea data alla camera apostolica
Aquistato in Valtriano all'arcivescovado staiora 2000 di terra lavoratia
Raquistato 1200 staiora di terra pratata e padulescha nelli paduli d'Asciano, teneane in feudo el comune di Campo già e alla data al signor Ruberto in feudo

C. 2 RECTO

Ridotto li huomini d'avanti a ricognioscere el comunale dall'arcivescovado.
Item, tutte le case e vigne e possessioni volessino fare nel comunale o nel feudo, debbono ricognioscere da detto arcivescovado e da quello tenerla
Fatto el conte di Lari feudatario della corte e iurisditione di detto luogho dell' arcivescovado e per chagione di ciò pagano l'anno uno porcho salvaticho
In detto luogho riavute alcune possessioni
In Petrignano e Luchagnano riavute possessioni perdute
Al Bagno ad'Aqua raquistato piu possession e beni erano perduti

A Malaventre e Nodicha fatto quel medesimo
Trovato el rame nelle iurisditioni dell'arcivescovado e nella corte delle Noci
Raquistato una buona parte della corte di Ripabbella che teneano gli huomini di Montescudaio
Aquistato case in Rasignano
Aquisto terreni nella machia del padule, teneano ocupati questi da Castelnuovo
Fatti multi terreni occupati ricognioscere livellari dell'arivescovado
Item, aquistoltene [struck out:alcune] buona quantità di nuovo

APPENDIX III

WILL OF FILIPPO DE' MEDICI

Transcribed by Maria Ausilia Pisano
ASF, Mediceo Avanti il Principato, F. 81, doc. 22

cc.123r–126v

/c.123r/ Copia

In Dei nomine, amen. Sit omnibus manifestum qualiter dominice incarnationis anno millesimo quadringentesimo septuagesimo quarto, indictione ottava, die ventiquattro mensis ottobris more ac solitam consuetudinem notariorum Pisarum, tempore sanctissimi in Christo patris et domini domini Sexti divine providentie Pape quarti. Cum iam pridem et longo lapso animo reverendus in Christo patre et dominus dominus Filippus de Medicis de Florentia sancte Pisarum ecclesie archiepiscopus Dei et apostolice sedis gratie Sardinee et Corsice primas et dicte sedis in eis legatus, ut ipse suo proprio asseruit ore in presentia mei notarii infrascripti et infrascriptorum testium fuerit intentionis et propositi aliquam facere impensam piam ac devotam ac Deo amabilem, tam de pecuniis et redditibus sui archiepiscopatus quod etiam de nonnullis bonis et stipendiis iam dudum perventis ante promotionem sui archiepiscopatus, et idem propositum ideo distulerit, quia dubius erat anceps quo in loco dicte ecclesie cathedralis et sui archiepiscopatus aut membris dicte ecclesie dictam impensam faceret et tandem, Deo inspirante, iam parvo tempore elapso, deliberaverit dictam erogationem facere ad ampliationem, augumentum et maiorem devotionem in iungendum sanctissimo et unico in orbe edifitio Campi Sancti civitatis Pisarum. Quod ingnoscitur esse membrum /c.123v/ nobile dicte alme ecclesie pisane, ideo idem ipse reverendissimus dominus Philippus archiepiscopus, per viam dispensationis, distributionis et erogationis et omni meliori modo, forma et iure, quibus melius posse et ex certa eius scientia et non per aliquem iuris vel facti errorem, pure, libere, inrevocabiliter et inter vivos elargendo, voluit, disposuit et ordinavit et obligavit et fidem sua adstrinsit, promictendo ac conveniendo mihi notario infrascripto ut publica persona presenti, stipulanti ac recipienti vice ac nomine totius capituli et canonicatus dicte ecclesie Pisarum et pro omnibus etiam aliis quorum interest ac interesse poterit in futurum facere, constituere et edificare seu fieri construi et edificari facere suis sumptibus de redditibus dicti sui archiepiscopatus, seu pecunia et aliis rebus mobilibus reductis seu redigendis de redditibus predictis quam etiam de aliis mobilibus pretiosis acquisitis ante dictam sui promotionem, in dicto et circa dictum edifitium dicti Campi Sancti unam cappellam[1] in capite dicti edifitii versus crucifixum in eo loco in quo est designatum certum signum in forma volte, in muro de sinopite in a[.]i[..]s constructura et edificio quanta quantitas expendi debeat, cum effectu que sufficiat ac suppleat ad honorificentiam ac sufficientiam dicte cappelle, secundum congruitatem ac condecentiam dicti dignissimi ac sanctissimi loci campi Sancti et ipsam cappellam sic fundandam et, postquam sic fundata et edificata et constructa fuerit, dotare et pro dote ipsius cappelle constituende in bonis immobilibus emendis de dictis / c.124r/ redditibus suis et bonis mobilibus ut supra, adeo quod etiam redditibus dicte cappelle possint sostentari cappellani in sufficienti numero prout ipse deliberavit, ut sic continue ibidem habeant cotidie offitium celebratum et missas secundum ritum et ordinationem fiendum per eum ad laudem omnipotentis Dei et pro remissione peccatorum suorum, infra tempus ac terminum annorum duorum. Et, si contingat sive contigerit modo aliquo predicta non fieri vel fieri non possent modo aliquo, sua aliqua causa sive casu aut eventu quod dictum dominum archiepiscopum ex nunc fiat, ex tunc et ex hinc prout ex nunc et ad hos ut omnia predicta habilius detentioni mandentur, valuit, disposuit ac ordinavit idem dominus archiepiscopus, per viam distributionis et dispensationis et erogationis predicte, pure et libere et simpliciter et inrevocabiliter et inter vivos elargendo, dando et concedendo et donando omnia mobilia bona per eum empta, habita et acquisita consistentia tam in argento et in generali etiam pannis laneis cuiuscumque materiei quam laneis et vestibus eiusdem domini reverendissimi archiepiscopi existentibus ac consistentibus tam in archiepiscopatu Pisarum quam extra, tantum excepta cappa de rosato meliori dicti reverendissimi domini archiepiscopi que non veniat in presenti donatione sive instrumento non comprehendat et cetera. Sicque donavit et inrevocabiliter dedit et concessit dicte cappelle et fabrice construende et mihi notario infrascripto presenti et, /c.124v/ ut publica persona, stipulanti ac recipienti pro eadem cappella et fabrica et pro omnibus ac singulis quorum interest et poterit interesse in futurum et quod ipsaque bene vendantur et dentur bona fide et sine fraude voluit, commisit, ordinavit atque disposuit ut supra per spectabilem militem dominum operarium pisane maioris ecclesie qui est, vel pro tempore fuerit, dictis casibus vel aliquo eorum evenientem et per nobiles viros Thanai de Medicis de Florentia, fratrem dicti reverendissimi domini archiepiscopi, Antonium vocatum Morettum, Berardi de Vivario et Leonardum Antonii de Vanagollis cives et mercatores pisanos vel duos ex eis in quibus intervenire debeat dictus Thanai et, sine ipso, predicta aut inscripta pro aliis fieri non possint quibuscum predicta ut supra dedit amplam, plenam et liberam patentem et mandatum cum libera administratione duraturam et duraturum etiam post dicti reverendissimi domini archiepiscopi mortem plus offerenti. Et de pecuniis exigendis ex dictis bonis mobilibus, ut supra constituatur et perficentur et construi e perfici debent dicta cappella et in ea constituatur altare et tabula una depingatur et fiat de aurato cum cruce in medio depicta et a latere imago Virginis Marie et ab alio imago sancti Filippi et cum omnibus ornamentis, paramentis, calice, messale et aliis necessariis omnibus ad dictam cappellam beate memorie condecentiam et nobilitatem loci prout inter eos videbitur, et in ea fiat in marmore sepulcrum et sepultura nomine dicti domini archiepiscopi et ponantur arma in eisdem ipsius domini archiepiscopi et intituletur la cappella /c.125r/ della Croce, in qua cappella construenda et edificanda et emi ornamentis et fornimentis et sepultura expendatur et expendi debeat id et tantum quod ac quantum dictis domino Antonio, Thanai, Antonio et Leonardo vel duobus ex eis interveniente cum uno semper dicto Thanai videbitur ac placebit eorum arbitrio e voluntate et quod de et ex pecaniis reservantibus ultimam dictam expensam fiendam pro dicta cappella per supradictos dominum Antonium, Thanai, Antonium et Leonardum vel duos ex eis interveniente semper in uno ipsorum duorum ipso Thanai posse super ac bona in mobilibus ex redditibus quantum habeant substentari ibidem cappellani perficiendi et eligendi de ipsis inscriptis dicte cappelle et predicta fieri et exequi debeant et exequantur infra tempus et terminum annorum duorum dictis casibus vel aliquo eorum ut supra et quos fructus, redditus et proventus dictorum bonorum et ipsa bona habeant ac debeant regi, gubernari et locari per operarium pisane maioris ecclesie perpetuo qui pro tempore fuerit et erit in offitio et ex pecaniis redigendis per ipsum operarium ex dictis fructibus ac proventibus habeant ac debeant substentari, ut infra, cappellani dicte cappelle videlicet quod tot ibidem preficiantur et eligantur et deputentur capellani[1] ut sit quilibet cappellanus /c.125v/ habeat et habere possit florenos triginta librarum quattuor monete currentis valute pro quolibet floreno et singulo anno hoc modo, videlicet ex qualibet edomada [*sic*: hebdomada] ac quolibet de sabbata eiusque edomade eiusque anni debeant precipere singuli a dicto operario qui pro tempore erit tantam tantam (diplografia) summam pecuneatam prout tanget pro rata dictorum triginta florenorum dividendo dictam summam de edomada in edomadam prout supra que rata tamen debeat solvi cuilibet cappellano, casu quo afficerent, ut infra dicitur, et alia non habeat nec conloquatur modo aliquo et quod teneantur ac obligati sint qualibet de ipsi et quolibet eorum unam missam plenam mortuorum pro anima sua in perpetuum, exceptis diebus veneris, qualibus diebus diceretur celebrari debeant et teneantur missam unam dedicatam pro anima dicti reverendissimi domini archiepiscopi, adveniente casu mensis, et una missa semper qualibet die cum offitio solempni cantate in dicta cappella singule teneantur et obligati sint de dictis missis et quod cappellani predicti debeant et possint eligi ac deputari tantum per dictum reverendissimum dominum archiepiscopum ipso veniente et non per alium et deinde, post eius mortem, debeant eligi ac presentari per fratrem Tanai de Medicis, eo mutata tantum et, post eius mortem, per suos filios masculos et descendentes ex linea masculina in perpetuum et quod dicti cappellani sic eligendi sint ac esse debeant cives Pisarum tamen ac pisani dicti et non alii quoquo modo /c.126r/ possint eligi vel deputari; et quod debeant institui ac confirmari per capitulum dicte maioris ecclesie Pisarum, videlicet eligendi post dicti reverendissimi archiepiscopi obitum. Que omnia ac singula suprascriptus reverendissimus dominus Filippus archiepiscopus per solempnem stipulatum convenit ac praemisit mihi Guaspari Iohannis notario infrascripto presenti ac, ut publica persona, stipulanti ac recipienti, predicta fabrica sic construenda et pro omnibus et singulis quorum interest, intererit et poterit in futurum quorumlibet interesse perpetuo per se ac suis successoribus firma, rata et grata habere et tenere ac habituram et ipsa aut aliquod eorum aut dictam donatam, modo aliquo casu sine ingenio contradici vel excogitari posse non revocare, ad penam dupli valenti dictorum bonorum vel dupli eius vendi pro tempore ageretur solempni stipulatum premissa in singulis capitulis, partibus ac menbris hiis contrarius in solidum, que pena tenens commictatur et peti ex exigi possit ac valeat cum effectu quanto in aliquo esset quolibet contractum sine ventum aut predicta non sinantur plenaria observatur, et dicta pena commissi soluta ex acta vel non predicta, omnia et singula firma ac rata maneant et perdurent pro quibus omnibus ac singulis scriptis et infrascriptis perpetuo ac firmiter observandis et adimplemdis et predicta pena solvendo, si commissa fuerit et quotiens commicti contingat, obligavit inde sic dictus reverendus dominus archiepiscopus et successores suos et bona omnia presentia et Ventura mihi notario infrascripto presenti ac recipienti ut supra, renunptians in predictis omnibus, /c.126v/ et singulis excepitione non facta dicte donationis ac non sic vel aliter celebrati gratius dicti mali metus causa infectum actum, omni quod alii iuri legum ac statutorum auxilio iuri ac legi dicenti generaliter renunptians non sufficere seu non valere, cui quidem reverendissimo domino archiepiscopo presenti ac predicta omnia guarentanti sicque fieri valenti precepi ego notarius ac iudex ordinarius infrascriptus probe mihi liceat ac licet suam formam supradictorum quorumcumque locorum de guaranti[gi]a loquentium, quatenus predicta omnia ac singula supra presenti premissa faciat, adimpleat ac observet in omnibus ac per omnia ut supra premissa continetur ac scriptum est. Et dedit ac concessit licentiam, auctoritatem ac mandatum mihi Guaspari Iohannis notario infrascripto, predicta omnia ac singula extradendi ac roborandi ad sensum cuiuscumque sapientis substantia tamen facti non mutata totiens quotiens fuerit opportunum productum in iuditio sive non productum, sine alicuius indiciis offitialis sine curis licentia sive obtentu et tantum me notarium infrascriptum rogavit ut inde de predictis conficerem instrumentum et plura traderem, que petentibus quorum interesset instrumentum ac infrascripta. Actum Pisis in camera primi solarii palatii dicti domini archiepiscopi ac archiepiscopatus Pisarum, presentibus domino Iohanne de Alamannis plebano plebis Vallis Gratiole de Calci Pisarum comitatus ac Pisarum diocesis et presbitero Thomasio olim magistri Bonaini rectore ecclesie Sancti Cristofori Kinsica testibus ad predicta vocatis specialiter ac rogatis suprascriptis anno, indictione, die, mense ac tempore.

[In the left margin: Haec subscriptio notarii apparet unde copiavi.]

Ego Guaspar Iohannis olim ser Guglielmi de Franchis pisanus civis et imperiali auctoritate iudex ordinarius ac notarius predictus omnibus et cetera.

APPENDIX IV

DOCUMENTS FOR THE APSE MURALS IN THE CATHEDRAL OF SPOLETO

Archivio di Stato, Spoleto, Archivio dell'Opera del Duomo di Spoleto, Registro 4 (formerly no. 1), 1465–1505.

c.105 recto (formerly c. 116 recto):

Uscite del'anno 1466. Camerlingo ditto Giordano [di Tommaso] et Operali ditto Cesari [de Angelo] e Vanni [di Girolamo]

+Adì 11 di gennaro 1466

Pagose di volontà di ditti operali ad Dominicho d'Antonio Schiavo f. _ s. XX: sono per facetura di telari per impannare due finestre

f. __ s. 20 d.__

+Adì 18 del ditto

Pagose di volontà di ditti ad maestro Battista da Civitello s. X, sonno per acconciatora dello serrame per l'uscio d'andare all'organi

f. __ s. 10 d. __

+Adì 20 del ditto

Pagose di volontà di ditti ad maestro Giacho lombardo f. 1 s. XX, sonno per acconciatora del camino della sacrestia f. 1 s. 20 d. __

+Adì ditto

Pagose di volontà di dittiad maestro Battista da Cappello: f. 1 s. XXX: sono per telari fece [struck out: nelle rose del frontespizio] per impanarle finestre

f. 1 s. 30 d. __

+Adì ditto

Pagose di volontà di ditti ad uno prete figl[i]olo di Battista di Puccio da Spoliti f.X, sonno per legname comparato da lui per imbossolare la sacrestia

f. 10 s. __ d. __

+Adì ditto

Pagose di volontà di ditti ad facchino da Cascia f.III, sonno per vettura di migliara 3 di mattono portò all'Opera f. 3 s. __ d. __

+Adi 8 di febraro

Pagose di volontà di ditti operali ad Venanzo di Solebancho f. CV s. XL, sonno che li se dero comparasse per ditta Opera oro batttuto, azurri oltramarini et altre cose f. 105 s. 40 d. __

+Adi 5 di marzo

Pagose di volontà di ditti ad messer Andrea delo Cioppo et messer Io. Antonio, canonici, s. XXXII d. VI, sono loro mandati ad Montefalcho

f. __ s. 32 d. 6

+Adì primo d'aprile

Pagose di volontà di ditti ad Micchiorre di Beneditto da Spoliti f. V, sonno per li fatti della heredità di Iohannolo pertenente a ditta Opera e ad lui

f. 5 s. __ d. __

+Adì 19 del ditto

Pagose di volontà di ditti ad done Pasquale da Ponte s. XXV, sonno per uno paro di battici da sonare el venerdì sancto

f. __ s. 25 d. __

+Adì 23 del ditto

Pagose di volontà di ditti ad ser Tholomeo da Spoliti f. III, sonno per uno testamento trasse di Antonio di Tomaxo, pertenente all'Opera

f. 3 s. __ d. __

+Adì ditto

Pagose di volontà di ditti ad Mattio di Langilo f. VIIII, sonno per parte del prezo montaranno le seppolture fa nella cappella se dice di messer Marino

f. 9 s. __ d. __

138. 77. 6

C. 105 VERSO

+Adì 25 d'aprile 1466

Pagose di volontà di ditti ad Dominicho d'Antonio Schiavo f. II, sonno per telari fece da ponersi nelle rose del frontespizio per impannarle

f. 2 s. __ d. __

+Adì primo di magio

Pagose di volontà di ditti ad Andrea, maestro di mattuni, f. V, sonno per coppi tolti da lui per la ditta Opera, cioè per coppi 2000

f. 5 s. __ d. __

+Adì ditto

Pagose di volontà di ditti Operali ad Tomaxo di Giachovo da Spoleti f. III s. V, sonno li pagò ad frate Filippo, dipintore di Firenze, per condurlo a Spoleti per pegnere la tribuna f. 3 s. 5 d. __

+Adì ditto

Pagose di volontà di ditti ad frate Filippo, dipintore di Firenze, f. VIIII, sonno per chortesia fattali venendo a Spoliti e per spese per la sua retornata

f. 9 s. __ d. __

+Adì 24 del ditto

Pagose di volontà di ditti ad mastro Battista da Campello f. X, sonno per parte del prezo montarà uno titto locatoli a ffare sopra la tribuna

f. 10 s. __ d. __

+Adì 26 del ditto

Pagose di volontà di ditti ad li frati di Sancto Salvatore f. II s. XLVII d. VI, sonno per parte del prezo montano perteche dui di prete comparate da loro f. 2 s. 47 d. __

+Adì 31 del ditto

Pagose di volontà di ditti ad Micchione di Beneditto da Spoliti s. LV, sonno che s'è pagato al ditto come procuratore del'Opera contra le heredi di cittadino f. __ s. 55 d. __

+Adi ditto

Pagose di volontà di ditti ad mastro Andrea fornacchiaio ditto sopra, f. IIII, sonno per parte di quello montano coppi 3000 tolti da lui

f. 4 s. __ d. __

+Adì ditto

Pagose di volontà di ditti ad Andrea dalle Valli f. III s. XII d. VI, sonno per coppe 50 da calcina tolte da lui, per s.6 d. 3 coppa

f. 3 s. 12 d. __

+Adì ditto

Pagose di volontà di ditti ad li frati di Sancto Salvatore f. III s. XII d. VI, sonno per ultimo pagamento di dui perteche di prete, comparate da loro

f. 3 s. 12 d. __

+Adì 2 di g[i]ugno

Pagose di volontà di ditti Operali ad Lionello da Chamoro f. I s. XIIII, sonno per pagare scotti dati ad frate Filippo dipintore dal ditto

f. 1 s. 14 d. __

+Adì 7 di g[i]ugno

Pagose di volontà di ditti ad Ciecho di Lucha da Spoli[ti] f. II, sonno per parte del prezo monta la capella della imagine f. 2 s. __ d. __

+Adì 15 del detto

Pagose di volontà di ditti ad Pucciatto di Mattiolo da Spoliti f. I s. XX, sonno per portatore di prete da Sancto Salvatore ad Sancta Maria

f. 1 s. 20 d. __

46 .66. 6

C. 106 RECTO

+Adì 20 di g[i]ugno 1466

Pagose di volontà di ditti ad Ciecho di Lucha da Spoliti f. XX, sonno per parte del prezo monta la cappella della ymagine, quali danari habbe per le mani di don Filippo, presenti ser Giovanni di Lucha et P[i]er Nichola di Manzolo f. 20 s. __ d. __

+Adì ditto

Pagose di volontà di ditti al sopradetto Ciecho f. V, sonno per parte della ditta cappella della ymagine, quali foro delli danari tenner in deposito don Filippo, presenti ditti f. 5 s. __ d, __

+Adì ditto

Pagose di volontà di ditti ad Piernichola di Manzolo da Spoliti f. X, sonno per parte del prezo monta el posto da ponersi l'organi f. 10 s. __ d. __

+Adì 21 del ditto

Pagose di volontà di ditti ad Mastro Battista da Campello f. IIII, sonno per parte del titto fa sopra la tribuna f. 4 s. __ d. __

+Adì ditto

Pagose di volontà di ditti ad ser Nicholà ser Pierangelo da Ciselli x. VII d. VI, sonno per misuratora di uno pezo di terra venduto ad Andreuccio della Valle di Sancto Pietro f. __ s. 7 d. 6

+Adì ditto

Pagose di volontà di ditti ad Marino merciaro f. II s. XV, sonno per braccia 39 di panno canavaccio per impannare le rose del frontespizio di Sancta Maria, et per una groppera da cavallo se camparo per frate Filippo tornando ad Firenze f. 2 s. 15 d. __

+Adì 23 del detto

Pagose di volontà di ditti ad Ciecchо di Lucha da Spoliti f. VI s. XXV, sonno per coppe 100 di calcina si comparò da Galiotto di messer Miliaolus, i quali si pagaro per parte della cappella della imagine f. 6 s. 25 d. __

+Adì 26 del detto

Pagose di volontà di ditti ad Scenzio albergatore da Chammoro f. IIII s. V, sonno per scotti dati ad frate Filippo dipintore, quali si pagaro per lui ad maestro Tomaxo in coppe 9 di orgio f. 4 s. 5 d. __

+Adì 27 del ditto

Pagose di volontà di ditti operali ad Piciacchio alias Lorenzo f. III, sonno per portatore di rena e prete alla ditta opera f. 3 s. __ d. __

+Adì detto

Pagose di volontà di ditti ad Pier Marcho di Damiano f. II s. XX, sonno per dui libri grandi se compararo da lui per scrivero intrata e uscita e debitori

f. 2 s. 20 d. __

+Adì detto

Pagose di volontà di ditti ad maestro Battista da Campello f. I s. XII d. Vi, sonno per legname comparo per lo titto sopra la tribuna

f. 1 s. 12 d. 6

57. 89

C. 106 VERSO

+Adì 27 di g[i]ugno 1466

Pagose di volontà di ditti Operali ad maestro Battista da Campello f. V, sonno per parte di quello monta lo titto sopra la tribuna f. 5 s. __ d. __

+Adì 28 del ditto

Pagose di volontà di ditti ad ser Philippo da Sellano f. I s. L, sonno per fare trare uno testamento in publica forma fatto per uno da Sellano quale lassò danaro all'Opera f. 1 s. 50 d. __

+Adì 2 di lugl[i]o

Pagose di volontà di ditti ad Pier Nichola di Manzolo da Spoleti f. XXII s. V, sonno per facetora dell'oscio della cappella della imagine, quali s'ebbero dal vichario di Monsignor f. 22 s. 5 d. __

+Adì 2 [struck out: 6] del ditto

[in margin: frate Filippo ducati 50]

Pagose di volontà di ditti ad frate Filippo depintore di Firenze f. LXXVII s. LXXXXV, sonno per parte et arra di ducati 700 doverà haere per depegnere la tribuna, quali habbe in ducati 50 papali et bolognini 18, vagl[i]no a bolognini 62 per ducato, che in questo modo foro accattati, cioè rendendo moneta al prestatore, volse a ragione di bolognini 62 per ducato

f. 77 s. 95 d. __

+Adì 15 del ditto

Pagose di volontà di ditti operali ad ser Gabriello di ser Nofrio s. 5, sonno per comparare carta per scrivere relitti fatti ad ditta opera f. __ s. 5 d. __

+Adì 19 del ditto

Pagose di volontà di ditti ad maestro Battista da Campello f. VII s. XVIII d. VI, sonno per parte del prezo montarà el titto da farsi per lui sopra la tribuna

f. 7 s. 18 d. VI

+Adì 20 del ditto

Pagose di volontà di ditti ad maestro Battista ditto f. IIII, sonno per muratora de certi cossetti di muro fece murare in nome delli Operali per ditto titto

f. 4 s. __ d. __

+Adì 24 del ditto

Pagose di volontà di ditti ad Pier Andrea di Taratetta da Spoleti s. XXV, sonno per far reponere una campana nel campanile, quale cadde venendo Monsignore f. __ s. 25 d. __

+Adi ditto

Pagose di volontà di ditti ad Matteo di l'Angilo da Spoleti s. L, sonno per parte de quel montaranno le seppolture che fa nella cappella se dice di messer Marino, quali se pagaro per lui ad Piciacchio per portare rena

f. __ s. 50 d. __

+Adì ditto

Pagose di volontà di ditti ad Sancto da Cascia f. III, sonno per vettura di 3000 coppi portò ad ditta opera f. 3 s. __ d. __

+Adì 26 del ditto

Pagose di volontà di ditti ad Lorenzo dello Pretarello f. I s. LX, sonno per vergoni de ferro, comparati da lui per ponere nel posto delli organi quali hebbe in coppi dui di grano, recivi da Mariano di Fecharmo

f. 1 s. 60 d. __

+Adì ditto

Pagose di volontà di ditti ad mastro Battista da Campello f. II s. LXXV, sonno per parte di quel montarà el titto da farse per lui sopra la tribuna

f. 2 s. 75 d. __

125. 83. 6

C. 107 RECTO

+Adì ultimo di lugl[i]o 1466

Pagose di volontà di ditti operali ad maestro Battista da Campello f. I s. XXV, sonno per levatura delle ferrate stavano alla cappella della imagine, quali s'è pagato per lui ad Domenicho d'Antonio f. 1 s. 25 d. __

+Adì ditto

Pagose di volontà di ditti ad mastro Battista da Campello f. I, sonno per parte di tutti lavorii allocateli e da farli per lui fine ad ditto dì, cavatone lo imbossolare della sacrestia f. 1 s. __ d. __

+Adì 13 d'augusto

Pagose di volontà di ditti ad Lorenzo dello Pretarello f. X, sonno per virgoni di ferro comparati da lui, da ponersi per scambio di monacelle nel titto grande sopra la tribuna f. 10 s. __ d. __

+ Adì 16 del ditto

Pagose di volontà di ditti ad Antonio da Lucano f. II s. XXV, sonno per muratura di certo muro sopra la tribuna, per lo titto da farsi per maestro Battista da Campello f. 2 s. 25 d. __

+Adì ditto

Pagose di volontà di ditti ad certi lombardi f. I, sonno per smuratura d'una cossa di muro era lato la cappella della imagine, et portatura di pietre

f. 1 s. __ d. __

+Adì ditto

Pagose di volontà di ditti operali ad Dominicho lombardo s. XLV, sonno per sgomberare la chiesia e acconciatura in certi lochi in dì della festa

f. __ s. 45 d. __

+Adì ditto

Pagose di volontà di ditti ad Giovanni lombardo f. I s. XXV, sonno per acconciatura delle scali di San Giovanni, donde si cavaro li marmi per l'uscio della imagine f. 1 s. 25 d. __

+Adì ditto

Pagose di volontà di ditti ad Giovanni Guercio lombardo f. II s. XXV, sonno per murare sopra la tribuna per lo titto da farsi per maestro Battista

f. 2 s. 25 d. __

+Adì ditto

Pagose di volontà di ditti ad Mattio de l'Angelo et Polinoro di Girardino s. LXXV, sonno per parte di quel montaranno le soppulture da farsi per loro et per intridere calcina f. __ s. 75 d. __

Adì 17 del ditto

Pagose di volontà di ditti ad Mattio di Sacho, s. XL, sonno per uno ligno d farse uno carritto f. __ s. 40 d. __

Adì 20 d'augusto

Pagose di volontà di ditti ad Venanzo di Solebancho da Spoleti f. X s. XXXVII d. VI, sonno per resto di robbe portate da Venetia, cioè per balle 6 di piombo, M [migliaia] 4 doro battuto, oncie 10 1/2 d'azzurro oltramarino, quali robbe montano con gabella vettura et altre spese ducati 74 veneziani e bolognini 43, delli quali habbe ditto Venanzo como appare in questo a uscita a c. 116, ducati 68 veneziani cioè f. 105 s. 40. Resta ditti f. 10 s. 37 d. 6 f. 10 s. 37 d. 6

30. 97. 9

C. 107 VERSO

+Adì 26 d'augusto 1466

Pagose di volontà di ditti ad Lorenzo dello Pretarello da Spoliti s. VIIII d. VI, sonno per as[s]e tolte da lui per l'uscio d'andare all'organi

f. __ s. 9 d. 6

+Adì ditto

Pagose di volontà di ditti al sopraditto Lorenzo f. VIIIIs. XXXV, sonno per altri vergoni di ferro tolti da lui per ponere nel titto grande sopra la tribuna, in servigio di monacelle. Pexaro [struck out: detti vergoni libre 497 per s. 48] montano f. 19 s. 88. Et più per libre 53 di ferro adoperato per lo racconciare el posto delli organi per facetura de [in margin: certe stanglie de ferro da ponere a traverso sopra lu titto della tribuna e lavorato dal dicto Lorenzo, monta f. 22 s. 45, li quali tutti ha auti, come appare in questa uscita, in 4 partite]

f. 9 s. 35 d. __

+Adì detto

Pagose di volontà di ditti ad mastro Battista da Campello per parte de Bercello, monta el titto da farse per lui sopra la tribuna

f. 1 s. 15 d. __

+Adì ditto

Pagose di volontà di ditti al sopraditto s. LXXV sonno per parte di quello monta el titto da farsi per lui sopra la tribuna f. __ s. 75 d. __

+Adì ditto

Pagose di volontà di ditti al sopradetto f. III per parte di quello monta el titto da farsi per lui sopra la tribuna. Quali se pagaro[no] di suo volontà ad Piertoniaxo di Marinagl[i]o f. 3 s. __ d. __

+Adì 27 del ditto

Pagose di volontà di ditti ad Persicho di Pinacchio da Spoletio f. V, sonno per parte de portatora e valuta di 2600 mattoni portò ad ditta opera i quali hebbe in coppe 10 di grano f. 5 s. __ d. __

+Adì 28 del ditto

Pagose di volontà di ditti ad Permattio di Caracosa s. XXV, sonno li pagò ad li molinari per macenatora delle olive dell'opera f. __ s. 25 d. __

+Adì ditto

Pagose di volontà di ditti ad Piergeronimo di Cristofano s. LXXXXV, sonno per coppi se compararo da lui e per stagno si adoperò in recolare le campane sopra lo coro f. __ s. 95 d. __

+Adì 2 di settembre

Pagose di volontà di ditti ad Pertomaxo di Marinagl[i]o s. VII d. VI, sonno per misuratora d'uno pezo di terra venduta ad Antonio d'Augustino da Teggi
f. __ d. 7 d. 6

+Adi ditto

Pagose di volontà di ditti ad una persona sono s. XV sonno per scangiare ducati et monete a f. larghi quali si mandono ad frate Filippo
f. __ s. 15 d. __

+Adì ditto

Pagose di volontà di ditti ad Giovanni lombardo s. XXX, sonno per portatore di marmi per luscio della imagine dal vescovato alla ecchiesia
f. __ s. 30 d. __

+Adì 3 del ditto

Pagose di volontà di ditti ad Ciecho di Lucha da Spoliti f. II, sonno per parte de quel monta la cappella della imagine da farsi per lui
f. 2 s. __ d. __

23. 7

C. 108 RECTO

+Adì 5 di settembre 1466

Pagose di volontà di ditti ad uno Sanctuccio s. VII d. VI, sonno per sgomberatura di terrino de Sancta Lucia f. __ s. 7 d. 6

+Adì 6 del ditto

Pagose di volontà di ditti ad Manzetto di Giovanni s. XXX, sonno per acconciare certi posti di campane nel campanile f. __ s. 30 d. __

+Adì ditto

Pagose di volontà di ditti ad Gregorio di Angeluccio da Spoliti s. XXV, sonno per una scale se comparò da lui f. __ s. 25 d. __

+Adì 8 del ditto

Pagose di volontà di ditti ad Ciccho di Lucha da Spoliti f. X, sonno per parte de quel montarà uno cottimo datoli ad cavare uno condutto dereto alla ecclesia verso la roccha f. 10 s. __ d, __

+Adì 12 del ditto

Pagose di volontà di ditti ad Pier Francescho speziale s. V, sonno per uno capretto di carte comparato da lui f. __ s. 5 d. __

+Adì 20 de ditto

Pagose di volontà di ditti ad ser Pier Angelo da Caselli s. L, sonno per misuratura del muro fatto per Ceccho della capella della imagine f. __ s. 50 d. __

+Adì ditto

Pagose di volontà di ditti ad Ceccho di Lucha da Spoliti s. L, sonno per parte di quel monta la cappella della imagine da farsi per lui, quali se pagaro per lui a ser Pierangelo per la parte sua per misurare detta cappella f. __ s. 50 d. __

+Adì 21 del ditto

Pagose di volontà di ditti ad Piermattio di Caracosa f. II s. L, sonno per mandarlo ad Firenze per frate Filippo dipintore f. 2 s. 50 s. __

+Adì 23 del ditto

Pagose di volontà di ditti ad Ciecho di Lucha di Spoleti f. III, sonno per parte di quello monta la cappella della imagine, fatta per lui, quali habbe in coppe 4 di grano per le mani di Piermattio f. 3 s. __ d. __

+Adì 27 de ditto

Pagose di volontà di ditti ad mastro Battista da Civitella s. XV, sonno per acconciare telari delli posti delle campane f. __ s. 15 d. __

+Adì ditto

Pagose di volontà di ditti ad Ciecho di Lucha f. I, sonno per parte de quel montarà la cappella della imagine, fatta per lui f. 1 s. __ d. __

+Adì ditto

Pagose di volontà di ditti ad Ciecho di Lucha f. III, sonno per parte di quel montarà la cappella della imagine, fatta per lui, quali habbe da Morichone di Domenicho in coppe 6 di grano a bolognini 60 coppa, delle quali era debitore detto Dominicho per uno cottimo f. 3 s. __ d. __

21. 32. 6

C. 108 VERSO

+Adì primo d'ottobre 1466

Pagose di volontà di ditti ad maestro Giacho lombardo s. LXXV, sonno per spianare el terrino nella cappella della imagine f. __ s. 75 d. __

+Adì ditto

Pagose di volontà di ditti ad frate Filippo dipintore di Firenze f. LXXVI s. XXV, per parte di ducati 700, per depintora della tribuna i quali se lli mandaro per Piermatteo di Carachosa, quali se pagaro per le mani di Vannozo di Giovanni di Firenze; foro f. 50 larghi, vagl[i]on a bolognini 61

f. 76 s. 25 d. __

+Adì 21 del ditto

Pagose di volontà di ditti ad Ciecho di Lucha da Spoliti f. XVII s. LXXVI, sonno per ultimo pagamento di quello monta la capella della imagine fatta per lui, quale monta secundo la rascione renduta per ser Pier Angelo da Caselli, quale dixe essere lo muro fatto per ditto Ciccho in decta cappella perteche 27, piedi 50, per f. 7 la pertecha, che montano f. 192 s. 50, delli quali appare haver hauti ad libro del mio camorlengato nel 1463, operali Vanni di Mesone et Lorenzo dello Pretarello, in più partite, et in questo libro nel 1465 et nel 1466 in più partite, in somma f. 173 s. 76, che resta havere f. 18 s. 76, della quale somma promixe lassare f. 1 fra tutto, como appare per mano di ser Pier Nofrio di ser Tolomeo. Si diè resta avere f. 17 s. 76, li quali detto Ciccho ha auti, presente Lodovicho di Nicholo da Pianciano et ditto ser Pier Nofrio da Spoliti

f. 17 s. 76 d. __

+Adì ditto

Pagose di volontà di ditti al sopraditto Ciccho f. III s. LXXV, sonno per uno pezo di muro fatto nel muro dereto alla ecchiesia verso la roccha, quale fo, secondo dixe ser Pier Angelo da Ciselli pedi 72 3/4, per f. 5 la pertecha

f. 3 s. 75 d. __

+Adì ditto

Pagose di volontà di ditti ad ditto Ciccho f. 1 s. LV, sonno [per] uno uscio fece e murò nella cappella della imagine, per andare all'organi

f. 1 s. 55 d. __

+Adì 5 ditto

Pagose di volontà di ditti ad Giovannio da Milano, balio, s. VII d. VI, sonno per essere mandato ad Valtarena f. __ s. 7 d.6

+Adì ditto

Pagose di volontà di ditti ad uno balio di Vescoato s. X, sonno per essere mandato ad Somma f. __ s. 10 d. __

+Adì 12 di novembre

Pagose di volontà di ditti ad Pier Matteo di Caracosa f. II s. LXXV, sonno per remandarlo un'altra volta ad Firenze per frate Filippo

f. 2 s. 75 d. __

+Ai ditto

Pagose di volontà di ditti ad Crostofano del'Angelo da Spoliti s. XLII, sonno per uno cocchiarono per colare piombo e per lena f. __ s. 42 d. __

+Adì 25 di novembre

Pagose di volontà di ditti ad Ciccho di Luca da Spoliti f. XL, sonno per parte di quello montarà uno condulto da farsi per lui dereto alla ecchiesia, et per uno pezo di muro da fornirsi per lui sopra la sacrestia verso la roccha, quali recivì in nome mio da Ruscitto di Bartolomeo per uno relitto fece Todisco, so fratello ad ditta opera f. 40 s. __ d. __

143. 41.

C. 109 RECTO

+Adì 27 di novembre 1466

Pagose di volontà di ditti ad Mattio dil'Angelo da Spoliti f. XI s. L, sonno per parte de quel montano le seppolture da farse per lui nella cappella se dice di messer Marino, quali habbe per noi da Andriuccio d'Angirillo per resto di quello dovia pagare per uno pezo di terra li se vendé

f. 11 s. 50 d. __

+Adì ditto

Pagose di volontà di ditti ad lo ditto Mattio f. I s. XL, sonno per parte di quel montaro le ditte seppolture da farsi per lui, quali habbe in coppe 2 di grano a bolognini 28 coppa volse se dagissero ad Polinoro di Gerardino

f. 1 s. 40 d. __

+Adì ditto

Pagose di volontà di ditti ad Cristofano di l'Angelo da Spoliti s. XXV, sonno per [struck out: acconciatora] mittitora vergoni di ferro mise nel titto grande sopra la tribuna, e per acconciatora di certe piastre di piombo et chiovi comparati per ditto, tutto f. __ s. 25 d. __

+Adì 28 del ditto

Pagose di volontà di ditti ad Pier Nichola di Manzolo da Spoliti, f. VI s. LX, sonno per parte di quel montarà el racconciare el posto dell'organi, quali hebbe in some 3 di grano, a bolognini 22 coppa f. 6 s. 60 d. __

+Adì ditto

Pagose di volontà di ditti ad Mattio dil'Angelo da Spoliti f. IIII, sonno per parte di quello monterò le seppolture da farse per lui in detto locho

f. 4 s. __ d. __

+Adì 29 del ditto

Pagose di volontà di ditti ad mastro Battista da Campello s. LXXXXII, sonno per ultimo pagamento de tutto quello dovene havere da ditta opera fine al presente dì cavatone lo 'mbossolare della sacrestia et uno titto datoli ad fare sopra la sacrestia della chiesia f. __ s. 92 d. __

+Adì ditto

Pagose di volontà di ditti ad Gentilischo nepo di don Giovan Paulo s. XLV, sonno per alcuni dì stette ad levare le ferrate delle imagine

f. __ s. 45 d. __

+Adì ditto

Pagose di volontà di ditti ad mastro Battista da Campello f. I, sonno per parte del titto da racconciarse per lui sopra la sacrestia f. 1 s. __ d. __

+Adì 6 di dicembre

Pagose di volontà di ditti ad Cristofano del'Angelo d Spoliti s. L, sonno per parte per acconciatura d'uno cavallo del titto e revoltatura nella camera di don Bonaccurso f. __ s. 50 d. __

+Adì 6 di dicembre

Pagose di volontà di ditti ad mastro Battista da Campello f. VI, sonno per parte del titto da racconciarsi per lui sopra la sacrestia f. 6 s. __ d. __

+Adì 7 di dicembre

Pagose di volontà di ditti ad Lorenzo dello Pretarello f. II, sonno per parte quello montaranno vergoni di ferro tolti da lui da ponererli nel posto dell'organi f. 2 s. __ d. __

+Adì ditto

Pagose di volontà di ditti al sopraditto Lorenzo f. I s. X, sonno per parte de sopraditti vergoni da ponersi in detto posto, e nel titto della chiesia quali habbe in coppe 2 di grano a bolognini 22 coppa, quale habbe per noi da Mariano di Fecarino per uno cottimo tene dell'opera

f. 1 s. 10 d. __

35.72. __

C. 109 VERSO

+Adì 8 di dicembre 1466

Pagose di volontà di ditti ad maestro Battista da Campello f. I s. XXV, sonno per ultimo pagamento di f. 8 1/4 monta el titto fatto per lui sopra la sacrestia delli quali ha 'uti f. 7 in dui partite, como appare in questo

f. 1 s. 25 d. __

+Adì ditto

Pagose di volontà di ditti ad Francescho di Martucio s. XII d. VI, sonno per trasinatora di dui costarecce da ponersi nel titto sopra la cappella della imagine

f. __ s. 12 d. 6

+Adì 11 del ditto

Pagose di volontà di ditti ad Caroso, balio del communo, s. XXXV, sonno per essere mandato ad Sellano per citare alcuni debitori dell'opera

f. __ s. 35 d. __

+Adì 13 del ditto

Pagose di volontà di ditti ad Giovanni alias Pazagl[i]a lombardo f. II, sonno per parte di quel montarà el mettere certi vergoni di ferro per scambio delle monacelle pel titto sopra la tribuna et per lo camino fatto nella sacristia

f. 2 s. __ d. __

+Adì 14 del ditto

Pagose di volontà di ditti ad Battista di Puccio, d Stefano di Gasparrina, ad Lorenzo di Pier Valente, per legname, ad Manzitto per ferro f. VIII s. XLVIII d. VI, sonno per essere adoperati in tre titti, cioè sopra la cappella della imagine, sopra la sacrestia, et uno nella canonicha, nella stanzia del lo priore f. 8 s. 48 d. 6

+Adì ditto

Pagose di volontà di ditti ad Dominicho d'Antonio f. II s. LXII d. VI, sonno per facitora del titto della cappella della ymagine et della canonicha sopra la stanzia del priore f. 2 s. 62 d. 6

+Adì ditto

Pagose di volontà di ditti ad mastro Andrea fornacchiaio per resto de' 3000 coppi a f. 3 1/2 lo migliaio, f. I s. L, montano f. X 1/2, de' quali appare havere hauti in 2 partite in questo f. 9 f. 1 s. 50 d. __

+Adì 16 del ditto

Pagose di volontà di ditti ad ser Lonardo di Matteo da Postignano s. L, sonno per alcune scripture tratte di suo mani in publica forma cioè testamenti nelli quali apparo essere lassati danari all'opera f. __ s. 50 d. __

+Adì ditto

Pagose di volontà di ditti ad ser Gabriello di ser Nofrio f. I s. XXV, sonno per haver cavati relitti fatti all'opera per mano di ser Moscato e ser Previsano suo fratello f. 1 s. 25 d. __

+Adì 18 del ditto

Pagose di volontà di ditti ad ser Pier Angelo di Falzarone s. L, per uno rogo per sua mano de una renuntiatione fatta all'opera da Licciardina, donna che fo di Sirio f. __ s. 50 d. __

+Adì 21 di dicembre

Pagose di volontà di ditti ad Pier Mattio di Caracosa f. XV s. XXXV, sonno per resto di suo salario dello stare all imagine, cioè per l'anno 1465 e per 1466

f. 15 s. 35 d. __

+Adì ditto

Pagose di volontà di ditti ad Piccione di Gregori f. __ s. LXXX, sonno per 200 mattoni prestò all'opera et per libre 3 di chiovi a s. 5 libra

f. __ s. 80 d. __

134. 73

C. 110 RECTO

+Adì 21 di dicembre 1466

Pagose di volontà di ditti ad Pier Mattio di Carachosa s. L, sonno per 3 dì stette in Firenze per aspattare frate Filippo la prima volta et per gire a Prato la seconda volta quando fo remandato per ditto frate Filippo f. __ s. 50 d. __

Adì 26 del ditto

Pagose di volontà di ditti ad Giovanni alias Pazagl[i]a lombardo f. I s. LXXXIII 1/2, sonno per ultimo pagaminto del mettere certi vergoni di ferro per scambio delle monacelle nel titto sopra la tribuna et per lo camino fatto per lui nella sacrestia f. 1 s. 83 d. 6

+Adì ditto

Pagose di volontà di ditti ad Pier Francescho di Giovanni s. LII 1/2 per dui cappie di ferro per lo catarcione da ponerse nell'uscio delle pontiche di piaza quale tene a pescione, et per copertura del titto d'essa

f. __ s. 52 d. 6

+Adì ditto

Pagose di volontà di ditti ad maestro Pier Nicchola di Manzolo f. 23 s. 35, sonno per l'ultimo pagamento di quello lo posto dell'organi per lo refarlo, cioè per ralugarlo, per l'uscio fatto nella cappella della imagine et per uno frontone fatto sopra di ditto uscio con l'arme di monsignore. Remasti d'accordo montano detti lavorii 139 soldi [?] delli quali appare haverne hauto dal libro f. 75 s. 65, computatoce uno cotano vendutoli dalli operali per f. 2, et a' libro uscita nella anno 1463 f. 40, somma f. 115 s. 65. Resta havere ditto f. 23 s. 35 f. 23 s. 35 d. __

+Adì ditto

Pagose di volontà di ditti ad Bartolo di Giacho s. LX, sonno per una costareccia comparata da lui da ponerse nel titto della cappella della imagine

f. __ s. 60 d. __

+Adì 30 del ditto

Pagose di volontà di ditti ad Picchio della Valle di Sancto Pietro s. LX, sonno per un'altra costareccia comparata da lui da ponerse nel titto della cappella della imagine f. __ s. 60 d. __

+Adì ditto

Pagose di volontà di ditti ad Cristofano del'Angelo di Biascio f. IIII s. XL, sonno per haver represse alcune piastre di piombo sopra lo muro del titto della chiesia, cioè in quelli lochi donde s'è levato le monacelle sopra la tribuna, cioè per parte, et per parte del suo salario deve havere per esserli dato a manutenere el titto per anni 7 a f. 5 l'anno f. 4 s. 40 d. __

+Adì ditto

Pagose di volontà di ditti ad Giuliano Pistillo s. LVII d. VI, sonno per panni et termintina et bolle comparate da lui per impannare finestre nella chiesia

f. __ s. 57 d. 6

+Adì ditto

Pagose di volontà di ditti ad Vannitto di Bartolomeo da Eggi s. XXV, sonno per 5 propagene poste da lui in pezo di terra dell'opera

f. __ s. 25 d. __

32. 63. 6

C. 110 VERSO

+Adì ultimo di dicembre 1467 [*sic*: 1466]

Pagose di volontà di ditti ad maestro Pier Nichola di Marchionne f. VI, sonno per parte di f. XI monta uno pilone da ll'acqua benedetta da farsi per lui

f. 6 s. __ d. __

+Adi ditto

Pagose ad ser Andrea di Bartolomeo s. L, sonno per scritture haute da lui di relitti fatti all'opera f. __ s. 50 d. __

+Adì ditto

Pagose di volontà di ditti ad ser Gian [. . . ?] f. VII s. XV, sonno per la particola del testamento di Lucha di Barnabeo Gual[tie?] camarlingo et per relitti fatti di suo mano pertinenti all'opera, de' quali n'à 'uti in grano f. 2 s. 75, come apare ad intrata e lo [?] f. 7 s. 15 d. __

+Adì ditto

Pagose di volontà di ditti ad ser Scipione di ser Mariano s. XXXVII d. VI, sonno per registratione d'una bolla di papa Nicchola, e per una procura in publica forma e altre scritture f. __ s. 37 d. 6

14. 12. 6

C. 111 RECTO

+Uscita dell'anno 1467, camerlingo detto Giordano et Operali detto Cesari de Angelo et Tomasso di Giacho di Pietro Paulo

+Adì 13 di genaro 1467

Pagose di volontà di ditti ad Cristofano del'Angelo s. XXXV, sono per uno cocchiaro ne[tto?] da colare piombo f. __ s. 35 d. __

+Adì 12 di febraro

Pagose di volontà di ditti ad Sanctuccio di Pietri di Palitto della Voltaddano s. LXVII, sonno per tavole comparate da llui, delle quali se ne fece una scala in canonicha f. __ s. 67 d. __

+Adì 19 di febraro

Pagose di volontà di ditti ad Pietri maestro di lengname f. 2 s. XII d. VI, sonno per sex banchi fatti per lui per ponerli in chiesia per sedere alle prediche

f. 2 s. 12 d. 6

+Adì ditto

Pagose di volontà di ditti ad Mariano [struck out: pasa?] s. L, sonno per una scala fece nel pergoro da predicare, per remettere la tavola nell'altare

f. __ s. 50 d. __

+Adì 21 del ditto

Pagose di volontà di ditti ad Cristofano [written above: di Broscio] et Cristofano di Ferro s. L et più s. XX d. VI, sonno per acconciatora del presello della canonicha et una scala in detta canonicha, cioè li s. 50 et li XII s. 6, per una giornata per recoprire il titto in canonicha f. __ s. 62 d. 6

+Adì ditto

Pagose di volontà di ditti alli ditto s. XI, sonno per chiodi comparati per detto lavorio f. __ s. 11 d. __

+Adì 26 del ditto

Pagose di volontà di ditti ad ser Bartholomeo di Mario s. LXX, sonno per piedi sex di tavole comparae da lui per fare banchi per uno telaro della rosa del frontespizio da farse per Mariano d'Antonio f. __ s. 70 d. __

+Adì ultimo del ditto

Pagose di volontà di ditti ad Pietro maestro di legname f. 1 s. 3 1/2, sonno per tre banchi fatti per lui per ponere in chiesia per sedere a predicha

f. 1 s. 3 d. 6

+Adì 2 di marzo

Pagose di volontà di ditti a Giovanni lombardo s. XVII d. VI, sonno per remettere la 'mpannata della rosa grande f. __ s. 17 d. 6

+Adì 7 di marzo

Pagose di volontà di ditti ad Ciambrocchio di Caxello s. XXII 1/2, sonno per otto de' corenti comparati da lui per fare uno celagio per impannare la rosa

f. __ s. 22 d. 6

+Adì ditto

Pagose di volontà di ditti ad Mariano s. LXVII d. VI, sonno per refacetora dello telaro impannato per la rosa del frontespizio f. __ s. 67 d. 6

+Adì ditto

Pagose di volontà di ditti al ditto Mariano f. II s. XXXII d. VI, sonno per sex banchi fatti per lui quali se posero in chiesia per sedere a predicha

f. 2 s. 32 d. 6

---

9. 49. 6

C. 111 VERSO

+Adì 14 di marzo 1467

Pagose di volontà di ditti ad Polinoro di Girardino et Matteo di Caratosa per loro et dui altri schiavi adoperati per poner banchi e legni in chiesia e tramutare per ponerli in piaza et tramutare certa calcina f. __ s. 50 d. __

+Adì ditto

Pagose di volontà di ditti ad Piero di Valtarina s. LXXV, sonno per tavole compartite da lui per fare banchi f. __ s. 75 d.__

+Adì 16 del ditto

Pagose di volontà di ditti ad Mattione di Lorenzo d'Acquaviuro f. VII s. L, sonno per coppe 150 di calcina a s. 5 coppa quale si tolse per bisogni dell'opera f. 7 s. 50 d. __

+Adì 17 del ditto

Pagose di volontà di ditti ad Lorenzo dello Pretarello s. XX, sonno per certi ferre per incontanaro el pilone dell'aqua benedetta, portò Pier Nichola f. __ s. 20 d. __

+Adì 21 del ditto

Pagose di volontà di ditti ad Pier Nichola di Micchione f. V, sonno per resto di f. XI per facetora d'uno pilone dell'aqua benedetta f. 5 s. __ d. __

+Adì 28 del detto

Pagose di volontà di ditti ad Polinoro di Gerardino et ad Mattios di Langelo s. LXII d. 6, quali sonno per reponere una pietra nell'altare del Corpo di Cristo e spazatora della [?] chiesia f. __ s. 62 d. 6

+Adì 16 d'aprile

Pagose di volontà di ditti ad Pier Nichola di Micchorre f. II, sonno per parte di una resicha che fa sopra lu titto della cappella della imagine f. 2 s. __ d. __

+Adì 21 d'aprile

Pagose di volontà di ditti operali ad Stefano di ser Aluvixi s. XXV, sonno per libre 5 di chiovi s'è comparato per refare lo telagio delle roxe dello frontespizio f. __ s. 25 d. __

+Adì 24 del ditto

Pagose di volontà di ditti ad Polinoro di Girardino s. X, sonno per farli spazare la casa data ad frate Filippo dipintore f. __ s. 10 d. __

+Adì 26 del ditto

[in margin: frate filippo ducati 15]

Pagose di volontà di ditti ad frate Filippo f. XXII s. LXXXVII d. VI in ducati 15 larghi, sonno per parte delli 700 ducati li si daranno per depegnere la tribuna quali li se pagaro in Spoliti, volze per remandarli in Firenze ad suo' garzoni f. 22 s. 83 d. 6

+Adì 5 di magio

Pagose di volontà di ditti ad Berella e Zuccharo f. I, sonno per uno magio, cioè una ligna se comparò da loro per fare lu ponte alla tribuna, per depegnere f. 1 s. __ d. __

+Adì ditto

[in margin: frate filippo ducato 1]
Pagose di volontà di ditti ad frate Filippo f. I s. L, sonno per parte delle duc. 700 se daranno per depentora della tribuna, volze se pagassero per lui ad Tadddea di Pier Mario per vino tolta da lei como appare per suo bollettino

f. 1 s. 50 d. __

+Adì 9 del detto

[in margin: frate filippo duc. 1 s. 57 d. 6]
Pagose di volontà di ditti ad frate Filippo f. I s. LVII d. 6, sonno per parte delli duc[ati] 700 li se daranno per depentora della tribuna, volse se pagassero per lui ad Maccorone dello Pupillo per XXI scotto habbe da lui come dece per suo bollettino f. 1 s. 57 d. 6

43 .87 .6

C. 112 RECTO

+Adì 11 di magio 1467

Pagose di volontà di ditti ad Cola pizicarolo s. LXXXX, sonno per di corda [written above: lire 27] comparata da lui per fare el ponte alla tribuna e per depegnerla f. __ s. 90 d. __

+Adì 13 di ditto

Pagose di volontà di ditti ad Zuccho et altri compagni f. I s. LII d. VI, sonno per un dì comparate da loro per fare el ponte alla tribuna per depengnerla

f. 1 s. 52 d. 6

+Adì ditto

Pagose di volontà di ditti ad Pier Andrea di Taratetto e compagni f. III, sonno per fattura del ponte se fa per depegnere la tribuna f. 3 s. __ d. __

+Adì 13 di ditto

[in margin: frate filippo bolognini 52]
Pagose di volontà di ditti a frate Filippo f. I s. XXX, sonno per parte delli f. [*sic*: ducati] 700 li se daranno per depegnere la tribuna, li quali li se dero in 2/3 di perpignano di grana, volse per uno paio di calze per Filippino suo

f. 1 s. 30 d. __

+Adì 16 di ditto

Pagose di volontà di ditti s. X, sonno per comparare uno paro di piccioni per donare ad frate Filippo f. __ s. 10 d. __

+Adì 17 di ditto

Pagose di volontà di ditti ad Cataruccio di Nicolo da Zano f. II s. XII, sono per tavole comparate da lui per fare el ponte alla tribuna, per dipignere, cioè per uno pugillo e piedi 18 f. 2 s. 12 d. __

+Adì 23 di ditto

Pagose di volontà di ditti s. XX quali diei ad Pier Mattio per comparare uno capretto per donare ad frate Filippo f. __ s. 20 d. __

+Adì ditto

Pagose di volontà di ditti ad uno prete da Sancta Maria, sacrestano, s. XI d. III, sonno per comparare una scala per gire nel campanile

f. __ s. 11 d. 3

+Adì ditto

[in margin: frate Filippo bolognini 50]

Pagose di volontà di ditti ad frate Filippo f. I s. XXV, sonno che si pagharo per lui ad uno vetturale per uno fardello portò di lui pesò libbre 120

f. 1 s. 25 d. __

+Adì 25 di ditto

Pagose di volontà di ditti ad maestro Gregorio di Martango f. IIII, sonno per uno pugillo et piedi 18 di tavole d'alvano per lire XI pugillo et piedi 71 di tavole di ulmo per lire X pugillo f. 4 s. __ d. __

+Adì ditto

Pagose di volontà di ditti Batista di Puccio f. I s. LXXXX, sonno per dui costarecce e una costarecciola per fare lo ponte per pegnere la tribuna

f. 1 s. 90 d. __

+Adì 27 di magio

Pagose di volontà di ditti ad Pierantonio di Taratetto f. II s. LXII d. VI, sonno per 34 decorenti, per 6 pianconcilli, per 1 pianconcillo, per 4 colonnelli, et per parte di 4 dì e mezo stette per fare el ponte alla tribuna

f. 2 s. 62 d. 6

---

19. 3. 3

C. 112 VERSO

+Adì 29 di magio 1467

Pagose di volontà di ditti ad Brunitto di Ciancho da Eggi f. I s. XXX, sonno per 37 decorrenti comparati da lui per bolognini 1 decorrente et per parete di 4 opere e meza bolognini 15 f. 1 s. 3 d. __

+Adì 30 di ditto

Pagose di volontà di ditti ad Bertaccino di Benedetto s. LXV, sonno per 7 colonnelli et 3 pianconcelli comparati da lui per fare lo ponte alla tribuna

f. __ s. 65 d. __

+Adì ditto

Pagose di volontà di ditti ad Crisanti s. XLVII d. VI, sonno per dui pianconcilli se compararo da lui per fare lo ponte alla tribuna

f. __ s. 47 d. 6

+Adì ditto

Pagose di volontà di ditti ad maestro Battista da Civitella s. XXXVII d. VI, sonno per fattura del ponte della tribuna, cioè per una opera e meza

f. __ s. 37 d. 6

+Adì ditto

Pagose di volontà di ditti ad Manzitto di Iovanni di Chiera s. XLV, sonno per parte della fattura del ponte della tribuna f. __ s. 45 d. __

+Adì ditto

Pagose di volontà di ditti ad maestro Battista da Campello f. I, sonno per fattura di certi trisperi da ponerese sopra al ponte per depegnere la tribuna et per uno pontecillo fecesi al posto delli organi allo ponte della tribuna, cioè per parte di dette cose et altro che farrà f. 1 s. __ d. __

+Adì ditto

Pagose di volontà di ditti ad Polinoro di Girardino s. XX, sonno per spazatura dello posto dell'organi e le scali per andare e portatore di calcinacci e per zappatura dell'orto di frate Filippo f. __ s. 20 d. __

+Adì primo di zugno

Pagose di volontà di ditti ad Giovanni di Nicholò s. LXXV, sonno per trasinare 8 lene da più lochi ad la chiesia per lo ponte per depegnere la tribuna f. __ s. 75 d. __

+Adì 5 del ditto

Pagose di volontà di ditti ad Bartoletto del'Angelo s. XXXVII d. I, sonno per libre 7 oncie 5 di bolloni tolti da luji per bolognini 2 libra per far lu ponte f. __ s. 37 d. 1

+Adì 6 del ditto

[in margin: frate Filippo s. 52 d. 6]

Pagose di volontà di ditti ad uno da Bazano s. LII d. VI, sonno per una coppa di grano se comparò per frate Filippo f. __ s. 52 d. 6

+Adì ditto

Pagose di volontà di ditti ad Marcho di Lucha per Giovanni di Sentio s. LXVIII d. IIII, sonno per tavole 14 comparate da lui per lo ponte f. __ s. 68 d. 4

+Adì ditto

Pagose di volontà di ditti ad l'Angelo di Giacho s. XX, sonno per 6 colondelli per fare lo ponte nella tribuna f. __ s. 20 d. __

+Adì ditto

Pagose di volontà di ditti ad Baptista di Puccio f. I s. XX, sonno per dui maggi 4 da correnti da scale se compararo da lui per fare lo ponte nella tribuna f. 1 s. 20 d. –

+Adì ditto

Pagose di volontà di ditti ad Ursino d'Angiluccio f. I s. XII d. VI, sonno per tavole comparate da lui per fare lo ponte per la tribuna f. 1 s. 12 d. 6

9. 30. 5

C. 113 RECTO

+Adì 8 di g[i]ugno 1467

Pagose di volontà di ditti ad Cola pizicharolo s. LX, sonno per corde comparate da lui per fare lo ponte nella tribuna f. __ s. 60 d. __

+Adì 9 di ditto

Pagose di volontà di ditti ad maestro Battista da Campello f. 1, sonno per resto del fornire el ponte e per cercare legname e trisperi fatti

f. 1 s. __ d. __

+Adì ditto

Pagose di volontà di ditti ad Pier Mattio di Carachoxa s. LXXX, sonno per essere operato a fare lo ponte f. __ s. 80 d. __

+Adì ditto

Pagose di volontà di ditti ad Battista da Campello s. XXIII, sonno per legname comparò per l'opera da più persone, et chiovi comperati

f. __ s. 24 d. __

+Adì 10 di ditto

Pagose di volontà di ditti ad Pinacchio s. X, sonno per parte della rena se compara da lui per intonachare la tribuna per pegnerla

f. __ s. 10 d. __

+Adì 16 del ditto

Pagose di volontà di ditti s. XII, sonno per una scaletta si comparò per adoperare nel ponte della tribuna f. __ s. 12 d. __

+Adì 17 del ditto

Pagose di volontà di ditti a dì uno dalle eppe s. XXIIII, sono per uno cassetta di carne salata si donò ad frate Filippo f. __ s. 24 d. __

+Adì ditto

[in margin: frate Filippo duc. 3 larghi]

Pagose di volontà di ditti ad frate Filippo f. IIII s. LVII d. VI, sonno in ducati 3 larghi per parte delli ducati 700 per depintura della tribuna, quali volze per dare a don Diamante per remandarlo ad Firenze

f. 4 s. 57 d. 6

+Adì 20 del ditto

Pagose di volontà di ditti ad Santo da Chascia s. XV, sonno per vettura di tavole portò da Beroiti a Spoliti f. __ s. 15 d. __

+Adì ditto

Pagose di volontà di ditti ad Giacho di Lorenzo s. LVII d. IIII, sonno per legname comparato da lui per lo ponte fatto in tribuna

f. __ s. 58 d. 4

+Adì ditto

Pagose di volontà di ditti ad G[i]acho di Palmuccio da Scorbizo s. XL, sonno per tavole d'ulmo comparate da lui per lo ponte fatto in tribuna

f. __ s. 39 d. __

+Adì ditto

Pagose di volontà di ditti ad Pier Marcho di Damiano s. XXV, sonno per chiovi comparati da lui per fare lo ponte in tribuna

f. __ s. 25 d. __

+Adì 23 del ditto

Pagose di volontà di ditti ad maestro Iaco[po] lombardo s. L, sonno per parte di quello de' avere per intonachatora e mattonatora di sopra alla cappella della imagine f. __ s. 50 d. __

9. 54. 10

C. 113 VERSO

+Adì 24 di giugno 1467

Pagose di volontà di ditti ad Langlo s. VII d. VI, sonno per dui de' corenti s'è comparato da lui per lo ponte se feci in tribuna

f. __ s. [struck out: vi] 7 d. 6

+Adì 27 di giugno

Pagose di volontà di ditti ad Tomaxo di Polo s. XX d. X, sonno per uno pianconcello si comparò da lui per lo ponte

f. __ s. 20 d. 10

+Adì ultimo del ditto

[in margin: frate Filippo bolognini 54]

Pagose di volontà di ditti Britio da Todi f. I s. XXXV, sonno per coppe 3 di grano si comparò da lui per dare ad frate Filippo

f. 1 s. 35 d. __

+Adì 6 di lugl[i]o

Pagose di volontà di ditti ad Polinoro di Girardino f. I s. VII d. VI, sonno per smoratora d'uno muro massicio era nella cappella verso la roccha et per portatore di mattoni da una cappella alla cappella delle ymagine

f. 1 s. [struck out: V] 7 d. 6

+Adì ditto

[in margin: frate Filippo bolognini 30]

Pagose di volontà di ditti ad frate Filippo s. LXXV, sonno per 2/3 di perpignano biancho pagati per lui, volze per uno paro di calze perpignane per Filippino f. __ s. 75 d. __

+Adì 7 del ditto

[in margin: frate filippo f. 46 1/2 larghi e bolognini 46 1/2 cioè f. 47 larghi e bolognini 16]

Pagose di volontà di ditti ad frate Filippo f. LXXII s. VII d. 6, sonno per M. [migliaia] 4 de oro e once 10 d'azurro oltramarino, quale li se dè per parte del suo pagamento per depegnere la tribuna f. 72 s. 7 d. 6

+Adì ditto

Pagose di volontà di ditti ad Giacho lombardo f. I s. LV, sonno per ultimo pagaminto di quello d'avere per intonachatora e mattonatora sopra la cappella della imagine f. 1 s. 55 d. __

+Adì 11 del ditto

[in margin: frate Filippo ducati 1]

Pagose di volontà di ditti ad frate Filippo f. I s. L, sonno che s'è pagato per lui ad Paulo Antonio per pescione di letti e tovagl[i]e tene delle soe, comenzando adì 27 d'aprile f. 1 s. 50 d. __

+Adì 25 di lugl[i]o

Pagose di volontà di ditti s. XXIII d. VIII, sonno per comparare II para di piccioni per donare ad frate Filippo dipintore

f. __ s. 23 d. 8

+Adì primo d'augusto

Pagose di volontà di ditti ad Brunotto di Iovanni s. XX, sonno per uno legno se comparò da lui per lo ponte della tribuna f. __ s. 20 d. __

+Adì 4 del ditto

Pagose di volontà di ditti s. IIII, sonno per popuni se compararo per donare a frate Filippo f. __ s. 4 d. __

+Adì 6 del ditto

Pagose di volontà di ditti s. X, sonno per bolluze se compararo da Brunetto per chiavare panno per impannare la rosa del frontespizio

f. __ s. 10 d. __

+Adì 7 del ditto

Pagose di volontà di ditti s. V, sonno per popuni si compararo per donare ad frate Filippo f. __ s. 5 d. __

+Adì 13 del ditto

Pagose di volontà di ditti ad s. XV, sonno per dare ad Mariano Pazo e maestro Iovanni per levare lo impannato dalle rose del frontespizio in nelle feste

f. __ s. 15 d. __

79. 35. 2

C. 114 RECTO

+Adì 17 di'augusto 1467

Pagose di volontà di ditti ad don Maschio di Iohanni f. III, sonno per [struck out: parte] lo suo salario per sonare l'organi in Sancta Maria del qual tanto toccha all'opera per l'anno 1467 f. 3 s. __ d. __

+Adì ditto

Pagose di volontà di ditti s. 5, sonno per dare ad uno balio portò uno comandamento ad li figl[i]oli di Verrione f. __ s. 5 d. __

+Adì ditto

Pagose di volontà di ditti f. I s. XL, sonno per dare a Pieriamato di Salustio per quindici tavole se compararo da lui per fare lo ponte nella tribuna f. 1 s. 40 d. __

+Adì 20 del ditto

Pagose di volontà di ditti f. II, sonno per braccia 40 di tela di purnano per s. 5 braccio quale se comparò da Marino merciaro per ponere denanti al ponte per pegnere la tribuna f. 2 s. __ d. __

+Adì 24 del ditto

Pagose di volontà di ditti ad Tomaxo di Paulo di Bonanno f. II, sonno quali pagò l'opera como heredi Caradonna, mogl[i]e che fo di Francesco di Vigl[i]-ardo, la quale lassò, como appare in suo testamento, f. 4 ad Rosata mogl[i]e del ditto Tomaxo, delli quali se toccha f. 2 all'opera et f. 2 a' locho di Sancto Salvatore f. 2 s. __ d. __

+Adì primo di settembre

[in margin: frate Filippo bolognini 50]

Pagose di volontà di ditti f. I s. XII d. VI, sonno per coppe 3 di grano a bolognini 15 coppa, et bolognini V pagai per lui per macinatora di ditto f. 1 s. 25 d. __

+Adì 2 del ditto

Pagose di volontà di ditti s. XV, sonno per frutti si compararo per donare ad frate Filippo f. __ s. 15 d. __

+Adì ditto

[in margin: frate Filippo bolognini 60]

Pagose di volontà di ditti f. I s. L, sonno in danari chontanti li se dero, dixe volerli per pagare chrocioli da mettere colori f. 1 s. 50 d. __

+Adì 5 del ditto

Pagose di volontà di ditti s. XX, sonno per rena sottile, portò Tomaxo di Battista per depegnere la tribuna f. __ s. 20 d. __

+Adì 10 del ditto

Pagose di volontà di ditti s. XXXV, sonno per chiovi et corde comparati da Salustio f. __ s. 35 d. __

+Adì 19 del ditto

Pagose di volontà di ditti s. XXX, sonno che si pagaro ad Gregorio lombardo per coprire el titto sopra la cappella della [i]magine f. __ s. 30 d. __

+Adì 24 del ditto

[in margin: frate Filippo ducati 1]

Pagose di volontà di ditti f. I s. L, sonno che se pagaro ad Paulo Antonio per frate Filippo per pescione di letti e tovagl[i]e tene delle soe, a bolognini 19 lo mese f. 1 s. 50 d. __

+Adì 28 del ditto

[in margine: frate Filippo ducati 1]
Pagose di volontà di ditti f. I s. L, sonno che se pagaro ad frate Filippo quali se diero ad Filippino como appare per una so' polixa f. 1 s. 50 d. __

15 .20 __

C. 114 VERSO

+Adì 3 d' [struck out: settembre] ottobre 1467
Pagose di volontà di ditti f. II ad Pier Giovanni di Battista per calcina vendè al'opera per depegnere f. 2 s. __ d. __

+Adì 9 d'ottobre
[in margin: frate filippo bolognini 60]
Pagose di volontà di ditti f. I s. L, sonno se pagaro ad frate Filippo depintore, quale li portai dixe volere per suo bisogni f. 1 s. 50 d. __

+Adì 17 di detto
Pagose di volontà di ditti s. XV, sonno per vettura di dui some de calcina da Ghano a Spoleti, quale si volze per dipegnare f. __ s. 15 d. __

+Adì 20 d'ottobre
Pagose di volontà di ditti f. VII s. XXV, sonno per 1500 coppi a f. 3 1/2 migliaio, et per mattoni 1000 a f. 2 lo migliaio, quali si comporaro da Andrea d'Antonio lombardo f. 7 s. 25 d. __

+Adì 22 del ditto
[in margin: frate Filippo bolognini 60]
Pagose di volontà di ditti f. I s. L ad frate Filippo dipintore, quali si pagaro per lui ad Bernardo da Migiana per lena li portò f. 1 s. 50 d. __

+Adì 24 del ditto
[in margin: frate Filippo bolognini 20]
Pagose di volontà di ditti s. L ad frate Filipo quali volse per comparare due cossetti di carne salata portò Pier Mattio f. __ s. 50 d. __

+Adì ditto
[in margin: frate Filippo bolognini 60]
Pagose di volontà di ditti f. I s. L ad frate Filippo, dixe volerli per sue bisogni, portò Filippino suo f. 1 s. 50 d. __

+Adì ditto
Pagose di volontà di ditti s. 6, sonno che si pagarò per dui asetti che si posero in una finestra sopra la tribuna f. __ s. 6 d. __

+Adì ultimo del ditto
Pagose di volontà di ditti s. XXX, sonno che si pagano per comperarare uno paro di capponi per donare a frate Filippo f. __ s. 30 d. __

+Adì ditto

Pagose di volontà di dittis. XXV, sonno che se pagarò ad maestro Giovanni d'Arezo per uno [above: uscio da] fenestra fece nel titto della ecchiesia
f. __ s. 25 d, __

+Adì 7 di novembre

[in margin: frate Filippo ducati 4 larghi]
Pagose di volontà di ditti f. 6 s. 10, sonno che pagaro ad frate Filippo dipintore, quali volse per mandare a Firenze f. 6 s. 10 d. __

+Adì ditti

Pagose di volontà di ditti s. 17 d. 6, sonno per legname che se comparò da Tomaxo per lo titto sopra all imagine f. __ s. 17 d. 6

+Adì 10 del ditto

Pagose di volontà di ditti f. III, sonno per 3 costareccie e 70 de corenti se compararo da Benedetto di Biascio, montaro d'accordo
f. 3 s. __ d. __

+Adì 15 del ditto

[in margin: frate Filippo bolognini 60]
Pagose di volontà di ditti s. I d. L, sonno che se dero ad frate Filippo quali li portai per suo bisogni f. 1 s. 50 d. __

25. 78. 6.

C. 115 RECTO

+Adì 18 di novembre 1467

[in margin: frate Filippo duc. 5 bol. 31]
Pagose di volontà di ditti f. VIII s. XL, sonno che pagaro ad frate Filippo dipintore quali habbe in coppa 24 di grano a bolognini 14 coppa
f. 8 s. 40 d. __

+Adì 23 del ditto

Pagose di volontà di ditti s. XV, sonno per uva appassita se comparò per donare a frate Filippo f. __ s. 15 d. __

+Adì 27 del ditto

Pagose di volontà di ditti s. LX, sonno per libre 2 di pennocchiati se compararo per donare ad frate Filippo f. __ s. 60 d. __

+Adì 28 del ditto

[in margin: frate Filippo bolognini 14]
Pagose di volontà di ditti s. 35, sonno che se pagaro ad frate Filippo, li volze per comparare uno paro di capponi per le mani di Michelangelo
f. __ s. 35 d. __

+Adì 10 di dicembre

[in margin: frate Filippo bolognini 60]
Pagose di volontà di ditti f. I s. L, sonno che si pagaro ad frate Filippo dipintore, quale volze per suo bisogni f. 1 s. 50 d. __

+Adì 19 di dicembre

[in margin: frate Filippo bolognini 21]
Pagose di volontà di ditti s. LII d. VI, sonno che si pagaro ad frate Filippo, cioè in 1 libra di pennochiati con spezie, s. 30 in 1/8 di pille, s. 5 in cellini, s. 2 1/2 in 1 paro di starne s. 15 f. __ s. 52 d. 6

+Adì ditto

[in margin: frate Filippo bolognini 20]
Pagose di volontà di ditti s. L, sonno che se pagaro ad frate Filippo quali volze se pagassero ad Bernardo da Gagiano per lena li portò

f. __ s. 50 d. __

+Adì 24 del ditto

Pagose di volontà di ditti f. II s. LXXXXV, sonno per uno titto fatto per maestro Battista da Campello, cioè per legname s. 95 et per opere f. 2

f. 2 s. 95 d. __

+Adì 30 del ditto

Pagose di volontà di ditti s. XXV, sonno per calcina per depegnere la tribuna, se comparò d[a] G[i]ovanni di Nicholò f. __ s. 25 d. __

+Adì 30 di dicembre

Pagose di volontà di ditti ad Pier Mattio d[a] Cararosa f. VI s. LXXII 1/2, sonno per parte di f. 10 del suo salario per l'anno 1467 che resta haver f. 3 s. 76, quali f. 6 s. 92 d. 5 habe in coppe 2 1/2 di grano di bolognini 13 coppa, e barile 3 di musto a bolognini 15 lo barile, et f. 5 in danari contanti

f. 6 s. 92 d. __6

+Adì 31 ditto

[in margin: frate Filippo duc. 1 s. 3 d. 9]
Pagose di volontà di ditti ad frate Filippo f. I s. XLII d. VI, sonno che li pagai per lui a Pier L[i]onardo cimatore per panno et cimatora d'esso e per fodere e cositura ad Lucha cimatore bolognini 5 1/2 somma

f. 1 s. 56 d. 3

+Adì ditto

Pagose di volontà di ditti alo priore di Sancta Maria s. LXX, sonno per legname comparò ditto priore per una scala se fece in canonica

f. __ s. 70 d. __

24. 41. 3.

C. 115 VERSO

+Adì ditto 1467

Pagose di volontà di ditti ad Giovanni di G[i]aro spiziale s. XV, sonno per libre 3 di bolloni tolge più tempi sonno Pier Andrea di Taratetto per fare el ponte nella tribuna f. __ s. 15 d. __

+Adì ditto

Pagose di volontà di ditti a Buno s. XXXII, sonno per dui pari concelli se compararo per fare uno titto in canonicha f. __ s. 32 d. __

+Adì ditto

Pagose di volontà di ditti f. III s. VII d. VI, sonno per resto di f. 10 del salario di Pier Matteo per stare alle imagine f. 3 s. 8 d. 2

3. 55. 2

[struck out: +Adì 18 del ditto
Pagose di volontà di ditti f. XXVI, sonno perche si pagaro ad Simone di ser Giovanni per vedere uno testamento di ser Iohanni di messer Giaco per lo imteresse dell'opera]

C. 116 RECTO

Uscita del 1468, Camarlingo ditto Giordano di Tomaxo et Operali ditti Tomaxo di Giacobo et Cesari d'Angilo

+Adì 16 del ditto [gennaio]

[in margin: frate Filippo]
Pagose di volontà di ditti f. II, sonno che pagaro ad frate Filippo dipintore quali si pagaro per lui ad Bernardo da Baiano per lena hauta da lui
f. 2 s. __ d. __

+Adì 23 del ditto

Pagose di volontà di ditti f. II s. XL, sonno che se pagaro ad maestro Battista da Campello quali sono per legname comparo per lo titto verso la roccha, cioè f. 1 s. 40 et f. 1 per opere del ditto f. 2 s. 40 d. __

+Adì 30 di genaro

[in margin: frate Filippo]
Pagose di volontà di ditti ad frate Filippo dipintore f. 1 s. 25, sonno in 3/4 di panno ruscio pagai per lui per uno paro di calze tolze per Filippino et in bolognini 16 tolze contanti per pagare scarpe f. 1 s. 25 d. __

+Adì 4 di febraro

[in margin: frate Filippo]
Pagose di volontà di ditti ad frate Filippo dipintore s. XLVIII d. VI, sonno che si pagaro per lui ad Paulo Antonio per resto di quello dovia havere per la pescione del letto e tovaglie havia da lui f. __ s. 48 d. 6

+Adì ditto

Pagose di volontà di ditti ad Paulo Antonio s. XX, sonno per certi panni ci prestò per coprire dinanti alla tribuna quali si tennero 4 mesi a s. 5 lo mese
f. __ s. 20 d. __

+Adì 10 del ditto

Pagose di volontà di ditti s. XV, sonno per una zappa da intredere calcina, quale fece maestro Antonio dello Seichiaio f. __ s. 15 d. __

+Adì ditto

[in margin: frate Filippo]
Pagose di volontà di ditti ad frate Filippo f. LXXVI s. XXV, quali volze per mandare a Firenze per comparare una caxa in Prato, et più bolognini 50 quali si pagaro per cambiare moneta a fiorini larghi che costarono bolognini 62
f. 77 s. 50 d. __

+Adì 3 [*sic* 13?] di febraro

[in margin: frate Filippo]
Pagose di volontà di ditti ad frate Filippo f. III, quale portò per Matteo volze per suo bisogni f. 3 s. __ d. __

+Adì 14 di marzo

Pagose di volontà di ditti f. I s. XXX, sonno che si pagaro in libre 10 di chiovi, bolognini 20, e per revoltare la trasanne della porticha s. 7 d. 6 et bolognini 20 ad maestro Batista per magisterio del titto fece nella canonich, e bolognini 9 s'è comparato 1 paio di gagline per donare ad frate Filippo; quali f. 1 s. 30 s'ebbero da Pierfrancexcho di Iohanni di Paulo, como appare ad intrata
f. 1 s. 30 d. __

+Adì 21 di marzo

Pagose di volontà di ditti ad Gintilisco per maestro Battista per remettere lo telaio nelle rose del frontespizio f. __ s. 45 d. __

88. 73. 6

C. 116 VERSO

+Adì 23 di marzo 1468

Pagose di volontà di ditti ad Simone lombardo s. LXXV, sonno per recoprire el titto sopra le camore della canonicha f. __ s. 75 d. __

+Adì 26 di marzo

Pagose di volontà di ditti s. LXXV ad Margarita di Giacho di Palitto per legname diè per sconto di f. 2 lassò ditto Giacho
f. __ s. 75 d. __

+Adì ditto

[in margin: frate Filippo]
Pagose di volontà di ditti s. LXXII d. VI ad frate Filippo i quali ebbe in vino da Margarita di Giaco di Palitto la quale diè per sconto di f. 2 lassò ditto Giacho f. __ s. 72 d. 6

+Adì 11 d'aprile

Pagose di volontà di ditti s. L, sonno che se pagaro ad uno da Spello per marmi da paramentare si comparò da lui f. __ s. 50 d. __

+Adì 12 del ditto

[in margin: frate Filippo]

Pagose di volontà di dittis. s. XV, sonno che si pagaro ad frate Filippo, volze se dagessero ad uno da Spello per crocioli tolze da lui f. __ s. 15 d. __

+Adì 16 del ditto

Pagose di volontà di ditti s. XXV, sonno per comparare uno capritto per donare ad frate Filippo portò Pier Mattio f. __ s. 25 d. __

+Adì ditto

Pagose di volontà di ditti f. II, sonno che se pagaro ad Cristofano del'Angelo per parte di quello de'avere per mantenere el titto di Sancta Maria f. 2 s. __ d. __

+Adì ditto

[in margin: frate Filippo]

Pagose di volontà di ditti f. I s. L, sonno che se pagaro ad frate Filippo, portò Filippino, dixe volere per suo bisogni f. 1 s. 50 d. __

+Adì 26 del ditto

[in margin: frate Filippo]

Pagose di volontà di ditti f. I s. XXV, sonno che se pagaro ad frate Filippo quali pagai per lui ad Pier Mariano di maestro Brascio per cose tolte da lui per la sua Infermità f. 1 s. 25 d. __

+Adì ditto

Pagose di volontà di ditti s. 5 sonno che se pagaro ad Coraza per sgombrare la ecclesia f. __ s. 5 d. __

+Adì ditto

Pagose di volontà di ditti s. VIII sonno che se pagaro ad Simone lombardo per portatora di C coppi da casa d'orcio ad Sancta Maria f. __ s. 8 d. __

+Adì 9 di magio

Pagose di volontà di ditti s. XXX, sonno che se pagaro ad maestro Iacopo lombardo per acconciatora d'una seppultura nella cappella si dice di messer Marino f. __ s. 30 d. __

+Adì 14 di magio

Pagose di volontà di ditti s. XXV, sonno per uno capretto per donare a frate Filippo f. __ s. 25 d. __

+Adì ditto

Pagose di volontà di ditti [above: ad Cristofano del'Angelo] f. I, sonno per parte d'uno lavorio fa sopra lo muro della tribuna cioè per levare certe monacelle et ponere piumbo f. 1 s. __ d. __

+Adì ditto

[in margin: frate Filippo]

Pagose di volontà di ditti f. I s. XL, sonno che se pagaro ad frate Filippo volse per pagare una soma di grano f. 1 s. 40 d. __

10. 95. 6

C. 117 RECTO

+Adì 18 di maggio 1468

[in margin: frate filippo]

Pagose di volontà di ditti f. III sd. VIII, sonno che si pagaro in carlini 22 piccioli ad frate Filippo, volge per mandare ad Roma don Diamante quando fo mandato cerchando da Monsignore di Vicenza

f. 3 s. 8 d. __

+Adì 19 del ditto

Pagose di volontà di ditti f. III, sonno che se pagaro ad don Nofrio per lo salario suo per sonare l'organi per quello toccha all'opera, cioè per l'anno 1468 f. 3 s. __ d. __

+Adì 28 di ditto

Pagose di volontà di ditti s. XLII, sonno per vitro si comparò da Francesco di Pontano cioè spera spirilli f. __ s. 42 d. __

+Adì 3 di g[i]ugno

[in margin: frate Filippo]

Pagose di volontà di ditti f. I s. L, sonno che si pagaro ad frate Filippo volze per suo bisogni portali io ad casa sua f. 1 s. 50 d. __

+Adì 17 di g[i]ugno

[in margin: frate Philippo]

Pagose di volontà di ditti f. I s. LXXXVII d. VI, sonno che si pagaro ad frate Filippo volze per dare ad Paulo Antonio per pescione dello letto tenne frate Filippo letto e tovagl[i]a mesi 7 per bolognini 19 mese e finiti ditti 7 mesi paga per pescione dello letto bolognini 15 lu mese f. 1 s. 87 d. 6

+Adì 18 del ditto

Pagose di volontà di ditti f. XXXVIIII, sonno per parte di f. 50 resta ad avere per Nichola per paramentare la cappella se dice di messer Maringo

f. 39 s. __ d. __

+Adì 23 del ditto

[in margin: frate Philippo]

Pagose di volontà di ditti f. VI, sonno che se pagaro ad frate Filippo quali habbe quando me parti per la moria f. 6 s. __ d. __

[in margin: frate Philippo]

Et a dì detto f. II s. LXX, sonno che se pagaro per lui ad Lorenzo albergatore per vettura d'uno ronzino per gire ad Firenze don Diamante che stette dì 27, monta a bolognini 4 lu dì f. 2 s. 70 d. __

+Adì [blank] di luglio

[in margin: frate Filippo]

Pagose di volontà di ditti f. VII, sonno che se pagaro ad frate Filippo, quali li portai io da Bazano f. 7 s. __ d. __

+Adì [blank] d'augusto

[in margin: frate Filippo]

Pagose di volontà di ditti f. VII s. LXII 1/2, sonno che se pagaro ad frate Filippo quali li portò per Matteo d'Amelia in f. 5 larghi

f. VII s. 62 d. __

+Adì 29 di settembre

[in margin: frate Filippo]

Pagose di volontà di ditti f. I s. 50, sono che se pagaro ad frate Filippo quali li portai da Bazano f. 1 s. 50 d. __

+Adì ultimo di settembre

[in margin: frate Filippo da lui]

Pagose di volontà di ditti f. XXIIII s. XLVII, sonno che se pagaro ad frate Filippo quali se pagaro per lui ad Pierangelino di Matteo per robbe tolte da lui, cioè azurri, stagni e altri coluri, diè al ditto f. 18, lo resto in danari contanti f. 24 s. 47 d. __

+Adì 8 d'ottobre

[in margin: frate Filippo]

Pagose di volontà di ditti f. VII s. XLI d. III, sonno si pagaro ad frate Filippo, quali habbe per noi da Ricciardo di Stefano per cose tolte da lui

f. 7 s. 41 d. 3

Somma ha 'uto ditto frate Filippo sine al presente dì f. 444 s. 80 d. 3, sonno ducati papali a bolognini 61 ducati 290 s. 55.

105. 58. 3

C. 117 VERSO

+Adì 12 d'ottobre 1468

[in margin: frate Filippo]

Pagose di volontà [di] ditti f. CXXII, sonno che si pagaro ad frate Filippo dipintore [crossed out: et per p] e quali ebbe in ducati 80 [written above: larghi] et più per comparare ditti ducati f. 1 s. 62 d. 6, sonno in tutto [crossed out: quali dixe volera] per mandare ad Firenze per oro e azurri et altri colori

f. 123 s. 62 d. 6

+Adì 12 di novembre

Pagose di volontà di ditti ad Pier Matteo d'Amelia garzone di frate Filippo f. III, sonno per tramotare lo ponte della tribuna f. 3 s. __ d. __

+Adì 17 di novembre

[in margin: Pinotto per la pesione]

Pagose di volontà di ditti d Pinotto di G[i]uliano s. LXXV, sonno per parte della piscione della caxa si tolse per frate Filippo f. __ s. 75 d. __

+Adì 18 di novembre

Pagose di volontà di ditti s. XXVI, sonno che se pagaro ad Simone di ser Giovanni per vedere el testamento di ser Giovanni di messer Giacho per lo interesse dell'opera f. __ s. 26 d. __

+Adì 26 del ditto

Pagose di volontà di ditti s. LXII d. 6, sonno che se pagaro ad Tomaxo di Battista per calcina portò per depegnere la tribuna

f. __ s. 62 d. 6

+Adì ditto

[in margin: frate Filippo]

Pagose di volontà di ditti f. I s. LII d. 6, sonno che se pagarò ad frate Filippo quali habbe per pagare ½ braccio di rosato f. 1 s. 52 d. 6

+Adì 2 di dicembre

[in margin: frate Filippo]

Pagose di volontà di ditti f. I s. LXIIII d. VI, sonno che se pagaro ad frate Filippo depintore, quali pagai per lui ad Pier Matteo di Marmangilo per cose tolze da luyi quando stetto amalato f. 1 s. 64 d. 6

+Adì 10 dicembre

Pagose di volontà di ditti f. VI s. X d. V, sonno per parte di ducati 6 piccioli da darse ad Simone di ser Giovnni per lo testamento di ser Giovanni di messer Saccho. Et ad ser Michelangelo di Urbano per scriptura et tragetura d'esso in publica forma f. 6 s. 10 d. 5

+Adì ditto

Pagose di volontà di ditti s. XXVII d. VI, sonno per uno paro di capponi se comparò per donare ad frate Filippo f. __ s. 27 d. 6

+Adì 16 di dicembre

[in margin: frate Filippo]

Pagose di volontà di ditti ad frate Filippo f. IIII s. LXVIIII d. IIII, sonno che l'abbe per noi da Piccione di Gregori per cose tolte da lui

f. 4 s. 69 d. 4

+Adì ditto

Pagose di volontà di ditti ad Piccione di Gregori f. VI s. XLII d. VIIII, sonno per più cose tolte da lui come appare a libro suo f. 6 s. 42 d. 9

+Adì ditto

Pagose di volontà di ditti f. I s. XXII, sonno che si compararo pedi 68 di tavole per apparare el ponte per depegnere f. 1 s. 22 d. __

+Adì ultimo di dicembre

Pagose di volontà di ditti s. XXX, sonno che se pagaro ad Santo da Cascia per vettura di mattoni si portaro per fare uno camino in camora di don Pier Giacho

f. __ s. 30 d. __

+Adì ultimo di dicembre

Pagose di volontà di ditti f. X quali se pagaro ad Pier Matteo di Caracosa per lo salario suo di stare alle imagine, cioè per l'anno 1468 delli quali f. X ha 'uti contanti f. 5 et f. 5 [crossed out: per intratti] auti per intrata di danari et musto, hauto dell'opera, come appare alla intrata f. 10 s. __ d. __

160. 44.

C. 118 RECTO

+Adì ultimo di dicembre 1468

Pagose di volontà di ditti s. LXV, sonno che se pagaro ad Retundo di Montarona per certi de' correnti se compararo da lui per lo ponte nella tribuna f. __ s. 65 d. __

Uscita dell'anno 1469, Operali ditti Tomaxo et Cesari

+Adì 18 di genaro 1469

Pagose di volontà di ditti f. XI s. LXXXXVI d. VI, quali sonno che se pagaro ad uno mastro G[i]achovo fabricatore quale mandò monsignore per fare la cappella di Sancta Maria, quali danari li se dero per merito della sua venuta f. 11 s. 96 d. 6

+Adì 23 del ditto

[in margin: frate Filippo]

Pagose di volontà di ditti f. II s. X, sonno che se pagaro ad frate Filippo quali volze se pagassero ad Lodovicho di Niccholo per coppe 3 di grano comparò da lui a bolognini 28 coppa f. 2 s. 10 d. __

+Adì 28 del ditto

[in margin: Piciotto per pesione]

Pagose di volontà di ditti f. III, sonno per pagare ad Piciotto di Iuliano per parte della pescione della caxa t[i]ene frate Filippo quali pagai per lui ad Pier Lonardo di Iohanni f. 3 s. __ d. __

+Adì ditto

[in margin: frate Filippo]

Pagose di volontà di ditti f. II s. LXXXX, quali sonno che se pagaro ad frate Filippo dipintore volze per comparare una soma di grano comprò Bernardo f. 2 s. 90 d. __

+Adì 28 del ditto

Pagose di volontà di ditti s. XXII d. VI, sonno che si pagaro ad uno lombardo per mondatura del condutto va per la piaza di Sancta Maria et per vettura di uno cavallo si adoperò f. __ s. 22 d. 6

+Adì 30 del ditto

Pagose di volontà di ditti f. VII, sonno che se pagaro ad ser Michelangelo d'Urbano per farli trane in publica forma lo testamento di Francesco d'Angelitto et uno codicillo f. 7 s. __ d. __

+Adì ditto

Pagose di volontà di ditti s. XII d. VI, sonno che se pagaro ad uno lombardo per remoratora di certe fenestre nella tribuna f. __ s. 12 d. 6

+Adì 4 di febraro

Pagose di volontà di ditti s. X, sonno che se pagaro ad uno lombardo per sgomoratora di certe prete di una caxa caschò dell'opera f. __ s. 10 d. __

+Adì 11 di febraro

Pagose di volontà di ditti s. XXVII 1/2, sonno che se pagaro in uno paro di capponi per donare a frate Filippo f. __ s. 27 d. 6

+Adì 18 di febraro

Pagose di volontà di ditti f. III ad Michelangelo di Cristofano per parte del suo salario per manutenere el titto di Sancta maria f. 3 s. __ d. __

+Adì 24 di febraro

Pagose di volontà di ditti s. XXXVII d. VI, quali se pagaro ad Pier Andrea di Taratetta per reponere l'impannati nelle rose del frontespizio

f. __ s. 37 d. 6

+Adì 24 del ditto

Pagose di volontà di ditti f. IIII s. L, sonno che se pagaro ad Mariano di Nicholo et a Tomaxo di Battista per refare lu martello della campana grossa di Santa Maria f. 4 s. 50 d. __

+Adì ultimo del ditto

[in margin: frate Filippo]

Pagose di volontà di ditti f. III, sonno che se pagaro ad frate Filippo portò per suo bisogni f. 3 s. __ d. __

39. 21. 6

C. 118 VERSO

+Adì primo d'aprile 1469

[in margin: frate Filippo]

Pagose di volontà di ditti f. [crossed out: IIII] V s. V, quali se pagaro ad frate Filippo cioè f. 3 s. 5 abbe don Diamante che li portai io a Firenze quali volse se dagessero ad Dominicho dipintore et f. I abbe frate Filippo ala bancha di Pinbello f. 5 s. 5 d. __

Et più ditto dì ad Mattione per some 16 di lena li fici portare f. I

+Adì ditto

Pagose di volontà di ditti s. 40, sonno per uno serrame et ase se compararo per uno uscio se fece nel ponte dove pegne frate Filippo

f. __ s. 40 d. __

+Adì 8 del ditto

[in margin: mastro Giacho et mastro Francescho]

Pagose di volontà di ditti f. X, sonno che dero ad maestro Giacho et mastro Francischo fabricatori della cappella fanno in Sancta Maria habbero in 2 partite come appare in uno foglio [crossed out: di mio] hanno di mia mano

f. 10 s. __ d. __

+Adì ditto

Pagose di volontà di ditti s. XII, sonno che se pagaro ad lo figl[i]o di Pier Matteo per portatora di calcina per pegnere la tribuna
f. __ s. 12 d. __

+Adì 10 del ditto

Pagose di volontà di ditti s. X ad don Biondo per acconciare le seppulture delle trasanne f. __ s. 10 d. __

+Adì 15 del ditto

[in margin: frate Filippo]
Pagose di volontà di ditti f. III, sonno che se pagaro ad frate Filippo dipintore quali se pagaro per lui allo priore di Sancto Pietro per una soma di grano comparò da lui f. 3 s. __ d. __

+Adì 26 del ditto

[in margin: frate Filippo]
Pagose di volontà di ditti f. IIII s. L, sonno che se pagaro ad frate Filippo dipintore, volse per suo' bisogni f. 4 s. 50 d. __

+Adì ditto

[in margin: organi]
Pagose di volontà di ditti f. III, sonno che se pagaro ad don Nofrio per lo salario suo per sonare l'organi f. 3 s. __ d. __

+Adì 29 del ditto

Pagose di volontà di ditti s. XX, sonno per some dui di calcina se comparò da Bertoletto per depegnere la tribuna f. __ s. 20 d. __

+Adì ditto

[in margin: maestro Giaco e maestro Francescho]
Pagose di volontà di ditti f. V, sonno che se dero ad mastro Giacho et mastro Francischo fabricatori delle cappelle di Sancta Maria quali volse mastro Francescho dixe per comperare grano f. 5 s. __ d. __

+Adì ditto

[in margin: per Lonardo e Dolce]
Pagose di volontà di ditti s. L, sonno che se pagare ad per Lonardo di Ruberto et Dolce d'Angerello per sgomberare le terrino di Sancta Maria
f. __ s. 50 d. __

+Adì 4 di magio

[in margin: frate Filippo]
Pagose di volontà di dittif. VI s. XX, quali sonno che se pagaro ad frate Filippo dipintore quali pagai ad don Diamante per lui e per lo ditto ad Antonio da Monte Lione per uno tappeto comparo da lui f. 6 s. 20 d. __

+Adì 6 del ditto

Pagose di volontà di ditti f. I s. XXII 1/2, sonno per coppe XX di calcina se comparò da Andrea d'Ant[oni]o da Patricho vollese per dipignere la tribuna et rendise allo spedale per calcina vecchia se tolse da lui
f. 1 s. 12 d. 6

+Adì 9 del ditto

[in margin: per Lonardo et Dolce per levare terrino di Sancta Maria]
Pagose di volontà di ditti f. II, sonno che se pagaro ad per Lonardo di Berto et Dolce per levare lo terrino di Sancta Maria quando se fecero le cappelle
f. 2 s. __ d. __

+Adì 10 del ditto

[in margin: frate Filippo]
Pagose di volontà di ditti f. 6, quali se pagaro ad frate Filippo et per lui ad don Ciriolo per 8 coppe di grano habbe da lui in Schiagino a bolognini 30 coppa
f. 6 s. __ d. __

47. 19. 6

C. 119 RECTO

+Adì 10 di magio 1469

[in margin: maestro Giaco et maestro Francesco]
Pagose di volontà di ditti f. XII, sonno che se pagaro ad maestro Francesco et maestro Giacho fabricatori delle cappelle quale portò maestro Francesco dixe per comparare pane et vino et per dare ad fabri f. 12 s. __ d. __

+Adì 12 di magio

Pagose di volontà di ditti di ditti f. III, sonno che se pagaro ad dui schiavi per sgomborare terreno della chiesia quando si fecero le cappelle
f. 3 s. __ d. __

+Adì 15 del ditto

[in margin: frate Filippo]
Pagose di volontà di ditti f. III, sonno che se pagaro ad frate Filippo volse se dagessero ad don Diamante quando andò a Roma
f. 3 s. __ d. __

+Adì 17 del ditto

[in margin: frate Filippo]
Pagose di volontà di ditti f. II s. LXXX, sonno che se pagaro ad frate Filippo quali se pagaro per lui ad ser Pietro Paulo per una soma di grano a bolognini 28 coppa f. 2 s. 80 d. __

+Adì 20 del ditto

Pagose di volontà di ditti f. II s. LX, sonno che se pagaro alle redi di Pier Nichola di Manzolo per resto del paramentare la cappella di messer Marino quali se pagaro per lui ad Vallarino e ad Pietri per cose tolse di bottega
f. 2 s. 60 d. __

+Adì ditto

Pagose di volontà di ditti s. XVII d. 6, sonno che se pagaro per comparare uno capretto per donare ad frate Filippo f. __ s. 17 d. 6

+Adì ditto

[in margin: frate Filippo]
Pagose di volontà di ditti f. I s. L, sonno se pagaro ad frate Filippo portò per lui Matteo d'Amelia dixe volere per suo bisogni f. 1 s. 50 d. __

+Adì 26 del ditto

[in margin: frate Filippo]
Pagose di volontà di ditti f. III s. XX, sonno che se pagaro ad frate Filippo et per lui ad Liuccio G[i]udeo per panno carfagno dixe haver tolto da lui per una camera per admira f. 3 s. 20 d. __

+[Adì] ultimo del ditto

[in margin: frate Filippo]
Pagose di volontà di ditti s. LXV, sonno che se pagaro ad frate Filippo et per lui ad frate Servadio di Sancto Augustino per vino tolto da lui
f. __ s. 65 d. __

+Adì 5 di zugno

[in margin: frate Filippo]
Pagose di volontà di ditti f. I s. L, sonno che se pagaro ad frate Filippo portò Matteo per suo bisogni f. 1 s. 50 d. __

+Adì 8 del ditto

[in margin: maestro Giaco e maestro Francescho]
Pagose di volontà di ditti s. LXXV, sonno che se pagaro ad maestro Francescho et maestro Iaco fabricatori delle cappelle et per lui ad Iohanni di Franco da Monte Martano per prete li portò f. __ s. 75 d. __

+Adì 22 de zugno

[in margin: frate Filippo]
Pagose di volontà di ditti f. III, sonno che si pagaro ad frate Filippo portò lui dixe volere per suo' bisogni f. 3 s. __ d. __

+Adì 24 del ditto

Pagose di volontà di ditti f. I s. LX, sonno che se pagaro ad certi da Patrico per some 30 di calcina che se compararo per rendere ad don Ruscotto che l'avia prestate f. 1 s. 60 d. __

+Adì 28 del ditto

[in margin: frate Filippo]
Pagose di volontà di ditti f. II s. XL ad frate Filippo quali se pagaro per lui ad don Filippo per alcune cose comparò da lui f. 2 s. 40 d. __

C. 119 VERSO

+Adì 3 di lugl[i]o 1469

[in margin: frate Filippo]
Pagose di volontà di ditti f. LXXXXIII quali sonno che se pagare ad frate Filippo le quali pagò per l'opera Tomaxo di Giacho per danari contanti habbe da lui et vino et olio
f. 93 __

+Adì 6 del ditto

[in margin: frate Filippo]
Pagose di volontà di ditti f. XI s. LV, sonno che se pagaro ad frate Filippo et per lui ad Langelo dello Ruscio ducati 6 papali per panno tolse da lui et f. 2 s. 40 ad Lodovico di Nicolò per una soma di grano tolse da lui

f. 11 s. 55 __

+Adì 8 del ditto

Pagose di volontà di ditti s. XXXV, sonno che se pagaro ad uno fabro per dui ase se compararo da lui per adoperare nell'uscio della cappella della imagine

f. __ s. 35 __

+Adì 8 di lugl[i]o

[in margin: maestro Francesco et maestro Iaco]
Pagose di volontà di ditti f. XXI, sonno che si pagaro ad maestro Francescho et maestro G[i]acho fabricatori delle cappelle f. 21 s. __

+Adì 14 del ditto

[in margin: frate Filippo]
Pagose di volontà di ditti f. __s. LX, sonno che se pagaro ad frate Filippo et per lui ad Tomaxo di Giacho per uno paro di caponi comparò da lui portò Filippino f. __ s. 40 __

+Adì 18 del ditto

[in margin: frate Filippo]
Pagose di volontà di ditti f. __ s. LX, sonno che se pagaro ad frate Filippo portò Filippino dixe volere per comparare capponi f. __ s. 60 __

+Adì 22 del ditto

[in margin: frate Filippo]
Pagose di volontà di ditti f. I s. L, sonno che se pagara ad frate Filippo portò Filippino quando stava infermo f. 1 s. 50

+Adì 26 del ditto

[in margin: frate Filippo]
Pagose di volontà di ditti f. I s. L, sonno che se pagaro ad frate Filippo et per lui ad mastro Nicholo per haverlo medicato et per lui a Pier Mascetto

f. 1 s. 50

+Adì 31 del ditto

[in margin: frate Filippo]
Pagose di volontà di ditti f. I s. L, sonno che se pagaro ad frate Filippo portò Filippino

f. 1 s. 50

+Adì 10 d'augusto

[in margin: frate Filippo]
Pagose di volontà di ditti f. 15, sonno che se pagaro ad frate Filippo dixe volere per comparare azurri portò per Matteo di sua volontà f. 15 s. __

+Adì 11 del ditto

[in margin: frate Filippo]
Pagose di volontà di ditti f. 9 s. LXVIII, sonno che se pagaro ad frate Filippo et per lui ad me Giordano per some 9 di pititti 34 di vino comparò da me
f. 9 s. 68 __

+Adì ditto

[in margin: frate Filippo]
Pagose di volontà di ditti f. VII s. XX, sonno che se pagaro ad frate Filippo et per lui ad me Giordano per panno monachino pagò per Pier Matteo d'Amelia f. 7 s. 20

+Adì 14 d'augusto

[in margin: Pinotto per la pescione della caxa]
Pagose di volontà di ditti f. III s. LXXV, sonno che se pagaro ad Giovanni di Iuliano per resto di f. 7 s. 50 monta la parte li toccha della pescione della caxa si tenne a pescione per la stantia di frate Filippo, cioè per ¾
f. 3 s. 75 __

+Adì 15 di ditto

Pagose di volontà di ditti f. V s. LXII d. VI, sonno che se pagaro ad Antonio Schiavo suo compagno per sgomboratura de terreno della cappella
f. 5 s. 62 d. 6

+Adì 16 del ditto

[in margin: maestro Francesco et maestro Iaco]
Pagose di volontà di ditti f. I s. LII d. VI, sonno che se pagaro ad maestro Francischo et per lui ad Marin Iohanni per Antonio da Campagnano
f. 1 s. 52 d. 6

174. 18.

C. 120 RECTO

+Adì 19 d'augusto 1469

[in margin: maestro Giaco et maestro Francescho]
Pagose di volontà di ditti f. XXX, sonno che se pagaro ad maestro Giaco e maestro Francesco portò maestro Francesco dixe volere per comparare grano per dare ad magistri f. 30 __

+Adì ditto

[in margin: maestro Giacho e maestro Francesco]
Pagose di volontà di ditti f. XV s. 80, sonno che se pagaro ad maestro Giacho e maestro Francesco portò per loro maestro Andrea per mattoni dati alli ditti quali abbe in ducati 10 viniziani a [?] 79 sonno f. 15 s. 80
[in margin: frate Filippo]

+Adì 21 del ditto

Pagose di volontà di ditti f. V s. LXXXIIII, sonno che se pagaro ad frate Filippo et per lui ad Paulo Antonio per resto della pescione del letto tene da lui

che l'à tenuto fine al presente dì misi 28 cioè misi 7 a bolognini 19 lo mese et misi 21 a bolognini 15 lo mexe che monta f. 11 s. 26 per tempo paxato
f. 5 s. 84 __

+Adì ditto

Pagose di volontà di ditti f. II s. L, sonno che si pagaro alle heredi di Pier Nichola di Manzolo per resto de havere per paramentare la cappella se dice di messer Marino et per lui ad Pier Francischo di Giovanni f. 2 s. 50

+Adì 23 del ditto

[in margin: maestro Giacho et maestro Francischo]

Pagose di volontà di ditti f. III s. XX, sonno che se pagaro ad maestro Giacho et maestro Francischo et per loro ad Pietro Paulo di Vangnilista bolognini 68 per ferro auto da lui et bolognini 60 per loro ad Paulangelo di Giacho per carne auta da lui f. 3 s. 20

+Adì 26 del ditto

[in margin: maestro Giacho et maestro Francischo]

Pagose di volontà di ditti f. I s. V, sonno che si pagaro ad maestro Giacho et maestro Francischo et per loro ad Piero di Luca dalli Roselli per vettura di prete f. 1 s. 5

+Adì ditto

Pagose di volontà di ditti f. I s. LXXX, sonno che se pagaro ad Cerescio di Battagl[i]a da Berate per uno posillo de tavole di olmo se compararo da lui per fare ponte et armatura per le cappelle f. 1 s. 80 d. __

+Adì 2 di settembre

[in margin: maestro Giacho et maestro Francischo]

Pagose di volontà di ditti f. X, sonno che se pagaro ad maestro Giacho et maestro Francischo dixe volere per soi bisogni f. 10 s. __ d. __

+Adì ditto

Pagose di volontà di ditti s. LVIIII d. VI, sonno che se pagaro ad Langilo di Giacho per 15 de corenti e fascie 4 d'assari se compararo da lui per fare l'armadura delle cappelle f. __ s. 59 d. 6

+Adì 5 di [struck out: d'augosto] settembre

[in margin: maestro Giacho et maestro Francischo]

Pagose di volontà di ditti f. 1 s. 50, sonno che se pagaro ad maestro Giacho et maestro Francischo et per loro ad Roscio volse per dare ad uno suo garzone per andare a Roma di volontà di Lionardo f. 1 s. 50 d, __

+Adì ditto

[in margin: maestro Giacho et maestro Francischo]

Pagose di volontà di ditti f. IIII, sonno che se pagaro ad maestro Giacho et maestro Francischo portò Lionardo dixe volere per pagare vetture di prete
f. 4 s. __

+Adì 6 del ditto

[in margin: maestro Giacho et maestro Francischo]

Pagose di volontà di ditti f. 1 sonno che se pagaro ad maestro Giacho et maestro Francischo et per lui ad maestro Andrea dalli mattoni et per lui ad Manzitto dallo Pogiolo per vettura di mattoni f. 1 s. __

77. 28. 6

C. 120 VERSO

+Adì 10 di settembre 1469

[in margin: frate Filippo]

Pagose di volontà di ditti f. IIII s. XXXV, sonno che se pagaro ad frate Filippo et per lui ad Gagio hebreo per rescotere uno p [?] d'azurro da lui

f. 4 s. 35

+Adi 27 di settembre

Pagose di volontà di ditti s. XXX, sonno che se pagaro ad maesro Antonio dello Secchia et Saperuso dello Gelfone per uno serrame se mise nell'uscio della imagine f. __ s. 30

+Adì 30 di settembre

[in margin: frate Filippo]

Pagose di volontà di ditti f. II, sonno che se pagaro ad frate Filippo et per lui ad Sforza di Domo per vino tolze da lui f. 2 s. __

+Adì 30 di settembre

[in margin: maestro G[i]acho]

Pagose di volontà di ditti f. I s. LXXV, sonno che se pagaro ad maestro Giacho et per lui ad maestro Andrea Mattonaso et per lui ad Pasquitto d'Antonio da Sancto Brizio per vettura di mattoni f. 1 s. 75 __

+Adì primo d'ottobre

[in margin: pescione della caxa pagata ad Bilia]

Pagose di volontà di ditti f. II s. L, sonno che se pagaro ad Bilia di Sentio per la rata li toccha della pescione della casa se tolze per dare ad frate Filippo

f. 2 s. 50 __

+Adì 4 d'ottobre

[in margin: maestro Giacho]

Pagose di volontà di ditti f. IIII, sonno che se pagaro ad maestro Giacho portò Lionardo dixe volero per comprare biada per muli f. 4 s.

+Adì ditto

Pagose di volontà di ditti s. XXXV, sonno che se pagare ad certi lombardi per mattonare la cappella della imagine f. __ s. 35 __

+Adì ditto

Pagose di volontà di ditti s. LXXV, sonno che se pagaro ad Pasquitto da Sancto Brizo per tavole se compararo da lui per fare l'armadure per le cappelle

f. __ s. 75 __

+Adì 6 del ditto

[in margin: maestro G[i]acho]

Pagose di volontà di ditti f. IIII, sonno che se pagaro ad maestro G[i]acho portò Lionardo dixe per vole[re] dare ad Pietri fornaio per vino tolto da lui

f. 4 s. __

+Adì 10 del ditto

[in margin: frate Filippo]

Pagose di volontà di ditti f. II s. XV, sonno che se pagaro ad don Diamante et Filippino et per loro ad preti et a frate et vicini per lo exequio di frate Filippo f. 2 s. 15 __

+Adì ditto

[in margin: frate Filippo]

Pagose di volontà di ditti f. XX s. L, sonno che se pagaro ad frate Filippo et per lui ad Tomaxo di Giaco e G[i]ordano di Tomaxo per panni tolti da loro

f. 20 s. 50

+Adì ditto

[in margin: maestri Giacho]

Pagose di volontà di ditti f. V, sonno che se pagaro ad Lionardo per mastro G[i]acho dixe volere per suo' bisogni f. 5 s. __

+Adì 11del ditto

[in margin: frate Filippo]

Pagose di volontà di ditti f. IIII s. XI d. VIIII, sonno che se pagaro ad don Diamante e Filippino et per lui ad Gaio per 284 fogli d'oro per bolognini 58 centinaio, monta f. 4 s. 11 d. 9

+Adì ditto

Pagose di volontà di ditti s. X pagaronse ad Antonio Schiavo per sgomberatura di terreno se cavò della soppultura di frate Filippo

f. __ s. 10 d. __

+Adì 12 del ditto

[in margin: frate Filippo]

Pagose di volontà di ditti s. XLVII d. VI, sonno che se pagaro ad don Diamante e Filippino e per loro ad Antonio da Monte Lione per una berretta negra se comparò da lui f. __ s. 47 d. 6

52. 34. 3

C. 121 RECTO

+Adì 14 d'ottobre 1469

[in margin: maestro Giacho]

Pagose di volontà di ditti f. I s. LXXII d. VI, sonno che se pagaro ad maestro Giacho et per lui ad maestro Andrea el quale volse dare ad lo figl[i]o di Capoccio da Magiano per vettura di 4000 mattoni portò

f. 1 s. LXXII d. VI

+Adì ditto

[in margin: maestro Giacho]

Pagose di volontà di ditti f. X, sonno che si pagaro ad maestro Giacho portò Lionardo dixe volere per pagare ad garzoni f. 10 s. __ d.

+Adì ditto

[in margin: mestro Francesco et maestro Giacho]

Pagose di volontà di ditti f. IIII, sonno che se pagaro ad maestro Francesco et maestro Giacho et per lui ad fraticello di Marco per vino tolsero d lui

f. 4 s. __ d.

+Adì 18 del ditto

[in margin: maestro Giacho]

Pagose di volontà di ditti f. X, sonno che se pagaro ad maestro Giacho et per lui ad maestro Andrea dalli Mattoni di volontà di Lionardo

f. 10 s. __

+Adì ditto

Pagose di volontà di ditti f. I s. VIIII, sonno che se pagaro d Battista da Beroite per pezi 61 di tavole se compararo da lui per fare l'armadura della cappella

f. 1 s. 9

+Adì 19 del ditto

[in margin: frate Filippo]

Pagose di volontà di ditti f. III, sonno che se pagaro ad Filippino portò lui dixe volere per pagare la fattura del mantello e suo' altri bisogni

f. 3 s. __

+Adì 20 del ditto

[in margin: maestro Giaco]

Pagose di volontà di ditti f. X, sonno che si pagaro ad maestro Giacho portò Lionardo dixe volere per pagare beccari et altri suo' bisogni

f. 10 s. __

[in margin: frate Filippo]

+Adì 21 del ditto

Pagose di volontà di ditti f. V s. XXX, sonno che se pagaro ad Filippino et per lui ad maestro Giovanni medico per cose tolte per la infermità di frate Filippo f. 5 s. 30 __

+Adì 23 del ditto

[in margin: frate Filippo]

Pagose di volontà di ditti s. XXXII d. VI, sonno che si pagaro ad Filippino et per lui ad Sforza di Domo per resto di piatti 110, di vino comparo da lui, cioè s. XX, et s. XII d. VI ad Giacoangelo sartore per facitura di uno paro di calze di perpignano biancho f. __ s. 32 d. 6

+Adì 27 del ditto

[in margin: maestri Giacho]

Pagose di volontà di ditti f. III s. LX, sonno che se pagaro ad maestro Giacho et per lui ad maestro Antonio dello Secchiagio per facitura di ferri

f. 3 s. 60 d. __

+Adì 28 del ditto

[in margin: maestro Giacho]
Pagose di volontà di ditti f. X, sonno che si pagaro ad maestro Giaco portò Lionardo dixe volere per suo bisogni f. 10 s. __ d. __

+Adì ditto

Pagose di volontà di ditti f. I s. XXX, sonno che se pagaro ad don Pier Giacho di Iohanni perchè fe' fare una fenestra in camera suo
f. 1 s. 30 d. __

+Adì ultimo di detto

[in margin: maestro Giacho]
Pagose di volontà di ditti f. VI, sonno che se pagaro ad maestro Giacho portò Lionardo dixe volere per coparare grano f. 6 s. __ d. __

66. 34.

C. 121 VERSO

+Adì 2 di novembre 1469

[in margin: frate Filippo]
Pagose di volontà di ditti f. III s. XIIII d. VI, sonno che se pagaro ad Filippino in dui ducati d'oro, uno viniziano uno largho dixe volere per comparare uno gabbano f. 3 s. 14 d. 6

+Adì detto

[in margin: maestro Giacho]
Pagose di volontà di ditti f. XXX s. XXVII, sonno che se pagaro ad maestro Giacho et per lui ad maestro Francesco da Bologna quali habbe dal ditto maestro Giacho remasti d'accordo insieme di quel tanto restara havere del lavoro ditto maestro Francescho, quale di volontà loro s'è retratto del detto lavoro, et ditto maestro Giacho disobliga lo ditto Francesco et chiamasi obligato lui solo del tutto el lavoro. Quali f. 30 s. 27 se li pagaro in ducati 19 veneziani e bolognini X. Presenti don Dominicho priore di Sancto Andrea et Ciavatto di Pietri da Spoleti f. 30 s. 27 d. __

+Adì detto

[in margin: maestro Giacho]
Pagose di volontà di ditti f. IIII, sonno che se pagaro ad maestro Giacho portò Lionardo, dixe volere per bisogni di caxa f. 4 s. __

+Adì 4 del detto

[in margin: frate filippo]
Pagose di volontà di ditti f. II s. L, sonno che se pagaro ad Filippino et per lui ad Bernardo da Bagiano per lena li vendè più tempi sonno
f. 2 s. 50 __

+Adì detto

Pagose di volontà di ditti f. __ s. L, sonno per certo lengname se compararo da Pierangelo da Pompagnano per adoperarse nella cappella

f. __ s. 50

+Adì 6 del detto

Pagose di volontà di ditti s. XXXVII d. VI, sonno che se pagaro ad Filippo lombardo per 3 dì stette ad lavorare in camera di don Pier Giacho

f. __ s. 37 d. 6

+Adì 7 del detto

[in margin: maestro Giacho]

Pagose di volontà di ditti f. I s. LXXV, sonno che se pagaro ad maestro Giacho et per lui ad maestro Andrea, et per lui ditto ad Manzitto dallo Pogola per vettura di mattoni et ditto ad don Pasquale f. 1 s. 75 __

+Adì 11 del detto

[in margin: maestro Giacho]

Pagose di volontà di ditti f. X, sonno che si pagaro ad maestro Giacho, portò Lionardo dixe volere per dare ad loro garzoni f. 10 s. __

[in margin: maestro Giacho]

+Adì 21 di novembre

Pagose di volontà di ditti f. XV, sonno che si pagaro ad maestro Giacho portò lui contanti f. 12 s. 90, et f. 2 s. 10 in braccia 3 1/2 di panno cilestro per Bologna f. 15 s. __

+Adì 22 del detto

Pagose di volontà di ditti f. __ s. XV, sonno che se pagaro ad uno lombardo per certo acconcio fece in canonica f. __ s. 15

+Adì 29 del detto

[in margin: frate Filippo]

Pagose di volontà di ditti f. III s. XI, sonno che se pagaro ad Filippino et per lui ad Pier Urbano di Battista per cera se tolze da lui per fare lo exequio di frate Filippo f. 3 s. 11 __

+Adì detto

[in margin: frate Filippo]

Pagose di volontà di ditti f. I s. LVIII, sonno che sse pagaro in ducato 1 viniziano ad Filippino dixe volere per pagare maestro Giovanni di maestro Gregorio f. 1 s. 58 __

72. 37. 6

C. 122 RECTO

+Adì 29 di novembre 1469

[in margin: maestro Giacho]

Pagose di volontà di ditti f. VI, sonno che se pagaro ad mastro Giacho quali habbe per noi dal'Angelo di Cataruccio dixe volere per pagare Nofrio per calcina tolze da lui f. 6 __

+Adì detto

[in margin: frate Filippo]
Pagose di volontà di ditti f. II s. LII d. VI, sonno che se pagaro ad Filippino et per lui ad Lucha di Colantonio, cioè bolognini 54 per vino tolze da lui e bolognini 47 per panno tolze da lui per calze f. 2 s. LII d. VI

+Adì primo di dicembre

[in margin: frate Filippo]
Pagose di volontà di ditti f. I s. L, sonno che se pagaro ad Filippino, portò lui, dixe volere per bisogni di caxa f. 1 s. 50 __

+Adì detto

[in margin: frate Filippo]
Pagose di volontà di ditti f. III s. XXVII ½, sonno che se pagaro ad Filippino et per lui ad Pier Simone di ser Valentino per some dui et petitti 30 di vino vermiglio comparò da lui per le mani di Pier Matteo ad ragione di bolognini 50 soma f. 3 s. 27 d. 6

+Adì 2 del detto

[in margin: maestro Giacho]
Pagose di volontà di ditti f. IIII, sonno che si pagaro ad maestro Giacho quali li habbe per noi da l'Angelo di Cataruccio dixe volere per bisogni di caxa, portò Ruscio f. 4 s. __

+Adì 5 di dicembre

[in margin: maestro Giacho]
Pagose di volontà di ditti f. XV s. XL, sonno che se pagaro ad maestro Giacho quali habbe in f. X d'oro a b[olognini] 77 per ducato, portò Luruscio dixe volere per dare al maestro Dominico lombardo f. 15 s. 40 __

+Adì detto

[in margin: maestro Giacho]
Pagose di volontà di ditti f. I s. XXX, sonno che se pagaro ad maestro Giacho e per noi da Ambrosino pizicarolo per coxe tolte da lui f. 1 s. 30__

+Adì 8 di dicembre

Pagose di volontà di ditti f. II s. XXXII 1/2, sonno che se pagaro ad Pier Giovanni di Battista e Nicholo suo fratello per quanta calcina hanno portata per depegnere, che forono coppe 45 a bolognini 2 coppa, et per sacchetti 216 di rena sottile, che montano f. 4 bolognini 38, delli quali n'ànno hauti come appare ad una uscita al loro f. 20 in altra partita s. 62 d. 6
f. 2 s. 32 d. 6

+Adì 11 del ditto

Pagose di volontà di ditti f. XXVII, sonno che se pagaro ad maestro Giacho portò Ruscio dixe per volere dare ad garzoni f. 27 s. __

+Adì del ditto

Pagose di volontà di ditti f. I s. XX, sonno che si pagaro ad maestro Andrea per certi mattoni se compararo da lui per adoperarli in camera di don Piccione
f. 1 s. 20

+Adì 16 del detto

[in margin: frate Filippo]

Pagose di volontà di ditti f. I s. L, sonno che se pagaro ad Filippino, portò lui dixe volere per bisogni di casa f. 1 s. 50

66. 6

C. 122 VERSO

+Adì 18 di dicembre 1469

[in margin: maestro Giacho]

Pagose di volontà di ditti f. XIIII s. LI, sonno che se pagaro ad maestro Giacho, portò Ruscio, et per lui ad G[i]ordano di Tomaxo per panni tolti da lui como appare nel suo fogl[i]o f. 14 s. 50 __

+Adì detto

Pagose di volontà di ditti s. XX, sonno che se pagaro ad Bertolitto nepo[te] di don Morichitto per fattura di certi ferri se misero nella tribuna per potere appichare cortine f. __ s. 20 __

+Adì detto

Pagose di volontà di ditti s. VI, sonno che si pagaro ad Andrea merciaro per certe anella da uscio per lascio delle ymagine f. __ s. 6 __

+Adì 24 del detto

[in margin: frate Filippo]

Pagose di volontà di ditti f. I s. L, sonno che si pagaro ad Filippino quali portò lui dixe volere per suo' bisogni f. 1 s. 50

+Adì detto

Pagose di volontà di ditti s. XXVII d. VI, sonno che se pagaro per comparare uno paro di capponi per donare ad Filippino f. __ s. 27 d. 6

+Adì detto

Pagose di volontà di ditti s. XL, sonno che se pagaro ad certi garzoni per sgomborare la tribuna del legname si levò del ponte f. __ s. 40 __

+Adì 27 del detto

Pagose di volontà di ditti f. I s. II 1/2, sonno che si pagaro ad Pier Marcho spetiale per una scatola di coliandri si compararo da lui per donare ad frate Filippo quando venniso in casa sua Antonio del Pullagiolo et Pier Ignoverate f. 1 s. 2 d. 6

+Adì 29 del detto

[in margin: frate Filippo]

Pagose di volontà di ditti f. II s. IIII, sonno che si pagaro ad Filippino volle per dare ad frate G[i]ovanni quando venne ad Spoleti l'ultima volta f. 2 s. 4 __

+Adì ultimo del ditto

Pagose di volontà di ditti f. __ s. XXVII d. VI, sonno che se pagaro adì uno per fare certi busci nella tribuna per mettere ferri d'attacchare cortine f. __ s. 27 d. 6

+Adì detto

Pagose di volontà di ditti f. I s. L, sonno per una costareccia si comparò da Placito di Gisach quale fo per fare lo ponte alla tribuna f. 1 s. 50

+Adì detto

[in margin: frate Filippo]

Pagose di volontà di ditti f. III s. VIII, sonno che se pagaro ad Filippino in f. 2 d'oro volsero per dare ad frate Giovanni f. 3 s. 8

+Adì detto

[in margin: frate Filippo]

Pagose di volontà di ditti f. II s. LXXXV d. 6, sonno che se pagare ad Filippino et per lui ad Pier Matteo spiziale per cose tolte da lui per la infirmità di frate Filippo cioè lire 12 s. 8, et per some 6 di legna bolognini 15

f. 2 s. 85 __

+Adì detto

[in margin: frate Filippo]

Pagose di volontà di ditti f. VIIII s. XXIIII, sonno che se pagaro ad Filippino in ducati 6 dixe volere per dare ad Simone quando tornò ad Firenze

f. 9 s. 24

+Adì detto

[in margin: maestro Giacho]

Pagose di volontà di ditti f. VI, sonno che se pagaro ad maestro Giacho portò Ruscio quali habbe per noi da l'Angelo di Cataruccio adì 27 di genaro come appare ad suo fogl[i]o f. 6 s. __

+Adì detto

Pagose di volontà di ditti s. LXX, sonno che se pagaro ad ser Carlo di messer Tomaxo per copie de examinationi di testimonii del testamento di ser Giovanni quali habbe dal' Angelo di Cataruccio f. __ s. 70

---

43. 64. 6

C. 123 RECTO

+Adì ultimo di dicembre 1469

Pagose di volontà di ditti f. I, sonno che se pagaro ad don Diamante per disfacimento del ponte quando si finì la dipintura della tribuna

f. 1 s. __ d. __

C. 123 VERSO

Al nome di Dio adì 6 di iennaro 1470

Uscita de dicta opera, Operali Iordano de Tomaxo Mastelleri et ser Michelangelo di Crelano, de tutti denari che de volontà delli sopradicti, per me publico camarlingo predicto se pagaranno per qualunque ratione per bisogno di dicta opera etc.

Pagose di volontà di dicti operali ad Pieragnolo de Dominicho de Valtarena per dui panconcelli et certe pranche comparate da dicto operate nello [?] della canonica soldi trena cioè f. __ s. 30

+Adì 20 di gennaro

Pagose di volontà di dicti f. uno ad [?] 50 per fiorino ad Mariano di Antonio da Spoliti che levò li arbori dalla tribuna de dicto chesia per parte di sua faticha dicti f. 1 s. __ d. __

+Adì 27 del dicto

Pagose di volontà de dicti s. 25 ad Pier Andrea de [?] da Spoleti per una scala venduta per lui alli operali proximi passati, dicti f. __ s. 25 d. __

+Adì primo de febraro

Pagose di volontà di dicti f. uno ad Mariano de Antonio sopradicto per resto della levatora de' sopradicti arbori dalla tribuna et acconciatura della campana grossa et de uno colonnello per la spera et una fenestra nella cappella delle ymagine dicte f. 1 s. __ d. __

+Aì 3 del decto

Pagose di volontà di dicti s. 55 ad Cecho di Cinque da Spoleti per decorrenti et altro legname comperato da lui per lli operali passati, dicti

f. __ s. 55 d. __

+Adì dicto

Pagose di volontà di dicti ad Dolce da Bucillo dalla Badia cherico in dicta chesia per parte de uno coptimo ad sgommerare prete et terrino della nave dalle cappelle nove, ditti f. __ s. 20 d. __

+Adì 7 del dicto

Pagose di volontà di dicti s. 15 ad Barolomeo lombardo che tramutò nel[la] piazza certa quantità di calcina de dicta opera, dicti

f. __ s. 15 d. __

+Adì 15 del dicto

Pagose di volontà di dicti s. 30 ad Dolce da Bucillo sopradicto per parte de dicto coptimo dàtoli a sgommorare dicte prete et terra della nave delle cappelle nove, dicti f. __ s. 30 d. __

4. 50. 0

C. 124 RECTO

+Adì 23 del dicto

Pagose di volontà di dicti Operali f. ducentodece s. trenta ad b[olognini] 50 per fiorino per comandamento ali dicti facto per lui vicario di Monsignore di Spoliti come appare per manu de ser Golino di Iohanni notaro della camera episcopale ad don Diamante de [blank] garzone de fra Filippo pentore fiorentino per ultimo et finale pagamento della depentura della tribuna in dicta chesia cioè dicti f. 210 s. 30 d. __

+Adì 27 del dicto

Pagose di volontà di dicti f. uno l [?] XX, ad Dolce da Buciello comprimario predecto [?] de dicte prete et [?] da levarse de dicta chiesia della nave delle cappelle nove dicti f. 1 s. 50 d. __

+Adì primo di marzo

Pagose di volontà di dicti s. 45 ad Chascio di Tomaxo de Orsolino et forono facti [?] per l'asse da titto d'essa curia dati ad Francesco da G [?] et compagni operali già passato della decta opera dicti f. __ s. 45 d.

+Adì 3 de marzo

Pagose di volontà di dicti s. L ad Pierantonio chericho in Sancta Maria et a Pier Lonardo del'orto e a Montelione cherico in dicta chesia per parte del suo coptimo da sgonmorare terreno et prete delle cappelle nove li dicti

f. __ s. 50 d.

+Adì 15 de marzo

Pagose di volontà di dicti s. 14 ad Michelagnolo disse voleva per tre some de legna comparate per lui per gettare piastre di pionbo per dicta opera dicti

f. __ s. 14 d.

+Adì 22 de marzo

Pagose di volontà di dicti s. 20 ad Michelagnolo di Cristofano sopradicto disse voleva per some quattro de legne comparato per lui per gettare piastre di piombo per dicta opera f. __ s. 20 d.

+Adì 23 del dicto

Pagose di volontà di dicti Operali f. dui a [b?] 50 per fiorino ad Michelagnolo di Cristofano per parte di sua provisione per la manutentione del ticto della dicta chiesia come appare decti a libro de memorie da me a c. 139 decti

f. 2 s. __ d.

+Adì 7 de aprile

Pagose di volontà di dicti s. 12 d. 6 ad Sentio de Barchi per uno pianconcello per dicta opera tolse Mariano d'Antonio monta dicti

f. __ s. 12 d. 6

+Adì 7 del dicto

Pagose di volontà di dicti s. 30 ad Mariano de Antonio mastro de legniame per parte de certe copere date per lui in dicta chesia li dicti

f. __ s. 30 d. __

+Adì 10 del dicto

Pagose di volontà di dicti f. tre et mezzo a [?] 50 ad Pierantonio cherico et a Pier Lonardo de Berto chericho in Sancta Maria per resto e final pagamento della somma di fiorini sey promissi alli dicti et ad Dolce [?] per sgonmoratora de terra et prete delle cappelle nove in dicta chiesia li dicti

f. 3 s. 50 d. __

C. 124 VERSO

+Adì 13 d'aprile 1470

Pagose di volontà di dicti f. XI s. X ad mastro Iacho da Pietrasancta porto Ruscio suo fattore disse volere per pagarne f. VIIII s. X ad messer Antonio canonico per vino tolto da lui et f. II per dare ad Ambrosino pizzicarolo per robbe aute da lui li dicti f. 11 s. X

+Adì 16 d'aprile

Pagose di volontà di dicti f. uno s. X ad Polinoro di Gerardino et ad Pier Lonardo de Berto che sgomborarono [?] et prete dalla nave delle cappelle nove in dicta chiesia li dicti f. 1 s. X d.

+Adì 19 d'aprile

Pagose di volontà di dicti s. 40 ad messer Andrea canonico Spoletino procuratore de dicta opera per spese facte per lui in due fiate quando è andato ad Montefalco et ad [?] ad excotere maltolutti incerti in dicti locchi li dicto f. __ s. 40 d.

+Ai 21 d'aprile

Pagose Baptista di Puccio de volontà di dicti s. trenta disse erano fassi cinque d'assari portò Mariano d'Antonio per lo titto della chiesia li dicti f. __ s. 30 d.

+Adì 21 del dicto

Pagose di volontà di dicti s. XXVII ad Mariano d'Antonio per lo acconciamento del titto della chiesia nella nave verso la roccha li dicti f. __ s. 27 d.

+Aì 23 del dicto

Pagose di volontà di dicti s. V allo balio dello episcopato che citone ad instantia de' dicti operali certi debitori de dicta opera li dicti f. __ s. 5 d.

+Adì 26 de aprile

Pagose di volontà di dicti f. I s. 55 ad mastro Iacho da Pietrasancta portò Russio suo factore disse volere per pagare che cusì se pagarono ad Ferrone de Geronimo da Patricho per vettura de some sessanta de calcina li dicti f. 1 s. 55

+Adì 7 de magio

Pagose di volontà di dicti f. 2 ad Polimero di Gerardino et Pier Lonardo de Ruberto che cavarono uno fosso dereto alla tribuna per sciaquare certa aqua dicti f. 2 s.

+Adì 7 del dicto

Pagose di volontà di dicti f. 1 ad Polimero de Garardino et Pier Lonardo di Ruberto per rempitura della sepultura de ser Tolomeo li dicti f. 1 s. __

+Ai 9 del dicto

Pagose di volontà di dicti f. 1 ad Redolfino magistro di legname per tavole comparate da lui per lu ticto da farse sopra al Salvatore nel frontespizio de dicta chiesia lavora Mariano d'Antonio f. 1 s. __

+Adì 10 del dicto

Pagose di volontà di dicti f. 1 ad Boccio per tavole comparate da lui per lu ticto et trasanna da farsi sopra al Salvadore del frontispizio li dicti

f. 1 s. __

+Adì 10 del dicto

Pagose di volontà di dicti f. 3 s. __ d. __ ad Russchio factore de mastro Iacomo dalla Cappelia per coppe otto di grano hebbe ditto Russchio da Pier Mattio dalle ymagine li dicti come appare ad intrata in questo a c. 14

f. 3 s. __

22. 77. 0

BIBLIOGRAPHY

Abbate, Francesco, "Il monumento a Ladislao di Durazzo," in Roberto Paolo Ciardi et al., eds., *Le vie del marmo; Aspetti della produzione e della diffusione dei manufatti marmorei tra quattrocento e cinquecento*, Florence: Giunti, 1992, pp. 17–22.

Ackerman, James, "'Ars sine Scientia Nihil Est': Gothic Theory of Architecture at the Cathedral of Milan," *Art Bulletin*, vol. 31, 1949, pp. 84–112.

Adinolfi, Pasquale, *La via sacra o del papa*, Rome: Monaldi, 1865.

Ahl, Diane Cole, *Benozzo Gozzoli*, New Haven and London: Yale University Press, 1997.

Ahl, Diane Cole, "Da Roma a Montefalco," in Toscano and Capitelli, eds., *Benozzo Gozzoli, Allievo a Roma, maestro in Umbria*, pp. 181–87.

Ahl, Diane Cole, "Frescante a San Fortunato," in Toscano and Capitelli, eds., *Benozzo Gozzoli, Allievo a Roma, maestro in Umbria*, pp. 93–105.

Ahl, Diane Cole, "Camposanto, Terra Santa: Picturing the Holy Land in Pisa," *Artibus et historiae*, vol. 24, 2003, pp. 95–122.

Ahl, Diane Cole, *Painting in Fifteenth-Century Italy: "This Splendid and Noble Art,"* New Haven and London: Yale University Press, 2023.

Ahl, Diane Cole, and Gerardo de Simone, eds., *Le arti a Pisa nel primo Rinascimento/The Arts in Pisa during the Early Renaissance*, ed., *Predella Monografie*, nos. 13–14, Pisa: Edizioni ETS, 2016 [2018].

Alberti, Leon Battista, *On Painting and On Sculpture. The Latin Texts of De pictura and De statua*, ed. Cecil Grayson, London: Phaidon, 1972.

Alexander, Jonathan J. G., "'Jerusalem the Golden': Image and Myth in the Middle Ages in Western Europe," in Kühnel, ed., *The Real and Ideal Jerusalem in Jewish, Christian and Islamic Art*, pp. 255–64.

Amadore, Duccio di, *Il Cincturale*, ed. and trans. Cesare Grassi, Prato: Società Pratese di Storia Patria, 1984.

Amato, Pietro, *De vera Effigie Mariae: Antiche Icone Romane*, Milan: Mondadori, 1988.

Ames-Lewis, Francis, ed., *Cosimo 'il Vecchio' de' Medici, 1389–1464*, Oxford: Clarendon Press, 1992.

Ammannati Piccolomini, Jacopo, *Lettere (1444–1479)*, ed. Paolo Cherubini, Rome: Ministero per i beni culturali e ambientali, Ufficio centrale per i beni archivistici, 3 vols., 1997.

Andaloro, Maria, "Il mosaic di Solsterno," in Benazzi and Carbonara, eds., *La cattedrale di Spoleto*, pp. 213–19.

Andreani, Laura, "Regesti," in Benazzi and Carbonara, eds., *La cattedrale di Spoleto*, pp. 465–67, docs. nos. 85–174.

Andreatta, Emanuela, et al., eds., *Benozzo Gozzoli e l'architettura*, Florence: Edam, 2002.

Andreotti, A., et al., "The Wall Paintings of the Monumental Cemetery of Pisa: The War, the Restoration, the Conservation," in Antonio Sgamellotti et al., eds., *Science and Art: The Painted Surface*, Cambridge: Royal Society of Chemistry, 2014, pp. 193–209.

Angeli, Fabrizio Alessio, and Elisabetta Berti, *Abbazia delle Tre Fontane*, Rome: Associazione Culturale Sesto Acuto, 2007.

Angelis, P. de, "Un frammento di sacra visita della diocese spoletina del 1465," *Archivio per la storia ecclesiastica dell'Umbria*, vol. 3, no. 1, 1916, pp. 440–50.

Antonelli, Giovanni, ed., *Statuti di Spoleto del 1296*, Florence: Olschki, 1962.

Arias, Paolo Enrico, Emilio Cristiani, and Emilio Gabba, *Camposanto Monumentale di Pisa: Le Antichità*, Pisa: Pacini Editore, 1977.

Ariès, Philippe, *The Hour of Our Death*, New York: Alfred A. Knopf, 1981.

Arnoldi, Francesco Negri, "L'attività romana di Giovanni Dalmata," in Maria Grazia Bernardini and Marco Bussagli, eds., *Il '400 a Roma: La rinascita delle arti da Donatello a Perugino*, Milan: Skira, vol. 1, pp. 41–47.

Auffarth, Christoph, "Paradise Now – but for the Wall Between: Some Remarks on Paradise in the Middle Ages," in Gerard Luttikhuizen, ed., *Paradise Interpreted; Representations of Biblical Paradise in Judaism and Christianity*, Boston: Brill, 1999, pp. 168–79.

Aujoulat, Norbert, *Lascaux: Movement, Space, and Time*, New York: Abrams, 2005.

Azzolini, Monica, and Isabella Lazzarini, eds., *Italian Renaissance Diplomacy: A Sourcebook*, Durham: Institute of Medieval and Early Modern Studies, 2017.

Bacci, Michele, *Pro remedio animae: Immagini sacre e pratiche devozionali in Italia centrale*, Pisa: Edizioni ETS, 2000.

Bacci, Michele, et al., eds., *Journeys of the Soul; Multiple Topographies in the Camposanto of Pisa*, Pisa: Edizioni della Normale, 2020.

Baert, Barbara, *A Heritage of Holy Wood: The Legend of the True Cross in Text and Image*, trans. Lee Preddy, Leiden: Brill, 2004.

Bailo, Marina, et al., *Viaggiatori stranieri a Pisa dal '500 al '900*, Pisa: Nistri Lichi, 2003.

Bandini, Fabrizio, "A Comparison of Agnolo Gaddi's painting technique in the fresco cycle of the Cappella Maggiore with Cennino Cennini's Il libro dell'arte," in Frosinini, ed., *Agnolo Gaddi and the Cappella Maggiore in Santa Croce in Florence*, pp. 271–82.

Banti, Ottavio, *Jacopo D'Appiano. Economia, società e politica del Comune di Pisa al suo tramonto (1392–1399)*, Livorno: Il Telegrafo, 1971.

Banti, Ottavio, *Le iscrizioni delle tombe terragne del Camposanto di Pisa*, Pontedera: Bandecchi and Vivaldi, 1998.

Banti, Ottavio, "A proposito del 'Iohanne magistro edificante' 'architetto' del Campo Santo di Pisa," *Critica d'arte*, 8th ser, vol. 75, nos. 53–54, 2013 [2015], pp. 101–8.

Banti, Ottavio, "Le iscrizioni della cattedrale," in Garzella et al., eds., *La Cattedrale di Pisa*, pp. 111–19.

Baracchini, Clara, and Enrico Castelnuovo, eds., *Il Camposanto di Pisa*, Turin: Eiunadi, 1996.

Barolsky, Paul, "The Visionary Experience of Renaissance Art," *Word and Image*, vol. 11, 1995, pp. 174–81.

Bartlett, Robert, *Why Can the Dead Do Such Great Things? Saints and Worshippers from the Martyrs to the Reformation*, Princeton: Princeton University Press, 2013.

Battistoni, Marta, "Antonio di Jacopo dalle Mura, orafo e operaio del Duomo di Pisa, 1461–1488," *Bollettino storico pisano*, vol. 63, 1994, pp. 131–48.

Battistoni, Marta, *L'Opera del Duomo di Pisa: Il patrimonio e la sua gestione nei secoli XII–XVI*, Pisa: Pacini Editore, 2013.

Baxandall, Michael, *Giotto and the Orators*, Oxford: Clarendon Press, 1971.

Baxandall, Michael, *Painting and Experience in Fifteenth-Century Italy*, 2nd ed., Oxford: Oxford University Press, 1988.

Becherucci, Luisa, and Giulia Brunetti, *Il Museo dell'Opera del Duomo di Firenze*, 2 vols., Milan: Electa, 1971.

Belting, Hans, *Die Oberkirche von San Francesco in Assisi: Ihre Dekoration als Aufgabe die Genese einer neuen Wandmalerei*, Berlin: 1977.

Belting, Hans, "The New Role of Narrative in Public Painting of the Trecento: *Historia* and Allegory," in H. Kessler et al., eds., *Pictorial Narrative in Antiquity and the Middle Ages*, Washington, DC: National Gallery of Art, 1985, p. 151–70.

Belting, Hans, "Remarks on Communal Paintings in Siena and Pisa," *Studia artium orientalis et occidentalis*, vol. 2, 1985, pp. 11–16.

Belting, Hans, "Icons and Roman Society in the Twelfth Century," in Tronzo, ed., *Italian Church Decoration of the Middle Ages and the Early Renaissance*, pp. 27–41.

Belting, Hans, "Das Bild als Text: Wandmalerei und Literatur im Zeitalter Dantes," in Belting and Blume, eds., *Malerei und Stadtkultur in der Dantezeit*, pp. 23–64.

Belting, Hans, *The Image and Its Public in the Middle Ages: Form and Function of Early Paintings of the Passion*, trans. Mark Bartusis and Raymond Meyer, New Rochelle, NY: A. D. Caratzas, 1990.

Belting, Hans, *Likeness and Presence; A History of the Image before the Era of Art*, trans. Edmund Jephcott, Chicago: University of Chicago Press, 1994.

Belting, Hans, and Dieter Blume, eds., *Malerei und Stadtkultur in der Danbtezeit: Die Argumentation der Bilder*, Munich: Hirmer Verlag, 1989.

Benassi, Paolo, and Marco Ciatti, et al., eds., *Officina Pratese: Tecnica, Stile, Storia*, Florence: Edifir, 2014.

Benazzi, Giordana, "Le storie della Vergine," *Art e dossier*, no. 51, 1990, pp. 16–23.

Benazzi, Giordana, "Le 'storie della Vergine' di Filippo Lippi nel Duomo di Spoleto. Alcune considerazioni dopo il restauro," in Cristina Acidini Luchinat et al., eds., *Scritti per l'Istituto Germanico di Storia dell'Arte di Firenze*, Florence: Casa editrice Le Lettere, 1997, pp. 125–32.

Benazzi, Giordana, "Le storie della Vergine di Filippo Lippi," in Benazzi and Carbonara, eds., *La cattedrale di Spoleto*, pp. 261–77.

Benazzi, Giordana, "Filippo Lipi a Spoleto. Tempi, costi, materiali e collaboratori," in Benassi et al., eds., *Officina Pratese: Tecnica, Stile, Storia*, pp. 77–92.

Benazzi, Giordana, and Giovanni Carbonara, eds., *La cattedrale di Spoleto*, Milan: Federico Motta Editore, 2002.

Benazzi, Giordana, and E. Lunghi, eds., *Pierantonio Mezzastris: Pittore a Foligno nella seconda metà del Quattrocento*, Foligno: Edizioni Orfini Numeister, 2006.

Benazzi, Giordana, and Paolo Virilli, *Filippo Lippi nel Duomo di Spoleto 1467–1469; Notizie dopo il restauro*, Spoleto: Panetto & Petrelli, 1992.

Bent, George, *Public Painting and Visual Culture in Early Republican Florence*, Cambridge: Cambridge University Press, 2016.

Bernacchioni, Annamaria, "Family Alliances, Merchant Companies: The Alberti, Agnolo Gaddi and the Cappella Maggiore of Santa Croce," in Frosinini, ed., *Agnolo Gaddi and the Cappella Maggiore in Santa Croce*, pp. 35–45.

Berrtelli, Carlo, "L'Enciclopedia delle Tre Fontane," in *Paragone*, vol. 20, no. 235, 1969, pp. 24–49.

Berti, Marcello, "The Pisa Company: A Difficult Political Context," in Nigro, ed., *Francesco di Marco Datini*, pp. 281–320.

Besserman, Lawrence, *The Legend of Job in the Middle Ages*, Cambridge, MA: Harvard University Press, 1979.

Beyer, Andreas, and Bruce Boucher, eds., *Piero de' Medici 'il Gottoso,'* Berlin: Akademie Verlag, 1993.

Bianchini, Giuseppe, *Notizie istoriche della sacratissima cintola*, Prato: Vestri, 1822.

Binski, Paul, *Medieval Death: Ritual and Representation*, Ithaca: Cornell University Press, 1996.

Bisori, Guido, "Gli ordinamenti di un comune toscano nei primi del 1500," *Archivio storico pratese*, vol. 5, 1925, pp. 104–26.

Bisticci, Vespasiano da, *Le vite*, ed. Aulo Greco, Florence: Istituto Nazionale di studi sul rinascimento, 1970.

Bizzocchi, Roberto, "Politica fiscale e immunità ecclesiastica nella Toscana medicea fra Repubblica e Granducato," in Hermann Kellenbenz et al., eds., *Fisco religione stato nell'età confessionale, Annali dell'Istituto storico italo-germanico*, Bologna: Il Mulino, 1989, vol. 26, pp. 355–85.

Bizzocchi, Roberto, "Vescovi e potere politico nello stato regionale fiorentino fra quattrocento e primo cinquecento," in Giuseppina de Sandre Gasparini et al., eds., *Vescovi e diocese in Italia dal XIV alla metà del XVI secolo*, Rome: Herder, 1990, vol. 2, pp. 957–64.

Black, Robert, "Cosimo de' Medici and Arezzo," in Ames-Lewis, ed., *Cosimo 'il Vecchio' de' Medici*, pp. 33–47.

Black, Robert, ed., *Studio e scuola in Arezzo durante il medioevo e il rinascimento: I documenti d'archivio fino al 1530*, Arezzo: Accademia Petrarca di lettere, arti e scienze, 1996.

Black, Robert, "Education and the Emergence of a Literate Society," in John Najemy, ed.,

Italy in the Age of the Renaissance, 1300–1550, Oxford: Oxford University Press, 2004, pp. 18–36.

Bloch, Amy, *Lorenzo Ghiberti's Gates of Paradise: Humanism, History and Artistic Philosophy in the Italian Renaissance*, Cambridge: Cambridge University Press, 2016.

Blume, Dieter, *Wandmalerei als Ordenspropaganda: Bildprogramme in Chorbereich franziskanischer Konvente Italiens bis zur Mitte des 14. Jahrhunderts*, Worms: Werner'sche Verlagsgeschellschaft, 1983.

Boccaccio, Giovanni, *The Decameron*, trans. Richard Aldington, New York: Garden City, 1930.

Bodner, Neta B., "The Baptistery of Pisa and the Rotunda of the Holy Sepulchre: A Reconsideration," in Bianca Kühnel, et al., eds., *Visual Constructs of Jerusalem*, Turnhout: Brepols, 2014, pp. 95–105.

Bodner, Neta B., "Earth from Jerusalem in the Pisan Camposanto," in Renana Bartal et al., eds., *Between Jerusalem and Europe: Essays in Honour of Bianca Kühnel*, Leiden: Brill, 2015, pp. 74–93.

Bolli, Guerriero, *L'abbazia di San Cassiano nel monastero narnese di Belisario*, Terni: Diocesi di Terni-Narni-Amelia, 2010.

Bolzoni, Lina, "La predica dipinta: Gli affreschi del 'Trionfo della Morte' e la predicazione domenicana," in Baracchini and Castelnuovo, eds., *Il Camposanto di Pisa*, pp. 97–114.

Bolzoni, Lina, *The Web of Images: Vernacular Preaching from Its Origins to St. Bernardino da Siena*, trans. C. Preston and L. Chien, Aldershot: Ashgate, 2004.

Bonaini, Francesco, "Breve degli Anziani di Pisa," *Archivio storico italiano*, vol. 6, no. 2, 1845, pp. 635–812.

Bonaini, Francesco, "Memorie inedite intorno alla vita e ai dipinti di Francesco Traini e ad altre opere di disegno dei secoli XI, XIV e XV," *Annali delle università toscane*, vol. 1, part 1, 1846, p. 569.

Bonaini, Francesco, *Statuti inediti della Città di Pisa dal XII al XIV secolo*, Florence: G. P. Vieusseux, 1854.

Bonfioli, Mara, "Un importante restauro: L'icone del Duomo di Spoleto," *Spoletium*, vol. 24, no. 27, 1982, pp. 35–38.

Bonfioli, Mara, "L'Icona del Duomo di Spoleto: Nuovi contribute alla sua storia," *Spoletium*, vol. 33, 1988, pp. 17–25.

Bonfioli, Mara, "La reliquia della croce del Duomo di Spoleto," *Spoletium*, vols. 31/32, nos. 34–35, 1990, pp. 55–60.

Bonfioli, Mara, "La 'santissima icone,'" in Benazzi and Carbonara, eds., *La cattedrale di Spoleto*, pp. 185–87.

Bonfioli, Mara, "Per la storia dell'icona di Spoleto. Documenti," in Vittorio Casale et al., eds., *Scritti di archeologia e storia dell'arte in onore di Carlo Pietrangeli*, Rome: Edizione Quasar, 1996, pp. 237–42.

Bonfioli, Mara, "Qualche appunto sull'iscrizione metrica latina sotto il mosaico della facciata del Duomo di Spoleto," in *Temi e Metodi. Arte d'Occidente. Studi in onore di Angiola Maria Romanini*, Rome: Ed. Sintesi informazione, 1999, pp. 1001–11.

Bonfioli, Mara, and Elisabetta Ermini, "Premesse ad un riesame critico dell' 'icone' del Duomo di Spoleto, in *Atti del IX congresso internazionale di studi sull'alto medioevo*, Spoleto, 1983, pp. 821–36.

Borsi, Stefano, Francesco Quinterio, and Corinna Vasic Vatovec, *Maestri fiorentini nei cantieri romani del quattrocento*, Rome: Officina Edizioni, 1989.

Borsook, Eve, "Fra Filippo Lippi and the Murals for Prato Cathedral," *Mitteilungen des kunsthistorischen Institutes in Florenz*, vol. 19, 1975, pp. 1–148.

Borsook, Eve, *The Mural Painters of Tuscany*, 2nd ed., Oxford: Clarendon Press, 1980.

Boskovits, Miklós, *Pittura fiorentina alla vigilia del Rinascimento 1370–1400*, Florence: Edam, 1975.

Boskovits, Miklós, *The Painters of the Miniaturist Tendency*, in Offner, Steinweg et al., eds, *A Critical and Historical Corpus of Florentine Painting*, sec. 3, vol. 9, Florence: Giunti, 1984.

Boskovits, Miklós, *Gemäldegalerie Berlin, Frühe Italienische Malerei*, Berlin: Gebr. Mann, 1988.

Boskovits, Miklós, "La bottega del Beato Angelico tra Firenze e Roma, e la formazione di Benozzo Gozzoli," in Toscano and Capitelli, eds., *Benozzo Gozzoli, Allievo a Roma, maestro in Umbria*, pp. 133–41.

Botticelli, Guido, *Metodologia di restauro delle pitture muali*, Florence: Centro Di, 1992.

Bourdua, Louise, *The Franciscans and Art Patronage in late Medieval Italy*, Cambridge: Cambridge University Press, 2004.

Bozzoni, Corrado, and Giovanni Carbonara, "Il quattrocento e il cinquecento: Ulteriori sviluppi," in Benazzi and Carbonara, eds., *La cattedrale di Spoleto*, pp. 103–9.

Braudel, Fernand, Giovanni Cherubini, et al., eds., *Prato, Storia di una città*, 6 vols., Florence: Le Monnier, 1986–93.

Brenk, Beat, *The Apse, the Image and the Icon*, Wiesbaden: Reichert Verlag, 2010.

Brown, Alison, "Lorenzo de' Medici's New Men and Their Mores: The Changing Lifestyle of Quattrocento Florence," *Renaissance Studies*, vol. 16, no. 2, 2002, pp. 113–42.

Brown, Peter, *The Cult of the Saints: Its Rise and Function in Latin Christianity*, Chicago: University of Chicago Press, 1981,

Brucker, Gene, "The Medici in the Fourteenth Century," *Speculum*, vol. 32, 1957, pp. 1–26.

Brucker, Gene, "A Civic Debate on Florentine Higher Education (1460)," *Renaissance Quarterly*, vol. 34, 1981, pp. 517–33.

Bruni, Bruno, *La Rocca di Spoleto: Studi per la storia e la rinascita*, Milan: Silvana Editoriale, 1983.

Bullard, Melissa, "In Pursuit of Honore et Utile: Lorenzo de' Medici and Rome," in Gian Carlo Garfagnini, ed., *Lorenzo il Magnifico e il suo mondo*, Florence: Olschki, 1994, pp. 123–42.

Bullough, David, "Burial, Community and Belief in the Early Medieval West," in Patrick Wormald, ed., *Ideal and Reality in Frankish and Anglo-Saxon Society*, Oxford: Basil Blackwell, 1983, pp. 177–201.

Bulman, Louise, "Artistic Patronage at SS. Annunziata: 1440–1520," PhD dissertation, Courtauld Institute, 1971.

Burchard of Mount Sion, *A Description of the Holy Land*, trans. A. Stewart, London: Palestine Pilgrims' Text Society, 1896.

Burgalassi, Silvano, *San Ranieri attraverso nove secoli di storia pisana*, Pisa: Edizioni ETS, 2004.

Burnam, Reneé K., "Le vetrate del Duomo di Pisa," *Annali della Scuola Normale Superiore di Pisa*, serie iv, quaderno no. 13, 2002.

Burnam, Renée K., "The Lost Stained-Glass Windows of the Camposanto of Pisa and Fifteenth-Century Florentine Politics," in Molly Bourne and A. Victor Coonin, eds., *Encountering the Renaissance*, Ramsey, NJ: WAPACC Organization, 2016, pp. 327–38.

Burresi, Mariagiulia, and Antonio Caleca, *Affreschi medievali a Pisa*, Pisa: Pacini Editore, 2003.

Burroughs, Charles, *From Signs to Design: Environmental Process and Reform in Early Renaissance Rome*, Cambridge, MA: MIT Press, 1990.

Byrne, Joseph Patrick, "Francesco Datini, 'Father of Many,'" PhD dissertation, Indiana University, 1989.

Cadogan, Jean K., *Domenico Ghirlandaio: Artist and Artisan*, New Haven and London: Yale University Press, 2000.

Cadogan, Jean K., "The Chapel of the Holy Belt in Prato: Piety and Politics in Fourteenth Century Tuscany," *Artibus et Historiae*, vol. 60, 2009, pp. 107–38.

Cadogan, Jean K., "Agnolo Gaddi and His Family: A Florentine 'Success Story,'" *Zeitschrift für Kunstgeschichte*, LXXIV, 2011, pp. 153–76.

Cadogan, Jean K., "Agnolo Gaddi's Career and the Opera del Duomo in Florence," in Frosinini, ed., *Agnolo Gaddi and the Cappella Maggiore in Santa Croce in Florence*, pp. 55–71.

Cagianelli, Cristina, ed., *Il Palazzo dell'Arcivescovado*, Pisa: Edizioni ETS, 2021.

Caleca, Antonio, "Costruzione e decorazione dalle origini al secolo XV," in Baracchini and Castelnuovo, eds., *Il Camposanto di Pisa*, pp. 13–48.

Campbell, Stephen, ed., *Artists at Court: Image-Making and Identity, 1300–1550*, Boston: Isabella Stewart Gardner Museum, 2004.

Campbell, Stephen, *The Endless Periphery: Towards a Geopolitics of Art in Lorenzo Lotto's Italy*, Chicago: University of Chicago Press, 2019.

Canali, Ferruccio, "La 'domus sapientiae' di Pisa e Lorenzo il Magnifico: Novità tipologiche e stratificazioni d'ornato tra Leon Batista Alberti e Giuliano da Sangallo (1471–92)," in Daniele, ed., *Le dimore di Pisa*, pp. 83–90.

Cannon, Joanna, *Religious Povety, Visual Riches: Art in the Dominican Churches of Central Italy in the Thirteenth and Fourteenth Centuries*, New Haven and London: Yale University Press, 2013.

Capitelli, Giovanni, and Graziano Alfredo Vergani, eds., *Benozzo Gozzoli: A Growing Workshop*, Milan: Silvana Editoriale, 2003.

Cardella, Lorenzo, *Memorie storiche de' cardinali della Santa Romana Chiesa*, Rome: Stamperia Pagliarini, 1793.

Cardini, Franco, *In Terrasanta: Pellegrini italiani tra medioevo e prima età moderna*, Bologna: Il Mulino, 2002.

Cardini, Franco, "Identità cittadina, mariodulia e culto delle reliquie. Il 'caso' pratese," in Paola Maffei et al., eds., *"Honos alit artes": Studi per settantesimo compleanno di Mario Ascheri*, Florence, 2014, vol. 2, pp. 177–85.

Cardini, Franco, "San Ranieri a Gerusalemme tra pelegrinaggio e crociata," in Castelli and Ceccarelli Lemut, eds., *Intercessor Rainerius ad Patrem*, pp. 95–99.

Carl, Doris, "Il ritratto commemorativo di Giotto di Benedetto da Maiano nel Duomo di Firenze," in Margaret Haines, ed., *Santa Maria del Fiore. The Cathedral and Its Sculpture*, Fiesole: Cadmo, 2001, pp. 129–47.

Carl, Doris, *Benedetto da Maiano: A Florentine Sculptor at the Threshold of the High Renaissance*, 2 vols., Turnhout: Brepols, 2006.

Carl, Doris, "Zu Francione und den Brüdern da Sangallo. Ihre Partnerschaft im Licht neuer Dokumente," in A. Belluzzi et al., eds., *Giuliano da Sangallo*, Milan: Officina Libraria, 2017, pp. 169–85.

Carocci, Sandro, *Vassalli del papa: Potere pontificio, aristocrazie e città nello stato della chiesa (XII–XV secolo)*, Rome: Viella, 2010.

Carocci, Sandro, "The Papal State," in Andrea Gamberini and Isabella Lazzarini, eds., *The Italian Renaissance State*, Cambridge: Cambridge University Press, 2012, pp. 69–89.

Carratori Scolaro, Luigina, *Le visite pastorali della diocese di Pisa*, Pisa: Pacini Editore, 1996.

Carratori, Luigina, and Michele Luzzati, "'Forestieri' a Pisa nella second metà del Quattrocento," in Rinaldo Comba et al., eds., *Strutture familiari, epidemie, migrazione*, Pisa: Edizioni scientifiche italiane, 1984, pp. 389–400.

Carratori, Luigina, "Il Capitolo della cattedrale nelle vicende pisane della fine del Trecento e degli inizi del Quattrocento," *Bollettino storico pisano*, vol. 56, 1987, pp. 1–68.

Casagrande, Giovanna, *Religiosità penitenziale e città al tempo dei comuni*, Rome: Istituto Stoico dei Cappuccini, 1995.

Casalini, Eugenio, *Michelozzo di Bartolommeo e l'Annunziata di Firenze*, Florence: Convento della Santissima Annunziata, 1995.

Casalini, Eugenio, *Una icona di famiglia*, Florence: Convento della Santissima Annunziata, 1998.

Casini, Bruno, "I fuochi di Pisa e la prestanza del 1407," *Bollettino storico pisano*, ser. 3, vol. 27, 1958, pp. 156–272.

Casini, Bruno, "Contribuenti pisani alle taglie del 1402 e 1412," *Bollettino storico pisano*, ser. 3, vols. 28–29, 1959–60, pp. 90–318.

Casini, Bruno, *Il Catasto di Pisa nel 1428–29*, Pisa: Giardini, 1964.

Casini, Bruno, *Aspetti della vita economica e sociale di Pisa dal catasto del 1428–29*, Pisa: S.E.I.T., 1965.

Casotti, Count Giuseppe Maria, "Lunario istorico pratese del Conte Giuseppe Maria Casotti," ed. Ruggero Nuti, *Archivio storico pratese*, vol. 8, no. 4, 1929, pp. 158–78; vol. 9, no. 1, 1930, pp. 16–24; no. 2, pp. 64–71; vol. 9, no. 3, 1931, pp. 124–35; no. 4, pp. 170–80; vol. 10, no. 1, 1931, pp. 17–29; no. 2, 1932, pp. 61–69; no. 3, pp. 107–22; no. 4, pp. 163–72; vol. 11, no. 1, 1933, pp. 26–30; no. 2, pp. 89–94; no. 3, pp. 121–29.

Cassandro, Michele, "Commercio, manifatture e industria," in Braudel et al., eds., *Prato, storia di una città*, vol. 1, part 1, pp. 396–462.

Cassidy, Brendan, "The Assumption of the Virgin on the Tabernacle of Orsanmichele," *Journal of the Warburg and Courtauld Institutes*, vol. 51, 1988, pp. 174–80.

Cassidy, Brendan, "Artists and Diplomacy in Late Medieval Tuscany: The Case of Giotto, Simone Martini, Andrea Pisano, and Others," *Gesta*, vol. 51, 2012, pp. 91–110.

Cassuto, Umberto, *Gli ebrei a Firenze nell'età del Rinascimento*, Florence: Galletti and Cocci, 1918.

Castelli, Patrizia, and Maria Luisa Ceccarelli Lemut, eds., *Intercessor Rainerius ad Patrem: Il santo di una città marinara del XII secolo*, Pisa: Pacini Editore, 2011.

Castelli, Patrizia, and Maria Luisa Ceccarelli Lemut, eds., *L'invenzione di Ranieri il taumaturgo tra XII e XIV secolo: agiografia ed immagini*, Pisa: Pacini Editore, 2013.

Castelli, Patrizia, "Ranieri da cantore a santo taumaturgo: agiografia e immagini di propaganda civica e religiosa nella città di Pisa (secoli XII–XIV)," in Castelli and Ceccarelli Lemut, eds., *L''invenzione' di Ranieri il taumaturgo tra XII e XIV secolo: agiografia ed immagini*, pp. 57–72.

Castiglione, Roberto, "Pisa e l'Opera di Santa Maria del Fiore di Firenze: I rapporti fiscali dal 1416 al 1430," *Bollettino Storico Pisano*, vol. 81, 2012, pp. 1–25.

Cavaciocchi, Simonetta, "Francesco Datini and the Painters," in Nigro, ed., *Francesco di Marco Datini*, pp. 217–34.

Cavalca, Domenico, *Volgarizzamento delle vite de' Santi Padri*, 6 vols., 2nd ed., Milan: Tipografia di Gio. Silvestri, 1853–54.

Cavalca, Domenico, *Le Vite de' S.S. Padri*, ed. Carmelina Naselli, Turin: Unione Tipografico-Editrice Torinese, 1926.

Cavallaro, Anna, "Benozzo Gozzoli e Antoniazzo Romano nel Lazio Meridionale," in Anna Cavallaro and Stefano Petrocchi, eds., *La pittura del quattrocento nei feudi caetani*, Rome: Edizioni di Storia e Letteratura, 2013, pp. 269–90.

Cavallaro, Anna, and Stefano Petrocchi, eds., *Antoniazzo Romano Pictor Urbis*, Milan: Silvana Editoriale, 2013.

Cavallaro, Anna, and Stefano Petrocchi, eds., *La pittura del quattrocento nei feudi caetani*, Rome: Edizioni di Storia e Letteratura, 2013.

Ceccarelli Lemut, Maria Luisa, "La città e i santi: Pisa tra XII e XIII secolo," in Castelli and Ceccarelli Lemut, eds., *Intercessor Rainerius ad Patrem*, pp. 33–52.

Cennini, Cennino, *Il libro dell'arte*, ed. Fabio Frezzato, Vicenza: Neri Pozza Editore, 2003.

Cennini, Cennino, *Il libro dell'arte*, ed. and trans. Lara Broecke, London: Archetype, 2015.

Ceriana, Matteo, "Il portico rinascimentale e l'opera di Ambrogio Barocci a Spoleto," in Benazzi and Carbonara, eds., *La cattedrale di Spoleto*, pp. 289–303.

Cerretelli, Claudio, "La piazza ed il palazzo del comune dal XIII agli inizi del XIV secolo," *Prato, storia e arte*, vol. 77, 1990, pp. 7–44.

Cerretelli, Claudio, "La Pieve e la Cintola: Le trasformazioni legate alla reliquia," in Martini, ed., *La Sacra Cintola nel Duomo di Prato*, pp. 89–162.

Cerretelli, Claudio, "La Madonna della Cintola a Prato," in Paolucci, ed., *Colloqui davanti alla Madre: Immagini mariane in Toscana tra arte, storia e devozione*, Florence: Mandragora, 2004, pp. 81–90.

Cerretelli, Claudio, "Tre cappelle per la sacra Cintura," in Lapi Ballerini, ed., *Agnolo Gaddi e la Cappella della Cintola*, pp. 63–73.

Cerretelli, Claudio, "L'architettura della chiesa," in Cerretelli, Fantappiè, et al., eds., *Il Duomo di Prato*, pp. 57–145.

Cerretelli, Claudio, "Bettino, la cintola, e la prima veduta del Duomo di Prato," *Prato, storia e arte*, vol. 121, June 2017, pp. 17–31.

Cerretelli, Claudio, "La sacra cintola e il suo scrigno: La pieve di santo Stefano dal XII alla fine del XIV secolo," in De Marchi and Mavarelli, eds., *Legati da una cintola*, pp. 40–57.

Cerretelli, Claudio, Renzo Fantappiè, et al., eds., *Il Duomo di Prato*, Florence: Le Lettere, 2009.

Chambers, David S., "Cardinal Francesco Gonzaga in Florence," in Peter Denley et al., eds., *Florence and Italy: Renaissance Studies in Honour of Nicolai Rubinstein*, London: Committee for Medieval Studies, 1988, pp. 241–61.

Chambers, David S., "A Cardinal in Rome," in Robert Black and John Law, eds., *The Medici: Citizens and Masters*, Cambridge: Villa I Tatti, 2015, pp. 205–17.

Chareyron, Nicole, *Pilgrims to Jerusalem in the Middle Ages*, trans. W. Donald Wilson, New York: Columbia University Press, 2005.

Cherny, Robert *Victor Arnautoff and the Politics of Art*, Urbana: University of Illinois Press, 2017.

Chiodo, Sonia, "*Painters in Florence after the 'Black Death': The Master of the Misericordia and Matteo di Pacino*," in Offner, Steinweg, et al., eds., *A Critical and Historical Corpus of Florentine Painting*, sec. 4, vol. 9, Florence: Giunti, 2011.

Chiodo, Sonia "Comparative Analysis and Historical Context," in Frosinini, ed., *Agnolo Gaddi and the Cappella Maggiore in Santa Croce in Florence*, pp. 73–83.

Chittolini, Giorgio, *La formazione dello stato regionale e le istituzioni del contado*, Turin: Einaudi, 1979.

Ciaconius, Alphonso [Alphonso Chacón], *Vitae et res gestae pontificum Romanorum et S.R.E. cardinalium ab initio nascentis Ecclesiæ usque ad Urbanum VIII. Pont. Max*, 4 vols., Rome: De Rubeis, 1677.

Ciappelli, Giovanni, and Patricia Rubin, eds., *Art, Memory, and Family in Renaissance Florence*, Cambridge: Cambridge University Press, 2000.

Ciardi, Roberto Paolo, "Il Quattrocento," in Claudio Casini et al., eds., *Scultura a Pisa tra Quattro e Seicento*, Pisa: Cantini, 1987, pp. 12–110.

Ciardi, Roberto Paolo, "'Ars marmoris': Aspetti dell'organizzazione del lavoro nella Toscana ocidentale durante il Quattrocento," in Enrico Castelnuovo, ed., *Niveo de marmore*, Genoa: Colombo, 1992, pp. 341–49.

Ciardi, Roberto Paolo, "'Quest'insigne dormentorio de' morti': Chiesa, cimitero, museo," in Baracchini and Castelnuovo, eds., *Il Camposanto di Pisa*, pp. 57–68.

Ciatti, Marco, "Gli affreschi della Cappella della Cintola," in Martini, ed., *La Sacra Cintola nel Duomo di Prato*, pp. 177–92.

Ciccaglioni, Giovanni, "Patrimonio culturale e formazione territoriale nella Toscana fiorentina: Il caso pisano," in Denise La Monica et al., eds., *Municipalia. Storia della Tutela: Patrimonio artistico e identità cittadina: Pisa e Forlì (sec. XIV–XVIII)*, Pisa: Edizioni ETS, 2010, vol. 1, pp. 91–100.

Cipollaro, Costanza, *Agnolo Gaddi e la leggenda di Santa Croce: La cappella maggiore e la sua decorazione pittorica*, Foligno: Cartei & Bianchi, 2009.

Cirulli, Beatrice, "Note sulla cappella Albertoni all'Aracoeli a Roma e la Vergine in Gloria della collegiate dell'Assunta a Sermoneta (1456–58)," in Toscano and Capitelli, eds., *Benozzo Gozzoli, Allievo a Roma, maestro in Umbria*, pp. 230–37.

Clarke, Georgia, *Roman House – Renaissance Palaces: Inventing Antiquity in Fifteenth-Century Italy*, Cambridge: Cambridge University Press, 2003.

Clarke, Georgia, and Fabrizio Nevola, eds., "The Experience of the Street in Early Modern Italy," *I Tatti Studies in the Italian Renaissance*, vol. 16, nos. 1/2, September 2013, pp. 47–55.

Clarke, Paula, *The Soderini and the Medici: Power and Patronage in Fifteenth Century Florence*, Oxford: Oxford University Press, 1991.

Clayton, Mary, *Cult of the Virgin Mary in Anglo-Saxon England*, Cambridge: Cambridge University Press, 1990.

Coden, Fabio, "Sguardo d'insieme all'architettura umbra del Duecento," in Enrico Menestò, ed., *L'Umbria nel XIII secolo*, Spoleto: CISAM, 2011, pp. 333–420.

Cohn, Samuel K., Jr., *The Cult of Remembrance and the Black Death*, Baltimore: Johns Hopkins University Press, 1992.

Cohn, Samuel K., Jr. "Collective Amnesia: Family, Memory and the Mendicants," in Ciappelli and Rubin, eds., *Art, Memory and Family*, pp. 277–80.

Cole, Bruce, "The Interior Decoration of the Palazzo Datini in Prato," *Mitteilungen des Kunsthistorischen Institutes in Florenz*, vol. 13, 1967, pp. 61–82.

Cole, Bruce, *Agnolo Gaddi*, Oxford: Oxford University Press, 1977.

Collareta, Marco, "Le vetrate," in Gabriella Garzella et al., eds., *La Cattedrale di Pisa*, Pisa: Pacini Editore, 2014, pp. 211–17.

Colvin, Howard, *Architecture and the After-Life*, New Haven and London: Yale University Press, 1991.

Connell, William, and Andrea Zorzi, eds., *Florentine Tuscany: Structures and Practices of Power*, Cambridge: Cambridge University Press, 2000.

Convenevole da Prato, *Regia Carmina*, ed. and trans. Cesare Grassi, Milan: Silvano, 1982.

Cooper, Donal, "Redefining the Altarpiece in Early Renaissance Italy: Giotto's 'Stigmatization of Saint Francis' and Its Pisan Context," *Art History*, vol 36, 2013, pp. 686–713.

Cooper, Donal, and Janet Robson, *The Making of Assisi*, New Haven and London: Yale University Press, 2013.

Cordella, Romano, "Un opera inedita di Giovanni Dalmata a Norcia," in *Acta Historiae Artium Academiae Scientiarum Hungaricae*, vol. 27, 1981, pp. 233–46.

Cordella, Romano, "Aggiunta all'articolo 'Un opera inedita di Giovanni Dalmata,'" *Acta Historiae Artium Academiae Scientiarum Hungaricae*, vol. 28, 1982, pp. 265–66.

Costa, Berta, "Amministrazione di Pisa e aspetti della vita pisana al tempo di Lorenzo il Magnifico," PhD dissertation, University of Pisa, 1950–51.

Crabb, Ann, *The Merchant of Prato's Wife: Margherita Datini and Her World, (1360–1423)*, Ann Arbor: University of Michigan Press, 2015.

Cristiani, Emilio, *Nobilità e popolo nel comune di Pisa*, Naples: Istituto italiano per gli studi storici, 1962.

Crociani, Lamberto, "Culto mariano in Santa Maria del Fiore," in Timothy Verdon and Annalisa Innocenti, eds., *La cattedrale e la città: Saggi sul Duomo di Firenze*, Florence: Edifir, 2001, vol. 1, part 1, pp. 431–39.

Czarnecki, James, "Antonio Veneziano: A Florentine Painter of the Late Trecento," PhD dissertation, Indiana University, 1978.

Da Morrona, Alessandro, *Pisa illustrata nelle arti del disegno*, vol. 1, Pisa: Francesco Pieraccini, 1787.

Daniele, Emilia, ed., *Le dimore di Pisa: L'arte di abitare; i palazzi di una antica repubblica marinara dal medioevo all'unità d'Italia*, Pisa: Alinea Editrice, 2010.

Dante Alighieri, *The Divine Comedy*, trans. Geoffrey Bickersteth, Oxford: Basil Blackwell, 1981.

Danti, Cristina, ed., *La Trinità di Masaccio: Il restauro dell'anno duemila*, Florence: Edifir, 2002.

Dati, Goro, *L'Istoria di Firenze dal 1380 al 1405*, ed. L. Pratesi, Norcia: Tonti, 1904.

Davies, Jonathan, *Florence and Its University during the Early Renaissance*, Leiden: Brill, 1998.

Davies, Paul, "The Lighting of Pilgrimage Shrines in Renaissance Italy," in Thunø and Wolf, eds., *The Miraculous Image in the Late Middle Ages and Renaissance*, pp. 57–80.

Davis-Weyer, Caecilia, *Early Medieval Art 300–1150; Sources and Documents*, Toronto: University of Toronto Press, 1986.

DeLancey, Julia A., "Shipping Colour: *Valute*, Pigments, Trade and Francesco di Marco Datini," in Jo Kirby, et al., eds., *Trade in Artists' Materials: Markets and Commerce in Europe to 1700*, London: Archetype Publications, 2010, pp. 74–85.

Desjardins, Abel, "Mémoire sur la politique extérieure de Louis XI et sur ses rapports avec l'Italie," *Mémoires présentés par divers savants à l'Académie des inscriptions et belles-lettres de L'Institut de France*, 1st series, vol. 8, part 2, 1874, pp. 1–36.

Desjardins, Abel, and Giuseppe Canestrini, *Négociations diplomatiques de la France avec la Toscane*, vol. 1, Paris: Impr. Impériale, 1859.

Diedrichs, Christof, "Wahrnehmung des mittelalterlichen Kirchenraums," in Christina Lechtermann and Carsten Morsch, eds., *Kunst der Bewegung: Kinästhetische Wahrnehmung und Probehandeln in virtuellen Welten*, Bern: Lang, 2004, pp. 267–84.

Dizionario biografico degli italiani, 98 vols., Rome: Istituto della Enciclopedia Italiana, 1960–2020.

Dodge, Barbara Kathryn, "Tradition, Innovation, and Technique in Trecento Mural Painting: The Frescoes and Sinopie attributed to Francesco Traini in the Camposanto in Pisa," PhD dissertation, Johns Hopkins University, 1977.

Dolfi, Waldo, *Vescovi e Arcivescovi di Pisa: I loro stemmi e il palazzo*, 2 vols., Pisa: Opera della Primaziale Pisana, 2000.

Donati, Fulvia, "Storia della Collezione; Raccolta delle opera antiche," in Salvatore Settis, ed., *Camposanto Monumentale di Pisa: Le Antichità*, vol. 2, Modena: Edizioni Panini, 1984, pp. 12.

Donati, Fulvia, "Il reimpiego dei sarcofagi; profilo di una collezione," in Baracchini and Castelnuovo, eds., *Il Camposanto di Pisa*, pp. 69–96.

Donati, Fulvia, and M. Cecilia Parra, "Pisa e il reimpiego 'laico': La nobilità di sangue e d'ingegno, e la potenza economica," in Bernard Andreae and Salvatore Settis, eds., *Colloquio sul reimpiego dei sarcofagi romani nel medioevo*, Marburg: Verlag des Kunstgeschichtlichen Seminars, 1984, pp. 103–32.

Draper, James David, *Bertoldo di Giovanni, Sculptor of the Medici Household*, Columbia: University of Missouri Press, 1992.

Dunford, Penelope, "Iconografia della Dormizione e dell'Assunzione della Vergine Maria nell'arte rinascimentale italiana," *Arte Cristiana*, 63, 1975, pp. 284–98.

Durandus, Guillelmus, *Rationale Divinorum Officiorum* [1284], ed. A. Davril and T. M. Thibodeau, 2 vols. Turnout: Brepols, 1995–98; trans. Timothy Thibodeau, *The Rationale Divinorum Officiorum of William Durand of Mende*, book 1, New York: Columbia University Press, 2007; books 2–3 Scranton: University of Scranton Press, 2010; books 4–5 Turnhout: Brepols, 2013–15; trans Janet Gentles, 6 vols., Bedford: Paschal Light, 2019; French translation, with commentary, in *Rational ou Manuel des Divins Offices de Guillaume Durand*, trans. Charles Barthélemy, 5 vols., Paris: Louis Vivès, 1854; Italian translation of the first book in *Manuale per comprendere il significato simbolico delle cattedrali e delle chiese*, trans. Rosanna Campagnari, Rome: Edizioni Arkeios, 2000.

Echols, Mary, "The Coronation of the Virgin in Fifteenth Century Italian Art," PhD dissertation, University of Virginia, 1976.

Egidi, Pietro, ed., *Necrologi e libri affini della provincia romana*, Rome: Forzani, vol. 1, 1908; vol. 2, 1914.

Elam, Caroline, "Art and Diplomacy in Renaissance Florence," *RSA Journal*, Vol. 136, 1988, pp. 813–26.

Elliot, Alison Goddard, *Roads to Paradise: Reading the Lives of the Early Saints*, Hanover: University Press of New England, 1987.

Eroli, Giovanni, *Notizie de' vescovi Eroli estratte dalle vite de' Narnesi illustri*, Terni: Polsenli, 1852.

Eroli, Giovanni, *La Coronazione di Maria Vergine del Ghirlandaio e la Madonna del Libro di Raffaello*, Narni, 1880.

Eroli, Giovanni, *Descrizione delle chiese di Narni e suoi dintorni*, Narni: Petrignani, 1898.

Eubel, Conradus *Hierarchia Catholica Medii Aevi*, vol. 2 (1431–1503), Monasterii: Sumptibus et Typis Librariae Regensbergianae, 1950.

Even, Yael, "Paolo Uccello's John Hawkwood: Reflections of a Collaboration between Agnolo Gaddi and Giuliano Pesello," *Source: Notes in the History of Art*, vol. 4, 1985, pp. 6–8.

Fantappiè, Renzo "Nascita e sviluppo di Prato," in Braudel et al., eds., *Prato, storia di una città*, vol. 1, part 1, 1991, pp. 79–299.

Fantappiè, Renzo, "Storia e 'storie' della Cintola," in Claudio Martini, ed., *La Sacra Cintola nel Duomo di Prato*, Prato: Claudio Martini, 1995, pp. 41–60.

Fantappiè, Renzo, "Da pieve a cattedrale," in Cerretelli, Fantappié, et al., eds., *Il Duomo di Prato*, pp. 16–25.

Fantappiè, Renzo, "Per la storia del Sacro Cingolo," *Archivio storico pratese*, vol. 87, 2011 [2013], pp. 133–77.

Fanucci, Miria, Michele Luzzati, and Lionel Lovitch, *L'estimo di Pisa nell'anno del Concilio (1409)*, Pisa: Pacini Editore, 1986.

Farnedi, Giustino, et al., *Monasteri benedettini in Umbria: Alle radici del paesaggio umbro*, Cesena: Centro Storico Benedettino Italiano, 2014.

Fausti, Luigi, "Il portico del Duomo di Spoleto; nuovi documenti," *Bollettino della regia deputazione di storia patria per l'Umbria*, vol. 22, 1917, pp. 339–44.

Fausti, Luigi, "Le pitture di Fra Filipo Lippi nel Duomo di Spoleto," *Archivio per la storia ecclesiastica dell'Umbria*, 3, 1915, pp. 1–36.

Felici, Alberto, "The Scaffolding for the Frescoes of the Cappella Maggiore," in Frosinini, ed., *Agnolo Gaddi and the Cappella Maggiore in Santa Croce in Florence*, pp. 203–15.

Feliciantonio, Vitorio di, "Palazzo Vecchio de' Medici," in Karwacka Codini, ed., *Architettura a Pisa nel primo periodo mediceo*, pp. 162–65.

Fengler, Christie Knapp, "Bartolo di Fredi's Frescoes in San Gimignano," *Art Bulletin*, vol. 63, 1981, pp. 374–84.

Fernedi, Giustino, and Nadia Togni, *Monasteri Benedettini in Umbria*, Cesena: Centro Storico Benedettino Italiano, 2014.

Fioravanti, Gianfranco, "Il convento e lo Studium domenicano di Santa Caterina," in Lucia Battaglia Ricci et al., eds., *Pisa crocevia di uomini, lingue e culture: L'età medievale*, Rome: ARACNE, 2009, pp. 81–95.

Fiumi, Enrico *Demografia movimento urbanistico e classi sociali in Prato*, Florence: Olschki, 1968.

Florio, John, *Queen Anna's World of Words*, London: Melch. Bradwood, 1611.

Folda, Jaroslav, "Jerusalem and the Holy Sepulchre through the Eyes of Crusader Pilgrims," in Kühnel, ed., *The Real and Ideal Jerusalem in Jewish, Christian and Islamic Art*, pp. 158–64.

Foster, Philip, "A Study of Lorenzo de' Medici's Villa at Poggio a Caiano," PhD dissertation, Yale University, 1974.

Foster, Susanna, "The Ties That Bind: Kinship Association and Marriage in the Alberti Family 1378–1428," PhD dissertation, Cornell University, 1985.

Fra Mariano da Firenze, *Itinerarium Urbis Romae*, ed. Enrico Bulletti, Rome: Pontificio istituto di archeologia cristiana, 1931.

Franceschi, Franco, and Gloria Fossi, eds., *La grande storia dell'Artigianato*, vols. 1–3, Florence: Giunti, 1998–2000)

Frati, Marco, "La piazza del Duomo di Pisa. Un millennio di miracoli," in Garzella et al., eds., *La Cattedrale di Pisa*, pp. 47–59.

Freedberg, David, *The Power of Images, Studies in the History and Theory of Response*, Chicago: University of Chicago Press, 1989.

Freuler, Gaudenz, *Bartolo dei Fredi Cini*, Disentis: Desertina Verlag, 1994.

Frey, Carl, *Die Loggia dei Lanzi zu Florenz*, Berlin: Hertz, 1885.

Friedman, David, *Florentine New Towns: Urban Design in the Late Middle Ages*, Cambridge, MA: MIT Press, 1988.

Frommel, Christoph Luitpold, "Francesco del Borgo," *Römisches Jahrbuch für Kunstgeschichte*, vol. 21, 1984, pp. 71–164.

Frommel, Christoph Luitpold, *Architettura e committenza da Alberti a Bramante*, Florence: Olschki, 2006.

Frommel, Sabine, and Gerhard Wolf, *Architectura Picta nell'arte italiana da Giotto a Veronese*, Modena: Franco Cosimo Panini, 2016.

Frosinini, Cecilia, ed., *Agnolo Gaddi and the Cappella Maggiore in Santa Croce in Florence: Studies after Its Restoration*, Milan: Silvana Editoriale, 2014.

Frosinini, Cecilia, ed., *Progetto Giotto: Tecnica artistica e stato di conservazione delle pitture murali nelle cappelle Peruzzi e Bardi a Santa Croce*, Florence: Edifir, 2016–17.

Frosinini, Cecilia, and Roberto Bellucci, "'Di greco in latino.' Considerazioni sull'underdrawing di Giotto, come modello mentale," in Marco Ciatti, ed., *L'officina di Giotto. Il restauro della Croce di Ognissanti*, Florence; Edifir, 2010, pp. 167–77.

Frugoni, Chiara, "Altri luoghi, cercandi il paradiso," *Annali della Scuola Normale Superiore di Pisa*, Classe di Lettere e Filosofia, 3. Ser. vol. 18, 1988, pp. 1557–643

Frugoni, Chiara, *A Distant City*, trans. W. McCuaig, Princeton: Princeton University Press, 1991.

Fubini, Riccardo, ed., *La toscana al tempo di Lorenzo il Magnifico*, vol. 3, Pisa: Pacini Editore, 1996.

Fujikawa, Mayu, "Florence's Territorial Hegemony in the Eyes of Foreign Dignitaries: The Cappella della Sacra Cintola in Santo Stefano, Prato," in Lilian Zirpolo, ed., *The Chapels of Italy, from the Twelfth to the Eighteenth Centuries: Art, Religion, Patronage, and Identity*, Woodcliff Lake, NJ: WAPACC Organization, 2010, pp. 177–203.

Fulton, Rachel, "Quae est ista quae ascendit sicut aurora consurgens? The Song of Songs as the Historia for the Office of the Assumption," *Mediaeval Studies*, vol. 60, 1998, pp. 55–122.

Fusco, Giuseppe, *L'Opera della Primaziale attraverso i tempi*, Pisa: FF. Nistri, 1908.

Gamberini, Andrea, and Isabella Lazzarini, eds., *The Italian Renaissance State*, Cambridge: Cambridge University Press, 2012.

Gardner, Julian, "The Decoration of the Baroncelli Chapel in Santa Croce," *Zeitschrift für Kunstgeschichte*, vol. 34, 1971, pp. 89–114.

Gardner, Julian, "Pope Nicholas IV and the Decoration of Santa Maria Maggiore," *Zeitschrift für Kunstgeschichte*, vol. 36, 1973, pp. 1–50.

Gardner, Julian, *The Tomb and the Tiara: Curial Tomb Sculpture in Rome and Avignon in the Later Middle Ages*, Oxford: Clarendon Press, 1992.

Gardner, Julian, "The Louvre Stigmatization and the Problem of the Narrative Altarpiece," in *Patrons, Painters and Saints: Studies in Medieval Italian Painting*, Aldershot: Variorum, 1993, pp. 217–47.

Gardner, Julian, *Giotto and His Publics: Three Paradigms of Patronage*, Cambridge, MA: Harvard University Press, 2011.

Gardner, Julian, *The Roman Crucible: The Artistic Patronage of the Papacy 1198–1304*, Munich: Hirmer Verlag, 2013.

Gardner, Julian, "Papal Exactions, Royal Gifts and Fashionable Cardinals: The Curial Clientele for Opus Anglicanum c. 1300–1370," in M. A. Michael, ed., *The Age of Opus Anglicanum*, New York: Brepols, 2016, pp. 22–35.

Garrison, Edward, *Italian Romanesque Panel Painting*, Florence: Olschki, 1949.

Garzella, Gabriella, Antonino Caleca, et al. eds., *La Cattedrale di Pisa*, Pisa: Pacini Editore, 2014.

Geary, Patrick, *Furta Sacra*, 2nd ed., Princeton: Princeton University Press, 1990.

Geary, Patrick, "The Historical Material of Memory," in Ciappelli and Rubin, eds., *Art, Memory, and Family in Renaissance Florence*, pp. 17–25.

Gentili, Lamberto, et al., *L'Umbria; Manuali per il territorio: Spoleto*, Rome: Edindustria, 1978.

Gherardi da Volterra, Jacopo, "Il diario romano di Jacopo Gherardi da Volterra," ed. E. Carusi, in Giosu Carducci and Vittorio Fiorini, eds., *Rerum Italicarum Scriptores*, 2nd ed., vol. 23, part 3, Città di Castello: Casa Editrice Lapi, 1904.

Giani, G, "Documenti su antichi pittori pratesi," *Archivio storico pratese*, vol. 2, 1917, pp. 70–74.

Gilbert, Creighton, "What Did the Renaissance Patron Buy?," *Renaissance Quarterly*, vol. 51, 1998, pp. 367–91.

Gill, Meredith, "'Where the Danger Was the Greatest': A Gallic Legacy in Santa Maria Maggiore, Rome," *Zeitschrift für Kunstgeschichte*, vol. 59, 1996, pp. 498–522.

Gill, Meredith, *Angels and the Order of Heaven in Medieval and Renaissance Italy*, Cambridge: Cambridge University Press, 2014.

Giorgi, Manuela de, *Il Transito della Vergine*, Spoleto: Centro Italiano di Studi sull'alto Medioevo, 2016.

Giurescu, Ena, "Trecento Family Chapels in Santa Maria Novella and Santa Croce: Architecture, Patronage, and Competition," PhD dissertation, New York University, 1997.

Giusti, Maria Adriana, "Architetture a Pisa nella seconda metà del Quattrocento," in Morolli et al., eds., *L'architettura di Lorenzo il Magnifico*, pp. 197–207.

Giusti, Maria Adriana, "Il 'palazzo vecchio' di Pisa," in Morolli et al., eds., *L'architettura di Lorenzo il Magnifico*, pp. 208–9.

Gnoli, Umberto, *Pittori e miniatori nell'Umbria*, Spoleto: C. Argentieri, 1923.

Goldschmidt, R. C., *Paulinus' Churches at Nola – Tests, Translations and Commentary*, Amsterdam: N.v. Noord-Hollandsche uitgevers maatschappij, 1940.

Goldthwaite, Richard, *The Building of Renaissance Florence*, Baltimore: Johns Hopkins University Press, 1980.

Goldthwaite, Richard, *Wealth and the Demand for Art in Italy, 1300–1600*, Baltimore: Johns Hopkins University Press, 1993.

Grassi, Cesare, "La Storia del Sacro Cingolo," in Martini, ed., *La Sacra Cintola nel Duomo di Prato*, pp. 23–39.

Grégiore, Réginald, *San Rainerius di Pisa (1117–1160) in un ritratto agiografico inedito del secolo XIII*, Pisa: Pacini Editore, 1990.

Grosso, Franco del, "Origine del culto alla Madonna d'Impruneta e suoi rapporti con la città di Firenze," in *Impruneta, una pieve, un paese*, "Quaderni di storia urbana e rurale," vol. 2, Florence: Salimbeni, 1983, pp. 33–77.

Guardabassi, Mariano, *Indice-guida dei monumenti pagani e cristiani riguardanti l'istoria e l'arte esistenti nella provincia dell'Umbria*, Perugia: Boncompagni, 1872.

Guarini, Elena Fasano, "Città soggette e contadi nel dominio fiorentino tra Quattro e Cinquecento: il caso pisano," in Mario Mirri, ed., *Ricerche di storia moderna*, Pisa: Pacini Editore, 1976, vol. 1, pp. 1–94.

Guarini, Elena Fasano, ed., *Storia della civiltà toscana, vol. 3: Il principato mediceo*, Florence: Le Monnier, 2003.

Guarino, Francesco, et al., *Abbazie benedettine in Umbria*, Perugia: Quattroemme, 2008.

Guasti, Cesare, *Due legazioni al Sommo Pontefice per il Comune di Firenze presedute da Sant'Antonino Arcivescovo*, Florence: Bianchi E. C. Barbera, 1857.

Guasti, Cesare, *Lettere di un Notaro a un Mercante del secolo XIV*, 2 vols., Florence: Le Monnier, 1880.

Guasti, Cesare, *Santa Maria del Fiore: La costruzione della chiesa e del campanile*, Florence: M. Ricci, 1887.

Guazzini, Giacomo, "Commissioni artistiche tra Prato e Pistoia, anno 1400: Un'apertura per il vescovo Andrea Franchi ed il fratello Bartolomeo," in Benassi et al., eds., *Officina Pratese: Tecnica, stile, storia*, pp. 211–28.

Guerri, Domenico, *La corrente popolare nel rinascimento: Berte burle e baie nella Firenze del Brunellesco e del Burchiello*, Florence: Sansoni, 1931.

Guicciardini, Francesco, *Storia d'Italia*, ed Silvana Seidel Menchi, 3 vols., Turin: Einaudi, 1971.

Guidotti, Alessandro, "Battiloro e dipintori a Firenze fra Tre e Quattrocento: Bastiano di Giovanni e la sua clientele (dal Catasto del 1427)," in Cristina De Benedictis, ed., *Scritti di storia dell'arte in onore di Roberto Salvini*, Florence: Sansoni, 1984, pp. 239–49.

Guizzelmi, Giuliano, *Historia della Cinctola della Vergine Maria*, ed. Cesare Grassi, Prato: Società Pratese di Storia Patria, 1990.

Gurrieri, Francesco, and Cristina Acidini Luchinat, *La Cattedrale di Santa Maria del Fiore a Firenze*, 2 vols., Florence: Giunti, 1994–95.

Gutmann, Joseph, "Abraham in the Fire of the Chaldeans: A Jewish Legend in Jewish, Christian and Islamic Art," *Frühmittelalterliche Studien*, vol. 7, 1973, pp. 342–52.

Hager, Hellmut, *Die Anfänge des italienischen Altarbildes*, Munich: Schroll, 1962.

Haines, Margaret, "Firenze e il finanziamento della cattedrale e del campanile," in Timothy Verdon, ed., *Alla riscoperta di piazza del Duomo in Firenze, vol. 3: Il Campanile di Giotto*, Florence: Centro Di, 1994, pp. 82–83.

Haines, Margaret, ed., *Santa Maria del Fiore: The Cathedral and Its Sculpture*, Fiesole: Cadmo, 2001.

Halbwachs, Maurice, *The Collective Memory*, trans. Francis Kitter and Vida Ditter, New York: Harper and Row, 1980.

Hall, Marcia, ed., *Artistic Centers of the Italian Renaissance: Rome*, Cambridge: Cambridge University Press, 2005.

Hamburger, Jeffrey, "The Visual and the Visionary: The Image in Late Medieval Monastic Devotions," *Viator*, vol. 20, 1989, pp. 161–82.

Hamburger, Jeffrey, and Anne-Marie Bouché, *The Mind's Eye: Art and Theological Argument in the Middle Ages*, Princeton: Princeton University Press, 2006.

Hankins, James, "Cosimo de' Medici as a Patron of Humanistic Literature," in Ames-Lewis, ed., *Cosimo 'il Vecchio' de' Medici*, pp. 69–94.

Harris, Michael, "Urban Totems: The Communal Spirit of Black Murals," in James Prigoff and Robin Dunitz, eds., *Walls of Heritage, Walls of Pride: African American Murals*, Rohnert Park: Pomegranate Communications, 2000.

Hatfield, Rab, "Some Unknown Descriptions of the Palazzo Medici in 1459," *Art Bulletin*, vol. 52, 1970, pp. 232–49.

Heinzelmann, Martin, *Translationsberichte und andere Quellen des Reliquienkultes*, Turnhout: Brepols, 1979.

Helas, Philine, and Patrizie Tosini, eds, *Tra Campidoglio e curia: L'ospedale del SS. Salvatore ad Sancta Sanctorum tra medioevo ed età moderna*, Milan: Silvana Editoriale, 2017.

Herlihy, David, *Pisa in the Early Renaissance: A Study of Urban Growth*, New Haven and London: Yale University Press, 1958.

Herrmann-Mascard, Nicole, *Les Reliques des saints: Formation coutumière du'un droit*, Paris: Klincksieck, 1975.

Holmes, George, "Cosimo and the Popes," in Ames-Lewis, ed., *Cosimo 'il Vecchio' de' Medici*, pp. 26–27.

Holmes, Megan, "The Elusive Origins of the Cult of the Annunziata in Florence," in Thunø and Wolf, eds., *The Miraculous Image*, pp. 111–12.

Holmes, Megan, *The Miraculous Image in Renaissance Florence*, New Haven and London: Yale University Press, 2013.

Iacobilli, Ludovico, *Vite de'santi e beati dell'Umbria e di quelli i corpi de'quali riposano in essa provincia*, 3 vols., Foligno: Agostino Alterii, 1661.

Iannella, Cecilia, "Civic Virtues in Dominican Homiletic Literature in Tuscany in the Thirteenth and Fourteenth Centuries, *Medieval Sermon Studies*, vol. 51, 2007, pp. 22–32.

Iannella, Cecilia, "Il ciclo pittorico di San Ranieri in Camposanto nel contesto storico pisano," in Castelli and Ceccarelli Lemut, eds., *Intercessor Rainerius ad Patrem*, pp. 167–77.

Iogna-Prat, Dominique, et al., ed., *Marie: Le culte de la Vierge dans la société Médiévale*, Paris: Beauchesne, 1996.

Ito, Takuma, *La vetrata nella Toscana del Quattrocento*, Florence: Olschki, 2011.

Joannides, Paul, *Masaccio and Masolino: A Complete Catalogue*, London: Phaidon, 1993.

Jugie, Martin, *La mort et l'assomption de la Sainte Vierge*, Città del Vaticano: Tipografia Poliglotta Vaticana, 1954

Kaftal, George, *The Iconography of the Saints in Tuscan Painting*, Florence: Sansoni, 1952.

Karwacka Codini, Ewa, "Il palazzo della Sapienza a Pisa: della sua edificazione rinascimentale," in Bartolomeo Azzaro, ed., *L'Università di Roma 'La Sapienza' e le università italiane*, Rome: Gangemi, 2008, pp. 235–46.

Karwacka Codini, Ewa, "La Sapienza," in Karwacka Codini, ed., *Architettura a Pisa nel primo periodo mediceo*, pp. 48–61.

Karwacka Codini, Ewa, ed., *Architettura a Pisa nel primo periodo mediceo*, Pisa: Gangemi editore, 2010.

Karwacka Codini, Ewa, "Dimore nobiliari a Pisa e metamorfosi del volto urbano nel period mediceo," in Daniele, ed., *Le dimore di Pisa*, pp. 43–54.

Kent, Dale, *Cosimo de' Medici and the Florentine Renaissance: The Patron's Oeuvre*, New Haven and London: Yale University Press, 2000.

Kent, Francis W., "The Making of a Renaissance Patron of the Arts," in Alessandro Perosa, ed., *Giovanni Rucellai ed il suo zibaldone; A Florentine Patrician and his Palace*, vol. 2, London: Warburg Institute, 1981.

Kent, Francis W., "Lorenzo de' Medici at the Duomo," in Timothy Verdon and Annalisa Innocenti, eds., *La Cattedrale e la Città: Saggi sul Duomo di Firenze*, Florence: Edifir, 2001, vol.1, pp. 341–68.

Kent, Francis W., *Lorenzo de' Medici and the Art of Magnificence*, Baltimore: Johns Hopkins University Press, 2004.

Kent, Francis W., "Sainted Mother, Magnificent Son; Lorenzo de' Medici and the Love of Women," in Francis W. Kent, *Princely Citizen: Lorenzo de' Medici and Renaissance Florence*, ed. Carolyn James, Turnhout: Brepols, 2013, pp. 67–104.

Kent, Francis W., *Princely Citizen: Lorenzo de' Medici and Renaissance Florence*, ed. Carolyn James, Turnhout: Brepols, 2013.

Kessler, Herbert, "Caput e speculum omnium ecclesiarum: Old St. Peter's and Church Decoration in Medieval Latium," in Tronzo, ed., *Italian Church Decoration in the Middle Ages and Early Renaissance*, pp. 119–46.

Kessler, Herbert, and Joanna Zacharias, *Rome 1300: On the Path of the Pilgrim*, New Haven and London: Yale University Press, 2000.

Killerby, Catherine Kovesi, *Sumptuary Law in Italy 1200–1500*, Oxford: Clarendon Press, 2002.

Kinney, Dale, *S. Maria in Trastevere from its Founding to 1215*, New York: New York University, 1975.

Kitzinger, Ernst, "A Virgin's Face: Antiquarianism in Twelfth-Century Art," *Art Bulletin*, vol. 62, 1980, pp. 6–19.

Klapisch-Zuber, Christiane, *Carrara e i maestri del marmo*, trans. Bruno Cherubini, Massa: Palazzo di S. Elisabetta, 1973.

Kleinberg, Aviad, *Flesh Made Word: Saints' Stories and the Western Imagination*, trans. J. Todd, Cambridge, MA: Harvard University Press, 2008.

Knight, Cher Krause, *Public Art: Theory, Practice and Populism*, Oxford: Basil Blackwell, 2008.

Knight, Cher Krause and Harriet F. Senie, eds., *A Companion to Public Art*, Cichester: John Wiley & Sons, 2016.

Kogman-Appel, Katrin, "The Second Nuremberg Haggadah, a Stylistic and Iconographic Analysis," PhD thesis, Hebrew University, Jerusalem, 1993.

Kogman-Appel, Katrin, "Coping with Christian Pictorial Sources: What Did Jewish Miniaturists *Not* Paint?," *Speculum*, vol. 75, 2000, pp. 816–58.

Kogman-Appel, Katrin, "Hebrew Manuscript Painting in Late Medieval Spain: Signs of a Culture in Transition," *Art Bulletin*, vol. 84, 2002, pp. 246–72.

Kogman-Appel, Katrin, *Illuminated Haggadot from Medieval Spain: Biblical Imagery and the Passover Holiday*, University Park: Pennsylvania State University Press, 2006.

Kosegarten, Antje Middeldorf, "The Origins of Artistic Competitions in Italy," in *Lorenzo Ghiberti nel suo tempo: Atti del convegno internazionale di studi*, Florence: Olschki, 1980, vol. 1, pp. 167–86.

Kosegarten, Antje Middeldorf, "Situazioni conflittuali nei rapporti tra artisti, committenti e operai intorno al 1300," in Margaret Haines and Lucio Riccetti, eds., *Opera: Carattere e ruolo delle fabbriche cittadine fino all'inizio dell'età moderna*, Florence: Oschki, 1996, pp. 371–92.

Kosegarten, Antje Middeldorf, "Florentiner Statuen von 'Uomini illustri' aus dem frühen Quattrocento; Versuch über die Fassade von S. Maria del Fiore," in Marion Ackermann, et al., *Kunst und Geschichte: Festschrift für Karl Arndt zum seibzigsten Geburtstag*, Munich: Deutscher Kunstverlag, 1999, pp. 41–91.

Krautheimer, Richard, *Lorenzo Ghiberti*, 2nd ed., Princeton: Princeton University Press, 2 vols., 1970.

Kreytenberg, Gert, "Giovanni d'Ambrogio," *Jahrbuch der Berliner Museen*, vol 14, 1972, pp. 5–32.

Kreytenberg, Gert, *Der Dom zu Florenz: Untersuchungen zur Baugeschichte im 14. Jahrhundert*, Berlin: Gebr. Mann, 1974.

Kreytenberg, Gert, "Giovanni Fetti und die Porta dei Canonici des Florentiner Domes," *Mitteilungen des Kunsthistorischen Institutes in Florenz*, vol. 20, 1976, pp. 127–58.

Kreytenberg, Gert, "Tre cicli di apostolic dell'anitca facciata del Duomo fiorentino," *Antichità viva*, vol. 16, 1977, pp. 13–29.

Kreytenberg, Gert, "Die Figurekonsolen der Loggia dei Lanzi," *Mitteilungen des Kunsthistorischen Institutes in Florenz*, vol. 24, 1980, pp. 275–82.

Kreytenberg, Gert, "La Decorazione del Duomo nel Trecento e la genesi della scultura fiorentina," in Margaret Haines, ed., *Santa Maria del Fiore: The Cathedral and Its Sculpture*, Fiesole: Cadmo, 2001, pp. 47–58.

Kreytenberg, Gert, "Piero di Giovanni Tedesco; Ein Deutscher Bildhauer in der Florentiner Dombauhütte am Ende des 14. Jahrhunderts," *Städel-Jahrbuch*, n.s. vol. 20, 2009, pp. 55–90.

Kühne, Hartmut, *Ostensio Reliquiarum: Untersuchungen über Entstehung, Ausbreitung, Gestalt und Funktion der Heiltumsweisungen im römisch-deutschen Regnum*, Berlin: de Gruyter, 2000.

Kühnel, Bianca, ed., *The Real and Ideal Jerusalem in Jewish, Christian and Islamic Art*, Jerusalem: The Hebrew University, 1997–98.

Ladis, Andrew, *Taddeo Gaddi*, Columbia: University of Missouri Press, 1982.

Lang, Piero Hans, *Cosimo de' Medici; Die Gesandten und die Condottieri*, Padeborn: Ferdinand Schöningh, 2009.

Lanza, Antonio, *Firenze contro Milano: Gli intellettuali fiorentini nelle guerre con i Visconti (1390–1440)*, Anzio: De Rubeis, 1991.

Lapi Ballerini, Isabella, ed., *Agnolo Gaddi e la Cappella della Cintola; la storia, l'arte, il restauro*, Florence: Edizioni Polistampa, 2009.

Lapi Ballerini, Isabella, "Per onorare la sua preziosissima Cintola," in Lapi Ballerini, ed., *Agnolo Gaddi e la Cappella della Cintola*, pp. 39–41.

Lapi Ballerini, Isabella, "La Cappella della Cintola," in De Marchi and Mavarelli, eds., *Legati da una Cintola*, pp. 58–71.

Lasinio, Carlo, *Pitture a fresco del Camposanto a Pisa intagliate da Carlo Lasinio*, Florence: Molini, 1812.

Lasinio, Giovanni Paolo, and Giuseppe Rossi, *Pitture a fresco del Camposanto a Pisa disegnate da Giuseppe Rossi ed incise dal Prof. Cav. G. P. Lasinio*, 2nd ed., Florence: Tipografia all'Insegna di Dante, 1832.

Lavin, Marilyn Aronberg, "The Stella Altarpiece: Magnum Opus of the Cesi Master," *Artibus et historiae*, vol. 22, 2001, pp. 9–22.

Lazzarini, Isabella, *Communication and Conflict: Italian Diplomacy in the Early Renaissance, 1350–1520*, Oxford: Oxford University Press, 2015.

Lazzarini, Vittorio, "Libri di Francesco Novello da Carrara," *Atti e memorie della R. Accademia di Scienze, Lettere ed Arti in Padova*, vol. 18, 1902, pp. 25–33.

Lazzerini, Luigi, "Benozzo Gozzoli e la fraternita dei fiorentini di Pisa," in Ahl and de Simone, eds., *Le arti a Pisa nel primo Rinascimento / The Arts in Pisa during the Early Renaissance*, pp. 231–49.

Lentes, Thomas, "Inneres Auge, äusserer Blick und heilige Schau. Ein Diskussionsbeitrag zur visuellen Praxis in Frömmigkeit und Moraldidaxe des späten Mittelalters," in Klaus Schreiner and Marc Müntz, eds., *Frömmigkeit im Mittelalter: Politisch-soziale Kontexte, visuelle Praxis, körperliche Ausdruksformen*, Munich: Fink, 2002, pp. 179–220.

Leone, Giorgio, *Icone di Roma e del Lazio*, Rome: L'Erma di Bretschneider, 2012.

Lightbrown, Ronald, *Donatello and Michelozzo: An Artistic Partnership and Its Patrons in the Early Renaissance*, London: Miller, 1980.

Lillie, Amanda, "Lorenzo de' Medici's Rural Investments and Territorial Expansion," *Rinascimento: Rivista dell'Istituto Nazionale di Studi sul Rinascimento*, 2nd ser., vol. 33, 1993, pp. 53–67.

Lillie, Amanda, "Giovanni di Cosimo and the Villa Medici at Fiesole," in Andreas Beyer and Bruce Boucher, eds., *Piero de' Medici 'il Gottoso,'* Berlin: Akademie Verlag, 1993, pp. 189–205.

Lippi, Lorenzo, "L'orazione di Lorenzo Lippi per l'apertura dell'Università di Pisa," ed. Vito Giustiniani, *Rinascimento: Rivista dell'Istituto Nazionale di Studi sul Rinascimento*, 2nd ser., vol. 4, 1964, pp. 265–84.

Lippincott, Kristen, "Giovanni di Paolo's 'Creation of the World' and the 'thema mundi,'" *Burlington Magazine*, vol. 132, 1990, pp. 460–68.

Lironi, Gaetano, *Notizie storiche sul culto della B. Vergine che si venera nella Chiesa metropolitana di Spoleto*, Rome: Tipografia Poliglotta, 1877.

Lironi, Gaetano, *Memorie storiche sul culto e sulle vicende orientali della SS. Icone della Beata Vergine che si venera nella Chiesa metropolitana di Spoleto*, Foligno: Stabilimento di Pietro Sgariglia, 1881.

Litta, Pompeo, *Famiglie celebri italiane*, Florence: 1 ser., vol. G–O, Milan: Presso Paolo Emilio Giusti stampatore, 1819.

Little, Lester, *Religious Poverty and the Profit Economy in Medieval Europe*, Ithaca: Cornell University Press, 1978.

Lloyd, Joan Barclay, "The Medieval Murals in the Cistercian Abbey of Santi Vincenzo e Anastasio ad Aquas Salvias at Tre Fontane, Rome, in Their Architectural Settings," *Papers of the British School at Rome*, vol. 65, 1997, pp. 287–348.

Lloyd, Joan Barclay, *SS. Vincenzo e Anastasio at Tre Fontane near Rome: History and Architecture of a Medieval Cistercian Abbey*, Kalmazoo: Cistercian, 2006.

Löhr, Wolf-Dietrich, and Stefan Weppelmann, eds., *"Fantasie und Handwerk": Cennino Cennini und die Tradition der toskanischen Malerie von Giotto bis Lorenzo Monaco*, Berlin, Gemäldegalerie, 2008.

Lombardi, Suzanne Woodbury, "Politics and Humanism in the Depression Era Frescoes of Victor Arnautoff," MA thesis, University of California, Berkeley, 1984.

Long, Pamela O., "Power, Patronage and the Authorship of Ars," *Isis: Journal of the History of Science*, vol. 88, 1997, pp. 1–41.

Long, Pamela O., *Artisan/Practitioners and the Rise of the New Sciences 1400–1600*, Corvallis: Oregon State University Press, 2011.

Long, Pamela O., "Trading Zones in Early Modern Europe," *Isis*, vol. 106, no. 4, 2015, pp. 840–47.

Lucciardi, D., "Federigo Visconti Arcivescovo di Pisa," *Bollettino storico pisano*, vol. 1, 1932, pp. 7–47; vol. 2, 1933, pp. 7–37.

Lumbroso, Matizia, and Antonio Martini, *Le confraternite romane nelle loro chiese*, Rome: Fondazione Marco Besso, 1963.

Lunghi, Elvio, "I cicli pittorici, le opere d'arte medievali e la cappella di Sant'Anna," in Benazzi and Carbonara, eds., *La cattedrale di Spoleto*, pp. 241–45.

Lupi, Clemente, "Sulle origini del Camposanto di Pisa," *Notizie d'arte*, vol. 2, 1910, pp. 10–20.

Luzzati, Michele, "Filippo de' Medici Arcivescovo di Pisa e la visita pastorale del 1462–1463," *Bollettino storico pisano*, vols. 33–35, 1964–66, pp. 361–408.

Luzzati, Michele, "Un arcivescovo Mediceo del quattrocento pisano," *Comune di Pisa: Rassegna periodica di informazioni*, vol. 3, no. 4, 1967, pp. 22–29.

Luzzati, Michele, "Il sepolcro del maestro medico Ligio Ammannati nel Camposanto pisano," *Rassegna periodico culturale e di informazione*, vol. 5, 1969, nos. 6–8, pp. 31–38.

Luzzati, Michele, *La casa dell'ebreo: Saggi sugli ebrei a Pisa e in Toscana nel medioevo e nel rinascimento*, Pisa: Nnistri-Lischi, 1985.

Luzzati, Michele, "Caratteri dell'insediamento ebraico medievale," in Michele Luzzati, ed., *Gli ebrei di Pisa (secoli IX–XX)*, Pisa: Pacini Editore, 1998, pp. 1–44.

Luzzati, Michele, "Su due ritratti di Filippo de' Medici arcivescovo di Pisa (1461–1474)," *Bollettino storico pisano*, 3rd ser, no. 71, 2002, pp. 193–98.

Mack, Charles, "Studies in the Architectural Careeer of Bernardo di Matteo Ghamberelli called Rossellino," PhD dissertation, University of North Carolina at Chapel Hill, 1972.

Maginnis, Hayden B. J., *Painting in the Age of Giotto: A Historical Reevaluation*, University Park: Pennsylvania State University Press, 1997.

Magnuson, Torgil, *Studies in Roman Quattrocento Architecture*, Stockholm: Almquist and Wiksell, 1958.

Majarelli, Stanislao, and Ugolino Nicolini, *Il Monte dei poveri di Perugia*, Perugia: Banco del Monte di Credito, 1962.

Émile Mâle, *L'art religieux du XIIIe siècle en France*, Paris: Armand Colin, 1923.

Mallett, Michael, "The Sea Consuls of Florence in the Fifteenth Century," *Papers of the British School at Rome*, vol. 27, 1959, pp. 156–69.

Mallett, Michael, *The Florentine Galleys in the Fifteenth Century*, Oxford: Clarendon Press, 1967.

Mallett, Michael, "Pisa and Florence in the Fifteenth Century: Aspects of the Period of the First Florentine Domination," in Nicolai Rubinstein, ed., *Florentine Studies: Politics and Society in Renaissance Florence*, London: Faber and Faber, 1968, pp. 403–41.

Mancinelli, Fabrizio, et al., *Michelangelo: La Cappella Sistina*, 3 vols., Città del Vaticano: Edizioni Musei Vaticani, 1994.

Maniura, Robert, "Persuading the Absent Saint: Image and Performance in Marian Devotion," *Critical Inquiry*, vol. 35, 2009, pp. 629–54.

Maniura, Robert, *Art and Miracle in Renaissance Tuscany*, Cambridge: Cambridge University Press, 2018.

Mann, C. Griffith, "From Creation to the End of Time: The Nave Frescoes of San

Gimignano's Collegiata and the Structure of Civic Devotion," PhD dissertation, Johns Hopkins University, 2002.

Marchesi, Giorgio Viviano, *La galleria dell'onore ove sono descritte le segnalate memorie del sagr'ordine militare di S. Stefano p. e m. e de' suoi cavalieri colle glorie antiche e moderne dell'illustri loro patrie e famiglie dentro e fuori d'Italia*, Forli: Fratelli Marozzi, 1735.

Marchi, Andrea De, "Prato 1338: Una pala risarcita di Bernardo Daddi, una città che cresce sotto il segno della cintola," in De Marchi and Mavarelli, eds, *Legati da una cintola*, pp. 13–29.

Marchi, Andrea De, ed., *Santa Maria Novella; La Basilica e il Convento*, vol. 1, Florence: Mandragora, 2015.

Marchi, Andrea De, "Prato e la sacra Cintola: Mitopoiesi civica e nuove forme della devozione, all'incrocio fra la Chiesa e il mondo," *Iconographica*, special issue, 2021, pp. 15–24.

Marchi, Andrea De, and Cristina Gnoni Mararelli, *Legati da una cintola*, Florence: Mandragora, 2017.

Marchini, Giuseppe, *Il Duomo di Prato*, Milan: Electa, 1957.

Marchini, Giuseppe, *Il Tesoro del Duomo di Prato*, Prato: Cassa di risparmi, 1963.

Margolis, Oren, and Brian Maxson, "The 'Schemes' of Piero de' Pazzi and the Conflict with the Medici (1461–2)," *Journal of Medieval History*, vol. 41, 2015, pp. 484–503.

Margolis, Oren, *The Politics of Culture in Quattrocento Europe: René of Anjou in Italy*, Oxford: Oxford University Press, 2016.

Marino, Eugenio OP, "Iconologia del ciclo 'Via Paradisi' di Giovanni di Bartolomeo Cristiani: 'Penitenze' e 'Regno di Dio' tra medioevo e umanesimo," in *Memorie Domenicane*, vols. 8–9, 1977–78, pp. 249–339

Martines, Lauro, *The Social World of the Florentine Humanists, 1390–1460*, Princeton: Princeton University Press, 1963.

Martines, Lauro, *April Blood: Florence and the Plot against the Medici*, Oxford: Oxford University Press, 2003.

Martini, Claudio, ed., *La Sacra Cintola nel Duomo di Prato*, Prato: Claudio Martini, 1995.

Martini, Giuseppe, *Theatrum Basilicae Pisanae*, 2nd ed., Rome: Antonii de Rubeis, 1728.

Martino, Raffaella, "Gli atti di elezione e investitura degli Operai dell'Opera del Duomo di Pisa nei secoli XIII e XIV," tesi di laurea University of Pisa, 2002.

Mathews, Karen Rose, et al., eds., *A Companion to Medieval Pisa*, Leiden: Brill, 2022.

Mattei, Antonio, *Ecclesiae Pisane Historia*, Lucca: Typographia Leonardi Venturini, 1772.

Mauss, Marcel, *The Gift: The Form and Reason for Exchange in Archaic Societies*, trans. W. D. Halls, New York: W. W. Norton, 1990.

Maxson, Brian, *The Humanist World of Renaissance Florence*, Cambridge: Cambridge University Press, 2014.

McAllister, Amber, "Narrative and Allegory in the Genesis Fresco Cycle in the Chiostro Verde, Santa Maria Novella, Florence," PhD dissertation, University of Georgia, 2003.

McHam, Sarah Blake, *Pliny and the Artistic Culture of the Italian Renaissance*, New Haven and London: Yale University Press, 2013.

McLean, Alick, "Sacred Space and Public Policy: The Establishment, Decline and Revival of Prato's Piazza della Pieve," PhD dissertation, Princeton University, 1993.

McLean, Alick, *Prato: Architecture, Piety and Political Identity in a Tuscan City-State*, New Haven and London: Yale University Press, 2008.

Medici, Lorenzo de', *Scritti scelti*, ed. Emilio Bigi, 2nd ed., Turin: UTET, 1965 (reprinted 1977).

Medici, Lorenzo de', *Lettere*, 18 vols, ed. Nicolai Rubinstein, et al., Florence: Giunti-Barbèra, 1977–2021.

Medici, Lucrezia Tornabuoni de', *Lettere*, ed. Patrizia Salvadori, Florence: Olschki, 1993.

Meiss, Millard, *Painting in Florence and Siena after the Black Death*, Princeton, Princeton University Press, 1951.

Meiss, Millard, Ugo Procacci, et al., *The Great Age of Fresco: Giotto to Pontormo*, New York: The Metropolitan Museum of Art, 1968.

Melis, Federigo, *Aspetti della vita economica medievale*, Siena: Monte dei Paschi, 1962.

Menichella, Anna, "Il maestro delle Tre Fontane," in Angiola Maria Romanini, ed.,

Atti della IV settimana di studi di storia medioevale dell'università di Roma, 1983, pp. 477–85.
Mercati, Silvio, "Sulla santissima icone del Duomo do Spoleto," *Spoletium*, vol 3, no. 1, 1956, pp. 3–6.
Mercati, Silvio, *Collectanea Byzantina*, vol 2, Bari: Dedalo Libri, 1970.
Metelli, Cecilia, "Vicende decorative prima e dopo il rifacimento barberiniano," in Benazzi and Carbonara, eds., *La cattedrale di Spoleto*, pp. 335–39.
Meyvaert, Paul, "The Medieval Monastic Claustrum," *Gesta*, vol. 12, 1973, pp. 53–59.
Michelagnolo di Cristofano da Volterra, "Le Mirabili et inaldite belleze e adornamenti del Camposanto di Pisa," in I. B. Supino, ed., *Il Camposanto di Pisa*, Florence: Alinari, 1896, pp. 301–17.
Migne, J. P., ed., *Patrologiae Latinae Cursus Completus*, 221 vols., Paris : Jacques-Paul Migne, 1844–65; reprinted Paris: Garnier, 1865–80.
Milanesi, Gaetano, "Il viaggio degli ambasciatori fiorentini al re di Francia nel MCCCCLXI descritto da Giovanni di Francesco di Neri Cecchi loro cancelliere," *Archivio storico italiano*, ser. 3, vol. 1, part 1, 1865, pp. 7–62.
Milanesi, Gaetano, *Delle nozze di Lorenzo dei Medici con Clarice Orsini nel 1469, informazione di Piero Parenti Fiorentino*, Florence: Bencini, 1870.
Milanesi, Gaetano, *Nuovi documenti per la storia dell'arte Toscana dal XII al XV secolo*, Florence: Dotti, 1901.
Milanesi, Gaetano, and Carlo Milanesi, eds., *Il libro dell'arte o trattato della pittura di Cennino Cennini*, Florence: LeMonnier, 1859.
Miniati, Giovanni, *Narrazione e disegno della terra di Prato di Toscana [1594]*, Prato: Vestri, 1827.
Mirri, Mario, ed. *La città e il contado di Pisa nello stato dei Medici (XV–XVII secoli)*, Pisa: Pacini Editore, 2000.
Molho, Anthony, "The Brancacci Chapel: Studies in Its Iconography and History," *Journal of the Warburg and Courtauld Institutes*, vol. 40, 1977, pp. 50–98.
Molho, Anthony, "The State and Public Finance: A Hypothesis Based on the History of Late Medieval Florence," in Julius Kirshner, ed., *The Origins of the State in Italy*, Chicago: University of Chicago Press, 1996, pp. 106–9.
Moretti, Simona, "Spoleto. Chiesa di San Paolo inter vineas," in Mara Bonfioli, ed., *Corpus della pittura monumentale bizantina in Italia*, vol 1: Umbria, Rome: Edizioni Quasar, 2012.
Mori, Maria Luisa, *La dominazione fiorentina a Pisa dal 1451 al 1469*, Pisa: Orsolini-Prosperi, 1936.
Morolli, Gabriele, Cristina Acidini Luchinat, and Luciano Marchetti, eds., *L'architettura di Lorenzo il Magnifico*, Milan: Silvana Editoriale, 1992.
Morolli, Gabriele, "La domus cardinalis di Filippo de' Medici, arcivescovo di Pisa. Una 'prova generale' del nuovo palazzo umanistico all'antica di metà quattrocento: tra Vitruvio e Alberti," in Daniele, ed., *Le dimore di Pisa*, pp. 55–82.
Morolli, Gabriele, "'Aethereasque domus (. . .) pinxit': Benozzo Primo illustratore delle istituzioni albertiane di architettura," in Andreatta et al., eds., *Benozzo Gozzoli e l'architettura*, pp. 23–40.
Moroni, Gaetano, *Dizionario di erudizione storico-ecclesiastica*, Venice: Tipografia Emiliana, 1843.
Moroni, Maria Laura, "Itinerari a Spoleto," in Saverio Ricci, ed., *Piermatteo d'Amelia e il rinascimento; itinerari in Umbria*, Milan: Silvana Editoriale, 2009, pp. 14–17.
Morpurgo, Salomone, "Le epigrafi volgari in rima del 'Trionfo della Morte' del 'Giudizio Universale e Inferno' e degli `Anacoreti' nel Camposanto di Pisa," *L'arte*, vol. 2, 1899, pp. 51–87.
Morris, Colin, "San Ranieri of Pisa: The Power and Limitations of Sanctity in Twelfth-Century Italy," *Journal of Ecclesiastical History*, 45, no. 4, 1994, pp. 588–99.
Moskowitz, Anita, *The Sculpture of Andrea and Nino Pisano*, Cambridge: Cambridge University Press, 1986.
Mouridi, Doula, "A Deesis Icon in the Art Museum," *Record of the Art Museum, Princeton University*, vol. 28, 1968, pp. 13–28.
Mueller, Reinhold, *The Venetian Money Market: Banks, Panics, and the Public Debt, 1200–1500*,

Baltimore: Johns Hopkins University Press, 1997.

Muir, Edward, *Ritual in Early Modern Europe*, 2nd ed., Cambridge: Cambridge University Press, 2005.

Müntz, Eugène, "L'architettura à Roma durante il pontificato di Innocenzo VIII," *Archivio storico dell'arte*, vol. 4, 1891, pp. 60–63, 363–70, 456–68.

Müntz, Eugène, *Les arts a la cour des papes pendant le XVe et le XVIe siècle*, part 1, Paris: Ernest Thorin Editeur, 1878; part 2, 1879 ; part 3, 1882.

Nagel, Alexander, *Michelangelo and the Reform of Art*, Cambridge, MA: Harvard University Press, 2000.

Nagel, Alexander, and Christopher Wood, *Anachronic Renaissance*, New York: Zone Books, 2010.

Najemy, John, *A History of Florence 1200–1575*, Chichester: John Wiley & Sons, 2008.

Narkiss, B., *The Golden Haggadah, a Fourteenth Century Illuminated Manuscript in the British Museum*, 2 vols., London: Eugrammia Press, 1970.

Nees, Lawrence, *Early Medieval Art*, Oxford: Oxford University Press, 2002.

Nelson, Jonathan, and Richard Zeckhauser, eds, *The Patron's Payoff: Conspicuous Commissions in Italian Renaissance Art*, Princeton: Princeton University Press, 2008.

Nelson, Robert, "Appropriation," in Robert Nelson and Richard Shiff, eds., *Critical Terms for Art History*, 2nd ed., Chicago: University of Chicago Press, 2003, pp. 59–62.

Nessi, Silvestro "Il Duomo di Spoleto nel secolo XII," *Spoletium*, vol. 10, 1966, no. 12, pp. 31–36.

Nessi, Silvestro, "Restauri antichi e recenti alle mura e alle porte di Spoleto," *Spoletium*, vol. 22, 1977, pp. 19–36.

Nessi, Silvestro, *Nuovi documenti sulle arti a Spoleto: Architettura e scultura tra romanico e baroco*, Spoleto: Banca popolare di Spoleto, 1992.

Nessi, Silvestro, "La cattedrale nella storia diocesana," in Benazzi and Carbonara, eds., *La cattedrale di Spoleto*, pp. 66–73.

Nethersole, Scott, *Art and Violence in Early Renaissance Florence*, New Haven and London: Yale University Press, 2018.

Ng, Aimee, Alexander Noelle, et al., *Bertoldo di Giovanni: The Renaissance of Sculpture in Medici Florence*, New York: The Frick Collection, 2019.

Niccolai, Alberto, *Palazzi, ville e scene medicee in Pisa e nei dintorni*, Pisa: Editrice Mariotti, 1914.

Nigro, Giampiero, *Il Tempo liberato: Festa e svago nella città di Francesco Datini*, Prato: Istituto Internazionale di Storia Economica "F. Datini," 1994.

Nigro, Giampiero, ed., *Francesco di Marco Datini: The Man the Merchant*, trans. Isabelle Johnson, Florence: Florence University Press, 2010.

Nora, Pierre, "Mémoire collective," in J. Le Goff, R. Chartier, and J. Revel, eds., *La Nouvelle Histoire*, Paris: Retz, 1978, pp. 398–401.

Nora, Pierre, "Between Memory and History: Les Lieux de Mémoire," *Representations*, vol. 26 Spring, 1989, pp. 7–24.

Norman, Diana, *Siena and the Virgin*, New Haven and London: Yale University Press, 1999.

Norman, Diana, *Siena and the Angevins 1300–1350: Art, Diplomacy, and Dynastic Ambition*, Turnhout: Brepols, 2018.

Novelli, Alessandro, and Lucilla Vignoli, *L'arte a Narni tra medioevo e illuminismo*, Perugia: Era Nuova, 2004.

Novelli, Alessandro, and Lucilla Vignoli, "Il cardinale Berardo e Benozzo di Lese: Ipotesi di un rapport di committenza," in Novelli and Vignoli, eds., *L'arte a Narni tra medioevo e illuminismo*, pp. 70–72.

Novello, Roberto Paolo, "Tarsie di Guido da Seravallino per il Duomo di Pisa," *Bollettino storico pisano*, vol. 55, 1986, pp. 129–47.

Novello, Roberto Paolo, "Le tarsie lignee," in A. Peroni, ed., *Il Duomo di Pisa*, Modena: Panini, 1995, vol. 3, p. 301–12.

Novello, Roberto Paolo, "Baccio Pontelli a Pisa: una rilettura," in Gabriele Donati and Valeria Genovese, eds., *Forme del legno: Intaglio e tarsie fra gotico e rinascimento*, Pisa: Edizioni della Normale, 2013, pp. 81–92.

Nuti, Ruggero, "La consacrazione dell'altare del Sacro Cingolo," *Archivio storico pratese*, vol. 12, no. 2, 1934, pp. 73–75.

Nuti, Ruggero, *La Fiera di Prato attraverso i tempi*, Prato: Associazione turistica pratese, 1939.

Nuti, Ruggero, "Aspetti di Prato nel Medioevo: La Piazza della pieve," *Archivio storico pratese*, vol. 27, 1951, pp. 45–68.

Nuti, Ruggero, "Aspetti di Prato nel Medioevo, II: Il Palazzo del Popolo," *Archivio storico pratese*, vol. 29, 1953, pp. 25–48.

Nuttall, Paula, *From Flanders to Florence*, New Haven and London: Yale University Press, 2004.

O'Malley, John, *Praise and Blame in Renaissance Rome*, Durham: Duke University Press, 1979.

O'Malley, Michelle, *The Business of Art: Contracts and the Commissioning Process in Renaissance Italy*, New Haven and London: Yale University Press, 2005.

O'Malley, Michelle, *Painting under Pressure: Fame, Reputation, and Demand in Renaissance Florence*, New Haven and London: Yale University Press, 2013

Offner, Richard, Klara Steinweg, Miklós Boskovits, et al., eds., *A Critical and Historical Corpus of Florentine Painting*, 30 vols., Florence: Giunti; New York: Institute of Fine Arts, 1930–2011.

Oliver, J., "Image et dévotion: Le Rôle de l'art dans l'institution de la Fête-Dieu," in André Haquin, ed., *Fête-Dieu (1246–1996): Actes du colloque de Liège*, Louvain: Collège Erasme, 1999, vol. 1, pp. 153–72.

Orlandi, Maria Luigia, *Benozzo Gozzoli a Pisa: I documenti (1468–1495)*, Pisa: Pacini Editore, 1997.

Orlandini, Nicoletta, "Economia e società a Pisa alla metà del XV secolo," 2 vols., Tesi di laurea, University of Pisa, 1984–85.

Os, Henk van, "The Assumption in Sienese Painting," *Studies in Early Tuscan Painting*, London: Pindar, 1992, pp. 173–279.

Ottaviani, M. Grazia Nico, *Rocche e fortificazioni nello stato della chiesa*, Naples: Edizioni Scientifiche Italiane, 2004.

Ottosen, Knud, *The Responsories and Versicles of the Latin Office of the Dead*, Aarhus: Aarhus University Press, 1993.

Ousterhout, Robert, "Flexible Geography and Transportable Topography," in Kühnel, ed., *The Real and Ideal Jerusalem in Jewish, Christian and Islamic Art*, pp. 393–404.

Paatz, Walter, and Elisabeth Paatz, *Die Kirchen von Florenz*, 6 vols., Frankfurt: Klostermann, 1940–54.

Palmizi, Alessandro Taidelli, "Galeazzo Maria Sforza a Firenze: L'ospite d'onore," *Art e dossier*, vol. 27, no. 285, 2012, pp. 60–63.

Panofsky, Erwin, "Imago Pietatis," in *Festschrift für M. J. Friedlander zum 60. Geburtstag*, Leipzig: Seemann, 1927, pp. 261–308.

Panofsky, Erwin, *Tomb Sculpture: Four Lectures on Its Changing Aspects from Ancient Egypt to Bernini*, New York: Harry N. Abrams, 1964.

Paoli, Emore, "I santi titolari della cattedrale: l'Assunta e san Primiano," in Benazzi and Carbonara, eds., *La cattedrale di Spoleto*, pp. 60–65.

Paoli, Marco, "Un aspetto poco noto della scultura trecentesca pisana: la lapide sepolcrale con ritratto," *Antichità viva*, vol. 21, nos. 5–6, 1982, pp. 38–47.

Paolucci, Antonio, ed., *Colloqui davanti alla Madre: Immagini mariane in Toscana tra arte, storia e devozione*, Florence: Mandragora, 2004.

Parenti, Daniela, ed., *Giovanni da Milano: Capolavori del gotico fra Lombardia e Toscana*, Florence: Giunti, 2008.

Parimoo, Ratan, et al., eds: *The Art of Ajanta*, 2 vols, New Delhi: Books & Books, 1991.

Park, Marlene, and Gerald Markowitz, "New Deal for Public Art," in Harriet Senie and Sally Webster, eds., *Critical Issues in Public Art: Content, Context and Controversy*, Washington, DC: Smithsonian Institution Press, 1992, pp. 128–41.

Partner, Peter, *The Lands of St. Peter: The Papal State in the Middle Ages and the Early Renaissance*, Berkeley: University of California Press, 1972.

Passavanti, Jacopo, *Lo Specchio di Vera Penitenza*, 2 vols., Florence: P. Fraticelli, 1843.

Pasternak, Nurit, "Together and Apart: Hebrew Manuscripts as Testimonies to Encounters of Jews and Christians in Fifteenth-Century Florence," PhD dissertation, Hebrew University, Jerusalem, 2009.

Pastor, Ludwig von, *Storia dei papi*, 4 vols., 4th ed., trans. Angelo Mercato, reprint, Rome: Desclée, 1961.

Pastor, Ludwig von, *Ungedruckte Akten zur Geschichte der Päpste*, Freiburg im Breisgau: Herder, 1904.

Pasut, Francesca, and Johannes Tripps, eds., *Da Giotto a Botticelli; Pittura fiorentina tra Gotico e Rinascimento*, Florence: Giunti, 2008.

Pavan, Paola, "Gli statuti della società dei Raccomandati del Salvatore ad Sancta Sanctorum 1331–1496," *Archivio dlela Società Romana di Storia Patria*, vol. 101, 1978 [1980], pp. 35–96.

Pavan, Paola, "La confraternita del Salvatore nella società romana del Tre- Quattrocento," *Ricerche di storia religiosa di Roma*, vol. 5, 1984, pp. 81–90.

Pecchai, Pio, *L'Opera della Primaziale Pisana*, Pisa: F. Mariotti, 1905.

Pelagatti, Gioacchino, *Il Sacro Cingolo Mariano in Prato*, Prato: Giachetti, 1895, 2nd ed., Prato: Bechi, 1937.

Pellegrini, Marco, "Ascanio Maria Sforza: La creazione di un cardinale 'di famiglia,'" in Giorgio Chittolini, ed., *Gli Sforza, la chiesa lombarda, la corte di Roma*, Naples: Liguori, 1992, pp. 215–89.

Pentcheva, Bissera, *Icons and Power: The Mother of God in Byzantium*, University Park: Pennsylvania State University Press, 2006.

Perry, Rebekah, "The Medieval Inchinata Procession at Tivoli: Ritual Construction of Civic Identity in the Age of the Commune," *Journal of the Society of Architectural Historians*, vol. 76, 2017, pp. 36–62.

Pestilli, Livio, and Ingrid Rowland, et al., eds., *"Napoli è tutto il mondo." Neapolitan Art and Culture from Humanism to the Enlightenment*, Pisa: Serra, 2008.

Petralia, Giuseppe, "1406: Il dissolversi di una società tardocomunale come premessa alla costruzione di uno stato toscano," in Tognetti, ed., *Firenze e Pisa dopo il 1406*, pp. 123–35.

Petralia, Giuseppe, "Pisa Laurenziana: Una città e un territorio per la conservazione dello 'stato,'" in Fubini, ed, *La Toscana al tempo di Lorenzo il Magnifico*, pp. 955–80.

Petrucci, Francesco, *Santissima Annunziata*, Rome: Fratelli Palombi, 1992.

Piattoli, Renato, "Un mercante del trecento e gli artisti del tempo suo," *Rivista d'arte*, ser. 2, vol. 11, 1929, pp. 221–53, 396–437, 537–79; vol. 12, 1930, pp. 97–150.

Piccirillo, Michele, ed., *In Terrasanta: Dalla Crociata alla Custodia dei Luoghi Santi*, Florence-Milan: ArtificioSkira, 2000.

Picotti, G. B., *La giovinezza di Leone X: il Papa del Rinascimento*, Milan : Hoepli, 1928.

Picotti, G. B., *La Dieta di Mantova e la politica dei veneziani*, Trento: Università degli studi di Trento, 1996.

Pieper, Jan, *Pienza; Il progetto di una vision umanistica del mondo*, London: A. Menges, 2002.

Pietrangeli, Carlo, ed., *Santa Maria Maggiore a Roma*, Florence: Nardini Editore, 1988.

Pisani, Linda, *Francesco Traini e la pittura a Pisa nella prima metà del Trecento*, Milan: Silvana Editoriale, 2020.

Pius II (Aeneas Sylvius Piccolomini), *Commentaries*, books 6–9, trans. Florence Alden Gragg, *Smith College Studies in History*, vol. 35, 1951; ed. and trans. Margaret Meserve and Marcello Simonetta, Cambridge, MA: Harvard University Press, vol. 1, books 1–2, 2003; vol. 2, books 3–4, 2007.

Pius II (Aeneas Sylvius Piccolomini), *Orations "Messis quidem," "Quamvis non dubitamus." "Vocati estis," and "Maxima" of Pope Pius II (5 and 8 March, 1460, Siena)*; Michael von Cotta-Schønberg, ed. and trans., Copenhagen, 2015.

Platina (Bartolomeo Sacchi), *The Lives of the Popes from the Time of Our Saviour Jesus Christ, to the Reign of Sixtus IV, 1421–1481*, trans. Paul Rycaut, London: Christopher Wilkinson, 1685; ed. and trans. William Benham, London: Griffith, Farran, Okeden and Welch, 1888.

Pliny the Elder, *Natural History*, ed. H. Rackham, 10 vols., Cambridge, MA: Harvard University Press, 1938–63.

Poeschke, Joachim, *Die Kirche San Francesco in Assisi und ihre Wandmalereien*, Munich, 1985.

Poeschke, Joachim, *Italian Frescoes: The Age of Giotto 1280–1400*, New York: Abbeville Press, 2005.

Poggi, Giovanni, "La Cappella del Sacro Cingolo nel Duomo di Prato e gli affreschi di Agnolo Gaddi," *Rivista d'arte*, vol. 14, 1932, pp. 355–76.

Poggi, Giovanni, *Il Duomo di Firenze: Documenti sulla decorazione della chiesa e del campanile, tratti dall'archivio dell'opera*, 2 vols., ed. Margaret Haines, Florence: Edizioni Medicea, 1988.

Polzer, Joseph, "Who Is the Master of the Crucifixion in the Camposanto of Pisa?," *Studi di storia dell'arte*, vol. 21, 2010, pp. 9–40.

Pope-Hennessy, John, *The Robert Lehman Collection I: Italian Paintings*, New York: The Metropolitan Museum of Art, 1987.

Popple, Alessandra, "Il restauro della cappella della cintola," in Lapi Ballerini, ed., *Agnolo Gaddi e la Cappella della Cintola*, pp. 135–57.

Potenti, Alessandra, *Uomini, villaggi, terreni: Aspetti economici e demografici delle campagne pisane del quattrocento*, Pisa: Pacini Editore, 2002.

Prampolini, Giacomo, *L'Annunciazione nei pittori primitivi italiani*, Milan: Hoepli, 1939.

Proto Pisani, Rosana Caterina, "Una pieve, un comune rurale, un santuario," in Proto Pisani, Rosana Caterina, ed., *Il Museo di Santa Maria all'Impruneta*, Florence: Salimbeni, 1996, pp. 14–21.

Quinterio, Francesco, "La costruzione della torre di Babele," in Andreatta et al., eds., *Benozzo Gozzoli e l'architettura*, pp. 53–62.

Quinterio, Francesco, *Giuliano da Maiano, "grandissimo domestico,"* Rome: Officina Edizioni, 1996.

Ratté, Felicity, *Picturing the City in Medieval Italian Painting*, Jefferson: McFarland and Company, 2006.

Rava, Eleonora, *"Volens in testamento vivere": Testamenti a Pisa, 1240–1320*, Rome: Istituto storico italiano per il medio evo, 2016.

Raveggi, Sergio, "Protagonisti e antagonisti nel libero commune," in Braudel, ed., *Prato: Storia di una città*, vol. 1, part 3, pp. 614–759.

Réau, Louis, *L'Iconographie de l'art chrétien*, 3 vols., Paris: Presses universitaires de France, 1955–59.

Redi, Fabio, *Pisa come'era: Archeologia, urbanistica e strutture materiali (secoli V–XIV)*, Naples: Liguori, 1991.

Redi, Fabio, "I palazzi pisani nel medioevo. Una lettura archeologica e tipologica delle strutture superstiti," in Daniele, ed., *Le dimore di Pisa*, pp. 33–42.

Regni, Claudio, "La rocca di Spoleto tra impegni finanziari e rappresentazione del potere," in Ottaviani, ed., *Rocche e fortificazioni nello stato della chiesa*, pp. 213–33.

Renner, Stefanie, *Die Darstellung der Verkündigung an Maria in der florentinischen Malerei von Andrea Orcagna bis Lorenzo Monaco*, Bonn: Lemmens, 1996.

Renzoni, Stefano, *Il Camposanto monumentale di Pisa*, Pisa: Pacini Editore, 2020.

Richa, Giuseppe, *Notizie istoriche delle chiese fiorentine [1759]*, reprint Rome: Multigrafica Editrice, 1972.

Richards, Lily, "Saint Ranieri of Pisa: A Civic Cult and Its Expression in Text and Image," in Joanna Cannon and Beth Williamson, eds., *Art, Politics, and Civic Religion in Central Italy 1261–1352*, Aldershot: Ashgate, 2000, pp. 179–235.

Richardson, Carol, *Reclaiming Rome: Cardinals in the Fifteenth Century*, Leiden and Boston: Brill, 2009.

Ringbom, Sixten, *Icon to Narrative: The Rise of the Dramatic Close-up in Fifteenth Century Devotional Painitng*, Abo: Abo Akademi, 1965.

Ringbom, Sixten, "Devotional Images and Imaginative Devotions: Notes on the Place of Art in Late Medieval Piety," *Gazette des Beaux-Arts*, ser. 6, vol. 73, 1969, pp. 159–70.

Roberts, Ann, *Dominican Women and Renaissance Art: The Convent of San Domenico of Pisa*, Aldershot: Ashgate, 2008.

Rochon, André, *La jeunesse de Laurent de' Médicis*, Paris: Les Belles Lettres, 1963.

Rohault de Fleury, Georges, *Les monuments de Pise au moyen age*, Paris: A. Morel, 1866.

Röll, Johannes, "Un'opera ignota di Giovanni Dalmata: Il monument Fusconi a Norcia," *Spoletium*, vols. 36–37, 1992, pp. 72–75.

Röll, Johannes, *Giovanni Dalmata*, Worms: Werner, 1994.

Romagnoli, Alessandra Bartolomei, ed., *Francesca Romana; La santa, il monastero e la città alla fine del medioevo*, Florence: Edizioni del Galuzzo, 2009,

Romagnoli, Margherita, "La dimora di un mercante pratese nel XIV secolo, parte II," *Arte Cristiana*, vol. 97, 2009, pp. 19–30.

Romanini, Angiola Maria, "La storia architettonica dell'abbazia delle Tre Fontane a Roma. La Fondazione cistercense," in Benoît Chauvin, ed., *Mélanges Anselme Dimier*, vol. 3, Pupillin (Arbois): B. Chauvin, 1982, pp. 653–95.

Romano, Serena, *La basilica di San Francesco ad Assisi: Pittori, botteghe, strategie narrative*, Rome: Viella, 2001.

Romano, Serena, "I Colonna a Roma: 1288–1297, in Sandro Carocci, ed., *La nobilità romana nel medioevo*, Rome: École française de Rome, 2006, pp. 291–312.

Romano, Serena, *Apogeo e fine del medioevo 1288–1431, La pittura medievale a Roma 312–1431; Corpus e Atlante*, vol. 6, Milan: Jaca Book, 2017.

Ronzani, Mauro, "Arcivescovi, chiesa cittadina e comune a Pisa nella prima metà del trecento," *Bollettino storico pisano*, vol. 57, 1988, pp. 11–38.

Ronzani, Mauro, "Il 'cimitero della chiesa maggiore pisana': Gli aspetti istituzionali prima e dopo la nascita del Camposanto," *Annali della Scuola normale superiore di Pisa, Classe di lettere e filosofia*, ser. 3, vol. 18, no. 4, 1988, pp. 1665–90.

Ronzani, Mauro, "'Figli del comune' o fuorusciti? Gli arcivescovi di Pisa di fronte alla città-stato tra la fine del Duecento e il 1406," in Giuseppina de Sandre Gasparini et al., eds., *Vescovi e diocesi in Italia dal XIV alla metà del XVI secolo*, Rome: Herder, 1990, vol. 2, pp. 773–827.

Ronzani, Mauro, "La formazione della Piazza del Duomo (secoli XI–XIV)," *Bollettino dell'Istituto storico artistico orvietano*, vols. 46–47, 1990–91 [1997], pp. 19–134.

Ronzani, Mauro, "Dal 'cimitero della chiesa maggiore di Santa Maria' al Camposanto," in Baracchini and Castelnuovo, eds., *Il Camposanto di Pisa*, pp. 49–56.

Ronzani, Mauro, *Un'idea trecentesca di cimitero: La costruzione e l'uso del Camposanto nella Pisa del secolo XIV*, Pisa: Edizioni Plus-University Press, 2005.

Ronzani, Mauro, "L'Opera del Duomo nel medioevo," in Garzella et al., eds., *La Cattedrale di Pisa*, pp. 37–44.

Roover, Raymond de, *The Rise and Decline of the Medici Bank*, New York: W. W. Norton, 1966.

Rossi, Adamo, "Di una cappella fabbricata a Spoleto nel Cinquecento per la santa Icone," *Giornale di erudizione artistica*, vol. 2, 1873, pp. 218–22.

Rossi, Adamo, "Documenti per la storia della scultura ornamentale in pietra," *Giornale di Erudizione artistica*, vol. 3, 1874, pp. 153–55.

Rossi, Vittorio, "L'Indole e gli studi di G. di Cosimo de' Medici. Notizie e documenti," *Atti della Accademia nazionale dei Lincei. Rendiconti, classe di scienze morali, storiche e filologiche*, ser. 5, vol. 2, 1893, pp. 129–50.

Rowlands, Eliot, "Filippo Lippi and His Experience of Painting in the Veneto Region," *Artibus et Historiae*, vol. 19, 1989, pp. 43–52.

Rubin, Miri, *Corpus Christi: The Eucharist in Late Medieval Culture*, Cambridge: Cambridge University Press, 1991.

Rubinstein, Nicolai, *The Government of Florence under the Medici*, 2nd ed., Oxford: Clarendon Press, 1997.

Ruda, Jeffrey, *Fra Filippo Lippi: Life and Work*, London: Phaidon, 1993.

Ruschi, Pietro, "Antico e moderno nell'architettura dipinta di Benozzo Gozzoli," in Andreatta et al., eds., *Benozzo Gozzoli e l'architettura*, pp. 41–48.

Russo, Daniel, "Les représentations mariale dans l'art d'Occident: Essai sur la formation d'une tradition iconographique," in Iogna-Prat et al., eds., *Marie: Le culte de la Vierge dans la société Médiévale*, pp. 173–291.

Rutherford, Richard, *The Death of a Christian: The Rite of Funerals*, New York: Pueblo, 1980.

Saalman, Howard, "Early Renaissance Architectural Theory and Practice in Antonio Filarete's 'Trattato di Architettura,'" *Art Bulletin*, vol. 41, 1959, pp. 89–106.

Saalman, Howard, "Santa Maria del Fiore: 1294–1418," *Art Bulletin*, vol. 46, 1964, pp. 471–500.

Saalman, Howard, *Filippo Brunelleschi: The Cupola of Santa Maria del Fiore*, London: Zwemmer, 1980.

Sacchetti, Franco, *La battaglia delle belle donne, Le lettere, Le sposizioni di vangeli*, ed. Alberto Chiari, Bari: Laterza, 1938.

Sainati, Giuseppe, *Diario Sacro Pisano*, 2nd ed., Siena: Editrice S. Bernardino, 1886.

Salvadori, Patrizia, "Lorenzo de' Medici e le communità soggette tra pressioni e resistenze," in Fubini, ed., *La toscana al tempo di Lorenzo il Magnifico*, pp. 891–906.

Salvadori, Patrizia, "Florentines and the Communities of the Territorial State," in Connell et al., eds., *Florentine Tuscany*, pp. 207–24.

Salvadori, Patrizia, *Dominio e patronato: Lorenzo dei Medici e la Toscana nel Quattrocento*, Rome: Edizioni di storia e letteratura, 2000.

Sanpaolesi, Piero, Mario Bucci, and Licia Bertolini, *Camposanto Monumentale di Pisa: Affreschi e sinopie*, Pisa: Opera della Primaziale Pisana, 1960.

Sansi, Achille, *Degli edifici e dei frammenti storici delle antiche età di Spoleto*, Foligno: P. Sgariglia, 1869.

Sansi, Achille, *Storia del commune di Spoleto dal secolo XII al XVII*, 2 vols., Foligno: P. Sgariglia, 1879.

Sardo, Ranieri, *Cronaca di Pisa*, ed. Ottavio Banti, Rome: Istituto Palazzo Borromini, 1963.

Sartori, Antonio, "La cappella di S. Giacomo al Santo di Padova," *Il Santo*, vol. 6, 1966, pp. 267–359.

Sartori, Antonio, *Documenti per la storia dell'arte a Padova*, Vicenza: Pozza, 1976.

Saturno, William, et al., *The Murals of San Bartolo, El Petén, Guatemala Part 1: The North Wall.* Ancient America 7, Barnardsville: Boundary End Archaeology Research Center, 2005.

Schmitt, Jean-Claude, "L'Exception corporelle: à propos de l'Assomption de Marie," in Hamburger and Bouché, eds., *The Mind's Eye: Art and Theological Argument in the Middle Ages*, pp. 151–85.

Seidel, Max, "Studien zu Giovanni di Balduccio und Tino di Camaino," *Städel-Jahrbuch*, vol. 5, 1975, pp. 37–84.

Seidel, Max, "Building a Cathedral at the Time of the Crusades: On the Iconography of the Architectural Complex of the Primaziale of Pisa," in Max Seidel, *Italian Art of the Middle Ages and the Renaissance*, vol. 2, Venice: Marsilio Editore, 2005, pp. 49–70.

Sguerzo, Elsa Marantonio, *Evoluzione storico-giuridica dell'istituto della sepoltura ecclesiastica*, Milan: Giuffrè, 1976.

Sigal, Pierre-André, *L'Homme et le miracle dans la France médiévale (XIe–XIIe siècle)*, Paris: Cerf, 1985.

Silva, Pietro, *Pisa sotto Firenze dal 1406 al 1433*, Pisa: A. Valenti, 1909.

Silva, Pietro, *Il Governo di Pietro Gambacorta in Pisa e le sue relazioni col resto della Toscana e coi Visconti*, Pisa: FF. Nistri, 1910.

Silvestrelli, M. R., "Dal maestro di Cesi a Piermatteo d'Amelia: Aspetti della cultura figurativa nell'Umbria meridionale tra XIV e XV secolo," in Bruno Toscano, ed., *La pittura nell'Umbria meridionale dal Trecento al Novecento*, Terni: Provincia di Terni, 1993, pp. 27–43.

Simoncini, Giorgio, *Roma: le trasformazioni urbane nel quattrocento*, 2 vols., Florence: Olschki, 2004.

Simoneschi, Luigi, *Ordinamenti suntuari pisani per gli anni 1350, 1386*, Pisa: Mariotti, 1889.

Skerl del Conte, Serena, *Antonio Veneziano e Taddeo Gaddi nella Toscana della seconda metà del Trecento*, Udine: Campanotto, 1995.

Smith, Christine, *The Baptistery of Pisa*, New York: Garland, 1978.

Smith, Christine, *Architecture and the Culture of Early Humanism*, New York: Oxford University Press, 1992.

Snowden, Frank, *The Conquest of Malaria; Italy, 1900–1962*, New Haven and London: Yale University Press, 2006.

Solberg, Gail, "The Madonna Avvocata Icon at Orte and Geography," in Andrew Ladis and Shelley Zuraw, eds., *Visions of Holiness: Art and Devotion in Renaissance Italy*, Athens:

Georgia Museum of Art, University of Georgia, 2001, pp. 123–35.

Spallanzani, Marco, and Giovanna Gaeta Bertelà, *Libro d'inventario dei beni di Lorenzo il Magnifico*, Florence: Associazione Amici del Bargello, 1992.

Sperandio, Bernardino, *Chiese romaniche in Umbria*, Perugia: Quattroemme, 2001.

Sperandio, Francesco, *Sabina sagra e profana antica e moderna*, Rome: Zempel, 1790.

Stinger, Charles, *The Renaissance in Rome*, Bloomington: Indiana University Press, 1985.

Stinger, Charles, "Italian Renaissance Learning and the Church Fathers," in Irena Backus, ed., *The Reception of the Church Fathers in the West*, Leiden and New York: Brill, 1992, vol. 2, pp. 473–510.

Storia di Prato, 2nd ed., 3 vols., Prato: Edizioni Cassa di risparmi, 1981.

Stubblebine, James, *Assisi and the Rise of Vernacular Art*, New York: Harper and Row, 1985.

Sumption, Jonathan, *Pilgrimage: An Image of Mediaeval Religion*, Totowa: Rowman and Littlefield, 1975.

Supino, I. Benvenuto, *L'arte del rinascimento nella primaziale di Pisa: I maestri d'intaglio e di tarsia in legno, i pittori e gli scultori*, Rome: Tipologia dell'Unione Cooperativa Editrice: 1893.

Supino, I. Benvenuto, *Il Camposanto di Pisa*, Florence: Alinari, 1896.

Supino, I. Benvenuto, *Arte Pisana*, Florence: Alinari, 1904.

Syson, Luke, "Bertoldo di Giovanni, Republican Court Artist," in Stephen Campbell, et al., eds., *Artistic Exchange and Cultural Translation in the Italian Renaissance City*, Cambridge: Cambridge University Press, 2004, pp. 96–133.

Sznura, F., "Edilizia private e urbanistica in tempo di crisi," in Braudel et al., eds, *Prato, storia di una città*, vol. 1, part. 1, p. 342.

Tanfani-Centofanti, Leopoldo, *Notizie di artisti tratte dai documenti pisani*, Pisa: Enrico Spoerri, 1897; reprint Bologna: Forni, 1972.

Tanzini, Lorenzo, "Tuscan States: Florence and Siena," in Gamberini and Lazzarini, eds., *The Italian Renaissance State*, pp. 99–101.

Tazartes, Maurizia, "Anagrafe Lucchese II: Michele Ciampanti, Il maestro Stratonice," *Richerche di storia dell'arte*, vol. 26, 1985, pp. 18–26.

Taube, Karl, et al., *The Murals of San Bartolo, El Petén, Guatemala, Part 2: The West Wall.* Ancient America 10. Barnardsville: Boundary End Archaeology Research Center, 2010.

Tekippe, Rita, "Pilgrimage and Procession: Correlations of Meaning, Practice, and Effects," in Sarah Blick and Rita Tekippe, eds., *Art and Architecture of Late Medieval Pilgrimage in Northern Europe and the British Isles*, Leiden: Brill, 2005, pp. 693–751.

Thompson, Augustine, *Cities of God: The Religion of the Italian Communes 1125–1325*, University Park: Pennsylvania State University Press, 2005.

Thompson, Nancy, "The Franciscans and the True Cross: The Decoration of the Cappella Maggiore of Santa Croce in Florence," *Gesta*, vol. 43, 2004, pp. 61–79.

Thunø, Erik, and Wolf, Gerhard, eds., *The Miraculous Image in the Late Middle Ages and Renaissance*, Rome: Erma di Bretschneider, 2004.

Tintori, Leonetto, and Millard Meiss, *The Painting of the Life of St. Francis in Assisi, with Notes on the Arena Chapel*, New York: New York University, Institute of Fine Arts Conservation Center, 1962.

Toccafondi, Diana, "Legati da una Cintura: Devozione, culto e potere a Prato dal medioevo all'età contemporanea," in Martini, ed., *La Sacra Cintola nel Duomo di Prato*, pp. 61–74.

Toesca, Pietro, *Storia dell'arte italiana: Il medioevo*, 2 vols., Turin: Unione Tipografico-Editrice Torinese, 1927–51.

Tognetti, Sergio, ed., *Firenze e Pisa dopo il 1406: La creazione di un nuovo spazio regionale*, Florence: Olschki, 2010.

Toker, Franklin, "Building on Paper: The Role of Architectural Drawings in Late-Medieval Italy," *L'art et les révolutions: XXVIIe Congrès international d'Histoire d'art*, vol. 8, Strasbourg: Société alsacienne pour le développement de l'histoire de l'art, 1992, pp. 31–50.

Tolaini, Emilio, *Forma Pisarum, Storia urbanstica della città di Pisa*, Pisa: Nistri-Lischi, 1979.

Tolaini, Emilio, "Camposanto di Pisa: Progetto e cantiere," *Rivista dell'Istituto Nazionale d'archeologia e storia dell'arte*, 3rd ser., vol. 17, 1994, pp. 101–46 [reprinted, with slight revisions in Emilio Tolaini, *Camposanto di Pisa: progetto e cantiere: La forma architettonica e la decorazione plastica*, Pisa: Edizioni ETS, 2008].

Tolaini, Emilio, *Pisa: la città e la storia*, Pisa: ETS, 2007.

Tolaini, Emilio, "Quando i sarcofagi entrarono in Camposanto," *Critica d'arte*, vol. 33/34, 2008, pp. 51–56.

Toniolo, Giuseppe, et al., *Il Museo dell'Opera del Duomo a Pisa*, Milan: Silvana Editoriale, 1986.

Thomasberger, Edith, "Beobachtungen über die Fresken der Hiobsgeschichte im Camposanto," *Storia dell'arte*, vol. 62, 1988, pp. 25–27.

Toscano, Bruno, *Spoleto in pietre: Guida artistica della città*, Spoleto: Azienda del turismo, 1963.

Toscano, Bruno, *Il Duomo di Spoleto. La piazza vicende e guida artistica del monumento*, Spoleto: Ente Rocca di Spoleto, 1969.

Toscano, Bruno, "L'antico altare del Duomo di Spoleto," *Spoletium*, vol. 50/51, new series nos. 6/7, 2013–14, pp. 99–111.

Toscano, Bruno, and Giovanna Capitelli eds., *Benozzo Gozzoli, Allievo a Roma, maestro in Umbria*, Milan: Silvana Editoriale, 2002.

Trachtenberg, Marvin, "On Brunelleschi's Old Sacristy as Model for Early Renaissance Church Architecture," in Jean Guillaume, ed., *L'Église dans l'architecture de la Renaissance*, Paris: Picard, 1995, pp. 9–39.

Trexler, Richard, "Ritual Behavior in Renaissance Florence: The Setting," *Medievalia et Humanistica*, n.s., vol. 4, 1973, pp. 125–44.

Trexler, Richard, *Public Life in Renaissance Florence*, Ithaca: Cornell University Press, 1980.

Tripps, Johannes, "Tendencies of Gothic in Florence: Andrea Bonaiuti," in Offner, Steinweg, et al., eds., *A Critical and Historical Corpus of Florentine Painting*, section 4, vol. 7, part 1, Florence: Giunti, 1996.

Tronci, Paolo, *Memorie istoriche della città di Pisa*, Livorno: Bonfigli, 1682; repr., Bologna: Forni, 1967.

Tronzo, William, "The Prestige of St. Peter's: Observations on the Function of Monumental Narrative Cycles in Italy," *Studies in the History of Art*, vol. 16, 1985, pp. 93–112.

William Tronzo, *The Via Latina Catacomb: Imitation and Discontinuity in Fourth-Century Roman Painting*, University Park: Penn State University Press, 1986.

Tronzo, William, "Apse Decoration, the Liturgy and the Perception of Art in Medieval Rome: S. Maria in Trastevere and S. Maria Maggiore," in Tronzo, ed., *Italian Church Decoration of the Middle Ages and Early Renaissance*, pp. 167–94.

Tronzo, William, ed., *Italian Church Decoration of the Middle Ages and Early Renaissance*, Bologna: Nuova Alfa, 1989.

Ughelli, F., and N. Coleti, *Italia sacra*, Venice: Sebastianum Coleti, 1717.

Varagnoli, Claudio, "Il Seicento: La cattedrale barberiniana," in Benazzi and Carbonara, eds., *La cattedrale di Spoleto*, pp. 111–21.

Vasari, Giorgio, *Le vite* [1550], ed. Luciano Bellosi, Turin: Einaudi, 1986; *Le vite de' più eccellenti pittori scultori ed architettori scritte da Giorgio Vasari pittore Aretino* [1568], ed. Gaetano Milanesi, 9 vols., Florence: Sansoni, 1906, repr. 1973; trans. Gaston de Vere, New York: Knopf, 2 vols., 1996.

Vauchez, André, "Patronage of Saints and Civic Religion in the Italy of the Communes," Daniel Bornstein, ed., trans. Margery Schneider, *The Laity in the Middle Ages*, Notre Dame: University of Notre Dame Press, 1993, pp. 153–68.

Verde, Armando, *Lo Studio Fiorentino 1473–1505: Ricerche e documenti*, 6 vols., Florence: Istituto Nazionale di Studio sul Rinascimento, 1973–2010.

Verdier, Philippe, *Le Couronnement de la Vierge*, Montréal: Institut d'études médiévales Albert-le-Grand, 1980.

Verdon, Timothy, "Michelozzo e lo spazio della preghiera: Il 'Tempietto' della Santissima Annunziata," in Gabriele Morolli, ed., *Michelozzo scultore e architetto*

(1396–1472), Florence: Centro Di, 1998, pp. 171–77.

Verdon, Timothy, "L'Incarnazione e la città del fiore: L'Annunciazione nell'arte fiorentina," *Arte cristiana*, vol. 88, 2000, pp. 227–30.

Verdon, Timothy, "La Santissima Annunziata: storia, arte, spiritualità," in Timothy Verdon, ed., *Alla riscoperta delle chiese di Firenze, 4. Santissima Annunziata*, Florence: Centro Di, 2005, pp. 9–32.

Veronensis, Gasparis, *De gestis tempore Pontificis Maximi Pauli secundi*, ed. G. Zippel, in Giosu Carducci and Vittorio Fiorini, eds., *Rerum Italicarum Scriptores*, 2nd ed., vol. 3, part 16, Città di Castello: Casa Editrice Lapi, 1904.

Vignoli, Lucilla, "Il Cardinale Berardo Eroli e la decorazione della cappella di San Bernardino a Narni," in Benazzi and Lunghi, eds., *Pierantonio Mezzastris*, pp. 193–217.

Vigo, Pietro, *Una festa poplare a Pisa nel Medioevo. Contributo alla storia delle costumanze italiane*, Pisa: Mariotti, 1888.

Virilli, Paolo, "I dipinti di Filippo Lippi nell'abside del Duomo di Spoleto," in S. Rinaldi, ed., *Tecniche della pittura murale dall'alto medioevo al quattrocento*, Viterbo: 1998, pp. 32–37.

Von der Osten, G., "Job and Christ: The Development of a Devotional Image," *Journal of the Warburg and Courtauld Institutes*, vol. 16, 1953, pp. 153–58.

Voragine, Jacobus de, *The Golden Legend*, trans. William Ryan, 2 vols., Princeton: Princeton University Press, 1993.

Vossilla, Francesco, *La Loggia della Signoria: Una galleria di scultura*, Florence: Edizioni Medicea, 1995.

Waley, Daniel, *The Papal State in the Thirteenth Century*, London: Macmillan, 1961.

Walter, Christopher, "Two Notes on the Deesis," *Revue des études byzantines*, vol. 26, 1968, pp. 311–36.

Walter, Christopher, "Further Notes on the Deesis," *Revue des études byzantines*, vol. 28, 1970, pp. 161–87.

Wallace, William, *Michelangelo at San Lorenzo: The Genius as Entrepreneur*, Cambridge: Cambridge University Press, 1994.

Wallace, William, *Michelangelo, God's Architect: The Story of his Final Years and Greatest Masterpiece*, Princeton: Princeton University Press, 2019.

Wanrooij, Marzia Casini, Claudio Cerretelli, et al., *Sacre Suggestioni: Museo dell'Opera del Duomo di Prato*, Prato: Cariprato, 2001.

Warner, Marina, *Alone of All Her Sex: The Myth and the Cult of the Virgin Mary*, New York: Knopf, 1976.

Warnke, Martin, *The Court Artist: On the Ancestry of the Modern Artist*, trans. David McLintock, Cambridge: Cambridge University Press, 1993.

Warr, Cordelia, and Janis Elliott, eds., *Art and Architecture in Naples 1266–1713: New Approaches*, Oxford: Basil Blackwell, 2010.

Watanabe, Yumi, "Filippo Lippi's Frescoes at Spoleto, Cardinal Eroli, and the Immaculate Conception," *Mitteilungen des Kunsthistorischen Instituts in Florenz*, vol. 64, 2023, pp. 220–29.

Webb, Diana, *Patrons and Defenders: The Saints in the Italian City-States*, London: Tauris Academic Studies, 1996.

Webb, Diana, *Saints and Cities in Medieval Italy*, Manchester: Manchester University Press, 2007.

Webster, Sally, and Sylvia Rhor, "Modern Mural Painting in the United States: Shaping Spaces/Shaping Publics," in Knight and Senie, eds., *A Companion to Public Art*, pp. 75–92.

Weissen, Kurt, "I banchieri fiorentini ai concili di Costanza e Basilea," in Lorenzo Tanzini and Sergio Tognetti, eds., *"'Mercature è arte': Uomini d'affari toscani in Europa e nel Mediterraneo tardomedievale,"* Rome: Viella libreria editrice, 2012, pp. 81–95.

Weitzmann, Kurt, *The Monastery of St. Catherine at Mount Sinai: The Icons*, vol. 1, Princeton: Princeton University Press, 1976.

Weppelmann, Stefan, *Spinello Aretino und die Toskanische Malerei des 14. Jahrhunderts*, Florence: Edifir, 2003.

Westfall, Caroll William, *In this Most Perfect Paradise: Alberti, Nicholas V, and the Invention of Conscious Urban Planning in Rome, 1447–55*, University Park, Pennsylvania State University Press, 1974.

Wieruszowski, Helene, "Art and the Commune in the Time of Dante," *Speculum*, vol. 19, 1944, pp. 14–33.

Wilkinson, John, *Jerusalem Pilgrimage 1099–1185*, London: The Hakluyt Society, 1988.

Wischnitzer-Bernstein, Rachel, "Jüdische Legendenstoffe bei Benozzo Gozzoli," in *Feschrift zum 70. Geburtstage von Moritz Schaefer*, Berlin, 1927, pp. 271–74.

Wolf, Gerhard, *Salus Populi romani: Die Geschichte römischer Kultbilder im Mittelalter*, Weinheim: VCH Verlagsgesellschaft, 1990.

Wolff, Martha, ed., *Kings, Queens and Courtiers: Art in Early Renaissance France*, Chicago: Art Institute of Chicago, 2011.

Zaccagnini, Gabriele, "San Ranieri: Profilo storico e agiografico," in Castelli and Ceccarelli Lemut, eds., *Intercessor Rainerius ad Patrem*, pp. 53–71.

Zaccagnini, Gabriele, *La vita di San Ranieri: Analisi storica, agiografica e filologica del testo di Benincasa: Edizione critica dal codice C181 dell'Archivio Capitolare di Pisa*, Pisa: GISEM, 2011.

Zaccaria, Raffaella Maria, "Nicola di Vieri dei Medici," in Roberto Cardini et al., eds., *Alberti e la cultura del quattrocento*, Florence: Edizioni Polistampa, 1997, vol. 1, pp. 418–23.

Zanardi, Bruno, *Il cantiere di Giotto Le storie di San Francesco ad Assisi*, Milan: Skira, 1996.

Zanardi, Bruno, *Giotto e Pietro Cavallini*, Milan: Skira, 2002.

Zervas, Diane, ed., *Orsanmichele a Firenze, "Mirabilia Italiae,"* Modena: Panini, 1996.

Zorach, Rebecca, *Art for People's Sake: Artists and Community in Black Chicago, 1965–1975*, Durham: Duke University Press, 2019.

Zorzi, Andrea, "L'inquadramento di Pisa e del suo territorio nel dominio fiorentino," in Tognetti, ed., *Firenze e Pisa dopo il 1406*, pp. 85–107.

INDEX

The page numbers in *italics* indicate Figures.